N COMPUTER SYSTEMS AND T█████████████████████████████████ONS

Video training courses are available on the subjects of these books in the
James Martin ADVANCED TECHNOLOGY LIBRARY from Deltak Inc.
1220 Kensington Road, Oak Brook, Ill. 60521 (Tel: 312-920-0700).

MANAGING
THE DATA-BASE
ENVIRONMENT

TELEPROCESSING
NETWORK
ORGANIZATION

DISTRIBUTED FILE
AND DATA-
BASE DESIGN ←→ STRATEGIC
DATA-PLANNING
METHODOLOGIES

SYSTEMS ANALYSIS
FOR DATA
TRANSMISSION ←→ DESIGN AND STRATEGY
FOR DISTRIBUTED
DATA PROCESSING

COMPUTER
DATA-BASE
ORGANIZATION

(second edition)

INTRODUCTION
TO COMPUTER
NETWORKS ←→ COMPUTER NETWORKS
AND DISTRIBUTED
PROCESSING

PRINCIPLES
OF DATA-BASE
MANAGEMENT

INTRODUCTION
TO
TELEPROCESSING

PRINCIPLES OF
DISTRIBUTED
PROCESSING

AN END-USER'S
GUIDE TO
DATA BASE

Books On   Books On   Books On

DESIGN OF REAL-TIME
COMPUTER SYSTEMS

Prentice-Hall
Series in Automatic Computation
George Forsythe, editor

The author lecturing on the design of real-time systems.

Prentice-Hall, Inc.,   Englewood Cliffs, New Jersey

DESIGN OF REAL-TIME
COMPUTER SYSTEMS

James Martin

STAFF MEMBER
SYSTEMS RESEARCH INSTITUTE
IBM CORPORATION

Current printing (last digit):

27   26   25   24   23   22   21   20

Library of Congress Catalog Card Number: 67-18923
Printed in the United States of America

PRENTICE-HALL INTERNATIONAL, INC., *London*
PRENTICE-HALL OF AUSTRALIA, PTY. LTD., *Sydney*
PRENTICE-HALL OF CANADA, LTD., *Toronto*
PRENTICE-HALL OF INDIA PRIVATE LIMITED, *New Delhi*
PRENTICE-HALL OF JAPAN, INC., *Tokyo*

PREFACE

The trend in the use of data processing is towards larger, more integrated systems. The computing equipment now available is enabling many organizations to combine functions that were previously done separately, and large geographically-dispersed systems are now being installed.

Data transmission links are speeding the flow of business and technical information. With massive random-access files the dreams of management information systems can be realized—if only the necessary systems analysis can be done. In many fields, man is acquiring a new relationship with the machines through the use of remote displays and terminal devices.

As these trends spread, systems designers are faced with an increasingly difficult task. Many disciplines now have to be welded together into the building of one system. Communication networks need to be planned. An often massive and changing bank of data must be organized. The behaviour of the terminal users must be studied and a means devised that will enable them to communicate with a complex system. The terminal hardware and software must together form a "language" by means of which the users and the computer interact. Reliability becomes a more vital issue and techniques must be devised for lessening the troubles caused by hardware failures. Instead of having one machine chewing its way through a fixed sequence of data we can now have a far-flung system in live interaction with an ever-changing environment. Complex supervisory Programs must co-ordinate this varied and unpredictable activity.

The design calculations become much more complex. The runs on early batch-processing computers could be timed precisely because records of a known length were processed in a field sequence. Now inputs occur at times not precisely predictable, often at the whim of the many human users. Queues build up. There are peaks of high activity. The design calculations need techniques such as queuing theory and simulation, and will give answers in terms of probabilities.

This book emphasizes real-time commercial systems with their special problems and dangers. However, many of the techniques described apply also to other types of system. Some non-real-time systems today face many of these problems.

Throughout this wide-ranging design process it is important that a sense of perspective be maintained. Some members of the design team must understand the whole system, and how decisions in one area have impact on the planning in others. This book, therefore, attempts to range over all of the disciplines involved, and necessarily in a mere 630 pages covers many of them in an introductory fashion.

This book is intended for both the analysts and programmers employed in the detailed aspects of systems implementation, and for those whose interest is less technical—such as general management, many students, and, in some cases, computer salesmen. The latter will have less interest in parts such as Section V which are more detailed. The former will probably find the second half of the book the most useful.

Part of the book is intended as a design *handbook*. The formulas and curves in Chapter 6 and Section V constitute a tool for use in systems design. These, along with the check-list of design questions in Chapter 39 and the summaries of design approaches in other parts may be useful for repeated reference. It is hoped, therefore, that this book will be owned by data processing professionals rather than meeting the sad fate of only being borrowed from a library and read once.

J. M.

ACKNOWLEDGEMENTS

Any book about the state of the art in a complex technology draws material from a vast number of sources. There are many acknowledgements that should accompany a book of this nature. The development of the techniques described has been the result of the creativity and labor of a very large number of persons. Most of the techniques are now coming into common computer usage, but the work that has led to these methods was originated on certain pioneering projects which include amongst others, SAGE, Project Mercury, American Airlines SABRE System, Pan American Airways PANAMAC System, British Overseas Airways Corporation's BOADICEA project, the New York Stock Exchange System, IBM's PARS project, and a variety of savings bank, production control and message switching systems. To the many systems engineers and programmers who contributed to this body of inovation, the author is indebted.

An author is also indebted to his own educators. Much of my understanding of the queuing theory used in Section V came from the technical reports produced in IBM by Mr. P. Seaman and his associates, and was improved by the brilliant lecturing of Dr. J. E. Flanagan at IBM's Systems Research Institute. The author learned PL/1 from Dr. G. Weinberg. Dr. Weinberg's excellently written *PL 1 Programming Primer*, McGraw Hill, New York, 1966, is highly recommended for beginners.

Mr. R. B. Edward's staff helped enormously in typing and reproducing the manuscript. The author is particularly grateful to Miss Cora Tangney for her help in this. The most patient assistance in assembling this work was given by Miss Kathleen Hill (see Fig. 8.2).

Parts of the manuscript were read and valuable criticisms made by Mr. P. Vince in London, and Mr. C. T. Fike, Dr. J. E. Flanagan and Mrs. E. Schaefer in New York. The long-suffering students of IBM's Systems Research Institute also used the manuscript and made many corrections. To all these the author is indebted.

J. M.

CONTENTS

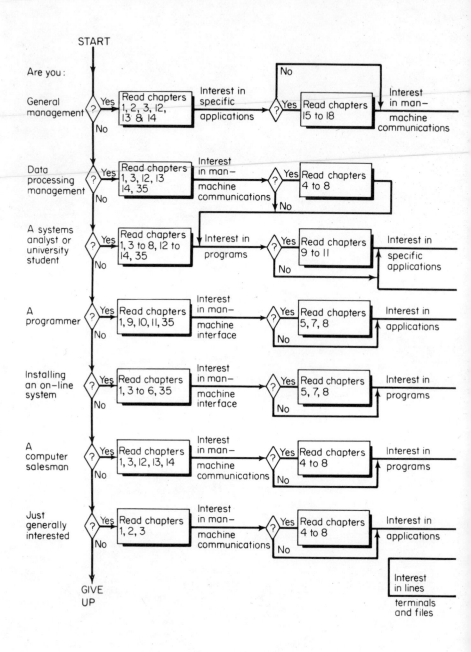

START

Are you:

General management — Yes — Read chapters 1, 2, 3, 12, 13 & 14 — Interest in specific applications — Yes — Read chapters 15 to 18 — No — Interest in man-machine communications
No

Data processing management — Yes — Read chapters 1, 3, 12, 13 14, 35 — Interest in man-machine communications — Yes — Read chapters 4 to 8 — No
No

A systems analyst or university student — Yes — Read chapters 1, 3 to 8, 12 to 14, 35 — Interest in programs — Yes — Read chapters 9 to 11 — No — Interest in specific applications
No

A programmer — Yes — Read chapters 1, 9, 10, 11, 35 — Interest in man-machine interface — Yes — Read chapters 5, 7, 8 — No — Interest in applications
No

Installing an on-line system — Yes — Read chapters 1, 3 to 6, 35 — Interest in man-machine interface — Yes — Read chapters 5, 7, 8 — No — Interest in programs
No

A computer salesman — Yes — Read chapters 1, 3, 12, 13, 14 — Interest in man-machine communications — Yes — Read chapters 4 to 8 — No — Interest in programs
No

Just generally interested — Yes — Read chapters 1, 2, 3 — Interest in man-machine communications — Yes — Read chapters 4 to 8 — No — Interest in applications
No

GIVE UP

Interest in lines terminals and files

HOW TO READ THIS BOOK.

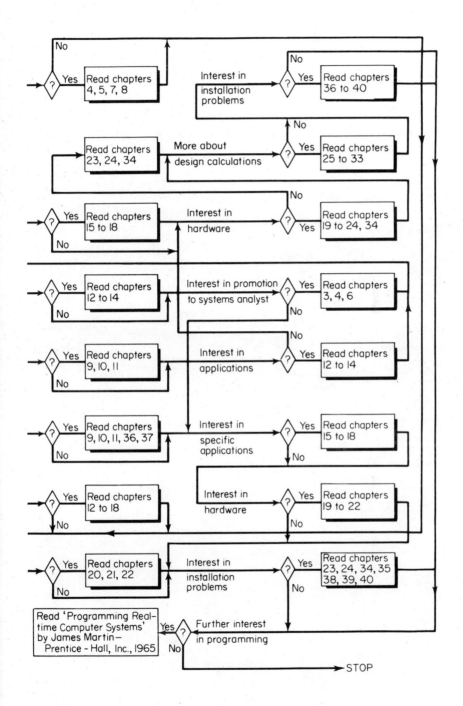

SECTION I

INTRODUCTION

1 INTRODUCTION

Computers have been installed in the past which could make decisions in microseconds but did not produce information *where it was needed, as fast as it was needed.*

The elegantly styled machine, in a plant-adorned room, shimmered its console lights faster than the eye could follow, but management could not find out the latest stock figures. A customer at a bank window could not withdraw the cash he wanted immediately. A scientist had a twenty-four hour wait to receive the results of his small calculation. An airline desk did not have enough information to book the seat a traveller wanted, and, in general, facts and figures received from the computer were too late to control what was happening *at that moment.*

The problem was threefold. *First,* it took the data a long time to reach the computer. They sometimes had to pass through a variety of clerical, mail, or delivery processes before reaching the machine. *Second,* the data-processing mechanisms were not organized so that the computer could turn its attention immediately to any transaction that might need it. Data were stored sequentially on tapes or in other files which had to be scanned, merged, and sorted. The computer could not obtain facts or figures at random the instant it needed them. Instead a lengthy cycle of preplanned operations had to be worked through. *Third,* it took a long time to relay the results back to the person or process where they were to be used.

Thus the computer, lightning fast though it was, was surrounded by a system, or organization, which could not in any sense keep pace with it.

Today, however, all data can be instantly available to the computer via direct-access files. Telecommunication lines can link the computer to any point and speed the flow of data to and from the machine. The users, many miles away, can be provided with keyboard or display devices which they operate

3

in a "conversational" manner if necessary, and suddenly become face to face with the machine.

With such a system business management can maintain instant-by-instant *control* over what is happening, rather than make separate and inaccurate adjustments with large time intervals between them. The system can deliver information where it is wanted *when* it is wanted.

To a large extent, then, this book is concerned with the speed at which a data-processing system reacts. However, as will be seen, there are by-products of the speedy reaction which can change the whole nature of data processing. A live interaction between the thought processes of human beings and the data-handling power of machines can be built up to achieve a result more powerful than could be obtained by either of these alone.

Systems described as "on-line" and "real-time" are now installed in many organizations. In these, data may be entered directly into the computer system from the environment it works with, and results relayed back. A wide variety of devices have been built for sending data from a distant location to the computer and for receiving its reply. These are referred to in this book as *terminals*.

The terminals may be in the computer room or may be a long way away, connected to the computer by telephone line or other form of telecommunication link. They may be on the shop floor of a factory, on the counter of a bank, in a warehouse or a supermarket, in the general manager's office, in fact anywhere within an organization. There are many different types of terminals, and they can be designed to fit as naturally as possible into their environment.

The operator of a terminal, whoever he may be, sends data to the computer. These may be an enquiry or may be information to be processed. The computer deals with them, sometimes immediately, sometimes not, and a reply may or may not be sent back to the operator. Sometimes a computer sends data "unsolicited" to a terminal. Items of data transmitted are referred to throughout this book as *messages* or *transactions*. An on-line system may transmit batches of data as well as single items.

Messages arriving at the computer from its terminals may be processed immediately, or they may be stored for later processing. Often a message is processed and a reply returned to the terminal within seconds. Transactions often update records immediately rather than being stored on serial files, such as tape or card, for later "batch processing" and sorting.

The telecommunication lines may be "on-line" or "off-line" to the computer. On-line means that they go directly into the computer with the computer controlling the transmission. Off-line means that telecommunication data do not go directly into the computer but are written onto magnetic tape or punched into paper tape or cards for later processing.

An on-line system may be defined as one in which the input data enter the computer directly from the point of origination and/or output data are trans-mitted directly to where they are used. The intermediate stages of punching data onto cards or paper tape or of writing magnetic tape or off-line printing are largely avoided.

The terminals on a computer system may be designed for human operation, or they may utilize technical equipment to collect data automatically. They may, for example, read thermocouples, strain gauges, or other instrumentation. They may send a signal to the computer whenever an item is finished on a machine tool. They may enable the computer to count objects passing detectors on a production line. A very wide variety of devices is in use for collecting data at their source and for delivering the results of the computation where they are needed.

If the computer reacts to its input data quickly, completes its processing, and takes action within a short period of time, the term "real-time" is sometimes used.

A real-time computer system may be defined as one which controls an environment by receiving data, processing them, and taking action or returning results sufficiently quickly to affect the functioning of the environment at that time.

Real-time is a term that is defined differently by different authorities. The question of "response time" may enter into the definition. Response time is the time the system takes to react to a given input. If a message is keyed into a terminal by an operator and the reply from the computer is typed at the same terminal, *response time may be defined as the time interval between the operator's pressing the last key and the terminal's typing the first letter of the reply.* For different kinds of terminals, response time may be defined similarly, *the interval between an event and the system's response to the event.*

Some authorities use the term "real-time" to imply a response time of a few seconds. Others expand the definition to include any response which controls the minute-by-minute or hour-by-hour functioning of an environment. Still others claim that no system should be called "real-time" unless the response is within milliseconds as with a missile homing on an evasive target. This book is not going to enter into the semantic argument. Some of the systems discussed will give a response time of seconds; others, longer.

In using a computer to control a set of operations a low response time is usually necessary. The speed of response differs from one type of system to another according to the needs. In a system for radar scanning a response time of milliseconds is needed. Airline reservation systems in operation give a response time of about two seconds. A warehousing control system may have a response time of thirty seconds. In a system used for controlling a paper mill a five-minute response time may be adequate. On some systems the response time is higher than this, perhaps half an hour or more, but above this it is certainly arguable whether the system should still be described as "real-time".

Most commercial installations with earlier generations of machines have exclusively used batch processing. Several hundred transactions would be grouped into a batch. In a punched-card installation many trays of cards would be fed through one machine before the setup of that machine was changed for the next function it would perform. The "batch" would then have to wait for the next operation to be performed on it, possibly a sorting or merging operation ready for another "run." Similarly with the use of magnetic tape on computers, large tape files would be processed with one program before the file was sorted and made ready for the next operation. It is economic to have large batches. A cycle of operations, perhaps a weekly cycle, is adhered to, which means that it takes a long time before any one particular transaction is processed.

Now, instead of operating run by run, and printing out results which will be read at a later time, the computer can deal with transactions immediately if necessary or in an hour or so if that is good enough. It can complete all the processing associated with one transaction at one time.

It can provide management with information *when* they ask for it. It can give quick answers to enquiries about the status of an account or the creditworthiness of a customer or the amount of an item in stock. The answer will not be a week out of date but up to the minute. Each transaction reaching the computer center or entered into a distant terminal can receive individual treatment. If the item gives rise to exceptional conditions, these can be dealt with immediately, and, if someone in the organization needs to be informed as a result, there is no delay.

Techniques are necessary to achieve minute-by-minute control of a commercial situation in the same way that control is maintained over, say, a chemical plant. The computer may schedule work through a factory and reschedule it whenever new requirements occur or the situation on the shop floor changes. It can control the selling of airline seats all over the world. It can enable customers entering *any* branch of a bank to withdraw cash from their accounts, while protecting against insufficient funds. Immediate insurance quotations can be given and claim reporting and payments handled more quickly. Salesmen's orders from all over the country can be processed in time for the following day's production. Traffic in a turbulent city has been speeded up by computers maneuvering it into groups of vehicles and changing traffic lights at the best moment, and in a similar way the events in an industrial process can be regulated in an optimum manner.

This is real-time.

The benefits of such control are not necessarily the traditional saving of manpower. Often the benefits accrue from increased efficiency, better customer service, or more profitable utilization of facilities.

How many customers are lost to competition because you cannot give them an immediate reply? What would be the increase in profitability if your work could be organized to give a machine-tool utilization of 60 instead of 50 per cent? How much more money would an airline make if it had one more passenger on each flight with empty seats? To what extent could overproduction and underproduction be avoided by up-to-the-minute planning? Could immediate processing of data result in a reduction of inventory cost? These are the benefits of tight control and quick reactions in an organization.

Perhaps one of the most fundamental changes in the work of a systems analyst with the equipment available today from that of the analyst with the earlier generations of computers is that he must evaluate what reaction time is needed for each function the computer is to perform.

In order to control a situation a certain reaction time is needed. How fast this must be depends upon the pattern of activity being controlled. In order to control the steering of a car, a man reacts to visible input in a second or so. Certain exceptional conditions demand a faster reaction time! In controlling the temperature of a room heated by a log fire, however, he may make adjustments to the fire every quarter of an hour or so, depending upon whether he is feeling too warm or too cold.

Similarly in situations that are controlled by a computer, the response time needed depends upon the mechanism being controlled. The control of a rocket launching needs responses in milliseconds. For the control of an engine on a test bed, seconds will be adequate. For most dynamic administrative processes, a response in an hour or so will be enough, but certain exceptional conditions may need quicker action than this. When "conversation" occurs between man and machine, the latter must react ideally in about a second or two.

Not every function needs to be carried out quickly. Much of the data-processing work in an organization has no immediacy about it, and the conventional methods of batch processing can be used. For certain functions a reaction time of less than twenty-four hours would be desirable if it could be obtained. For example, it would be of value in some companies if the previous day's cost figures for manpower, and in certain cases also for materials, could be presented to management each morning. Unusual delays or expenses might be highlighted by the data-processing system quickly enough to do something about them. Orders for certain types of products should be processed quickly. This is especially true of perishable goods or products in which there is a highly competitive market. Stock record updating and the control of stock levels need to be done also within a twenty-four hour period with certain types of stock in order to minimize the inventory held while ensuring that that stock does not run out. There are many administrative functions which need a reaction time within one day.

Some functions, on the other hand, require a very fast response time. When *enquiries* are made of the computer, the answer will usually be required quickly. Management may be making the enquiry, and they cannot afford to be held up. In other cases the enquirer may have a customer on the telephone or at a sales desk.

The picture, then, that this book describes may be of an information-processing system capable of reacting at different speeds to different events. There may be a wide spectrum of differing reaction times. Less urgent work will form a background constantly giving way to jobs that must be tackled within a short period. All work will be interrupted by transactions or enquiries that must be dealt with in real time with a reaction time of seconds or possibly minutes. The computer must be capable of handling *multiple interrupts*. The transactions needing a fast response time must break into programs doing less immediate work. They may break in only at predetermined check points, or they may be able to interrupt another job at any point if the response is to be very fast.

Some systems are entirely, or almost entirely, real-time. Occasionally the real-time and non-real-time parts of the processing are done on separate computers, perhaps sharing the same file units.

The mass of data that the computers must maintain and have access to is planned in an integrated fashion. The file units are chosen and organized so that the data can be found, read, and modified sufficiently fast.

Telecommunication links speed the flow of data throughout the organization. They place the computer center within easy reach of all parts of a company. In certain more spectacular schemes, such as one designed for British Overseas Airways Corporation, the computer has been made immediately accessible to locations all over the world.

Enquiries can be addressed to the computers and answers received almost immediately. The enquiries may simply demand the display of information on the files. They may need calculation performing or a search making for certain facts. New and exciting possibilities are opened up by programming the computers so that users can carry out more elaborate conversations with the machine.

Terminal devices and display units are specially designed to provide an efficient *man-machine interface*. Programs are written so that a relatively unintelligent operator with no knowledge of computers can communicate with the machine and the machine will check his actions and tell him immediately if it detects any errors. On the other hand, a highly intelligent operator with a thorough knowledge of computers and much skill at programming might use the system. He might enter or modify programs at a terminal. He might construct simulation models, modify PERT planning networks, and so on. A combination of the skilled use of human intelligence, coupled with the best of machine capabilities, is a very potent mixture, the full potentialities of which will probably take decades to develop, or even to understand.

Time sharing will be used so that the slow use of a computer by a human terminal operator does not delay the machine processing. The operator sits at his desk equipped, perhaps, with a typewriter, or keyboard and display screen, attached to a computer many miles away. He has at his fingertips the power of a large computer with banks of data files. But he also has time to think. He is never holding up the computer which is racing ahead with other work. Possibly dozens, or even hundreds, of operators, are all using terminals at the same time.

The mass of different programs that are needed will be stored in backing files, such as drums or disks. When the computer needs a program it will read it into its core storage to execute it—permanently in core there will be an *executive program* which organizes all the activity. The executive program will read other programs into core when they are needed. It will enable different programs to operate in parallel. The aims of a dynamic data-processing system today, then, are likely to involve the tying together of different decisions or actions so that some process can be carried out more efficiently. Functions that before were done on separate computer runs may be linked, for example, doing stock control at the same time as prebilling. Elements of an operation that are separated by distance, such as the allocation of trucks to jobs in a trucking concern, or cars on a railroad may be coupled together. Data may be collected from many different points and correlated in sufficient time to control some process. This may be a business process like the selling of airline seats, or an operational process, such as the scheduling of work through a factory, or a technical process, such as the testing of a jet engine with many instruments.

The real-time system may disseminate information from its files to persons making enquiries or carry out processing to give quick answers to questions. It may enable state and local governments to integrate their record keeping. It may be installed to give speedier action in some situation, for example, bank customers queuing to draw cash in their lunch hour, or two airplanes on a possible collision course over an airport. It may be installed simply because it is the cheapest way of handling data-transmission links. It will enable companies or departments too small to own a computer to share the cost of a distant machine and rent the terminals for their work.

Perhaps most important of all, real-time processing is going to be a part, sometimes a small part, of information-handling systems in numerous types of organizations.

Some of the work in a company is likely to be commercial batch processing; some, scientific calculations; some, real-time; but everywhere the trend is toward a computer or network of computers that integrates these different types of processing. This is likely to involve large "random-access" files and multiprogramming techniques. The programs on the system will constantly interrupt one another to give the desired response times.

It will be designed to decrease management planning cycles, to maximize turnover, to make the best use of an organization's facilities, and to provide information where and when it is wanted. It will enable an organization to deal with urgent orders rapidly or dispatch spare parts at the time they are requested, and so on. A company with a well-planned information-handling system will be able to react quickly in changing business circumstances.

This represents a change to a higher degree of automation. In making this change the programs have become more complicated because they now handle many functions over which there was manual control before.

The transactions may flow to the computer on communication lines and be stored by the machine in a queue ready for processing. The machine will load its own programs, do the work, and print the results or transmit them back. There is less changing of tape reels and setting of switches. In some systems the complete cycle of control happens automatically, without human intervention.

This change is, in a sense, the computer's "growing up." It is no longer one machine in one room with an operator making it perform a succession of functions. It is now an autonomous system carrying out all or most of its functions by itself. It can access the data it requires from its on-line files. It can check its own work and its input and, to a large extent, deal with errors. It may be one computer or many computers talking to each other. By means of telecommunication links it spreads its tentacles throughout the organization it is working in, and its nerve endings may be anywhere in a factory, or anywhere in a city, or, on the largest systems, all around the world. It communicates directly with the human beings who need its assistance, not second or third hand.

Sir Leon Bagrit in the BBC Reith Lectures of 1964* said that automation in its true sense is brought to full fruition only through a thorough exploitation of its three major elements, communication, computation, and control —the three "C's." In many data-processing installations today, computation is emphasized, but mechanized communication and control have been neglected.

A dramatic increase in the usefulness of computers is brought about when the systems analyst has in his bag of tools telecommunications, feedback control, man-machine communications, and where necessary, real-time processing.

This book discusses the equipment, the configurations, the techniques, and design calculations. It points out the technical problems that have been met with on such systems and indicates solutions to these. It discusses the

---

*Sir Leon Bagrit, *The Age of Automation*. London: Weidenfeld and Nielson, 1965.

schedule and procedures needed in installing such a system. The book concentrates mainly on techniques when a fast reaction time is needed. It discusses the applications, the economics, and the design of real-time systems in commercial usage.

2 THE BASIC BUILDING BLOCKS

Let us begin by summarizing the types of equipment available from which a data-processing system may be built up. Readers familiar with current computing hardware may skip this chapter.

In the punched-card era before computers, an installation was designed by assembling separate machines, such as calculators, tabulators, sorters, collators, and summary punches. Large installations had hosts of clanking machines with girls pushing trolleys of cards between them.

This proliferation was cleaned up considerably by the advent of the computer. One general-purpose machine replaced many punched-card devices. However, the computer steadily became more complicated. Its peripheral devices became more numerous, and again we became faced with a kit of construction-set parts that could be connected together in many configurations. Almost every month now more devices are added to the collection. This is especially true now that telecommunication facilities can be on-line. It is steadily being discovered that anything from a typewriter to a blast furnace can be on the other end of a telephone line.

Later chapters discuss in detail considerations necessary in selecting the hardware. It is much more difficult to carry out design calculations for a complex network of equipment than for separate punched-card machines or for a single general-purpose computer.

The main types of hardware, as listed in Fig. 2.1, are as follows:

1. *The Computers*

The computer is the heart of the system, performing the calculations and the logic and data manipulation. To a large extent it will control the other equipment on the system. There is often more than one computer in a system. If separate computers are used, they may or may not be connected

12

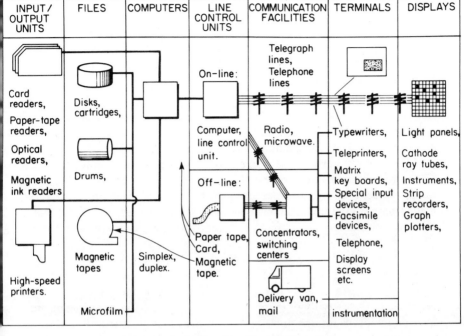

INPUT/ OUTPUT UNITS	FILES	COMPUTERS	LINE CONTROL UNITS	COMMUNICATION FACILITIES	TERMINALS	DISPLAYS
Card readers, Paper-tape readers, Optical readers, Magnetic ink readers, High-speed printers.	Disks, cartridges, Drums, Magnetic tapes, Microfilm	Simplex, duplex.	On-line: Computer, line control unit. Off-line: Paper tape, Card, Magnetic tape.	Telegraph lines, Telephone lines Radio, microwave. Concentrators, switching centers Delivery van, mail	Typewriters, Teleprinters, Matrix key boards, Special input devices, Facsimile devices, Telephone, Display screens etc. instrumentation	Light panels, Cathode ray tubes, Instruments, Strip recorders, Graph plotters,

Fig. 2.1. The main types of hardware available.

and capable of sending data to each other and interrupting each other. Often the link between them is purely manual.

There is a variety of different features on present-day computers. Most machines have "optional" instructions or mechanisms. The features desirable for different types of real-time computation are discussed in Chapter 19. It is particularly important that machines of the correct speed and core size should be used. Often the core needs to be expanded, or the machine speeded up when it is installed and in use. The capacity of a real-time system cannot be increased merely by working another shift. It is necessary therefore to use a truly *modular* computer. The computer itself should be regarded as a unit in the system which can be modified or taken out and replaced by a bigger or faster unit. For this reason most manufacturers now have a range of "compatible" computers, compatible meaning that the programs from one can run on the others without having to be rewritten.

2. The Files

The data-processing system must store a large amount of information. It may be stored in such a way that the computer can read it when it needs to without human intervention, or it may be stored on shelves on a medium such as magnetic tape or magnetic cartridges. Ideally, we would like every record to be accessible instantaneously to the computer, so that the appropriate files could be read or updated while a transaction was being processed. In actuality the file units make a record accessible in about five to five hundred milliseconds.

If the computer can read any record in a file at random in this time scale, the file is referred to as a "random-access," or "direct-access," unit. The main types of random-access files are magnetic drums, magnetic disks, and cartridges of magnetic strips or cards. Large core memories are attached to some computers and described as random-access units. They are generally too expensive, however, for the filing of records.

Magnetic tape provides a cheap form of storage. An unlimited number of records on magnetic tape can be stacked away on shelves. This is *not* random-access storage because, to find a record at random from a reel loaded onto a tape unit, the machine must search the reel serially. It would have to scan the reel, inspecting each record to see if it was the correct one. The normal method of using magnetic tape is to sort the records into a desired order so that they can be processed sequentially.

With some random-access files the recording surfaces, for example, the disk faces, are permanently in position. The total amount that can be stored is limited to the capacity of these surfaces. With others the recording medium may be removed, for example, a pack of disks may be lifted off and stored on shelves. An interchangeable recording media adds to the flexibility of the system as different records can be on the random-access file at different times. The on-line capacity of the file is, of course, limited, but off-line any

Fig. 2.2. The IBM 2314 file unit. Eight high capacity removeable sets of disks plus a ninth spare unit to increase system availability.

Fig. 2.3. The UNIVAC unidisc. A small removable random-access file.

quantity can be stored. Furthermore, if a file unit breaks down, the records can be transferred to a different unit. Some disk and cartridge units have removable recording media. Drums and other types of disk units do not.

Two time factors are important when considering files: first, the time it takes to find a record, and second, the rate of data transfer. The former is referred to as the access time. It will depend upon factors, such as the rotation time of a drum or the time taken to position a magnetic strip over a reading head. Some disk files have to move their reading heads physically in order to locate a record. This is referred to as "seeking" and takes a time ranging from sixty to five hundred milliseconds.

The most important characteristics of typical files are given in Table 2.1.

3. *Input/Output Units*

Input/output units fall into two categories, those for dealing with a mass of data, and those for handling single items or a small number of items.

Table 2.1

	Tapes	Magnetic Card Cartridges	Disks with Moving Heads	Disks with one Head per Track	Drums with Moving Heads	Drums with one Head per Track	Large Core
Random-access?	No	Yes	Yes	Yes	Yes	Yes	Yes
Removable Recording Media?	Yes	Yes	Yes or No	No	No	No	No
Typical Access Times:	Minutes	50–600 msec	20–200 msec (some much longer)	10–20 msec	20–150 msec	10–20 msec	8 μsec
Typical Capacity One Unit (in million characters):	20	600	200	∞	1000 (Univac, Fastrand II)	∞	∞
Typical Cost per Character:	Low	Fairly low	Low to medium	Medium to high	Low to medium	Medium to high	Very high

For massive input, there are card readers, paper-tape readers, optical readers of documents with marks or characters, magnetic-ink character readers, and so on. For massive output, high-speed printers are used. Fast output punches are also used. Since all these devices are slow by comparison with computer speeds, they are sometimes not connected to the main computer. They may be on a separate inexpensive computer which converts cards to magnetic tape for input to the main computer and prints magnetic-tape output. However, with many modern machines they *are* attached and work in such a way that their operation is fully overlapped with other computing. For output of data which will be read only by the computer, magnetic tape is usually used.

Fig. 2.4. Sperry Rand Corporation's UNIVAC DCT-2000 Data Communications Terminal, a combination card punch, high-speed printer and card reader, control unit and operator's console. It can send and receive information via voice-grade telephone lines at speeds of 300 characters per second. The printer, at left, can be ordered separately should printed output alone be required.

Input and output of single transactions or small groups of transactions is done by a variety of different machines. These are discussed on page 20 under the heading of "Terminals," because almost all of these devices can operate at the other end of a telecommunication line as well as operating in the computer room.

4. *Telecommunication Facilities*

Data-processing technology took a great leap forward when the computer became able to use the telephone. Digital data suitable for computer digestion can be transmitted over the telephone network as easily as the sound of the human voice. Some of the large telecommunication firms already derive a large proportion of their business from data transmission rather than voice transmission.

Virtually any telecommunication media can be used by the computer. The facilities provided differ mainly in the speed at which transmission occurs. The most commonly used facilities are telephone and telegraph lines, telephone channels being considerably faster than telegraph. Transmission faster than single telephone line can be obtained by grouping lines together or using the "wide-band" facilities offered by the telephone companies. Microwave transmission and coaxial cable circuits provide very fast point-to-point links. The majority of applications do not yet need transmission as fast as this, but it is in use where large volumes of data have to be sent quickly. Microwave transmission dishes are shown in Fig. 20.2. Short-wave radio is also used in locations or situations where the fixture of telecommunication wires or stationary microwave aerial dishes is impractical. It has been considered, for example, for transmission from moving buses in a city and for transmission from men in a railroad marshalling yard. Short-wave radio links are much slower than microwave and need elaborate error-detection circuiting if they transmit data, because of the noise that is encountered.

Noise occurs much more frequently on any telecommunication link than on other parts of the computer circuitry. Stray electrical impulses induced into the lines or originating in switchgear cause "bits" of data to be lost or erroneously added. The crackles you may hear on your telephone could change data being transmitted over that line. For this reason, error-detection circuitry and automatic facilities for retransmission are used on most data-transmission links. Some teleprinters and other devices do not have error-detection circuitry. This is the reason for the small errors often found in teleprinter messages.

Three types of facilities are mainly in use today:

1. *Low-speed lines* giving speeds of below 200 bits per second. Many telegraph circuits available permit transmission at only 45 to 75 bits per second.

2. *Voice grade lines* giving speeds up to 4800 bits per second. These include the telephone circuits over which the human voice is normally transmitted.

3. *High-speed links* giving speeds greater than 4800 bits per second.

Each of these facilities may be *simplex*, *half duplex*, or *full duplex*. Simplex means that transmission can occur in one direction only. Half duplex means that transmission can occur in either direction, but only in one direction at one time. Full duplex means that transmission can occur in both directions at the same time.

Given these parameters and a definite cost, the physical nature of the link has little or no effect on the system design providing the noise level is acceptably low. A line between two points operating at 2400 bits per second may consist of overhead telephone lines, a share of a coaxial cable, or a share of microwave circuit. This is the problem of the common carrier, such as American Telephone and Telegraph Company or Western Union in America, or the General Post Office in England, or the Postes Telegraphes et Telephones in France.

The communication lines may be privately owned or leased from a telecommunication firm. The public network is used with some machines so that one dials up the computer and establishes the connection before transmitting.

5. Line Control and Buffering Devices

Many communication lines can enter one computer system, and all may be transmitting at once. One line may have several input/output devices attached to it, and several man-machine conversations may be going on in parallel. All of this activity has to be controlled, and the computer system has to provide temporary storage for the transactions being received and transmitted.

The main computer may be able to control the transmission while it is carrying out its other processing. Alternatively, a separate computer or lesser device may be used, and this feeds data a character at a time or a message at a time to the main computer.

Some form of line control may be needed at a remote location. A device is sometimes used which accepts data from several low-speed lines and pumps it over a high-speed line to the computer. The converse happens with outgoing transmission. This remote *store-and-forward concentrator* lessens the length of communication lines used and so lowers their cost.

Other devices concerned with the communication line network are exchanges, switching centers, and computers for routing message traffic in a large organization. These are discussed in Chapter 20.

Often the communication lines are not on-line to the computer. Data arriving at the computer center may be punched into cards or paper tape; they may be written directly onto magnetic tape or stored on disks. This is possible when no fast response is needed to the terminal locations. Generally speaking, for a small number of lines, the cost of off-line telecommunication facilities are lower than on-line for a small number of lines. For a large number of lines it becomes cheaper and easier to use on-line communications.

The economics of the communication facilities are very much tied up with what response time, or turn-around time, is needed. For a response time in minutes on-line facilities are demanded. For a response time in hours off-line facilities are good enough if they are in fact cheaper than on-line.

A turn-around time of eight hours or so, depending upon distance, may be attainable using automobiles or delivery vans. If two days or so is acceptable, the mail services might provide the cheapest answer.

6. *Terminals*

A vast and ever-growing array of devices can be attached to communication lines for transmitting data to a computer. These can be devices into which data are entered by human operators or which collect data automatically. Data collected automatically may be in analogue form, such as temperature or pressure readings; it may be in the form of impulses, as from flowmeters or devices for counting. Whatever form, if it is sent over telecommunication lines, it is first converted to digital characters. Analogue-digital converters are used either remotely or on the computer site if the computer is close to the instrumentation.

Similarly, the output devices can be analogue, impulse-controlled, or

Fig. 2.5. Bell System Dataspeed. Tape transmission system. A remote location can be dialed and data transmitted at voice line speed.

digital. They can present information for human use, or they can control machines, valves, or other devices automatically.

Terminals for human use may be typewriters or other keyboard machines. They may permit a two-way conversation with the computer or be a remote equivalent of the computer-room input/output devices. Paper-tape readers and card readers may provide input over communication lines. Printers may provide the output. Figure 2.5 shows a Bell System terminal for transmitting data from paper tape over a dialed line. Figure 2.6 shows a Honeywell

Fig. 2.6. A Honeywell Data Station which combines several input and output devices into single remote communications terminals that can be linked to a distant computer over telephone lines. The modular terminal can (left to right) optically scan bar-coded documents, read paper tape, print at high or medium speeds, read punched cards (unit behind operator), and punch paper tape depending upon the devices connected to it.

Data Station which can carry out a variety of operations. This operates over a voice line at about 1200 bits per second. It can scan bar-coded documents, read cards and paper tape, punch paper tape and print.

Terminals which give real-time answers to human operators must be designed to give the most efficient man-machine interface. The operators obtain their *image* of the system from the terminals they are using. These devices should present information in a form that is as familiar as possible and should respond sufficiently adroitly to avoid making the operator impatient.

The latter is especially so if the operator is a burly manual worker, for example, who is likely to thump the machine if it does not respond to his pressing the keys.

The information given to the operator may have to be in *hard-copy* form, or it may not. If not, a versatile device like a cathode-ray tube may form the terminal (Fig. 2.7), or a telephone might be used. Various means have been devised for making the computer talk with a human voice. At first this was regarded as a cute piece of laboratory showmanship, entertaining but of no practical value. Now, however, it is being installed by many firms because it is the cheapest way to make the computer give information over the telephone network. On some systems an almost unlimited number of human-voice words may be stored in digital form on the files. A person wanting information from the machine dials it on the telephone. After establishing contact he dials his enquiry in a coded form. The machine assembles appropriate words in reply and speaks them clearly over the telephone.

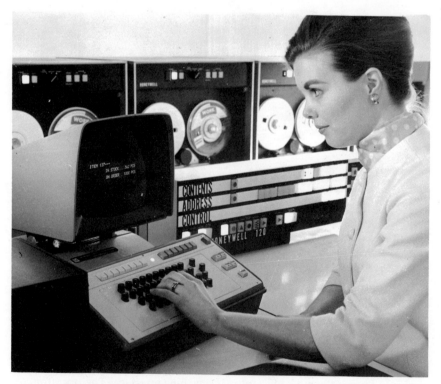

Fig. 2.7. A Bunker-Ramo display seen here with a Honeywell 200 computer. Like other terminals this can be hundreds of miles from the computer, connected by telephone line.

Table 2.2

Document Transmission Terminals	Human-input Terminals	Answer-back Devices and Displays
Paper-tape readers/punches	Keyboard-like typewriter	Typewriter
Card readers/punches	Special keyboard	Printer
Magnetic-tape units	Matrix keyboard	Teleprinter
Badge readers	Lever set	Passbook printer
Optical document readers	Teleprinter	Display tube
Microfilm	Telephone dial	Light panel
Plate readers	Push buttons	Graph plotter
	Light pen with display tube	Strip recorder
	Facsimile machine	Dials
	Plate reader	Telephone
	Badge reader	Facsimile machine

Table 2.2 lists some of the devices in use for input of data from documents, and for human input and replies. Many terminals use combinations of the facilities listed, and a great variety of shapes and sizes exist. Some systems use big display boards as their output, so that they give information to a large number of people at once. Group displays may be used so that the computer may be interrogated by a member of the group.

3 BASIC
TECHNIQUES

Two types of approach have been used in commercial data processing for some time—batch processing and in-line processing. The majority of installations still exclusively employ the former. Large batches of transactions are gathered together and sorted so that they can be run in parallel with a tape or card file in the same sequence. Cards may be pulled from card files and merged with the transaction cards ready for processing. After the run, decollating or more sorting may take place so that the batch can be run in parallel with another file. In large commercial installations doing batch processing, a high proportion of the time is taken up in sorting.

IN-LINE PROCESSING *In-line* processing was introduced and used in the late 1950's on machines, such as the IBM 305 RAMAC, and then on more elegant computers. Here the data were held in random-access storage so that any record could be read or updated in less than a second—without any time-consuming sorts having to take place. As soon as a transaction was punched into a card, it could be processed and all the relevant files updated. A simple *in-line* system is illustrated in Fig. 3.1. Orders from customers are used for preinvoicing and stock control. Cash transactions are processed. An order card contains a customer number and several part numbers with the quantities ordered. The computer looks up the appropriate customer and stock records and updates these. It composes and prints an invoice. If the stock drops below preset reorder points, a reorder card is punched. If, for some reason, an item on the customer's order cannot be met, another exception card is punched. Similarly, cash transactions cause appropriate fields in the customer records

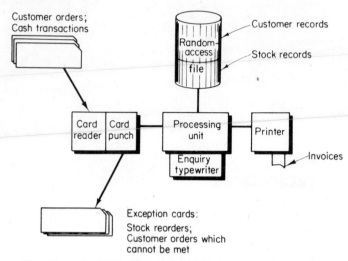

Fig. 3.1. A simple "in-line" system. This and the following three figures illustrate the kind of progression that has taken place in this type of data processing in the last eight years.

to be updated. The customer orders and cash transactions could be mixed in the same input deck, but often this would not be done as it might cause the computer to have to reload programs.

A run of this type on an in-line machine was usually slow compared with a run on a batch-processing machine because the references to the random-access file were time consuming. However, lengthy sorting operations were avoided, and there was no need to organize the processing into a cycle of operations which might spread over several days. Each order could be processed very shortly after it was received. The records in the files were kept up to date, and enquiries could be made to them at any time by means of the enquiry typewriter. The data-processing programs had certain points written into them at which they could be interrupted by an enquiry. The appropriate record from the file was typed out in answer to the enquiry.

TELECOMMUNICATION LINKS The random-access files in use today are a vast improvement on the early ones, and a simple extension to the in-line concept has been made by permitting the input cards to be entered and the enquiries typed at a distance from the data-processing center. The card reader, typewriter, or other input/output devices may be at the other end of telecommunication links. When telecommunication links are used, they may or may not be connected directly to the computer. A directly connected link, as stated earlier, is referred to as an on-line link; otherwise it is off-line. (The confusing similarity between the terms on-line and in-line does not convey a relationship in their meaning.)

Figure 3.2 shows a system in which transactions arrive from distant depots or warehouses on paper tape and replies are returned in the same manner, as with a teleprinter network. Whereas the data-transmission links are still off-line, the system permits a number of enquiry stations to be used on-line. On some systems the on-line units must be within a few thousand yards of the computer on multicore or coaxial cable. Such units are usually within the same building or factory, and it is referred to as an "in-plant" system. Units on the other end of telephone or telegraph lines are referred to as "out-plant."

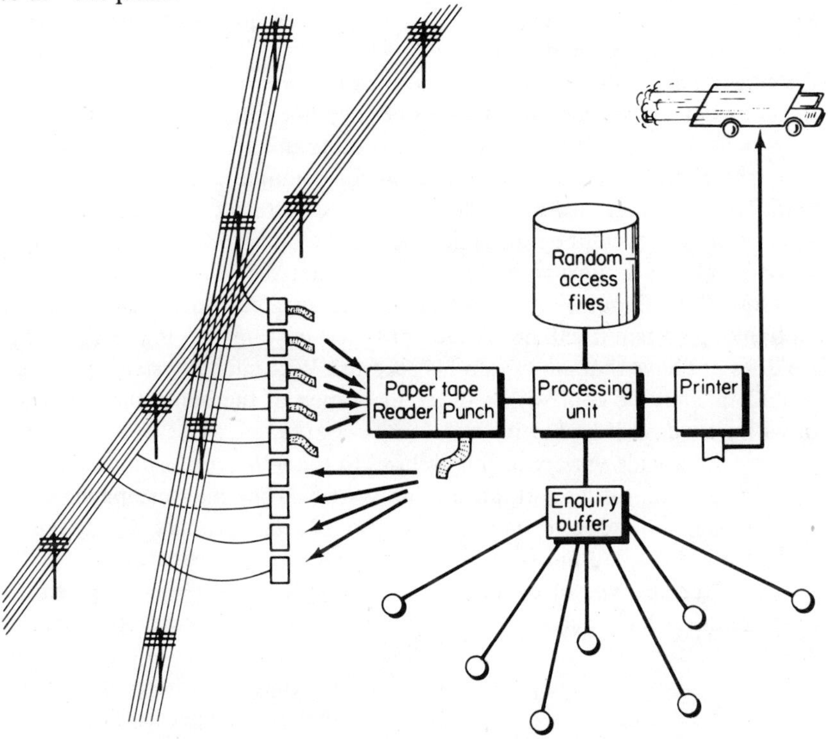

Fig. 3.2. Off-line data transmission links; on-line, in-plant enquiry stations.

The processing of transactions from paper tape in this system is still in-line. The processing of enquiries is real-time, as an answer is given while the enquirer is at the enquiry unit. The distinction between in-line and real-time processing becomes rather blurred, and some people in commercial data processing have used the term real-time to refer to the systems here described as in-line. Others reserve the term real-time for all on-line data-transmission systems, though the processing in an on-line system could look very similar to that in the system in Fig. 3.1. There is, however, a fundamental distinction between a system which *must* give an answer within a certain short period and a system which stacks transactions for processing as soon as it works its way to them. This is discussed further in the next chapter.

ON-LINE
SYSTEMS

In a system with many more data-transmission links than in Fig. 3.2, the handling of paper tape becomes congested. Furthermore, the cost of the paper-tape units with adequate checking and retransmission facilities plus the cost of their operators becomes greater than the cost of taking the communication lines directly into the computer. The system therefore becomes on-line, rather than off-line.

There are many other reasons for using an on-line system. Validity checks can be made on transactions at the time they are entered, and so mistakes can be picked up immediately while the distant terminal operator is in contact. The terminal can be used for enquiries or for communicating with the computer. The computer can be instructed to take certain types of action. The computer may process the transaction before the operator leaves the terminal and so check for any exceptional conditions that the operator may be able to do something about. For example, it may check a customer's credit status. In a banking system it will notify a teller that a customer trying to withdraw cash does not have that amount in his account. With such a system, although the account may be kept with a different branch of the bank, the customer can withdraw cash if he has it.

There are a wide variety of possibilities in the *terminals*, or units that are used for communicating with an on-line system. They may use paper tape, cards, or magnetic tape or have only keyboards and printers. Cathode-ray tubes or other display units are used. Terminals are tailored to the specific needs of a certain type of operator of industry; for example, savings banks use terminals which automatically update customers' passbooks. Airlines have terminals specially designed for booking seats. A variety of transmission speeds are possible, ranging from those of teleprinters to those of fast line printers, or ranging from paper-tape to magnetic-tape speeds. The speeds in use today on conventional telegraph and telephone circuits range from 6 characters per second to about 400 characters per second. Faster speeds than about 400 characters per second today need more than one telephone channel, but there is no fundamental problem in obtaining much higher speeds with grouped lines or microwave links.

Figure 3.3 illustrates a possible on-line development of systems in Figs. 3.1 and 3.2. The main plant computer now receives data or enquiries directly from its terminals. It will answer enquiries almost immediately but may stack other data on the magnetic tapes so that they wait their turn for processing. A *data-collection system* is also on-line to the computer, providing up-to-the-minute shop-floor data for production scheduling, answering delivery enquiries, and so on. A subsidiary factory, too small to afford its own com-

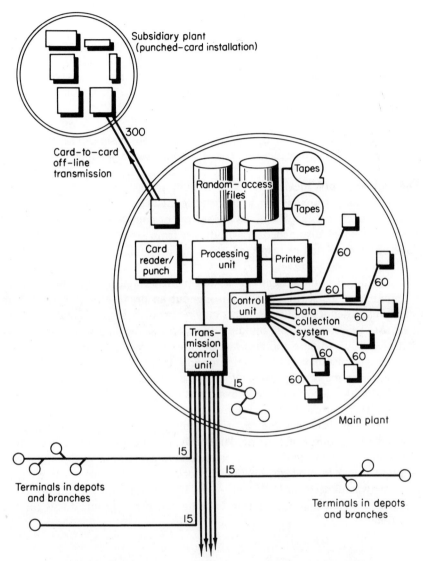

Fig. 3.3. On-line terminals in branches and depots. An in-plant data collection system. An off-line card-to-card link with a subsidiary factory. Figures are typical transmission speeds in characters per second.

puter, has a punched-card installation. The versatility and power of this is increased by having an off-line card-to-card transmission link to the computer center. The cards are processed by the computer, with a low priority, and the results sent back on card.

DATA
COLLECTION
SYSTEM

Many companies had their first introduction to data transmission from an in-plant data-collection system. Having successfully installed applications, such as payroll, invoicing, accounts, and so on, the data-processing team looked toward the production side of the business. They found that many of the procedures being run used data which were out of date. Often, also, they were inaccurate. To rectify this, terminals were installed on the shop floor.

A data-collection system can be on-line or off-line. If it is off-line, cards or paper tape are punched for later machine processing. The shop-floor terminals can be card readers, workmen's badge readers, paper-tape readers, or often special data-collection devices. Robust and easy-to-use keyboards and numeric entry devices have been built to be operated by workmen. Often the data transmission is unidirectional. The terminals are used for reporting such facts as when jobs are started or completed, what goods have been received or dispatched or withdrawn from stores, when certain items have been completed or inspected, what the availability of machine tools is, and so on.

A data-collection system can be out-plant as well as in-plant and such terminals may be scattered wide throughout an organization. Terminals in warehouses, depots, and sales offices may report orders, shipments, deliveries, inventory levels, and so on, building up records at the data-processing center that give an up-to-date and accurate picture, which is used for planning and control. The installation of a computer and data-collection system has often resulted in a major improvement in the accuracy with which records are kept and with which facts are known. It is often only when a firm has gone through this exercise that it realizes how inaccurate its information was before. The inefficiencies and chaotic planning that such a system can reveal have proved a source of surprise. Higher management did not realize before how much workers' time was idle or underemployed, how much capital was tied up in work in progress, how much stock was unnecessary, or how much business was unnecessarily turned away. This type of system can bring the manner in which the organization is being run precisely into focus for the first time.

CLOSING
THE LOOP

Data collection is only a first step toward the use of a computer in helping to control an organization. However it is an essential and often difficult first step. As with the process-control systems summarized in Chapter 13, a computer-assisted system of management control must start with some means of forming an up-to-date and, so, constantly changing set of records describing the situation to be controlled. The computer must form an image of the situation as in Fig. 13.5. The second step is to formulate the decision rules needed to improve the situation. Whereas on a process-control system this may not be possible until after the data have been collected, on an administrative scheme it may be part of the initial plan; and so the third step of "closing the loop," or setting up means of controlling what is happening, may begin as soon as the methods of collecting data have been installed and "debugged."

With relatively simple processes, such as reordering stock from a known manufacturer or issuing a work ticket stating the next job to go on a machine tool, the controlling action may be automatically taken by the computer. However, many of the controlling actions will still be management decisions but with management making use of the computer as an aid to decision making. The computer becomes a management information system and has two types of communication with the men who use it.

Firstly it produces reports, formulated as clearly as possible and highlighting exceptional conditions or areas that need attention, rather than producing an overwhelming mass of routine figures. These may be printed on a high-speed printer at the computer center or transmitted directly to where they are needed. Work tickets may be printed by typewriters on the shop floor or in the foreman's office; bills of lading may be printed by teleprinters at depots; exceptional conditions which should be dealt with urgently may be printed in a manager's office. Lengthy reports needed in distant plants may be transmitted there and printed on printers of higher speed than typewriters.

Secondly, the computer may operate in a conversational mode. Management, foremen, sales, and other personnel may make enquiries, inspect information in the computer's files, possibly ask the computer what would be the effect of certain types of decision, and possibly modify the records in the machine. The computer may print out status messages for management or supervisors when certain points are reached in a process. The men in question may change the levels at which this occurs, saying, for example, "Give me a report when batch 126 is completed," or "Print out the booking status when 120 seats have been sold." The possibilities in man-machine communications are endless.

CENTRALIZATION OF INFORMATION   The information that is acquired using a data-collection system, or, indeed, other means of input to the data-processing center, is likely to be of value, not to one functional department of a firm or organization, but to several. Likewise the data on the files are of value to different departments. The use of the computer is likely therefore to cut across the formal divisions between departments. It would be wrong to have, as has sometimes happened in the past, one data-processing setup for the accounts department, one for production control, and so on.

A centralized information-processing group is needed to serve *all* the various departments. This will have the advantage of:

1. Reduction of duplication in data collection. If a data-collection system is used, its value is enhanced if it serves as many departments as possible.

2. Reduction of duplication in records kept. A compact file organization can be designed that serves all departments and minimizes file reference times.

3. The accessibility and usefulness of the data available can be increased.

4. The operation of the firm can be optimized by tying together separate decisions.

In a very large organization it may be more difficult to cut across departmental lines, but the value of doing so is greater. In a Rand Corporation research study* on the data-processing needs of state and local government, the value of centralizing the vast files that are kept becomes clearly apparent. In an organization this large, centralization of the files does not necessarily imply centralization of processing, provided that high-speed telecommunication facilities are available.

SUPERVISORY PROGRAMS   In a system which carries out many functions, for example, that in Fig. 3.3, there can be much activity going on in the computer at the same time or almost at the same time. There are real-time enquiries to be answered, transactions from terminals which may be dealt with as they arrive or may be stacked and then processed as soon as possible, cards to be processed with lower priority, and in fact, many other jobs which are important but do not need a fast response time. All of this activity must continuously be scheduled and controlled by the computer as it is happening. Priority decisions must be made moment by moment to decide what the computer is to attend to next. The many different input/output activities must be coordinated, and interrupts, which will be occurring constantly, must be dealt with. All of this is the work of a *Supervisory Program* or a set of Supervisory Programs. These are also referred to by names such as Control Program, Monitor, Executive, Operating System, and so on, but will be referred to consistently throughout this book as Supervisory Programs.

There are two types of program in the final working system—those which carry out the required data processing, referred to throughout this book as

*Edward F. R. Hearle and Raymond J. Mason, *A Data Processing System for State and Local Government*, a Rand Corporation research study. Englewood Cliffs, N.J.: Prentice-Hall, Inc., 1963.

Application Programs, and those which coordinate and augment these, the Supervisory Programs. The Supervisory Programs carry out the input/output operations and some of the "housekeeping" functions needed by the Application Programs. They perform the fairly elaborate work of controlling the data-transmission links. The programmers writing the Application Programs can think of the Supervisory Programs almost as part of the machine system. They are not programming merely a computer, but a computer plus a set of Supervisory Programs. In this way the Application Programs can be written almost independently of one another and can operate together in a machine carrying on as much simultaneous activity as that in Fig. 3.3.

MULTIPROGRAMMING   A computer with a number of telecommunication links will often be receiving and transmitting on several at once. It may be logging these transactions on tape or disk, or reading them from tape or disk, or merely using core for this. The telecommunication activity will be going on at the same time as processing. In this sense the machine will be doing *multiprogramming*, rather like a batch-processing computer reading cards to tape or tape to printer at the same time as doing the processing.

There are, however, requirements for these machines to do a much higher degree of multiprogramming than this. The early in-line machines were inefficient because a random-access file reference took half a second or so and the processing took much less than this. The processing unit had to sit idle much of the time while the disk-file unit was clonking its seek arm up and down, or in and out. Modern random-access files execute their seek more quickly, but to the computer which thinks in microseconds it still seems a long business. Therefore, to reduce computer idle time as much as possible, several seeks may be overlapped and several transactions processed in parallel. As soon as the handling of one transaction reaches a point at which no more processing can be done until a file reference is completed, work starts on the next transaction.

To differentiate this type of processing from other meanings of the word multiprogramming, the term *multithread* processing is used. A "thread" is the sequence of actions that are necessary to process one transaction. Multithread means that several threads are partially completed at one time. The early in-line machines were all single thread in their operation, and indeed many in-line and real-time computers still are today. Some restrict the number of threads that can be going on at once, others do not. In some of the large and fast real-time systems, as many as twenty transactions may be in core, partially processed, at one time. The threads may each need different programs, and the transactions being processed at once may be of different types. An elaborate set of Supervisory Programs is needed, and on a system with a high degree of multithread operations it needs to be efficiently written or a considerable wastage of core and time will result.

SHARED COMPUTERS   When different people use such a system, it is possible for them to be quite independent of one another. They may be using different records and different programs. This, of course, becomes expensive, and the cost of different response times must be taken into consideration, as discussed in the next chapter.

The question of different users having independent access to a large machine becomes attractive to organizations or groups within an organization who cannot afford their own computer. They may be faced with the alternative of either owning a small and very limited computer or punched-card installation or having a part share of a large machine. They could, of course, have the use of a large machine if they went to a data center or service bureau, but this, while useful, entails waiting perhaps one day, or maybe several days. A part share of an on-line machine gives them a terminal in their own plant or office which behaves almost as though they had their own computer. Furthermore, they can have their own data stored in the files of the computer and quickly accessible. A small firm has just the same need for a fast response time as a large firm, and this may be the only way it can be achieved economically.

Separate small banks have arranged to share the same computer, each bank having its own on-line terminals. Separate stockbrokers have discussed the possibility of using a centralized computer. Subsidiary firms within a group or divisions within an organization have combined their computing. But, at the time of writing, the vast potentialities of this technique lie largely untouched. There has been talk of computer centers being set up with large numbers of on-line users, each of whom would be too small to own even a punched-card installation. This would enable the computer manufacturers to penetrate a vast market that is today unavailable to them. The grocer on the street corner, the small bank, the new business could all have a terminal on their premises and a minute share of a distant computer. Data processing, once the rich man's prerogative, is coming to the masses.

LINKED COMPUTERS   Figure 3.4 shows the type of computer arrangement that a number of medium-sized and large firms have today. The main plant in this illustration has a powerful data-processing center using random-access files and tape. The laboratories have a large scientific computer. Some of the sub-

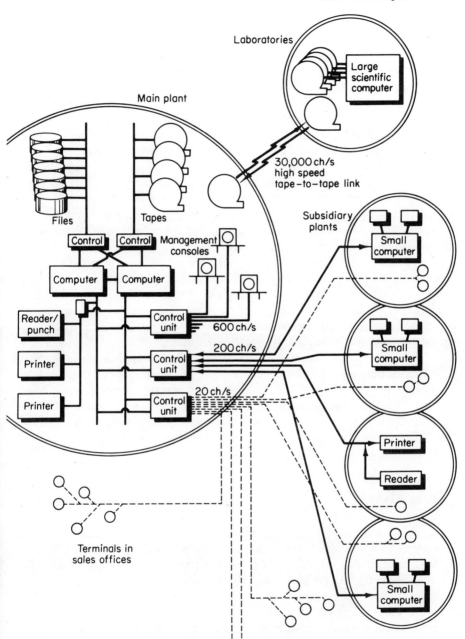

Fig. 3.4. Large computer center at main plant with links to computers in subsidiaries and laboratory. Figures are typical transmission speeds in characters per second.

sidiary plants have small card computers which they use for routine work, such as payroll and invoicing. The small plants use the large computer at the main plant for production scheduling and other jobs needing a machine with a larger core and random-access files. Some of these jobs need a fairly fast response and produce a fair quantity of printing, so the small computer is directly connected to the large computer and the small computer's printer is used. The smallest plant of those on the diagram does not have a computer. It has a medium-speed card reader and printer attached to the main plant's computer, and this does all the data-processing work of the plant.

Management members in the main plant are provided with on-line cathode-ray tubes to give them the best means of communicating with the computer. A network of enquiry terminals is used in sales office, depots, and subsidiary plants. Some of the messages from the subsidiary plants need a reply which takes a considerable amount of printing, and so this is returned, possibly a little delayed, on the printer of their computer.

The laboratories have a large scientific computer which uses an operating system such as a FORTRAN monitor. The engineers and market research staff at the main plant make considerable use of this, and their programs and data are transmitted by a high-speed magnetic-tape link. It is convenient for this to be off-line. Engineers at the subsidiary plants can also use it by sending their data to the main plant for retransmission.

With many real-time and on-line systems two computers are used. This increases the certainty of receiving a reply as, when one computer breaks down, the other comes on-line. It does not necessarily mean that one computer sits idle, because the installation is usually planned so that machines share the load or so that the on-line machine has other work to do. Various configurations designed for increasing the system's reliability are discussed in Chapter 5.

TIME SHARING   In scientific and engineering work, programs are often run once only, and, in contrast to the repetitive processing of commercial work, much of the computer's time is occupied in program testing. The scientists who use such a machine may have little interest in programming as an art but want to get their programs written, debugged, run, and then perhaps modified, as quickly as possible. A program may have a number errors in it when it is written and need a dozen or so quick shots on a computer with a few minutes' manual inspection between each to make it workable. It is often the case that a scientist has to wait six hours, twenty hours, or even two or three days in order to receive the results of a computer run. This has been overcome by setting up *time-shared* computers, in which many programmers use the computer at once, sitting at real-time consoles, or terminals. The terminals, as before, can be a long way from the computer.

A Supervisory Program makes the computer devote a portion of time to each terminal operator in turn. It may scan around all of the terminals in a few seconds. The user sees the results of his run in minutes rather than hours or days. A program which may have taken two weeks and much desk effort to debug before may now be completely finished within an afternoon. The scientists are now able to make much more use of the machine than before. Time sharing of this type is discussed in Chapter 6.

LARGE NETWORKS   The network of terminals in many installations is quite small, and each can be on a communication line going directly to the computer. Others, however, have many terminals; some, over a thousand. Certain organizations have a large number of teleprinters which must communicate with each other and, now, also with the computer.

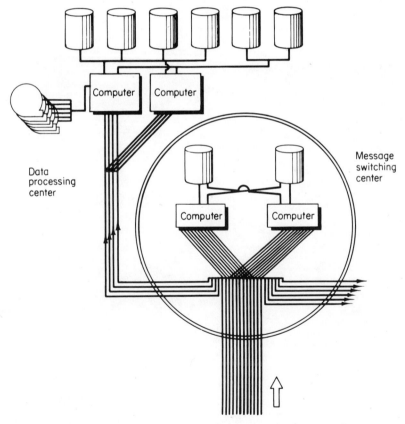

Fig. 3.5. A message-switching center passing a portion of its traffic onto the data-processing center.

Some form of *exchange* or *store-and-forward unit* may be used on a large network. Sometimes a *message-switching center* is used which is, itself, a real-time computer. It analyzes the routing instructions on all the transactions sent to it, stores them, and sends them to those teleprinters or terminals in the organization that need to receive them. It communicates directly with the data-processing center and controls the communications network. Such a computer may be part of the data-processing center or may be separate, as in Fig. 3.5.

These concepts are discussed in Chapters 15 and 20.

4 RESPONSE TIME

Many of the considerations discussed in this book are in some way connected with the response time, or turn-around time, that a user obtains from a computer system.

Response time, as discussed earlier, is the time a system takes to respond to a given input. For an operator using a terminal keyboard in real time, it may be defined as the interval between the operator's pressing the last key of the input message and the terminal's switching on lights or typing the first character of the reply. For different kinds of systems it may be defined similarly: the interval between an event and the system's response to the event. In a chemical plant it may be the interval between reading instruments and making appropriate adjustments to valves, heaters, and so on; in a factory it may be the interval between management's requesting certain information and receiving it, or the interval between facts' becoming available and their being processed; in a laboratory, the interval between a scientist or engineer's completing a FORTRAN program and seeing its results.

Ideally one would like the response time of all data processing to be very short. However, this is too costly and one has to compromise, evaluating where a fast response is needed and where it is not. Systems worth calling real-time may respond in seconds or minutes; other on-line systems may take an hour or so before a transaction is processed. Systems with off-line data-transmission links may possibly take several hours. When a periodic batch-processing job cycle is used, the work may have to wait its turn for several days, and when the mail is used for sending transactions to the computer, the response will also take days.

The decision to use data-transmission links is really a question of response time. There are other, slower means of bridging distances which are cheaper than data transmission. When very large volumes of data need to be sent, as is the case on some systems, it may even be quicker *not* to use a communication line. If five million characters have to be sent over a voice grade line with equipment that can handle about 250 characters per second, this takes approximately six hours. Higher-speed facilities may be too expensive, and a station wagon might cover the distance in less time.

Similarly, the use of random-access file units is often decided upon because of the required response time. When serial data files with a low activity ratio are to be processed, random-access units may give a cheaper system configuration than the use of tapes; but often these units are selected because they permit random processing and hence give a fast turn-around time.

It is possible when examining the various available system configurations to work out the *cost* of having different response times. If this is done, the *value* of different response times should also be considered. This is more difficult because often so many intangibles are involved, such as the value of improved customer service, the value of giving management up-to-the-minute information whenever they want it, and the improvements that result from shortening an organization's reaction time. Figures 4.1 and 4.2 illustrate how the cost of systems giving different response times may vary. They also indicate how the value of the system may vary with its response time. In

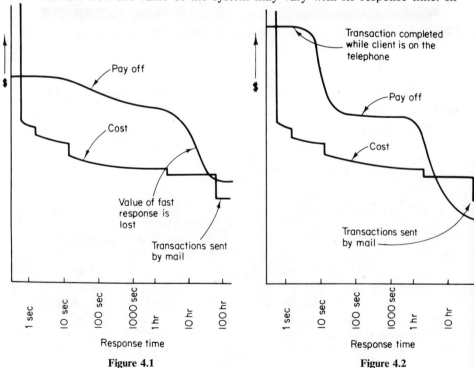

Figure 4.1   **Figure 4.2**

some applications the value of having a fast, or real-time, response is considerably greater than that of a slow response. In other applications the payoff curve would be flatter, less dependent on response time.

The various functions carried out by one system often need different response times. The curves in Figs. 4.1 and 4.2 are likely, therefore, to be an oversimplification. *The systems analyst, when making his study, should determine what response time each of the various functions of the system requires.* Some systems may need a very fast processing of urgent transactions and enquiries, processing in an hour or so of other transactions, and a background of processing with no urgency.

**TYPES OF
RESPONSE TIME**   The response-time requirements commonly found may be divided into the following categories:

1. *Immediate.* Systems controlling a technical process may need to give a very fast response to certain events. A microswitch closing or a pressure's being exceeded may cause an immediate interruption of the program being run. A program to deal with the condition would be executed to give the fastest response possible.

2. *Conversational.* People may be using the computer in a conversational manner, for example, to answer enquiries, to make an airline booking, to debug a program, or to process a bank transaction while the customer stands at the window. In this case the response time must be geared to human reaction time. Less than one second is unnecessarily fast. More than fifteen seconds is too long, and the human terminal operator will become impatient. If the operator is carrying on a complex conversation with the computer, the response needs to be fairly fast (in human terms). Some of the airline systems that record all the necessary details about passengers making bookings were ordered with a contract saying that they must react to 90 per cent of the transactions in less than three seconds.

From the terminals the operators of a system gain an image of its capability. It is sometimes thought desirable to impress the user of the system with its slickness by giving a response of half a second or so—still long in computer terms. Sometimes this is no more expensive than a three-second response. However it may be more expensive, so the programming and throughput considerations need to be examined before such a decision is made.

3. *As soon as is convenient.* Some transactions from terminals may need to be processed quickly, within minutes or seconds if possible, but are not geared to the speed of a human conversation. A manager may say on a terminal, "Print me a report on so-and-so as soon as is convenient." A teletype message reaching an airline reservation system will not need an immediate answer back, as do conversational messages from the agent sets,

but should update the seat availability records as soon as is convenient in the computer's operations. An item received and filed by a message-switching computer should be routed to its destinations without much delay, but there is no need for a three-second response.

4. *Deferred, on-line.* Some computers receive jobs from the computer room and/or from distant terminals which can wait in a queue of jobs to be processed in an in-line manner. When the computer receives them, it stores them on a backing file such as tape or disk and works its way down to them on a basis of priority. It will not be constantly executing and reloading different programs for them as with transactions needing a fast response. One job might be to deal with a small batch of transactions, and the computer will not begin another such job until this is completed. Nevertheless the system will be designed so that the job queues do not become too large and the items will normally not have to wait longer than an hour or so.

5. *Within one day.* With many types of transaction it is desirable to complete the processing on a daily basis. Orders received this morning may be answered by today's last mail. Cost figures may be produced daily. Tomorrow's truck schedule may be determined by today's events. This degree of speed could be met by a tight cycle of batch processing, though often in-line processing will be needed. The collection and distribution of the necessary data will usually need data transmission and will certainly need this if long distances are involved.

6. *Long time available.* Some functions have no urgency and can take their place in a weekly, or longer, batch cycle. Such transactions can be sent by mail.

SYSTEM OPERATION

As well as evaluating the response time needed for the various functions that the system performs, the system's analysis team must understand the effect that different response times have on the operations of the computer. Sometimes a short response time is as easy or, what is more important, as inexpensive to achieve as a longer one; sometimes not.

Some real-time systems have high peaks of traffic at certain times of the day. A savings bank, for example, with teller terminals at the bank counter, has a flood of customers coming in during the lunch hour. Again, some real-time systems have momentary peaks of transactions lasting for only a few seconds because many terminal operators all happen to use the system at the same moment(see Fig. 24.3,p.339).If the response-time requirements are to be rigorously adhered to during these peaks, then a faster computer and/or larger core will be needed than during nonpeak operation. If, however, the peak can be flattened by delaying some transactions or some of the functions until after the peak has passed, then a more economic system is possible.

A fast response to random transactions can need a larger core and faster hardware because programs are needed at random and may have to be fetched into core. If a slower response could be tolerated, transactions needing the same program could be queued until that program is in core. This will depend upon the variation in transaction types and the amount of program they need.

Again, if transactions are processed at random, the time for seeks on the random-access files will be fairly long. If the transactions are queued, it may be possible to reduce the seek time by processing transactions which relate to a given part of the file together.

Systems with a high throughput of real-time transactions need an elaborate Supervisory Program to control their actions. This may allow many simultaneous seeks and file references and a high degree of multiprogramming. With such a Supervisory Program the system may give a response time of a second or so unless it becomes seriously overloaded. Often in such a system a response time of ten seconds would be no less expensive than one of one second.

A smaller system may process only one real-time item at a time. Here, the queuing of transactions, giving a slower response, may be of value in increasing the total throughput of the system or allowing it to perform more non-real-time work.

When different transactions reaching the system need different response times, *a means of allocating priorities* of processing is needed. This is a normal function of the Supervisory Programs. A system may be handling a *job stream* of items for low-priority in-line processing for which a response time of an hour is adequate and at the same time dealing with urgent items needing a fast response. All the transactions arrive on the transmission lines. The low-priority ones are put in the job stream, and the urgent ones are lined up for immediate processing.

As well as different functions having different response times, different *places* may also differ. It is often too expensive to give all locations of the same type an on-line terminal. A bank, for example, may put terminals in its main branches but not in its very small ones because the cost would be too high. The small branches must keep their own customer records (this is especially so in Europe) or telephone a location with a terminal if a customer tries to withdraw more than a certain sum of money. Similarly an airline may have expensive agent sets in its big sales offices but non-real-time teleprinters in small offices or remote parts of the world.

A study of the data flow needed in an organization for its computer system must place different response-time values on different functions and different locations. These will be determined by economics and by the mechanisms needed for control.

5 TIME-SHARING SYSTEMS

Most real-time systems with manually operated terminals are time shared, meaning that more than one user is using them at the same time. When the machine pauses in the processing of one user's item, it switches its attention to another user.

The term *time-sharing*, however, is commonly used to refer to a system in which the users are *independent*, each using the terminal as though it were the console of a computer and entering, testing, and executing programs of his own at the terminal. The work on programs of one terminal user is quite unrelated to the work or programs of other users. It is this meaning of the term which is discussed in this chapter and which is now common usage.

In many of the systems discussed in this book, the users do not *program* the system at the terminal, neither are the users entirely independent. They are each *using* the programs in the computer in a related manner. They may, for example, be insurance or railroad clerks possibly using the same programs and possibly using the same file areas. In the time-shared systems discussed below, the computing facility is being divided between separate users who can program whatever they wish on it, independently of one another.

There are three categories of on-line system differing by the degree of independence of the users:

1. Systems which carry out a carefully specified and limited function, for example, a banking system or a factory information system.

2. Systems in which programmers can program anything they wish at the terminals providing they all use the same language, an interpreter or compiler for this being in the machine.

3. Systems in which programmers can program anything using a variety of different languages. The latter two types of system are, in effect, dividing

up the computing facility "timewise" and giving the pieces to different programmers to use.

ON-LINE
PROGRAMMING
In the early days of computers it was common to sit down at the console of the machine to debug a program. When the machine stopped or went into a loop because of a program error, the cause of the trouble could be found there and then, and often corrected on the spot. The effect of corrections could be investigated as they were made, and only occasionally did the programmer retire from the machine to carry out a major rethinking of his program.

Those who have become accustomed to working with a computer in this deliciously wasteful manner, perhaps at night in the silent gloom of a computer factory, know that it can have significant advantages. The debugging will be over relatively quickly. The direct communication with the machine helps users to locate and correct errors and rapidly to test the validity of their thinking. Short sections of program can even be written at the console typewriter more quickly than away from the machine.

Such methods of testing rapidly gave way to more organized techniques. Decks of cards for testing, along with suitable control cards to instruct the machine what to do, are handed to an operator who feeds the computer with a batch of jobs. The programmer receives an indication of what happened to his program along with a core print-out if necessary. He may have to submit

Fig. 5.1a. A program is being checked out here on a teleprinter connected to a distant GE-235 time-sharing computer in GE's Manhattan Information Processing Center. Forty such users can employ this system simultaneously. Some of the calculations for drawing the curves in Chapter 26 were performed on this system.

Fig. 5.1b. When the machine's replies are lengthy, faster man-machine conversation can take place with a display terminal such as this GE Datanet-760* display unit.

the program many times before all the errors are corrected, and the wait between each attempt may be long.

The computer is too expensive to allow one user to monopolize it in the way described above. Direct man-machine interplay is not normally practical when the machine costs $100 per hour and the man earns $6 per hour. On the other hand, if forty men could use the machine independently at the same time, the economics would look very different. This is possible with *time-sharing* techniques.

With time-sharing, the users may be at the other end of telecommunication links and may each have consoles, typewriters, card readers, or other terminals connected to the computer. Each user regards and operates his terminal much as though it were a computer and input unit and *as though* he had the computer all to himself. Time-sharing is used for testing and writing programs as well as for executing them. The terminals of a time-shared system may be all in one organization, or the computer may be shared by different firms.

REASONS FOR TIME-SHARING   There are three main reasons for using a time-shared system:

1. *Cost.* Time-sharing permits users who could not afford their own computer to have a part share in a machine. As communication lines give them fast access to it and fast replies, it can behave much as though they had a machine on their own premises. Bulk input/output,

*Registered trademark of the General Electric Company.

for example, high-speed printing, will be limited on their premises by the speed of the communication lines used. However, economical and accessible computing services can be provided for scientific, engineering, and business groups previously unserved.

2. *Low turn-around time.* On a batch-processing system or a system with a lengthy job queue, the turn-around time can be long. It is still longer if the computer is remote from its users. To obtain a run on a heavily loaded computer may take half a day. If the data has to be sent and returned by station wagon, this may be a day; by mail, two or more days. Off-line transmission links have been installed to bridge both long and short distances. On-line batch systems are also in use so that the work is entered directly into the computer's job stream on disk or tape. On-line batch systems may reduce the turn-around time to an hour or so, depending upon how heavily loaded the system is and how long individual jobs run. However, on a time-sharing system we are generally talking about conversational turn-around times of only a few seconds and problem-solution times measured in minutes. The programmer can locate and correct half a dozen bugs in an hour rather than a week. The engineer or scientist can solve problems while sitting at the terminals of the system.

3. *Conversational mode of operating.* The user at the terminal is once again in direct contact with the machine. He can use the power of the machine to supplement his own thinking as in the old days when he might have had a computer all to himself. He is even better off now because he can use modern languages and the computer probably has a large random-access store in which elaborate Supervisory Programs, compilers, and all manner of program routines are kept. He can experiment with his programs at the terminal, testing the effect of modifications. For example, he can change parameters or logic elements of a simulation program and observe the effects of this. Man-machine interaction is being shown to expand vastly the creative power of skilled users.

The conversational mode of operating or programming a computer is likely to be of less value, perhaps, to the professional programmer than to the scientist, engineer, or statistician who occasionally needs a computer during the course of his work and is not necessarily interested in programming as an art in itself. To these men the help they can obtain from such a system and the fact that they can solve a problem in one continuous session with the machine are of great value in their work. They can see their results immediately and experiment with their approaches—for often the work of such men is experimental in nature. They can inject their own judgment and decision power while the computer is effectively at their fingertips.

TIME
DIVISION

The time-sharing computer must allocate a portion of its time to each of its users in turn. If it is designed so that it can have up to forty terminals in use at one time, for example, it may have a Supervisory Program which permits not more than one-quarter second to be spent on each terminal. It might scan the terminals in a given sequence, and, if it does not complete attending to a terminal in one-quarter second, then it leaves this terminal and its program, and will return to it where it left off on the next scan. This means that the longest time a terminal operator can be kept waiting for a simple conversational reply is ten seconds, but normally the time will not be nearly as long as this because most of the terminals on a scan do not occupy the computer for more then a very small fraction of a second.

Terminals which *need* a fast response because they are operating conversationally may be given priority over terminals for which a longer job is being executed. The Supervisory Program will then have two lists of work to be done: first, terminals needing conversational attention if any and, second, terminals for which a program is being executed or about to be executed. When the Supervisory Program finishes attending to any terminal, it will scan the former list first.

There are many possible variations of the means of dividing the time of the computer between different users. Different priority schemes are used. Usually an interval timer interrupts any program that is occupying the machine for too long so that adequate response times can be given to other users.

Different users will need different programs. Some of the programs may be permanently in core, such as those for carrying out routine editing of terminal input and sending routine replies. Others will be brought into core when needed from a backing file, or, if assembled or modified in core, they will be stored on a backing file for later use. As the processing unit switches its attention between the terminals using it, the programs, or some of the programs, will be ping-ponged backward and forward between the backing store and the core in which they are executed.

The files mainly in use for this are drums, disks, and large core memories. Disks, with their larger capacity but slower access time, may be used to keep a library of programs which users may ask for, or to store programs which users have entered and will need later. Drums, smaller but fast, may be used for temporarily storing programs and data that are in use and continually being transferred to and from core. Drums, like disks, have a rotation time which is long in computer terms, so a program cannot be immediately brought into core when it is needed. The computer must wait until the drum rotates to the correct position to begin reading in the program. Large core memory units, though more expensive than drums, have the advantage that no wait is involved.

SUPERVISORY PROGRAMS

The Supervisory Programs, sometimes referred to as a Monitor on time-sharing systems, schedule the work, coordinate the allocation of storage and other   facilities between the users, govern the reading in and out of temporarily stored data, and control the telecommunication facilities.

The scheduling of the sequence of operations must be done so as to maximize the utilization of the more critical system components and to maintain the required response time to all of the terminals. Control will normally be returned to the scheduling routine whenever work for one terminal is completed or when a program is interrupted by the interval timer. The scheduling routine then decides which of the various jobs requiring the computer's attention to carry out next.

Different terminals require programs occupying different amounts of core storage. Some will need only a very small program; others will need most of the core on the machine. The optimum method of allocating core is therefore not easy to determine. Programs will normally be "relocatable," meaning that they can be executed from any position in core. A program can thus be interrupted at the end of its time period, dumped on to the backing store, and at a later time brought back into core *in a different location*. Its execution continues from this new location as though no break had occurred. There are a number of different ways of achieving relocation of programs. The easiest makes use of special registers on the machine.

As the programs used are of different lengths, it may be necessary to slide them down to one end of the core each time a program is finished with or taken from core. This prevents finished programs from leaving irregular-sized "holes" which are difficult to fill. Alternatively, the core and programs may be divided into fixed-length blocks. A lengthy program would occupy several blocks and would branch from one block to another via a table saying where the blocks were in core at that time.

TYPES OF
OPERATION
The time-sharing systems now in use operate in a number of different ways. The terminals may be used to transmit and test programs before execution, or they may send data to be operated on by programs already in the files of the system. The operation may be batch, in which the input is edited, checked, and, if necessary, corrected in real-time, and then stored in a batch job stream for execution as soon as possible; or it may be "immediate," in which case execution as well as perhaps editing, compilation, and testing of the program takes place straightaway.

Some systems permit programs to be compiled in various different languages and provide most of the services that a normal computer center would give. For example, Project MAC at Massachusetts Institute of Technology gives many simultaneous users facilities for entering at distant terminals programs written in many different languages. They may assemble and test these programs and call for production runs, receiving the results on a local remote printer.

Other systems are more limited and permit use of only one language but with special on-line debugging facilities. IBM's QUICKTRAN is a language specially designed for time-shared systems to be programmed like FORTRAN and have facilities to help in on-line use. This permits three modes of operation:

1. *Command mode.* In this mode the terminal is used like a powerful calculating machine in which expressions to be evaluated are typed in a symbolic manner. The computer checks their validity and types back the results.

2. *Program mode.* Programs in the FORTRAN-like language can be keyed in on line. Many nonprofessional programmers' errors are format or clerical errors. These are picked up as the input is being keyed in, a statement at a time. The program can then be assembled and tested. Errors can be corrected by changing only those statements that need to be changed. The program can then be executed. It can be stored in the system's files for later use or subsequent modification. Immediate execution or modification of programs already in the files can be obtained.

3. *Batch mode.* This mode allows data or programs to be entered into the computer's job stream for remote batch processing. Partial programs or jobs may be accumulated on the files until a complete job is ready for running. Results will be delivered back to the terminal when convenient.

QUICKTRAN PROCESSOR

The compiler in the QUICKTRAN system, as with other such time-sharing systems, is a program which translates the terminal user's source language into a form in which it can be interpretively executed by the computer or translated back into the source language. The latter is used to facilitate source-language debugging.

The language is designed so that, as well as using FORTRAN statements, the terminal operator has a set of statements to help debugging, at the terminal, and editing of this program. The user can display any part of his program and make modifications, such as insertions, replacements, and deletions. If he has made a number of changes, he can reserialize his program. The language also contains operating statements which provide the user with the functions normally available on a computer console.

He can therefore operate the terminal as though he were sitting at a computer and no one else were using it.

INEFFICIENCY

Programming and operating a computer in a time-shared manner as described above is not as efficient a use of the machine as batch processing. The total throughput is lower, perhaps 30 or 40 per cent lower on some systems, though others are claiming considerably greater efficiency than this. Because of this, professional programmers submitting programs for batch operation will always make better use of the computing facilities than if terminals are used in a real-time manner. The advantage of time-sharing operations are being proved largely with the mass of engineers, scientists, and other computer users who have neither the time nor skill of the professional programmer. To these people time-sharing techniques are making the computer a more practical tool for solving their problems. It has now become easily accessible and fast to use. Furthermore, real-time man-machine interaction is allowing many exciting results to be achieved that were hardly possible with off-line procedures.

The use of *conventional* languages, compilers, and control programs *also* reduces the efficiency of the machine usage. They lower the total possible throughput and cause machines to be ordered with larger cores than they would otherwise have, Their use, however, has become generally accepted almost everywhere because they increase the ease with which results can be obtained from the computer. The same is happening with time-shared operations.

It seems certain that remote terminals will be used extensively in this way in the years ahead. The facilities to dial a distant computer and use it in a time-shared manner for simple data processing, scientific calculations, information retrieval, or elaborate problem solving will take some years to grow up. Stand-alone computers are likely to put up a good fight with time-sharing because the new Large Scale Integration circuitry will make it possible to build small computers at much lower cost than today. If more than 10,000 of one machine can be sold, Large Scale Integration circuitry can be mass-produced very inexpensively. However, many users will require access to centralized files, and hence time-sharing. Sooner or later such facilities will be as common as telephone service is today.

6 RELIABILITY AND STANDBY

Reliability of the equipment is an important consideration in any computer installation; however, in a situation which needs a real-time computer it is likely to be much more vital.

If a batch-processing computer breaks down and takes two hours to repair, this is normally not too serious. The staff who run it may perhaps have to work overtime to complete the day's processing. However, if a real-time system is out of action for two hours, the organization or control of a situation which depends upon it will be disrupted. There will no longer be guidance in the control of a process. There will no longer be seat availability information at the fingertips of an airline clerk or share information available to a broker. Customer files kept by the distant computer will be temporarily inaccessible.

The seriousness of a system interruption is often related to the response-time requirements. With the categories of response time listed in Chapter 4, systems needing immediate and conversational response times are seriously disrupted by two-hour interruption. Systems with "as soon as is convenient" responses may find a two-hour interruption not too catastrophic. "Deferred-on-line" and "within-one-day" systems can accept breakdowns of two hours, but not twenty-four hours.

There are basically three ways of planning for hardware failures:

1. *Duplication of equipment.* When one computer fails, a second one takes over its work. When one piece of equipment ceases to function, a second one is switched in. This is expensive. It still does not give 100 per cent reliability because the second piece of equipment may fail also. It would be more reliable to use three computers, but even more expensive.

2. *Fallback procedures.* Most faults that develop will be in one component of the system and will not be a complete failure of the entire system. Fallback

means that the system modifies its mode of operation to circumvent the error. In so doing it may give a degraded form of service but still carry out the urgent part of its job. A system may be designed with more than one computer, spare file units, and alternative data paths so that some type of fallback can be used whenever a single component failure occurs. A system may have a hierarchy of fallback procedures to deal with different eventualities, each circumventing an interruption of the more important functions of the system. The term "fail softly" is used to mean that, when a component goes out, the system uses an alternative means of processing rather than failing completely. It may then give a degraded service, but this is "graceful degradation" rather than a total collapse of the system. Any functions for which a fast response is not mandatory may be temporarily shelved.

3. *Bypass procedures.* When a system does fail and terminals become inoperative, the terminal users must still have some means of dealing with the situations that confront them. The bank teller must still be able to deal with customers who come in and ask to withdraw money. The insurance clerk, the shop foreman, and the telephone sales girl must have some standby procedure that enables them to carry on their work without real-time assistance from the computer.

The computer may make periodic print-outs of the key information in its files in anticipation of failure. These may be transmitted to the terminal operators at night or when the terminal is not in use. In a bank, for example, the balances of all branch accounts containing more than $500 may be printed at that branch, so that no amount greater than this will be paid out without checking.

Alternatively, the terminal operator may make a telephone call to a central location to obtain key information. The terminal may be used off-line to obtain human replies from a central location. In most cases the terminal operator carries on as best as possible, and the computer sorts out what has happened when it comes back on the air. When the computer is used to control the events that are happening in an optimum fashion, the events will still go on when the machine has failed but will no longer be optimized. The non-optimum bypass procedure in such cases represents a loss in revenue which may be roughly calculable.

Different functions in a system often have different reliability requirements, just as they have different response-time requirements. *When doing a survey, the systems analyst should examine each function to be performed and assess what reliability is required.* He may conclude that certain functions are vital, and immense problems would be caused if the system failed to perform them. These, therefore, need to be made as fail-safe as possible in the system design. Other functions are less vital, and it may be possible to calculate how much it is worth spending on improving their reliability. From this basis the design of the system may then proceed.

CONFIGURATIONS THAT IMPROVE RELIABILITY   No computer configuration is absolutely reliable, no matter how much money is spent on it. By duplicating or triplicating the units of the system the probability of failure can be reduced to a very small amount. Simple duplexing has doubled the cost of some of the real-time computer centers that have been installed. Today this is still unavoidable in many systems *dedicated* to a real-time job that must have very high reliability. However, other installations use two or more computers in such a way that they are fully occupied with less vital work which can stop when one of them breaks down, leaving the others to carry on the real-time work.

Figure 6.1 illustrates a number of common configurations using two computers. In the top two systems, when computer *B* breaks down, computer *A* may be able to take some limited action on its own. However, when computer *A* breaks down, all on-line telecommunication transmission will cease unless the communication lines can be temporarily attached to *B*, as is sometimes possible. However, off-line data transmission can still go on and forms a valuable standby procedure. There is a tendency today to replace systems like these with one computer now that better telecommunication facilities and the requisite software are becoming available on most computers; however, this makes the system even more vulnerable to failure.

In the *shared file system*, *A* may be able to handle all or most of the real-time work by itself. If *A* fails, off-line data transmission must be used unless the communication lines can be switched across to *B*.

The *parallel* or *load-sharing system* is valuable for real-time work and is often used with more than two computers. In the system illustrated, the two computers are needed to handle the peak traffic. During off-peak hours one of them can handle it, leaving the other free for other work, preventive maintenance, and program testing. If one computer fails at off-peak times, there is no degradation of the real-time performance. However, if this happens during a peak period, the one computer left can only carry out certain of the real-time functions.

The *duplex* configuration is a common one. The hardware needed for the real-time job is exactly duplicated so that a switchover can occur if the on-line system fails. The off-line system is available for other work, though it may be abruptly interrupted for switchover. Most of the large airline reservation systems use this configuration.

The *twin* system at the bottom of Fig. 6.1 is used when high reliability and certainty of results are vital. It is used for the BMEWS, Ballistic Missile Early Warning Systems, and was used for the manned space flights of Projects Mercury and Gemini. The input goes into both computers and is processed identically. If the results do not agree, this indicates a failure in one computer. Still more reliable would be the use of triplet computers as two of the three should give identical results (unless a highly unlikely double failure occurs).

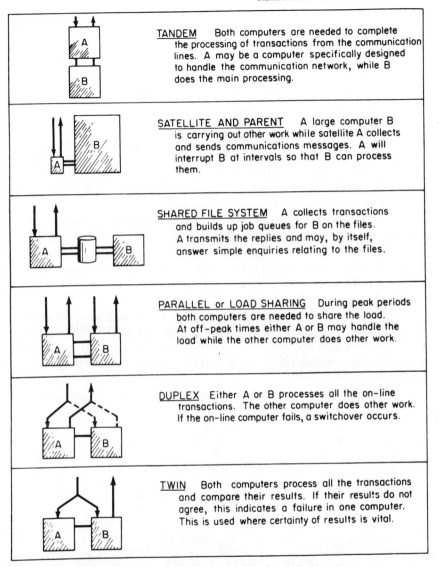

Fig. 6.1. Examples of configurations using two computers.

This is used in certain vital process or guidance control systems. It is to be used with four computers, assuming one may be out for maintenance, in the American moon-shot program.

These illustrations are an oversimplification of the problem of finding a configuration that gives standby facilities. As well as considering the processing unit, other system components and especially communication equipment must be considered.

Figure 6.2 gives an illustration of a tandem system, showing its peripheral units. For the normal processing load, both computers are needed. Computer *A* is a machine designed to handle telecommunication facilities. It receives the transmitted data, checks it, edits it, possibly queues it, and delivers transactions to computer *B*, which is ready to process them. Computer *B* can "read" a transaction from computer *A* as easily as it can obtain a card from its card reader.

When computer *B* breaks down, computer *A* is left on its own and can take two types of action. It can log the transactions on its files ready for processing when *B* comes back "on the air," or it can attempt a limited form of processing itself on a small proportion of the messages. It can read *B*'s files and so may be able to answer urgent enquiries.

When computer *A* breaks down, the communication input cannot enter the system in the normal way. Computer *B* may, however, be designed so that it can handle one or a small number of lines, possibly through a console attachment. The operator can then switch different lines into computer *B* as urgent requirements arise. Alternatively, paper tape may be punched and this fed to computer *B*.

The files also are partially duplicated in Fig. 6.2. If one file or file channel fails, the urgent data are available on the duplicate unit. This means that, whenever these data are updated, two copies must be written. If one file is off the system for a period, time must be spent updating it when it is returned to the system.

A tandem arrangement like this is generally not very satisfactory for giv-

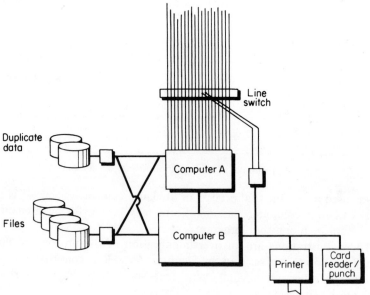

Fig. 6.2. A tandem system with limited fall-back facilities.

ing real-time reliability, though it is often better than a single computer and cheaper than a duplex system. Figure 6.3 shows a duplex system. This type of configuration is found in many of the early real-time systems for commercial work, for example, the airline reservation systems. The files in this illustration are completely duplicated. If either line control unit, computer, file channel, or any file fails, the system can switch to a combination that still carries on the complete real-time job. For real-time work only one computer is in use at any one time; the other computer may therefore do other work which may be suddenly interrupted.

Duplexing the file units is expensive and complicates the Supervisory Programs dealing with file failure and recovery from failure. Files have now been developed from which the recording media can be removed and stored on the shelves like tape reels. Such files are usually designed so that, whenever a failure occurs, the recording media, such as a pack of disks or a magnetic-strip cartridge, can always be removed and placed on a different file unit.

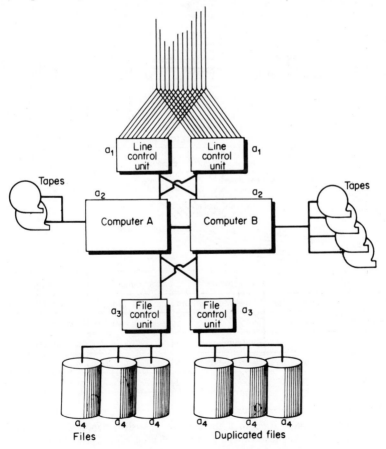

Fig. 6.3. A duplex system with duplicated data files.

It is then not necessary to duplex all the file units, but merely to have one or more standby ones in case of failure.

As well as the two-computer combinations shown above, there are a variety of configurations possible, and installed, with three or more computers. Figure 6.4 shows a three-computer system in which a computer doing non-real-time work is included in the configuration. This work may be invoicing, accounting, and so on, which was done before the real-time system was installed and now remains largely unchanged. The computer doing it, however, is linked into the real-time configuration to increase its reliability; and this also improves the ease with which accounting data are entered.

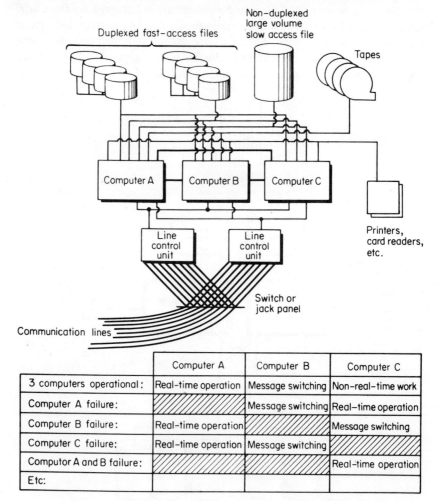

	Computer A	Computer B	Computer C
3 computers operational:	Real-time operation	Message switching	Non-real-time work
Computer A failure:	/////////	Message switching	Real-time operation
Computer B failure:	Real-time operation	/////////	Message switching
Computer C failure:	Real-time operation	Message switching	/////////
Computor A and B failure:	/////////	/////////	Real-time operation
Etc:			

Fig. 6.4. Illustration of a three-computer system handling real-time work, message switching, and batch processing. The real time work is given the highest priority when failures occur.

Message switching is also done by a separate computer, probably using a package set of programs provided for this. If one of the three computers fails, the non-real-time work is suspended and appropriate computer switchover takes place. If two computers fail, only the real-time work continues and messages to be rerouted by the message-switching programs must wait.

There are, of course, endless variations of this theme and illustrations in other chapters of this book show configurations planned to give standby or fallback facilities when units fail, for example, Fig. 3.4 on page 37, Fig. 3.5 on page 39, Fig. 16.2 on page 215, and Fig. 22.1 on page 315.

POLYMORPHISM   To arrange units of a system in a string—for example, line control unit, computer, and channel, or file control unit and file, or tandem computers, as in Fig. 6.5—gives low reliability because, if any one unit in the string fails, the whole string is out of action. The arrangement in Fig. 6.6 is better because cross switching can circumvent the failure of any one unit.

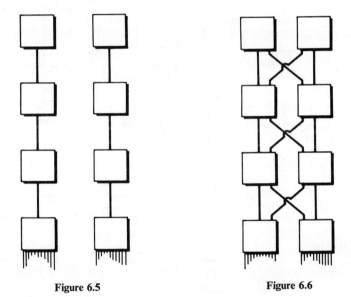

Figure 6.5   Figure 6.6

It is the design philosophy in some systems to have multiple use of relatively small hardware units so that the over-all availability of the system is high. Sometimes a number of small computers are used. Sometimes the core, the channel controls, the channels, and the processing units are all separately switchable. A system which permits many changes in this way to circumvent failures is referred to as "polymorphic." The required degree of polymorphism for an application must be decided. Figure 6.7 and 6.8 show polymorphic systems in which the core storage is separate from the processing units. Channel controllers permit a flexible means of interconnecting input/output units, core storage units, and processing units. Data from any channel may enter any core unit at the same time as other processing is taking place. Any data path between core units, processing units, or channel controllers may be disconnected with a set of manual switches. These are also used for parti-

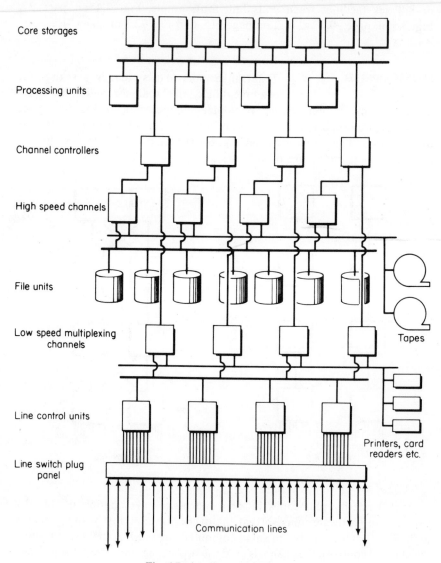

Fig. 6.7. A polymorphic system.

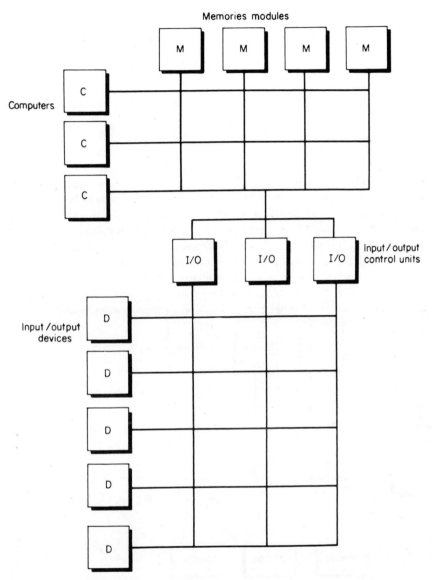

Fig. 6.8. The Burroughs D825 modular data processing system designed for real-time applications.

tioning the system if desired. The system can sense the setting of these switches.

Figure 6.8 shows a typical configuration of the Burroughs D 825 system. This system was designed primarily for real-time applications such as message switching. If a system needs 16,000 words of memory—four modules—it will probably be designed with five modules. Similarly one extra processing unit and input/output controller may be added. If more than the one redundant module fails the system is still at least partially operational. It is claimed that total down-time of a fraction of an hour per year can be attained in this way.

When programs are executed in such a system, their references to core, to files, or to input/output units must be translated, as the unit to which they refer may have been switched. This is necessary even within one core storage when relocatable segments of program are used, which may be located anywhere in the core.

On a system with many possible interconnections the switching mechanism itself can become complicated, and its reliability needs to be examined. This is especially so if the switching operates automatically or under program control. A centralized switch unit as in Fig. 6.9 may be a relatively weak link in the system. Instead, some form of *distributed switching* is needed as in Fig. 6.10. Here there are two "tails" to each storage shown. A polymorphic system may have *multiple tails* from different channels and processors. If a channel should fail, the storage unit is still accessible by other channels, and, if a storage fails, the channel can still address other storage units.

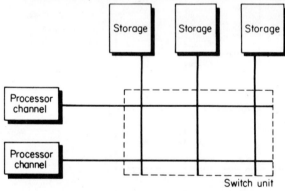

Fig. 6.9. Centralized switching.

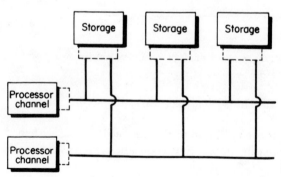

Fig. 6.10. Distributed switching.

It is likely that on some computers of the future, polymorphism will be taken much further than is shown in Figs. 6.7 and 6.8. In general the smaller the element sizes and the larger the number of alternate paths, the greater will be the reliability of the system. Alternate logic paths within the computer circuitry may well be provided as well as alternate paths between units.

The main problem of polymorphic configurations is that, the larger the number of switchable paths, the more complicated the Supervisory Programs or circuits for controlling the flow of data become. Various actions and references of the computer must be interpreted according to how the data paths are switched. The fallback, failure, and recovery procedures become very complicated. The systems in Figs. 6.7 and 6.8, for example, need very elaborate Supervisory Programs for handling these. There is a break-even point beyond which further complication of the system is not worthwhile.

SUPERVISORY PROGRAMS   In the various configurations illustrated in this chapter, Supervisory Programs must assist in the switchover and fallback procedures. These are likely to be used for some or all of the following functions:

1. Monitoring the system, checking its accuracy and that all units are operating; detecting the need for a switchover.

2. Initiating the switchover. This may be a switch between computers, files, or input/output units or a switch to an alternate communication line.

3. Rerouting the data when a switch has occurred; for example, converting a "logical" file address used by the Application Program into a machine address for the unit on which that data file is now located.

4. Substituting alternative types of units; for example, writing printer output onto tape temporarily when a printer fails.

5. Copying new file records onto a duplicate file unit, in real time, after a period of file fallback.

6. Ensuring that no transactions are lost during the switchover period or that no files are mistakenly updated twice.

7. Notifying the terminal operators that the system may be off the air for a minute or more while switchover takes place; asking them to repeat any transactions that were received in core but not completely processed when switchover occurred.

8. Communicating with the computer operator: notifying him of the machine status; instructing him to operate switches, change file cartridges, and so on; acting on his instructions to initiate switchover.

The switchover process may be automatic, or it may be manual. Parts of it may be automatic, such as the selection of alternative communication lines or alternative files, and the remainder manual. Again, switchover may be able to take place immediately, or it may have to wait until the alternative computer or unit has been made ready. A file cartridge may have to be transferred, or the alternative computer may have to reach a check point in other work it is performing.

There are thus different speeds possible in the switchover process. Typical times for switchover are as follows:

1. Automatic switchover   1 to   15 seconds
2. Manual switchover,
   immediate   10 to 120 seconds
3. Manual switchover after
   changing file cartridges   2 to   5 minutes
4. Manual switchover readying
   standby computer   2 to   10 minutes

When one operator has to change a number of file cartridges to a different unit or set of units (as might happen with the file in Fig. 23.1, p. 329), the time may become as long as a quarter of an hour, and it may pay to use more than one highly drilled operator. The time that can be allowed for the switchover process is related to the response-time requirements of the system and should be planned at the same time as this. If manual switchover is used, the operator must be sufficiently alert to execute it quickly. The computer may be equipped with a buzzer which it sounds to alert the operator.

When the configuration of the system is changed, either to execute preventive maintenance on a unit or because a unit has failed, the system must, as far as possible, maintain the illusion to the terminal operators that a normal configuration exists. The terminal operator should not have to modify his way of working because the configuration has been modified. The illusion must be maintained not merely to the users of the system but also to the Application Programs, which are written by programmers who do not normally consider fallback and switchover. These are normally functions of the Supervisory Programs. The data reaching the system and the actions of the Applications Programs are intercepted accordingly.

RELIABILITY
CALCULATIONS
When desirable reliability criteria have been decided upon, it must be determined whether the possible configurations meet this. This is a calculation that often can only be performed by the manufacturer of the equipment, because only he has the relevant performance figures of the units. Often, however, the user of the equipment can make a sensible estimate of the failure rate of the individual components, and from this can make a judgement of the validity of the design.

In determining the *availability* of the system, two figures are needed for each of its units, the *mean time between failures* and the *mean time to repair*. *The maximum time to repair* may also be of interest. The first of these figures is dependent entirely upon the unit. The latter two are dependent to some extent upon the skill and location of the engineer. If the engineer is not permanently on site but has to be contacted and may have to cross a crowded city when the machine breaks down, this will decrease the over-all system availability. If there is only one engineer and the failures occur sufficiently frequently to place concurrent demands on him, this will increase the mean time to repair which can then be calculated by examining the mean time to repair of the units. The time to repair a unit can thus be *dependent* upon the other units.

The availability of the system or of a unit may be defined as

$$\text{Availability} = \frac{\text{mean time between failures}}{\text{mean time between failures} + \text{mean time to repaire}}$$

The mean time between failures of a typical second-generation computer might be 100 hours, and mean time to repair, 2.5 hours. This gives an availability of 0.976.

When the availability figures for the various units are known or estimated, it is necessary to calculate the availability of the complete system. There may be many different ways of configurating the system, each of which would give a different *system availability*.

Let a = availability. Then the availability of a system composed of two units *in series* having availabilities a_1 and a_2 (Fig. 6.11) is

$$a = a_1 \times a_2 \qquad\qquad (6.1)$$

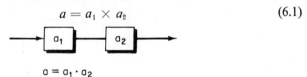

$$a = a_1 \cdot a_2$$

Figure 6.11

The availability of two units *in parallel* having availabilities a_1 and a_2 and of which one must be available (Fig. 6.12) is

$$a = 1 - (1 - a_1)(1 - a_2) \qquad\qquad (6.2)$$

$$a = 1 - (1 - a_1)(1 - a_2)$$

Figure 6.12

The availability of many systems may be analyzed with these two formulas.

If the computers in Fig. 6.1 have availabilities of 0.976, then the tandem system has an availability of 0.953 and the duplex system has an availability of 0.9994. If the duplex system is operational for 12 hours per day, 5 days a week, it will, then, be unavailable for 1.87 hours in 1 year.

Most systems are more complicated than this to analyze as they consist of a number of files, control units, multiplexors, etc., each having different relations to one another, and different availability figures. A systems engineer doing a reliability analysis usually knows the availability figures for each unit or subsystem. He can then arrange these in different combinations so as to produce a system with the required over-all availability.

Using the above two formulae, the availability of this system (Fig 6.13) is

$$a = a_1 a_2 a_3$$

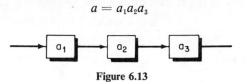

Figure 6.13

The availability of three units in parallel, where one in three must be operational (Fig. 6.14) is

$$a = 1 - \{1 - a_1\} \{1 - [1 - (1 - a_2)(1 - a_3)]\}$$
$$= a_1 + a_2 + a_3 - a_1 a_2 - a_2 a_3 - a_1 a_3 + a_1 a_2 a_3 \qquad (6.3)$$

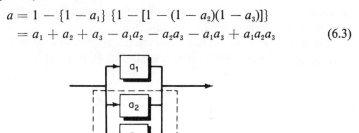

Figure 6.14

If there are a number of units of availability $a_1, a_2, a_3, a_4, \ldots$, all of which *must be in operation* for the system to be available, then the availability is $a_1 a_2 a_3 a_4 \ldots$ This might apply, for example, to file units. Another type of configuration for which availability figures may need to be calculated is one in which a certain number of a set of units must be working, for example four tape units out of five, or two files out of three.

Let us consider three units with the same availability, a_1, of which two must be working, and evaluate the probability of this.

The system availability, $a =$ the probability that three out of three units will be working + the probability that two out of three units will be working.

The probability that three out of three units are working $= a_1^3$

The probability that two specific units are working and the third is not working is $a_1^2(1 - a_1)$, but there are three ways in which two units could be working, therefore the probability that any two out of three units are working is $3a_i^2(1 - a_1)$

∴ The system availability is

$$a = a_1^3 + 3a_i^2(1 - a_1) \tag{6.4}$$

Similarly, for three units out of four we get

$$a = a_1^4 + 4a_i^3(1 - a_1)$$

For $N - 1$ units out of N we get

$$a = a_i^N + Na_i^{N-1}(1 - a_1) \tag{6.5}$$

For $N - 2$ units out of N we get

$$a = a_1^N + Na_i^{N-1}(1 - a_1) + \frac{1}{2} N(N - 1)a_i^{N-2}(1 - a_1)^2 \tag{6.6}$$

and so on for $N - 3$ units out of N, etc.

Using such formulas the availability of any system may be determined, knowing the availability of its components.

Take the systems in Figs. 6.5 and 6.6, for example. Suppose that the availability of each of the components drawn as squares is 0.95. If the operation of the system in Fig. 6.5 depends upon one or another of the strings of units working, its system availability will be

$$1 - (1 - 0.95^4)^2 = 1 - (0.1855)^2 = 0.9656$$

The availability of the system in Fig. 6.6 on the other hand is

$$[1 - (1 - 0.95)^2]^4 = 0.9975^4$$
$$= 0.9900$$

Sometimes it helps to redraw a system configuration to make it clearer what reliability formulas should be applied. For example, Fig. 6.3 might be redrawn as shown in Fig. 6.15.

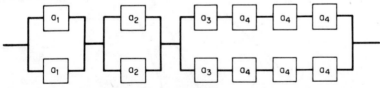

Figure 6.15

The assumption is inherent in this drawing that either one or the other group of three files must be available *as a whole*. The reliability is then:

$$a = [1 - (1 - a_1)^2][1 - (1 - a_2)^2][1 - (1 - a_3 a_i^3)^2]$$

On many such systems, however, it would not be correct to assume that the group of files must be available as a whole, but rather that file A must be available either from one group or the other, that file B must be available either from one group or the other, and the same with C.

In this case we can have two possibilities: Firstly, both file control units are working. The probability of this is a_3^2. The availability of files A, B, and C together in this case is $a_3^2 [1 - (1 - a_4)^2]^3$.

Secondly, one file control unit is working and the other is not, the probability of this is $a_3(1 - a_3)$. The availability of the files A, B, and C together in this case is $a_3(1 - a_3) a_4^3$.

The total availability of the file system is therefore

$$a_3^2\{1 - (1 - a_4)^2\}^3 + 2a_3(1 - a_3)a_4^3.$$

The availability of the over-all system is then

$$a = \{1 - (1 - a_1)^2\}\{1 - (1 - a_2)^2\}[a_3^2\{1 - (1 - a_4)^2\}^3 + 2a_3(1 - a_3)a_4^3]$$

Figures 6.16 and 6.17 show curves giving the relation between the availability of units and the availability of the system for various configurations. Each unit in this sketch is assumed to have the same availability. The availability of most systems is towards the top of these curves, and here the difference between a system with some redundancy and one without is the most significant.

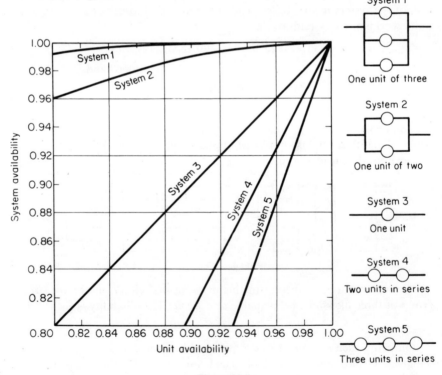

Figure 6.16

Cross switching as in system 3 in Fig 6.17 increases the realiability and it would be more increased if there were more than two units in the string, as is usually the case. The switch itself is sometimes the only unit which is not duplicated. If this is a simple manually operated switch, its reliability is often very high. However, if it is a complex switch operated under program control it could be the weakest link in the chain.

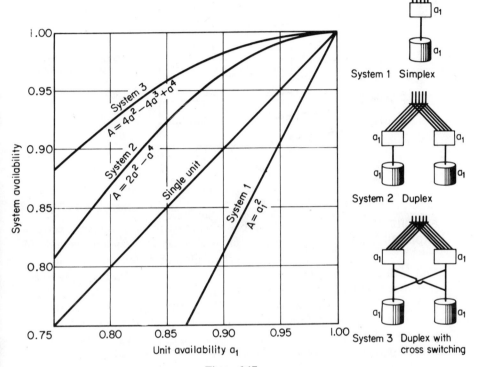

Figure 6.17

Figure 6.18 illustrates a system in which part is duplex and part is not, the figure shows that at the top end of the availability curves the availability of the system is almost entirely dependent on the availability of the non-duplex unit or subsystem. This subsystem may be a communication link or terminal. There would be no point in expensively duplexing the computing equipment unless the availability of the communication link or terminal was improved. However, I have known it be recommended to duplicate a line control unit on a system with one computer. This would be of practically no value, especially as the line control unit is considerably more reliable than the computer as it usually consists of similar circuitry in smaller quantity.

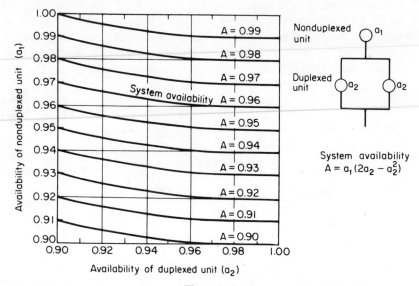

Figure 6.18

FAILURE PROBABILITIES The probability that a piece of complex electronic equipment will fail in a given time period follows approximately an exponential distribution. This is discussed further in Chapter 26. It can be proven mathematically* that if a machine consists of a *large* number of independent components, each with its own pattern of failure and replacement, then the distribution of the time between failures tends to be exponential as the number of components and the time of operation increases. This gives us a convenient way of calculating the probability of a system failing in a given time period. If we know the mean time to failure, we can calculate the probability of failure in a given time.

This is illustrated in Fig. 6.19. The time between consecutive failures is here written as t_f. The mean time to failure is the mean of t_f: $\bar{t}_f$. The curve shows the probability that the time between consecutive failures is less than T months, where T is plotted along the horizontal axis. The mean time to failure as shown on the curve is about 0.22 months.

This is an exponential curve, and so we have the probability that t_f is less than or equal to T:

$$P(t_f \leqslant T) = 1 - e^{-T/\bar{t}_f}$$

Thus if the mean time to failure is 0.22 months, then the probability of

---

J. Soc. Indust. & Appl. Math., Vol. **8** (December 1960). R. F. Derrick, "The Failure of Complex Equipment."

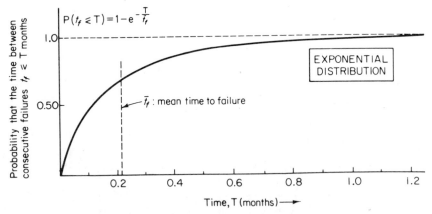

Fig. 6.19. The failure distribution of complex equipment. It is assumed that there are a large number of components, independent of each other, and each having their own pattern of failure and replacement. These components make up the equipment for which the curve is drawn.

the system failing in a period of 0.4 months is:

$$P(t_f \leqslant 0.4) = 1 - e^{-0.4/0.22} = 0.862$$

The probability of it running without a failure for 0.4 months is $1 - 0.862 = 0.138$. Again, if the mean time to failure is 300 hours, the probability of the system failing on one particular day (24 hours) is:

$$P(t_f \leqslant 24) = 1 - e^{-24/300} = 0.077$$

Suppose that this system has a peak period which lasts for five days. It is very heavily loaded for 9 hours in each of these five days. It would be very inconvenient if the system went out of action during any of these nine-hour periods. The user may wish to calculate the probability of this happening:

$$1 - P(t_f > 9)^5 = 1 - e^{-\frac{9 \times 5}{300}} = 0.139$$

The probability may seem too high. If so, additional redundancy may be built into the equipment.

Figure 6.20 gives a curve, drawn on two scales, which the reader may use to assess, quickly, the probability of failure in a given period of time. For example, a system has a mean time of failure of 100 hours. What is the probability of it failing in the next 10 hours? To read this from the curve we examine the horizontal axis at point (T/mean time to failure) $= 0.1$, and read off the Scale B curve that the probability of failure in this time period is 0.095.

More sophisticated methods of reliability analysis exist. *Simulation* programs are used for examples in which the probabilities of different times

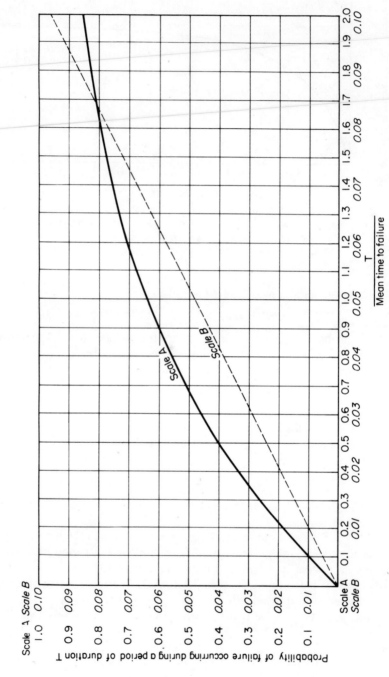

Fig. 6.20. Curves for evaluating the probability of failure during a given period.

74

between failure and times to repair may be quoted, and the probabilities of given system interruptions are listed.

Some manufacturers have proprietary programs which include in their data reliability figures for their various units and components. In this way the anticipated performance of proposed configurations may be analyzed.

FUNCTIONAL AVAILABILITY   With many of the better-designed systems one cannot talk simply about the system working or not working. Often when a unit fails the system *partially* works. In this case the most meaningful figure to calculate is *functional availability* which might be defined as "The probability that an input transaction is handled according to certain criteria." The system may have different functional availability figures for different transactions. It may have different figures for peak load to those for average load. The figures may vary considerably with the criteria specified for the successful handling of a transaction.

This may arise from the fact that certain files are duplicated, while others are not. The system may be designed to carry out only the vital part of processing a transaction when a failure occurs. It may only process certain transactions when a failure occurs, and log the others on tape for later action.

If a system with two file types, A and B, can normally process five types of transaction of equal importance, but when file unit A fails can only handle four, it may be said to have a "capability" of 80 per cent when this failure occurs. The functional availability is then:

a_F = (capability when all files are working) × (probability of this)
   + (capability when file A fails) × (probability of this)
   + (capability when file B fails) × (probability of this)
   + (capability when file A and B both fail) × (probability of this), etc.

This type of calculation can be extended to many units.

Such a figure can be useful, as an indication of how often a terminal operator will receive the reply she wants, or it can be misleading. Whatever the figure, a well thought out means of "graceful degradation" should be aimed at giving attention to the prime needs of the operator when the various units fail.

The relatively simple reliability calculations described in this chapter should be regarded as an essential part of the design process of an on-line system. In a commercial system, different functions demand differing degrees of reliability. By using quick reliability calculations the systems engineer may examine many variations of hardware configuration and attempt to relate the cost of differing degrees of reliability for different system actions to the business economics which make them desirable.

7 THE MAN-MACHINE INTERFACE

In the systems discussed in this book, man may communicate directly with the computer, and the computer communicates with man.

In the past it has usually been a highly trained computer-room operator, and no-one else, who pressed the machine's buttons and typed data into it. Today, however, we see the spectacle of terminals being pounded by heavy-fingered factory workers, harassed salesgirls, and impatient scientists and managers. People who do not understand the machinery at all have to operate it. Sometimes we see very highly intelligent personnel sitting in front of a cathode-ray tube or teleprinter, allowing a powerful computer to help them in their thinking, or making use of its message data storage.

There are a variety of reasons for communication between man and machine. Operators may be sending data to the computer. They may be asking questions of it or searching for information. The machine may require human assistance in its processing and may make a request for this when necessary. It may be unable to handle exceptional conditions. It may be requesting the benefits of certain specialized human experience. In some cases, as in the use of a computer as a teaching machine or as an aid in a design process, a complex conversation may take place between the system and its users.

The best way of carrying out certain difficult types of processing and making certain decisions is neither to use a computer alone nor human means alone, but to use an optimum combination of the two. Language translation is an example of this. Human translation alone is slow; machine translation alone is either very expensive or else inaccurate. The optimum can be a combination of the two, in which the machine rapidly produces a rough translation and a man scans it, correcting the machine's imperfections. The same is true in many real-time situations. A real-time computer used for production control may not make all of the decisions about the routing of jobs through the shops, for example. It may demand management intervention at certain points so that human experience can be used. Again, the setting of booking limits on multistop airline flights may be an operation in which the intervention of flight controllers is desirable. The flight controllers have experience of the booking patterns that can occur at various times on various routes, and this experience can be used by the machine to improve the loading of multileg flights.

The use of human intervention at given points in processing or decision-making operations may spring from an admission that certain operations are too difficult to program yet or are unprogrammable economically. On the other hand, it may spring from a desire to keep a human check on certain actions initiated by the computer. An "operator guide" system, as opposed to a "closed-loop" system, for process control gives the safety of a human link, and erroneous computer actions, if they occurred, would be detected. Some systems process teletype or similar messages sent to them from distant offices, and certain of the transactions are unprocessable. They may, for example, contain comments in English which the computer cannot interpret. The computer will give the unprocessable message to a group of attendants who will re-enter it in a processable format or will take other appropriate action.

A common form of man-machine communication is that in which *enquiries* are made of the computer. The enquiry may require simply the displaying of a record from the files. It may require some processing to be done by the computer, and possibly several records will be examined for this. In some cases the user will need to browse, examining many records before he obtains the information he is seeking. A library system is one in which browsing is needed. The user looks through a list of titles and then a number of abstracts to locate literature on the subject he is interested in. In commercial applications also it may be necessary to carry out a man-machine search in order to find required facts.

Terminals may be used for direct entry transactions to be processed at a computer center. It may not be necessary for the processing to occur within seconds. A time lapse of an hour or more may be satisfactory. In this case the transactions may be collected off-line at the computer center. In some systems, for example, workmen use terminals to send production information. The data transmitted are punched into cards for subsequent entry into a computer. One of the advantages to be gained, however, from on-line entry is the control of human errors. A transaction received by the computer is checked in every way possible, and, if there is any error, an indication is made to the operator while he is there. The checking program may be used on an interrupt basis. On the other hand, a small satellite computer or stored-program multiplexor may handle the terminals, as in Fig. 6.1, without interfering with the main processing.

Catching human errors at their source at the time they are made is a major advantage of certain on-line processing systems. A large scientific computer used in a time-shared manner gives many interesting uses of man-machine communication.

The use of a computer *in real-time* by skilled and intelligent human beings who are deliberately trying to exploit its powers rather than use it for a clerical or administrative purpose has given rise to many exciting results. Problem solving of a variety of types has been carried out in this way. The user can vary his approach to problems according to the results he obtains at the terminal.

A visual display screen, such as a cathode-ray tube, can be particularly useful in some situations. The user can scan through quantities of data quickly until he finds what he is searching for or obtains clues to where he might find it. Using a "light pen" he can point to certain parts of a display and have them enlarged . If a mathematical process produces a curve on the screen, he might be interested in a certain portion of the curve and will instruct the computer to enlarge this.

The display screen has been used to speed up the production and modification of engineering drawings. The drawings are produced on a display screen by an engineer with a light pen, using a library of computer routines to help him. Similarly, the display screen has been used for setting and correcting page copy for printers. The combination of an information retrieval system with computer routines for making various types of analysis can have many powerful applications. Users may test the validity of assumptions or theories about the information stored. Management may explore the effect of sales changes, stock control actions, and so on. The systems so far in operation give only a glimmering of the potential that is possible with the hardware available today.

TYPES AND CONFIGURATIONS OF TERMINAL

The types of terminals and displays that are used are an important factor in designing the man-machine interface. These devices create the image of the system to the persons using it.

As far as possible the terminals should use methods familiar to the user. They may perhaps resemble typewriters or adding machines. They should use message formats and language already known to the user. The keys or lights may be labelled with terms familiar in the user's business.

A wide variety of terminal types are available, as listed in Chapter 2. Some of these produce hard copy; others do not. The decision must be made whether a print-out is needed. If not, a terminal using a telephone or a cathoderay tube may suffice.

Another important decision is whether a given operator can modify the computer records. Only responsible operators can be allowed to do this, and then the process must be carefully controlled. Some terminals have a lock and key. The operator taking actions that will change records must first turn his key.

An installation using several terminals may be planned so that only some of them can be used to modify file records. A terminal configuration is shown in Fig. 7.1 in which only one operator and terminal can change records. This terminal is more expensive than the others. Its operator is more experienced and highly trained. When the other operators, who may perhaps be answering telephone calls, wish to modify a record, details will be written on a card which travels on the conveyor belt to the main terminal. This configuration lowers the over-all terminal cost, gives added security, and enables the organization to use mostly unskilled terminal operators.

The main terminal may also be used as a *supervisor's terminal.* It is useful for a supervisor to be able to duplicate any messages on his terminal so that he may check the work of, or give asistance to, any of the other operators.

When, as in this case, telephone calls must be routed to the first free operator, there are a number of ways of organizing this. A small exchange is sometimes used, but this is expensive. Calls may be routed to the first free operator by the main exchange in the building; or an automatic device may be used by which every operator knows when a call is waiting because a red light flashes, and the first operator to become free deals with the call.

A display may be set up in a *semipermanent* fashion, giving the status of some situation. Panels of lights are sometimes used for this, and a computer changes the lights when necessary. Such a display can be read by many people rather than just one operator.

When a computer requires human attention, or human assistance, terminals must be arranged so that it can obtain this. It is normal for a com-

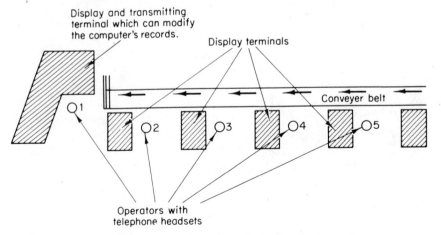

Fig. 7.1. Operators 2 to 5 use their display terminals to answer telephone enquiries. If they originate transactions which must update the computer records, these are sent to operator 1. Operator 1 is more responsible highly trained. He has a more expensive terminal. A time lag in the entry of transactions is permissible.

When the computer reaches a point at which human intervention or decision is needed, it obtains this from a group of controllers at on-line consoles.

Details are keyed into a remote console by agents who normally deal with the public.

Fig. 7.2. Three-way conversation.

puter to demand attention from its operator, possibly using a console type-writer; but here it is asking for assistance from personnel with some experience or skill, but not necessarily any knowledge of the computer's operation. *Human-decision consoles* will be planned so that these personnel can reply to the computer's messages. The computer may type out messages on a remote terminal and expect an answer to these to enable it to complete some processing.

Figure 7.2 illustrates a three-way conversation. Members of the public ring the organization, and their requests are dealt with by girls wearing telephone headsets and equipped with terminals connected to a computer. This telephone-answering office may be many miles from the computer. In some working systems it is on the opposite side of the Atlantic, for example. The computer may need human assistance to deal with a small proportion of the transactions. It will obtain this from the personnel on the human-decision consoles, as shown. If this human link in the processing occurs in real-time while the customer is on the telephone, it must be fast and well organized. Often, however, a reentry into a human-decision console need not be made immediately but can wait for ten minutes or an hour or more. The computer may build up a queue of items needing human attention at a terminal. Sometimes this human decision itself can only take place after a conversation between the man in question and the computer.

ERROR CONTROL   One of the uses for a human-decision console in some systems is as a means of repairing damaged or invalid messages. A message received, for example, on a teletype circuit may have an error caused, perhaps, by an operator. To a human being it is clear what was meant by the message, but the computer cannot determine this. Undecipherable messages may therefore be given to a console operator to clean up, and only occasionally must retransmission be demanded. Immediate communication with the person entering the data is the easiest way to deal with errors which can be caught as they are made. However, if paper tape is transmitted some time after the message was composed, it may be more difficult to return it to its sender for correction, and so a "repair line" at the computer center is of more value.

On a well-designed system, as much of the error control as possible will be automatic. Noise errors on the communication line, for example, will be detected by parity or longitudinal redundancy checks and retransmission obtained automatically without human intervention. There are some errors however, where human intervention *is* required, and these are mainly errors caused by human mistakes. An operator may send a message with an incorrect format. She may spell a customer's name differently on different occasions. She may type a part number or account number incorrectly. The computer should be programmed with every error-detection device that can be thought of, and, when a human error is detected, it will be logged and the originator asked to correct it immediately if possible.

The detection of human errors *as they are made* is of great value on some real-time systems. It can have a considerable psychological effect on the operators and so lessen the incidence of error. Just as immediate reinforcement of correct answers in a learning process improves the retention of the learning, so immediate detection of errors can improve the accuracy of the operator. The correct attitude, however, must always be enforced by supervisors. Operators must be instructed not to make errors, otherwise they can lapse into the view, "It doesn't matter if I make errors because the machine always catches them!"

One interesting form of error control that is used on some systems is a check on name spelling. A record is held in the computer that has a client's name in it. When an enquiry is made from a terminal relating to that client, the operator may spell the name incorrectly. The machine will inform her that there is no name of that spelling, but may scan the other clients in the same category to see what names are similar. The machine will print these out for the operator possibly in order of decreasing similarity.

As well as making format and validity checks, the controls used must ensure that no transactions are lost. The methods of doing this, as discussed in Chapter 35, include the use of group totals and the sequential numbering of messages.

Very careful operator procedures must be laid down for use when components of the system fail. The machine must be programmed to give an operator every help possible during this difficult period. The operator procedures must be adhered to rigorously to ensure that no messages are lost and no records are updated twice by mistake.

MAN-MACHINE LANGUAGE   The first essential for man and machine to be able to converse is that they should use a common language.

This is one of the main problems that stands in the way of a widespread and sophisticated use of man-computer communication. It is a problem that affects both programming or "software" design, and the design of terminals. There are a number of approaches to making men and machines converse at present. Some of these are as follows:

1. *Use of the Computer's Language*

A programmer may communicate with the machine, using its own language or a variation of the language designed for on-line use. Often a higher-level language is used, such as FORTRAN, which is designed to use statements similar to mathematics.

This is the most versatile way to communicate with the computer but it is also very slow. A complete program must be entered, compiled, and debugged before the machine will reply. Nevertheless, the use of terminals on-line to a time-sharing machine and a language designed for on-line work, examples of which are discussed briefly in subsequent chapters, permit some problems to be solved more quickly than ever before.

2. *Use of a Problem-Oriented Language*

Conventional computer languages are not sufficiently familiar or easy to use for most of the people who would like to solve problems on an on-line terminal. Various languages have been written to express certain specific types of problem to a computer. For example, IBM's COGO is a language for expressing problems in coordinate geometry. It is used by civil engineers, is very quickly learned, and is difficult to make mistakes with.

Much work needs to be done on languages for use by people who are not trained programmers and have no interest in programming for its own sake.

3. *Use of the Terminal as a Calculating Machine*

A "problem-oriented" language of wide applicability is one which enables the user to evaluate mathematical expressions. There are several of these in use. Expressions to be evaluated may be keyed into the terminal in such a way that the computer can immediately interpret them, evaluate them,

Fig. 7.3. A "problem-oriented" terminal. The terminal was especially designed for this application. It enables Holiday Inn clerks throughout America to communicate with their nationwide reservation system.

and type back the results. The language uses a notation similar to the notation the user is familiar with. An example of this is given in the next chapter.

4. Use of Special-Purpose Keys

Just as a language may be problem-oriented, so a terminal can be designed to tackle one well-defined job rather than be general in its usage. Sometimes the best way of designing a system, if it can be afforded, is to use both a problem-oriented language and a problem-oriented terminal.

Figure 7.3 shows a terminal design for one specific application. It was decided that the best way to design the communication between a hotel clerk and a distant computer used for reservations was to build a special purpose terminal with keys that perform all the desired actions.

The example earlier, in which mathematical expressions are evaluated with a general-purpose terminal that is equally well used for invoicing or sending cables, can be tackled elegantly with a special-purpose terminal. Terminals have been built to be used like a calculating machine by people with no knowledge of computers. A wide variety of mathematical problems can be stated on the keys. In one terminal answers appear in lights in front of the user.

Another approach which needs no major reengineering is to relabel the keys of an existing terminal such as a typewriter or teleprinter. Figure 7.4 shows a typewriter-like keyboard in which the letters are always typed in in lower shift. Mathematical functions labelled on the keys above the letters are typed in in upper shift. Numbers may also be typed in in upper shift, and so, without taking the keyboard out of upper shift, mathematical problems may be expressed. Figure 7.5 shows how the same keyboard could be labelled to carry out an airline reservation function. This keyboard is part of either a typewriter or cathode-ray tube agent set. The terminal illustrated in Fig. 15.6 and discussed in Chapter 15 is an example of a terminal specially engineered for one job. This terminal is cheap and expresses in a very simple manner the limited range of facts that its operator must communicate to the computer.

There are many other examples of problem-oriented terminals with keys and other devices which permit certain precisely defined actions to be taken. A given record in the files may be displayed. Lights may be lit against a matrix card on certain conditions. A customer's account may be updated and details printed. This is not scintillating conversation, but it has many sound commercial uses and meets the demand often made on a terminal, that it must be very simple to use.

5. Use of Special Coding

More versatile than special keys can be special coding. The computer can be programmed to attach meaning to certain characters or abbreviations keyed into a terminal or teleprinter. Messages will be sent consisting, first,

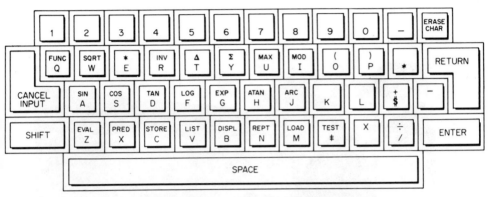

Fig. 7.4. Typewriter keyboard labelled for mathematical work.

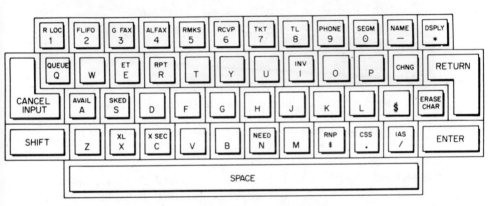

Fig. 7.5. Typewriter keyboard labelled for airline reservations.

of an *action code* or word and, then, of data to be processed using the program associated with that action code. The computer can display information on a cathode-ray tube or a typewriter and number items in such a way that they are easily referred to by the operator in responding messages. Using this technique, means can be built up of carrying out fairly elaborate conversations about specific and carefully defined situations. The terminal, again, may be specially labelled with the action codes for the job. It is possible to use masks for labelling the keyboard so that the same terminal can be used for different tasks.

It is likely that language and terminal developments for on-line applications in the years to come will considerably enhance the potentialities of man-machine communication. Much research is under way on interaction languages. Chapter 8 gives some illustrations of simple man-machine conversations in use today.

Fig. 7.6. Everything from bar charts to engineering drawings can be called up in seconds on display screens such as this. Here a sales chart is being displayed in IBM's Los Angeles Data Center.

THE FUTURE   The examples discussed above are taken from systems now operating. In addition to these, there have been many which clearly indicate that the future of man-machine communications will produce some startling and powerful results. There are certain thought processes which will always remain in the domain of *human* rather than machine activity. Others, however, are better done by machine. When the two can be efficiently combined the result is more powerful than either process on its own.

The computer can store vast quantities of data and retrieve individual items quickly. It can carry out well-defined calculations or logic processes at enormous speed. It can keep files up to date and take controlling actions at the moment they are required. In it, a repertoire of procedures can be built up, which do not become distorted or forgotten as in the human brain. The human brain, or the other hand, can select goals and criteria, select approaches, detect relevance, formulate questions and hypotheses. It can handle the unforeseen.

With the logic power of the computer and the mass information retrieval available to it, the capability of the human brain for tackling certain types of problem can become immensely greater. The human operator may formulate hypotheses and immediately test them on the data concerned. The computer can help formulate and evaluate the effect of management policies. It can assist in producing engineering drawings or PERT charts or simulation programs. It can help in planning complex schedules. It can help programmers write programs, keying them directly into a terminal and changing them where necessary as they go along. It is possible that in the future, complex programs and computer software will be produced with the aid of on-line terminals.

Much research is needed, and is being done, on the combined use of man and real-time computers. Using time-sharing techniques, a man may use a part share in a powerful computer and its files at a fraction of the cost of the whole system. The term *man-machine symbiosis* has been coined to describe this new type of thinking—part machine, part human.

Among the possibilities that are now becoming reality are the following:

Designers of various types can use computers to assist them. A circuit designer, for example, may store details of all the components available to him and quickly make the computer investigate the effect of various arrangements or modifications. An architect or bridge engineer can use a display tube to produce plans, fitting elements of the design together and modifying the results as required, A linkage of steel girders in a building or a bridge may be built up on a display screen, and the computer will place figures by each indicating the results of stressing calculations. The designer may change his linkages and investigate the stresses caused by different loadings and so optimize his design. General Motors has done much work on the use of graphic real-time computing in automobile design. The designer sketches surfaces on a screen with a light pen, and can very rapidly making changes in this way. The computer will fit a mathematical expression to the surface and then "rotate" the surface on the screen so that the designer may observe its shape from all viewpoints. The computer will apply constraints that are forced by mechanical or manufacturing considerations, and the designer will adjust his shapes to achieve a compromise within the constraints that must apply.

If these processes were done by hand or with a batch-processing computer they would take a long time—so long that the designer would be restricted in the full use of his imagination or inventive ability. Most design processes are 1 per cent inspiration or art, and 99 per cent calculation and the laborious working out of detail. The object of using a real-time computer for design is to take away as much as possible of the tedious work and enable the designer to observe as quickly as possible the effects of his ideas. In a trial-and-error process, if there are three months between the trial and the error, the designer can lose much of his original ideas. Where it is possible to explore the effect of these ideas in real-time, much more fruitful and exciting thinking can sometimes be stimulated.

Similarly *simulation models* may be "built" at a display terminal to investigate the passage of work through a factory, the flow of traffic through a city, or any other situation capable of being simulated. A standard simulation language may be used for this, the model being tested as it is built. The effect of different actions may be investigated using such models. A model of the functioning of an organization may be permitted to grow until it steadily becomes a more accurate representation of the behavior of the organization. Sales forecasts may form inputs to a model used for planning. The effects of different policies may be investigated, and experiments carried out with the model. As in a design process, the work of building a simulation model today can be long and laborious. If somebody asks, "What would be the effect of doing so-and-so," the answer may come two months later. This is too slow for many purposes, especially in the racing turmoil of the commercial world. To demonstrate to management that quick and effective answers can be obtained from simulation, real-time methods may be needed.

The surprising effectiveness of computers used for *teaching* has already been demonstrated. Many pupils can be handled at once, and different subjects taught. The computer gives individual treatment to students and modifies its behavior according to their progress in a much more adaptable way than simpler machines. A device with a teleprinter or, better, a display screen can be used as the terminal. Perhaps one day a device like a domestic television set will be rentable at home and be connected to a distant computer over the telephone line. Films as well as static displays might be used in the teaching process, and perhaps the device could also receive "dial-up" television when not being used for self-education!

The computer used in this way becomes a type of storehouse for human learning and thinking. An effective teaching program can be used throughout the world in many types of computer and is likely to be constantly improved as student reactions are observed. Languages for writing teaching programs are now being developed so that a professional educator with little knowledge of computers can write them. As the potentialities of this become understood and developed it is likely that many educators throughout the world will set to work writing and improving computerized instruction courses.

Information retrieval also is an area in which human knowledge will be made increasingly accessible and usable. Banks of data on certain subjects will grow in the years and decades to come. In the future, after an enormous quantity of coding and classification work has been done, the biochemist will be enabled to check what reports have been written on a particular topic, the lawyer will have the mass of literature he needs electronically available to him, and the patent agent will be enabled to carry out a search in real-time. Again the quantity of data in computer-scannable form will build up over the decades. It would be of value *now*, to standardize a procedure whereby all technical reports are written accompanied not only by a title and an abstract, but also by a *data index* for information-retrieval purposes. A standard dictionary of content words would be used, which could constantly be added to. There would be a major subject category, such as "physics," a subdivision of this, such as "superconductivity," and sub-subdivisions, such as "Meissner effect." A number of words relating to the contents of the report would be in its data index, and relationships between the words might be indicated. In searching for reports on a given topic the user would carry on a two-way conversation with the distant computer. The computer might suggest more precise categorizations of what he was seeking. He might browse through many data indices, titles, and abstracts before he found what he wanted.

Doctors will one day make use of a distant computer as a help in diagnosis. A patient's symptoms will be transmitted to the distant machine. The machine will make suggestions to the doctor and perhaps ask for additional information. Already electrocardiagram signals have been sent over the telephone lines to a computer for remote analysis. This is only a small beginning of things to come. The computer will not in any way replace the human qualities of the doctor, but it would add to his limited store of information. Here again the computer will carry on a type of information-retrieval work, but probably with more logical or analytical programming in it than straightforward information retrieval. For use with patients in hospitals, real-time computers have startling possibilities. Various measuring instruments attached to a patient have been used experimentally on-line to a computer. The computer can monitor the patient's condition, help in diagnosis, and help in medical research. To the layman this appears a particularly alarming form of man-machine interface!

The boardroom or *management control room* in industry in the future may be designed with computer display panels and enquiry consoles like a military war room. The potentialities for providing help to management and displaying pertinent facts at the appropriate time are great. As with the other applications indicated above, the limitation is no longer in the hardware. It is in the programming and the organization of the vast quantities of information involved.

Much of the development in the years to come will probably be in the area of languages, especially languages for on-line use. Now we have this immensely powerful tool available to us, it is important to extend its use to the maximum number of people. We must develop languages that the scientist, the architect, the teacher, and the layman can use without being computer experts. The language for each user must be as *natural* as possible to him. The statistician must talk to his terminal in the language of statistics. The civil engineer must use the language of civil engineering. When a man learns his profession he must learn the *problem-oriented languages* to go with that profession.

If we give teachers throughout the world the right computer language for them, they will build *libraries* of teaching programs. If we give circuit designers the right language for them, they will make computers design circuits. If we give the medical profession the right language, they will give a doctor far more information at his fingertips than one individual could ever have today.

It now becomes apparent that we are going to need a *public* use of computers. People everywhere must be able to dial up a computing facility appropriate to their needs. They may have a portion of a file reserved for them in a distant machine. The grocer on the street corner will transmit the paper tape from his cash register and have his accounts done. A bank branch will transmit a record of the day's transactions (adequate security will be maintained). An engineer will do his routine calculations on a teleprinter or on a terminal that looks like a desk calculating machine. Computer programmers will develop programs on line, and many problem-oriented programs will be available to architects, market researchers, and other professional people. Banks of data and programs will be available for information retrieval and teaching, and many more exotic uses of man-machine symbiosis will be possible.

Some form of *public utility* is needed for this. Just as we can pick up a telephone today, so in the future we will be able to dial up and use a computer. Probably the computer will also prepare the bills for its users. Experimental and as yet rather limited computer centers of this type are being set up today. These will grow and multiply and interlink. A countrywide and probably a worldwide network of computers that can be dialed up on the existing telecommunication facilities will be available to us before many years have passed.

This technology is bringing the computer to the masses. People everywhere will be able to participate in using and building an enormous quantity of "computerized" information and logic. We are at the beginning of a chain reaction. The ingredients already exist. The fuse has been lit. It is clear that we now have a tool so powerful that it will take many decades for us to use it to its full potential. But its full potential is far beyond our cleverest imagination today.

8 CONVERSATIONS WITH A COMPUTER

This chapter illustrates some of the man-machine conversations that occur when operators use the real-time systems discussed in this book. For clarification of the illustrations below, the data the operator keys in are in **heavy print,** and the computer responses in *italics.*

First, a simple example, an invoice is prepared on a typewriter-like terminal. The operator keys in only the customer number and the part numbers and quantities, as shown in Fig. 8.1. The computer prints the rest in front of her. The computer extends the invoice, records the data in its customer files, makes adjustments to the stock records noting whether any reordering is needed, and deals with any exceptional conditions such as credit limit exceeded. Most operator errors can be controlled as they occur. Self-checking numbers may be used for customer numbers and part numbers (see Chapter 35). The operator can enter special rates or comments if necessary.

The use of self-checking numbers is valuable on on-line terminals for controlling errors. Alphabetic descriptions may also be used to help in checking. For example, if a storekeeper makes an enquiry about the number of 25-volt solenoids in stock and should key in **Q5288317 BN**, requesting the computer to type out the quantity of the items of that number, he may make a mistake and the conversation looks as follows:

Q5288137 BN
PAINT CARNIVAL RED   206 GALLON DRUMS

He then sees immediately that he has typed in the wrong digits.

BONNINGTON COSMETICS
287—9 Castle St., London, S.W.17.

| 0023108 | Sold to
THE DRUGGIST
BENTYRE ROAD,
BUDE, CORNWALL | Deliver to
THE DRUGGIST
BENTYRE ROAD,
BUDE, CORNWALL | Invoice |

Territory	Invoice date	Invoice No.	Order No.	Despatch method	Despatch date	P. Tax Reg. No.
09	30.04.65	20048	587691	VAN	17.01.64	

Quantity	Item No.	Item description	Retail price incl. tax		Net price per doz		Purchase tax		Goods value		
120	211	PERFUME COLUMBINARY W9	4	6	26	0	6	19	5	13	0	0
24	615	NAIL ENAMEL STRIPPER	3	11	21	6	1	3	1	2	3	0
8	513	NAIL ENAMEL RACING RED	4	9	26	0		9	4		17	4
12	223	HAND CARE MY SKIN	5	9	32	6		17	5	1	12	6
		DISCOUNT									17	8

56	Total quantity

Total purchase tax		Total goods value	
9	9	3	16	15	2

Total due for payment 26 4 5

Figure 8.1

AIRLINE RESERVATIONS   The early airline-reservation systems which handled passenger names and details on-line all used terminals with typewriters, but it is likely that many of those installed from now on will use cathode-ray tube display terminals as these are faster and in many cases cheaper than typewriters. The following example is taken from Pan American Airways' PANAMAC system. An agent in Picadilly London, England, shown in Fig. 8.2, is conversing with an IBM 7080 computer in New York at the same time as handling a customer. The responses from across the Atlantic are typed after a pause of about a second.

The agent selects a matrix card relating to the journey the passenger wishes to make and fits it into place in the terminal shown in Fig. 8.3. She presses keys above the card to indicate to the computer the departure point of the flight. She also keys in the date on which the customer wants to fly

Fig. 8.2. Pan American Airways agent in London conversing with a computer in New York.

and the number of seats required and presses a key indicating that she wants to know the *availability* of such seats. The computer checks the validity of this date. Lights at the side of the card light up to indicate those flights which meet the requirements.

The agent passes this information on to the customer. The customer selects a flight he would like to travel on, and the agent presses a button adjacent to one of the lights which came on. She presses a key indicating that she wishes to sell these seats, and the computer decreases the record of seat availability by the appropriate number. The computer now prints out details of the sale on the terminal type-writer as shown in Fig. 8.3.

If the customer had wanted to make a longer journey of several segments, the print-out might look as shown in Fig. 8.5.

The agent will compare these print-outs with the customer's requests to ensure that the correct itinerary has been booked. She

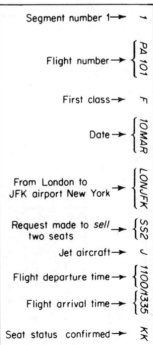

Segment number 1 ⟶ 1

Flight number ⟶ PA 101

First class ⟶ F

Date ⟶ 10MAR

From London to JFK airport New York ⟶ LONJFK

Request made to *sell* two seats ⟶ SS2

Jet aircraft ⟶ J

Flight departure time ⟶ 1100

Flight arrival time ⟶ 1335

Seat status confirmed ⟶ KK

Figure 8.3

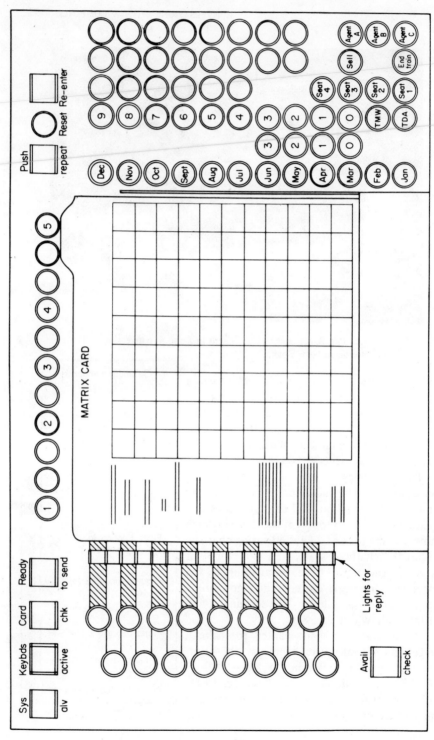

Fig. 8.4. Matrix card.

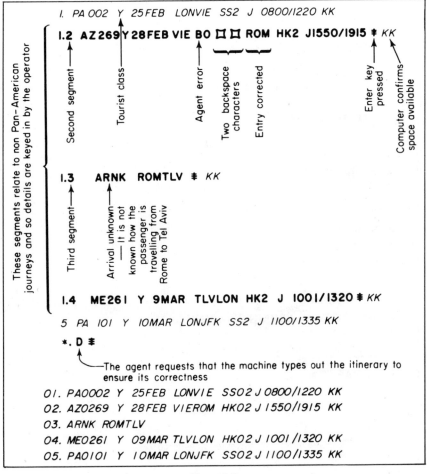

Figure 8.5

must then enter his name and other relevant details. The keyboard for doing this is basically a typewriter keyboard, but the top row of keys also has labels, NAME, PHONE, REVD, RMKS, and so on, for entering passenger details.

The conversation with the machine might go as shown in Fig. 8.6, in which General and Mrs. H.F. Owen-Evans are booking a return trip to New York.

Certain entries are obligatory. If for example the agent left out the telephone entry, the computer would reply:

TELEPHONE ENTRY OMITTED

If the passenger has no telephone, the agent must type in:

4 NIL

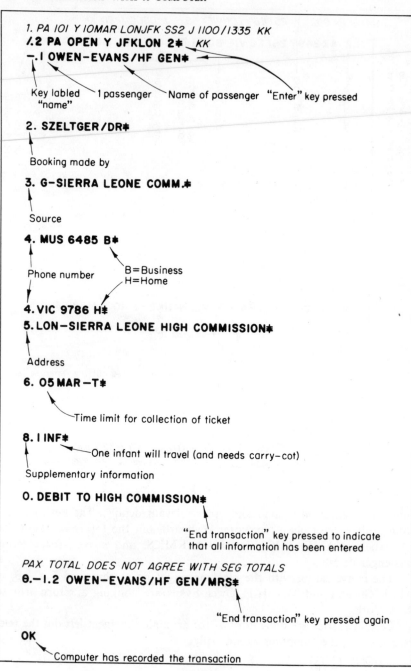

1. PA IOI Y IOMAR LONJFK SS2 J IIOO/I335 KK
/.2 PA OPEN Y JFKLON 2∗ KK
−.I OWEN−EVANS/HF GEN∗

Key labled   1 passenger   Name of passenger   "Enter" key pressed
"name"

2. SZELTGER/DR∗

Booking made by

3. G−SIERRA LEONE COMM.∗

Source

4. MUS 6485 B∗

Phone number   B=Business
                H=Home

4. VIC 9786 H∗
5. LON−SIERRA LEONE HIGH COMMISSION∗

Address

6. O5 MAR−T∗

Time limit for collection of ticket

8. I INF∗

One infant will travel (and needs carry−cot)

Supplementary information

O. DEBIT TO HIGH COMMISSION∗

"End transaction" key pressed to indicate
that all information has been entered

PAX TOTAL DOES NOT AGREE WITH SEG TOTALS
θ.−I.2 OWEN−EVANS/HF GEN/MRS∗

"End transaction" key pressed again

OK

Computer has recorded the transaction

Figure 8.6

When the entry is correct the machine will file it away, typing out the message **OK**, and, if General or Mrs. H.F. Owen-Evans comes into a Pan American office or phones up about the trip, the first action of the agent will be to display their "passenger name record" as shown in Fig. 8.7.

One of the main advantages of using a cathode-ray tube display for man-machine conversation is that the response can come back very rapidly. The typewriter, operating, as it does, at speeds of about fifteen characters per second or less, produces information at a much slower rate than that at which a human being can digest it. The telephone lines used for data transmission can pour out written information at speeds roughly equivalent to human scanning and speaking rates. A display tube on a telephone line is therefore a better facility for conversing with a machine, particularly when the subject is one about which the machine has a lot to say.

A display tube used for the above airline reservation work could dispense with the somewhat clumsy matrix-card reader and its associated keys (Fig. 8.3). The information on the matrix cards would be kept in the computer files, and so updated centrally rather than at local offices.

The conversation between man and machine in making a booking might now look something like that shown in Fig. 8.8. The agent selects the flight she wants (Fig. 8.9), and the computer condenses the contents of the screen to one line, eliminating all the unwanted data (Fig. 8.10). If the desired flight had not been among the four shown, the girl would have asked for further possible flights to be displayed.

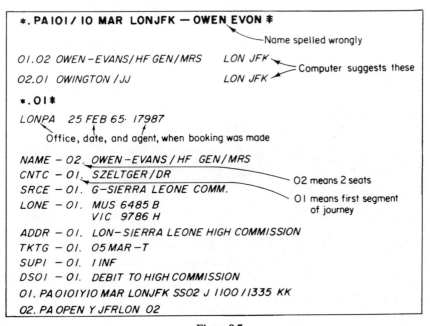

Figure 8.7

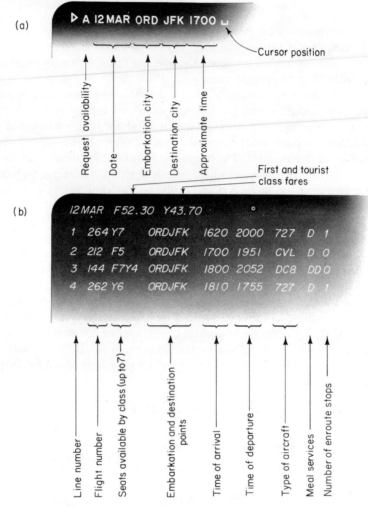

Figure 8.8

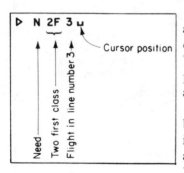

Figure 8.9

The agent can now enter passenger details as before. The computer acknowledges receipt of each detail line by displaying an asterisk. When an agent makes a mistake which is picked up by the computer, she modifies it and the screen is cleaned up appropriately.

When an agent displays an itinerary booked previously in order to make a change in it, the computer will give her as much help as possible. She may wish to change segment 3, so she types in:

X3.

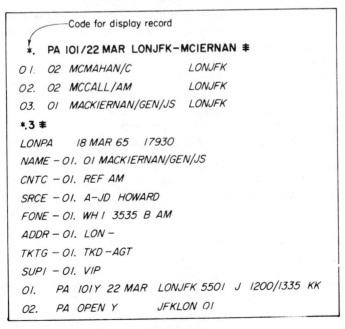

1   144F 12MAR ORDJFK HS2 1800 2050

Figure 8.10

The computer then flashes the message on the screen:

NEXT SEGMENT ENTRY REPLACES 3

She then types in the change, and, as always, the computer checks it. When the agent and the passenger are satisfied with the change, she displays the amended passenger record, and so condenses and cleans up the information on the screen.

In attempting to display or modify the record of a passenger who telephones or calls in the airline office, the girl operating the terminal may spell the name incorrectly, or differently to have it as originally input. The computer will then automatically display similar names on that flight, as in Fig. 8.11. If the computer does not find the correct name at the first attempt, the operator will tell it to search further.

Many codes other than those illustrated are used on an airline reservation system. The array of codes is complicated for the agent to learn and so must be made as similar as possible to codes she already knows and understands.

Code for display record

*. PA 101/22 MAR LONJFK-MCIERNAN *

01. 02 MCMAHAN/C   LONJFK

02. 02 MCCALL/AM   LONJFK

03. 01 MACKIERNAN/GEN/JS LONJFK

*.3 *

LONPA   18 MAR 65   17930

NAME - 01. 01 MACKIERNAN/GEN/JS

CNTC - 01. REF AM

SRCE - 01. A-JD HOWARD

FONE - 01. WH1 3535 B AM

ADDR - 01. LON -

TKTG - 01. TKD -AGT

SUPI - 01. VIP

01.   PA 101Y 22 MAR LONJFK 5501 J 1200/1335 KK

02.   PA OPEN Y   JFKLON 01

Figure 8.11

A standard set of teletype codes is in use in the airlines, and the new on-line language is constructed so as to resemble this. It is a general principle when designing any such language that it should be *as natural as possible* for the operator to use. As much familiarity as possible must be built into the codes.

CALCULATIONS Time-sharing systems are enabling engineers and other personnel to do calculations, although they have no detailed knowledge of programming. Here the language used must be simple and familiar, as in the example in Fig. 8.12 from the Rand Corporation's JOSS, based amazingly on a 1951–53-built Johnniac computer.

1.1 TYPE X, SQRT(X), LOG(X), EXP(X), (X+0.25)/X IN FORM 1.

FORM 1:

— _·_____ _·____ _·___ _·____

DO STEP 1.1 FOR X = 1(1) 4.

1	1.00000000	0.00000	2.7183	1.25000
2	1.41421356	0.69315	7.3891	1.12500
3	1.73205081	1.09861	20.0855	1.08333
4	2.00000000	1.38629	54.5982	1.06250

Fig. 8.12. This illustration appeared in the *New Scientist*, May 27, 1965, in an article by Dr. Arthur L. Samuel of IBM.

A typical example of what an engineer or statistician might want to use a terminal for is the drawing of curves, such as those in Chapter 26 of this book. The author used a teleprinter, such as that in Fig. 5.1, connected to a distant GE 235 computer to do the calculations for these curves. An illustration of his "conversation" with the machine is shown in Fig. 8.13, in which the data for drawing Fig. 26.15 are calculated. The results were obtained within about 20 minutes of going to the teleprinter—much quicker than with a conventional data center, or with a calculating machine.

IBM's QUIKTRAN system used a language with a format like the already familiar FORTRAN, thus:

$y = A(x + ut)$ would be written $Y = A*(X + U*T)$

$E = mC^2$ would be written $E = EM*C**2$

[*EM* is written rather than *M* to make the variable floating point rather than fixed point.]

$E = mC^2 \left(\dfrac{1}{\sqrt{1 - u^2/c^2}} - 1 \right)$ would be written

$E = EM*C**2*(1./SQRT(1. - U**2/C**2) - 1.)$

$P = \dfrac{A + 2T(U - \sin^2 x)}{N}$ would be written

$P = (A + 2.*T*(U - (SIN(X))**2))/N$

Floating point numbers can also be expressed. Thus,

1.458×10^9 would be written   1.458E9

2.6×10^{-18} would be written   2.6E-18

The terminal operator wishing to evaluate an expression in this mode might type in

BASE = 2.E−9∗50. ∗(ALOG(2.∗50./10.)−1. + 10./50.)

and the terminal would replay

BASE = 0.15025850E−06.

As far as possible the machine would pick up errors in input; thus,

Q = (2./(3.1416∗10.)∗∗0.5∗SIN (10.)

would receive the reply

ERROR PARENTHESES NOT IN BALANCE

The operator would then type

Q = (2./(3.1416 ∗10.))∗ ∗ 0.5 ∗SIN (10.)

and receive the reply he sought

Q = 0.13726357E − 00

On the QUIKTRAN system errors are pointed out where possible at the time each statement is typed in. This can speed up the writing of a bugfree program and shorten the time taken to obtain results.

As on the other time-sharing systems, the user may either type in simple calculations rather like using a calculating machine or may type in a complete program as in Fig. 8.14. Figure 8.14 shows a period spent by the author at a QUIKTRAN terminal doing the calculations needed to draw the curves in Fig 26.16. Note that the program can be interrupted during its execution to make changes.

Figure 8.15 shows a scientist at work using a terminal of the type QUIKTRAN uses. In this illustration it is connected not to a QUIKTRAN system but to a time-shared IBM 7094 at M.I.T.

Programs may in this way be composed and edited on real-time terminals of time-sharing systems. Figure 8.16 gives an example of this on a FORTRAN II program written with the software for Digital Equipment Corporation's PDP-6.

Not all remote computing need be this complicated, as we see in Fig. 8.17. Here is a New York City high school student doing her homework with the help of an IBM computer 50 miles away. The device she is using is like a normal Touch-Tone telephone keyboard. It has twelve keys instead of the ten that are conventional on a telephone. They are labelled as in Fig 8.18. (Note that each key has two possible meanings. The key "8" can be used to

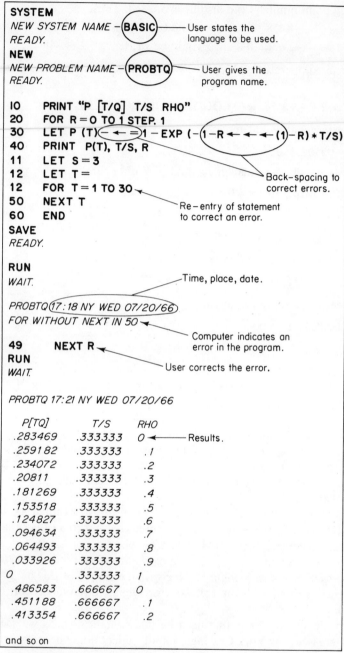

```
SYSTEM
NEW SYSTEM NAME – (BASIC)——— User states the
READY.                          language to be used.
NEW
NEW PROBLEM NAME – (PROBTQ)——— User gives the
READY.                          program name.

 IO    PRINT "P [T/Q] T/S RHO"
 20    FOR R = O TO 1 STEP. 1
 30    LET P (T)(– ← =)1 – EXP (–(1–R ← ← ← (1)– R) * T/S)
 40    PRINT  P(T), T/S, R
 11    LET  S = 3
 12    LET  T =                        Back–spacing to
 12    FOR  T = 1 TO 30                correct errors.
 50    NEXT T                 Re–entry of statement
 60    END                    to correct an error.
SAVE
READY.

RUN
WAIT.                         Time, place, date.

PROBTQ(17:18 NY WED 07/20/66)
FOR WITHOUT NEXT IN 50
                              Computer indicates an
 49      NEXT R              error in the program.
RUN
WAIT.                         User corrects the error.


PROBTQ 17:21 NY WED 07/20/66

     P[TQ]        T/S      RHO
    .283469     .333333    0 ←——— Results.
    .259182     .333333    .1
    .234072     .333333    .2
    .20811      .333333    .3
    .181269     .333333    .4
    .153518     .333333    .5
    .124827     .333333    .6
    .094634     .333333    .7
    .064493     .333333    .8
    .033926     .333333    .9
   0            .333333    1
    .486583     .666667    0
    .451188     .666667    .1
    .413354     .666667    .2

and so on
```

Fig. 8.13. A teleprinter connected remotely to a GE 635 computer is here used by the author to do the calculations for plotting the curves in Fig. 26.13.

```
101.  – READY          PROGRAM  PROBQ
102.  + READY     1    DIMENSION  R (50)
102.  + RJECT         THIS STATEMENT MUST NOT BE NUMBERED
102.  + READY          DIMENSION  R (50)
103.  + READY          DIMENSION  P (50, 100)
104.  + READY     5    DO 26 N = 1, 10
105.  + READY    10    X = 0
106.  + READY    11    DO 22  I = 1, 50
107.  + READY          R(I) = X
108.  + READY          X = X + .02
109.  + READY          Z = R(I)
110.  + READY    15    DO 20 K = 1, N
111.  + READY    20    Z = Z – (1.– R(I)) *R(I) * *K
112.  + READY    22    P(I, N) = Z
113.  + READY          PRINT 23, N
114.  + READY    23    FORMAT (2HN =, 13)
115.  + READY          PRINT 26, (P(I, N), I = 1, 50)
115.  + RJECT         STATEMENT 26 PREVIOUSLY DEFINED OR REFERRED TO AS
                      EXECUTABLE
115.  + READY    24    PRINT 25, (P(I, N), I = 1, 50)
116.  + READY    26    CONTINUE
117.  + READY    25    FORMAT (10(F 6.3))
118.  + READY          IF (N –10) 30, 32, 32
119.  + READY    30    GO TO 10
120.  + READY    32    DO 26 N = 20, 100, 20
121.  + READY          GO TO 10
122.  + READY          START (0)
```

Errors are picked up statement by statement as the program is being typed in.

The program is executed as soon as it is entered.

```
114. = o 23    N = 1
116. = o 25    0.    0.000 0.002 0.004 0.006 0.010 0.014 0.020 0.026 0.032
116. =     2   0.040 0.048 0.058 0.068 0.078 0.090 0.102 0.116 0.130 0.144
116. =     3   0.160 0.176 0.194 0.212 0.230 0.250 0.270 0.292 0.314 0.336
116. =     4   0.360 0.384 0.410 0.436 0.462 0.490 0.518 0.548 0.578 0.608
116. =     5   0.640 0.672 0.706 0.740 0.774 0.810 0.846 0.884 0.922 0.960
114. = o 23    N = 2
116. = o 25    0.    0.000 0.000 0.000 0.001 0.001 0.002 0.003 0.004 0.006
116. =     2   0.008 0.011 0.014 0.018 0.022 0.027 0.033 0.039 0.047 0.055
116. =     3   0.064 0.074 0.085 0.097 0.111 0.125 0.141 0.157 0.176 0.195
116. =     4   0.216 0.238 0.262 0.287 0.314 0.343 0.373 0.405 0.439 0.475
116. =     5   0.512 0.551 0.593 0.636 0.681 0.729 0.779 0.831 0.885 0.941
114. = o 23    N = 3
116. = o 25    0.    0.000 0.000 0.000 0.000 0.000 0.000 0.000 0.001 0.001
114. 1 = o 23   N = 20
```

Fig. 8.14. Work carried out by the author at a QUIKTRAN terminal in order to draw the curves in Fig. 26.16.

```
116. = o 25    0.      0.000 0.000 0.000 0.000 0.000 0.000 0.000 0.000 0.000
116. =      2  0.000 0.000 0.000 0.000 0.000 0.000 0.000 0.000 0.000 0.000
116. =      3  0.000 0.000 0.000 0.000 0.000 0.000 0.000 0.000 0.000 0.000
116. =      4  0.000 0.000 0.000 0.000 0.000 0.001 0.001 0.002 0.004 0.007
116. =      5  0.012 0.019 0.031 0.049 0.078 0.122 0.189 0.290 0.442 0.668
111. =         XEQER EXECUTION RESULTS IN FLOATING POINT OVER/UNDER. FLOW
123. + READY          ALTER (10, 11)
105. + ALTER      10   X = .78
105. 1 + ALTER    11   DO 22 I = 40, 50
105. 2 + ALTER         ALTERX
123. + READY          START (32)
113. 1 = o 23   N = 20
116. = o 25    0.      0.000 0.000 0.000 0.000 0.000 0.000 0.000 0.000 0.000
116. =      2  0.000 0.000 0.000 0.000 0.000 0.000 0.000 0.000 0.000 0.000
116. =      3  0.000 0.000 0.000 0.000 0.000 0.000 0.000 0.000 0.000 0.000
116. =      4  0.000 0.000 0.000 0.000 0.000 0.001 0.001 0.002 0.004 0.007
116. =      5  0.012 0.019 0.031 0.049 0.078 0.122 0.189 0.290 0.442 0.668
113. 1 = o 23   N = 40
116. = o 25    0.    0.    0.    0.    0.    0.    0.    0.    0.    0.
116. =      2  0.    0.    0.    0.    0.    0.    0.    0.    0.    0.
123. + BREAK
123. + READY          ALTER (24, 24)
115. + ALTER      24   PRINT 25, (P( I, N), I = 41, 50)
115. 1 + ALTER         ALTERX
123. + READY          START (32)
113. 1 = o 23   N = 20
116. = 25   5  0.012 0.019 0.031 0.049 0.078 0.122 0.189 0.290 0.442 0.668
113. 1 = o 23   N = 40
116. = 25      0.000 0.000 0.001 0.002 0.006 0.015 0.036 0.084 0.195 0.446
113. 1 = o 23   N = 60
116. = 25      0.000 0.000 0.000 0.000 0.000 0.002 0.007 0.024 0.086 0.298
113. 1 = o 23   N = 80
116. = 25      0.000 0.000 0.000 0.000 0.000 0.000 0.001 0.007 0.038 0.199
113. 1 = o 23   N = 100
116. = 25      0.000 0.000 0.000 0.000 0.000 0.000 0.000 0.002 0.017 0.133
```

This error is corrected at the terminal as soon as it is revealed.

The program execution is interrupted by the terminal operator because he wants to make a change

Figure 8.14. (CONT.)

Fig. 8.15. An M.I.T. scientist, who like many of his colleagues, is used to using a powerful computer without moving from his desk.

tell the computer to repeat its answer.) The girl keys in details of the calculation she wants to perform and the computer replies by voice.

She keys in the digits and operators of the calculation. Each operator keyed in (except +) must be followed by an✻, in order that the computer can tell that it is an operator. She ends each operation by signalling ✻ ✻. Thus if she wishes to divide 3 by 14, she keys in:

3 7 ✻ 14 ✻ ✻   ("7 ✻" means divide)

and the computer speaks back over the telephone with a distinct human voice:

Your answer: Two. One. Four. Two. Eight. Five. Seven. One. Four. Two. . .

and so on for fourteen digits.

She keys 1 ✻ to mean "decimal point" thus to subtract 3.8692 from 14.908 she would key:

141 ✻ 908 0 ✻ 31 ✻ 8692 ✻ ✻ .

IJOB	Initialize job
ASSIGN DTA	Assign a DECtape
DEVICE DTA5 ASSIGNED	
CORE 1	Assign 1024 words of core
GET DTAØ: EDITOR	Load the editor
JOB SETUP	
START	Start the job
S5, MATRIX	Create a file called MATRIX on DECtape 5
I1Ø, 1Ø	Initialize sequencing at 10 and increment by 10
ØØØ1Ø **TITLE MATRIX**	
ØØØ2Ø **X = (A + B∗C)**	
ØØØ3Ø **DO 1 I = 1, 8**	
ØØØ4Ø **X = (A + B) ∗C**	
ØØ25Ø **END**	Leave incrementing mode
ØØ26Ø	
I 11	Insert line 11
ØØØ11 **DIMENSION A(8)**	
D3Ø	Delete line 30
P1Ø, 26Ø	Print lines 10 – 250
ØØØ1Ø TITLE MATRIX	
ØØØ11 DIMENSION A(8)	
ØØØ2Ø DO 1 I = 1, 8	
ØØØ4Ø X = (A + B)∗C	
⋮	
ØØ25Ø END	
E	End file
IC	Transfer control to monitor
KJOB	End the job

Figure 8.16

Fig. 8.17. Solving homework problems by computer. An inexpensive touchtone unit sends calculations to the computer. The computer replies by human voice.

The machine replies:

Your answer: One. One. Point. Zero. Three. Eight. Eight.

If she failed to write this all down and wants it repeated, she presses 8✳✳✳, and the machine repeats it.

The machine is equipped with temporary and permanent storage locations into which results may be placed with keys 2 and 3. The storage may be cleared with the "+" key. Using these storages, lengthy calculations may be performed. Thus if she presses 2✳0 this means "Place a number into temporary storage 0 for use in the next problem." If she presses 2✳7, this means "Place a number in permanent storage 7 for future use".

To calculate $\pi \times 3.78^2$, the sequence would be as follows:

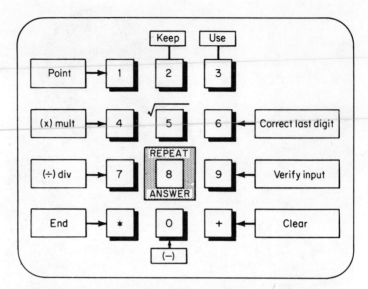

Fig. 8.18. The touch-tone telephone keyboard with overlay. The code on the overlay near each key serves to identify the various operations and instructions at the disposal of the user in performing her calculations.

31✱78 4✱ 31✱78 2✱0 ✱✱

Your answer: Holds One. Four. Point. Two. Eight. Eight. Four. Key your function.

4✱ 31✱ 1417 ✱✱

Your answer: Four. Four. Point. Eight. Eight. Nine. Eight. Six. Six. Two. Eight.

Similarly she may use the contents of, for example, permanent storage 9, by keying 3✱9.

If she makes mistakes which the computer can detect, it will inform her, as with other terminal systems, thus:

31✱78 4✱ 31✱78 2✱ ✱✱

A storage location has not been indicated. Please re-enter your problem and specify a storage location after the Use function.

31✱78 4✱ 31✱ 78 2✱97 ✱✱

You have specified a storage lacation which does not exist. Please re-enter your problem.

723 7✱3✱9 ✱✱

You have indicated a division by zero. Change your division and re-enter the problem.

723 7✱ 379 ✱✱

Your answer: One. Nine. Zero. Seven. Six. Five. One. Seven. One. Five. Three.

*Nine. Five. Seven. Your message has not been followed by the End function. Verify
your entry.*

9* **

Your entry: Seven. Two. Three. Divided by. Three. Seven. Nine.

A similar method has been used in simple commercial applications, for
example, checking a customer's credit in a department store.

PROBLEM-ORIENTED   Some languages are designed for one specific
LANGUAGE   type of calculation, or one type of problem. In
                        this way a problem can be made much easier to
tackle than by using a general language such as FORTRAN or ALGOL. Various
categories of engineering problems, for instance, can be given a *problem-
oriented* language which enable that particular problem to be tackled quickly
and easily. A remote computing system may have in its files many such
languages for different users, which can be called into operation from the
terminal. This approach holds great promise of widening the range of
scientists who use computers in their daily work.

A simple example of such a language is IBM's COGO. This is designed
as a very quick means of solving civil engineering coordinate geometry
problems. Figure 8.20 is an example of using COGO at a QUIKTRAN terminal.
This version of COGO has, in fact, been written in the QUIKTRAN language.*

Figure 8.20 is the work of a terminal user tackling the problem sketched in
Fig. 8.19. It is desired to find the area of the shaded portion of this diagram,
and other details of that area. First the operator calls in the COGO program
by typing **LOAD (COGO)**. He then starts the COGO program by typing
START (1) and this enables him to type in the known details of the map in
question as shown.

Conversation between man and machine can well be a somewhat one-
sided affair as the two have rather different talents. The computer can be
a prolific "talker." It can display masses of facts in natural language very
quickly, if so desired. It does not, however, have an equal flair for understanding what its human operators say. Usually they have to use messages
which are simple, perfectly accurate, and completely preplanned. Any deviation from this and the machine will abruptly ask its user to rephrase his
statement.

Figure 8.21 is a diverting illustration in which the computer is doing
most of the talking. A GE 635, at the same time it is conducting more serious
business with most of its users is playing "Black Jack" with one of its teleprinter operators.

*IBM manual on QUIKTRAN/COGO, Form H20-0204-0. International Business Machines
Corp., 1965.

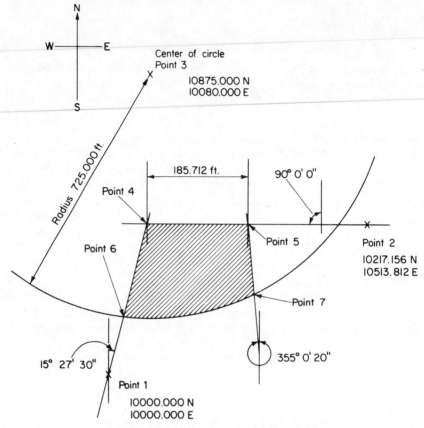

Fig. 8.19. A problem in civil engineering coordinate geometry: find details of the shaded area (see Fig. 8.20).

In many commercial applications it is, indeed, desirable to design the conversation language so that the operator keys in as little as possible, and the computer helps her with its high speed displays.

Take the case of passengers checking in at a bustling airport desk. A small cathode-ray tube terminal is used by the check-in agent to help in this process. It has connected to it a distant computer which has full details of the bookings made for the flight being checked in.

A lady by the name of Mrs Kirksieck-Schaefer turns up in the queue, somewhat harassed because she does not know whether her husband has checked in or not. If the language were designed so that the check-in girl, who is being pestered from all sides, had to type in the name of the passenger she would probably spell it wrong. Instead she types in **∗KI**, which means

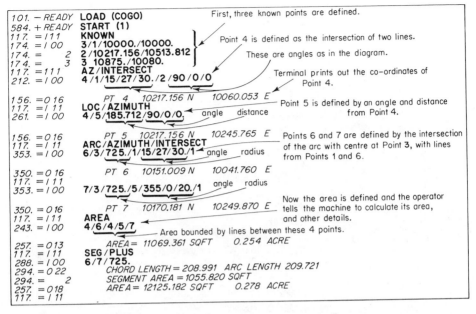

Fig. 8.20. Use of cogo on the problem in Fig. 8.19.

"display the passengers booked whose names begin with KI." The "$*$" character on the keyboard is labelled "display." The machine displays the relevant passengers who have not checked in yet:

Mr. Kirksieck-Schaefer has not checked in yet—his name is there on the screen. His wife decides to go ahead and check in without him. The check-in girl types **C2/F/E/4**. C means check-in. **2** refers to line 2 on the display above. **F/E/4** means that the passenger is female (a fact which will be used in plane weight and balance calculations), her initial is E, and she is checking in four bags. Possibly, it would be required to type the weight of the bags, (also for the weight and balance calculations) although probably not.

The computer now can identify the passenger. Details of this passenger including any comments that were made on the passenger's record when the reservation was made are displayed. A suggested seat number may also be displayed. This could be related as far as possible to a passenger's requests when the booking was made. (No airline is yet doing the latter but some are planning it.) The passenger may wish to have a different seat from the one he was assigned, and, if so, possibly a seat plan would be displayed on the screen with indications of the type of allocation so far made to different seats. When Mr Kirksieck-Schaefer turns up, the girl will have to make sure that he has a seat next to his wife.

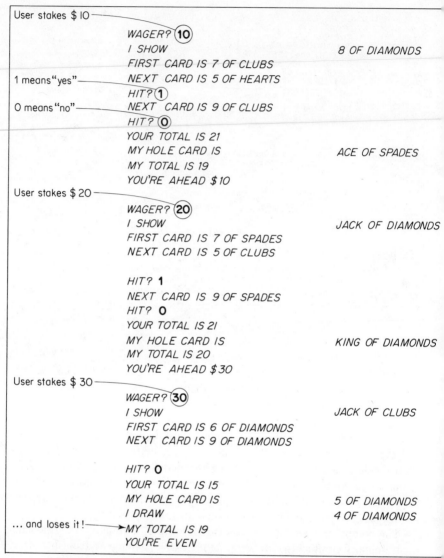

User stakes $ 10

WAGER? (10)
I SHOW   8 OF DIAMONDS
FIRST CARD IS 7 OF CLUBS

1 means "yes" —— NEXT CARD IS 5 OF HEARTS
HIT? (1)
0 means "no" —— NEXT CARD IS 9 OF CLUBS
HIT? (0)
YOUR TOTAL IS 21
MY HOLE CARD IS   ACE OF SPADES
MY TOTAL IS 19
YOU'RE AHEAD $10

User stakes $ 20

WAGER? (20)
I SHOW   JACK OF DIAMONDS
FIRST CARD IS 7 OF SPADES
NEXT CARD IS 5 OF CLUBS

HIT? 1
NEXT CARD IS 9 OF SPADES
HIT? 0
YOUR TOTAL IS 21
MY HOLE CARD IS   KING OF DIAMONDS
MY TOTAL IS 20
YOU'RE AHEAD $30

User stakes $ 30

WAGER? (30)
I SHOW   JACK OF CLUBS
FIRST CARD IS 6 OF DIAMONDS
NEXT CARD IS 9 OF DIAMONDS

HIT? 0
YOUR TOTAL IS 15
MY HOLE CARD IS   5 OF DIAMONDS
I DRAW   4 OF DIAMONDS
... and loses it! —— MY TOTAL IS 19
YOU'RE EVEN

Fig. 8.21. A GE 635 while conducting more serious business with most of its users is playing "Black Jack" with one of its teleprinter operators.

A variety of circumstances can occur during the check-in process. Some passengers arrive with no reservation. Some with reservations fail to arrive. Groups have to be handled. One passenger will ask to sit next to another who has checked in elsewhere, etc. The agent's actions should be designed so that she has the minimum of keying to do, as in the case above.

* KI		
1 KING	PAR	Y
2 KIRKSIECK — SCHAEFER	ROM	Y
3 KIRKSIECK — SCHAEFER	ROM	Y
4 KIELCZEWSKI	PAR	F
5 KIKUOKA KYOKO	PAR	F

Figure 8.22

UNTRAINED OPERATORS   For many of the conversations discussed above, the operator needs special training in the language he must use to converse with the machine. Certainly with QUIKTRAN and the airline reservation systems above, the operator needs careful tuition and some practice. Training, as will be discussed in a later chapter, is an important consideration in the implementation of a commercial real-time system.

It is also desirable, however, to devise "languages" in some applications for which the operator will need little or no training. He will need to be trained to use the terminal hardware, but once he knows this, what he keys into the machine becomes largely self-evident. We might, in fact, categorize our terminal operators into three groups.

(1) Programmers, such as those using QUIKTRAN, etc.
(2) Operators trained in a special language, who use the terminal uniquely for one particular application—e.g., airline reservations, etc.
(3) Operators who know how to work the terminal but who have had no special training in any "language" for conversing with the computer.

A major part of the computer manufacturer's revenue in the years to come is likely to be through terminal applications which "bring the computer to the masses." How fast this comes about will depend to a large extent on our success in devising simple means for the man in the street to communicate with a computer via a terminal—means which do not frighten away people who are not in the high I.Q. brackets, and people too busy to learn elaborate terminal "languages."

In industry, a terminal for administrative purposes or a terminal for providing management with information, will operate, not on one application, like the airline reservation terminals, but on a whole range of different applications. An office clerk may at one moment want to enquire about the status of a given order, and at another time enter details about payments

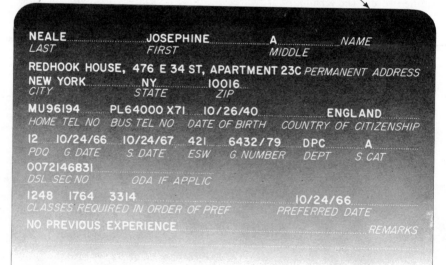

This screen is retrieved by the operator for data entry

The operator moves the cursor and "fills in" the blanks thus

Fig. 8.23. The bureaucracy of the future? This technique of "filling in forms" with the keyboard on the screen of an inexpensive display terminal, is one way an operator untrained in any special language can communicate with the system. It will often be any one step in a lengthier conversation.

received. He needs a simple means of doing a wide variety of different operations.

It is the dream of most of us to do away with administrative paperwork. Certainly, the administrative terminal systems now being planned in some big organizations will reduce paperwork drastically. It seems probable that, as these techniques spread, much of our future form-filling-in could be done with a typewriter-like keyboard and a display tube.

In Fig. 8.23 the operator is presented a "form" to fill in as part of the man-machine conversation. The keys on the keyboard enable her to move the "cursor" around the screen to any area that needs "filling in." She positions the cursor at the start of any of the dotted lines and then types her entry. The dotted lines are replaced by the characters she types. To speed them up, each entry starts on the first character of a line on the screen. The cursor can be moved quickly to these positions. When the screen-full is transmitted to the computer, only the characters she entered will be sent, along with the control characters indicating the beginning of a new line.

One single form is limited in the data it can handle, and more usually the cathode ray tube will display a sequence of screens, each screen dependent upon the previous operator entry. In this way, the operator is led down a logic "tree," until the requisite data is entered or the facts required are displayed, and often, as before, the computer will be doing much more talking than its operator.

Consider the following conversation in which a company has details of its customers and their orders stored in the computer files. A customer telephones, wishing to bring forward the delivery date of an order. The clerk sits at a terminal and the computer tells him to enter the customer number if known. However, the clerk does not have it immediately available. The conversation is shown in Fig. 8.24.

The order records are tied into a factory schedule which indicates that the requested delivery date cannot quite be achieved unless the priority is changed.

It is necessary for the terminal operator, as in other applications above, to identify himself, and to have some means of indicating to the computer that he has the authority to make the change to the records. This may be done by keying in a code number whenever he uses the terminal, or by using a hardware device which enables him to insert a unique card, or key, or badge.

Notice that the conversation above does not require knowledge of special codes or mnemonics on the part of the operator. The terminal always tells him precisely what to do. He need not learn any terminal "language." This differs considerably from the airline reservation examples given earlier. For the latter, it is common that the operators have a two-week training course. The operator of the administrative terminal in Fig. 8.24 may have to do such a wide variety of operations that the above means of conversing is

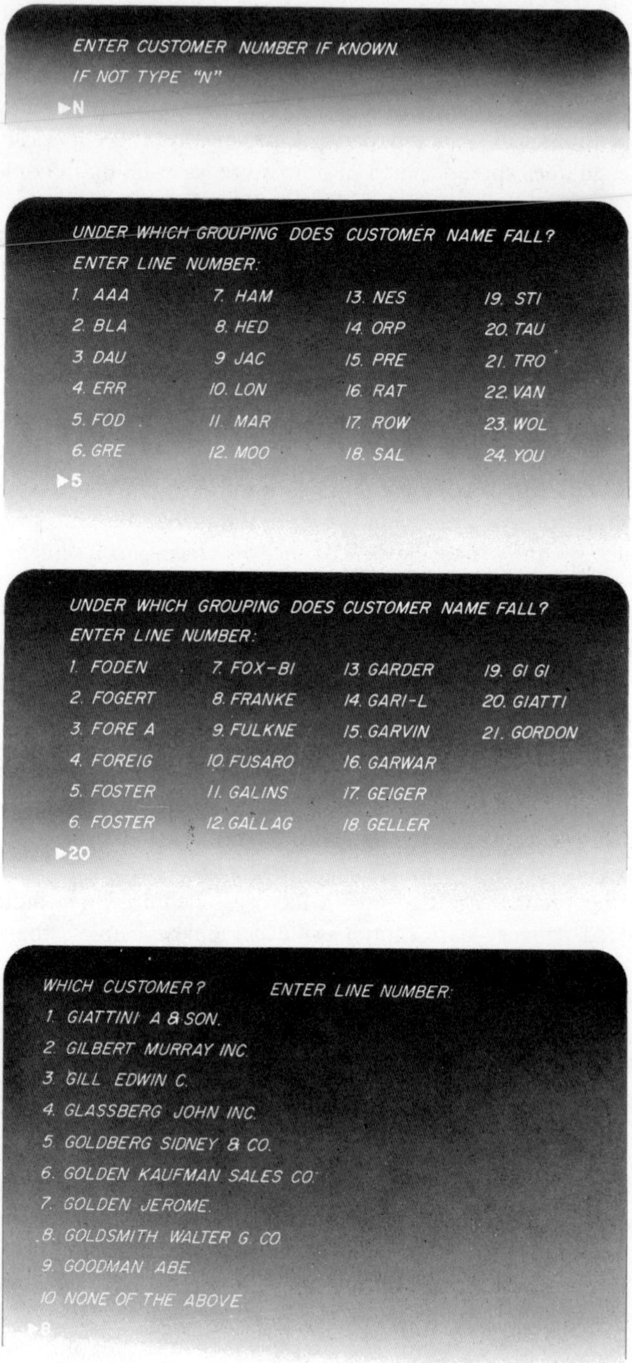

ENTER CUSTOMER NUMBER IF KNOWN.

IF NOT TYPE "N".

▶N

UNDER WHICH GROUPING DOES CUSTOMER NAME FALL?

ENTER LINE NUMBER:

1. AAA	7. HAM	13. NES	19. STI
2. BLA	8. HED	14. ORP	20. TAU
3. DAU	9 JAC	15. PRE	21. TRO
4. ERR	10. LON	16. RAT	22. VAN
5. FOD	11. MAR	17. ROW	23. WOL
6. GRE	12. MOO	18. SAL	24. YOU

▶5

UNDER WHICH GROUPING DOES CUSTOMER NAME FALL?

ENTER LINE NUMBER:

1. FODEN	7. FOX-BI	13. GARDER	19. GI GI
2. FOGERT	8. FRANKE	14. GARI-L	20. GIATTI
3. FORE A	9. FULKNE	15. GARVIN	21. GORDON
4. FOREIG	10. FUSARO	16. GARWAR	
5. FOSTER	11. GALINS	17. GEIGER	
6. FOSTER	12. GALLAG	18. GELLER	

▶20

WHICH CUSTOMER?   ENTER LINE NUMBER:

1. GIATTINI A & SON.

2. GILBERT MURRAY INC.

3. GILL EDWIN C.

4. GLASSBERG JOHN INC.

5. GOLDBERG SIDNEY & CO.

6. GOLDEN KAUFMAN SALES CO.

7. GOLDEN JEROME.

8. GOLDSMITH WALTER G. CO

9. GOODMAN ABE.

10. NONE OF THE ABOVE.

▶8

Figure 8.24

```
CUSTOMER NUMBER:    17-8341
GOLDSMITH WALTER G CO
745, OLD STONE HIGHWAY, SPRINGS,
EAST HAMPTON, NY., 11937
REPRESENTATIVE  K.B  JENKINS  #45731


PRESS  ENTER  IF  CORRECT
```

The clerk presses the ENTER key

```
WHICH INFORMATION IS TO BE CHANGED?
ENTER LINE NUMBER:
 1. NEW ORDER              9. INVOICE TO ADDRESS
 2. CANCEL ORDER          10. SHIP TO ADDRESS
 3. ORDER QUANTITY        11. CUSTOMER ADDRESS
 4. DELIVERY DATE         12. CUSTOMER NAME
 5. PRIORITY CODE         13. MISC INSTRUCTIONS
 6. ORDER DETAILS         14. REPRESENTATIVE DETAILS
 7. DISCOUNT              15. BRANCH OFFICE
 8. TAX DETAILS           16. OTHER
►4
```

```
WHICH ORDER IS TO BE CHANGED?
ENTER LINE NUMBER:
    ORDER #   ITEM#S                          ORDER DATE  DEL DATE
 1. 573824    87289   00241   00029   4/1/66    4/1/67
              00310   77139   04126
              00900
 2. 575931    00391   00700   00421  10/1/66    4/1/68
 3. 575828    00750   00900          12/1/66   12/1/67
 4. 579003    02107                   6/1/66    8/1/67
►2
```

```
ORDER NUMBER 575931
ITEM #S    DESCRIPTION                          QTY
00391      MAGNETIC D EXTRACTOR 7 BR             5
00700      LINK ADAPTOR ADDL                     5
00421      CTC DIRECT CONTROL                    5
ORDER DATE   10/1/66          DELIV DATE   4/1/68

ENTER NEW REQUIRED DELIV DATE   (XX/XX/XX)
►10/01/66
```

```
EARLIEST DELIVERY DATE POSSIBLE AT PRIORITY 3 IS
2/1/66
IF THIS IS REQUESTED ENTER "Y"
►Y
```

desirable. It is, however, used at the expense of a considerable increase in the number of characters that must be sent on the transmission lines from the computer. Such squandering of transmission line capacity could be prohibitively expensive for a far-flung airline reservation system. As always in such system design there is a compromise to be faced.

TEACHING   A further step to help the operator can be the inclusion of what is virtually a *teaching program* on-line. This can be useful with any of the three categories of operators listed above. When the operator fumbles or makes mistakes in his use of the terminal or its language, the computer can give him a few lessons on the spot. He can ask for assistance whenever there is something he would like explained.

A user of System Development Corporation's TINT language for on-line programming can ask the computer to explain any part of the language he has forgotten or is not familiar with. Thus,

? EXPLAIN RENUMBER

✱ *TO MAKE TINT RENUMBER YOUR PROGRAM LINES, TYPE:*
? *RENUMBER*

YOUR PROGRAM LINES WILL BE RESEQUENCED STARTING AT 1.00. THE SECOND LINE WILL BE 2.00, ETC.

However, if he asks it to explain something not in its vocabulary or if he spells the item incorrectly, it asks for clarification thus,

? EXPLAIN HOLLERITH VALUES

✱ *EXPLAIN WHAT?*

? EXPLAIN HOLLERITH

✱ *EXPLAIN WHAT?*

The Rand Corporation's JOSS system is briefer in demanding an explanation of input it does not understand and simply says,

Eh?

In the years to come, *teaching* is probably going to become a major application of time-shared computers. The indications to date are that it can be very efficient and quite fascinating for the pupil. Writing a good teaching program, however, that deals with all types of student reaction is lengthy and skilled work. The examples below represent a short extract from a course on statistics by a behavioral psychologist at IBM's Thomas J. Watson Research

Center. The experience of four students illustrates the differing response to the course material. Notice how the computer can vary its reaction in a way a simpler teaching machine can not.

Student No. 1:

> 51. Therefore, the shape of the sampling distribution of t depends on
>
> _____.
>
> **area**
>
> Remember that we have just seen that different size samples result in different distribution curves.
>
> **size**
>
> 52. Notice that the sampling distributions of t in Fig. 2 are all symmetrical, but not normal, with a mean of _____.
>
> **X**
>
> If we convert our scores to standard scores, what should the mean of the distribution be?
>
> **zero**
>
> 53. The means of the sampling distributions in the previous question tend to be 0 because all the raw scores have been converted to _____ scores.
>
> **z**
>
> This answer is partially correct but a more inclusive answer would be _____ scores.
>
> **t and z**
>
> What is another name for t and z-scores?
>
> **deviation**
>
> Since t and z-scores are standard scores which result in a mean of 0 for the distributions, the answer is _____ scores.
>
> **standard**
>
> 54. Now refer to the last page of this chapter in the text. There are two distributions with n's of 5 and 50. The curve based on an n of 5 is (Y/Z).

Student No. 2:

> 51. Therefore, the shape of the sampling distribution of t depends on _____.
>
> **n**
>
> 52. Notice that the sampling distributions of t in Fig. 2 are all symmetrical, but not normal, with a mean of _____.
>
> **zero**
>
> 53. The means of the sampling distributions in the previous question tend to be 0 because all the raw scores have been converted to _____ scores.
>
> **t**
>
> This answer is partially correct but a more inclusive answer would be _____ scores.
>
> **t and z**

What is another name for t and z-scores?
standard
54. Now refer to the last page of this chapter in the text. There are two
distributions with n's of 5 and 50. The curve based on an n of 5 is (Y/Z).

Student No. 3:

51. Therefore, the shape of the sampling distribution of t depends on _____.
number
52. Notice that the sampling distributions of t in Fig. 2 are all symmetrical,
but not normal, with a mean of _____.
0
53. The means of the sampling distributions in the previous question tend to
be 0 because all the raw scores have been converted to _____ scores.
z
*This answer is partially correct but a more inclusive answer would be _____
scores.*
standard
54. Now refer to the last page of this chapter in the text. There are two
distributions with n's of 5 and 50. The curve based on an n of 5 is (Y/Z).

Student No. 4:

51. Therefore, the shape of the sampling distribution of t depends on _____.
area
*Remember that we have just seen that different size samples result in differ-
ent distribution curves.*
tails
*Since the shape of the sampling distribution is dependent on sample size,
the best answer here is "n."*
52. Notice that the sampling distributions of t in Fig. 2 are all symmetrical,
but not normal, with a mean of _____.
n
*If we convert our scores to standard scores, what should the mean of the
distribution be?*
x
*Reflect back to the mean of the normal curve of z-scores for a possible
solution.*
0
53. The means of the sampling distributions in the previous question tend
to be 0 because all the raw scores have been converted to _____ scores.
standard
54. Now refer to the last page of this chapter in the text. There are two
distributions with n's of 5 and 50. The curve based on an n of 5 is (Y/Z).

Many members of the teaching profession still regard mechanized teaching as something that can only widen the gap in personal contact between teachers and pupils. Paradoxically, in actual practice with simple machines it has worked in exactly the opposite way. It takes the drudgery out of the teachers' hands and gives them far more time for individual contact where it is particularly needed. As with other real-time systems it can help the user to concentrate on those aspects of the work that are more uniquely human. The examples above were programmed with IBM'S *Computer Assisted Instruction* language,* a language that will enable a teacher with no detailed knowledge of computers to program a course of instruction and to improve upon it as he observes the reactions of students. It seems likely that, as teaching programs are built up over the years to come, they will be continuously improved upon by successive teachers observing their effect on varying classes of students.

The interaction between man and machine needs a language of some type. The illustrations in this chapter have been of some of the first attempts at achieving this. There is a vast amount of work to be done in the development of languages for different purposes and different professions. This is one of the most interesting areas of future software development.

*IBM manual on *Computer Assisted Instruction, Form* C24-3253-1. International Business Machines Corp., 1965.

9 THE ORGANIZATION OF DATA IN THE PROCESSING UNIT

Two factors complicate the flow of data in the processing unit of an on-line system. First, the system may be in use by human operators or geared to other events which are very slow compared with computer speeds. In this case, to use a fast processing unit's power efficiently, a high degree of multiprogramming may be needed. Secondly, events occur at times which are unpredictable; therefore, the sequence in which programs are executed changes constantly. The actions of the computer must be scheduled dynamically by the computer according to the needs of the moment.

TIMING   On conventional computer applications of the past the programmer has mapped out the utilization of time and core in detail when the programs were designed. On most on-line systems he cannot do this because of the randomness of events.

The following times are unpredictable:

1. The times at which external events occur. For example, the time when a human operator enters a message.

2. The times of clock interrupts. A clock may be set to make the computer perform some action at a given time and may interrupt it at a point which might be anywhere in a program.

3. The times of completion of input/output actions, especially for references to random-access files.

On a real-time system messages arriving at the computer from human operators or automatic input need a quick response. The allocation of time, core, channels, input/output units, and other facilities must therefore be done quickly by the Supervisory Programs.

The timing pattern varies from one type of system to another. Five simplified diagrams of timing patterns are shown in Figs. 30.1 to 30.5 on pages 470-473.

The diagrams are of systems planned for one specific application, rather than time-sharing systems in which the computer constantly switches its attention from one type of user to another.

Where random-access files are used with seeks occurring at random, these complicate the timing because the seek durations are long in comparison with processing. It is usually desirable for the processing unit to carry on with other work while a file reference is being made. This is illustrated in Fig. 30.2. Here, the processing of one transaction requires two file references, first on file channel A and second on file channel B, represented on the diagram by dotted lines. These references can be completely overlapped with processing: so can the input and output operations, also marked on the diagram by dotted lines. In many applications the ratio of dotted lines to processing time would be greater than in this diagram. Figure 30.3 shows several of these same transactions being processed in parallel and illustrates how multiprogramming is used to increase the throughput of a system in which input/output time would otherwise prevent full use of the processing unit. Figure 30.5 gives another example of this, and here the input is repetitive rather than random.

Some systems need a very high degree of multiprogramming. Others, for example, many small savings bank systems, are able to use slow processing units and avoid multiprogramming, as in Fig. 30.1.

Small systems or situations, for example, during program testing, in which one transaction is completed before the processing of another begins, as in Fig. 30.1, are referred to throughout this book as *single thread*. When more than one transaction, or thread, is processed in parallel, as in Fig. 30.3, the term *multithread* is used.

QUEUES   Input to an on-line system usually occurs at times independent of the state of current transactions in the processing units. Consequently queues build up, just as queues of automobiles build up at a gas station.

Transactions are kept waiting when they request data from the files. They may have to wait for the attention of the processing unit, for a file channel to become free, or for an output line to become available. There accumulate queues of requests for a file unit, queues of half-completed items, queues of items on which processing has not yet started, and so on.

A major part of the work of the Supervisory Programs on such systems is the building of queues for input/output units and files and queues of items requiring to be processed. Items are transferred to and from these queues according to considerations of timing and priority.

When new transactions arrive they cause an interruption in the processing and are let into core. If a separately programmed line control unit is used, they are assembled in this and a completed message is sent to the main computer. If this is not the case, they will have to be assembled in the main computer. Either way, a message arrives in the core of the main computer and waits there to be processed. If many messages arrive in the same short space of time, a *new-input queue* will build up of messages waiting. As the transactions arrive more or less at random the queues will occasionally grow long.

When the processing on one item proceeds, the need will probably be found to obtain or update information in a backing store. This will involve a wait of anything from 10 to 600 milliseconds if the request is serviced immediately. However, there may be other transactions already using that input/ output channel or waiting to use it. And so queues build up waiting for the channels. This constitutes too long a delay for a fast computer, and so it continues with other work, perhaps processing the next item in the new-input queue.

When the input/output request has been completed, work can start again on the processing of the transaction. It waits in a *work-in-progress* queue for the Supervisory Program to transfer control again to its Application Program.

As processing proceeds once more, the need may again arise for an input/ output operation, and the transaction finds itself again in a *channel-waiting queue*. This may happen several times, perhaps many times, in the life of a transaction. Finally, its processing is complete. An answer-back message is composed, or possibly several messages to different terminals, and the instruction is given to send these. Again there may be a queue because the channel to which the line control unit is attached is busy, and so the transaction waits in an *output queue*

There are thus four common types of queue, and these will be referred to consistently throughout this book with the names:

1. New-input queue
2. Channel-waiting queue
3. Work-in progress queue
4. Output queue

In technical literature the word "list" is sometimes used to mean the same as queue in this book.

There may be other types of queue, for example, an overflow queue in which items are temporarily stored on a backing store or tape because too many items have arrived at the computer at the same time, or a non-real-time queue containing items of lower priority contesting for processor time with the real-time transactions.

In the core storage a queue consists of a number of blocks of data. These are not necessarily sequential but may be scattered throughout the core. If they are scattered, they are connected by control words, as illustrated in Fig. 9.1. Here an area of core is divided into fixed-length blocks which are used for different purposes. The queues straggle across this area. The next block to be chained to the queue shown may be from anywhere in the area, depending upon which blocks are uncommitted at that time.

The control words may be in the blocks themselves so that the blocks are chained together as shown, or they may be in a separate index maintained by

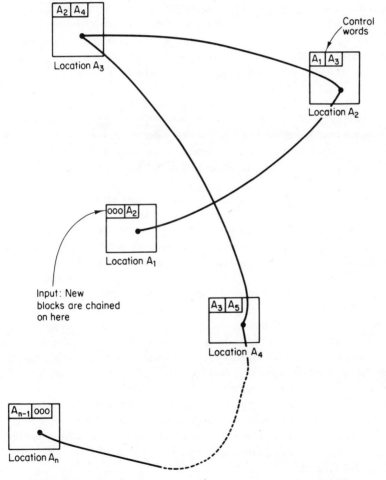

Fig. 9.1. An illustration of a typical queue. Items are scattered throughout core but chained together by means of control words.

the Supervisory Program. If they are in the blocks, the control word may be the first word in each block. It gives the location of the next block of the chain. For the last block in the list it will have a value such as 00000 to indicate that this is the end of the chain.

When a block is moved from one queue to another, for example, moved from the channel-waiting queue to the work-in-progress queue because an input/output request has been completed, the block itself is not moved in core. It merely has its control words changed so that it becomes a member of a different queue.

DYNAMIC CORE ALLOCATION   The above mechanism is an example of *dynamic core allocation*. In many on-line and real-time systems the use of core constantly changes as processing switches from one type of transaction to another. There are two ways in which core of this type may be allocated: fixed core allocation, or dynamic core allocation.

With the former, specific areas are set apart for specific tasks. There are fixed areas into which new messages may be read, fixed areas into which records are read from file, fixed areas for programs, and so on. When processing switches to a new transaction type an area of core allocated in a certain fixed manner may be dumped onto a backing store and replaced by a different area.

Dynamic core allocation divides an area of core up into blocks. Any free block may be allocated for different purposes according to the requirements of the moment. Blocks are allocated in some systems for programs as well as for data. A typical use of dynamic core allocation is in the buffering for data arriving on the communication lines. Messages of widely varying lengths may arrive at unpredictable times. It can therefore be very uneconomic to allocate a fixed area to each line. Rather, a pool of blocks is made available for buffering, and blocks are taken from the pool as and when required. A long message may occupy several blocks chained together like queue chaining above.

When dynamic core allocation is used, it is necessary for the Supervisory Program to know which blocks are free so that it may quickly allocate a block for a new function. This may be achieved by a simple device. All the uncommitted blocks are chained together to form a type of queue of their own, referred to here as *uncommitted-storage list* When a block becomes free, it is chained to this list. When the Supervisory Program requires a block for a new function, it takes the first in this list. Whatever mechanism is used for programming the other queues, the same may be used for the uncommitted-storage list (Fig. 9.2).

The Supervisory Program may keep a count of how many blocks are in the uncommitted-storage list. Whenever it takes a block from it or adds a block to it, it updates the count. If the count falls below a certain figure, the Supervisory Program knows that the system is in danger of running out of core, and so it takes some form of emergency action. There may be different levels of emergency action for different degress of shortage.

MAIN
SCHEDULING
ROUTINE

Except on systems, such as process control systems in which instruments are scanned cyclicly, or systems handling batch transmission, the events on an on-line system occur in an unscheduled manner. The demands on the system will vary from moment to moment in an unpredictable fashion. New inputs will arrive before the preceding ones have been dealt with. Urgent situations will arise in the middle of not-so-urgent processing.

At the center of most such systems there is, therefore, a scheduling routine which looks periodically at the current demands on the system and decides what program shall operate next. Control returns to this *main scheduling routine* sufficiently frequently to ensure that the demands on the system are met.

The sets of rules that are used for scheduling the work differ considerably from one system to another depending upon its needs. The scheduling routine scans the current status of messages or system functions and, according to its rules, transfers control to the required program. All the programs are in a sense subroutines of this top executive.

The sequence of processing in the system is thus a series of relatively short bursts of program execution. When each program finishes, it passes control to the main scheduling routine and this decides which program is to be exe-

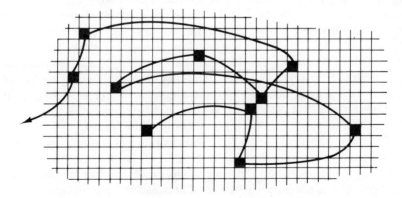

Fig. 9.2. *Uncommitted storage list:* The blocks not in use are chained together in the same way as a queue. New blocks are obtained from this chain, and released blocks are added to it.

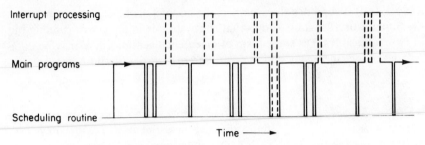

Fig. 9.3. At intervals the main scheduling routine decides what program to execute next, on a basis of the demands on the system at that moment.

cuted next. Superimposed upon this pattern are *interrupts*, illustrated in Fig. 9.3. In order to decide which segment of program is to be used next, some form of scheduling algorithm or set of rules must be used. This will be a function of parameters, such as the priorities of various tasks, the response times that are required, and the available equipment. The size of the main scheduling routine will depend upon the complexity of the set of rules used. It will differ very considerably from one system to another because their requirements differ.

A very simple example of a main scheduling routine is shown in Fig. 9.4. This piece of programming assumes that two categories of real-time transaction are waiting for the attention of the processing unit: new items which are now completely in core but on which work has not yet begun, and items on which work has begun but has been interrupted for some reason. The main scheduling routine scans these two queues, dealing first with work-in-progress items. It takes items from these queues and transfers control to the Application Program needed to process them. If there are no real-time items ready for further processing, it will see whether there is non-real-time work, such as tape processing or an on-line, non-real-time queue, to carry on with. This will be done only if there is a shortage of real-time work. Tests will be made as to the core storage and time that are currently available and, unless these exceed given amounts, no non-real-time work will be attempted. The available core may be checked by inspecting the count of blocks in the un-committed-storage list. The available time may be checked by inspecting a count of the number of transactions currently in the system.

If there are no items ready for processing and no non-real-time work, the computer cycles in a closed loop or waits for an interrupt to occur. As soon as an input/output or a file operation is completed or a new message enters the system, the item will be placed in one of the queues being scanned by the main scheduling routine, and this will transfer control to the next routine required to process the item. As soon as this program has finished or is held up waiting for an input/output or a file action, it will return control

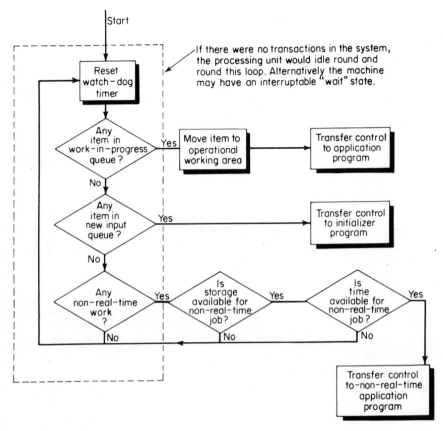

Fig. 9.4. A simple example of the central scanning loop of a supervisory program.

to the main scheduling routine. By this time, other interrupts may have resulted in further items being placed in the queues.

In this example no differentiation is made between the *priorities* of different real-time transactions. The main scheduling routine merely services the queues sequentially, first come first served. Input/output scheduling is done by a different routine when input/output interrupts occur. The type of central scanning loop of only a few instructions, described above, has served on many otherwise very complex applications. It is desirable that it should be as simple as possible because it is an overhead that may be used many times per second.

However, the main scheduling routine is likely to differ considerably from one application to another. Basically, a scheduling algorithm is needed for each application. This algorithm can be simple or can become very complex. It is a function of factors, such as

1. The priority structure between different tasks.

129

2. The precedence rules. Can one task interrupt another? Can one message pre-empt another?

3. How is the available equipment allocated? Are the input/output schedulers separate from the main scheduler?

4. What response times or deadlines must be met?

5. Are real-time work and non-real-time work combined?

Too complex a mechanism for scheduling gives rise to many difficulties in the implementation of the systems, especially in program and system testing.

TIME DIVISION

As shown in Fig. 9.3, the Application Programs cease periodically, and the main scheduling routine decides what is to be done next. There are two reasons that can cause a transfer to the main scheduling routine. First, the Application Program has finished all it can do for the time—either it is complete, or it can do no more until it receives the results of some file or input/output operation. Second, it has run for a long enough period of time, and control is taken away from it so that some other terminal can be serviced.

In the former case, if the system is giving a real-time response to a number of terminals, all of the segments of the Application Program must be fairly short in their execution time. In many systems for commercial work the program segments are all short. None take more than, say, fifty milliseconds, and so there is never any need to snatch control away from them. In a lengthy scientific program or process control system, control *may* be snatched away to deal with a situation that needs high-speed attention.

Probably the most frequent use of the second type of transfer is on time-sharing systems. Here, commonly, the user can enter any type of program to be compiled or executed. Some of these could occupy the system for a long enough time seriously to hold up other users if they ran to completion, and so they are not permitted to run for more than a short period, say a fifth of a second. The system's time is divided into *time slots*, and, at the end of the maximum time allowed to a program, it is interrupted and control given to the main scheduling routine so that, if other users need attention, they can be given it.

When the time-slot, or "quantum," for one user ends, it may be necessary to bring in a completely new set of data and programs for the next user. The conditions that existed for this user are restored exactly as they were when his programs were last removed from the computer a second or so ago. Processing and reading in the programs and data at the beginning of each time-slot can require an elaborate mechanism. The speed and efficiency with which the user's programs are "swapped" is a major factor in the design of a time-shared system. The means for bringing in new blocks or "pages" of program is referred to as the *paging mechanism*. This is discussed in Chapter 19.

Bringing in the new pages may be done entirely by programming or may be done partially by hardware. On any machine certain hardware features can help in speeding up this process. The bringing in of new programs will take place not only at the end of a time-slot, but also during the time-slot when a program is referred to which is not currently in core. In some cases, a user may write a program which is far too big for the current core of the machine; in this case, a paging mechanism will then move parts of the program in and out of core in order to execute it.

INTERRUPTS The term interrupt (different computers use different words, such as trap, derailment, or mode change) means that, because of a hardware event of some type, the program currently operating is temporarily stopped while a routine of higher priority is executed. When the *priority routine* is ended, control will normally return to the point at which the original program was interrupted, as in Fig. 9.3.

In some computers the original program cannot be interrupted at *any* point because this might cause a logic error under certain circumstances. Where desirable, instructions in it will be tagged, or marked, so that interrupts are inhibited. The interrupt will then have to wait until a nontagged instruction is reached in the program.

An interrupt is thus an automatic change in the program flow as a result of some condition arising in the data-processing system. Typical of the conditions that may cause an interrupt are the following:

1. *A signal that an input/output operation may begin.* For example, a line-control computer may signal that it is ready to transmit data to the central processing unit, or a file that has moved an access arm to a given location may signal that it is ready for a write operation to commence.

2. *A signal that an input/output or file operation is complete.* For example, when an input/output read or write is completed, the processing which was going on simultaneously with it is interrupted so that a priority routine can initiate a new read or write on that channel or unit without delay.

3. *A signal that an error or abnormal condition has been detected.* For example, a parity error in core or an input/output error will cause an interrupt to a priority routine for handling this condition rather than stop the computer, as it would have done on some older machines. A hardware feature, such as memory protection, will cause an interrupt if a program tries to reference a core-storage word beyond its specified area. Other types of program error may cause interrupts.

4. *A signal that indicates a special condition*, such as a timer reaching the end of its interval, or a real-time clock causing an interrupt at a given time.

An external signal from an operator or from equipment on-line to the computer may also cause an interrupt.

Some computers, particularly older machines, have only one level of interrupt. Others, as described in Chapter 19, have several levels so that a priority routine being carried out because of an interrupt may itself be interrupted by an event of still higher priority.

The main uses of interrupts on the systems being described are:

1. To keep the input/output units as busy as possible and thereby ensure that they are used efficiently.

2. To assist in obtaining a fast response time to real-time transactions.

3. To deal with emergency and error conditions and minimize the chance of their stopping the system.

INPUT/OUTPUT SCHEDULING   Let us look further at the question of keeping the input/output units busy.

In systems other than the simplest, the input/output activity is to a large degree independent of the main processing. The queues in the computer may be thought of as belonging to one of two categories: queues waiting for some type of input/output action, and queues of items waiting for processing. The latter are the queues scanned by a main scheduling routine such as that in Fig. 9.4 or more elaborate. The queues for input/output operations are, on most systems, scanned by a separate scheduling routine.

The input/output and file operations go on simultaneously with the processing and independently of it. When an input/output or file operation is completed, the processing will be interrupted so that the next job can be started on the unit in question as quickly as possible. The priority routine which deals with the interrupts will scan the queue of requests for that unit, if any, and initiate the next operation on it. When this is complete, the main processing will continue from where it was interrupted.

THREE TYPES OF ACTIVITY   On a typical system there are thus three types of activity going on, as illustrated in Fig. 9.5:

1. Normal Application Programs being brought into action by a scheduling routine on a basis of the priorities of jobs waiting to be processed.

2. Priority programs, the main purpose of which is to keep the files and input/output units efficiently utilized. These work down queues of requests made by the other programs for input/output activity. They are brought into play by an interrupt which occurs when an input/output unit is free and waiting for another item.

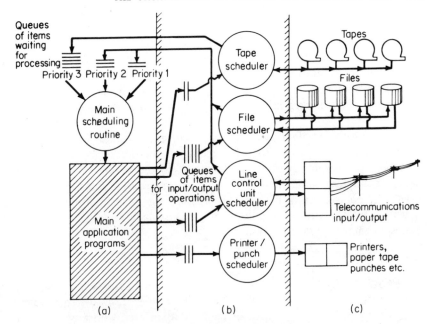

Fig. 9.5. (a) *Normal nonpriority programs.* (b) *Priority programs.* These operate when interrupts occur, to keep the input/output units fully utilized. (c) *Input/output operations.* These continue at the same time as the processing.

3. The input/output operations themselves which continue at the same time as the above processing, overlapped with it.

When an Application Program arrives at an input/output or file request, this operation will probably not be executed immediately because the channel or unit in question is busy. There may be other items earlier in the queue for this channel or unit. The supervisory input/output routine must therefore store the request for the operation in a place which the input/output scheduler will inspect later at a suitable time. Only in this way can the input/output units be kept continuously busy.

A list, or queue, of requests for operations on each unit and channel will be formed. A scheduling routine for the unit and a scheduling routine for the channel will inspect these when a new operation is to be started on a unit and channel. The Application Program making the request must furnish the following information:

1. A code giving the nature of the request, for example, write file in duplicate, or read tape.
2. The address of the input/output unit and channel.
3. The address or an identification of the record in the unit.
4. An address to tell the input/output routine where in core the item is that is to be read to or read from.

This information will be stored in a control word, and a table of such control words will govern the input/output and file routines.

When all the requests associated with one transaction are satisfied, this item will either be ready for further processing or be deleted from core, depening upon whether the last program segment used on it had terminated the work or not. If it had not, the block will be chained to the work-in-progress queue.

Input/output and file requests are not necessarily executed in the sequence in which they were requested. Movements of the access mechanisms, for example, take varying periods of time, and so the requests become completed at indeterminate times. The input/output routine must be ready to service the completion of file requests with no regard to the order in which they were made. It must be able to determine which request control word relates to each completed action.

MESSAGE
REFERENCE
BLOCKS

When multiprogrammed activity is taking place as described above, it is desirable to have one area of memory associated with any given job for the entire in-computer life of the job. It must contain any information unique to that message and necessary for its processing. When work on a message is interrupted while it waits for a file record to be found, the working data associated with it must not be destroyed. Such data could be stored in fixed locations set aside as working storage areas, but it is often convenient to use one of the blocks of relocatable storage as described above.

An area which belongs uniquely to a message for the duration of its life in the system is referred to in this book as a *message-reference block*. When a new message arrives, a message-reference block is allocated to it. The message itself is stored in that block, and during its passage through the system any relevant indicators or data are collected in the block. When the message has been processed and leaves the system, the block is freed for other work. If the block allocated is not large enough, another block may be chained to it, like a truck with a trailer. This might be done, for example, if teletype messages of great length are to be processed.

The message-reference block may be likened to a folder in a broker's filing cabinet. When a new client requires work to be done a folder is taken from the available folders and is devoted entirely to this client. When this client is finished with, the folder may be emptied and again be available for other work.

The contents of the message-reference block differ from one system to another. On some systems, the data related to a message are not all stored in one block, but in different areas of core; however, these areas are exactly equivalent to the message-reference block on other systems.

A message-reference block on a typical system may contain:

1. The original input message.
2. The address of the line and terminal from which it originated.
3. Working storage that can be preserved, if required, for the active life of the message.
4. A character giving the number of input/output requests to be completed for that entry. When this becomes zero, the entry may be placed in a queue ready for further processing.
5. In some control systems any input/output requests are defined by means of "request," or control, words, and these are stored in the message-reference block until the input/output is completed.

The detailed design of the message-reference block or equivalent will vary with such factors as how many input requests are in process at one time, how many levels of program in use at one time are to be recorded in the block, how much space the Application Programs require for storing data, and how long the messages are.

OPERATOR'S ASSEMBLY AREA
As well as having an area uniquely associated with each message, it is often necessary to have an area uniquely associated with each operator using the system or possibly with each transaction being processed. The processing of one commercial transaction may involve several messages; in other words, the operator carries on a conversation with the computer. In the case of scientific work the operator may occupy the machine on one problem for a long period of time with many messages passing to and fro in the course of this. It is therefore necessary to maintain continuity during the processing of one transaction or the solving of a problem as well as merely during each message.

Operator's assembly areas, or working areas, will therefore be maintained to provide this continuity. These will usually be kept on the backing store, as there will not be room for all of them in core.

When a message arrives, which is one in a sequence of messages relating to a given transaction or problem, a message-reference block will be created for it then and there, and, if the operator's assembly area is not in core at that time, it will be called in. In processing a transaction, the computer must have some way of knowing when this is complete. The operator may press an *end-transaction* key, or the computer may have some other way of deducing that it is finished. It will then file away relevant information and possibly release the operator's assembly area for other work.

The flow of work through a typical system is described step by step in Chapter 11, but first it is necessary to discuss the programs used.

10 THE PROGRAMS

In programming an on-line or real-time computer system and, indeed, other categories of complex computer installation, three kinds of program are needed: Application Programs, Supervisory Programs and Support Programs.

1. *Application Programs*

These are the programs that carry out the processing of transactions messages. They correspond to the data-processing programs of conventional applications and are unique to each system. They contain no input/output coding except in the form of macro-instructions which transfer control to an input/output control routine, or monitor, which on a real-time system is part of the Supervisory Programs.

2. *Supervisory Programs*

These programs, as stated in Chapter 3, coordinate and schedule the work of the Application Programs and carry out service functions for them. It is possible to consider the many Application Programs as subroutines of the main Supervisory Program. The Supervisory Programs handle input and output operations and the queuing of messages and data. They are designed to coordinate and optimize the machine functions under varying loads. They process interrupts and deal with error or emergency conditions.

The Supervisory Programs may be part of the standard software that is sold with the computer. IBM's 360 operating system, for example, provides the Supervisory Programs for many real-time applications. Sometimes, however, Supervisory Programs have to be written specially for a system or class of system. Some computers have no software suitable for "real-time."

136

3. *Support Programs*

The ultimate working system consists of Application Programs and Supervisory Programs. However, a third set of programs are needed to install the system and to keep it running smoothly. These are referred to in this book as Support Programs and include testing aids, data generator programs, terminal simulators, diagnostics, and so on. The manufacturer's software often provides some, but not all of the Support Programs needed.

The Application Programs are like the workers and plant in a factory, while the Supervisory Programs are like the office staff, management, and foremen. The Support Programs are like the maintenance crew, helping to install new plant and keep the machinery working.

Different terms are used by different organizations to describe these programs. The Application Programs are called "Operational Programs," "Problem Programs," "Processors," "Ordinary Processors," and so on. The Supervisory Programs are called "Control Programs," "Executive," "Monitors," and other names. A variety of terms are used for the Support Programs. In order to avoid confusion the terms Application, Supervisory and Support Programs are used exclusively throughout this book.

INTEGRATED RELATIONSHIP In writing programs for a batch-processing commercial application or for scientific calculations, the programs operate largely independently of one another. The work of one programmer does not interact with that of others, except in a very minor way when it uses the same records or input data. One of the big differences in real-time systems that have been designed to carry out a commercial, military, or complex technical function is that the programs all fit into an integrated system. They are all in the machine at the same time, and, although they are not all in core at once, many different combinations of them will be in core together. There are many different interactions between them. One program affects the functioning of others in many, and sometimes surprising, ways. *Time-sharing systems,* on the other hand, are designed so that the users are independent and there is no interaction between the programs in use for different transactions.

Building a real-time system for carrying out a complex function, such as airline reservations or production control, by its nature, demands a much greater degree of *teamwork* than lesser integrated systems in which often brilliant programmers can largely go their own way. Messages arrive at the computer at random times and require different programs to process them. The mix of programs that may be in core at any one time is, on some systems, almost infinitely variable. The relationships between them on integrated on-line systems can be so complex that some systems have never become

100 per cent debugged. When one program is changed, it can sometimes cause repercussions that echo throughout the entire system.

To further complicate the issue, it has often been the case that different parts of this tightly woven mesh of programs have been written by different teams working in different locations. Sometimes the Supervisory Programs are written by a team working for the computer manufacturer while the Application Programs are written by his customer, often miles away, sometimes in a different country. Where programs must fit together in this way, it is essential that the relationship between the programs is clearly defined at the outset. Programmers must be able to write the programs largely independently of each other, and therefore the interface between programs must be specified in detail. For example, the Application Programs use and continually refer to the Supervisory Programs. The latter must therefore be defined in detail and the means of linking with them specified before the work starts on the Application Programs. The definitions and linkages may be modified later, and, if there is any change, the Application Programmers must know about it.

SUPERVISORY PROGRAMS   It would be more correct to refer to a *set* of Supervisory Programs than to a single program. The nucleus of this system may be a central scanning loop, referred to in Figs. 9.4 and 9.5 as the *main scheduling routine* to which control is always returned when an Application Program or another Supervisory Program finishes its work. This central routine determines what work is to be done and transfers control to the appropriate program. The main scheduling routine could be regarded as the main program with Application Programs and other Supervisory Programs as subroutines to this. Some of these programs may themselves have subroutines. Application Programs will have subroutines which may be classed as other Application Programs or as Supervisory Programs, such as input/output routines.

With a well-written and well-defined set of Supervisory Programs, the Application Programmer is programming, as pointed out in Chapter 3, not merely a computer but a *computer plus supervisory system*. The supervisory system is generally designed to simplify the programming work. It frequently masks from the programmer the complex nature of the hardware. The programmer on some systems, for example, ignores the question of program block size or memory size. He knows nothing about the calling in, or relocation of, programs or what happens when interrupts occur. He is sometimes said to be programming a "virtual machine" which is different from the actual machine and is related to it by the compilers and Supervisory Programs which translate and run his program. The ICT ATLAS main memory appears to its programmer as all word-addressable, random-access storage. In actuality only a part is this. Similarly, the Burroughs B 5000 appears quite different to its user than is its real nature. These abstractions, virtual machines, are becoming more common, and certainly more necessary as computer operation becomes more complex.

A computer used for a conventional data-processing application normally follows a repetitive cycle of events, which may be planned and timed in detail by the programmer. Input and output operations are usually of a known length and time and may be balanced with each other and with the processing that is to be done.

In an on-line system this is unlikely to be true. Messages arrive at random times and are probably varied in their length and nature. The sequence of operations is unpredictable. However, the data are still to be handled in the minimum time, and computer facilities are to be used to their best. Events will occur in real time that cannot be built into any predicted timing pattern. Furthermore, failure of a machine component will necessitate immediate emergency procedures, and these may be automatic. In addition, in a large real-time system the volume and variability of messages received may be such that several transactions must be in the computer at once if reasonable efficiency of operation and the required response time are to be maintained. These transactions may require different programs.

For reasons such as these, the Supervisory Programs are used to continuously schedule the work, allocate core storage, and assess priorities, as this cannot now be done in advance in a rigid manner by the programmer.

Unlike Application Programs, which are generally written uniquely for each application, many generalized supervisory systems have been written which are intended to be usable in many applications. In this respect the supervisory system becomes much like part of the hardware. On large systems however, the requirements differ so much from one application to another, as described later, that many of the Supervisory Programs have been rewritten uniquely for individual applications. Standard computer software is written, usually, with a high degree of generality so that it can be used on a vast range of different types of systems. This high versatility introduces considerable inefficiencies in operation. Such software normally needs much more core and processing time than a tightly-written tailor-made program. A real-time system with a high throughput and fast response-time requirements may suffer because of this much more than a system with a small number of real-time transactions and slower response requirements. On the other hand, the small system may not be able to afford the excesses of core that a highly generalized Supervisory Program demands. However, the difficulties introduced by writing one's own Supervisory Program are considerable and where at all possible it is better to use a previously proven package and pay the additional hardware costs.

There is a wide difference in requirements for Supervisory Programs between the simple system with a few terminals, possibly not real-time, and a large multithread system with many real-time transactions being processed simultaneously. An on-line system without stringent response-time requirements may be able to complete the processing it is working on before attending to the communication lines.

FUNCTIONS OF SUPERVISORY PROGRAMS

The functions that are likely to be performed by the Supervisory Programs of a complex multiprogrammed system are listed below. Lesser systems will not require all these functions:

1. *Input/output control.* Scheduling the operations on input/output units and channels, checking for correct functioning, and so on.

2. *Communication line control.* Reading bits or characters from the line-control equipment and assembling them into messages. Controlling the terminals, and scanning them to detect whether they have something to send. Feeding messages bit by bit or character by character to the communication equipment. Error checking, and so on.

3. *Message setup services.* Giving an edited, checked-out message to the main programs and setting up a message-reference block in the required format.

4. *Handling displays.* For example, light-panel displays or cathode-ray tube displays which need repetitive scanning.

5. *Communicating with the operator.* Notifying the operator, possibly on the machine console, of error or exception conditions, requirements for tape changing, and so on. Permitting the operator to give instructions to the system.

6. *Scheduling the message processing.* Deciding which message to work on next, on a basis of priorities, response-time requirements, and other factors.

7. *Scheduling the machine functions.* Deciding which machine function is to be done when these conflict.

8. *Queue control.* Building queues of items or of requests for input/output operations. Working off the queues in the best sequence.

9. *Core storage allocation.* Assigning core to various functions as required.

10. *Allocation of other equipment.* As well as assigning core, it may be necessary to assign other components of the system to various functions as required.

11. *Communication between separate computers.* Transmitting data to, or receiving data from, another computer on a multicomputer system.

12. *Control of an off-line computer,* where this is a standby function as well as off-line processing and will take over when a failure occurs in the on-line machine.

13. *Linkage between programs and subroutines,* when these may be fixed in core or relocatable.

14. *Handling interrupts.* Analyzing the cause of the interrupt. Transferring control to the appropriate priority routine. Storing registers, switches, or data from the interrupted program to ensure that a logically correct return can be made.

15. *Selecting and calling in the required programs.* Deciding whether these are already in core or whether they must be read in. Deciding which used programs can be overwritten when core is needed.

16. *Retaining working data, registers, and so on,* when control switches from one program to another without an interrupt.

17. *Controlling time-initiated actions.* Initiating a given action at a predetermined clock time or after a given elapsed period.

18. *File security.* Ensuring, as far as possible, that file records are not overwritten incorrectly by testing programs or by errors in operational programs.

19. *Fault indication and reliability checks.* Taking appropriate action when errors of all the various types are detected.

20. *Diagnostics.* Operating on-line diagnostics for dealing with errors, for increasing confidence in the system, and for assistance to the equipment engineers.

21. *Switchover.* Organizing switchover to a standby computer when a failure occurs.

22. *Fallback.* Organizing a degraded mode of operation when a component of the system fails, for example, a file or a communication buffer. Switching to the twin in a duplexed file system. Organizing recovery from fallback, for example, returning a file to the system and updating records that would otherwise have been updated during its down period.

23. *Handling overloads.* Taking emergency action on a system which can be jammed by an overload.

24. *System testing aids.* Temporary routines to aid in real-time program debugging and the testing of the operational system.

25. *Performance monitoring.* Temporary routines to gather statistics on system performance.

LINK BETWEEN APPLICATION AND SUPERVISORY PROGRAMS

Control can pass from the Application Programs to the supervisory system in one of two ways. First there are interrupts, described briefly in the last chapter. These give control to a supervisory routine, usually for the purpose of handling some input/output operation, sometimes to handle error or other exception conditions in the system. Second, there are linkages which the programmer of the Application Programs deliberately writes into his programs. This linkage is generally in the form of a *macro-instruction*—one line of code which causes several or many instructions to be generated when the program is compiled.

At the time of writing, the programming languages being used for the Application Programs of most of these systems are at the *Assembly Program* level in which one line of code generates one machine instruction, except for macro-instructions which generate several or a whole routine. Higher languages, such as COBOL, are not in general use for real-time because they are imprecise in their use of core and do not yet have adequate linkage facilities to fit with a specially written Supervisory Program and be compiled into relocatable blocks of suitable length. Probably this deficiency will be overcome with some compilers by the time this book is published.

A set of accurately defined macro-instructions must be available for the Application Programmer to write into his coding. Some of the macro-instructions with the library routines necessary for compiling them will be part of the Supervisory Program package. Others will be written by the Application Programmers.

Much of the supervisory package thus consists of macro-instruction routines for inclusion in the computer's processor tape. Some computers may have standard routines for real-time work, written independently of specific applications. The user would then adjust the specifications of his supervisory routines when they are compiled in the same way that input/output control systems are compiled in conventional applications.

TYPICAL MACRO-INSTRUCTIONS   There is one type of macro-instruction that is referred to throughout the book. This is the macro-instruction which returns control to the main scheduling routine when a segment of Application Program has completed its work as described in the last chapter. This is here referred to as an "EXIT" macro. It may be at the end of the message processing, or it may not; it may be merely a temporary delay when no more processing can be done until a file record has been retrieved. Two separate macro-instructions are frequently used for these two cases, and in the description that follows these are called EXIT and WAIT respectively. Their use is illustrated in Fig. 10.1.

These and other typical examples of supervisory-package macro-instructions are described below. This set is typical of a small Supervisory Program written specially for a certain class of real-time system, rather than a fully general-purpose software package:.

1. WAIT

When an Application Program gives a file request and cannot do any more processing until this is complete, it must not hold up the processor.

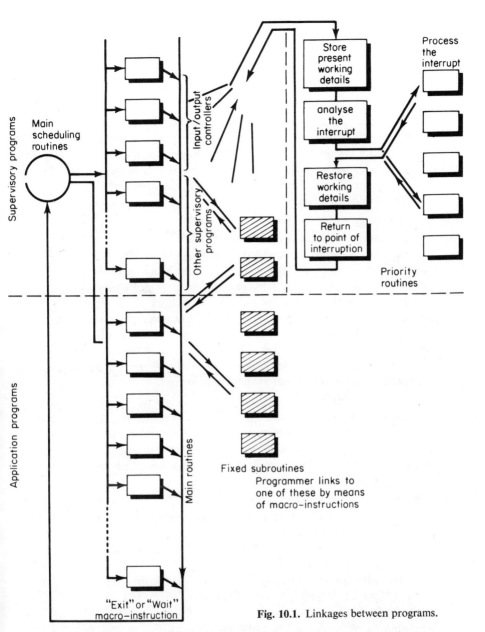

Store
present
working
details

analyse
the
interrupt

Restore
working
details

Return
to point of
interruption

Process
the
interrupt

Priority
routines

Main
scheduling
routines

Supervisory programs

Application programs

Input/output controllers

Other supervisory programs

Main routines

Fixed subroutines
Programmer links to
one of these by means
of macro-instructions

"Exit" or "Wait"
macro-instruction

Fig. 10.1. Linkages between programs.

In this and similar situations, the programmer writes a WAIT macro-instruction. The program location and conditions, which must be preserved for
restoring later, are stored in a suitable place, such as the message-reference
block, and control is transferred to the main scheduling routine. When an
input/output or file request is made, the input/output control routine may
increment a counter located, for example, in the message-reference block.
As each such operation is completed, this counter is decremented. When the
counter equals zero, the message-reference block is chained to an appropriate

queue ready for work again, and eventually the main scheduling routine will return control to the requisite Application Program.

2. EXIT

This is the last instruction in an Application Program, signifying that processing is complete. When this has been given, as soon as all input/output operations are complete, the Supervisory Program will release any working storage blocks held by this entry, including the message-reference block itself. Thus the life of the message in the computer is ended. Control will then return to other processing.

3. GET CORE

This macro is used when a storage block is required for the processing of a message. If the core is divided into blocks which are dynamically allocated, as described in the last chapter, a core block is removed from the uncommitted-storage list and is assigned to the message in question.

The count of the number of uncommitted blocks is determined, and, if this count falls below a certain level, this indicates that the system may be in danger of running out of core. The program then transfers control to a routine which will take corrective action. This corrective action may possibly be the completion of a partially processed message or the removal to disk of some of the Application Programs that are normally in core.

4. RELEASE CORE

This is the converse of GET CORE. It is, of course, important that core blocks should be released as soon as possible. There may therefore be macro-instructions which request both an output operation and a release of the associated core block, for example, a WRITE FILE would be given as a WRITE FILE and RELEASE CORE.

5. INPUT/OUTPUT MACRO-INSTRUCTIONS

A supervisory package may provide many input/output macro-instructions. Some typical ones are:

WRITE DISK, meaning seek disk record and write. The seek may be given separately from the write.

WRITE BOTH DISKS. On a system on which records are duplicated on different files for safety, this would write both of them.

READ DISK

READ DISK AND WAIT, a READ DISK combined with a WAIT.

WRITE DISK and RELEASE CORE, a WRITE DISK combined with a RELEASE CORE macro-instruction

READ TAPE, WRITE TAPE, REWIND TAPE, PUT or GET (with block or unblocking), and so on.

PRINT, TYPE, PUNCH A CARD, DISPLAY, and so on.

MESSAGE OUT. This might be used to transmit a message to the multiplexor.

OUTPUT TELETYPE. This is used separately from MESSAGE OUT when teletype messages are of a different length and nature.

All such input/output macro-instructions are likely to result in a request being given to an input/output scheduler, which is part of the Supervisory Programs. This routine will execute them as soon as is possible. Many may not be executed immediately because the input/output channel or unit is in use.

6. CREATE MESSAGE-REFERENCE BLOCK

A message-reference block, designed to contain all the details needed in the processing of a message and to save these throughout the in-system life of the message, is created in the required format. It may be desirable to split a transaction, producing duplicate message-reference blocks so that more than one output message may be sent.

7. MACRO-INSTRUCTIONS FOR TIME-INITIATED ACTIONS

These cause a designated program to be called in and used at a specified clock time. To use time-initiated macros, a special time-initiated supervisor routine will be needed.

8. LINKAGE MACRO-INSTRUCTIONS

There may be a variety of macro-instructions for making logical linkages between programs and subroutines and for saving data from one program for use by another.

9. LOGGING DATA AND DEBUGGING

Macro-instructions which may strictly be thought of as part of the Support Programs can be of great value in program testing, tracing system faults, and monitoring the performance of a system.

A CODING EXAMPLE To illustrate the use of the macro-instructions, a highly simplified piece of Application Program coding is shown in Fig. 10.2. Some macro-instructions of the types given above are included in it. The program is as follows:

When a message is received, two records must be found in order to process it. The file addressing is such that, when the record from file 2 is found, it might not be the correct one. In this case, an overflow address must be calculated and an overflow record read.

The processing will determine whether or not file 2 needs updating. If it does, the updated record is assembled and written. A reply to the message is assembled and sent.

To do this processing, the program must first obtain some core and set up a message-reference block. This is done with two macro-instructions as shown. It must then determine the addresses of the required file records, seek them, and read them. This is done with FIND macro-instructions, and these must be followed by a WAIT, so that the system can carry on with other processing while they are being found.

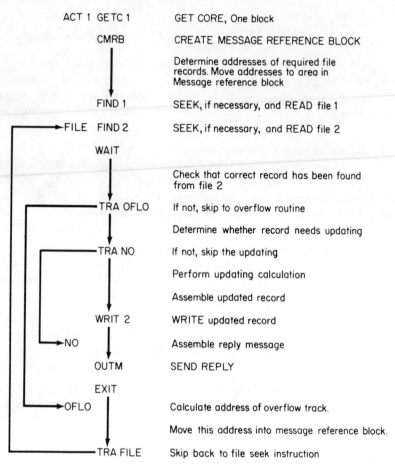

ACT 1	GE TC 1	GET CORE, One block
	CMRB	CREATE MESSAGE REFERENCE BLOCK
		Determine addresses of required file records. Move addresses to area in Message reference block
	FIND 1	SEEK, if necessary, and READ file 1
FILE	FIND 2	SEEK, if necessary, and READ file 2
	WAIT	
		Check that correct record has been found from file 2
	TRA OFLO	If not, skip to overflow routine
		Determine whether record needs updating
	TRA NO	If not, skip the updating
		Perform updating calculation
		Assemble updated record
	WRIT 2	WRITE updated record
NO		Assemble reply message
	OUTM	SEND REPLY
	EXIT	
OFLO		Calculate address of overflow track.
		Move this address into message reference block.
	TRA FILE	Skip back to file seek instruction

Fig. 10.2. Simplified illustration of coding showing typical control program macro-instructions.

Control is eventually returned to the program after the records have been read. The program checks that they are the right records and, if so, carries on processing. If the file 2 record is incorrect, the overflow location is found.

When the reply message has been sent, an EXIT is given. After the file actions are completed and checked, the EXIT releases the core that this processing used and this core may then be used by other messages. Thus the life of the message in the computer is ended.

LOCATION OF PROGRAMS Most real-time and on-line systems have too many programs to reside in core, and the majority of them are kept on a backing file. They are usually kept in a file in which they are quickly accessible, as some of them may be read into core very frequently. Sometimes drums rather than disks, which may be slower, are used for this. Sometimes a large backup core storage is used.

Careful planning is needed for the mechanism of calling the programs into core for use. The most frequently used programs and, especially, the main routines of the supervisory system are likely to be permanently located in core. The remainder may be cycled through core in a serial fashion or called in at random when required:

1. *Serial Read-in*

Program groups are brought into core in a serial fashion and recycled. When program group *A* is temporarily finished with, it is replaced by program group *B*. Program group *B* is followed by program group *C*, and so on, until program group *A* is again in core.

This scheme has the disadvantage of a long response time. The messages to be processed must wait until their particular program is in core. When a new program group is read into core, the new-input queue may be scanned and those messages requiring this group processed. If a response time of ten or twenty seconds is adequate, then this may be the simplest method of program read-in.

This is likely to be of value on a system with not too many messages and with Application Programs that run for a fair length of time. On a system requiring a large number of Application Programs each of which is quickly executed, random read-in, described below, is more likely to be used. A combination of serial read-in and random read-in will sometimes be the most economic.

2. *Random Read-in*

Programs are usually divided into segments, or "pages," and these pages are brought into core at random as required. When the processing of a message requires a program page, a Supervisory Program may check to see whether it is in core. If it is not, it is read in from disk or drum. Checking to see whether it is in core requires an operation, such as scanning a table and updating the table each time a program is read in. This may not be worthwhile, and on a system with a wide spread of Application Program usage, pages may be read in without this check, in which case some pages may be in core twice at one time.

Random read-in is useful where there is a large number of programs which are quick to execute and a fast response time is required. These criteria apply to many commercial systems, especially systems for making enquiries and updating records,.

Random read-in is generally more difficult to organize than the serial method. The program has to be located on the files, and the decision has to be made, concerning where in core it is to be read to.

On some applications, a combination of serial and random program read-in is used. Sometimes individual pages of program are called into core when needed. On other systems a complete *core load* of programs and data may be read in to tackle a particular job and possibly stored back on the file again sometime later.

Some computers have a relatively small but high-speed backing file, possibly drum or core, on, which the most frequently used pages are stored. The location and read-in of new pages may be programmed on conventional machines, but some computers have hardware to assist in *automatic page turning*, as discussed in Chapter 19. This may be particularly valuable on a time-sharing system where programs of certain users are constantly being moved in and out as the users are scanned.

REENTRANT
PROGRAMS

When processing a variety of input messages, one program may be "WAITing"—for a file action, for example—and at this time another transaction wishes to use the program. This can cause problems if the program is written in such a way that it modifies itself while being executed, or stores logic information for later use in a location other than the unique message-reference block.

Programs to be used by multiple transactions in this way must be carefully written so that no logic error can be caused by this. In particular, they must not modify themselves in such a way that, when control is taken away from them, another transaction can interfere with the modification.

Programs which can be entered by multiple transactions without inter-ference are referred to as *reentrant* programs. If a program is not reentrant, it may be necessary to have more than one copy of it in core at certain times in a multi-thread environment.

RELOCATABLE
PROGRAMS

Especially when random program read-in is used, it may be desirable to place a program in different locations in core at different times and execute it from these different locations. Programs which can be executed from different places in core are referred to as *relocatable*.

Dynamic core allocation is often used for programs, and so a program may be read from the file into an area that could be anywhere within the zone of dynamic allocation. It must then either be executed from this area, relo-catably, or be moved to a fixed area. The latter is slow and is not normally done on the latest computers (though one of the world's most complex airline reservation systems moves its programs at high speed to a fixed core location each time it executes them).

Many multi-programmed systems, on-line or otherwise, have to use relocatable programs. The programmer does not know where in core the program will operate from, so he writes it relative to core position zero. Hardware or software, or both, carry out the relocation.

There are, basically, two types of program relocation, static and dynamic.

Static program relocation means that the program is positioned in any selected area of core but not moved again until this particular execution of it is complete. The means will be set up for addressing it and its data in that location.

Dynamic program relocation means that the program may be moved before its execution is complete and operated from a different part of core. This is rather more complicated because the working data and conditions of the half-completed program must be preserved and reestablished elsewhere.

Dynamic program relocation is needed where the pressure of time is such that programs must be stopped before they have run their course in order to meet the response time required by other transactions. It is commonly used on *time-sharing systems*, in which the Supervisory Program allocates a given slot of time to each user's program, and, if the program is not completed when this interval ends, control is taken away from it and restored after the other active users have had their time-slots. As other users' programs come into core, the interrupted programs may have to be removed for the time being to make room for them. When it is read back into core, other current programs or data are occupying its old position, and it can be economic to leave them there and execute the program in question from a different location.

Alternatively the half-completed program may stay in core but not in its present position. It is slid down to one end of core to make room for new work. If all of the uncompleted programs were left where they were originally, they would leave irregular gaps throughout core as in a half-empty parking lot. Therefore they are all slid down to one end to make room, in case a big program has to be read in, which could not fit into these gaps. This is dynamic relocation.

The majority of commercial on-line real-time systems (at the time of writing) do not use, or need, dynamic relocation. Many use static relocation and many no relocation. The main reason for this is that most of them use programs that are broken into fairly short segments. Although the number of segments may be large and their interrelation complex, the time one program occupies core before a WAIT or EXIT is not normally more than, say, 100 milliseconds, and there is a programming rule that it should never be more than, say, 500 milliseconds. A program can therefore complete its operation before it is kicked out (although it may frequently be interrupted for supervisory reasons as discussed above).

A common way of handling relocatable programs on commercial or time-sharing systems where the Application Programs are not too complex is to use fixed-size blocks of program. These blocks can be marshalled in core and on the files more simply than variable-length blocks. Many systems therefore have program blocks, as shown in Fig. 10.1, with relocation between executions done as the block is read into core. When the program uses a branch (transfer) instruction or in any way refers to *itself*, it must know where itself is located. Suppose that it is written relative to core address 00000 and operated relative to core address 05000 because that is where it happens to be sitting in core; then, before execution, every instruction containing an address which refers to the program itself must be effectively modified by having 5000 added to it.

There are a number of different methods of achieving this. Undoubtedly the best is the use of a special hardware feature in the computer. The machine has a piece of hardware logic which automatically adjusts any address referring to the program by adding the contents of a *relation register* to that address. The appropriate value is loaded into the relocation register as the program is loaded into core.

Allied to the problem of program relocation is that of finding and reading-in a block of program from the backing files. Sometimes a program reference may be to a program which is not, in fact, in core. This processing will be intercepted at this point for the Supervisory Program to bring it into core.

**VIRTUAL
MACHINES**
With a well-designed compiler and supervisory system, the Application Programmer may know little or even nothing about program relocation and read-in. He may be instructed to divide his program into suitably sized blocks, or pages, and write macro-instructions to link them where required. The instruction addresses in each page may be relative to zero. The storage of these chunks of program and the conversion of their instruction addresses will all be handled by the software and are out of his hands.

Alternatively he may not even be concerned with pages. He may write his program as though he were writing for a machine in which he had the core all to himself. He is programming a virtual machine with a core large enough for his needs and possibly much larger than the physical machine. He programs it starting at address zero.

Similarly the programmer may be unconcerned with the specific input/output units. He defines the logical files he uses, within the constraints he is given, and may not worry whether they are on drum or disk or which particular unit. If he does address an input/output unit, he does not use an actual machine address but rather a *pseudo address* which the supervisory system can later translate into a specific hardware address. The unit in question may be different on different occasions because of failures, maintenance, load sharing, and so on, but this need not concern the Application Programmer.

The term *virtual machine* is thus used to mean one which appears simpler to the programmer than the actual machine. The software converts his programs appropriately, and the program testing aids produce results which relate to the virtual machine.

This process is becoming more and more desirable as complexities increase. In time-sharing systems, where the users may be writing quite unrelated programs which by chance may run on the same machine at the same time, it is essential. However it needs to be applied with caution if efficiency is a consideration. If a program runs over the edge of its page too frequently, this could waste much time in routines for changing pages, possibly bringing new pages from file into core. A programmer who determines his own page contents could to some extent stop this. A compiler probably would not. On a system for executing a specific set of functions, like most business systems, there is usually much interaction between the programs. Many inefficiencies can and usually do arise because of timing relationships, duplication of routines in core, unnecessary contention for channels or other facilities, unused pages in core, and a variety of overheads. It is a common experience that a working real-time business system can be tuned to improve its response time or decrease its processor utilization. Often, and especially with a complex system, the improvement found possible is startling. The author knows of more than one installation in which such polishing doubled the throughput.

We thus need a compromise between programming systems with Supervisory Programs that give the simplest virtual machines and those which allow the programmer of the team to strive for efficiency. The nature of the usage often determines where the compromise should be. The history of the subject to date contains examples of both extremes.

SUPPORT PROGRAMS   Finally, let us again mention the Support Programs. These are a vital part of the programming needed to put a real-time system "on the air." The man-years of effort they require is often substantial. But, like that part of an iceberg under the surface, they have sometimes not been viewed in their true significance by the teams planning and installing such systems.

A list of Support Programs for a typical real-time system will include such items as the following:*

*James Martin, *Programming Real-Time Computer Systems*. Englewood Cliffs, N.J.: Prentice-Hall, Inc., 1965.

System loading and initializing programs
Restart programs
Diagnostics
File reorganization programs
Fallback programs
Library tape and file maintenance programs
Data generation programs for program testing
File loading routines
Supervisory Program Simulators for use in testing
Application Program Simulators for use in testing
Operator set and line control unit simulators
Testing Supervisory Routine
"Introspective" testing aids
Core print programs
Debugging aids
Testing output analysis programs and sorts

11 THE FLOW OF WORK THROUGH A TYPICAL SYSTEM

To integrate and clarify the last two chapters, this chapter describes step by step what happens to a message in a typical on-line real-time system. This is a multithread system for carrying out commercial functions using a common data base. Time-sharing systems which do not have a common data base may have markedly different mechanisms.

An operator at a distant terminal sends a message to the computer, which is one of a group of messages needed to process a transaction or enable the operator to make a certain decision. The processing of the message is described with reference to Fig. 11.1.

Consider a message which needs the following action:

1. It must be logged on tape.
2. The appropriate *operator's assembly area* must be read into core from the backing store.
3. A record must be sought from the random-access files. It is not, however, directly addressable, and to locate it, table look-up must be done to determine the area of the files that must be sought.
4. The required area is to be sought and a *track index* read from it.
5. Another table look-up must be done on the contents of the track index to give the required record address.
6. The required record must be read into core.
7. A calculation needs to be done on the contents of the records, and details in the operator's assembly area must be updated.
8. A message is to be sent to the operator in reply.
9. The record must be updated and written back on the file.
10. The operator's assembly area must be written back on the file. There are too many operators using the system for there to be room to keep it in core until the next message relating to this transaction is received.

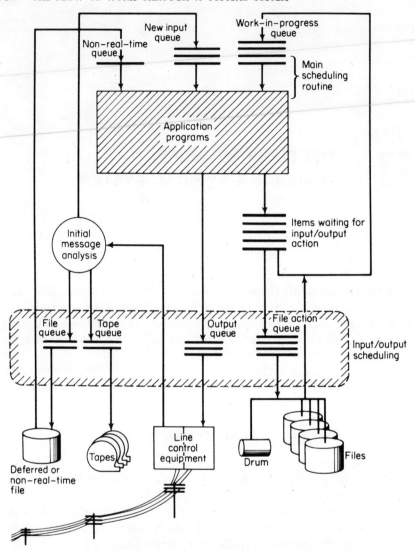

Fig. 11.1. The flow of data in a typical multi-thread real-time system.

The sequence of events in handling this message is as follows:

1. An *interrupt* occurs, and a *priority routine* detects that a message requires to be read in. It acquires a block of core from the *uncommitted-storage list* and initiates the read of the message into it. Control then returns to the interrupted program.

2. The reading in of the message from the communication lines continues at the same time as the computer is processing other work. When it is com-

pletely in the computer core, another *interrupt* occurs, signifying that this message is now ready for processing.

3. The *priority routine* answering this interrupt prepares the message for processing and does an *initial analysis* of what message type it is, in case it needs immediate attention. The priority routine performs a *validity or error check* on the message to ensure that it has been received correctly. If it is not correct, the priority routine will transfer control to an exception routine for dealing with the error.

The priority routine chains the block of storage containing the message into the *new-input queue.* If the message needs immediate attention, it will leave an indication for the main scheduling routine that this is the next message to be dealt with.

4. If the message does not require a real-time action but can be processed later at the computer's convenience, the routine doing the initial analysis will give a macroinstruction to write it on a file of *non-real-time work.*

5. The routine doing the initial analysis will also give a macro-instruction to write the message on tape for *logging* purposes.

6. Neither of the above two macro-instructions will necessarily cause an output operation to occur at that moment. They will set up *request words* for the action in question in the *tape-output queue* and *non-real-time file output queue.* Both such outputs may be written in blocks of more than one message. The macro-instruction will automatically arrange for this to happen. If a complete block now exists, the macro-instruction will attempt to write the block to tape or file. If not, this will occur when some later message arrives and the partially complete block remains in a buffer area in core. If the output unit or channel is busy, the output operation cannot occur now, but a program will be interrupted some time in the future and it will occur then as a *priority routine.*

7. At some later time the *main scheduling routine* works its way down to this message in the new-input queue. It transfers control to an *initializer routine,* which might be regarded as the first Application Program to work on the message.

8. The initializer converts the message's storage block into the format of a *message-reference block.* Again it may check the message for validity and initiate corrective action if there is an error in it. It analyzes the message to decide what *Application Program* is needed first and transfers control to this program by means of a linkage routine which is part of the Supervisory Program. It may be necessary to read the required Application Program in a backing file, in which case a file operation occurs as described below.

9. The Application Program executes a *table look-up* to find the area of the files that must be "sought." This table may be stored permanently in core storage, because it will be used by many messages.

10. The Application Program contains the macro-instruction to seek and read the *track index.* A *request word* for this is set up and stored in the

message-reference block. If the access arm or channel is busy or there are earlier requests for that arm, the requests is placed in the queue of requests for that channel and arm and will be executed later.

If duplexed files are used, only one need be read. The seek and read will probably occur on the first file to become available.

11. It is necessary for the Application Program also to read into core the *operator's assembly area* for this message. It contains a macro-instruction to seek and read this. Again a *request word* is set up, and again, if the arm or channel is busy, the request will be queued for execution later.

12. The Application Program can now do nothing until many milliseconds later when the necessary file reads are completed. It therefore contains a *WAIT macro-instruction*. This causes control to be returned to the main scheduling routine, and this will in turn give control to another application routine. The computer will perform other work while the above message waits.

13. At some later time some different program will be *interrupted* because one of the above seeks has been completed. The *priority routine* that services this interrupt will select a block from the uncommitted-storage list if necessary and commence a read of the record into it. It may read into the message-reference block.

14. Similarly, the other seek will be completed and the record read.

15. Still later, other routines will be interrupted because the reads are each completed. When this has been done the message again needs the attention of an Application Program and so the message will now become part of the *work-in-progress queue*. The priority routines will initiate the next operations on access mechanisms, for other message if any.

16. The *main scheduling routine* at some future time will detect this item in the *work-in-progress queue*. It will select the required Application Program which will still be in core, and transfer control to it.

17. The Application Program will execute a *table look-up* on the table contained in the *track index* that has been read in. This will tell it the address of the required track. It will then give a macro-instruction to read that track, followed by a WAIT. The reading sequence described above will occur again. The access arm may or may not have been reserved during this period. In other words, a reseek may or may not be required. On the large systems, it is often released because, otherwise, it could be tied up while a queue of other items is worked through. On small systems this may not be so.

18. The Application Program can at last carry out its processing of the message in question. It completes this, updates the record in core, updates the operator's assembly area, and composes a *reply message*.

19. A macro-instruction is then given to send out the replying message. A request word for this is set up and stored in the message-reference block. If the request cannot immediately be executed, the request will be placed in the *real-time output queue*.

20. Similarly, macro-instructions will be given to write the updated record on the file and to write back the *operator's assembly area*. If duplicated files are used, these will instruct the file-scheduler routine to write the updated records on both files. The output routines will check the records written and then release the core blocks that they occupied. Again these operations will be done by priority routines when the time is suitable.

21. Lastly an EXIT macro is given. This will be executed as soon as the final message has been sent and it has been verified that the transmission was correct. The message-reference block in core will be released for other work. Control is transferred to the main scheduling routine again for work on other messages.

This completes the life of the message in the system. The human operator will now read and think about the reply, taking a time which is long in computer terms. Eventually he may send another message, and the *operator's assembly area* will provide continuity with what took place above.

Finally he must send an *end transaction* signal which causes the Application Programs to complete their action, updating and checking any records associated with the transaction.

SECTION III

APPLICATIONS

12

BASIC FUNCTIONS
OF AN ON-LINE SYSTEM

This section of the book discusses applications of on-line or real-time systems. In this chapter the basic reasons for wanting to use real-time techniques are analyzed. The following chapter describes the use of real-time computers in an engineering environment controlling a technical process. This type of control has many analogies with the control needed, but often not achieved, in a commercial environment, and Chapter 14 discusses this parallel. The remaining four chapters in the section describe certain well-established applications of real-time, and the considerations necessary in planning these are examined.

The main benefits of the systems described in this book derive from different characteristics on different systems. On some the main advantages over earlier data-processing technology derive from the *telecommunications network*. This enables the system to extend its tentacles into areas of an organization previously untouchable. It speeds the flow of data through an organization and is the nervous system without which tight control and quick reactions cannot be obtained. On other applications the *random-access files* provide the main benefit. They give almost immediate access to any of the records the organization keeps. Files can be updated and necessary action taken quickly. Enquiries will receive up-to-date answers. These units break up the lengthy and cumbersome cycle of sorting and scanning. The *man-machine interface* gives a major benefit on other systems. A room full of airline sales agents or flight controllers all carrying on a high-speed and complex conversation with a computer is a most impressive sight. Again the facility for *control* may be the dominating advantage. To return processed data to an environment sufficiently quickly to control its operation opens up endless possibilities. This may be control of a chemical process in which the computer scans instruments and sets pressures, temperatures, and flows to their optimum value, or it may be control of the routing of work through a factory, control of the sequence of operations in a changing situation, even the control of traffic flow through a city by changing traffic lights at the best times. The computer has the facility to interrupt work it is doing and to switch to other programs as the circumstances demand.

The functions which a computer system will perform must be decided on *economic* grounds. The only sound reason for installing a computer in business is that, in some way, it will pay for itself and make a profit.

This might be difficult to assess with real-time applications, because often the saving will not be entirely a *tangible* one such as saving in manpower and equipment. There usually is a manpower saving, but the big payoff often comes through increased efficiency. The system may increase the flow of work that a given number of machine tools can handle. It may decrease inventories or cash holding. It may decrease the rolling stock a railroad needs to handle a given freight traffic. It may optimize the performance of a chemical plant. These savings, if they can be achieved, are likely to be much greater than manpower savings. As is illustrated in Chapter 14, an organization without tight controls tends to oscillate. This is true of a chemical plant, a factory and marketing organization, or even of a nation's economy. It would be true of a ship at sea or a house heating system or a man riding a bicycle, but here the control is tight and prevents major oscillations—usually! Oscillation in a large organization wastes money. Plant capacity and stock levels are higher than they need be. Demand can sometimes not be met.

Where there is a high degree of uncertainty, for example, if the product is such that the demand for it fluctuates, there is a greater need for a fast reaction time. If the produce is perishable, such as fashion items, frozen goods, or, in another sense, airline seats, there is again a need for speedy reactions. Keen competition in an industry can necessitate the speeding up of service to a customer. Without fast reactions a sale may be permanently lost.

As an organization becomes large, so it becomes more difficult to control and finds it more difficult to achieve fast reactions. This is true both of an organization that is large geographically, with branches or factories scattered over a wide area, and of one that is large administratively. The geographically dispersed organization needs data-transmission links in order to react quickly. The administratively large organization has economically sound reasons for *centralizing* many of its administrative functions. Centralized purchasing or stock administration, for example, can bring direct financial savings. Centralization, however, can and has in many cases produced a bulky, slow-to-move, bureaucratic administration. The use of computers planned to give the optimum reaction time can help to avoid this. The computer system must carry out the required processing as quickly as it is needed and must give information to management and other staff where and *when* it is needed. This necessitates the techniques described in this book.

The remainder of this chapter considers twelve basic reasons for using real-time techniques in commercial data processing. These are discussed with the over-all *economics* of the system in mind. How these functions have fitted together in actual systems can then be seen in the following chapters.

1. The Integration of Separate Functions, Decisions, and Files

There is pressure within the computer industry toward integrated data processing. It is economical to have one system for all the routine processing and decision making within an organization; also many types of decisions are made more efficiently if they are coordinated rather than made independently of one another. Integration of decision making is possible with the equipment that has now become available. Data from different sources are used for an over-all, up-to-date picture of the situation, and this is referred to in making the decision.

Centralization of warehouse control is an example. When an organization has many warehouses within one state or within one country, the inventory of these may be maintained centrally. Stocking of all warehouses will be planned by the one computer. By doing this, it is possible to reduce the inventory and make use of bulk buying. Store keepers will send to the computer details of goods entering and leaving their store and will be able to interrogate the centralized inventory records.

The warehouses could each be controlled separately by separate computers, but this would not result in smaller over-all stock holding. The combining of these functions demands, first, that it is possible occasionally to move stock from one warehouse to another if required and, secondly, that rapid communications facilities are available to the controlling computer.

The integration of files on a computer can give many advantages. It avoids the duplicate collection and storage of data that often exists in a less integrated system. Data that has to be collected for one function can often be used for another separate function.

A spectacular example of this saving is discussed in the Rand Corporation research study by Edward F.R. Hearle and Raymond J. Mason,* as mentioned in Chapter 3. The authors show how the files that have been kept separately in various government departments could be combined with great effect. They discuss the integration of many state and local government operations, using on-line systems.

2. Geographical Integration

Many organizations today have large distances between their plants or warehouses or branches. An argument that is constantly heard in industry is whether centralized planning or decentralized planning is the better for

---

*Edward F. R. Hearle and Raymond J. Mason, *A Data Processing System for State and Local Government*. Englewood Cliffs, N.J.: Prentice-Hall, Inc., 1963.

various organizations. There are many advantages of centralization, such as bulk buying with bulk discounts, inventory reduction, less duplication of effort, and staff savings. Where data processing is used, it is cheaper to have one centralized computer than many small computers at the branches. This can be done by using data-transmission links, and the method is now working successfully in many places.

A good example of this is the airline reservation systems, discussed in detail in Chapter 15. Bookings are made for the same flight in sales agents' offices in various parts of a country and various parts of the world. If these reservations are made independently of one another, overbooking or underbooking may result.

A man in Chicago may intend to book a seat on a flight from New York to London at the same time as a man in London attempts to make a similar reservation. Perhaps there is only one seat left on the plane and both of these men are sold that seat. The result is that the flight is overbooked. One of these reservations must be cancelled or a passenger will be kept waiting at the airport. Some airlines may reserve seats on the plane to meet this contingency, but this could result in the plane being underbooked if these seats are not used. Similarly many of the bookings made are subsequently cancelled. If all the sales agents do not quickly know about a cancellation, this may result in lost business.

An integration of these reservation decisions could avoid the above problems, and this has been done using on-line real-time computers connected by telephone or teletype lines to terminals in the sales agents' offices. The computer maintains an up-to-the-second image of the flight bookings. The sales agent interrogates this whenever he has enquiries from would-be passengers. If this integration of decisions results on average in an increased plane load of one passenger per flight the computer system has caused a substantial saving.

A scientific system needing geographical integration might be a defense system or a satellite-tracking system, where the reading of distant radars must be coordinated. The network of power stations feeding an electricity grid may be controlled centrally. The quantity of electricity they feed into the grid will be determined by the load on various areas.

3. *An Information Service*

A real-time system may be used to provide information about a service or a situation when it is required and where it is required. Management in a factory may obtain information about the order situation, the sales forecast, work in progress, and so on. The store keeper may find out whether an item is in stock in other stores in the same firm. Insurance companies may keep a centralized "black list" of certain types of client. The cashier may check the creditworthiness of a customer asking for credit (Fig. 12.1). Police

Fig. 12.1. An assistant at a department store telephones a computer to check the creditworthiness of a customer. She keys the customer's credit card number on a touch-tone telephone and the computer responds by voice.

may do a rapid check on the files to see whether there is any information against a man or a car that is suspect.

Information retrieval systems may be small, such as the retrieving of inventory details, or they may be large. Systems can be visualized that have to scan many documents in order to produce an answer to a given request. Such documents may take a very long time indeed to scan manually, and they may not be available when required.

Systems have been installed to give information about the technical reports and books in libraries. The user wishes to know what literature exists on a certain topic, say, "nuclear reactions between oriented target nuclei and polarized beams of X rays." He will type various *key words or phrases* into a terminal, such as "polarized," "X rays," or "oriented target." He may also type in the code of the subject category from a list of subjects, for example,

(a)

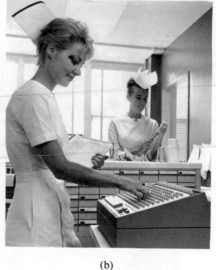

(b)

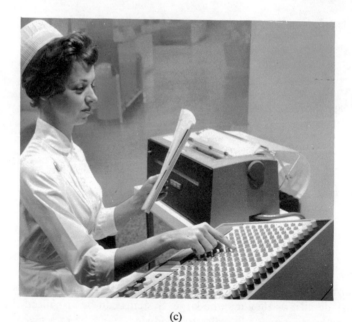

(c)

Fig. 12.2. The use of real-time terminals in a hospital: 12 steps or more can be involved in the routine filling of a medication order. The recording of this transaction can include seven written records which may be stored in different locations in the hospital. With the computer, all transactions can be centrally handled, controlled, and stored at one location. The ordering of drugs, lab tests, plasma, and special diets, the scheduling of operating rooms and X-rays, and immediate reports to doctors on their patient's progress can all be accomplished quickly, and form part of a *hospital information system*.

"nuclear physics" or a finer subdivision "nuclear reactions." The terminal will display the reference numbers and titles of all documents that have these key words in their title. Many of these will clearly be unsuitable. He will select those which look promising and ask the system to display an abstract of them. In this way he can find out what literature is available and know he can obtain it.

It is likely that in the future information-retrieval schemes will become an invaluable tool for professional men, such as doctors, lawyers, and scientists. They will browse quickly through documents flashed quickly onto a display screen.

The information requested may be static and unchanging, or only changing in a minor degree, for example, a library catalogue, or it may be constantly changing, such as the loading of machine tools on a shop floor. The information service may be an enquiry facility in a much larger data-processing scheme.

4. Data Collection

Perhaps the converse of an information service is a scheme for data collection. Often these must form two parts of the same system. A real-time system may collect information from the various points at which it becomes available and assemble this information to produce an image of a given situation.

Intelligence data or police data may be collected and filed. Details of work being done on the shop floor of a factory may be collected, for example, machine start and stop times or scrap values. Scientific data may be collected and assembled. A computer may be used to scan very rapidly all the instrumentation of a jet engine or a rocket-motor test bed. Frequently in designing a process control application, the first step is to collect a very large amount of data about the operation of the plant in question so that rules can be formulated about its operation and models constructed.

There are two categories of data collection: that initiated by the computer and that in which data are sent to the computer. Process control is an example of the former, in which the computer scans a set of instruments at preestablished intervals. An example of the latter is a system on which human terminal operators send data to the computer on an interrupt basis when they have it available.

Some systems have data collection as their sole function, but again it is more commonly combined with other functions. On a railroad, for example, a computer has been used to advise planners of the locations of all the various types of trucks. Each time a train moves, operators send details of this to a computer which correlates all the data.

5. Information routing

Communications between people and the dissemination of information become a problem in a big organization. It is desirable that many communications should be made faster than would be possible if the mail were used. Many large organizations have installed message-switching systems to transmit data rapidly to where they are needed. This application of computers is discussed in Chapter 17.

Solving the communications problem is an end in itself, but often it ties into the data-processing needs. There is often a strong case for linking the administrative message-routing system with the data-processing computers.

6. Speedier Action

A customer goes into a bank at lunch time to withdraw cash from his account. There is a queue of a dozen or more people, and each one of them is taking five minutes to be served. He waits for a while and then decides that it is going to take him too long to reach the counter. His lunch break is not long enough. In the evening the bank will be closed, and he cannot obtain the cash he needs. The real-time systems that are being installed in saving banks will relieve this situation, as discussed in Chapter 16. Customer service is improved, accuracy is improved, and perhaps the bank will be taking away customers from its competitors down the street.

There are many other examples where fast action is desirable. For example, fast answers to telephone enquiries may be an aid to sales. A national defense system must act very quickly. Many systems for controlling situations or operations need a fast response time. The computer may aid executives in quick decision making.

7. Fast Turnaround Time

Often, however, speedy response does not mean action in seconds or minutes, but action in an hour or so: or doing something today rather than in a week or a month's time. For example, decreasing a management planning cycle or dealing with urgent orders rapidly or dispatching spare parts at the time they are requested.

Single-transaction processing using random-access files, rather than the processing of large batches with intervening sorts, will give this. Sending transactions to the computer by telecommunication link rather than by mail may be desirable. However, the high degree of interruption between jobs which sometimes occurs on fast-response-time systems will not be necessary.

Time-sharing scientific systems aim to reduce the time taken to return results of program runs to the users. This may have a significant effect when certain decisions need special programming. In many business situations time is money, and time can be gained with a computer system designed to react quickly.

8. Control

The use of a computer to control an environment is perhaps one of the most significant uses of a real-time technology. It has been used to control

Fig. 12.3. The sport of kings is also becoming computerized. At New York Racing's Association's three tracks a pair of Honeywell 200 computers process all parimutual wagering—computing odds, totaling money pools, and computing all administrative costs. The real-time system also controls up to 600 ticket issuing machines—handling up to 1200 bets a second.

a paper mill or a job shop or a petroleum plant. It may control the usage of trucks in a trucking organization or even change traffic lights in a congested city.

Control, in the cybernetic sense of the word, is a great value in industry, as is discussed in the following two chapters. Such a system cannot normally be justified by cost displacement or staff replacement. It is justified by an increase in efficiency or an increase in the production of a given plant.

A system used for control reasons may combine several of the above headings. It may be necessary when setting it up to install first a data-collection system, which may not make a profit of its own. The data collected are analyzed, and methods are established for later closing the loop or guiding an operator.

The functions of control may be combined in a multiprogrammed manner with other computer functions.

9. Combining Manual and Computer Processing in an Optimum Fashion

Some types of processing or decision making are not best done either by machine alone or man alone, but by a closely knit combination of the two, as discussed earlier in this book.

The SAGE air defense network uses many operators working in conjunction with the computers. Some airlines have decided that the human experience of their flight controllers is something they cannot yet program into their computer system, and so their machine converses with these men when necessary. A similar arrangement is used in shop-floor production scheduling. It is likely to be so in a vast number of complex applications in the future.

10. Use of a Distant Computer

It is often of value for persons to have access to a computer elsewhere in their organization. They may use this for processing small programs, such as scientific calculations or simulation, for information retrieval, or as fallback for their own computer. Salesmen may dial up a distant computer for information or to key in their orders.

On a duplexed system, for example, message switching, the standby computer has been made available for use. It can be arranged that, when any machine in the organization breaks down, the requisite programs and data are sent to the message-switching machine on the communication lines available. If a decision of the organization has placed it in danger of not producing its payroll sheets on time, this standby is available.

11. Elimination of Intermediate Actions

In a conventional computer application, the data for the computer commonly has to be punched into cards or paper tape. The output of the computer is printed. In an on-line system, data may be entered directly into the computer at the points of origination. For example, a workman's badge reader or a time recorder may be used on the shop floor of a factory. A bank teller keys data directly into a terminal. Similarly, the output may be delivered where it is to be used. For example, the computer may operate a display screen or print directly on the passbook in a bank. If intermediate steps of punching and printing can be eliminated, this cuts the cost of a computer system and also helps to reduce errors. Data errors may be caught at their source.

The ultimate use of this can be direct transmission between one computer and another computer. Suppose that a computer in one division of a firm prints an invoice to obtain some goods from another division of the firm. The invoice is mailed to the other division, it is read there, and its contents punched into cards which are read by the computer. It will save money, time, and effort if the first computer can transmit the necessary data directly to a second computer over telephone lines. Eventually this direct communication between computers may take place between different firms as well as within one organization. When a computer in one firm decides upon the need to order a certain quantity of stock, how convenient it would be if it could ring up directly a computer in the supplier's organization and place the necessary order.

12. *Different Users Sharing One Machine*

A computer doing service bureau work for many users may have on-line terminals in the users' offices. A part share in a large computer could be very much more satisfactory for a user than to own his own small computer. Many firms, for example, have small computers for scientific calculations.

Applications have been devised in which many users share one large computer by means of multiprogramming. Programs and data may be entered directly into the large computer from terminals in the users' offices. Engineers may have a terminal in their laboratory.

Banks have successfully shared an on-line system, keeping their files rigorously separate. Stockbrokers have terminals in their offices connected to a distant computer. Supermarkets share credit-checking computers.

The sharing of a computer in this manner will eventually enable users, who today cannot afford to own a computer at all, to have a part share in a large and powerful machine. Plans have been drawn up to have hundreds of small users with quite different requirements sharing one computer system with large files. In the not too distant future the grocer on the street corner will probably have a cheap terminal which is connectable to a distant computer.

These are twelve of the reasons why real-time systems are used. The justification of any particular system may not be in one of these reasons, but in a combination of them. It will often be a system that combines real-time work with non-real-time.

13 THE REAL-TIME COMPUTER IN A TECHNICAL SYSTEM

Real-time computers were used for a variety of technical applications before they came into use in administrative and business systems. The application of predominantly scientific or technical procedures to administrative processes is proving valuable in a number of areas. The techniques used for *control* of technical processes are in many ways analogous to those needed for the control of business organizations and administrative processes.

In order to achieve control of an operation, whether it be a mechanical, electronic, or administrative operation, *feedback* is necessary. Data about the performance or results of the process are fed back to the mechanism for controlling it, so that the process may be adjusted to give the required performance.

Feedback control is one of the most widespread phenomena in nature. It governs the functioning of all living organisms; it controls the flow of electrons in electronic circuits; it provides the key to automation by enabling machines or processes to be governed without human intervention. A man driving his car is exercising feedback control over it. A missile homing on a target being steered using feedback, but operated by electronic rather than the human link. It manifests itself in the world all around us in thousands of ways.

Feedback-control theory is of prime importance to engineers in the design of control mechanisms for electronic or mechanized devices, for chemical plants, for reactors, for the stabilization of guns on moving tanks, and so on. The concept is also of value to physiologists studying the mechanisms of the human body. It is perhaps less obvious how it applies to industrial and administrative organizations, but here again, in order to control or stabilize what is happening, feedback control is needed. This concept applies to any kind of functioning organization, simple or complex. Many control systems, especially those found in nature, are too complex for scientists to define exactly what is happening. Control systems in living organisms are far more complex than those built by engineers. Administrative control systems are sometimes simply definable but in other cases are so complex that it is very difficult or impossible to define with precision what is happening.

To achieve control of a mechanism or situation, a *goal* or *desired state* must be specified. The devices used for control have the function of trying to achieve this objective. The objective may be to keep a temperature constant, to keep a missile on a desired trajectory, to maximize the output of a chemical plant, or to maximize the profit of an undertaking. The goal or desired state may be fixed, or it may in some cases be varying. If it is varying, it must continually be reestablished, dependent upon the changing conditions, and this may be done either by a human agency or by part of the mechanism itself. A man steering a car down an unknown road represents a control system the goal of which is changing; similarly, a factory responding to varying customer demands.

The state of the actual system will not normally be the same as the desired state. This difference may be referred to as the *error*. The difference sometimes exists because the goal is changing or because there are disturbing influences and the parameters affecting the system are changing. *Feedback control may be described as on operation which is designed to reduce the error, or bring the actual state of a system as close as possible to the desired state.* In order to do this, the error must be measured so that it can be used to trigger off an appropriate corrective action. An example of this is an electronic amplifier which may be stabilized by negative feedback. Consider a circuit designed to amplify a fluctuating input voltage V_{in} to produce an output voltage V_{out}. An amplifier may be used which gives a gain of A. Then

$$V_{out} = A V_{in}$$

However, because of the nature of the components used, A cannot be easily held constant and so variations in the amplification may occur or the amplification may fall off as the components age. To correct this, a small fraction B of the output is fed back negatively to the amplifier as shown in Fig. 13.1. The voltage fed back is $-BV_{out}$. The net input is, then,

$$V_{in} - BV_{out}$$

Therefore,

$$V_{out} = A(V_{in} - BV_{out})$$

Therefore the amplification achieved is:

$$\frac{V_{out}}{V_{in}} = \frac{A}{1 + AB}$$

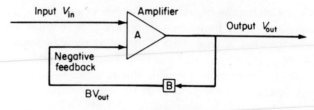

Figure 13.1

If $AB \gg 1$, then

$$\frac{V_{out}}{V_{in}} \approx \frac{1}{B}$$

In other words, the amplification has become almost independent of fluctuations in A. Stability has been gained at the expense of some loss in amplification.

Many cases exist of this simple form of negative feedback. The output V_{out} may be a velocity, for example, which is intended to be proportional to an input voltage V_{in}. A generator on the output shaft is used to feed back an opposing voltage BV_{out} so that the velocity is more accurately proportioned to V_{in} and independent of such parameters as changing friction.

In this simple example the signal fed back for control purposes is *continuous*. In others the output may be *sampled* at intervals, and the sample used for controlling the system. Some feedback control mechanisms only come into operation *when the output exceeds certain parameters*. A thermostat, for example, used for controlling the heating of a room will switch on the heater when the temperature falls below a given figure. As the temperature rises again above this figure the thermostat will switch off the heater.

The function which gives rise to the controlling action may be the *magnitude of the error*, or it may be the *rate of change of the error*, or both. The action taken may be simple, as in the cases above, or it may be the result of complex computation or table look-up. It becomes complicated when it must be based, not on one variable, but on many.

Feedback control is further complicated by the fact that time lags occur. There will be a time lag between the sensing of an error or a change in error and the corresponding action's being taken. There will be a second lag between the action's being initiated and the system under control's responding. On some systems the time lags are small compared with the rate of change of the parameters being controlled, and so they have little effect on the operation of the system. Other systems, however, have more inertia or the events affecting the system happen faster. The means of detecting or changing the system status may be slow. In these cases the time lags have a significant effect on the performance or stability of the system.

Figures 13.2 and 13.3 illustrate the difference between a quick-acting control system and one with a longer response time. The thermostat main-

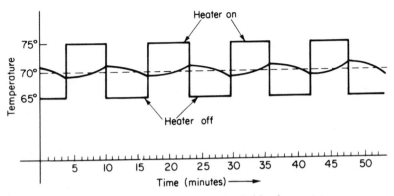

Fig. 13.2. Room temperature controlled by thermostat.

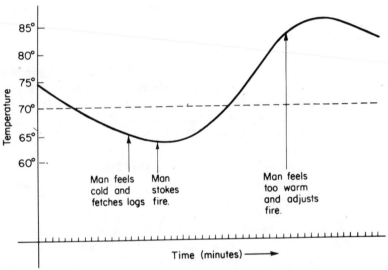

Fig. 13.3. Room temperature controlled by man stoking log fire.

tains the room at almost constant temperature, whereas the man permits large swings in temperature to occur because he does not act quickly or often enough. He waits until he feels cold and then loads logs on the fire, but it takes some time to bring the temperature back to 70°. It is characteristic of a human controller that, when he realizes that the *error* has become large, he overcompensates; he loads too many logs on the fire in an attempt to correct the error quickly and so causes the temperature to swing too high.

In this way *oscillations* about the desired state usually occur in a feedback control. They may be small and of no significance, or they may be large, wasteful, and even damaging. At worst, oscillations can steadily increase in magnitude so that the system becomes unstable. A *stable* system is defined

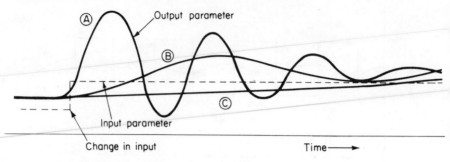

Fig. 13.4. A change in the input causes oscillations in the output which steadily die away.

as one in which, when a change occurs and oscillations ensue because of this, the oscillations die away steadily. An unstable system is one in which oscillations can increase in magnitude until the system breaks down or some other constraint limits the magnitude of the oscillations. Figure 13.4 illustrates an output parameter *A* of a stable system swinging and eventually settling to a new level because of a sudden change in an input parameter. If the input parameters were constantly varying, as is more often the case, the system would be oscillating constantly. Although it is a stable system, it may not meet its specifications because the magnitude of its oscillations is too great. A control system of different characteristics may give oscillations of a lower magnitude but possibly take longer to settle to the new level, as illustrated by curve *B* below. A heavily *damped* system may drift slowly to the new value, as in curve *C*. The heavily damped system may not react sufficiently quickly to achieve what is required. On the other hand, large oscillations can be undesirable and uneconomic. There are thus two objectives of most control systems, first, to reduce the error in order to give steady or optimum performance and, second, to do this quickly but without gross oscillations.

Situations in which computers are used for feedback control are likely to be considerably more complex than the above illustrations. There may be many variables involved, and achieving an optimum performance may be a matter of obtaining a correct relationship between many factors. Most feedback devices at present in operation are relatively simple in their functioning. They consist of simple mechanisms, such as a thermostat or steam-engine governor, or of electronic devices which produce signals proportional to the magnitude of a systems error or its rate of change. In a large plant there may be many such devices. An array of dials and controls is brought together in a control room for the scrutiny and operation of a human operator, as illustrated in Fig. 13.5. The operator makes adjustments to the running of the plant according to preset rules.

This human adjustment will not, in most plants, produce the best possible

Figure 13.5

operation. It will produce an operation that keeps the plant running and which has, in the past, been acceptable, as tighter control has been too difficult to achieve. However, it will be rather like comparing a thermostat operation with the human setting of temperature, as in Figs. 13.2 and 13.3. Greater profit will arise from the capability of always operating closer to the optimum. Swings like those in Fig. 13.3 represent a waste of money.

Where a large number of relatively simple feedback controllers are used, these may be replaced by one computer system. The computer can govern large numbers of settings at the same time.

Measurements of such quantities as flow rates, pressures, and temperatures are taken by the computer. They are converted into digital form by an analogue-digital converter, and the computer calculates what actions are necessary. The computer can then send to the plant signals which control what is happening by opening or closing valves, adjusting heaters, operating switches, and so on.

The instruments and controls are not necessarily close to the computer. The computer may control points widely separated by using instrumentation attached to telecommunication links. It has been used in this way, for example to control the flow of liquids in a nationwide pipeline. It has been used to link distant radar installations to a command and control center.

The majority of industrial processes are *complex multivariable systems.* To achieve an optimum state, many parameters must be measured and correlated so that a suitable combination of actions is taken. It is in this type of situation where the value of the computer becomes apparent. Simpler electronic or other control devices cannot achieve a sufficiently high degree of correlation or carry out the complex decision-making needed to optimize such processes. Generally a desired state for such a system is decided upon and controls are preset to achieve this state. This does not usually give the best possible performance, because the best setting of all the controls is not known and it may not be known whether the state aimed at can, in fact, be achieved at all. The more complex the system and the greater the number of variables, the more difficult it is to achieve efficient control in this way.

177

Furthermore, the system does not usually stay in one condition. Disturbing influences change the required settings. The demands on the system may change, and the input may change. Sudden events in the system may require quick action to be taken.

A process control system using a computer, then, is often one in which many instruments are scanned at intervals and other factors defining the process are recorded; some fairly complex decision making is carried out on these figures, and, as a result of this, adjustments are made to the operation of the process. The adjustments may be made hour by hour, minute by minute, or, on some operations, second by second. In addition, exception conditions in the process must be dealt with quickly if they arise. This is illustrated in Fig. 13.6.

Examples of this are a chemical or petroleum plant in which the process must be governed to give the maximum production under different circumstances; a steel strip mill in which red-hot bars race across the plant and are rolled and cut to different widths and lengths according to what customer orders are on the books at that time; a jet-engine test bed in which the running of engines at various settings may be governed and monitored, with calculations on the data collected being displayed to the engineers controlling the tests.

Often a computer-based control system does not dispense with the human plant operators. Except where a reaction time of less than a minute is needed,

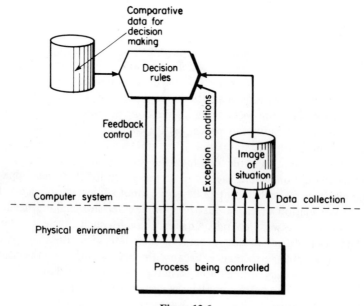

Figure 13.6

the human operators may still set the knobs and switches which govern the running of the plant. They set them, however, on the basis of information supplied by the computer. Such a computer system is referred to as an *operator guide* system. It is *open loop*, as opposed to *closed loop* in which the computer directly controls the plant settings. An open-loop control system is in some ways safer than a closed-loop one because a gross computer error will be recognized as such by the operator and will not cause damage to the plant. There are, however, automatic means of safeguarding against damage in a closed-loop system. A further, and often more important, advantage of an operator guide system is that the operator can keep the plant operating when the computer breaks down. This saves the expense of duplicating the computer. The plant will not be run at optimum performance during computer breakdown, but at least it will keep going, and this is more economic than having to shut it down.

A basically open loop system may have certain closed loops to deal with emergency situations or situations in which a response faster than a human reaction is desirable.

Setting up the decision rules for the control of a complex multivariable system is usually a lengthy and difficult project. A set of *designed experiments* may be used to establish how the input variables affect the output of the system. In a chemical plant, for example, we may control such factors as the mixture of reacting ingredients, the reaction time, the flow rates, the pressures, and the temperatures. There will be a number of disturbing influences that change with time. For example, the quality of the input substances may change, the required output quality may change, or factors concerning the plant itself may drift as in the case of parts wearing or catalysts becoming contaminated. In order to optimize the performance of the plant, the computer must continually evaluate what are the best settings. It may do this by using formulas that have been devised or by examining sets of tables.

Establishing the formulas or setting up the tables may be done by *mathematical methods*, by *experimental observation*, or by *simulation*.

Many operations which warrant the use of a computer for feedback control are too complex to analyze satisfactorily by mathematics. In this case a large amount of data may be collected on the actual performance of the plant. This will be analyzed and curves and tables drawn up to indicate how it behaves under different conditions. An experimental approach may be possible for this, in which certain factors are fixed and the effect of varying others systematically is measured. Often the computer and its instrumentation must be installed before this can be done adequately, and so the first phase of an installation may be a possibly non-profit-making, *data-collection phase*. As soon as sufficient data have been collected and analyzed to establish suitable decision rules for governing the plant's performance, the computer may enter a second phase in which it controls the plant's operation. This is often open-loop control to begin with. Closed-loop control may follow after the system has been proven error free and confidence has been established. There can thus be three phases:

Phase 1:   Data collection
Phase 2:   Open-loop control
Phase 3:   Closed-loop control

The use of *simulation* means that a model of the system to be controlled is built in the form of a computer program. The model will behave in many respects like the actual system and so may be used for predicting the behavior of the system under different circumstances. Simulation models are used for a variety of different purposes and are discussed in Chapter 25. They may be used to help in setting up the decision rules that a real-time computer will use and are particularly valuable where the system in question cannot itself be experimented with. The model can be varied and experimented with easily and endlessly. A model may be programmed, for example, for the flow of work through a factory, the rolling and cutting of steel bars in a strip mill, or the movement of trains on a railroad. Systems in which discrete events occur, possibly at unpredictable times, in which queues form and delays occur, may be tackled by simulation as analytical techniques can be very limited.

On many technical systems the collection and analysis of data is an end in itself, without any feedback. On a rocket-motor test bed, for example, the scanning of the instrumentation and analysis of the test performance may be done by a real-time computer. The equipment for detecting particles on a nuclear accelerator may be coupled to a computer. The scientists using very expensive equipment or test beds can obtain an immediate indication of the results of their experiments in this way and so know quickly whether they can pass on to the next operation or what the next operation shall be. A major justification of such a system may be that greater utilization can be made of the expensive facility. The duration of each operation may be much shorter and also the interval between operations is shorter. A test cell might, for instance, cost $5000 per hour to operate. The use of a computer purchased at $300,000 may enable three times as many tests to be carried out with that equipment.

On defense systems or systems for tracking space shots, the rapid analysis and display of information detected can be the objective. Data from radar or other installations may travel long distances over telecommunication lines and be used by a computer to build an up-to-the-second picture of events taking place.

Often human intervention or human assistance is needed in such systems. The computers may use cathode-ray tubes or other displays for conversing

(a)

Fig. 13.7. At the Manned Spacecraft Center, Houston, Texas, NASA technicians control computer systems receiving streams of data about Apollo missions. The system converts masses of tracking and spacecraft status data into display information which is sent 800 miles over Bell System circuits to mission controllers at Cape Kennedy. At the same time, the IBM 360 computers send aiming directions back to the tracking sites around the world.

(b)

with skilled human specialists. In some sets of events a combination of human action and computer action is needed. The men responsible for action's being taken may use the computer as a tool to help them, requesting from it whatever, displays they need. The focal point of the decision making in a complex operation may be a *command-and-control center* where the resources of experienced men and a data-processing network are combined in the optimum fashion.

Most of the concepts outlined in this chapter are now beginning to have direct counterparts in administrative or business systems.

14

THE INFORMATION SYSTEM
IN A BUSINESS ENVIRONMENT

The early users of computers in business were concerned with the mechanization of administrative operations already being carried out by hand. They prepared payroll checks, made out bills and invoices, updated stock records, compiled information needed for product planning and sales forecasting, and so on. The economic justification of such machines lay largely in the diminishing of the clerical labor force.

A more difficult but more valuable use of computers lies in the *control* of the various mechanisms that make a business function. There are a number of different aspects of business operations that need to be controlled, such as stock ordering and expediting, the production of components and subassemblies, the scheduling of jobs on machine tools, the control of quality, and the making of sales or reservations. These individual controllable mechanisms link together to form an organization over which over-all control must be established.

There are many analogies between the feedback control discussed in the last chapter and the control needed here. As with the control of a chemical plant, it is seldom a single factor that needs adjustment, but rather a number of interrelated variables. The adjustment of one factor sometimes affects many others. The main difference between the control of an administrative process and that of a chemical or mechanical process is that it is usually far more difficult or impossible to reduce it to a mathematical formula. Idealistically one might dream of a set of tables or set of formulas representing the entire operations of, say, a manufacturing business. Terminals located wherever they might be required would carry current information to the computer, appropriate processing would be performed, and the machine would send back data to control the functioning of the organization. The computer would control the entire business in the way it might control a petroleum cracking plant. *This, of course is an impossibility.* While some of the simpler administrative mechanisms can be completely controlled, such as the ordering of appropriate quantities of stock at the correct time, others are too complex for this and in the foreseeable future will remain primarily human work.

Generally speaking, the higher the level of management that deals with a function, the more difficult automatic control is likely to be. It is relatively easy to control a kiln or a machine tool automatically. Control of the flow of work through a job shop is much more difficult. Higher business control and policy decisions will probably always remain human tasks.

At lower levels, control might be by computer, but possibly with human intervention. The computer may give instructions to personnel, such as foremen or plant operators, but may have its decisions occasionally overruled. At the higher levels, management may perform the controlling function entirely but call upon the computer for information or assistance.

The computer may, therefore, be making control decisions or may merely provide information for humans to make control decisions. A fast-reacting *management information system* is needed if management is to achieve tight control. The computer will collect data so that it always has an up-to-date picture of the situation. It will report facts to management when exceptional conditions arise or when certain preset levels are passed, avoiding as far as possible the voluminous print-outs that were characteristic of the early days in data processing. In addition, management will be given the facility to make enquiries about the current status of the operations— stock levels, the queue of work on given machine-tool groups, a customer's credit status, and so on. Enquiries may be made about the effect of taking certain types of action. What effect would it have if I rescheduled the work in such-and-such a way? Can this order be met from available stock? Is it worth ordering a large quantity of such-and-such an item because of present bulk discounts? What other items will fail to meet their completion date if this batch is to be finished by next Tuesday?

Feedback control in an administrative process attempts, as in a chemical plant or a missile guidance mechanism, to achieve the closest proximity to a defined objective or set of objectives. Because of time lags in the system, oscillations will take place, as illustrated in the previous chapter though we may now be talking about oscillations lasting weeks or months instead of seconds. It is necessary to minimize the deviation from the objective but to do this without incurring over-large oscillations.

The oscillations that take place in manufacturing and other distributing organizations are considerable. They are very wasteful of resources and usually insufficiently understood by management. Reducing the time lags involved with the use of fast-reaction computer techniques and telecommunications can do much to reduce the swings that occur.

Imagine a boy riding a bicycle along a winding country lane. If he is alert he may deviate only slightly from his intended course. If, however, he is blindfolded and steering by instructions from someone following, there will be time

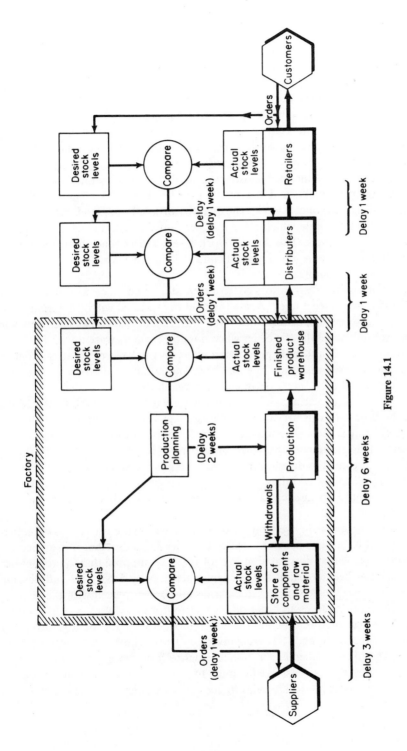

Figure 14.1

185

lag between his deviation from the best course and his correction of this error. Furthermore, when he realizes the error, he may overcompensate. Eventually be told to correct the overswing, but large oscillations will occur. If his informant or controller delays in giving him instructions the deviations will be larger; the longer the delay, the larger the error.

Jay W. Forrester in his work on *Industrial Dynamics** studies how similar swings occur in industrial organizations. Again oscillations are caused by delays in controlling the operations, and the size of the deviations depends upon the length of the delays, among other factors.

Consider the simplified illustration in Fig. 14.1. Customers are buying goods from retailers, and the retailers order new stock from distributors periodically, say, once a week. The quantity ordered each week may be calculated from a formula which takes into account the actual stock held and the desired stock levels. The desired stock levels will depend upon the rate at which customers are buying goods and the time it takes to replenish stock from the distributors.

Similarly, the distributors control *their* stock and place an order with the manufacturer once a week. Again the quantity ordered will be determined by a comparison of the actual stock levels with the desired stock. The factory in this example will fulfil the order when possible from its warehouse of finished products and establish its production plans on the basis of what is ordered. The factory will withdraw raw materials and components from its stores as required, and these must be replenished regularly.

There will be various delays in this process as shown in the figure. Many of the time intervals are unavoidable, such as the production time and the delivery times. However, some could be lessened, for example, those associated with decision making and the processing of information. It can be shown that the greater the delays, and in particular those associated with decision making, planning, and data processing, the greater the fluctuations that are likely to build up in such factors as stock levels, production, and work in progress.

An exaggeratedly oversimplified example will make it clear how fluctuations of this type can occur. Consider a retailer and a distributor in an organization such as that illustrated in Fig. 14.1. Let us suppose that the retail sales volume has been constant but suddenly increases by 5 per cent and observe the effect that this has on the stock levels and orders placed with the factory.

The retailer places an order on the distributor every week. Let us suppose that the size of this order is the difference between the desired inventory level for that item and the actual inventory level. The desired inventory level in this highly simplified illustration is equal to four times the average weekly sales figure. This is considered enough to prevent the retailer running out of stock. The average weekly sales figure is the average of the past ten weeks.

---

*Jay W. Forrester, *Industrial Dynamics*. Cambridge, Mass.: The M.I.T. Press, 1961. Professor Forrester discusses in depth the oscillations that occur in industrial organizations. He used a computer to simulate these and evaluate methods of feedback control.

Table 14.1. NO DATA-PROCESSING DELAY

Week	Retailer						Distributer				
	Sales	Average sales, last 10 weeks	Desired inventory	Actual inventory	∴Orders on distributer	Delivery to retailer	Average orders, last 10 weeks	Desired inventory	Actual inventory	∴Orders on factory	Delivery from factory
1	200	200	800	600	200	200	200	800	600	200	200
2	200	200	800	600	200	200	200	800	600	200	200
3	210	201	804	590	214	200	200	800	600	200	200
4	210	202	808	594	214	214	201	804	586	218	200
5	210	203	812	598	214	214	203	812	590	222	218
6	210	204	816	602	214	214	204	816	598	218	222
7	210	205	820	606	214	214	206	824	602	222	218
8	210	206	824	610	214	214	207	828	610	218	222
9	210	207	828	614	214	214	208	832	614	218	218
10	210	208	832	618	214	214	210	840	618	222	218
11	210	209	836	622	214	214	211	844	626	218	222
12	210	210	840	626	214	214	213	852	630	222	218
13	210	210	840	630	210	214	214	856	638	218	222
14	210	210	840	630	210	210	214	856	646	210	218
15	210	210	840	630	210	210	213	852	646	206	210
16	210	210	840	630	210	210	213	852	642	210	206
17	210	210	840	630	210	210	212	848	642	206	210
18	210	210	840	630	210	210	212	848	638	210	206
19	210	210	840	630	210	210	212	848	638	210	210
20	210	210	840	630	210	210	211	844	638	206	210
21	210	210	840	630	210	210	211	844	634	210	206
22	210	210	840	630	210	210	210	840	634	206	210
23	210	210	840	630	210	210	210	840	630	210	206
24	210	210	840	630	210	210	210	840	630	210	210

Tables 14.1 and 14.2. tabulate this. In week 3 in the tables the sales jump from 200 to 210 and they stay constant at this figure. The desired inventory level does not rise immediately as this might only be temporary; it is averaged out over ten weeks. As indicated in Fig. 14.1, there is one week's delay before the retailer receives the goods he ordered from the distributor. The figures for goods received in the seventh column of Table 14.1 indicate this by being one line lower than the equivalent figure showing the order for the goods.

These mechanisms apply in this simple illustration to the distributor ordering as well as to the retailer. They too order each week a quantity which is "desired inventory level minus actual inventory level," and their goods also take one week to be delivered (twelfth column).

Table 14.1 assumes no delay in data-processing or decision-making. A given stock position in Week 1 will result in an appropriate delivery of stock in Week 2. Table 14.2, however, assumes *one week's delay* in ordering, possibly because of the data-processing methods used. A given stock position in week 1 here results in the delivery of stock in week 3. It will be observed

Table 14.2. ONE WEEK'S DATA-PROCESSING DELAY

	Retailer						Distributer				
Week	Sales	Average sales, last 10 weeks	Desired inventory	Actual inventory	∴Orders on distributer	Delivery to retailer	Average orders last 10 weeks	Desired inventory	Actual inventory	∴Orders on factory	Delivery from factory
1	200	200	800	600	200	200	200	800	600	200	200
2	200	200	800	600	200	200	200	800	600	200	200
3	210	201	804	590	214	200	201	804	600	204	200
4	210	202	808	580	228	200	204	816	600	216	200
5	210	203	812	584	228	214	207	828	590	238	204
6	210	204	816	602	214	228	208	832	578	254	216
7	210	205	820	620	200	228	208	832	588	244	238
8	210	206	824	624	200	214	208	832	628	204	254
9	210	207	828	614	214	200	210	840	672	168	244
10	210	208	832	604	228	200	213	852	676	176	204
11	210	209	836	608	228	214	215	860	630	230	168
12	210	210	840	626	214	228	217	868	578	290	176
13	210	210	840	644	196	228	215	860	580	280	230
14	210	210	840	648	192	214	211	844	656	188	290
15	210	210	840	634	206	196	209	836	740	96	280
16	210	210	840	616	224	192	210	840	736	104	188
17	210	210	840	612	228	206	213	852	626	226	96
18	210	210	840	626	214	224	214	856	506	350	104
19	210	210	840	644	196	228	213	852	504	348	226
20	210	210	840	648	192	214	209	836	640	196	350
21	210	210	840	634	206	196	207	828	792	36	348
22	210	210	840	616	224	192	208	832	796	36	196
23	210	210	840	612	228	206	211	844	626	218	36
24	210	210	840	626	214	224	213	852	438	414	36

that, in the former case, no oscillations occur in the retailer's stock levels or order quantities. The stock steadily increases to the new level. The distributor's stock levels do, however, swing up higher than their final equilibrium level.

The same calculations with the same starting figures are done in Table 14.2, but with the stated delay. Now considerable swinging up and down occurs in the retailer's inventories and order figures, and these induce still larger oscillations in the distributor's inventories and order figures.

It is not suggested that inventory control systems as naive as this are likely to be common. The figures are used purely to provide a simple illustration. However, it is important to realize that *much more sophisticated schemes for determining the weekly orders will also give rise to such oscillations and that the magnitude of the oscillations will be affected by the lengths of the delays.* The reader is invited to retabulate the above illustrations using other formulas for determining the weekly order quantity and to note the effect of perhaps longer delays than those in the illustration. When a chain of events

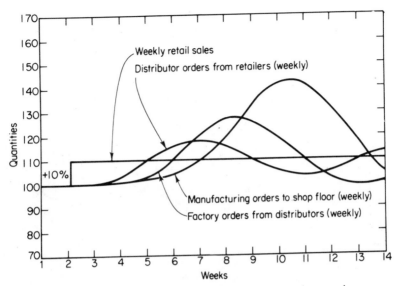

Fig. 14.2. Response of system to a sudden 10 per cent increase in sales.

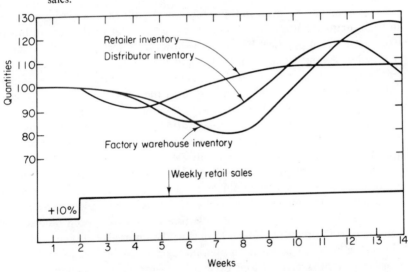

Fig. 14.3. Inventory variations in a system with long response time.

occurs such as that in Fig. 14.1, oscillations in an early link in the chain, such as the retailer's orders, will usually give rise to *bigger* swings farther down the chain. In Table 14.2 the retailer's ups and downs cause wide oscillations at the distributor's. The distributor's effect on the factory is even worse, and, usually, some way of leveling fluctuations has to be found at the factory.

Jay W. Forrester in his simulations of events that occur in actual industrial situations produced curves similar to those in Figs. 14.2 and 14.3. Figure 14.2 illustrates the orders that are placed in a retailer-distributor-factory system when a sudden change in sales volume occurs. Figure 14.3 illustrates

189

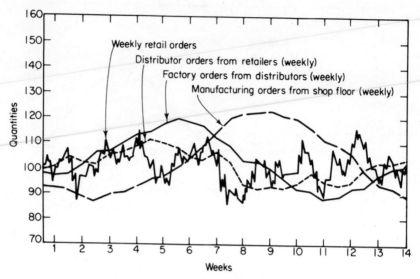

Fig. 14.4. Response of system to random variations in sales.

the swings in inventory levels in this situation. A sudden step in sales volume as in these figures is useful for illustrating the behavior of the system but is unlikely to occur in practice. Figure 14.4 shows the effect of a random variation in sales. Again oscillations occur, and a fluctuation with a frequency *characteristic of the system* rather than of sales is superimposed on the system.

Most organizational mechanisms, as with the electronic and mechanical systems discussed in the last chapter, have a tendency to oscillate with a frequency that is characteristic of the organization. The cycle time of the oscillations may be weeks, months, or even years, depending upon the time that elapses between an action and the results of that action. The oscillations in Table 14.2 have a cycle time that is three times the period between the stocks being ordered and stocks being delivered. There are thus peaks in inventory levels which occur once every six weeks. If the stock had taken three weeks to be delivered instead of two, the cycle time would have been nine weeks. When the time intervals are longer than this, the intervals between peaks will be longer. A factory's production planning and manufacturing time may be two or three months, giving a long cycle time. Forrester points out cases where swings caused by the organizational mechanism are interpreted quite incorrectly as being caused by seasonal fluctuations in sales.

In a country's economy the eventual effects of a credit squeeze or a stock market panic will not be felt until a year or two afterward. A trade cycle therefore develops with some years intervening between booms and depressions. All of these oscillations are very wasteful. They cause an excess of capital to be tied up in stock. They give rise to bad customer service. They cause periods of under-utilization of men and machines and at worse could cause unemployment and the laying off of workers.

One of the functions of management is to control an organization in such a way that it reacts to changes in the optimum manner. Any deviations from

190

the best performance objectives or criteria must be quickly detected and corrective measures applied. The organization must react quickly, but not over-react so that large oscillations are generated. The responses to a sudden change could be similar to those of Fig. 13.4. Too violent a response sets off large swings as in curve *A*. Too slow a response, as in curve *C*, is also disadvantageous. The optimum may be curve *B*. Here a slight overswing occurs, as in the distributor's inventory in Table 14.1, but this is soon corrected.

The mechanism for controlling the organization must be chosen to be as stable as possible. The simple mechanism used for determining the retailer's orders in Tables 14.1 and 14.2, could, surprisingly perhaps, easily become *unstable* if the delays in the system were too long. If the reader recalculates the table with a delay of *three* weeks so that a given stock position in week 1 results in an appropriate delivery of stock in week 4, he will find that the swings become uncontrollably large. A more stable means of calculating the weekly order quantity is needed. Here, in actuality, of course, a human mechanism for compensation would come into play. But not before a considerable waste had occurred.

The objective of management is to maximize profitability. For a given sales volume it is desirable to produce the items with the minimum men and machine tools and with the minimum capital tied up in stock and work in progress. For a given set of resources, such as capital equipment, it is desirable to maximize the goods produced, provided that they can be sold. If not, it is important not to overproduce. Oscillations of the types described above must be minimized, or they will cause overproduction at times, idleness at others. They will prevent a constant high level of efficiency being achieved. When work flows, in complex patterns, through a factory, as few machine tools as possible should be idle at any time. In an airline, when the last-minute flurry of bookings and cancellations takes place, as few seats as possible should be left unfilled, though the risk of overbooking must be minimized. On a railroad the cars should be maneuvered so as to give the maximum carrying capacity. Some of the control decisions needed to achieve these ends are complex. They require up-to-the minute information from many sources and fast processing of information. The control must be *tight*. Comparing, again, Figs. 13.2 and 13.3 in the last chapter, control should look more like the former diagram than the latter.

SITUATIONS NEEDING ON-LINE CONTROL There are certain types of situation and certain industries in which tight control is more important than in others. In these, on-line and real-time systems are apt to be of particular value. The following circumstances are likely to make this so:

1. *Fluctuating nonregular situations.* When the orders and production level are the same month by month and when the types of goods made do not often change. planning is relatively easy. The greater the degree of variabi-

lity and uncertainty, the greater the need for tight control. A factory making one-off items or small batches of work which are different day by day has a greater need of real-time scheduling than a factory making large batches with little change. Similarly, unpredictable sales, delivery, or other situations give a need for fast reactions.

A factory making steel tubes may have customers asking the prices of orders for tubes of many different shapes. The firm must have the ability to decide very quickly whether it can manufacture them by the requested date and at what price.

2. *Many items of large bulk or high unit cost* in an inventory may mean that large savings can be obtained from inventory reduction or centralization.

3. *Keen competition.* When customers can easily go elsewhere for goods, retailers must be constantly supplied with suitable quantities. In selling paint, for example, if a shop does not have the exact color a customer wants in one brand, he will take another brand. The airlines today are very conscious of the service they give, and, when a potential passenger makes an enquiry, he must be given an immediate answer or he may fly by another airline.

4. *Situations where a speedy reaction is needed or a sale is lost.* Quick price or delivery quotations may be needed, perhaps to customers on the telephone, to help sell. Some stockbrokers have installed real-time systems to help them buy stocks at a requested price.

5. *Situations with perishable goods*, such as perishable foods, theater tickets, or airline seats, must have quick action.

6. *Fashion goods* and popular books and records can have a sudden and very sharp upswing in certain items. If this is not met very quickly, much business may be lost. The same may apply to goods for which massive advertising is used.

7 *Goods in which a high turnover is needed to justify a high cost* may need a fast-reacting system to ensure this turnover.

8. *Firms covering a wide area* or with many branches may need data-transmission links to ensure that they are controlled in a coordinated fashion.

MANAGEMENT
INFORMATION
REQUIREMENTS

In order to achieve the management control discussed in this chapter, the following functions are required in the handling of information:

1. *A fast and accurate collection of all the data necessary to make the control decisions.* These data may have to come from widely separated points to the data-processing center.

2. *The fast making of control decisions,* Some of these decisions will be of a type that can be made automatically by computers. Others, because of their nature, will be human decisions, needing human ability and experience. However, using a computer can ensure that human decisions are made when needed and that the requisite information is available to the decision maker.

3. *A fast conveyal of the control decisions* to the point at which they are to be executed.

4. *A feedback of data to the decision makers* about the effect of their decisions, or feedback of knowledge about operations being controlled, so that adjustments can be made if necessary.

5. *A linking of separate events taking place in a sequence.* If a control decision at *A* is made, which is eventually going to affect a separate control decision at *B*, information about the events at *A* should be transmitted to *B* at the earliest possible time. Figure 14.1 provides an illustration of this, and also Figs. 14.2, 14.3, and 14.4, which relate to it. A retailer observes his sales figures and determines how much to order from the distributor. The distributor in this illustration observes these orders and decides how much to request from the factory. The factory production planning is based on the orders received from the distributor. Artificial fluctuations in the retailer's stocks and ordering cause larger fluctuations with the distributor. The distributor's fluctuations are yet again amplified by the mechanism with which the factory handles his orders. The resulting large swings in factory stocks and production could have been avoided in part if these decision-making processes had been linked and, in particular, if the retailer's sales figures had been considered in the planning of factory schedules. Any chain of control decisions like this should be linked, if possible, to avoid inefficient delays and oscillations.

Speed is important in all of the above processes if *tight* control is to be achieved. The larger the delays, the greater the possibility of severe variations from the optimum.

OPTIMUM COMBINATION OF COMPUTER AND HUMAN TALENTS   As was stated at the start of this chapter, complete control of a complex administrative process, such as running a factory, by computer alone is an *impossibility*. It is likely to remain so for the foreseeable future. The optimum system for handling and processing complex information is usually not entirely of computers, nor entirely of human beings. It is a careful combination of the best talents of both. It may be worth reexamining which functions in the ideal system are machine functions and which are still in the domain of man.

The computer and its peripheral equipment can carry out the following:

1. Rapid calculations, routine processing, fast editing and logic operations, optimum selection between multiple alternatives.

2. Fast reading of certain types of documents, fast reading of cards punched from documents, high-speed printing; hence fast preparation of invoices, orders, work tickets, checks, management reports, and so on.

3. The filing and maintenance of a vast bulk of information and the retrieval of information from the files, in a fraction of a second if necessary.

4. Scanning, sorting, and correlating of large amounts of information; searching for specific facts or correlations.

5. Collecting information very rapidly from many sources; accepting and checking manual input of information or documents from many sources. The sources may be at the other end of telecommunication links.

6. Fast distribution of information to many locations; distant print-outs or displays; the direct operation of machinery and chemical plant or other equipment.

7. Giving immediate answers to routine enquiries made in any location; facilitating man-machine conversations.

8. Surveillance, watching with an unfailing eye for exception conditions, potential causes of trouble, and situations needing human attention; notification of correct authorities using distant terminals.

9. The retention without loss of memory of routines that can be used again; the collection of information on which future action may be based. A computer system can be steadily improved and *tuned* as experience grows, to a degree not possible with human systems.

All of this forms a tool of great value in the managing of an organization and in other fields of human endeavor. Management will, of course, always be essential in dealing with human beings, but even in the handling of data the following tasks are still best done by man:

1. Handling unforeseen events; handling events of low probability.
2. Selecting goals and criteria.
3. Selecting approaches to a problem.
4. Recognizing patterns in events; detecting relevance.
5. Formulating questions and hypotheses. If man formulates a hypothesis, a computer might be used to test it.
6. Producing ideas; planning new products, new techniques, new business.

Many firms have begun the task of building an information system giving management the maximum help from automatic data processing. With the terminal equipment, display screens, and real-time techniques now available, man and computers are being made to work together much more closely than ever before. The possibilities of man-machine communication are great. However, the difficulties of building a complex management information system are formidable, and it is probably going to be decades before the potentialities of these techniques have been fully exploited.

15 AIRLINE RESERVATIONS

Many of the world's major airlines now have a real-time system for seat reservations. These systems, however, differ very widely in scope, function, complexity, and cost. Some airlines are on their second generation of real-time system, having started with a relatively simple one and later changed to a more complex and comprehensive system, often from a different manufacturer.

With the hardware available today it can be economic to include functions other than reservations in an airline real-time system. The planning now being done in several airlines is toward an airline *operating* system, of which reservations handling is a subset. The computer complex might handle real-time and non-real-time functions of revenue and cost accounting, crew scheduling, operation scheduling, scheduling of maintenance services, passenger check-in, load and trim calculations, spares inventory control, cargo handling, and so on. It might assist in flight planning and update flight plans while a flight is in progress. An airline operating system may include different computers in different parts of the world connected by communication lines. At the time of writing no such comprehensive system is operating and the problems ahead in achieving such a goal are enormous.

Building the programs and organization for such an integrated system will take many years. Some of the above functions will probably be working individually, possibly on separate machines, before such a comprehensive system is installed. This chapter discusses the data processing associated with reservations—from the moment a passenger first asks what flights are available to the time when he climbs on board the aircraft.

OBJECTIVES   There are three main objects in designing a reservation system:

1. To improve the service given to passengers and potential passengers.
2. To save staff in sales offices and in control offices where reservations are processed and space on aircraft is controlled.
3. To improve the load factor on flights.

If it handles cargo reservations, the objectives will be to save staff and to optimize the loading of cargo. Some systems have been planned with staff savings being the main or sole justification. However, a major payoff, where it can be achieved, is the potential increase in the loading of flights. Most airliners take off today with a large number of seats empty. Many airlines have an average load factor of only about 50 per cent. When this load factor can be increased by better reservation procedures or advertising, it gives a direct increase in revenue for the airline because the cost of flying a full plane is little more than that of flying a half-full plane. If a medium-sized airline can increase its load factor by one passenger per flight this represents an increase in annual revenue of more than a million dollars.

As reservations are being made, certain flights will become fully booked or so close to being fully booked that restrictions must be placed on further bookings. The flight is then referred to as a *critical flight*. However it is a characteristic of the airline business that in the two or three days before the flight leaves there will be a flurry of bookings and cancellations, and on many airlines the average seat sold is sold $2\frac{1}{2}$ to 3 times because of cancellations. For this reason booking limits need to be applied with caution. If the mechanisms for booking were perfect, the critical flights would take off 100 per cent full. However, in fact, they are commonly less than 90 per cent full. It might reasonably be expected that a computer using real-time space-control methods would increase the loading of critical flights from 90 to 95 per cent. If 10 per cent of all flights become critical, this represents an increase of 0.5 per cent in the airline's revenue. For a medium-sized airline, this may represent again about a million dollars per year. This argument applies more strongly to international flights than to flights within America, for example, for which there may be unbooked travellers waiting at the airport.

In addition the airline management should obtain valuable statistics for future route and flight planning. The system could indicate, for example, how much business is turned away and on what flights.

The introduction of a relatively simple real-time system in Eastern Airlines enabled it to cut its costs of passenger reservations by about 25 per cent and increase reservation operator efficiency by about 20 per cent. The load factors on criticial flights were increased from 90 to nearly 95 per cent.* Eastern Airlines subsequently ordered a more complex and comprehensive reservation system.

*Figures quoted in *Electronics Weekly* (London), Sept. 4, 1963.

**FUNCTIONS
OF THE
SYSTEM**

The reservation process starts when a potential passenger walks into a sales office or telephones to ask what seats are available or to ask for other flight information on a given route. The first function of the system will therefore be to enable a sales agent to give up-to-date information to the public. Many such people may be asking for seats on the same route all over the country or all over the world. A sales agent may say that seats are available when in fact they have just been sold by a different and far-away agent. To prevent overbooking, high-speed communications to a central coordinating office are required. The inventory of seats available may be kept up to date in a distant computer, and enquiries are made on this from the sales locations.

The potential passenger may then make a booking or several bookings that enable him to complete a journey. A ticket is made out, and the booking must be recorded. The booking will affect the number of seats available for other customers, and so the central inventory of seats must be updated. This is in effect a stock-control problem. It is a critical one because the stock item, an airline seat, is perishable. Once a flight departs, any seats that are left cannot be sold! It is further complicated by the large geographical area over which seats are sold. This is at its most extreme with an international airline. Seats on a flight from London to New York may be sold in Rome, Los Angeles, or Tokyo. The only way to have tight control over this kind of stock is by using fast communication facilities. They need to be fast because in the twenty-four hours before the plane takes off there will be a flurry of activity, many seats being cancelled, rebooked, confirmed from a waitlist, and so on. The sale of one seat can make the difference between a reasonable profit and a loss on a flight, and so control of the last-minute transactions is important.

Unfortunately, simple numerical stock control of airline seats gives rise to many errors. A passenger in his eagerness to ensure that he has a seat may become booked twice. His secretary may make a booking and he, himself, may ring up to confirm it. In one case in the author's experience a passenger was booked no less than fifteen times for one flight. Again, a passenger may cancel his bookings and by a mistake, on the part of the passenger or the airline clerk, they may be cancelled from the wrong flight. This can easily happen over the telephone. It leaves one flight with empty seats not open for sale and another in danger of being overloaded. A remedy for this problem is to use the passenger's name when modifying the inventory. When a booking is made on a flight, the names already booked are scanned to check that the booking has not already been made, and, when a cancellation is requested for a given flight, a check can be made that the passenger in question is, in fact, on that flight. It may be too big a job to scan the other passengers' names at the time the booking is made, and so they will be scanned at a later time, off line, and an appropriate authority notified of any suspected duplicates or mistakes.

This will reduce the number of "no-shows," that is, passengers booked who do not arrive at the airport desk to check in, and "no-recs," that is, passengers who do arrive but for whom there is no record.

Controlling the selling of seats in an optimum manner is much more difficult on airlines which have flights with several stops, and particularly difficult on long international flights which stop at points around the world and have few alternative flights. Consider a lengthy flight A-B-C-D-E for which the airline gains a considerable revenue from passengers who fly from A to E, but much less from those flying A to B, or B to C. It therefore wants to restrict the selling of one-, two-, and three-leg flights if there is a chance that they will prevent the sale of four- and five-leg flights on this route. However there probably will not be a plane full of passengers flying A to E, and so the restriction must be applied with caution. The pattern in which bookings build up and are cancelled will be quite different for different flights, and so each situation must be judged on its merit. Optimizing the revenue on these bookings is a complex problem in probability analysis that needs continuous real-time monitoring. It is a problem that no airline has yet solved completely satisfactorily.

EXISTING METHODS OF SELLING SEATS   Even in an airline which has installed a real-time system, some cities may be without terminal sets which tell them whether or not to sell seats at a given moment. There may be many locations in the world to which the computer will not be on-line in the foreseeable future, because the communication facilities are either nonexistent or too expensive. Again, a location may not have access to an on-line terminal because its volume of sales is too low. Some other means of controlling sales is needed in these locations.

The old, established methods used for this would still carry on in these places after the introduction of a computer. Methods in common use for this are as follows:

1. *Free Sale*

Space is sold freely at certain locations on certain flights without space-availability information being maintained. This cannot be allowed to occur at a location which may sell too large a volume of seats, and it must be stopped when a flight is near to becoming critical.

2. *Quota Sale*

A central space-control section gives allotments of seats on aircraft to various locations to sell. The size of the allotment is determined by a forecast of how much each location in question is likely to sell. When a location has sold all of its allocation, it may make a request for more space. A certain time, two or three days perhaps, before the flight takes off the location may change from quota sale on that flight to "sell and report."

3. Sell and Report

In this system each sale is reported to a central space-control section. When the seats on a flight become filled beyond a certain point the "flight controllers" observe this and may send status messages to the sales points placing restrictions on further selling. The restrictions may say, for example, that the office can sell no more seats on a flight without requesting permission or that it can sell no more than four seats without requesting permission.

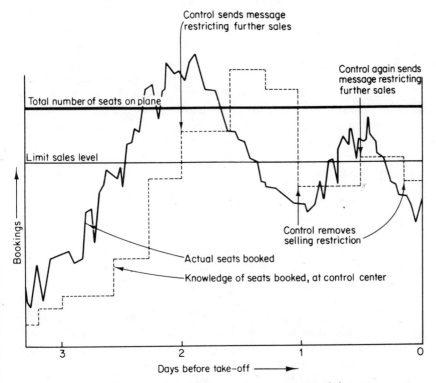

Fig. 15.1. The control of airline seat selling on a non-real-time system. A flurry of bookings and cancellations take place on a flight in the few days before it takes off. Where a time delay exists between the booking of seats and the placing of appropriate restrictions on booking from the control center, oscillations will occur in the manner described in the last chapter. The situation would be much more complex on a flight making several stops, with some passengers flying short journeys and others long, higher-revenue trips.

An internationally recognised standard code format is normally used for these messages.

Requesting permission may be a long process. Teletype messages from the sales office may take half an hour to reach the flight controller, or they may take half a day, depending upon the communication facilities available and the nature of the switching centers. The communication connections across the North American continent, Europe, or across the trans-Atlantic cable are generally fast and efficient; but this is not so to the Far East or Africa, and here "sell and report" has a long time lag.

Where there is a time lag before selling restrictions are placed or before they are effective, the bookings can swing beyond the authorized level. The restrictions are placed to correct this, and then too low a swing may occur before the control center knows about it, as shown in Fig. 15.1. Oscillations of this type occur in a similar manner to those described in the last chapter.

PASSENGER FILES   The airline sales offices must maintain a file on the passengers to whom seats are sold or who are waitlisted. The passenger is likely to contact the office again to cancel his flight or change his routing or ask questions about the booking made. He may have special requirements, such as the need to take a pet or baby or the need for special meals on the plane. The passenger may go to a different office from that at which he made the booking. If he is an American touring Europe, he may go into the Rome office to change his itinerary. The Rome office will have no record of his booking. They may be able to contact the office at which the booking was made but there will be considerable delay as teletype messages are sent and answered. In the worst case the passenger may not know the office where the booking was made. The total clerical labor involved in maintaining the passenger files in all the numerous sales offices is considerable. In the larger office difficulties can arise in this when manual filing is used. The filing clerks sometimes are unable to retrieve records on a customer.

It can be economic to automate this filing process, keeping the records centrally in a distant computer. The terminals and communication facilities used can be the same as those used for making bookings and answering availability queries. It is a large and complex step, however, because there are so many different functions that must be carried out to meet the variety of situations that can arise.

PASSENGER CHECK-IN   The final act of the reservations process takes place when the passenger arrives at the airport and checks in. A manifest is drawn up giving the names of all the passengers booked on the flight in question. This is transmitted to the airport check-in desk, and passengers are ticked off the list as they arrive. Last-minute alterations are liable to occur at the airport. Passengers may arrive for a given flight when they are not on the manifest. A flight may be cancelled and an attempt made to fit the passengers on other flights, possibly of other airlines. A passenger may arrive too late, and so on. A terminal at the airport desk connected to the distant computer can help in settling these problems and help in allocating the passenger a seat.

WEIGHT AND BALANCE

The passenger check-in process can be of more value if the weight and distribution of the load on the aircraft are taken into account. The freight to be carried by the aircraft, as well as the numbers of passengers, may vary in the brief period before takeoff. If fewer passengers travel, more cargo can be carried, and vice versa. It is valuable to have available an up-to-the-minute assessment of the permissible cargo load.

Records concerning the weight and balance in the aircraft may be set up in the computer files as soon as the flight is opened for check-in. An average value may be taken for the weight of a man, woman, and child. The bookings recorded will originally be used for setting up the weight and balance record. This is adjusted as the passengers check in with the weight of their baggage. Any updating of the booking records causes an updating of the weight and balance records. There is now no need to close the flight for weight and balance calculations half an hour or more before takeoff. Weight and balance control and passenger check-in take place simultaneously. When last-minute passengers arrive, the system will tell the check-in clerk whether they can be accepted for first or tourist class or whether they are acceptable as standby. If an attempt is made to check in a passenger too late, the reply will indicate that the flight is closed.

The advantages of having terminals at the airports to perform these functions are, then, firstly, a considerable saving in manpower is achieved by systems handling these functions. Secondly, it might be possible to close the flight later than otherwise and so last-minute occurrences may be dealt with. In some cases this will result in a greater passenger or cargo loading on the plane. Customer service is improved as the delay is less. Confusion caused by passengers arriving when there is no record of their booking can be dealt with more easily.

The calculation of the load and trim of an aircraft brings in fuel and cargo as well as passengers and their baggage. It therefore ties up with cargo reservations. It is of value to control the booking of cargo space on the same system as that for passenger bookings.

The outputs of the load control system may be warning of overload, cargo loading instructions, load and trim calculations given to the captain

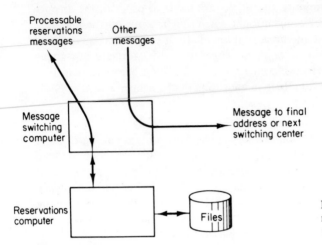

Fig. 15.2. Combination of message switching and reservations.

of the plane, boarding instructions telling the passenger-handling staff how many passengers should board, and messages about the load on the plane to stations on its route. All of this activity requires a large amount of data-message transmitting over telephone and teletype lines. This may need concentrators of the type described in Chapter 20. It will also involve message-switching centers handling the large amount of teletype traffic required. This may be within one country or in various parts of the world for an international airline. They may handle the traffic of one airline only, or they may handle several airlines. They will handle reservations traffic and other administrative traffic, so that some of the messages passing through them will be processable by computer; others not. Figure 15.2 illustrates the relationship of a message-switching computer to a reservations computer in a typical system.

SUMMARY OF SYSTEM FUNCTIONS   To summarize the problem, we list functions that may be automated in airline reservations. Although interrelated, these functions can be thought of separately and in many cases have to be automated separately.

Function 1. *Giving flight information* to distant sales points and, especially, answering availability requests.

Function 2. *Centralized inventory control* of seats booked and cancelled at distant locations. This has been done without passengers' names being used, but to be done efficiently these are needed to eliminate duplicate bookings and invalid cancellations.

Function 3. *Control of space allocation* to offices not directly on line to the computer. From a knowledge of the booking patterns on given routes, allotments of seats to be sold by various offices must be set and, as the bookings build up, status limits must be set.

Function 4. *Mechanization of passenger files.* These have previously been maintained manually in the sales offices. To keep them in the files of the distant computer and maintain them in a real-time manner, using the facilities needed for the above functions, will give major labor-cost savings and improve the service given to passengers.

Function 5. *Waitlisting, reconfirmation, checking ticket time limits,* and other operations concerned with manipulation of the passenger files. If, for example, a passenger does not reconfirm or collect his ticket when he should, the computer notifies the appropriate sales office.

Function 6. *Provision of special facilities for the passenger,* such as renting a car or booking hotels in a distant location or providing a baby carrier, wheelchair, or facilities for pets.

Function 7. *Message switching.* Airlines need large message-switching centers for routing off-line teletype bookings and other messages to the control points. Many of the teletype booking messages will be from other airlines. A computer can be used for this as part of the reservation system.

Function 8. *Passenger check-in at airports.* Manifests giving details of passengers are sent to the airport check-in desks. The check-in clerks have the facility to make enquiries on the distant computer and use this in allocating seats.

Function 9. *Load and trim* calculations done in a real-time fashion just before the airplane takes off can be combined with passenger check-in. Weights of passengers' baggage and estimated weights of passengers are used for the calculations. The results determine last-minute acceptance of cargo and passengers.

Function 10. *Cargo reservations* may also be controlled by the system, and the weight and approximate volume of cargo used in the load and trim calculations.

Not all of these functions are mechanized on all airline reservation systems. Today, however, it is probably economic to put all of them onto the same system in large airlines. Some airlines only mechanize function 3; others, functions 1 and 3; others, functions 1, 2, and 3. Many are now taking the complex step of mechanizing 4, 5, and 6. There is therefore a wide variation in cost and complexity between one airline reservation system and another. Some airlines use separate computers for message switching. Some use a separate system for functions 8 and 9. However, the more the functions can be combined onto one system, the more economic the operation becomes.

In thinking about each of these functions, the systems analyst or system designer must ask for each operation, "What is the response time needed for this?" and, "What degree of reliability is needed for this?" The answers to these questions have differed from one airline to another, and so here again there is a difference in the cost and complexity of the systems.

RESPONSE TIMES   Function 1 above needs a fast response time. The availability of seats or other information must be sent to the terminal while a customer waits behind a counter or at the other end of a telephone line, in conversation with a sales agent. It would be inconvenient if this took longer than twenty seconds. On most systems it takes less than three.

A man in Albany telephones the local office of an international airline and asks about seats on a journey, say to Cairo. The call is routed to New York on Telpak lines and reaches a sales agent with a real-time terminal connected, perhaps, to a computer in Europe. The agent sends an appropriate message to the computer as she talks to the man, and three seconds later she receives a reply indicating on which flight seats are available and on which the customer may be waitlisted.

If the man wishes to make a booking, there is slightly less need for doing this with a fast response time. It would be adequate if the booking were made in five minutes after the customer has rung off or even in two hours in most cases. In some airlines the inventory of seats booked is updated once per day—though this could result in lost passengers. If the inventory records are updated on a purely numerical basis, the terminal making availability requests can update them in three seconds or so with little extra cost. On the other hand, if passenger names are used when the inventory is updated, this would be much more expensive to do with the three-second response time. Some airlines keep two inventories, one updated numerically as rapidly as possible, and the other updated when teletype messages are received containing passenger details. The two inventories are compared at night or at off-peak periods, and the numerically updated one is adjusted for any discrepancies.

The response time for function 3 is geared to the speed at which messages can be sent to the distant sales offices over teletype. The response time for function 4, passenger-information retrieval, needs to be low if the data about a passenger are to be obtained while he is standing at the counter or is on the telephone. The response time for the various operations must be thought about in conjunction with the cost of the terminals and other equipment that is to be used. Some airlines give a response less than three seconds to almost every operation, and this is probably going to be the rule rather than the exception in the future.

RELIABILITY The computers or the files or other devices will fail every so often and will take a certain time to repair, perhaps two hours. The *mean time to failure* and *mean time to repair* can be predicted for the various units in the system, and so the overall failure rate of the system calculated as in Chapter 6.

Failure of the machinery is likely to cost the airline a certain amount of money. It may result in lost business, annoyance to passengers, inadequate loading of cargo, and so on. The probability of failure can be reduced greatly by duplicating certain parts of the equipment or designing fallback procedures so that vital parts of the work continue at the expense of nonvital parts. It must therefore be decided what degree of reliability it is economic to build into each of the operations.

In reservations the actions concerned with planes taking off in the next few hours are vital. Those concerned with the next few days are fairly important, and a quick answer is desirable. However, those relating to seats on planes for next week, next month, or next summer do not demand infallibility and no one will be very greatly inconvenienced if these cease to function for two hours or so. The bulk of the files do not hold data relating to the next few days, and so, perhaps, these need not be duplicated. If a customer rings up about his booking on a flight next week and the file holding his records is out of action, the sales agent can arrange to ring him back later. Similarly, if some of the communication lines are out or the computers are operating in a degraded fashion and only a fraction of the normal transactions can be transmitted and processed in real time, then the nonvital work may have to wait.

Of the functions listed, one that demands highest reliability is perhaps the load and trim calculating. This must be done shortly before takeoff, and it must be reliable, because if it fails the plane cannot take off in safety. The computer center may use two compatible computers, one large and one small. The small one is large enough to handle *only* the vital jobs if the large one fails. Many airlines, however, duplex *all* of the equipment on their system.

EXAMPLES OF TYPICAL SYSTEMS Figure 15.3 illustrates the processing of transactions on American Airlines SABRE System.

As a booking is made the passenger's name, home and business telephone numbers, ticketing arrangements, and other pertinent information are sent to the computer and stored on its disk files. This is done while the passenger is standing at the sales desk or is on the telephone to the sales agent. The computer checks the name with the booking to ensure, at that time, that it is not a duplicate booking. It checks also that all the desirable details for filing have been

(1) Passenger requests seat reservation by telephone or in person at ticket counter from any of nearly 1,000 American Airlines' agent positions serving more than 50 cities. (2) Agent places card listing all flights to AA designation specified by customer on display rack of desk-size console, keys in number of seats and date requested and presses "need" button.

(3) The operator sends a message over long distance lines to the SABRE computing center at Briarcliff, New York, asking for a seat on a specific flight.

(4) Computer instantly selects appropriate inventory record from its files. If requested seat is available, computer immediately flashes confirmation to agent and at same time automatically records the reservation and subtracts seat from inventory for the particular flight and date.

(5) If requested flight is not available, computer responds instantly by activating lights along side the card, thus informing agent of alternative flights that are open.

(6) Briarcliff center confirms sale by automatically typing out on printer in front of agent the flight number, date, number of passengers, departure and destination cities, and scheduled departure and arrival times. Agent then uses the console keyboard to type into computer record the passenger's name, home and business telephone numbers, ticketing arrangements, and other pertinent information.

(7) Computer automatically checks and confirms this additional data for completeness and electronically files the information as part of the passenger's record until his itinerary is completed, changed, or cancelled.

(8) The computer checks when the customer picks up his ticket, possibly at a different office, and ensures that the ticket time limit is observed.

Fig. 15.3. American Airlines SABRE system. [In addition to controlling seat inventory and maintaining passenger records, American's IBM system also: (A) Notifies agents when special action is required such as calling a passenger to inform him of a change in flight status. (B) Maintains and quickly processes waiting lists of passengers desiring space on fully-booked flights. (C) Sends teletype messages to other airlines requesting space, follows up if no reply is received, and answers requests for space from other airlines. (D) Provides arrival and departure time for all the day's flights.]

entered. In doing this, it enters into a conversation mode with the girl on the terminal many miles away.

Passengers will ring later to confirm, or change or cancel a booking. This happens with the majority of seats sold. While a passenger is on the telephone, the details of his booking will be retrieved from the system, and the agent will make the desired changes. The appropriate seat inventory will be reduced when cancellations or changes are made. The system will check that this is a valid reduction: that the seat being cancelled has in fact been booked. Tight checks and controls ensure that the many errors which occur on a noncomputerized airline reservation system cannot happen here.

The response time of the system to each agent's action must be low enough to permit efficient conversation with the computer while talking to a passenger on the telephone. The American Airlines' contract with IBM says that 90 per cent of all messages must have a response of less than three seconds. In fact, on the working system most of them receive a reply in about one second.

The reliability of the system must be very high. It would lose American Airlines' business if the system was "down" and details of passenger bookings were unobtainable. Every component at the computer center is duplicated, and almost all offices have more than one terminal.

The processing and filing of passenger names in real-time is expensive and complicated. Four-fifths of the massive random-access files are devoted to passenger details. Numerous programs are needed because so many exception conditions arise, and such a variety of situations must be catered for.

Other airlines followed American's lead in setting up a system that handles all details of the reservations process in this way. Pan American has installed a system that is even more spectacular because it is worldwide (see Fig. 15.4). Today many airlines are installing what is sometimes thought of as a "third generation" airline system using graphic display terminals instead of terminals operating at typewriter speed. The cost of such a scheme is high, although it is rapidly becoming less.

Many smaller airlines are thinking of a cheaper, less comprehensive system. This is particularly so with airlines outside the United States and Europe, for example, in South America and Africa. Here many airlines are less profitable than those in the United States. They are often supported by their country's government and prestige enters into the economics.

Figure 15.5 shows a reservation scheme less costly than SABRE and Fig. 15.6 shows an inexpensive terminal which handles numeric transactions only. This system handles reservations and also load control at major airports. It maintains a passenger detail file but does not enter into a conversation mode with the sales agents.

An on-line sales office has a fast response from the computer for availability requests and numerical bookings. The terminal for obtaining this is

She's got your number.

She's got your name. Telephone numbers. Ticket. And, your diet, if it's a special one. She's got all the poop on you, if you're flying with us.

Who is our brainchild? She's Boadicea. The most advanced computer system in the entire airline business. (We named her after a British queen who lived back in AD 60. A real lady tiger who proved to be somebody to have on your side.)

How does she work for you? Well, let's say you want to fly our VC10 to Britain. She'll tell you what's available on the day you want to leave. Reserve and confirm a seat for you. All in 3 seconds. Around the world she can do the same. And, if you ever have to use a connecting airline, she'll make arrangements in seconds.

But, say, suddenly you need to change flight dates. Up to 11 months in advance she can tell you what planes and seats are available, plus their arrival and departure

times. Then reschedule you in moments.

You wish hotel reservations and a hired car? Okay. They're made.

You want information on international currency, entry visas and vaccinations? She'll tell you all.

You want to take your baby with you? Or Fido? She'll arrange for a bassinet. Let you know if there's available space for Fido in the cabin.

And, when you take off, she'll check your baggage in, count how many pieces you have, and make sure it all flies with you. She'll make sure your plane has the most favorable winds so that you can arrive in the shortest time possible. (If your plane is delayed in stack-up, she'll contact anyone who'll be waiting for you.)

Come meet Boadicea. The most sophisticated woman in the whole world. Maybe **BOAC** the most beautiful, too.
TAKES GOOD CARE OF YOU

British Overseas Airways Corporation, 530 Fifth Ave., 25 Broadway, New York. MU 7-1600. 762 Broad Street, Newark. MI 3-8860.

Fig. **15.4.** Customer service: an example of an airline's advertising. The original design and proposal for this system was done by the author.

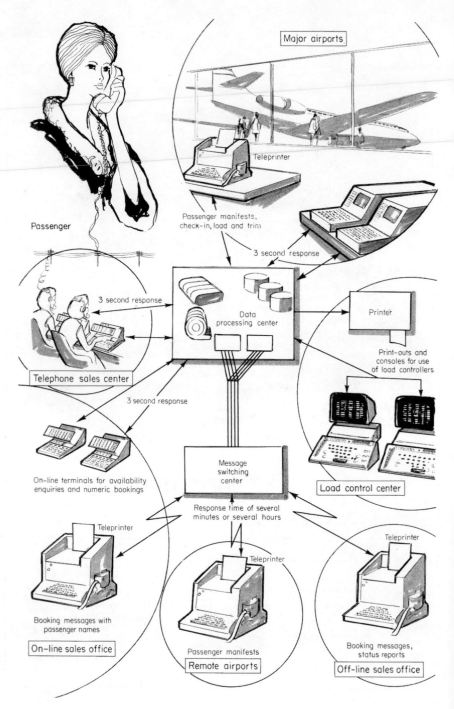

Fig. 15.5. Illustration of an airline reservation system which gives fast answers to availability enquiries but does not give fast access to passenger detail files.

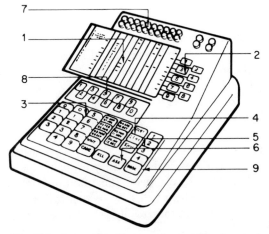

Fig. 15.6. A simple and inexpensive real-time terminal manufactured by Standard Telephone & Cables Ltd., London. It is installed in SAS and BOAC offices and in both these airlines it is soon to be replaced by more advanced terminals.

When operating, the user inserts a flight plate (1) giving flights to the destination in question. She keys in the segment of the flight (2), date (3), class (4), and number of seats (5). She depresses the ASK button (6), and the computer will send back lamp signals (7), thus:

> Green lamp: *The seats requested are available on these flights*
> Red lamp: *Not available*
> Red and green lamp: *Make teletype request*

She selects a flight indicated by the green lamp using key (8) and depresses the BOOK key (9) to make a booking. The booking must then be confirmed by teletype.

used by the sales agent while she talks to a customer. The passenger name and other details, however, will be written down manually as they always have been; when the booking is completed, they will be transmitted over a teletype network to the computer. This may take some time, as the message must pass through switching centers. If there is a query on the message, the computer will send it back, also over the relatively slow teleprinter network.

The computer will check the names of passengers booked on an off-line run to ensure, as far as possible, that no duplicate bookings are made or invalid cancellations deducted from the seat inventory. This will be a less exact process as errors are no longer caught at their source.

It may be necessary to keep two separate inventories: one up-to-date second by second, but likely to be inaccurate because purely numerical booking figures are used; the other hours out-of-date but more accurate. These would be correlated at off-peak periods.

With this system the sales office must still keep its own file of passenger records. Part of the justification of SABRE was the manpower saved in doing this. If a sales office wants to obtain information about a passenger filed in the computer or ask whether certain bookings can be made, it must do this by teletype and the answer may take several minutes or several hours to come back.

In the system illustrated, sales offices without availability terminals on line still have a teleprinter, as indeed they probably had before the computer was installed. This gives them the quota-sale and sell-and-report facilities described above. These will now be controlled by status messages from the computer, which automatically sets selling limits when the sales reach certain figures.

Handling exceptional conditions and possibly the sending of certain status messages will be done by load controllers. The diagram shows these having terminals with cathode-ray tubes. They also have a printer for providing them with flight-status listings. The load controllers are men with considerable experience of the airline's reservations problems. Certain situations needing more human experience than can be built into the programs may be referred to them. A small proportion of the teletype messages reaching the computer will not be machine processable. These are displayed or printed so that the load controllers can take the required action. Again, certain error conditions in messages received can be dealt with by the load controllers with returning the message in question to its source.

Whereas, on this system, the distant sales offices cannot operate in conversation mode with the computer, the load controllers *can*. As with many data-processing situations, the best solution is one which combines the abilities of a machine and an experienced man in the optimum combination.

16 BANKING

Another field in which the usage of on-line computers has become well established is banking. Banks and other financial establishments are using data transmission, on-line or off-line, to send transactions from branches to a central computer installation. Real-time terminals are being used on bank counters to check customers' balances and sometimes to produce statements or process the customer transactions on line.

SAVINGS BANKS
Among the first banks to install real-time systems were medium-sized savings banks. Some of these were entirely within one building, some with two or three branches, some with twenty or thirty branches. The tellers at the bank counters were equipped with terminals connected to a computer either in the same building or in a distant building, usually the bank's main branch.

The customer's recording document in such savings banks is a passbook. When he deposits money in his account or withdraws it, the transaction is entered in the passbook by the bank teller. Interest added is also written there. The terminal is designed so that the passbook fits into it, and a printing mechanism writes in the appropriate place. Figure 16.1 shows such a terminal. Figure 16.2 shows customers in a savings bank where these terminals are in use.

If a customer at the bank counter wishes to withdraw money from his account, for example, the teller keys in his account number, the sum to be withdrawn, and probably the old balance as recorded in the passbook. He then aligns the passbook in the slot provided so that the printing mecha-

213

Fig. 16.1. A savings bank passbook and the window machine it fits into. This terminal is manufactured by the National Cash Register Company and is in use in many savings banks.

nism will print a reply in the correct position and presses a key which indicates that now a reply may be printed. The computer, on receiving this message, seeks and reads the appropriate account record from its random-access files It checks that the old balance does in fact agree with that recorded as being the balance which should be in the bank. There may have been other transactions not yet written in the book, or there may be interest not yet added. If so, these are printed before the current transaction. The sum of the current transaction is then deducted from the balance, and a line is printed in the passbook representing this transaction. Figure 16.3 illustrates a page of a typical savings bank passbook updated as described.

In addition to printing on the passbook most banking terminals also print on a roll of paper that is used by the teller. This gives him a record of all transactions and enables the computer to communicate with him. If, for example, the old balance he keys in does not agree with that in the record, the computer will notify him. If the customer tries to withdraw an amount greater than that in his account or an amount that violated some stop conditions, the computer will inform the teller but not print in the passbook.

The keyboards on savings bank terminals frequently do not have alphabetic keys, although they do have some special-purpose keys. The teller may use numeric codes to indicate transaction types and send other special messages to the computer. It is, however, of advantage if the printer does have alphabetic characters, as the machine can then type English-language messages to the teller and more easily indicate pertinent conditions of the account being processed.

In addition to keeping the account records, the machine files the total of the cash and other transactions handled by each teller. The terminal may have a lock on it for security reasons, and, when more than one teller uses the terminal, there must be a simple way for him to indicate which one he is. The tellers' totals will be used for balancing the cash at the end of the day.

The on-line processing will end when the bank closes each day, and the computer will then carry out balancing and listing runs. A record will be kept

Fig. 16.2. Customer transactions being processed on-line in Long Island City Savings Bank. Thirty window machines like these in five offices are linked to a National Cash Register 315 computer.

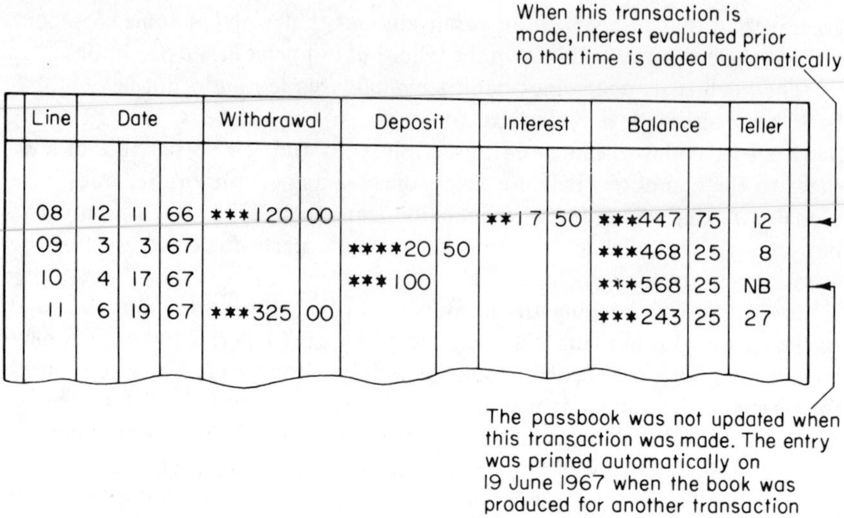

When this transaction is
made, interest evaluated prior
to that time is added automatically

Line	Date			Withdrawal		Deposit		Interest		Balance		Teller
08	12	11	66	***120	00			**17	50	***447	75	12
09	3	3	67			****20	50			***468	25	8
10	4	17	67			***100				***568	25	NB
11	6	19	67	***325	00					***243	25	27

The passbook was not updated when
this transaction was made. The entry
was printed automatically on
19 June 1967 when the book was
produced for another transaction

Fig. 16.3. A page from a savings bank paybook updated on an
on-line terminal.

throughout the day of all the transactions that occur. This will be sorted
and appropriate totals produced for cross-checking and balancing. If any
discrepancy is found, all transactions entered by the particular teller may
be listed and compared with the roll of paper printed by the appropriate
teller terminal to determine the reason for the difference. A savings journal,
an account activity report, and other reports may be produced at the end of
the day. An *audit trail* will be written, possibly on tape, which, with the teller
tapes, gives all data that are needed for auditing.

In addition to handling savings account withdrawals and deposits, a
system of this type can handle a variety of other functions which the savings
bank may deal with. Loan payments may be handled on line. The teller
would enquire about the current status of a loan account when necessary,
and the computer may tell him of some exception condition, such as payments
in arrears or unpaid penalities. He then refers the customer to a special department or to the branch manager. Similarly, mortgages, school accounts,
payroll, cost accounting, and so on, may be handled by the system, Such
saving bank systems are among the closest so far to *total systems*, integrating
all the data handling of an organization.

ADVANTAGES   As with most commercial computer applica-
                                tions, this system in usually intended to give
staff savings. Its cost is not usually however, *entirely* justified on staff savings.
In many banks the staff saving have been surprising small or nonexistent.

Organizations that have installed such a system have justified it on other advantages, as follows:

1. *Improved customer service.* Tellers can deal with customers more quickly. They do not have to leave their windows to refer to files or ledgers. They do not have to look up and write unposted interest or dividends or other items not yet recorded in the passbook. These are added automatically. One teller can now usually deal with all the customer's needs. The system can reduce the queuing which takes place at the bank counter and which can become too great at lunch times or other peak periods.

Surprisingly, perhaps, one still sees long queues in some banks that have installed real-time teller systems. These banks have sometimes saved money by reducing the number of tellers and teller positions needed and are prepared to allow queues to form at peak periods.

2. *Any-window, any-branch service.* A customer may now go into any on-line branch of the bank to withdraw money or make other transactions. Previously he could only go to the branch that kept his records. Inside a bank, he can go to any teller at any window bacause they all now have access to all savings records. All terminals display hold or special conditions, and all terminals add unposted items and interest.

3. *Increased security and accuracy.* A system of this type with well-designed balancing procedures and controls should be more accurate than earlier methods. The system will make careful checks before the records are updated, verifying, for example, the account number, which may be a self-checking number, and its odd balance. It will keep a check on teller actions and cash totals. Normally, balancing and other end-of-day procedures will be fast and exact. If an error does slip through, it can be quickly found by comparing the printed roll from that teller's terminal with a chronological transaction list for that teller produced by the computer. The printed roll records every clerical action the teller takes. Control totals and teller totals are developed by the computer and by the terminal and may be compared at any time.

The facility has been built into some systems for the customer to use a "password" when he makes a transaction. This is a unique number which he alone knows and which is recorded on his record in the system. He may, perhaps, use his driving license or social security number. Unless the correct password is quoted at the bank counter, the computer will not permit the transaction to be completed.

4. *Immediate updating of records.* Records are updated the instant each transaction occurs.

5. *Computer control of hold conditions.* Hold and other special conditions are continously monitored by the computer and so cannot be violated. A means for rapidly dealing with exceptional cases can be built into the system. If a teller or supervisor thinks it may be desirable to contravene a hold

condition, the system can give him a means of immediately contacting a control position where such a decision might be made.

6. *Saving of time.* The branches' books have to balance each day before the staff can go home. Before the use of computers this took considerable time and sometimes meant personnel working overtime searching through columns of figures for an error. It can now be done quickly, and errors are less likely. In some banks the leaving hour has been stabilized, and the turnover of staff, especially women, has fallen. This opens up the possibility of longer opening hours. Some banks are staying open longer in the evening. The Bowery Savings Bank, in New York, for example, closes its main counter area at the traditional 3 P.M., but a small area with a few terminals remains open until late.

7. *Better utilization of space.* The floor space needed for a teller and terminal is low compared with that previously needed for files, records, and clerks. Also more customers can be served by one teller. Windows lettered for different purposes are no longer needed. Floor space is very expensive in some financial districts of large cities, and the saving can be considerable. A bank may greatly increase its activity without extending its premises. It becomes possible to open a new branch in a very small area, such as a kiosk in a hotel lobby or bustling railway station, with only one teller and a terminal.

RELIABILITY   In a financial institution it is, of course, vital that the computer does not make mistakes, and the system must be designed for maximum accuracy. Controls on accuracy, very necessary here, are discussed in Chapter 35.

If the computer or any part of the system fails, it is important that there must still be some means of handling transactions for customers arriving at the bank counters. Some savings banks have installed duplex computers for reliability reasons. For the smaller bank, however, this can be hard to justify economically, and a less expensive standby procedure is needed.

Let us suppose that the computer or the communication line fails for a period of, say, two hours. How does the teller handle his transactions? The design of the terminal can help considerably in standby procedures. First, the roll of paper on which it prints all the teller's actions and which acts as a means of verifying transactions when the terminal was on line now becomes a record of all transactions made off line. When the computer is on the air again, the teller will enter everything on this roll, indicating to the computer that these were off-line transactions.

Secondly, the terminal may be equipped with its own accumulator, which updates the old balance and maintains teller cash totals. The IBM 1062, for example, has two accumulators which maintain the net cash position for two tellers and a third one which the teller uses to work out the new balance when the terminal is off line. The third acts as a communication buffer storage when the terminal is on line, improving the efficiency of line utilization and enabling the user to key in one item while the previous one is being printed. As soon as a failure occurs, the teller makes the terminal print out its control totals showing the net cash. These will have also been recorded in the computer files up to the time when the failure occurred. The terminal counters still accumulate net cash totals during the ensuing period of off-line operation, and, when the computer becomes usable again, the teller again prints the totals. These two sets of totals act as a control for the transactions processed off-line.

In this way complete audit control is achieved. The terminal accumulation of cash totals before and after off-line operation must agree with the teller totals kept by the computer. This checks that all account records on disk are correctly updated, if a little late.

It will be desirable for the teller, when operating off-line, to look up information on certain accounts. Periodic listings may be provided for this purpose by the computer and delivered to the branches. Listings may be made of all accounts or only of certain key accounts. They may give only balance information, or they may give dividends, interest, or other account data. If a customer wishes to withdraw money when the computer is down, the teller may look up the last listing as a check. Often, however, he will only do this if the customer wishes to withdraw more than a certain sum.

CHECKING ACCOUNTS

So far we have discussed only savings banks or institutions in which the customer produces a passbook. With these it is often convenient to process the transaction in real-time. In banks handling checking accounts there is also a need for centralized files and computers, though not necessarily for real-time transaction processing. Here, checks can only be drawn on one branch of the bank. If a customer goes into a branch and asks to withdraw money, he must make out a check, and before the clerk hands over any cash he will enquire to see whether the man has enough in his account. If the bank has no centralized file, this may mean a long-distance telephone call to the man's branch.

A checking account bank may therefore process its checks using in-line processing (as described in Chapter 5) of data sent over transmission lines and data from a magnetic-ink, character-recognition check sorter and reader. The customer's account will be kept centrally on random-access files, and the branches may have the facility to make real-time enquiries about the account. In some banks a customer requesting a statement receives it from a typewriter-like terminal on line to a distant computer. Figure 16.4 illustrates a possible configuration. Other banks, seeking inexpensive terminals, have considered dial-up voice answerback as a means of obtaining details about a customer's account.

The types of information that are kept on a central file accessible from

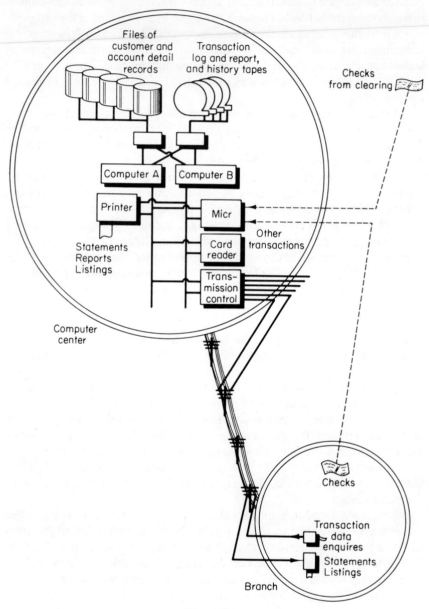

Figure 16.4

enquiry stations may differ from one system to another. Some may contain complete customers' details, such as name, address, occupation, coding, personal data, account history, and Social Security number in the United States. The customer record will probably contain pointers to relevant account records. These may contain master information, such as balance, charges, and in Europe, overdraft limit and standing orders; and detail information such as the details of each transaction not yet printed on a statement. In addition, the files may contain records relating to mortgages, commercial loans, installment loans, saving accounts, safe deposits, so on.

Some banks, on the other hand, while making an extensive use of data transmission, are not giving real-time access to a central file. Data to be processed centrally may be punched into paper tape and transmitted in batches to the computer center. Batches of about a hundred transactions, say, may be sent with a batch total. The batch total is checked and possibly other checks are made in real-time, but, once the batch is known to be correct, it waits in a stack of jobs for processing. Such data transmission may be on-line or off-line, but with the control programs available on many machines today it is often cheaper and more convenient for it to be on-line. Statements resulting from these transactions may be mailed centrally, and listings, statements, and exception reports may be transmitted back to the branch, possibly at night.

As with other applications, there is a range of possibilities between off-line batch data transmission and a fully integrated real-time system.

17 MESSAGE SWITCHING

This chapter describes the use of a computer for relaying messages and data between points in an organization. Every organization with activities in more than one place has a need to send messages and data between these places. As the pace and complexity of business increase, it is necessary or advantageous to send information faster than is possible by mail. Telecommunication systems enable large volumes of information, formerly delayed by distance, to be received, processed, and acted upon earlier.

Locations wishing to communicate with each other could send data directly by teleprinter links. However, where there are a large number of widely separated locations, the cost of communications can be reduced by using some form of message-switching system. Consider the points illustrated in Fig. 17.1. These represent terminals located in eight different cities.

One solution to providing telecommunication links between these would be to have direct communications between every pair of points as in Fig. 17.2.

An alternative, which uses far fewer communication lines, is to connect all the points to a switching device as shown in Fig. 17.3.

The larger the number of locations, the greater the saving in line costs

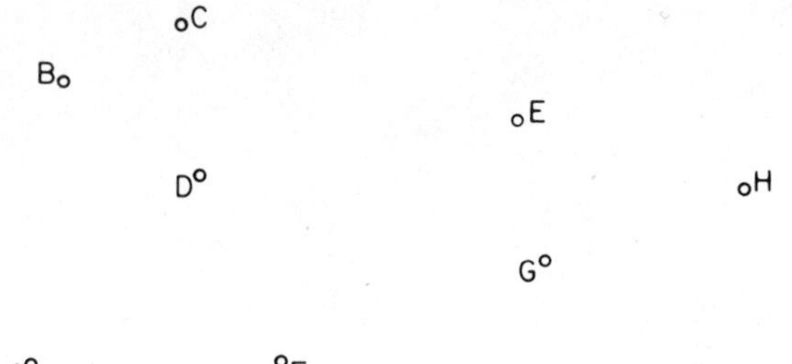

$_oC$

B_o

$_oE$

D^o $_oH$

G^o

A^o ^oF

Figure 17.1

222

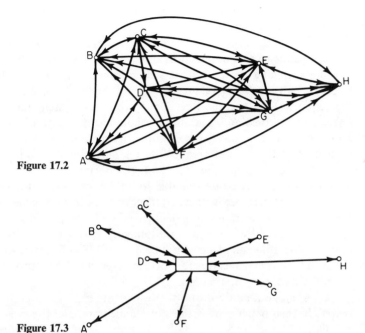

Figure 17.2

Figure 17.3

when a switching center is used. A further reduction in line costs is achieved by using *multidrop* lines, in which one line connects several terminals (Fig. 17.4). This could be done if the traffic volume was not too high. It is necessary that the switching center can address the terminals individually and that one terminal on a line respond only to messages addressed to it and not to those for other terminals. This is discussed in more detail in Chapter 20.

A variety of means are in use for switching messages. A small number of lines may be handled by a manual exchange in which an operator makes jack-plug connections as required. Similarly, automatic exchanges, like a telephone exchange, are in use, in which the switching is done by relays.

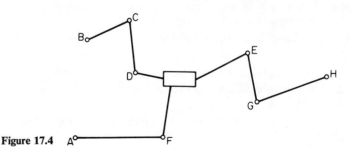

Figure 17.4

However, with a large volume of traffic it becomes desirable to store messages at the switching center.

Suppose that, in Fig. 17.4, terminal A wishes to send a message to terminal C, but the line to C is occupied by other traffic to or from terminals B, C, or D. The switching center cannot send the message until the line becomes free. A small localized system may be able to hold the message at A until the requisite lines become free. To do this, the system must receive and analyze the address and establish a communication path before the data are sent. This could be done, for example, by dialing and receiving a "busy" tone if the line was not free. With a large system handling many more locations and lines than in Fig. 17.4, the delays can become considerable at times, and it may be undesirable to hold a message at the terminal for a long time. Furthermore, with a system covering a large area and with different types of communication equipment, it may not be practical to analyze the address and establish a communication path, if available, before the data are sent. Dialing, for example, may not be possible. To circumvent this difficulty, the switching center receives the message regardless and stores it until it can be sent to its correct destination.

A system commonly in use for doing this is a *torn-paper-tape switching center*. In this, paper tape is the storage medium, and the switching is done manually. Figures 17.5 to 17.8 give illustrations of a typical torn-paper-tape switching center. As messages arrive at the center, they are punched into paper tape. There is normally one punch to each communication line for receiving messages. Similarly, there will be one paper-tape reader for each communication line for sending messages. The messages punched into tape will be preceded by the address or addresses to which they are to be sent. Girls operating this type of switching center will tear off the messages received, read the address to which they are to be sent, and place them on the appropriate transmitting paper-tape reader.

Queues of transactions will develop in such a system. If a large number of messages are received in a short period on one line, these will sit in a wire basket waiting for the girls to inspect them. Similarly, a temporary high load on an outgoing line will result in a number of pieces of torn paper tape waiting to be transmitted on that line (Fig. 17.7). A large switching center of this type may employ as many as sixty girls to keep it in operation.

A computerized switching center may be considered to be an automation of the system just described. Its advantages over a torn-paper-tape center are:

1. Much faster delivery of messages.
2. Automatic handling of transmission errors.
3. Elimination of operating errors.
4. Analysis of messages may be made and automatic actions taken if required.

Fig. 17.5. A typical torn-paper-tape switching center.

Figure 17.6

Fig. 17.7. A queue of messages waiting to be transmitted.

Figure 17.8

225

5. For message volumes above a certain limit, it is cheaper because of staff savings.

Its advantages over an electromechanical exchange are:

1. On large systems it gives faster delivery of messages.
2. Automatic handling of transmission errors is provided.
3. Routing a message to several different destinations can be done easily.
4. High-priority messages can be recognized and transmitted immediately.
5. Analysis of messages may be made and automatic actions taken if required.
6. For systems above a certain level of complexity, it is cheaper.

In general, any switching center that handles 6000 messages per day would probably be best operated with a computer. Some networks with a much *lower* traffic volume than this are switched by computer.

One of the largest commercial message switching centers is the Collins Radio System at Cedar Rapids, Iowa. This uses 10 computers, 24 hours of every day to switch airline messages. Its volume totals more than 200,000 messages per day.

The single computer may have one disadvantage over the above methods. If a computer failure occurs, the entire exchange is out of action until it is repaired. Most of the likely failures in the other methods put out only one line or, at worst, a few lines. The mean time to repair the computer when it fails may be of the order of two hours. On some networks a break of two hours is tolerable. On others it is not. If it is not, two computers must be used, giving a *duplexed* system, so that if one fails the other takes over. On some systems the duplexing may not be as wasteful as it sounds because the standby computer may run data-processing or other programs. Some organizations have deliberately sited the message exchange next to a data-processing center for this reason. The data-processing computer may interrupt its work only for the occasional period when the message-switching machine has failed. Certain computer operating systems permit message switching to go on at the same time as other data processing on the same machine.

Some message-switching systems have special *no-break power* supplies to maintain operation when mains power fails. Direct-current motor-driven alternators may be used, driven off a direct-current battery which is kept fully charged by being floated across the mains. Such a system can provide at least two-hours electricity supply when the mains fail. This gives ample time to start up a secondary diesel electric set to keep the battery charged.

The facilities desirable on a message-switching computer are a small random-access file for the temporary storing of messages being routed, and a serial-access file, often magnetic tape, for logging messages if they are to

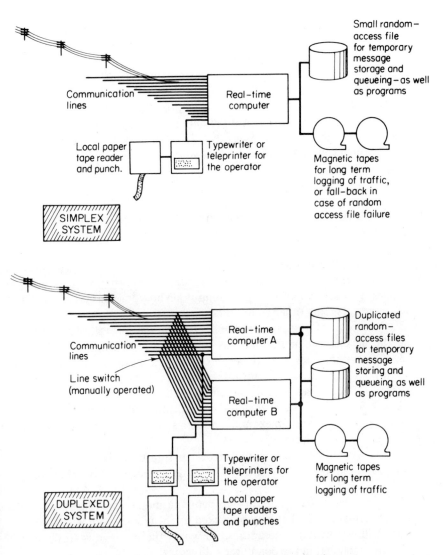

Fig. 17.9. Possible configurations for a message-switching system.

be kept for a long period of time. It must, of course, have the facilities for handling all the various types of communication lines used. The core size usually varies from about 40,000 to 200,000 characters, or the equivalent in binary words. Computer characteristics recommended for real-time in Chapter 19, are desirable for a message-handling computer. Figure 17.9 sketches typical configurations.

In a data-processing system, message switching may be thought of along with the other work and regarded as one element of the complete system. In this case it may be done by a separate line control computer which feeds messages also to the main computers; or one computer may handle message routing and data processing at the same time, in parallel. When message switching was first performed by computer, it was usually done by stand-alone machines dedicated to this function. However as multiprogramming and Supervisory Program techniques are improving, more and more systems combine message switching with some data processing. If a system handles, say, 2000 messages per day, even a small computer will be left with much idle time which can be absorbed in other work.

FUNCTIONS OF THE SYSTEM

To explain in detail what can be involved in message switching, the functions that a system performs are listed below:

1. The system will accept messages from distant terminals. The terminals are often teleprinters and paper-tape readers, but other devices may be used such as card readers and special input keyboards. The system may also accept messages from other computers.

2. On receipt of a message it will analyze the message's header to determine the destination or destinations to which the message must be sent.

3. The system may analyze the header for a priority indication. This will tell the program that certain messages are urgent. They must jump any queues of messages and be sent to their destination immediately.

4. It may analyze the header for an indication that some processing of the message is necessary, for example, statistical information from the message may be gathered by the system.

5. The system will detect any errors in transmission of the incoming message and request a retransmission of faulty messages. This retransmission may be automatic.

6. It will detect format errors in incoming messages as far as possible. Types of format errors that may be picked up include the following:

   (a) Address invalid. The address to which the message is to be sent is not included in the computer's directory.

   (b) Excessive addresses. There are more than the given maximum number of addresses allowed.

   (c) Incorrect format. An invalid character, for example, the control character, appears in the message in an incorrect location.

   (d) A priority indicator is invalid.

   (e) Originator code error. The address of the originator is not included in the computer's list.

   (f) Incorrect character counts.

7. The system will store all the messages arriving and will protect them from possible subsequent damage.

8. It will take messages from the store and transmit them to the desired addresses. One message may be sent to many different addresses. In doing this, it will not destroy the message held in the store. The store is thus a queueing area for messages received and messages waiting to be sent.

9. The system will redirect messages from the store and send them to the terminals requesting them. It may, for example, be asked to resend all messages from a given serial number or resend a message with a specified serial number.

10. Systems in use store messages in this manner for several hours or, on some systems, several days. Any message in the store is immediately accessible for this period of time.

11. The system may also maintain a permanent log of messages received. This will probably be done on a relatively inexpensive medium, such as magnetic tape, and not on a random-access file.

12. If messages are sent to a destination at which the terminal is temporarily inoperative, the system will intercept these messages. It may automatically reroute them to alternative terminals which are operative. On the other hand, it may store them until the time that the inoperative terminal is working again.

13. It might intercept messages for other reasons. For example, the system may be programmed to send a message to a location of an important person although he may be moving from one place to another. The person in question will leave his current location with the computer, and the computer will divert messages for him to that location. The system may handle messages on a priority basis. There may be one urgent priority level so that these messages are sent before any others. Some systems have more than one level of priority, priority level 1 being transmitted before priority level 2, priority level 2 being transmitted before priority level 3, and so on. The system may notify the operator in the event that any priority queue becomes too great.

A simple system may have no priority scheme, messages being handled on a first-in-first-out basis.

14. The system will maintain an awareness of the status of lines and terminals. It will be programmed to detect faulty operation on terminals where possible, to make a log of excessive noise on lines, and to notify its operator when a line goes out. The system will maintain records of any faults it detects.

15. On a well-planned system the messages should be given serial numbers by the operator sending them. The computer will check the serial numbers and place new serial numbers on the outgoing messages. When serial numbers are used, the system can be designed to avoid the loss of any message.

This is especially important in the event of a computer failure or of a switch-over in a duplex system.

16. At given intervals, perhaps once an hour, the system may send a message to each terminal quoting the serial number of the last message it received from that terminal. The terminal's operator will then know that the switching system is still on the air.

17. The system may conduct a statistical analysis of the traffic that it is handling.

18. It may be programmed to bill the users for the messages sent. It may, for example, make a small charge per character sent from each terminal and bill the terminal location appropriately.

19. It will produce periodic reports of its operation for its operator. These may include reports on the status of all facilities, error statistics, reports giving the number of messages in each queue, message counts, and so on.

The computer will be programmed in such a way that the operator may make a modification to its action, for example, change the routing of messages to certain destinations in the event of line outages.

The program to carry out these functions will reside mainly in core, though exception routines may be on a drum or disk to be called in when wanted, for example, when handling emergencies or line outages. Also in core will be a set of tables giving the addresses of the terminals and the lines they are on. This will enable the computer to find the correct terminal for a message with a certain destination code. Other tables will indicate the status of each line and whether there are messages waiting to be transmitted down it.

The organization of the files of messages is a major design question in this type of system. The queues of messages that are kept on the files vary from one period to another. But messages must be written on the files and retrieved from them in the minimum time. On a disk file in which the read/write heads are physically moved to seek a record, the data must be placed so that the seek times—relatively long in terms of computer speeds—are not too long.

A common method of organizing such files is to allocate areas for each output terminal. As messages are received, they are written sequentially in these areas. These are rather like the pigeonholes for letters in a club or college common room. When the attendant receives letters, he places them in the pigeonholes of the persons who are to receive them. If a pigeonhole becomes full because many letters are received for one person, an overflow area will be available. The computer will send messages from these areas to where they are required. If the retrieval of any message is demanded, the machine can search the appropriate "pigeonhole" for this message.

The active area of the file at any one instant will be relatively small. As the day proceeds and messages are sent, the active area may move across the file in such a way that the seek times within that area are always small.

Where the originating points and destinations of messages are widely separated geographically, the cost of lines for the system will be high. Any means of cutting down the line cost should be considered. For networks above a certain size it becomes economic to have more than one computer for message routing. A large organization is likely to have computers at several distant locations. Commonly these are at centers of the organization's operation and so could conveniently handle message routing. Some firms have used such points as relay stations for message routing. In Fig. 17.10 computer A is the main message-switching machine with the capacity to store a day's traffic on a random-access file and to perform all the functions outlined above. If computer A had communication lines to all the terminals shown in the diagram with, say, not more than three locations on one line, to avoid overloading the lines, the lines would cost much more than those shown. Computers B, C, D, and E are needed in places shown for other work. They are therefore made to perform a dual function, and part of the day they relay message traffic as well as doing their other work.

Computer A is a system dedicated to message switching. Computers B, C, D, and E are not dedicated and do not carry out all the functions that A performs. They merely pass on communication-line traffic as a secondary job, just as a computer may do a tape-to-printer or card-to-tape job secondary to its main processing. Any retrieval of past messages or interception of messages will be done by A, not by B, C, D, and E. With this system, if location K wishes to send a message to location Z, it will be passed by computer E down the high-speed line to computer A. A will determine its routing from that point on and carry out any processing that may be needed on it. A will send it down the high-speed line to computer D which will route it to terminal Z. If location K wishes to send a message to location G on this system, the message may also have to go via A. This will give the high-speed lines a higher load than if E itself switched the message to G. For this reason it may be economic to use larger programs in E which carry out all the functions described above if the distances involved are very large, as for example on a world-wide network. This will probably increase the cost of E as it will need more core storage and a random-access file capable of storing the traffic handled by E for a period of some hours. On the other hand, the most economic solution might be to have a simple routing program in E and send the message to A and back.

Communication links of this type between the data-processing centers in an organization can have many uses. When one computer becomes overloaded, data or programs can be transmitted to an alternative machine.

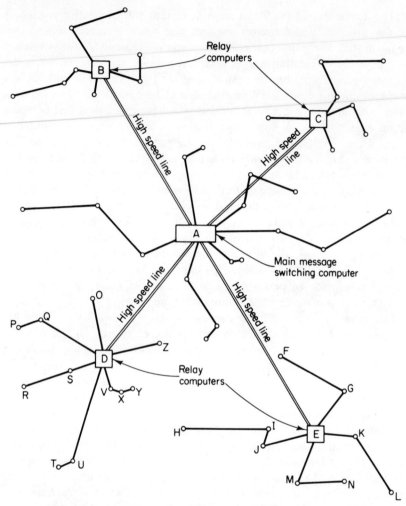

Fig. 17.10. A large network with very long distances may use more than one computer for message routing.

One machine may keep a central file of data that can be used by other machines. Persons at any of the terminals can have direct access to distant central files or distant computers. A location with no computer can transmit programs to be executed to a distant machine.,

If the message-switching machine is duplexed, the off-line computer of the pair may be used to give a service to the organization and may be used as a standby in case of failure of other distant computers. If a computer fails and cannot perform some vital work, the job may be transmitted to the switching center.

Data-processing systems and message-switching facilities can thus become very much interlinked. Message-switching facilities can be an integral part of larger real-time systems or can operate independently of other data processing. It is apparent that the needs of many large organizations are an integrated network of computers and data-transmission facilities.

18 MANUFACTURING CONTROL

The applications discussed in the last three chapters can be fairly similar from one organization to another; sufficiently similar, in fact, for some computer manufacturers to offer packages of Application Programs. Manufacturing firms, on the other hand, differ widely in their methods and their needs.

Figure 18.1 illustrates some of the common elements of a manufacturing process. There are, of course, other elements that need to be controlled, not shown on the diagram, such as costing, accounts, sales, and advertising and other data processing applications such as payroll. The diagram shows those functions that are the most likely candidates for in-line processing or real-time techniques, as opposed to serial processing.

The events in the production cycle are never exactly predictable, and so, in order to maintain control over the various stages in the production process, it is desirable that data about goods received, operations completed, items that transfer location, and so on, are *fed back* to the computer (dotted lines and circles in Fig. 18.1). The computer constructs and updates records of the status of the events that must be controlled. These may be records giving the levels of stock and details relating to the reordering of stock, records giving the status of each customer order, records giving details of the loading of each machine, and records relating to the work given to each employee.

In general, each type of facility that is employed in the production process may have a record giving its current status or loading, and the jobs to be done at each work center may be recorded with indications of priority. These records are kept up to date. They may be used either by the computer or by management and foremen in planning, scheduling, progress chasing, re-ordering, and so on. The computer will use them for such functions as

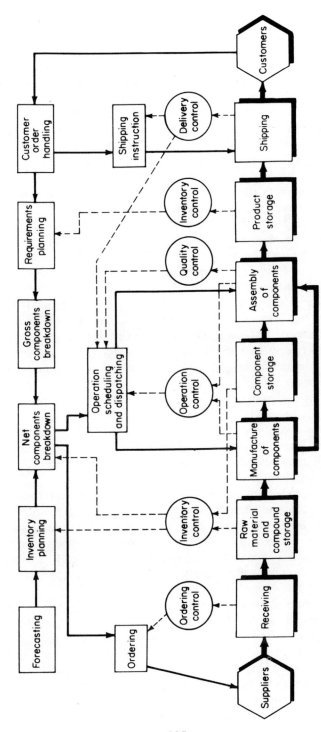

Fig. 18.1. Elements in manufacturing control.

producing work tickets, giving instructions to operatives, giving loading instructions, handling new orders, and notification of exception conditions or situations that have become critical and need expediting. Management will use them for displaying the facts they need for decision making.

This type of mechanism may be used in the operation, not only of a manufacturing process, but of any environment in which a large number of discrete events must be controlled in order to achieve certain results.

In a railroad, for example, the movement and use of the cars must be constantly rescheduled to convey the maximum quantity of goods in an acceptable time with the minimum cost. Details of each car, its contents, its actual movements, and its future intended movements would be stored in the computer files, and these records would be used by the computer or by management, or more probably by both, to optimize the operation. In an airline, the scheduling of aircraft operations, crew movements, and maintenance is a severe problem aggravated by circumstances that cannot be planned for in detail, such as the need to ground aircraft for unscheduled maintenance, crew change due to sickness, fog, and other hold-ups. At the time of writing, it has not been tackled by computers, but several airlines are directing their sights on it. They may possibly use the same transmission links as for reservations traffic. It is a problem that in some respects is analogous to manufacturing control. The analogy can also be seen in other types of industry.

A systems analyst in determining the extent to which on-line or real-time techniques are needed in such situations, must think about the time scale on which events take place. The time taken for manufacturing, for example, varies widely from one industry to another. In some firms the main criterion is using the machines fully. In others it is desirable to rush orders through the production shops as quickly as possible.

In many production shops the events that must be controlled occur in rapid succession, even though individual jobs take several hours. The control system that governs these must be at least as dynamic as the events it is controlling. A typical system needs to respond in three seconds or so to human enquiries and data input, but need not respond in seconds to events taking place on the shop floor. Rescheduling, new job allocation, or other response to events may be fast enough if it happens in half an hour, say.

We therefore usually need a computer system with two or three levels of activity going on: an almost immediate response on an interrupt basis to on-line human and sometimes nonhuman input; a queue of jobs that need to be tackled fairly quickly but not immediately, on a random basis, some jobs possibly having higher priorities than others; and a background activity of work for which there is no time pressure. In addition, a real-time clock may trigger off other activities at preset intervals.

The system, as with others we have discussed, will need fairly fast random access to a large amount of data and will have to call programs into core as and when it needs them. Serial processing from tape would not be satisfactory.

Let us illustrate these concepts by examining in more detail the control of the shop-floor manufacturing operations in a factory. Consider a factory in which batches of items or single items are made. These have to be worked on by a succession of work centers, machine tools, or machine tool groups, as shown diagramatically in Fig. 18.2. The number of items in a batch varies very widely in factories of this type and depends upon the nature of the product, the length of time to change the set up of a machine tool, the value of work in progress, and other factors.

For the purposes of this description, let us define a job as the work done on a batch of items by one of the squares in Fig. 18.2, either a machine tool or work bay with one worker, or sometimes a group of similar machine tools. Each batch or item will follow a route through the factory such as those indicated by the dotted lines.

The items vary in nature and frequency in a manner that cannot be predicted exactly. It is therefore not possible to keep all of the machine tools or work centers occupied all of the time. In many factories, some machine tools are as little as 50 per cent utilized. If the machine tool utilization is high, the queues of items waiting for them will become greater. This lengthens the production time and ties up more capital in work in progress. It is desirable that these queues should be kept small or nonexistent. If the time each job spent on each machine was known exactly, and if the time

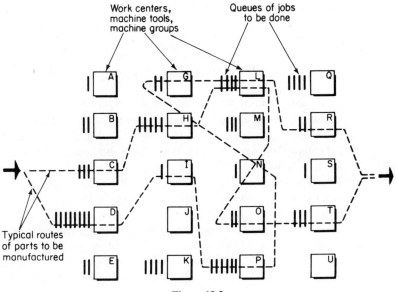

Figure 18.2

to move between machines and the machine setup times were known, the progress of items through the factory could be planned with the minimum of conflict. An optimum schedule could be computed. However, it is almost never possible to operate with this mathematical precision. The times are not predictable exactly, and the entire process is filled with unforeseeable occurrences.

It is the large number of unforeseeable events that make it necessary to tackle this scheduling problem and those in other fields in a dynamic fashion. If all was predictable, the computer could set up a timetable for events and movements, and everything would follow it. But deviations from the timetable occur constantly, and one hold-up in the complex pattern of movements of jobs between machines either holds up every other job or sets off a chain reaction of deviations that rapidly makes the timetable unworkable.

In actuality, a factory shop floor cannot be controlled inflexibly. Machines will always break down. Tools will become dull. Operators will take longer on some jobs because they are tired. The foreman will want to use an apprentice who can only tackle certain items. Men will fall sick. Material will fall short of specifications. And the foremen will only respect the instructions given by a computer system if it is flexible enough to deal with such circumstances.

As with any real-time system, if the users start to ignore the data or instructions given by the machine, the system is a failure. To achieve the necessary flexibility some means of *data collection* must be installed to inform the computer of the current status on the shop floor. Typical data-collection terminals in a factory are shown in Fig. 18.3. These terminals operate in real time, but, as is discussed later, this is not always essential for the means of data collection. When an employee finishes an operation, he will use some such means to send details to the computer. The computer will update its records accordingly and either then or later reschedule if necessary or issue new instructions.

The computer, using its information on the current shop status, allocates jobs in an optimum fashion. It may issue only one job at a time, or it may issue lists of jobs. The foremen, working from these instructions, govern the flow of work through their departments. When each job is done, details are reported back to the computer. If jobs, and especially urgent jobs, are not completed when expected, the computer can give instructions to chase these.

The computer controlling a manufacturing process in this way can work in much the same manner as a human controller would if he had the capability. In a small factory manufacturing only a few products, the production manager or owner may allocate the jobs to be done and can quickly give new instructions each time his schedule is disrupted. If an urgent order comes in, he can rush it through. *He knows the status of everything on the shop floor —orders, machines, and men. He knows his customers and can directly implement his own management policies.* As his factory grows bigger, however,

Fig. 18.3. Terminals on a factory shop floor. (a) An IBM 1050 printer. (b) An RCA data collection terminal at Lockheed.

(b)

he begins to lose touch. He can no longer know at first hand the status of everything on the shop floor. He divides the factory into separate departments, and different men now control each department. However, this causes inefficiencies because decisions are made in one department without knowledge of the situation in other departments. A solution to a problem in one place may cause hold-ups, overloading, idle men and machines, or other problems elsewhere. The larger the factory, the worse this difficulty becomes. Furthermore, information delays begin to be serious. In a large factory, when an unscheduled event occurs in the shop, there will be a long time lag before the office knows about this and can decide what to do about it. Usually, therefore, the decision of what to do is taken on the shop floor but without a knowledge of the factors which ought to affect this decision.

In an attempt to solve this problem partially, progress chasers are introduced. These men will follow up critical situations in detail. They will chase urgent orders from department to department. However, the isolated chasing of urgent orders delays other orders. It certainly does not lead to a full utilization of resources or a minimization of the capital and costs involved in work in progress. It is not uncommon to see a progress chaser talking to a foreman and the foreman exasperatedly listing all the other urgent jobs that are waiting for machining.

THE RECORDS THAT MUST BE KEPT

To use a computer system for shop control we need to store in its files those facts which the manager of the very small factory kept in his head or in his notebook. We must be able to collect these facts quickly and correlate them. We must then continually analyze the situation to determine what action is needed. This has become too complex to do centrally *without* the use of data processing, but it is only by doing it centrally as in the very small factory that events can be controlled efficiently.

Basically three categories of record are needed: records relating to each order, records relating to each employee who works on the order, and records relating to each machine or work center. The details of these may differ considerably from one factory to another. Here are some typical examples.

1. *Order Records*

When an order is released for production, this record (Fig. 18.4) will be created, giving details of the operations that must be performed on the item. As the item progresses through the shop, the various fields will be updated. The record will be deleted from the file when the item is completed, although it may be written to tape for later historical analysis.

In order that these records may be set up quickly, the files may contain master records giving all the fixed data for a given type of product. They would list the operations to be performed, giving setup times, run times as a function of quantity, tool requirements, material requirements, and other fixed data. The computer could then construct and display the order record, given part number, completion date, and quantity. The start times for various

Part number	Order number	Order quantity	Batch quantity	Priority code	Start date	Finish date	Work in progress value	Material code	Material quantity	Confirmation	
										Material	Tools

Operation number	Operation type	Department number	Machine number	Batch quantity	Job time	Set-up time	Set-up reqts	Tool reqts	Planned time		Actual time		Scrap value	Status
									Start	Finish	Start	Finish		
Operation 1														
Operation 2														
Operation 3														
Operation 4														
Operation 5														
Etc.														

Complete.
In process.
In queue.
Scheduled.
Emergency hold up.

Fig. 18.4. Order record.

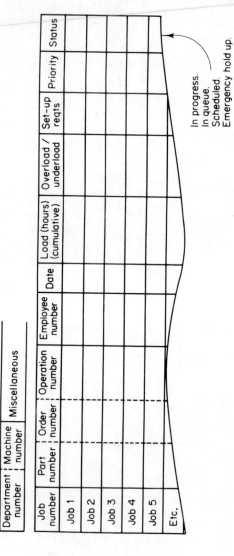

Fig. 18.5. Machine record.

242

operations would be rescheduled according to the events taking place on the shop floor, as described below.

2. Machine Records

There would be one of these records, as in Fig. 18.5, for each of the squares in Fig. 18.2, that is, for each machine, machine-group work center, or other facility. Normally the first entry in the list of jobs would be the job being set up or worked on by the machine. The third and subsequent entries *may not yet be allocated;* in other words, no work tickets have yet been issued for them as some unforeseen event may make it necessary to reschedule them. The lists represent, then, the computer's present schedule, or queue of jobs, for each machine, details of which may have to be changed. They give the foreseeable loading on the machines and so can be used to tell management what further orders can be met or what delivery dates are reasonable.

There is no need to put more details of each operation in the machine record, as the order number/operation number acts as a pointer to the appropriate part of the order records.

3. Employee Records

There will be one of these records, illustrated in Fig. 18.6, for each employee who works on the orders. Each employee record may contain only two job entries, the job he is currently working on and the next one waiting for him. The next job would not be allocated until he reports the completion of his present one.

The record contains the number of hours and the amount of overtime he has worked and so contains the basic data for payroll processing.

Employee number	Name	Job classification	Customary machine number	Hours worked	Hours overtime	Miscellaneous

Job number	Part number	Order number	Operation number	Department number	Machine number	Status
Job 1						
Job 2						

Direct labor.
Indirect labor.
Vacation.
Absent.
Union meeting.

There may be only two jobs allocated at one time

Fig. 18.6. Employee record.

Again the order number/operation number acts as a pointer to the part of the order records which gives more details of each operation.

DATA COLLECTION FROM THE FACTORY FLOOR
In order to keep these records up to date, events taking place on the shop floor must be continually reported to the computer. There are basically three ways of doing this:

1. On-line terminals on the shop floor which may or may not give a real-time response (Fig. 18.3). When an employee completes a job, he enters details in the nearby terminal, giving, for example, employee number, order number, operation number, a code indicating the type of transaction, and possibly scrap values, possibly number of pieces received. Commonly an entry is made when the job is started as well as when it is completed. The computer adds the time at which the transaction is made.

2. In many factories terminals are used in this way, transmitting to a central location, but they are not on line to a computer. Instead, a card is punched at the central location and may be fed to a computer.

3. The reporting may be manual. The workmen fill in details on a work ticket or operation card. They must now fill in the start time and stop time as well as the other information.

These means of reporting are used for the jobs performed and also, if necessary, for job movements within the factory and for the setting up of machines and sometimes for the maintenance or repair of machines.

The choice of reporting method depends to a large extent upon the *response time* that is needed to maintain efficient control over the factory in question. When reporting documents are filled in manually, it is probable that these will not be collected until the end of the day. The control center will analyze them on the following morning. For many factories this does not permit tight control. The use of terminals shortens the reporting cycle to an extent where different and tighter control methods can be used. A significant increase in the productivity of the shop floor may result.

On-line terminals permit a somewhat shorter reaction time than off-line terminals. The computer will be informed immediately about the status of urgent items and can assist in expediting without necessarily upsetting the schedules of other work.

ACCURACY
Another important factor is the accuracy with which data are received from the shop floor. Workmen usually make a considerable proportion of mistakes in writing or keying employee numbers, part numbers, and so on. The system needs to be

designed so that, as far as possible, it avoids updating records and changing schedules on the basis of wrong information.

The on-line terminal with a real-time response has the advantage that it can catch workers' input errors when and where they occur. For example, when the computer receives the employee number, it seeks the employee record and checks that order number and operation number are in fact the ones that this employee should be working on. If an error is detected it may flash a light or in some other way notify the employee at the terminal. He can attempt to correct the entry. Psychologically it is advantageous to alert an employee to his error at the time he makes it. Alternatively a discrepancy notice may be sent to key personnel on the shop floor.

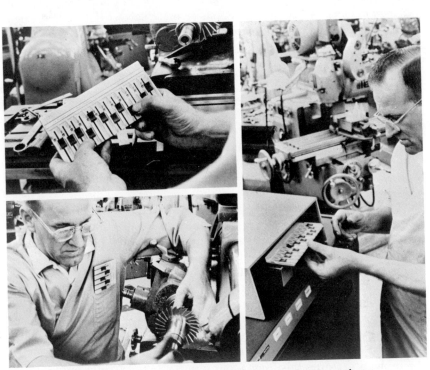

Fig. 18.7. Production information travels from the factory employee to the computer in seconds by means of a data cartridge, a pocket-sized recording device used with the IBM 1030 data collection system. At his work location, the employee logs information by manipulating small levers on the plastic cartridge (upper left). The cartridge then can be conveniently carried in the employee's pocket (lower left) until he is ready to transmit information to the computer. This is done by inserting the cartridge in one of the system's reporting stations (right).

Key personnel *must* be informed of certain exception conditions. For example, if a machine setup was reported, but not the subsequent operation, an employee may have forgotten to report the operation. If the quantity of parts report is different from the quantity sent, this should be investigated. If an operation has overrun the maximum time allowed, the foreman should be notified.

The design of the terminal can have an effect on the accuracy of reporting. An employee may identify himself, for example, by inserting a badge in the terminal. The employee number is automatically sensed and cannot be miskeyed. A punched card or other means of conveying digital data, such as the plastic data cartridge in Fig. 18.7, may accompany the order in its passage through the factory. The employee uses this to enter the order number/part number, which again prevents error. Whatever the methods, tight control on the factory-floor reporting, both as regards time and accuracy, is desirable.

GIVING INSTRUCTIONS TO THE FACTORY FLOOR

As well as collecting data from the factory floor, it is necessary to give instructions to the factory floor. The same three basic approaches apply: on-line terminals, off-line terminals, and documents which are delivered off-line manually. Again the reaction time and the tightness of control desired indicate the need.

Using off-line manual methods the computer may print a list each day of jobs to be done by each work center or each machine. The list would be in the sequence in which they should be run. It would indicate the priorities of different jobs. The foreman could vary the order in which jobs were done if he needed to. The priority codes would indicate to him which were the most important. Each day's list would contain more jobs than could be completed in order to leave the foreman some freedom of choice. The foreman should, as far as possible, keep to the sequence on the list, as deviations from it would affect the work of other departments. The computer could, if desired, be programmed to compare the actual jobs performed each day with those on its schedule. Too large a deviation could be investigated.

In many factories this twenty-four hour cycle time could be drastically improved upon. A more frequent reaction to the changing conditions on the shop floor would give better machine utilization, better control of rush orders, and lower work in progress. Terminals may be used on the shop floor to change the foreman's instructions as and when needed, and the foreman would inform the computer of any changes he wants to make.

A very flexible method of control is for the computer to allocate a new job for each machine or work center (squares in Fig. 18.2) only when the last-but-one job is reported complete. Each new job assignment is printed out on a typewriter near the work center. There are always two jobs issued for each machine at any one time, the job presently in progress and the next job to be done. This second one is issued in advance so that it could be prepared for, the parts moved, the machine tools obtained, and so on. If for some reason this assignment cannot be performed, there is time to allocate another one. The queues of operations indicated in Fig. 18.2 and in the machine record in Fig. 18.5 are in the files of the computer but, with the exception of the first two, the jobs are not yet allocated to the shop floor. The computer reshuffles the job sequence when any circumstance makes this desirable. The foreman can change the job sequence if he wants to. Some firms prefer to have three or four jobs always waiting at a time to give the foreman this freedom. If the sales manager storms in and says, "I don't care what the damned computer says, I want this order tomorrow," this need can be fed to the computer and it can reschedule accordingly.

SCHEDULING   We have now discussed the files and the mechanics of passing data to and from the shop floor. A major question that remains is how the job sequence is to be determined in an optimum manner.

Before a job can be released, it is essential that a machine that can execute it is available and also the man to operate the machine, and that the tools that are to be used on the machine and the raw material or parts are available. There may be several jobs wanting the same machine or the same tools, and only one can be allocated at a time. With many items to manufacture, each requiring several jobs (Fig. 18.2), there can be an almost endless number of different ways of sequencing the work.

1. Machine Utilization

It is desirable to achieve maximum utilization of each machine or work center, and the desirability of this is related to the cost of maintenance, overhead, and depreciation of that facility. The machines, and especially the expensive ones, should be kept as fully utilized as possible. Temporary bottlenecks which lower the throughput of work should be avoided and, in particular, bottlenecks which leave expensive facilities idle. Knowing the times that jobs are expected to take, a job sequence can be worked out which gives the maximum productivity, and this can be dynamically adjusted when circumstances arise in actual operation that affect the issue.

2. Value of Work in Progress

In some factories a large amount of money is tied up in partially completed work. There are overheads associated with storing work in progress, as well as the capital cost itself. This can be lessened by selecting the optimum sequence in which jobs should be completed.

When high-value and low-value jobs are contending for the same length machine time, the high-value jobs should be done first. However, where jobs that can be completed quickly are contending with similar-value jobs that take longer, the former should be done first. Suppose that a choice has to be made between two jobs for a machine, a $3000 job that will take 12 hours and a $2500 job that will take 4 hours. Let us multiply the value of the two jobs by the time they are held for this operation:
If the $3000 job is done first,

$$\$3000 \times 12 + \$2500 \times (12 + 4) = \$76,000$$

If the $2500 job is done first,

$$\$2500 \times 4 + \$3000 \times (12 + 4) = \$58,000$$

It is here best to do the job with the short completion time first, even though this holds up the expensive one.

The time to move items between one machine and another is sometimes long. This should be taken into consideration also in the scheduling. Often the time items spend waiting between operations is considerably greater than the duration of the operations themselves. When large queues of work are allowed to build up, as is seen in many factories, the work-in-progress cost becomes high. The scheduling method should aim at reducing these queues and again take the value of the items into consideration in doing this.

Again, if the item being manufactured is part of a larger assembly, its delay might hold up this much more expensive item. It is desirable that the various components come together to be assembled on schedule. An item which is part of a larger assembly may be given priority over other items.

3. *Setting up the Machines*

Setting up a machine to do a particular job may be a difficult or lengthy process. This further complicates the scheduling considerations. It can be expensive and undesirable to change the setup frequently, and so jobs needing a similar setup may be done together. This may be especially desirable if the jobs are small, and short-duration jobs may be batched together. Sometimes an employee other than the machine operator is needed to set up the machine. This would be shown in the setup fields of the machine record (Fig. 18.5). The cost of using similar setups may outweigh other considerations.

4. *Customer Order Date*

The above considerations have been related to the efficiency of the shop floor. It is also necessary to take the customer into account. If an order is needed by a certain date and the dates in the job queue in the machine record fall behind this date, exception action will be needed to move the schedule of this item forward. In practice, however much planning takes place, many factories have rush orders which must be pushed as fast as possible through their operations. Early delivery may conflict with considerations for high productivity.

5. Start Date

The scheduling process must establish a date on which the work commences. Some factories work backward from the order delivery date to establish the *latest* date at which production can start and still deliver on time. This ties up the least capital in stock and finished goods. On the other hand, other management policies use the *earliest* date, filling any available machine capacity, in hope that other orders will be obtained. If there is plenty of slack in meeting the delivery date, the priority of the item's jobs may be low.

It would obviously be very complicated to schedule for the optimum efficiency even if the situation were static. In the turbulent ever-changing environment of an actual factory, it is much more difficult. It is important that the system is constructed in a flexible manner so that the computer's schedule can be changed if operating circumstances make it desirable.

SIMULATION   The scheduling must be based on estimates of the times needed to complete the various operations, machine setups, and movements of items. These are derived from the *standard times* which factories have used long before the computer era.

If it is possible to make up a schedule for actual operational conditions, it is also possible to do it for hypothetical conditions, and this may sometimes be valuable. Management may ask questions such as, "What would be the effects on other work of accepting such-and-such an order?" or, "Could this delivery date be quoted on this item?" A hypothetical rescheduling could be done to answer these questions, building up a new set of records equivalent to those in Figs. 18.4 and 18.5.

In this way the shop floor can be *simulated* using programs similar to those for actual scheduling. Management, possibly using a visual display screen, can explore the implications of possible courses of action.

RUSH ORDERS AND EMERGENCY SITUATIONS   The computer using on-line terminals in the way discussed can be programmed to "chase" situations needing surveillance. It can be unfailingly dogged in its pursuit of urgent matters and will not forget anything owing to the pressure of other crises.

For example, it may follow the progress of a rush order, ensuring that the various operations are started and completed as scheduled. If one of these falls behind, it will quickly inform the foreman in question or a dispatcher whose job it is to follow up such situations.

The computer may store in its files a table of situations that it is to monitor. The real-time clock may interrupt the machine every half hour, say, or at a time interval which suits the factory in question. When the computer has finished the item it is processing, it will at that time inspect the table of situations and examine the appropriate operation sections of the order records (Fig. 18.4) to see whether the jobs in question have been reported as started or finished on time. If not, it will print a notice on an appropriate terminal.

Another situation that needs following up is an invalid report received from the shop floor. Suppose that a job is omitted or that material is moved to the wrong job center. Or suppose that a worker makes a mistake in reporting and does not correct it. The computer will type out a notice immediately to the appropriate foreman and will put this item on its table of situations to be monitored. If the situation has not been corrected by the next time the table is scanned, it will again type out a report asking for action to be taken. Similarly if a job is held up because of lack of a tool or material's running out, it can be put on the surveillance list.

This type of surveillance can be programmed to guarantee that nothing is forgotten and that urgent situations or orders receive the attention they should. It continues steadily through periods of peak shop-floor activity and carries over from one shift to another regardless of changes of personnel.

FLEXIBILITY   Many of the situations that arise cannot be dealt with quickly. It is no use merely putting them on a surveillance table. The foreman needs to make some major change in the schedule. This may happen, for example, when a machine breaks down, when the need for an engineering change is discovered, or when a decision is made to scrap a batch of material. The foreman may want to stop work completely on a particular item for the time being. He may know that the jobs to be done on the item could be tackled in a different sequence, and this would avoid holding up the item. It may become necessary to split a batch, doing part of it now and part later, maybe because some of the material is not up to specification.

The system must be programmed so that any such changes can be made, either by the foreman or, more likely, by a central control group who operate with the computer. The control group may communicate with the computer by means of a visual display terminal. On many systems operating today, they do this simply by the entry of punched cards; however, display terminals improve the man-machine communication, enabling them to have any facts displayed they need to.

Production or other management may also have a display terminal, though it is usually desirable not to allow them to make changes in schedules or other details except via the control group.

It is the flexibility that can be programmed into a real-time system such as this that makes it a major step forward over earlier ways of using computers The system can be adjusted continually to suit the needs of the operating environment. Such an application can become very complex and take several years to develop fully. However, after having studied a large shop floor, or other operating application, controlled by the confusion of methods depending on humans with their forgetfulness, temperament, and limited logic, one realizes that real-time computer control has an appeal which is aesthetic as well as financial.

SUMMARY OF ADVANTAGES   To conclude, let us summarize the main advantages of an on-line system for shop control.

1. It will increase the throughput of the shop and increase the utilization of the machines and other facilities.

2. It will reduce the capital tied up in work in progress.

3. It can be linked into an inventory control system to help minimize inventory .

4. It can help to ensure that delivery dates are met.

5. It can help the shop react quickly to changes in demand or to urgent situations.

6. It can be linked into a costing system and help to reduce costs. It can maintain an hour-by-hour control over production costs if so desired.

7. It reduces clerical work on the shop floor and in the control center. It saves clerical staff, dispatchers, and workers' time.

8. It prevents situations' being overlooked. There are no forgotten instructions. Items maintain their correct priority through all operations. Management policies are continuously implemented.

9. It can help to achieve shorter delivery times.

10. It can be used to help answer management questions about the status of orders, the possibility of producing additional orders, or meeting of stated delivery dates.

11. Foremen are left more time for training and supervising.

12. The optimum action can be taken when machines break down or other emergencies happen.

SECTION **IV**

HARDWARE

19 THE COMPUTERS

This chapter discusses the features that are used on present-day computers for on-line and real-time work. The following chapters discuss the telecommunication facilities and peripheral equipment.

The suitability of a computer for an on-line system is of course dependent on the suitability of the input/output gear that it can have attached to it. For example, some computers can have cheap disk storages with removable disks, others cannot. Some computers can handle telecommunication lines without special engineering. Providing they can have the requisite peripheral equipment, the majority of computers on the market today *could* be used for on-line or real-time work. There is not necessarily anything unique about a real-time computer. However, there are some desirable features for such work which many computers do not have. It is possible, often, to program around or in some way do without these features. But, just as it can be inefficient to program mathematical work on a machine designed for commercial data processing, so it can be inefficient to do real-time work without the aid of certain hardware features.

The higher the volume of real-time transactions, the more desirable it is to have a machine well equipped to handle real-time. If the system handles only an occasional real-time enquiry superimposed on other processing, then it does not matter greatly if the processing of this is inefficient. However, a system dedicated to handling only real-time messages should be equipped to handle them efficiently, and, if the volume is high and multiprogramming needed, it could be a serious handicap not to have the features that facilitate this.

What then are the desirable features of a real-time computer?

1. *Expandability*

First, the computer must have enough storage and a high enough processing speed. The requirements for this have proved remarkably difficult to estimate on some real-time projects. If there are any doubts about whether the estimates made are large enough *the computer should be such that more core storage can be added and possibly the speed increased without the programs having to be rewritten.*

The need for an increase in storage or speed commonly arises, not only from inaccuracies in estimating, but from a natural growth of the system. When the load on a non-real-time computer increases, this means that the computer works for a longer period of time each day. This cannot be so on a real-time system because transactions have to be dealt with as they arise. If a real-time machine is to do additional work beyond a certain design limit, it must increase its processing power by the use of more core storage or by an increase in processing speed. A machine should be selected which can do this with ease. *On many systems this may prove to be one of the most important of the requisite computer features,* but it is often neglected because of inability to foresee the future demands on the system or the programming complexities that will be encountered.

2. *Open-ended System*

It may also become desirable to make additions to, or improvements in, the peripheral equipment. More communication lines may be added, or the file capacity may be enlarged. It may be necessary to improve the speed of access to part of the files, perhaps by adding drums. The computer needs to be "open-ended" so that any likely additional equipment can be added without a major upheaval, particularly in programming.

3. *Interrupts*

Most computers today have an interrupt system. This means that certain events happening in the system, such as the arrival of a new message or the completion of an input/output operation, will cause the computer to interrupt its current program and execute a different program which "services" the interrupt. When the interrupt has been dealt with, the computer will return to the program which was interrupted and continue with it as though nothing had happened.

Although some real-time systems of the past have worked without an interrupt mechanism, this is generally undesirable on any system other than the simplest. To operate without an interrupt mechanism, the external events that would otherwise cause interrupts must, instead, set latches (switches). These latches must be tested *regularly*, by instructions added to all the operational programs, to see whether an interrupt has occurred.

The interrupt mechanism varies considerably from one machine to another. In assessing the interrupt facilities of a machine there are three main criteria to examine. First, what different types of interrupt does it have? Second, how automatic is the handling of interrupts? And third, can a program servicing an interrupt be interrupted itself by an event of higher priority; in other words, are there multiple levels of interrupt?

The types of interrupt that are desirable on a real-time system are as follows:

(a) *Input/output interrupts.* When a peripheral unit requires attention from the central processing unit, it may interrupt it. The main advantage of this is that the peripheral units can then be kept continuously busy. The times of input/output operations are not necessarily known to the programmers, and so any other method of controlling the peripheral units means that they must be inspected frequently by the program or else they will not be kept fully utilized. This is particularly true with random-access files. The seek or the positioning of the read/write mechanism or the rotational delay of a disk or drum is relatively long compared with computer speeds and varies widely in length. It is desirable on any system which is not underutilized that the files are kept continuously in use. On complex systems with a large amount of file activity these can form the main timing bottleneck. Consequently, as soon as a seek or read/write operation is completed, the computer should be interrupted so that it can give the next operation to the file or channel in question.

The alternative to the use of this type of interrupt would be to program an inspection of the input/output units periodically.

(b) *External interrupts.* On many systems it is desirable for some external event other than the input data messages to force its way fairly quickly to the attention of the computer. For example, it may be necessary that a clock interrupt the computer at a given time of day or after a given period. One computer may need to interrupt another computer. An operator may need an easy means of interrupting the machine to make it modify its action. In a technical application, the making or breaking of a contact or some emergency condition in a plant may have to capture the computer's immediate attention.

(c) *Interrupts which facilitate nonstop operation.* It is usually desirable that a real-time system should operate without stopping. Conditions which would stop most first-and second-generation non-real-time computers should here cause an interrupt instead. The programs then attempt to deal with the cause of the interrupt. Rather than stop the machine, they will circumvent the condition, if at all possible, so that there is no interruption of the vital work. For example, circuitry errors would have caused an older computer to halt. They may cause a real-time machine to execute *diagnostic programs* to analyze the nature of the error, which may be only a transient one that does not repeat itself. If it is a "solid" error, which always repeats itself, the system may be designed to take some alternative action as directed by the programs. It may function in a degraded or fallback mode of operation.

When a computer or other piece of equipment is found to have become faulty, the system may execute a *switchover* to an alternative computer or device. The switchover may be automatic or manual, performed by the operator. If it is automatic, the system must have an interrupt mechanism suitable for control of this.

In a duplexed system a standby computer may perform constant checks on the health of the operational computer. It may interrupt it at preset intervals, send a message to it, and check that the correct reply is received. If it is not, investigations are initiated. The interrupt facility here helps to guarantee continuity of correct operation on a system where this is vital.

The functioning of the system may be disrupted by program logic faults. These may be triggered by rare coincidences of timing, such as a particular sequence of messages or actions, or they may be caused by new and unperfected programs. To a limited degree a good interrupt facility can protect the system from these. It may, for example, be used with the watchdog timer and memory protection features described below. In one of the most reliable computers operating today, no less than seven levels of interrupt are used to circumvent system failures.

In general, good interrupt facilities can enable the system to operate in a nonstop fashion under most adverse circumstances. This use of interrupts cannot generally be programmed around. If the interrupt facilities are not on the machine, there is no way of achieving the same result.

(d) *Program condition interrupts.* Interrupts may be caused by certain conditions in the programs, such as exceptional results, invalid use of instructions, or a divisor field being zero. Unexpected accumulation overflows also may cause an interrupt. The actions the programs take when these interrupts occur will depend upon the circumstances.

As well as surveying the types of interrupts on a proposed computer, it is desirable to see how automatically it handles them. In computers without an interrupt facility the above conditions may just set a latch (switch), which is inspected by the programs in their own time, perhaps at a convenient check point. When a program is interrupted, this does not occur at its own time. Control may be wrenched away from it at any time. Some investigation of the interrupt must take place immediately, and usually the interrupt is completely serviced at that time, rather than later at the convenience of the interrupted program. The interrupt program must be able to return control to the interrupted program at the exact point at which it broke off. On some computers this is automatic, while on others the interrupt program must record where the interrupted program stopped and transfer back to that point.

Similarly, the interrupt program must restore exactly any conditions that existed in the old program when control broke away. The interrupt program may need to use registers, accumulators, latches, and so on, that the old program was using. The contents of these must be recorded and later restored before the old program resumes its work. Again, some computers store most of the useful registers and latches automatically; others do not. If a computer does not do this automatically, latches, and so on, must be stored by programming. This can be time consuming. On one application using a computer with a storage-cycle time of 4.5 microseconds per character, it was estimated to take about 1 millisecond per interrupt. If the speed of the application is such that this time loss does not matter, the automatic storage of program status information is not essential but is a matter of programming convenience.

The analysis to determine the cause of an interrupt may also be done either by programming or automatically. Different types of interrupt may cause control to go to areas of core where different interrupt programs are located. If the program itself has to analyze what type of interrupt has occurred, this again is time consuming.

Most modern computers have more than one level of interrupt, that is, the interrupt program can itself be interrupted. This is particularly valuable, for example, for error interrupts. If a machine fault occurs when an interrupt program is already running, it is necessary to interrupt this and go to a higher-priority program which will deal with the fault, otherwise the machine will stop or carry on in error. Similarly a program error or unusual program condition, such as accumulator overflow, may interrupt an interrupt program. This is not so essential as the hardware error interrupt, but it is nevertheless valuable. The interrupt routine dealing with program errors may itself be interrupted because of a machine fault.

In considering interrupts other than those for handling errors, there may again be multiple levels. The lowest level of interrupt program may be that used for handling input and output. When an input/output device causes an interrupt, this level of program executes the required operations. On a process control computer, input/output may need a higher priority interrupt than this. On all real-time systems, certain conditions may require a faster response than this, and so it may be necessary to have a higher level of interrupt than the input/output one. This is desirable on systems with a high transaction throughput or systems on which a very fast response is needed to certain messages or situations.

The higher interrupt may handle external conditions, such as a contact being closed to indicate an emergency situation; an interval-timer interrupt which updates an internal clock to keep track of the time of day; or, on a machine with automatic core allocation for buffering incoming messages, a signal indicating that the available storage is running low.

The likely levels of interrupt are illustrated in Fig. 19.1. In selecting a

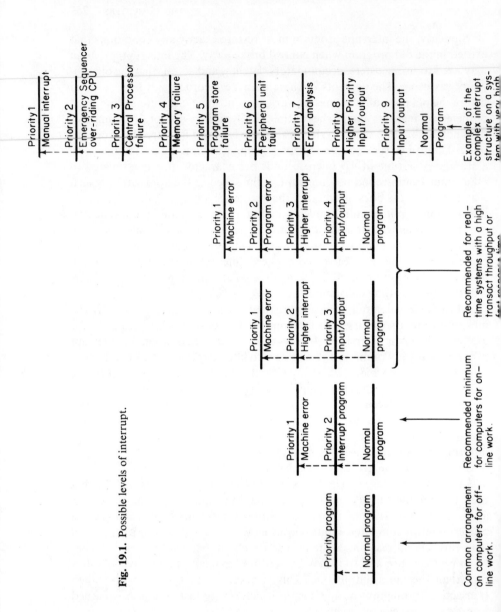

Fig. 19.1. Possible levels of interrupt.

Priority 1 — Manual interrupt
Priority 2 — Emergency Sequencer over-riding CPU
Priority 3 — Central Processor failure
Priority 4 — Memory failure
Priority 5 — Program store failure
Priority 6 — Peripheral unit fault
Priority 7 — Error analysis
Priority 8 — Higher Priority Input/output
Priority 9 — Input/output
Normal Program

Example of the complex interrupt structure on a system with very high

Priority 1 — Machine error
Priority 2 — Program error
Priority 3 — Higher interrupt
Priority 4 — Input/output
Normal program

Priority 1 — Machine error
Priority 2 — Higher interrupt
Priority 3 — Input/output
Normal program

Recommended for real-time systems with a high transact throughput or

Priority 1 — Machine error
Priority 2 — Interrupt program
Normal program

Recommended minimum for computers for on-line work.

Priority program
Normal program

Common arrangement on computers for off-line work.

260

machine for a particular application, it may be necessary to decide which of these are needed, or whether more levels are desireable.

4. Disable and Enable

When a *disable* instruction is executed, the program cannot from that point on be interrupted until an *enable* instruction is executed. With these two instructions the interrupt mechanism can effectively be shut off for a period of time. If this happens, an interrupt occurring is not lost but waits until the machine is able to deal with it. However it may not be possible for two interrupts on one channel to wait, and so the interrupt mechanism cannot be disabled for too long. There may be a finite probability of losing an interrupt. This could be dangerous. The author came across a case in which there was a finite probability of losing a character arriving on the communication lines.

The reason for using disable and enable instructions is that a logical fault may occur if certain parts of the coding are interrupted. For example, a priority routine may handle the interrupt caused by the arrival of a new message into a new-input queue. A nonpriority routine may remove items from this queue, also using chaining. If when chaining the last item in the queue a new message causes an interrupt, this can give rise to a logical error. Therefore for this brief period of time the interrupt mechanism should be disabled.

Some machines cannot disable interrupts. In this case care is needed in writing the Supervisory Programs to ensure that no logical conflict can arise between interrupt routines and normal routines.

5. Asynchronous Input/output

Input/output units should be asynchronous, that is, not time dependent on the central processing unit. The computer must not *stop* during an input/output operation, waiting for some function to be completed. The input/output operation should continue independently in time to the main processing, preferrably interrupting it on completion as outlined above.

The characteristics of the *channels* on the computer dictate to a large extent the over-all effectiveness of the input/output. The data rate, the overlap ability, the extent to which multiplexing can be accomplished, and the variety of functions that can be performed by the channel determine this. In some machines the channels can be regarded as essentially separate computers governing the input/output. In others they cause a considerable amount of interference with the main processing.

In addition to channels, the *control units* for input/output need attention. These units translate the commands from the computer into electromechanical action. Overlapping, buffering, storage of status conditions, switching ability, multiple-access ability are features the control unit may or may not have. Some control units have complex logical capabilities.

There is often much to be said for compatibility between the input/output units themselves. If they are made by different manufacturers, they may have different data formats, different control signals, different levels of buffering, different ways of identifying the end of record or end of message, different methods of demanding service or interrupting the computer, and so on. Input/output units designed to connect to the computer by a well-defined *standard interface* may give rise to less technical difficulties at installation time. The standard interface, however, is defined in much more detail by some manufacturers than others.

6. Input/output Buffer

To achieve efficient asynchronous input/output, buffers of some type are needed. Some computers are able to use the main core storage for buffering. Input from a peripheral unit enters core at the same time as processing is continuing, and vice versa on output.

The telecommunication lines have a particular need for buffers. Messages pour into the computer center on many systems at a rate largely independent of the processing. They must be put somewhere if the computer cannot handle them immediately. Furthermore, once the equipment has started to read a message, characters turn up at regular or irregular intervals until the message is complete. Somewhere the characters must be stored to form a complete message.

Telecommunication buffering is done on many systems in the core of the main computer as for other input/output, but other systems have separate telecommunication buffering. Some, in fact, use a separate special-purpose stored-program computer which handles all the communication lines. This passes fully checked and edited input messages to the main computer and receives output messages from it. The main computer treats it rather like any other input/output unit.

7. Dynamic Core Buffer Allocation

For the reasons given in Chapter 9, it is often desirable to use dynamic core allocation for buffering the messages from the communication lines. Some systems with short or fixed-length messages do not do this. If only a small number of messages are received or only one communication line is used at once, it may not be necessary. However, for a system which handles a large number of randomly generated messages or variable-length messages, it is less wasteful of core than fixed allocation.

It is possible to carry out dynamic core allocation on computers not designed with any special features to handle this. However, it is more efficient and needs rather less programming if the machine is equipped for it.

The computer may, for example, automatically chain together dynamically allocated blocks of core. It may automatically take the *next available block* from the available storage list. A register containing the address of the next available block may help it in this. One machine, for instance, allocates core in blocks of thirty-two characters, of which two are used for chaining. As characters come in one by one on a communication line, the machine automatically places each character in the next position in the appropriate block until the thirtieth position is reached. It then transfers the address of the next available block to the remaining positions, and also gives this to the register or word which tells the channel where to place the next character. The next character of that message then goes automatically into position in the new block. The new block contains the address of the block after that in the available storage list, and this is placed into the next-available-block register.

The converse happens on output, blocks being returned to the list of available blocks.

8. Program Relocation

Dynamic core allocation is used also for programs, though the mechanics of its operation are usually different from that above. It is found often on multi-programmed systems which are non-real-time as well as real-time.

A program may be executed at one time from one position in core and at another time from a different position. When the program modifies itself or branches (transfers) to itself, the instructions doing this must be capable of referring to the correct place regardless of where it is. Similarly other programs must be able to transfer to it correctly.

The programs may be written relative to core address zero—the programmer not concerning himself with where they will be in core when they are executed. They may be written in fixed-length blocks so that the control mechanism can more easily move them around in core according to the needs of the moment.

There are a number of ways to reference these *relocatable* programs. The best is with automatic relocation circuitry. This is becoming the most common method though many real-time systems have not had this. The computer is equipped with a piece of hardware logic which automatically adjusts any address referring to the program by adding the contents of a *relocation register, or base register*, to that address. The appropriate value is loaded into the relocation register as the program is loaded into core. The base register may be made nonprogrammable by the application programmers and allowed to be handled only by the Supervisory Programs.

Some machines have no relocation registers but do have *index registers*. An address in an instruction which refers to an index register has the contents of that register added to it. These may therefore be used for relocation in a manner similar to the use of relocation registers. This technique has the disadvantage (on machines without double indexing) that addresses which refer to the program cannot be indexed for purposes other than relocation. This is a serious handicap, as most machines use index registers for looping or branching, which they could not do at the same time as relocation.

On some systems, programs can be relocated only when they reach a WAIT instruction (see p. 142) or their execution is temporarily completed.

On others, it is desirable to relocate a program in the middle of its execution. If the program is broken off in the middle of execution it will be necessary to restore not only the core program but also the contents of any registers, switches, or accumulators it may have been using at that time. Because of the response-time demands of other users the program may be interrupted, removed from core to file to make room for other users' programs, and at a later time returned to core in a *different location*. The execution of the program then proceeds from where it left off. This relocation during execution is sometimes referred to as *dynamic relocation*. It may be done with relocation, or base, registers and appropriate software.

We thus have a number of different forms of program manipulating:

a. The relocation may have to wait until a natural break in the execution of the program, such as a WAIT macro-instruction, or it may be possible to kick it out of core at any time during its execution.

b. After it is kicked out (*rolled out*) it may be mandatory always to bring it back (*roll-in*) to the *same location* to continue its execution. Alternatively, it may have to continue its work from **any** location.

c. A further complexity is introduced if the programs are written in variable rather than fixed-length blocks. This will tend to leave irregular-sized gaps of unallocated core as programs are moved in and out, and it may be necessary to pack down the programs periodically to one end of core.

The decision between which of these techniques is to be used affects the choice of hardware needed to facilitate the techniques.

Some complex real-time and on-line systems have not used any form of program relocation. Certain large computers slide each program to a fixed area for execution. Other systems reassemble or modify programs appropriately as they enter core. However, these techniques waste much processing time on an otherwise efficient machine.

9. Indirect Addressing

A transfer to a program segment which is relocatable cannot be made directly. When programs branch to the relocatable program, they must know where it is. Some form of indirect addressing must be used. Certain computers have special hardware for indirect addressing, though others effect this by programming. If it is done by hardware, it will need an instruction with logic such as: "transfer to the instruction, the address of which is contained in location XXXXX"; on other machines the address field of any instruction may be tagged so that it means "the address which is contained in location XXXXX." The computer will have a list of addresses of all the programs in core.

10. *Automatic Program Read-in and Reference*

Most real-time systems, and especially time-sharing systems on which the users execute different types of programs, are constantly reading in programs from a backing store in which they are stored largely at random. The job of finding, reading-in, and referencing programs that are needed is executed frequently. Again it can be programmed on a machine which has no special hardware devices for this purpose. However, automatic features on some machines make it easier to program and faster in execution..

Ideally the application programmer would like to forget about such considerations. He writes his whole program whatever its size relative to core location zero, and lets the hardware plus software take care of program relocation, program storage on the files, and program read-in. This is, indeed, achieved on the best-designed systems. The user is then interested in the overheads needed to achieve it. How fast do program transfers occur? How efficiently is core used? How efficiently is the backing file of programs used (if this is in fact a limitation)?

The processor may couple its means of program relocation to its means of reading in programs. The hardware-software combination will (a) translate the user's logical address into the current machine address and (b) detect if the user is attempting to reference programs (or data) not in core and, if so, initiate the read-in of this. (c) Use some form of scheduling algorithm to determine the sequence of programs that are to be executed and read in. (d) Determine what program in core will be overwritten when a new one is read in.

These processes can be carried out entirely by hardware, however, on many machines they are only partially done by hardware, or not at all. The programs and frequently referenced data may be divided into fixed-length blocks or "pages," perhaps of the order of 4000 characters in size. If a *page* is not in core when referenced, it may be pulled in from a fast backing store. On some machines this is done automatically. The mechanism is sometimes referred to as *automatic page turning*.

When a program makes a reference to another program or data page, the machine must quickly decide where this page is. If it is in core it will be used immediately. If not, its read-in will be initiated, and control may be given to a different program while the read-in takes place.

The reference to new pages is sometimes referred to as *mapping*. Mapping may refer to the allocation of other resources in addition to core. The *mapping device* needs to be a fast device if references between pages occur very frequently. Mapping, whether done by hardware or software, generally needs a table look-up operation of some sort. There are two main types of mapping device. The first may use conventional core and conventional table look-up techniques. The scanning of the table may be implemented by hardware but otherwise it is conventional. The second may be done in *associative memory* or associative registers. Associative memory is addressed by content rather than by a location address. In this case, the content field used for addressing will be the page identification and the associative memory locations will be examined in parallel, and hence very rapidly, to discover the whereabouts and status of the page that is sought. With associative memory the location of the new page and the transfer to it can be done in the order of a microsecond on fast machines.

The IBM 360 Model 67, designed for time sharing, uses a group of eight associative registers, which the application programmer need know nothing about. Entries for eight pages giving their logical and physical addresses are stored in these. Whenever a reference to another page is made, they are examined. Most often, details of the new page will be found in the registers. If they are not, then a page table must be searched in the normal and slower manner. Details of *this* page when found will be entered into the associative registers. The associative registers thus contain details of the last eight new pages referenced. Most page references are to pages within this eight, especially if the computer is scanning users in a round-robin fashion, flip-flopping the programs they are using to and from a backing store. On some applications, a wider scanning range than eight may be desirable.

Each task attempted by the 360 Model 67 has a table in core giving details of all the pages to which it could refer. The pages are grouped into segments, each segment containing up to 256 pages. As a task is started, a further register, called the *table register*, is loaded with the address of the appropriate segment table. This can then be found quickly when necessary.

These hardware devices are simply means of speeding up the search for new pages of program or working data. Their value in effectively speeding up the processor depends on how much flip-flopping of programs occurs.

11. *Virtual Machines*

The discussion of program relocation and paging leads to the concept of "virtual machines," which was discussed briefly in Chapter 10. The programmer may program a "virtual machine" which is quite different from a physical machine. It may appear simpler. It may appear to have more core. It will certainly be a machine in which the complexities that arise from multiprogramming are hidden from the programmer. The mapping device will convert his references to virtual machine components into references to physical components, such as core, channels, references to registers, or other components of the processor. Many users may be using the machine in parallel or having their programs executed in parallel. This is illustrated in Fig. 19.2.

Some of the conversion between virtual and physical components will require mapping, perhaps using associative memory. This will be true of core and possibly also registers and file references. On the other hand some of the references to machine components will be primarily or entirely a matter, of scheduling. The programs wait their turn for the component in question—for example, channels and the processor itself.

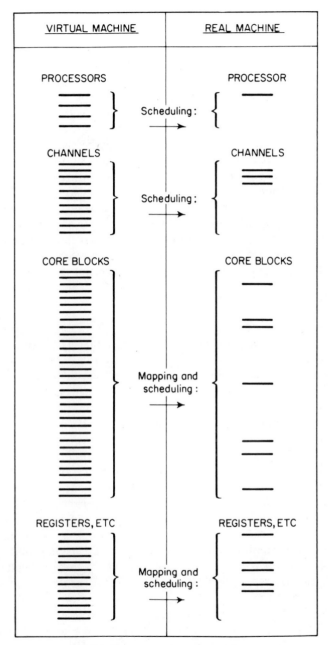

Figure 19.2 Virtual vs. real machine.

As an example of a use of a virtual machine, a programmer may define an array much larger than can be held in core. For example, in FORTRAN he may write **DIMENSION A (100,100,100)**. As he manipulates this he will constantly refer to virtual "pages" not in core. The mapping device will fetch them in when this happens.

So far we have been assuming that the pages are fetched in from a backing store, such as a fast drum. Although fast, such a device is very slow compared with the speeds of execution in the computer, and this gives rise to some of the complexity of paging and scheduling. Another approach that has been used is to have as the backing device a very large core unit with fast parallel access, and an extremely high-speed channel connecting it to the processor. If this is used, a major portion of the processor core may be changed with another section from the backing core very quickly. This is so, for example, on the CDC 6400. Such a configuration can act as a time-sharing system without the coexistence of programs in the processor core, and hence much of the elaboration of paging can be dispensed with. There will be no dynamic relocation, and no need for the elaborate protection of segments of program.

Such a technique is expensive in hardware but is fast and needs rather less complex Supervisory Programs. As the hardware cost is coming down fast and the development of software remains a major problem, we may see much more of this approach. Certainly, the concept of the *virtual* loom large in the computers of the future.

12. *Micro-programming*

Like mapping, scheduling can also be done either by hardware, or software, or by a combination of the two. It is possible to have a small segment of processor which can execute the frequently used scheduling algorithms very rapidly. *Microprogramming* using fast read-only storage may be used for this.

By means of microprogramming, a machine instruction of considerable complexity can be tailor-made to the system in question. In this way a sequence of operations may be coded into the hardware with the result that they are executed much more quickly than if they were programmed in the normal way. Algorithms for mapping, block chaining, or the central, and frequently entered, scanning loop of a scheduling routine (Fig. 9.4) might well, for example, be in the microcode. Other elements of the software might be microcoded where the increase in execution speed would make it worthwhile. Microprogramming has a potential in the difficult problem of real-time debugging, and also in monitoring the throughput and the loading on the various sections of a system. Without some hardware aid, it can be difficult to know how heavily loaded various facilities, such as channels, are becoming when the system is in operation.

The major use of microprogramming has so far been by the computer manufacturers. It is possible that the user could also employ this feature to advantage, possibly putting frequently used parts of the Application Programs in microcode, such as message editing, serial number checking, file-addressing algorithms, and so on. However, this has rarely been done to date.

13. *Memory Protection*

In a multiprogrammed environment it is important to ensure, as far as possible, that one program cannot interfere with others which are in core at the same time. Some of the programs may have errors which could cause them to destroy parts of core beyond that part intended for them. Some of the programmers may have failed to obey their rules. Protection from this, as rigorous as possible, is needed. It is necessary to build fences round each program so that, when one attempts to go astray, it cannot damage the others.

Memory protection is needed on machines for multithread operation. It is desirable to have it on any machine where a Supervisory Program and Application Programs run concurrently, but it is especially necessary on on-line real-time systems with users entering data at terminals. If, as on some time-sharing systems, the users enter or compose programs at the terminals, it is *vital* for the protection of other users.

Memory protection operates in different ways on different computers. One scheme is to use two registers giving the upper and lower boundaries within which the program must be confined. These are loaded for each program when it begins to operate, and, if it attempts to access core beyond these boundaries, an interrupt occurs. Another scheme divides core into blocks and each program must confine its activity to one block unless a formal transfer is made to a program operating in another block. Here the boundaries cannot be positioned as finely as with the above method, but nevertheless invalid transfers beyond the defined area are detected.

If an invalid transfer occurs, the program in question is interrupted and control passes to a priority program dealing with the cause of the error.

Some computers prevent reads from the protected areas as well as writes. Others only prevent writes. In general, the former gives a greater measure of protection but complicates the issue because some areas must be read from but never written on by the Application Programs, for example, areas containing the Supervisory Programs. Often write protection only is deemed adequate.

14. *Real-time Clock and Interval Timer*

The majority of real-time systems and many non-real-time on-line ones have a real-time clock or an interval timer, but again there are some that do not need it. Some computers have a real-time clock *and* a separate interval timer. Some have more than one interval timer. Such timing mechanisms usually tick on, independent of what the computer is doing. The real-time clock can be "read" by the computer and so the computer finds the elapsed time since it was last set. The interval timer may be set by the computer to time a given interval, and at the end of this it interrupts the computer.

These timing devices may be used for four functions:

(a) *Telling the time of day.* The computer may write the time on messages, for example.

(b) *Timing a given interval.* The computer may need to take some action if an event does not occur within a certain interval, for example, if an operator does not reply to a question in twenty seconds. On a time-shared system it may need to switch control back to the Supervisory Program every 200 milliseconds and so to ensure that every user's response-time criteria are met.

(c) *Initiating actions at given times.* The computer may have to send a certain message at a particular time of day. Periodically it will scan a table of this time-initiated work. Also, during its processing it may decide "if by 4 P.M. on Tuesday such-and-such an item has not been received, an exception report must be sent." It must then put this new item onto its time-initiation table. Sometimes a clock interrupt is used to initiate an action, and is given high priority by the Supervisory Programs.

(d) *As a watchdog timer.* To protect the computer from malfunctions, especially of the programs, a watchdog timer is needed as well as memory protection. This is particularly so on a multithread system. If one of the programs should start cycling in a closed loop, this would prevent others from obtaining attention. An interval timer may therefore be set, as in Fig. 9.4, every time the main scheduling routine is entered. It times out a given interval, say 500 milliseconds, unless it is reset by control's returning again to the main scheduling routine. If 500 milliseconds elapse without the main scheduling routine being entered, then something has gone wrong or a programmer has disobeyed the rules, and so an interrupt occurs. As with a memory-protection violation, control then passes to a priority program which deals with the situation.

If the machine has *one* interval timer, it is possible to program its use so that it carries on all of the above operations. It is easier, however, to use a separate clock and interval timer. When several intervals must be timed in parallel, more than one interval timer has been used on one machine. If only one timer is available, supervisory routines must accompany it to carry all the desired elements of timing in parallel.

15. *Switching*

It is common that these systems can switch units between computers to maximize the availability of the system, as discussed in Chapter 6, or to increase the flexibility of the system, giving different configurations for different parts of the work. Different computers however differ widely in their flexibility of switching and in the different configurations that are possible. See Figs. 6.1–6.10 on pp. 57 to 64. Figure 19.3, for example, shows an IBM 360 Model 67 system with manual partitioning switches allowing a variety of hardware combinations. The system can be used as a multiprocessing system in which the processing units combine to tackle a job or they may operate separately carrying on different functions. Each storage unit can be assigned to any processor or channel. Processors can share storage units if so desired.

The switching of components on such systems may be manual, or it may be done by the computers with suitable hardware. Many real-time systems find manual switching satisfactory. Automatic switching under program control will complicate the Supervisory Programs substantially.

If manual partitioning is used, as in Fig. 19.3, to break the path between various units when so desired, the processor must know what configuration is available to it. It must have a means of detecting which paths are open. This information will normally be held in tables by the supervisory system. If a program attempts to send data to a storage which is not available, an invalid address indication must result. On most machines an interrupt will take place, and the supervisory system will take appropriate action.

The system must have a physical means, however, of detecting the status of the paths so that undebugged Supervisory Programs can be tested and experimented with. A single wire containing an availability signal may be sampled for each path to indicate whether or not the path is open.

16. Checking

Good internal checking is most desirable on on-line systems, especially real-time. Thorough checking of all data transfers in the machine is needed. The checking should not stop the machine when an error occurs but initiate an interrupt as outlined above.

17. Facilities for Communication Lines

The digital information is transmitted on the communication lines a "bit" at a time. The messages to be transmitted must therefore be broken into bits and these sent at the speed of the line. Similarly, on receiving a message, bits are assembled one at a time into characters, and the characters are assembled into messages. Both the characters and messages must be error checked and the errors corrected if possible. Suitable control signals must be generated for operating the distant terminals at the correct times.

Depending upon the nature of the hardware in use, this may be done in the following ways:

(a) Entirely by programming.
(b) Entirely by electronic circuitry.
(c) Half and half, for example, with the electronics assembling bits into characters and the programs assembling characters into messages.

The communication lines may go straight into the main computer. When programs are needed to service the lines, the main programs will be interrupted for this purpose. There may be many such interrupts per second. Alternatively, the communication lines may terminate in a device which feeds characters to the main computer and accepts data characters and control characters from it. The main programs will then be interrupted to assemble characters into messages or feed characters to the line control equipment. Or, a third alternative, the communication lines may terminate in a separate device, often a subsidiary computer specially designed for the purpose, which feeds complete, checked-out, edited messages to the computer and receives complete messages for transmission.

The choice among these approaches may to some extent be indicated by

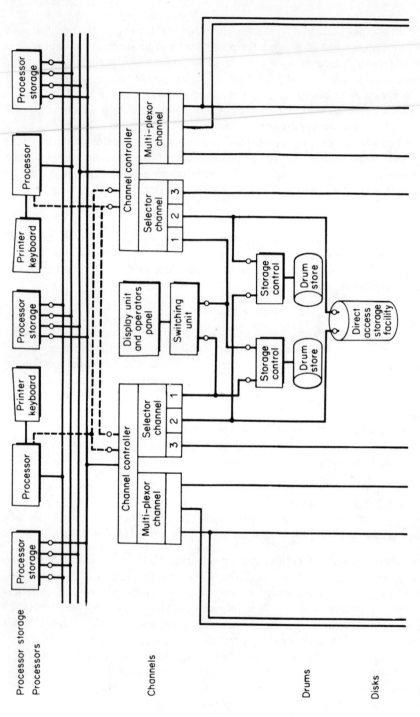

Processor storage

Processors

Channels

Drums

Disks

Processor storage

Processor

Printer keyboard

Processor storage

Printer keyboard

Processor

Processor storage

Channel controller

Multi-plexor channel

Selector channel

1 2 3

Display unit and operators panel

Switching unit

Storage control

Drum store

Storage control

Drum store

Direct access storage facility

Channel controller

Selector channel

1 2 3

Multi-plexor channel

272

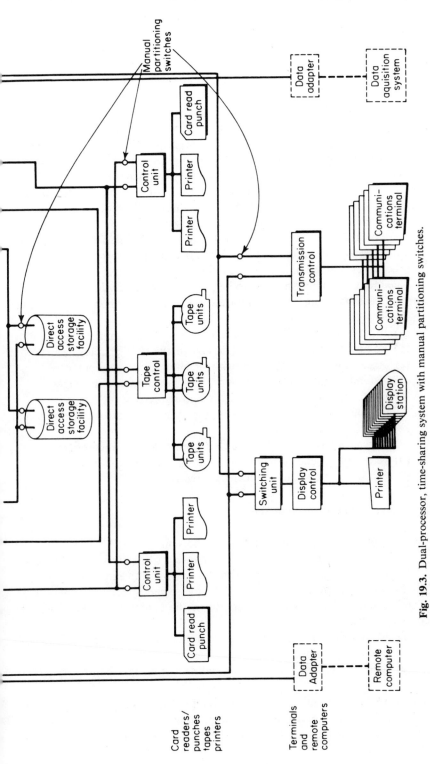

Fig. 19.3. Dual-processor, time-sharing system with manual partitioning switches. A configuration of IBM's 360 Model 67.

the number of communication lines that must be handled. If the system has only one communication line, this may go straight into the computer, or into a device with a buffer storage which automatically assembles or disassembles a complete message. If, however, there are fifty or a hundred communication lines, these may best be terminated in a separate *line control computer*, or *multiplexor*. For the sake of flexibility the multiplexor may be a stored-program computer capable of handling messages of any length and of controlling different numbers of lines. It would have an instruction set different from conventional computers and designed for the handling of communication lines. It may have the facility to log messages on its own random-access file or tape unit. It may send English-language messages to the terminal operators as part of its control procedures. Because it is a programmable unit, its procedures may be modified as circumstances demand.

The following functions have to be performed either by hardware or software for the handling of communication lines: First, when receiving data:

(a) Initiation and control of the reception of data from the lines.
(b) Polling terminals, described briefly in the next chapter.
(c) Receiving bits off the various lines entering the computer.
(d) Assembling bits into characters and characters into messages.
(e) Checking for transmission errors and requesting repeats.
(f) Editing out nondata characters, for example, control characters and backspace.
(g) Converting the coding of the characters to the computer code.
(h) Recognizing end-of-record and end-of-transmission chatacters.
(i) Storing and queuing the messages received.

Secondly, when transmitting data:

(a) Storing and queuing messages to be sent.
(b) Converting the coding of the characters to transmission-line code.
(c) Adding control characters if necessary for transmission.
(d) Initiating the transmission of the messages.
(e) Sending the appropriate bits down the communication lines at the correct intervals.
(f) Monitoring the sending process, repeating characters, or messages if errors occur.
(g) Signaling end of transmission and executing line control functions.

Most of these functions can be handled either by programming or hardware logic. If programmed in the main computer, they take some time away from the other processing. It may be preferable to handle polling and certain network control functions by programming so as to have the maximum flexibility for growth and change. Many on-line systems are likely to modify their transmission requirements frequently, adding terminals, rerouting lines, switching lines for fallback reasons, changing message priorities, and adapting to growth.

18. The Instruction Set

With any computer, on-line or not, the merits of different possible instructions can be argued about endlessly. The same criteria as in off-line computers generally apply, but there are certain types of instructions that are of value for on-line work.

Control of the transmission may use control words or characters, in which individual bits give the status of the lines or devices and instruct the controlling equipment what to do. If the computer manipulates the bits in such words or other control registers or uses bits for polling the terminals, it would be useful to have binary instructions with which this could be done easily. On the other hand, data arrive from most terminal devices and are transmitted character by character, and so it is useful to have character-manipulating instructions to take the characters when they are completely received and checked and pack them into messages, Many on-line computers have both bit-manipulation and character-manipulation instructions.

The computer may be receiving data from many communication lines at once. It must be able to interrupt what it is doing frequently to assemble the messages. An instruction is needed to examine each character quickly to see whether it is the end of message character.

It is usually desirable to code-convert the character from the code used on the transmission line, for example, Baudot, to the code used in the computer, for example, BCD. An instruction which uses automatically a table of equivalent characters will be helpful for this. On the IBM 360, for example, for the *translate* instruction the eight bits of a byte (character) are used to augment an operand address and so reference a list of bytes. The byte selected from the list replaces the original byte. This operation continues until the field in question is translated.

A further complication arises however in much data transmission because *figures-shift* or *letters-shift* characters are used to switch between one of two alternative codes. In this way figures and letters may be transmitted in a five-bit code giving only thirty-two possible combinations. When a letters-shift character is detected, the characters following are letters. When a figures-shift character is detected, the characters following are figures or special characters. A computer instruction which translates this form of code must detect the figures-shift or letters-shift characters and address one of two tables accordingly. This can be done with the IBM 360's "Translate and Test" instruction. This scans the input, translating as with the translate instruction, but each character is examined to determine the continuation of the operation.

Dynamic core allocation may be used for storing the input and output messages. With a large number of variable-length transactions this can give a much more economic use of core than fixed buffering. Certain instructions can facilitate the use of this. For example, when a dynamically allocated block becomes filled or an end-of-message character is received, an interrupt may occur which results in another available block being used. An instruction may use a *next-available-block register*.

In a similar way queues of items, either new items or work in progress or input/output requests, will be manipulated by the system. Certain instructions can help in queue manipulation, for example, automatic addressing of the next item wherever it may be in core, or automatic obtaining of a new core block and chaining it to the queue.

A greater or lesser degree of multiprogramming may be used on these systems. The programs are often relocatable. It is useful to have an instruction format which uses an appropriate base or relocation register automatically to access data or programs which change their location. The instructions may have a memory-protection key associated with them. Where *associative registers* or *associative memory* is used, a variety of instructions are possible for dealing with this.

A large number of interrupts will take place on most on-line systems, especially real-time systems. It is desirable to handle these completely automatically. However, if a machine does not do this, instructions can be executed to do it, for example, instructions which store all of the pertinent registers and restore them when the program in question again resumes control of the computer.

As with many of the features mentioned in this chapter, an on-line or real-time system could be programmed without most of these instructions. Some computers with a very poor instruction set for on-line work have been used successfully by programming around the deficiencies.

19. *Software*

Many users will exclusively use software provided by the manufacturer for telecommunication input/output and for queue chaining, interrupts, and so on. In this case, the difficulty of using the instruction set rests to a large extent with the manufacturer, and the user is more interested in examining the software provided. Are its facilities and its speed of operation good enough? Is it easy to use? Are its *macro-instructions* sufficiently comprehensive for what is to be done?

On many machines the hardware and associated software are becoming inextricably combined. It becomes almost valueless to assess the hardware without analyzing the supervisory system that goes with it. Some manufacturers have found that their service engineers, who used to concern themselves with the hardware alone, now need to know both the hardware and the software. This trend is likely to go further as the complexities increase.

Most users, especially small users, are finding it increasingly undesirable to write their own supervisory systems This is partly because of the manpower and professional skills involved, and partly because of the time involved and the difficulties of writing Application Programs when the supervisory system is not fully defined and of debugging Application Programs when the supervisory system is not fully debugged. It is only too easy to underestimate the complexities involved in developing this software. Supervisory Programs for systems with a high degree of polymorphism (such as those in Figs. 6.7 and 6.8) can be immensely complex, and as the degree of interswitchability increases this will become more so. Software development for such technology is running far behind the hardware development. When a computer user goes shopping, therefore, he is usually shopping not just for hardware but for a hardware-software combination.

The Supervisory Programs affect not only the performance of the system, the throughput, and the response time, but also the ease with which it is used. The programmer often appears to be programming, and wants to be programming, a *virtual machine* substantially different in many of its properties from the physical machine. The shopper must decide to what extent it is this virtual machine rather than the physical machine that he must scrutinize.

20 TELECOMMUNICATION FACILITIES

When designing a data-handling system, it is usually necessary to employ *existing* telecommunication facilities. This means, for example, that circuits and exchange equipment designed for *voice* transmission are adapted for sending data. The engineering of the transmission facilities was designed almost solely for telephone conversation without considering computer data. If they had been designed for data their engineering would be very different. It is thus a compromise to use them for data. The equipment and techniques needed to achieve this most useful compromise are discussed briefly in this chapter.

The services commonly used for data transmission are telegraph, telephone, microwave, and broadband telephone. When a telephone or telegraph circuit is used, this can itself utilize a variety of transmission media. Open-wire lines hanging from telegraph poles were the basis of most of the original carrier systems, but now these have been largely replaced by co-axial cable circuits and microwave.

Many voice channels can be carried by one coaxial cable circuit or a microwave link. Figure 20.1 shows a typical modern coaxial telephone cable which can carry some 11,000 telephone channels. Figure 20.2 shows a microwave radio tower in the foothills of the Rockies. Links of this type are used to carry one or more "groups" of 1800 voice channels. Both of these facilities may also carry television. Any of the individual voice channels may be used to carry computer data, or facilities of this type can carry bulk data at much higher speeds than are possible with a voice channel.

Less than 5 per cent of the circuit miles of the Bell System are now open-wire lines. Over long distances, radio, submarine cables, and now satellite transmission are used. Worldwide teletype links have been in use for some time for sending data which are machine processable.

Looking at the telecommunications map of a worldwide airline, one finds telegraph circuits carried across Europe and America by land line and across the Atlantic by submarine cable. Radio links bridge the Pacific and connect Europe to the Middle East, Far East, and Africa. All of these circuits carry machineable data messages, and message-switching centers—some automated, some not—relay the messages throughout the network. Where higher-speed transmission is needed, as on real-time reservations systems, voice-grade (telephone) lines are used, and these carry data across North America, Europe, and via the transatlantic cable, but not yet, at the time of writing, to the more remote parts of the world because of the expense of obtaining good quality lines there. Military and government installations do, however, have voice-grade transmission facilities circling the world.

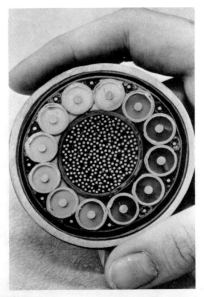

Fig. 20.1. A cross-section of a Western Electric telephone cable. Twelve coaxial units surround a core of conventional wire conductors. This can handle some 11,000 telephone conversations simultaneously, and any of these telephone channels could be used for carrying computer data.

As discussed in earlier chapters the transmission lines may enter the computer hardware on-line, or may be off line. Much data transmission is simply card to card, tape to tape, and so on.

Transmission lines are classed as simplex, half duplex, and full duplex.

Simplex lines transmit in one direction only.

Half-duplex lines can transmit in either direction, but only in one direction at once.

Full-duplex lines transmit in both directions at the same time. One full-duplex line is thus equivalent to two simplex or half-duplex lines used in opposite directions.

The speed of transmission is described in *bauds*, 1 baud normally being one bit of data per second. The speeds of telegraph lines are generally 45 to 75 bauds. Other low-speed lines are available at speeds of 150 and 180 bauds in America, and 100 and 200 bauds in Europe. Public telephone networks give 1200- to 2000-baud facilities, but where old plant is in use it may only be possible to achieve about 600. Private telephone circuits can give higher speeds than this up to about 4800 bauds or occasionally higher.

Fig. 20.2. A.T. & T. microwave radio links. Microwave links such as this now span many countries carrying voice and television channels. Such a link can carry one or more "groups" of 1800 voice channels.

Microwave and broadband telephone facilities are in use for transmission at speeds up to 25,000 or 50,000 characters per second and much higher could be achieved.

Most data transmission is serial by character and serial by bit. This is true of all the normal usage of telephone and telegraph lines discussed in this chapter. Transmission is sometimes used, often in-plant, that is parallel by bit; in other words, a different line circuit and associated electronics is needed for each bit in the character.

MODULATION   Data entering or leaving a computer or other data-processing machine is normally binary in form. In other words, it consists of two separate voltage levels, as in Fig. 20.3.

A variety of different codes are used, but always the data are in 1s and 0s

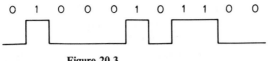

Figure 20.3

and the signal has a rectangular waveform of two voltage levels. Such signals can be transmitted between machines that are close together with no difficulty. However, if the circuit is long and the signalling speed is fast, the pulses become distorted as shown in Fig. 20.4.

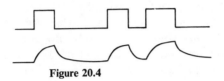

Figure 20.4

Binary pulses of this type were sent over the early teletype lines, but are very inefficient for the sending of data over a voice line. Instead a technique called *modulation* is used. There is a certain range of frequencies which will travel without much distortion over telephone circuits. A frequency of 1500 cycles per second, for example, is near the middle of the human voice range. *Modulation* employs these voice frequencies to carry data which would otherwise suffer too much distortion. Thus a sine wave of 1500 cycles per second, may be used as a *carrier* on which the data to be sent are superimposed in the manner shown in Fig. 20.5.

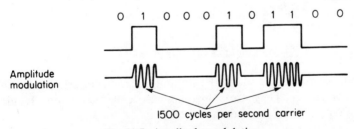

Fig. 20.5. Amplitude modulation.

Modulation achieves two ends: first, it reduces the effects of noise and distortion, and second, it increases the possible signalling speed. Using simple modulation devices, computer data can be sent without undue distortion over the voice circuits of the world.

Modulation is also used by the telephone companies to pack many voice channels into one high-frequency signal which can be sent over cables or microwave links. It is one of the techniques of "multiplexing" many voice channels on to one facility such as those in Figs. 20.1 and 20.2. In this case, it is the voice signal which is used to modulate the carrier wave. Many such carrier waves, separated in frequency by about 4000 cycles per second, are transmitted together. If we use modulation to send data over a voice channel on such a system, the data will thus pass through two modulation processes. In fact, there are often more than two, and the data waveform is manipulated by a variety of electronic processes before it eventually emerges after transmission in its original form. Figure 20.5 is an illustration of *amplitude modulation* in which a 1 is represented by the presence of the sine wave and a 0 by its absence. Other types of modulation are described below.

In order to achieve modulation, the binary output from the data-processing machine must enter a "modulator" which produces the appropriate sine wave and modifies it in accordance with the data. This produces a signal suitable for sending over voice circuits, and whatever manipulation the electronics do to the human voice, they can also do to this signal and the data will still be recoverable. At the other end of the communication line the carrier must be "demodulated" back to binary form. The circuitry for modulating and demodulating is usually combined into one unit, referred to by the abbreviated term *modem*.

The modem, a unit slightly larger than a domestic radio set, is connected to the data-processing machine, and it is then able to transmit data over normal telephone lines as in Fig. 20.6.

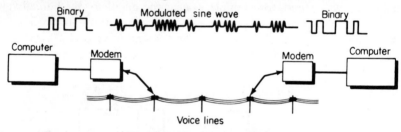

Fig. 20.6. The use of modems.

Modems are made both by the computer manufacturers, and by the telephone companies. They are sometimes also called *data sets*. Figure 20.7 shows a typical Bell System data set.

THREE TYPES OF MODULATION   Two other ways of modulating a sine wave carrier are now coming into more common use than amplitude modulation. These are referred to as *frequency modulation* and *phase modulation*.

1. *Frequency Modulation*

Instead of the 0 and the 1 being represented by two different amplitudes, they are represented by two different frequencies F_1 and F_2, as in Fig. 20.8.

Fig. 20.7. On the right at the rear is a typical Bell System data set. The girl is dialing a distant computer. When she hears a tone indicating that she has made a connection she will press the button behind the telephone dial labelled "DATA," and the terminal she is operating will then be in contact with the computer.

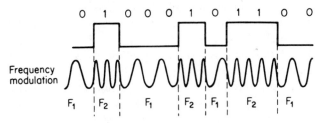

Fig. 20.8. Frequency modulation.

2. *Phase Modulation*

The 0 and the 1 are represented by sine wave carriers 180° out of phase with one another as in Fig. 20.9.

The previous figures all relate to binary transmission. It is possible however, to use a waveform with *more than two* states as the modulating waveform. This is shown for amplitude modulation in Fig. 20.10. "Di-bits" are used to give four possible states in the modulated waveform. This approximately doubles the transmission rate that can be achieved with the modem, but it also approximately doubles its susceptibility to noise. As amplitude modulation is already susceptible to noise, it is not normally used with this; however, it is frequently used with phase modulation.

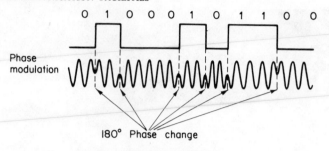

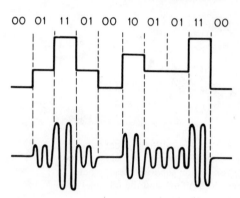

Fig. 20.9. Phase modulation.

Fig. 20.10. Amplitude modulation with four states. This gives a data rate theoretically twice as great as with two states but at least twice as susceptible to noise.

There is scope for much ingenuity in the design of modems and clever designs in recent years have increased the speed with which data can be sent over voice channels. Almost certainly this increase has not reached its final level yet. At the time of this writing, signalling speeds up to 2400 bits per second are in common use on *private leased voice lines*. Less frequently speeds up to 4800 bits per second are in use. In a few systems, experimental in nature, about 9600 bits per second is being achieved. However on *public lines* these speeds cannot normally be attained—partly because of lower line quality and partly because of *in-band signalling* which will be discussed. Common speeds on public lines are 600 and 1200 bits per second.

Increasing the possible speed of transmission by ingenious modulation techniques generally also increases the susceptibility of the system to noise. It also increases the complexity and cost of the modem. Frequency and phase modulation are generally less affected by noise than amplitude modulation. Usually phase modulation is the best of the three in this regard. As it has also been possible to achieve slightly higher speeds with some phase modulation techniques, this type of modem is now starting to be favored for data transmission. However, this type is usually the most complex and most expensive.

In selecting a modem for a system, the designer has to strike an appropriate balance between cost of modem, speed, and susceptibility to error.

On some systems, the terminals are slow as compared with line capacity, and so a slow and inexpensive modem may be selected. On others, the maximum protection against errors is needed. Where long and therefore expensive lines are in use it can be desirable to pack the maximum amount of data on to the lines, and so speed may be the prime consideration. It may be worthwhile to use the fastest modem even though it is more error-prone. An elaborate error-detection code may be used at the expense of some redundancy in the data, to compensate for the use of a modem which increases, perhaps doubles, the data speed. The increasing choice of mòdems on the market and in the laboratory, will give the systems engineer more scope in selecting between these criteria to suit his particular data-processing environment.

CIRCUIT PROPERTIES The speed of transmission possible varies from one voice circuit to another because of their physical characteristics. The 2400 bauds or more obtainable with phase modulation on a private line is usually not possible over a switched public network.

Attenuation of a carrier wave varies with frequency. Figure 20.11 illustrates this for a typical speech circuit. The amplifiers, equalizers, and other electronics are designed to give little attenuation over the frequencies between 300 and 3000 cycles per second because this is the range needed for the transmission of human speech. Outside this range, attenuation increases fast, and so such frequencies are of no use for data transmission. Some circuits are better than this. For example, telephone lines used to carry radio programs in some countries are designed and "equalized" so that equal attenuation and amplification occurs in the range of 50 to 5000 cycles per second.

On public telephone circuits certain frequencies are used for signalling. "Busy" and "number unobtainable" signals are needed. Supervisory signals are used to indicate that one switchboard desires to establish connection with another, and certain frequencies are designed to trigger off particular actions on the network. Frequencies used for these purposes must be avoided when the network is used for data transmission. The United States Bell System uses signaling at 2600 cycles per second. In some telephone systems signaling at 1000 cycles per second is used. Great Britain uses signaling at 600–750 and 2280 cycles per second. This is shown in Fig. 20.11 and leaves free only the frequencies between about 1000 and 2000 cycles per second for data transmission. The narrowing of the bandwidth available for data transmission means that the speed at which data can be sent over the public networks is less than an equivalent private leased line.

In addition to attenuation, *delay* also varies with frequency. This affects

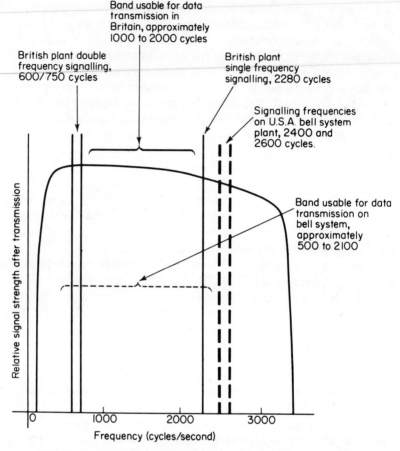

Fig. 20.11. Variation of signal strength with frequency after transmission on a typical voice line. In-band signaling frequencies on British telephone plant are shown as solid lines. Bell System signaling frequencies are shown as the dashed lines. The signaling systems prevent the entire voice band from being used for data.

phase modulation, and a carrier frequency must be selected so that this distortion does not interfere with the transmission of data. Also the amount of *noise* and interference varies from one circuit to another.

Because of these factors it is sometimes desirable to carry out *line tests* on the circuits in question when planning or installing a data-transmission system. These will indicate whether the modems selected will perform adequately and whether the noise level is acceptable.

**NOISE
AND ERROR
DETECTION**

We are all familiar with clicks, crackles, and crosstalk that are audible on the telephone. These cause little interference in human speech, but in data transmission they, and other distortions we cannot hear, cause the loss or addition of bits of information.

Noise on voice lines has many sources and, because most lines were not originally intended for data transmission, they were not specifically engineered to avoid it. Voltage surges are induced by dialling or relay operation in parallel or multiplexed circuits in the same cable. Batteries used in exchanges provide a common impedance giving noise pickup from other circuits. Old switch gear, atmospheric conditions, poor contacts, all give rise to noise which can add bits to, or remove bits from, the data being transmitted. As much of this interference gives rise to changes in amplitude, amplitude modulated signals are more badly affected by noise than signals sent with frequency or phase modulation. Whatever type of modulation is used, errors will occur in much greater numbers than can be acceptable in the majority of applications. They must therefore be detected and corrected.

To check that a message or character has been received correctly, it could be transmitted back to its origination point and compared with the original. An imperfect comparison will cause the data to be cancelled and re-sent. On most systems, however, error detection is done without duplicate transmission. Some form of *redundancy* is built into the messages so that, when they are received, they may be quickly inspected to see whether there is an error or not.

Different equipment for data transmission uses redundant bits for error checking in different ways. A parity bit may be added to each character, as on magnetic tape, and a longitudinal redundancy character used on each word or block or message. With some equipment, more than one character is formed and transmitted to make a check on a block of data. With some, parity bits on characters are not used. Some characters used in data transmission are coded so that only certain bit patterns are acceptable; for example, exactly four bits out of eight may be used for the coding. There are many algorithms in use for composing error-checking characters. They may be composed by program in the transmitting computer, or they may be constructed by hardware logic. Some are more efficient than others. The larger the ratio of redundancy bits to data bits, in general, the greater will be the proportion of transmission errors detected. However, too high a proportion of error-checking bits will slow down the transmission significantly. A compromise suitable for the application in question is needed.

A typical error rate over a good quality private line might be 1 in 10^6 characters in error, of which the error-detection code may pick up 99 errors, in 100, giving an undetected-error rate of 1 in 10^8 characters. Typical figures over switched public lines, where the noise factor is greater, might be 1 in 10^7 undetected error characters. Some lines can be markedly worse than these figures suggest, but also a greater degree of redundancy can be used to give greater protection.

ERROR
CORRECTION

Having discovered an error in a word or message it is necessary to correct it. There are two ways of doing this. First, sufficient redundant bits or characters may be sent not only to detect the error, but also to work out what the correct version should have been. To obtain sufficient accuracy, this may require a large proportion of redundant bits to be transmitted. Second, and this is the scheme normally used, an error signal may be returned to the transmitting hardware for that character, block, or message, to be retransmitted. It is necessary then, as discussed in the next chapter, for the transmitting device to hold the item in question, in a buffer or in other form, long enough for it to be retransmitted if desired.

The answer-back may consist simply of a yes/no message saying whether there was an error or not. On some equipment it consists of redundant bits derived by the receiving station, from which the transmitting hardware may determine whether the item was in error. An item with an error may be retransmitted more than once. If retransmission is requested more than a certain number of times, this may indicate something permanently wrong, and the machine will take exception action or notify its operator.

If a full-duplex circuit is used, it may be possible for the answer-back signal to return to the transmitting terminal at the same time as the next item is being sent. If a half-duplex circuit is in use, it must be sent back between each item.

Where the transmission lines are very long, as from the East to the West Coast of America or transatlantic, the time taken to receive an answer back becomes significant because of the physical transmission time. It is then desirable not to hold up transmission while waiting for an answer back or at least to minimize the number of such answer backs. Sufficient redundancy bits for error correction at the receiving end or answer-back messages relating to several blocks or items may become the most economic solution.

SYNCHRONOUS
VERSUS
ASYNCHRONOUS
TRANSMISSION

Data transmission can be either *synchronous* or *asynchronous*. With asynchronous transmission, sometimes referred to as "start/stop," one character is sent at a time. It is initiated by a start signal, shown in Fig. 20.12 as a 0 condition on the line, and terminated by a stop signal, here a 1 condition on the line.

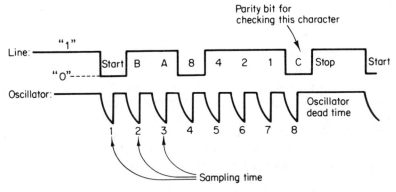

Fig. 20.12. Start-stop transmission.

The pulses between these two give the bits of which the character is composed and are sampled at regular intervals, usually determined by an oscillator in a manner such as that shown. Between characters the line is in a 1 condition. As a start bit switches it to 0, the oscillator starts its sampling.

Start/stop transmission is used, for example, on teleprinters and keyboard devices without a buffer, on which the operator sends characters along the line at more or less random intervals as she happens to press the keys. As the start pulse initiates the sampling, there can be an indeterminate interval between the characters. Start/stop transmission is also much used for continuous transmission, and it avoids any problems that might be caused by slight differences in frequency between the oscillators on the sending and receiving equipment.

The *C* bit in the illustration is a parity bit for checking purposes. Including this, the character must contain an even number of bits. However, noise bursts on communication lines are such that often two or more adjacent bits may be lost or picked up. In such cases *this simple parity check is inadequate* and needs to be backed up by a further check using additional error-detecting characters.

When two machines transmit to each other continuously, with regular timing, *synchronous* transmission may be used. Here the bits of one character are immediately followed by those of the next. The receiving and the transmitting devices have oscillators in exact synchronization, and so there is no need for start and stop pulses between the characters. This makes synchronous transmission more efficient than start/stop.

The oscillators determining the timing for the continuous transmission and reception of bits will, with machines in use today, drift very slightly apart in frequency. They are synchronized with each other at the start of each message, usually by a given bit pattern. If the message or record sent is long and goes on for more than a few seconds, their oscillators will be resynchronized.

In addition to giving faster transmission than start/stop, synchronous transmission is less susceptible to errors. The start pulses in start/stop transmission can be affected by noise. Synchronous transmission can tolerate a higher degree of jitter and distortion. For this reason, synchronous transmission is commonly used on higher-speed circuits. Synchronous terminals and control units are, however, usually more expensive than start/stop.

Bulk transmission of data, that is, tape to tape, card to computer, computer to computer, and so on, is often done by fast synchronous transmission. Relatively slow human keyboard action is often stop/start, though on this also, synchronous transmission may be employed *if the terminal has a buffer.*

CONCENTRATORS   It is often of value to use both synchronous and start/stop transmission in the same system's network. Operators using teleprinters or other keyboard devices may send data in an asynchronous fashion over low-speed, possibly teletype, lines to a collecting center, from which they are sent much more efficiently over a high-speed line to the computer, using synchronous transmission. Replies will travel back in a converse manner.

This is accomplished by means of a machine referred to as a *store-and-forward* device, or *concentrator*. A concentrator has a storage which it uses as a buffer to accept slow traffic from various locations simultaneously and, when it is complete, pump it at relatively high speed to the computer. Conversely it receives down its high-speed line messages for the locations it services and disseminates them to the terminals on the low-speed lines. The purpose of this is a saving in line costs and also sometimes a lowering of response times.

A typical concentrator is the IBM 1006, a machine which attaches to a voice grade line and has 4000 characters of core. It services up to thirty local lines, each of which has allocated to it a ninety-eight-character buffer in core. An operator with a terminal on a local line may slowly key a message into her terminal keyboard. When she completes the message, the last key she presses is labelled "enter." The 1006 then sends the message at high speed to the distant computer. It may receive a reply message from the computer in a second or less and start feeding this to a relatively slow-type head on the terminal. The actions of the 1006, its allocation of storage, its recognition of outgoing message addresses, and so on, are programmed by fixed wiring.

MULTIDROP   To lower the cost of the network of communi-
LINES   cation lines, it is often desirable to attach more than one terminal or more than one concentrator to a single line. A line, such as this, with several "dropoff" points is termed a multidrop line (illustrated in Fig. 17.4).

When several devices all share a communication line, only can one transmit at once, though several or all points can *receive* the same information. Each terminal must have an address of one or more characters, and it must have the ability to recognize a message sent to that address. A line may, for example, have twenty-six terminals with addresses *A* to *Z*. The computer sends down the line a message which is to be displayed by terminals *A*, *G*, and *H*. The message is preceded by these three addresses, and each terminal has circuitry which scans for its own address. Terminals *A*, *G*, and *H* recognize their addresses and display the message simultaneously. The other terminals do not recognize their address, and so ignore the message. The network may also have a "broadcast" code which causes all terminals on a line to display those messages preceded by it.

POLLING   For transmission in the other direction, several terminals may wish to transmit at the same time. Only one can do so, and the others must wait their turn. To organize this, the line will normally be polled. A *polling message* is sent down the line to a terminal saying, "Terminal *X*, have you anything to transmit? If so, go ahead." If terminal *X* has nothing to send, a negative reply will be received and the next polling message will be sent, "Terminal *Y*, have you anything to transmit? If so, go ahead."

Normally the computer organizes the polling. The computer may have in core a *polling list* telling the programs the sequence in which to poll the terminals. The polling list and its use determines the priorities with which terminals are scanned. Certain important terminals may have their address more than once on the polling list so that they are polled twice as frequently as the others. Certain terminals may always be polled before the others.

Some computers can receive and transmit on all their communication lines at the same time. Other hardware is more restricted, and only a certain number of lines may be in use at once. In the latter case the polling concept must be extended beyond one line, and the polling list will relate to several lines.

On long communication lines a different polling organization is used, referred to as *hub* or *hub-go-ahead polling*. Suppose that the distance between the computer and a group of terminals is very great. If the computer polls, "Terminal *A*, have you anything to transmit," and *A* replies, "No," and then the computer polls *B* and *B* replies, "No," and so on, the physical time taken to scan the terminals will become significantly great. Because of this, as shown in Fig. 20.13, if *A* has no data to send, it transmits the polling message on to *B*. If *B* has no data to send, it transmits the polling message on to *C*, and so on. If the last terminal on the line has nothing to send, it informs the computer.

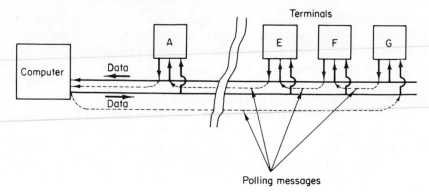

Fig. 20.13. Hub go-ahead polling.

CONFIGURATIONS OF COMMUNICATION LINES

Figure 20.14 shows various possible line configurations. It will be seen that, if multidrop lines are used (Fig. 20.14b), the line cost will be reduced, but there will be an added cost in the electronics ("stunt boxes") which recognize the terminal's address on the line and respond to polling messages. Multidrop configurations are more likely to be used where the lines are longer.

In addition to multidropping terminals, there may be more than one concentrator on a line, polled in a similar manner (Fig. 20.14c). Message-switching centers, as described in Chapter 17, are also in common use to cut down line costs (Fig. 20.14d) on very large networks. Where a terminal is not in constant use, the line to it may be sent through an *exchange*. The exchange may be private or public (Fig. 20.14e and f). The smallest private automatic exchanges are quite inexpensive. Several lines servicing a localized area may go to the exchange, and one line goes from it to the distant computer. If one line is using such a single path exchange, when another attempts to obtain a circuit through, an engaged condition will indicate to the second terminal that it must wait—just as when telephoning with the public exchanges. A system in which the terminals or lines are competing to obtain a circuit and the first one to find it free obtains it is called a *contention* system. Such a system, with terminals contending for a facility is less controlled than one in which the computer is polling.

Where a private exchange is used, the operator of the terminal trying to obtain a line may dial the exchange and obtain the line manually, or this may be done automatically by means of addressing characters at the start of each message.

Many systems send data over the public switched network. In the United States the common carriers permit much data-processing equipment to transmit using the public exchanges. Not all of this equipment is yet permitted by the European carriers, but there, also, use of the public network is rapidly

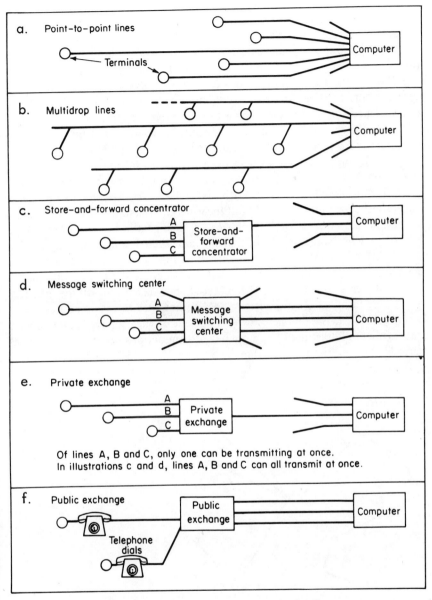

a. Point-to-point lines

Terminals

Computer

b. Multidrop lines

Computer

c. Store-and-forward concentrator

A
B
C

Store-and-forward concentrator

Computer

d. Message switching center

A
B
C

Message switching center

Computer

e. Private exchange

A
B
C

Private exchange

Computer

Of lines A, B and C, only one can be transmitting at once.
In illustrations c and d, lines A, B and C can all transmit at once.

f. Public exchange

Public exchange

Computer

Telephone dials

Fig. 20.14. Configurations of communication lines.

increasing. Telex, dial-up teletype operating at 50 bauds, is available through-out most of the world. The telephone-switched networks at up to 2000 bauds, are usable in certain countries. Intermediate-speed systems are also available, for instance, TWX at 150 bauds, in the United States. Such facilities are charged for on a time-used basis, which varies from one country to another.

Switched lines are generally economical when a terminal is geographically separated from the rest of the system or when its usage is infrequent. Point-to-point transmission of data from card to card, tape to computer, and so on, may require a line connection for only half an hour or so per day, and so it is cheaper to dial up on the public network than to lease a private line. If the usage was for more than a certain period, it would become cheaper to lease a private line. Some data-communication networks use both leased and switched lines, the latter being used for remote terminals or terminals with a very light usage. Sometimes the public network will be relied upon as a standby for times when line failures occur in the leased lines.

In designing a system with multidrop lines, exchanges, concentrators, and so on, the volumes of traffic and the response times required must be carefully considered. Long lines with too many dropoff points may be undesirable because of difficulties of fault location and reliability when one section of the line goes down. With the string of terminals in the left-hand side of Fig. 20.15, when some section of this line fails, there is a high probability that terminals farthest from the computer will be put out of action. The arrangement on the right-hand side reduces this likelihood somewhat, although it slightly increases the line cost. Other layouts may use a looped line, like that connecting terminal G on the left-hand diagram back to the computer.

In general, if the line layout is insufficient or the exchanges and concentrators are badly planned, large queues of transactions may develop at peak periods. This is discussed further in Section V of this book, "Design Calculations."

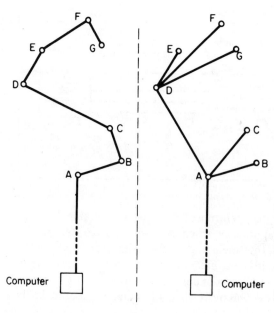

Fig. 20.15. Line configurations. The line layout on the left is slightly less expensive as the total line distances are less, but it is also more susceptible to line failures.

21 TERMINALS AND DISPLAYS

One of the important decisions in the planning of a computer with on-line facilities is the choice of suitable terminals. Sometimes it happens that this choice is rather neglected in the system design. There are so many difficult problems in the planning of an on-line system, such as computer speed and size, file organization, and fallback procedures, that the choice of terminals can be left low on the list of subjects that receive skilled attention. However, a poorly planned terminal configuration can have a serious effect on the efficient operation of a system. It can slow down the system, introduce errors, lessen the usefulness of the system, and significantly add to its over-all cost.

It is very desirable that the right terminals should be selected, because these are the link between the machinery and its human users. Whereas there are relatively few basic *types* of computer to choose from, there are a tremendous number of different terminal devices that can be attached to computers. The considerations necessary in selecting a terminal are outlined below. It is a choice that will ultimately affect every other part of the system.

The terminals may be automatic devices connected to machinery, plant, railroad lines, and so on. They may collect readings or signals from such equipment for processing, and after processing they may use signals from the computer for controlling the equipment. Alternatively, the terminals may be devices for human communication. A man may use the keyboard or other device for sending information to the computer. Similarly the computer may send information to the people using it. This information may be typed or displayed on screens or in lights. It may be spoken audibly, or other means of human communication may be used.

The information, whether from automatic devices or from manually operated keyboards, may be transmitted immediately to the computer or may be stored in some medium for transmission at a later moment. The preparation of data, in other words, may be *on-line or off-line*. Readings of instruments, for example, may be punched into paper tape which is later transmitted to the computer. Similarly data collected from manually operated devices may be punched into paper tape. In this case the terminal of the computer is an on-line paper-tape reader. The output also may make use of an interim medium, such as paper tape or punched cards, or it may directly control the environment in question. Very often it is necessary to make a printed copy of the computer output for later analysis. In this case part of the terminal equipment may be a typewriter or printer. Some illustrations of typical terminals are given on the pages in this and other chapters.

CHARACTERISTICS OF A DOCUMENT INPUT DEVICE

Input to the system may come directly from instruments or keyboards, or it may come from documents onto which the data have been transcribed. Let us first examine the characteristics of a document input device.

The documents to be read may be punched cards, paper tape, or other media onto which data can conveniently be transcribed. They may possibly be optical readers which read writing or marks on documents. Magnetic-ink character recognition might be used; other types of documents, such as a factory worker's badge, might be read. The factors that must be analyzed in selecting a terminal of this type are discussed below.

1. *Type of Media*

Careful thought must be given in the planning of a system to the selection of the best type of input media. Often paper tape is used in transmission systems because of its *low cost*. If it is used, the decision must be made: Will it be five-channel, seven-channel, or eight-channel paper tape? This will depend upon what checking facilities are desirable and upon whether the information transmitted is purely numeric, alphabetic, or alphanumeric with special characters, It may also depend upon the communication facilities available, for example, the line control unit at the computer center.

The media used may be one which necessitates *human attention* at the terminal. If small pieces of paper tape are transmitted, this will be so, but not so for a large reel of tape or a deck of punched cards loaded into a hopper and temporarily left unattended. The information transmitted may be partly from documents, such as cards or plates, and partly from the human-operated keyboards. If the keyboard is used along with the document reader, the terminal must be designed so that they can easily be operated in conjunction with one another.

2. Peak Traffic Volume

A thorough study must be done to determine the amount of data that will be transmitted by the terminal. The survey must indicate not only the average use of the terminal, but also how the volumes vary month by month, day by day, and hour by hour. The system must be designed to handle the peak traffic volume during the peak periods. It is necessary to have statistics on how rapidly the traffic builds up and dies away again. This may be important in order to determine what *queues* will develop. Traffic volume figures must be projected forward to indicate how the load on the terminal will vary after installation.

If the lengths of the message vary, information is needed on this. A histogram should be produced showing the frequency of occurrences of messages of different lengths.

3. Speed of Operation

A terminal of suitable speed must be selected, and this will be determined by the volume of traffic to be transmitted and by the speed of the communication lines available. Ideally a terminal will operate so that data are transmitted at the maximum rate the communication line allows, but this is not always possible, because of other factors in the terminal design. In considering speed, the number of terminals on one communication line must be evaluated.

4. Coding

The characters to be transmitted may be purely numeric or they may be alphanumeric or special characters. The information transmitted must be coded in a means that is compatible with the decoding equipment used at the line control unit.

5. Checking

The degree of checking that is carried out will depend to some extent upon the nature of the information being transmitted. If numeric data is being sent, it is usually of the utmost importance that this should be received accurately. The computer will process it and take decisions based upon it which will affect the basic records of the organization. With many types of information, repeated inaccuracy will cause chaos. A regular, though small, incidence of undetected errors can cause a steady deterioration of the data of the files. However if the system is routing *verbal* information from one terminal operator to another, then errors may not be so important. The receiving operator will recognize the errors and will take corrective action. The normal transmission of cables, for example, is an unchecked process, and, when cables are received with alphabetic errors, it is easy to spot these.

Usually the recipient can make sense of the cable or can ask for a retransmission.

For most types of data sent from an on-line terminal, automatic *error detection* is essential. On some terminals, if a character is in error, retransmission of that character is automatically requested a given number of times from a character buffer in the terminal. As well as automatic retransmission of characters, some systems have automatic retransmission of *messages*. On a paper-tape terminal this may mean the backspacing of a tape record for rereading. On a card terminal it may mean a mechanical design that can reread a card, as on the IBM 1050 terminal. Where the input cannot be reread easily or where the input is from a keyboard, retransmission of a message can occur only in a *buffer* at the terminal. If messages are persistently wrong, the system will have to notify the operator. It is very convenient to have a system that handles this automatically. However on some systems the expense may not be justified.

Automatic *error correction*, using sufficient redundancy bits to reconstruct an error message, is more of a luxury and is likely to be used only if retransmission is difficult or for some reason inefficient. If satellite transmission of data is used, for example, signals asking for retransmission might take too long because of the large distance, and so message reconstruction could become the most efficient method.

TERMINALS FOR MANUAL INPUT Most of the considerations above apply also to a terminal in which the input will be manual. However, when human beings are keying in data on line, many more considerations have to be looked into. We now have a man-machine interface, often real-time. This must be designed to be efficient and at the same time as convenient as possible for its operators to use. The terminal that is in some way inconvenient for human use will considerably impair the efficiency of this system. Some of the design considerations for a human-input terminal are discussed below:

1. *Volume*

Again the volume of traffic and the spread of message lengths at the peak hour must be estimated. However, with the terminal in human usage, peaks in traffic of smaller duration than one hour may need to be investigated. For some reason which is characteristic of the system, the terminal may be in very heavy use for a period of, say, ten minutes with a utilization much higher than average. A peak of this type may occur in a bank when customers come in at lunchtime, in a stockbroking system when a piece of news triggers off many enquiries, or in a factory when the workers are about to leave.

In considering the terminal with human input, one has to examine the habits of the people using it.

2. Type of Keys Provided

The terminal may have an alphabetic keyboard like a typewriter. It may have digits also. The digits may be in a 3 by 3 matrix so that they can be operated rapidly with one hand. Special characters may be needed, or special punctuation. Many terminals have special keys with meanings characteristic of that system, as keys with mathematical functions; date keys saying "yesterday," "today," and "tomorrow"; keys for sterling currency in England; and keys saying "one seat," "two seats," and "three seats," "first class" and "tourist class," "book," "cancel," and "confirm" on an airline reservations system. Again, many terminals have special control keys, such as "end of message," "cancel this transaction." Terminals using a cathode-ray tube have keys for manipulating or altering the data displayed on the screen. In many systems a single special character will replace the entering of a number of alphabetic characters or even replace a whole message. Elaborate special-purpose keyboards are used for creating certain types of man-machine interface as was described in Chapter 7.

The terminal may be designed so that the keys can alter their meaning from one transaction to another. A matrix of keys may be used over which a perspex sheet is placed which labels the keys according to requirements (Fig. 21.1). On airline reservations systems a card or plate of metal has been used which represents flights to a certain set of destinations (Fig. 15.6). When this card or plate is in place, the lights and keys which are lined up against it then represent the flights that are available and the cities to and from which they go. The card or plate itself has a number which is sensed by the terminal, and this number is transmitted to the computer as part of the input information.

Some terminals use levers or knobs rather than a keyboard. Some of the cheapest terminals make use of a telephone dial for input. A telephone, in fact, is sometimes used itself as a terminal to a real-time system. The telephone dial is used first for establishing communications with the computer and secondly for transmitting information. The ear-piece on the telephone may be used to receive a spoken reply from the computer. Telephone dials, however, are slow to use and prone to a surprisingly high number of operator errors. The types of keys provided depend to some extent on the language that is programmed for the man-machine communication. On many applications, as the systems analysts are working this out, they want to change the keys on the terminal. It is a good idea to use a terminal in which these keys *are* changeable, so that at least the key labels can be determined as the programs are being planned.

3. Use of Plates, Cards, and so on, in Combination with a Keyboard

On some systems it is desirable to transmit certain fixed information for which plates, cards, paper tape, and so on, may be used in conjunction with

Fig. 21.1. Plastic "keymats" are used on the IBM 1902 and 1903 to change the labeling of keys.

variable information which may be keyed into a keyboard. Alternatively the fixed information may be set up by means of levers or switches used in conjunction with a keyboard.

A card may be selected from a rack of cards and transmitted along with the keyed-in data. A workman may use a badge which is entered into a badge reader and its number transmitted along with keyed-in information. Analogue data from instruments may be transmitted, perhaps with manually entered data.

4. *Use of Data from the Computer in Combination with Keyed Input*

It is often necessary to add to or modify data which are already in the memory of a computer. In this case the data in question may be typed out or displayed in such a way that a minor modification to them can be made accurately and with as little new keyed input as possible. On a typewriter the sequence of operator actions might be as follows: First, he keys in a message requesting the computer to display the data that he wishes to add to or modify. He then presses a key with a label such as "duplicate"; this causes the typewriter to type a copy of the record displayed. It types as long as the duplicate key is depressed, and then, when it is released, the operator may key in the modification that he wishes to make and continue duplicating the remainder of the record. After the operator has established that the record is correct, it is reentered into the system.

When a two-way interchange between the computer and the terminal is used in this manner, a wide variety of possibilities exists for modifying the stored data by means of special keys or devices on the computer. Special keys are often devised which again are characteristic of the application in question.

5. Use of a Cathode-ray Screen or Similar Device

A cathode-ray tube display used in conjunction with a keyboard provides a more versatile way to modify data in the machine. Most cathode-ray tube and similar display terminals have a *cursor*. This is a visible point which can be moved by the operator to any position on the screen. The cursor is usually represented on the screen by a small star or triangle or a short dash underlining a character to which the cursor position currently refers. If an operator wishes to change a character in the middle of a display, he moves the cursor so that it refers to the character in question and he then takes appropriate action on the keyboard. The means for moving and utilizing the cursor differ from one device to another. Some screens have a "destructive" cursor, so that, as it is moved horizontally across the screen, it erases everything it passes over on that line. Others screen have non-destructive cursors.

Another device used in conjunction with a display screen is a *light pen*, a manually held pointer which can be directed accurately to any position on the screen. With this it is possible to "draw" on the screen, and many programming aids can be used to assist in perfecting the drawing. Keys can be used for making lines parallel, for duplicating parts of the drawing, for rotating, diminishing, enlarging, or deleting parts of the drawing, for adding components held in the computer's storage, and so on. A curve can be drawn on the screen, and the computer will devise a mathematical expression to fit the curve, adjusting the curve very slightly if necessary. A surface can be drawn—for example, metal panels in the design of a car body— and the computer will make the surface fit certain design constraints and rotate the image of it so that its designer may view it from all angles. A girder construction can be drawn and figures displayed on the screen giving the stresses on the girders in differing conditions.

An ingenious device that can be used like a light pen is a "desk pad" surface, such as that in Fig. 21.2. This is a printed circuit screen acting as a writing surface when pressed by an associated stylus, which the man in the illustration is holding in his hand like a pencil. The surface has a mesh

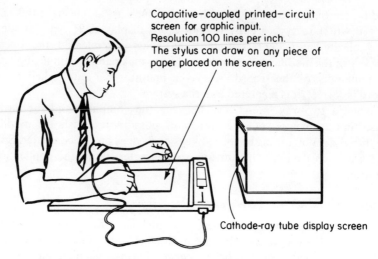

Capacitive-coupled printed-circuit screen for graphic input. Resolution 100 lines per inch. The stylus can draw on any piece of paper placed on the screen.

Cathode-ray tube display screen

Fig. 21.2. The Grafacon model 1010. A digit graphic input system manufactured by the Data Equipment Company.

of 100 lines to the inch, capacitive-coupled so that a piece of paper may be inserted between the surface and the stylus. The man can then draw on the paper, which may already have matter printed on it. Certain points on the writing surface may be given a special significance so that when the stylus touches them the computer takes certain actions. It may add axes to a graph, store what has been drawn, and so on.

This type of man-machine communication is very versatile, but it needs *a good input/output language to go with the terminal* and this often constitutes a major problem. The means by which the terminal communicates with the computer language needs to be carefully thought out, and the terminal must have adequate facilities for this. The hardware and software designs for complex man-machine interfaces such as these, especially when *graphic* communication is involved, need to be planned jointly to a large extent.

6. *Format Control*

When data are manually entered into a keyboard, it is necessary to insure that the computer interprets them correctly. When there is more than one field in a message, the computer must interpret the format and attach a correct meaning to each input character. A group of characters might be typed into a terminal in an airline reservation system giving a flight number, class, date, code for the airport of departure, code for the airport of arrival, departure time, and a code indicating what action the computer is to take. This might be typed in as one long string of characters. A different entry would also be a long string of characters but with a quite different meaning. Some of the fields might be variable in length. It is necessary for the computer to sort out the format of messages of this type.

One method of ensuring correct formats is to use preprinted stationery or templates so as to indicate the positions and sizes of the fields. This method can be inconvenient where there are many different types of input. It is also undesirable where the fields vary considerably in length.

Another method is always to key in fields in a given sequence and to put a hyphen or other symbol between the fields. Again the operator may enter the field label in a given code before entering the data. A field code or a message-type code can be useful when there are only a small number of fields in the message. However, with long messages, fields may be forgotten. If fields are separated only by hyphens, there is a danger that they might be entered in the wrong sequence.

Terminals for highly specialized purposes might have an elaborate means of controlling format; e.g., terminals for direct input of computer programs in their source language or direct input of simulator or similar programs might have a means of indicating to the operator that he has missed or miscoded any of the necessary fields.

Many systems designers hold the view that the human operators should do as little of the talking as possible in a man-machine conversation. Once the operator has initiated the conversation, the computer asks for what it needs, one item at a time. It checks each item as it receives it, and so problems of format control disappear. When the input messages would otherwise contain many fields, possibly of variable length, this approach is particularly desirable. To do this it is usually necessary to have a fast means of output, and a terminal with a keyboard and cathode-ray tube can be ideal.

The computer is certainly very versatile in its ability to talk and print natural language at the terminal, whereas it has difficulty in understanding other than the simplest messages from the operator. Its operator, furthermore, makes mistakes, and so the more simple-minded and controlled the operator's actions are, the better. Both in administrative systems such as that in Fig. 8.24, and in highly sophisticated systems, perhaps a scientist carrying out some type of information retrieval or hypothesis formulation, we find the computer doing more talking than the man.

If the nature of the conversation is recognized when the terminal is being designed, features can be included to simplify it. Much can be done, for instance, with two keys labelled "yes" and "no." In information retrieval the computer may be scanning report headings and flashing them at high speed on a screen. Most of them may not be what the operator is searching for, but an occasional one needs closer inspection. Keys telling the computer to "continue" or "stop" a process may similarly be desirable.

Systems in which conversation is facilitated by making the computer do much of the talking may result in a large quantity of data transmission. On a system with very long communication lines, this may be too expensive and transmission costs may be saved by making the operator do more of the work of formatting messages. In this case a different terminal design is needed.

7. Ease and Speed of Operation

It is necessary that some terminals be operated very quickly and easily. With others there is little or no need for speed in their operation. A terminal at a bank counter must be operated quickly because a customer is waiting for a reply. A data-collection terminal in a factory, which is only used infrequently, does not have the same requirement for speed unless it is used in such a way that queues of workers could be kept waiting, for example, to clock in at the start of the day. Terminals which handle a high volume of data must work rapidly, perhaps operated by touch typists. If a terminal is used to answer telephone enquiries, speed is usually essential because the answer required must be obtainable in a few seconds while the enquirer is on the telephone.

The type of operator has an effect on the terminal design. Some operators are highly trained in the use of a terminal. Others, such as factory hands or railroad workers, are less trained or less nimble-fingered and need a terminal which is easy to operate. Some terminals have to be operated by a touch typist in an office; others by a laborer on a building site.

The ease with which the terminal must be operated depends to some extent on what other work the operator is doing. Does she sit comfortably in front of the terminal all day, or does she only occasionally stand over it to make an entry? Does she use both hands, or is she holding a telephone in the other hand? Does she enter repetitive data by means of cards, plates, or other devices? Does an input transaction require a lot of thought and detailed checking? Does it require a conversation with the computer? In general the terminal should be designed or selected so that it fits in with the other actions of its operator as easily as possible.

8. Speed of Response

Does the operator require an answer back and, if so, how quickly? The answer back may be merely lights flashing on, or it may be a data message. If it is a long data message, such as a matrix of information or a listing of a number of items, then a typewriter may be too slow for this transmission and a display-screen device preferable. An elaborate conversation may need the speed of a display-screen device.

9. Terminal Environment

The surroundings of the terminal may be an important factor in its design. Does it have to fit into an elegantly designed showroom? Is it in an atmosphere of dust, or heat, or high humidity? Must it fit into a confined space or be placed on a bank counter? Will it be moved from one location to another? Is vibration a problem? Are there any restrictions on weight or electrical characteristics?

The packaging of the terminal is important in some applications but not in others. Terminals installed on the floor of the New York Stock Exchange, for example, needed careful packaging to meet limited space requirements. Terminals installed in a cellulose factory needed special flame proofing. Because of the inflammable atmosphere, sparks had to be suppressed. As some terminals are located in remote or small offices, this may affect the packaging needed.

Environmental illumination is an important consideration with a screen terminal. Can the screen contents be read without eye strain? The lettering must be sufficiently bright, sharp, large and flicker-free for the operator. If the operator uses the terminal eight hours a day, these considerations are especially important. A badly planned screen can easily give such an operator a headache.

10. *Visual Input Verification*

Three types of check might be made on the data manually entered into a terminal. First, these data may be visually displayed in some way so that the operator can check them. Secondly, the transmission itself will be checked automatically. And thirdly, certain programmed checks on the validity of the input might be made by the computer.

To enable the operator to check the input visually, it might be typed out or displayed on a cathode-ray tube before the computer processes it. If the terminal uses a set of slides or a matrix of keys, a complete message might be set up in these and examined by the operator before it is transmitted to the computer. The slides or keys will stay in position until the transaction is entered. If a device, such as a typewriter or display screen, is used, each character should print as it is keyed in. The operator can then watch the line of print as a visual check for errors. This, however, is not possible of all types of terminals, as the output printer might be connected to a computer by a communication line separate from that for the input device. In this case the printing of the input would require the computer to transmit this back to the terminal. This is likely to be impracticable, especially if many terminals are being used at once. Generally speaking, it is not a good idea to design terminals on a real-time system on which the operator cannot see what she keys in. Having the whole message visible in front of her helps considerably to reduce operating errors.

When an operator does make a mistake, she must be given an easy way to correct this error. She must be able to backspace and erase the last character transmitted or several previous characters. If the error occurred earlier in a long message, it is useful to be able to make a small correction without having to reenter the entire message. Control keys on the keyboards of some terminals give this facility.

11. Automatic Input Verification

There are various checks that can be made on the input to a real-time system. These are discussed in Chapter 35. Generally the checks rely on programming and organization, but there are a number of features that may be built into terminals to assist this.

The terminal may have some means of allowing the computer to indicate to the operator that a message is incomplete or invalid. This might be a printed message to the operator so that the terminal works in a conversation mode, or it might merely utilize an indicator such as a red light or a buzzer.

Batch totals or check totals might be used to ensure that no data are lost. These can be used whether transactions are entered in batches or whether they are entered singly. Quantities or account numbers or some other fields are added up by a control section and also by the computer to make sure that all the transactions have been received by the computer. This technique may be facilitated by the use of a mechanical counter on the terminal itself. Using the counter the operator can ensure that all the data have been received by the computer. On many systems the use of serial numbers is employed to ensure that no message has been lost. The adding of serial numbers to messages might be an automatic function of the terminal.

12. Security

It is usually desirable that unauthorized persons should not be able to interfere with the terminal or to enter data into it. On a banking system only an authorized teller should be able to send transactions to the computer. With the terminal in a stockbroker's office, it would be unfortunate if the cleaning lady could play with the system and inadvertently cause a transaction to be dealt with by the computer!

There are a number of ways of maintaining adequate terminal security. One of these is to place a lock on the terminal. A bank teller may have his own key, and every time he enters a transaction he must insert this key and turn it. Some banking terminals have two keys so that two separate tellers can use them.

Another way of maintaining security is to allow each terminal user to have a card or badge which he inserts into the terminal. Using this he must "sign in" before he can transmit data which are processed by the computer. When he has finished using the terminal, he must "sign out" similarly. The cards or badges used have different types of significance. Certain transactions may only be possible if a supervisor's card is inserted into the system. The system may operate in a training mode so that, when a trainee's card is inserted, the computer will respond to the terminal in all of its normal ways, but it will not change any of the records on its files.

13. Terminal Buffering

A buffer may be used on a terminal in order to save computer core, to save computer time, or to save time on the communication line. Whether or not a buffer is required for these purposes depends on the over-all timing and facility utilization. Where one communication line has many terminals attached to it, buffers on the terminals will increase the efficiency with which this line is used. The computer, in scanning the lines, can inspect the buffers to see when one of them has information to transmit. The buffer, however, is generally expensive on a terminal. The cost must be balanced against the savings.

A cheap form of buffer, as previously, may be the use of paper tape. A message is punched into paper tape, and this is placed on a tape reader to be read at the computer's convenience. This scheme is used on many message-switching systems. A buffer allows messages to be composed fully before being transmitted to the computer. If the message is long or complicated or takes a long time to compose, it may be worthwhile checking that it is correct before any of it is transmitted. If many long messages are sent to the computer without buffering at the terminal and the operator enters characters slowly, perhaps, because she is at the same time talking to a client on the telephone, then a large amount of computer core will be tied up in buffering the messages at the computer end of the communication lines. Partially completed messages will remain in core for a relatively long period before they are processed. When buffering is used, no single terminal will occupy the line for a long period of time, neither will it tie up the core of the computer for a long period.

Buffering on the terminal allows the operator to verify the message completely before transmitting it to the computer. Changes can be made or errors corrected without the computer being involved in this process and without the communication line being tied up.

14. Terminal Logic Ability

If core buffering is desirable at the terminal, this is expensive. It is possible to lower the cost by sharing a buffer between several terminals. The terminals may have a common control unit which carries out line control functions and buffering. This is shown in Fig. 21.3 This unit may be the *concentrator* discussed in the previous chapter. It may be on the same site as the computer or it may be remote so that it serves terminals in several locations.

It is normally desirable to have some logic associated with the terminal to facilitate the making of corrections by the operator, such as back-spacing, deleting, or correcting words or lines, and sometimes providing a variety of editing functions. The control unit of one terminal, for example, can reshuffle the entire contents of a page on the screen when a word is added or deleted.

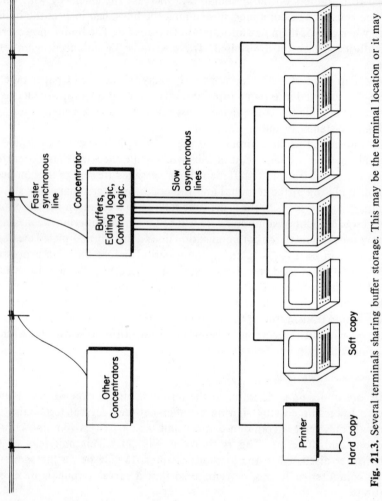

Fig. 21.3. Several terminals sharing buffer storage. This may be the terminal location or it may be remote. The terminals may be different sites. The quantity of logic in the concentrator varies. It is sometimes a small computer, possibly even with its own disk or drum file.

308

It is questionable whether these functions should be carried out at the terminal or in the central computer. It is usually cheaper to carry them out in the computer. The line load may be somewhat lessened if they are carried out at the terminal, however, and this may be significant, especially where long expensive lines are in use. More important, sometimes, the response to the operator's attempts to carry out editing operations will be immediate if they are done by the terminal or its control unit. Some terminals have a large amount of logic for re-formatting computer output. A message with compact data may be neatly expanded by the terminal into column and lines. Control characters in the message may govern tabbing, skipping, line spacing, and indenting, the adding of special characters, and so on. However, this expense at the terminal is probably not justified in the majority of applications.

DEVICES FOR OUTPUT OF INFORMATION
The output of information is often on the same machine as is used for input. This is the case with the terminals in many of the illustrations in this book. It is not always the case. An output printer or a display panel may stand alone with no input, just as an input device have may no output.

The terminal may give print-outs or displays which are to be read in real time as they are produced, or it may produce printing which is to be read at a later time. The printer on a conventional batch-processing system falls into the latter category, but, now, with telecommunications, the printer may be a long distance from the computer. Where the output is read as it is produced, the terminal may or may not be designed so that a man-machine conversation takes place.

Having determined the requirements for output terminals, the following considerations may affect its choice or design:

1. *Hard versus Soft Copy*

Is a printed or punched record of the transaction needed at the terminal location? Often this is not necessary, especially if the transaction is logged, for example, on magnetic tape, at the computer center.

The term "soft copy" is used to describe terminals which leave no permanent record. These fall into two categories, visual and audio. *Cathode-ray tubes* or other display devices are becoming popular. These can be fairly cheap devices that display information rapidly. If the data are more than, say, 100 characters they can be significantly faster than typewriter-like machines or teleprinters. Displays in pictorial or graphic form capable of quick comprehension may be used.

It is sometimes desirable to have a hard copy terminal backing up a group of soft-copy devices. A programmer using an on-line programming language may want a printer and punch so that his program may be printed or punched after he has modified it. He may also want a card reader to read it in again. A commercial installation may want some form of printed report, and in particular it may need regular print-out for stand-by purposes in case of system failure. The printer or punch may be attached to the same control unit as the soft-copy devices, as in Fig 21.3.

Alternatively *voice answer back* provides the cheapest possible output terminal as a normal telephone may be used. This type of reply may not be as clear as a visual display but is often adequate. The vocabulary of spoken words must be stored by the computer. Some machines store these in analogue

Fig. 21.4. An engineer gets a telephone reply from the IBM 7770 audio response unit. The 7770 obtains information from a computer in response to a dialed telephone inquiry and provides an answer over the telephone in the form of spoken words. The unit assembles the proper words from a recorded vocabulary stored on a magnetic recording drum (shown in uncovered panel), amplifies them and transmits them back over the dialing phone. Information needed to answer requests may be stored on the IBM 1311 disk storage drive —pictured at left—or on other storage units on the system.

form and have a limited vocabulary. They may be stored on a drum as with the unit in Fig. 21.4. Others store them in a digital format. The sound of human words is converted into computer digits or characters, and these can be converted back into clear understandable sound. The characters are then stored in the computer or on its files as normal computer records would be. An average-length human-voice word might take between 100 and 200 characters to store in this way. Sequences of human-voice words are composed by normal program instructions. Storing the words on tape or random-access files, the machine has thus an unlimited vocabulary.

2. Group versus Individual Displays

A display may be small and designed to be read by one individual, or it may be a large group display. The latter may be used at an operation control center, at a public location, such as an airport, or in a situation where several persons may discuss the display. One can foresee a board room or management control room of the future being equipped with a group display.

3. Amount of Data Displayed

If a display screen is used, the amount to be displayed at one time will affect its size. Where a typewriter or other continuous device is used, the amount is affected only by the timing requirements.

A display screen may be used with a program which slides the information on the screen up and down like a Biblical scroll. Use of certain keys can "wind" the scroll up or down in a flick. Similarly the image may be moved from side to side, or a graphic display can be enlarged or diminished to overcome the fact that the screen is a "window" of limited size. Some systems use a *video switching unit*, which enables operators to select different "channels" as on a television set and examine different displays generated by the computer. Some of the channels may be used also for visual observation using a television camera.

4. Timing

A device operating at typewriter speeds may be too slow for applications where lengthy messages or displays must be scanned quickly. A faster printer may be used, or a display screen. The display screen is very fast, but some screens have a lengthy erase cycle, which should be considered if conversational programming is used.

5. Operator Modification of Data

In many applications it is necessary for the operator to make modifications to records by displaying them, changing certain characters or factors, and sending them back to the computer. A typewriter or a display screen may be used for this, a keyboard working in conjunction with it as described in previous pages. Controls for easy modification of data must be built into the equipment, and also the programs must be written to give the operator the maximum help. If a display screen is used, controls for manipulating the cursor must meet the operator's needs.

6. Type of Data Displayed

To give maximum assistance to the terminal operator, the way in which the data are presented must be carefully thought about. They must be displayed in the form which he can understand most easily. This may be in a pictorial form. It may be in the form of light displays or bar charts or graphs. It may be tabulated, or it may be a verbal reply.

This may affect the equipment used. Display lights may be positioned beside a changeable matrix card. A graph plotting pen may be used. A display tube may be desirable for pictorial presentation, or a typewriter may be fitted with special characters.

Familiarity to the operator is important in designing the display, if this can be achieved. For example, in a process control application where a large control room full of meters has been partially replaced by computer-operated displays, it has been disadvantageous to use *digital* print-outs and tables. Some form of graphical or analogue presentation is preferable, as this is familiar to the operators.

7. Visual Suitability

The display size must be suitable for its audience. If a man sits immediately in front of a display screen with a bright sharp image, the lettering may be as small as the print of this book. If he is farther away or if the resolution is less good, it must be proportionately large. If two operators, for example, obtain quick answers from the same display screen, the writing must be large enough for this to be done efficiently.

The visual suitability of the display must be considered in relation to its environment. The brightness must be suitably greater than the ambient lighting. The contrast and accuracy must be sufficiently high; the distortion and flicker time sufficiently low.

8. System Activity Indicators

When programming, or carrying out some other activity, at an on-line terminal, there may be periods when the system is silent as the computer executes a program possibly interleaved with service to many other users. If the terminal is completely silent during this period the user often becomes restless, wondering sometimes if the computer is still paying attention to him. Terminals often have a "System Alert" light showing that the terminal is still connected to the distant computer. This is very useful but it is psychologically desirable also to have some means of indicating that the program is being run.

The terminal may for example, wink a light, make a soft bleeping noise or type a character at intervals. The signal for this could be sent to the terminal periodically in a similar way to a polling message. This activity has been referred to as "hand holding." Using the tones of a touch-tone telephone dial or data set, a variety of different sounds could be made, if so desired, to indicate to an impatient terminal operator what activity is being carried out. Audible sounds on some terminals, however, have proved distracting. If there is more than one operator and terminal in a room, they can become very annoying. It may be better if a silent means of indication is used.

9. Error Control

The means of detecting and correcting errors on computer output must be as efficient as on input. If the displays are on communication lines, careful checking for noise errors is normally needed, and, as with input, automatic retransmission of data in error is normally desirable.

In designing the use of terminals for man-machine interaction, programming and hardware considerations are very much interwoven. The programming language and the terminal design must combine to give the most *natural* tool to the user. The terminal and the way it is used must appear as familiar and easy to understand as possible. If in striving for this the program designer can modify the use of keys on a terminal, so much the better.

22 PLANNING THE DATA FILES

In a commercial data-processing application an approach to the survey which is often advocated is: *First plan the data files, then build the system around them.*

Before the advent of direct-access and random-access file units, the files were stored on media which were read sequentially, such as magnetic tape or punched cards. The files had to be sorted frequently to arrange them in a sequence suitable for processing. Deciding exactly what data fields should be kept on the files was, and always will be, a lengthy and detailed job that needed an intimate knowledge of the application, but planning the file equipment was relatively straightforward.

With file units designed for purely sequential processing, the main criterion to be examined is their speed. For in-line and real-time processing, other criteria become important. Direct-access or random-access files can, indeed, speed up sequential processing considerably. With many commercial systems, the optimum approach combines serial, in-line, and real-time processing, and so file design and file management has become a complex subject. Certainly the correct choice and organization of files has a great affect on the efficacy of a data-processing system.

It is desirable to integrate or centralize the files as far as possible. This is one of the aims of "integrated data processing." In some organizations different computer systems or different files have been used independently, when a combined approach would have reduced duplication of effort or duplication of storage. Sometimes data collected by one function could be used by others, but the persons concerned are not aware of their availability. Often political or procedural problems have prevented the sharing of computer files that would cut across a corporation's divisional or departmental barriers.

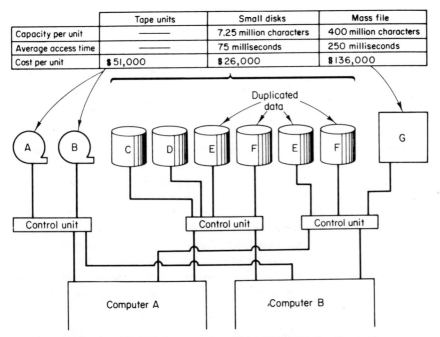

	Tape units	Small disks	Mass file
Capacity per unit	——	7.25 million characters	400 million characters
Average access time	——	75 milliseconds	250 milliseconds
Cost per unit	$51,000	$26,000	$136,000

Duplicated data

A B C D E F E F G

Control unit   Control unit   Control unit

Computer A   Computer B

Fig. 22.1. A file configuration in which: (1) frequently-referenced data (a small portion of the whole) is kept on separate fast-access files. (2) A vital nucleus of data is duplicated on separate files, enabling the most important real-time work to continue if a file breaks down. (3) Tapes are used for file security operations and sequential logging.

Data useful to one department may not be collected at all, although another department could do so easily as part of its regular operations. With the equipment and techniques now available it becomes increasingly important to tackle the file problem as a whole. Fast communications between one part of an organization and another and the use of the computer as a management information system enhance this need.

CHARACTERISTICS OF THE DATA AND ITS PROCESSING
There are certain characteristics in the data to be stored which indicate the file requirements. Let us first examine the nature of the data and its handling and from this draw conclusions about the types of hardware and techniques that are needed.

1. *Random or Sequential Processing?*

Many data-processing jobs are, by their nature, best done sequentially, scanning through a file in a given order. Payroll, for example, involves going through the employee list, extracting relevant information, and making up pay slips. There is no point in doing this other than in a serial computer run. There is no point in incurring lengthy random-access seeks.

315

Other jobs, however, have traditionally been done serially when a random approach could be of value. Stock updating, for example, is done in many firms by a sequential run that fits into the computer's cycle of sorting and processing and so may come around perhaps once a week. It is of value in some types of business to reduce this cycle time, to be able to check the latest stock position on certain items immediately, to reorder stock quickly when large orders come in or exceptional circumstances arise, and so on. This is especially so if the turnover rate is high, if the stock is perishable, if the demand for products fluctuates and is uncertain, or if the competitive situation is especially keen. With in-line processing the stock records may be checked and updated when each order is received. Access to stock records *at random* is necessary for this. There is not time to scan through a sequential file.

For some computer work, sequential processing cannot be considered. Most real-time jobs come into this category. When a computer must react within hours to an unanticipated situation, it is usually too time consuming to load a sequential file and scan through it. In production or operation scheduling, for example, the computer makes up an optimum timetable for the operations. Any unanticipated change, of which there may be many, must be fed to the machine so that it can modify the timetable if necessary. To do this it needs quick access to a variety of different records.

Systems for answering enquiries, booking seats, updating savings books at a bank counter, or carrying on a conversation with terminal operators demand quick, and therefore random, access to files.

However, only a small portion of the work may be real-time or in-line, and the same files may be used for other, possibly serial, processing. In this case, the files may be organized in such a way that serial scanning of them is possible.

2. *File-activity Ratio?*

In many files that are scanned sequentially, not every record is used. On a billing operation, for example, the customer file may be scanned, but only certain customer records are required and these may be a small proportion of the whole.

A file-activity ratio may be defined as

$$\text{File-activity ratio} = \frac{\text{Number of records read and used in one run}}{\text{Number of records scanned in that run}}$$

If the file-activity ratio is large, this run may be done, using a high-speed magnetic tape, in about the same time as using a direct-access device; and magnetic tape is a cheaper storage medium. On the other hand if the file-activity ratio is low, say 10 per cent, the direct-access device can skip the unwanted records. Most magnetic-tape units cannot skip but have to read all records scanned. The direct-access device therefore becomes faster than tape, and it may avoid lengthy sorting operations.

3. File Size

When serial files such as tape are used, there is no restriction on the amount of data that can be passed. One tape after another is loaded on to the computer until the whole file is processed. Some random-access devices do impose a restriction. The disks of an IBM 1302, for example, have a capacity of 234 million characters (for one unit with the maximum of two modules). If the file is larger than this, two units would be required.

Other random-access units, however, have an interchangeable recording medium. The disks or "bins," or cartridges may be removed, stored on a shelf like tape, and replaced by others. The restriction then is on what can be stored *on line;* there is no restriction on what can be stored on the shelf.

4. Record Sizes—Fixed or Variable Length?

How large are the records? Can small records be blocked to form large ones in order to make the best use of file characteristics. Are they fixed or variable length? Fully variable-length records can be handled easily on magnetic tape but not on all makes of random-access file.

5. Frequency of Reference

A record may be referred to many times, or it may be referred to infrequently. In many commercial files a small proportion of the records are referred to frequently, and a large proportion, not very often. For example 90 per cent of the stock movements may relate to 10 per cent of the items. In an airline 10 per cent of booking records may relate to flights taking off in the next week, but most of the activity—cancellations, rebookings, and enquiries—relate to these flights; 10 per cent of a bank's customers give rise to 90 per cent of the withdrawals and deposits. Similarly, some stock items hardly ever move; some bank accounts are hardly ever touched; some passengers book a year in advance and are never heard of again until the plane takes off.

The selection of the hardware and the placing of the data on it should, where possible, be such that the records used most frequently will be easy and quick to locate. If, in a stockbroker's system, processing is constantly being interrupted by enquiries or transactions relating to certain popular stocks, let these be stored where access to them can be in 20 milliseconds rather than 100 milliseconds.

Certain items on the files may be read *very* often, for example, programs, index records, and master records. These might be placed on a drum or other small quick-access file.

6. Speed of Reference

If an item is referred to frequently, it is usually desirable that the speed of obtaining it should be high. However, speed of reference can also be related to the desired response time. If the system must give its reply in a second or so, possibly because of the demands of conversation mode, and formulating the reply takes several seeks on channels where the queuing is high, then the seeks must not take long. On the other hand, if a response time of half an hour is good enough, the machine can stack the file requests and make infrequent excursions into the remoter areas of the files, collecting several records while it is there. Access to the remoter areas can be slow.

It is often necessary to have several access mechanisms. If the system under peak load must make thirty file references per second and each file reference takes 200 milliseconds on average, then the system must have at least six access mechanisms— $(30 \times 200)/1000 = 6$. If the type of file used can have only one access device, this means six or more file units.

It is often better to have a number of small file units rather than one large one. This increases the throughput capability of the system. It can also increase the reliability, because when one unit fails the others are still available.

To achieve an adequate processing rate, file accesses are often overlapped with one another. It is commonly necessary then to resort to multiprogramming.

7. *Single-transaction Access or Grouping?*

To scan through a file sequentially is quicker than random processing. Similarly to have access to a group of transactions at a time rather than to single transactions can be quicker. The group can be shifted into the optimum sequence for reading.

Does the nature of the application make it reasonable to have access to groups rather than to single transactions, so delaying the response? Often this is so. If it is, can the transactions be sorted into the best sequence before they enter the computer, or must this be done in core? If the transactions come from remote terminals, the sorting must be done in core. If they originate in the computer room, valuable computer time might be saved by entering cards in a small batch that has been sequenced on an off-line card sorter.

The pattern of seek times to different areas of a file unit differs from file to file. On some, presorting is more beneficial than on others.

8. *Ease of Addressing*

Like a reader locating a book in a library, the computer has to determine the whereabouts of an item on a random-access file. It may use an index rather like a library catalogue, or it may use other methods, as discussed in Chapter 27.

In some cases the data itself can make the addressing easy. For example, customer numbers may be allocated which *are* the machine address of the record in the files. Savings bank passbooks may have the machine address of the record printed on them, and the teller keys this in when entering a transaction. In other cases the data can make the addressing difficult. For example, given a date, passenger's name (which might be spelled wrong), and flight number (which the passenger might have forgotten), retrieve the passenger record.

To some extent the nature of the equipment can help in the file addressing. If a library catalogue is used, this, for example, can be kept in locations or on a separate file where it can be read quickly.

9. Number of Additions and Deletions

Some files are fairly static, that is, new records are not added very often, nor are records removed. The customers of a bank do not change very rapidly. The customers of an airline, on the other hand, do, and this file needs to be organized to cater to the change. Some files, such as a store of messages to be sent in a message-switching system, change constantly minute by minute.

A slowly changing file on a direct-access device can be reorganized periodically when the system is off the air so that the gaps left by deleted records do not cause a waste of space. A rapidly changing file must be organized so that the space left by deleted records can be filled by new ones as the need arises in real time.

In the latter case, the organization of the file may become steadily more inefficient. In other words, it takes longer to gain access to a record than it need because the records are not in the best locations. It should therefore be cleaned up periodically. This may be done when the system is not on the air, or it may be done, using multiprogramming, during the system's idler periods of operation. When there are few real-time transactions arriving, the computer may work through the files' indexes, moving records to fill up gaps.

10. Expandability

Is the file likely to grow? Will there be more stock items or railroad trucks or customers next year or in seven years' time? Almost certainly, yes. Can the present hardware hold the anticipated increase? If not, can more file units be added without upsetting the organization of the system?

11. Reliability of Access

If an access mechanism or channel or file unit breaks down, how will this affect the application? Sometimes it will be very disadvantageous to lose access to the records for two hours or so. If a channel fails, it may be possible to switch the file to a second channel. If a file fails, it may be possible to remove the recording media and place it on another unit. However, on many systems it has been necessary to duplicate some or all of the records.

Duplication of the data is expensive and brings programming problems concerned with fallback and keeping two sets of records up to date. The decision whether to duplicate is really an economic decision. How much is it worth to avoid losing the data for two hours? On some systems it is vital not to lose the records. On others it does not matter. Often it is worth duplicating a nucleus of the system on small, relatively inexpensive files. Many commercial systems can divide the files into a part which can be lost for two hours with no hardship and a part which it is vital to have in real time.

12. *Protection from Damage*

It may not be too harmful if records are inaccessible for two hours, but it would be disastrous if they were lost completely. They might be lost because of a hardware failure, a programming bug, or an operator error.

With good-quality modern files a hardware failure is *most* unlikely to damage the files. They are built to be fail safe. One's vision of the read/ write heads spraying red-hot iron filings from the disk surfaces is a nightmare that almost certainly will not happen. The nightmares that *can* be caused by programmers and operators are much worse. Most programmers deny categorically that their programs could damage the files. However in the unpredictable and always changing environment of a real-time system with data-transmission links, rare and subtle errors can appear, and these have been a cause of file damage on systems installed so far. Worse than this is the thought of an operator loading the files but using the wrong tapes to do so.

Damage to the files may happen very infrequently, but an insurance policy is needed for when it does. Detailed means of file reconstruction must be worked out and adhered to.

The traditional means of processing magnetic tape is to use "father" and "son" tapes. A record read from the father tape is updated and the new record written on the "son." The father tape is not erased. This provides security. If by accident the son is damaged, it can be reconstructed from the father. If the father is damaged, it can be reconstructed from *its* father. Such an approach is wasteful on a direct-access file system except when strictly serial processing is used on a file of high-activity ratio. With random processing or real-time processing it is impossible. Here the record is read, updated, and the new record written back in the same place, erasing the old one. Some other method of reconstructing the record is needed if it becomes damaged. The file may be "dumped" periodically and an "audit trail" left, that is, sufficient information written in temporary storage to reconstruct the changes that have been made to the record since the file was last dumped.

Very careful attention must be paid to any factor which might cause damage to the files. Safeguards will be built into the programs and means of checking the operator actions devised. File damage will therefore be a very rare event. Like a building catching fire, one hopes and expects it will never happen, but one *must* take precautions against it. The reconstruction procedures need not be slick and automatic, provided they can be made to work. The file must be dumped periodically onto some other storage media. How often it is dumped will vary from system to system—sometimes once a day, sometimes once a week, sometimes once a month, On a system with removable file cartridges or disks, a spare set may be stored, perhaps in a separate building. The data are copied on to these at intervals. Magnetic-tape units are frequently used for this. Some of the early IBM 305 RAMAC systems dumped their files on to 100,000 punched cards. Occasionally data-processing managers are content merely to print the files periodically, presumably hoping that, if damage occurs, it will be to a few records only; but printing a large file takes too long.

Similarly, with the audit trail, the possibilities are magnetic-tape logging, printing, recording on a spare file unit, or keeping the original source documents. If the messages reach the system through a message-switching computer, the logging file of this may be adequate security.

Whatever the method, file reconstruction techniques must be planned, and they may affect the file equipment required.

TYPES OF FILE   Some typical files in use today are as follows:

Card. High-security storage for programs and perhaps other vital data; may be kept away from the computer building to increase security.

Paper tape.
Cheapest medium for direct transmission over communication lines.

Magnetic tape.
Cheap mass-storage medium for large files serially processed; may be used on a random-access system for loading and dumping files, logging messages, keeping audit trails; for very fast off-line data transmission.

Small drums.
Capacity, up to 5 million characters; small backing store for programs or high-activity data; may hold addressing index to large random-access files.

Single disk.
Low-capacity backing store; interchangeable storage medium used for programs, small files, high-activity data. For example, inexpensive back-up program store of 3 million characters, interchangeable, average access time is half a second.

Small disk unit.
Interchangeable storage medium 7 million characters; seek requirement

of 50 to 200 milliseconds; 28,000 characters available without moving access arm; gives fast serial processing.

Large disk unit.
Capacity, 400 million characters; noninterchangeable disks; 900,000 characters available without moving access mechanism; access time, 40 to 180 milliseconds.

Large drum.
Fixed storage of a billion characters access time 30 to 50 milliseconds.

Magnetic card file.
Interchangeable cartridges of cards; 6 million characters on line; access time, 235 milliseconds; 24,000 characters available without need of reaccess.

Large magnetic-strip file.
Large random access file; 400 million characters on-line; interchangeable bins of strips; access time, 90 to 400 milliseconds 10,000 characters available without need of reaccess; can be used for fast serial processing.

Large core memory.
Relatively expensive temporary store with very fast access time; up to 8 million characters per unit; access time 8 microseconds.

EXAMPLE   Figure 22.1 shows a file configuration which illustrates some of the points discussed above. This configuration is used for a real-time system in which many of the transactions require a fast response of the order of seconds. The files are therefore mainly random access. Tapes, however, are used for certain serial processing and for security operations. A transaction log is dumped onto tape for later off-line analysis. Every night the files are dumped onto tape, and a file-check run is executed. This ensures that no file records have been inadvertently overwritten and provides a means of file reconstruction in the event of catastrophe.

The bulk of the data is held in the mass file *G*, which is a cheap but rather slow storage media. It would be too slow to keep all the items in that file; however, 70 per cent of the accesses refer to a relatively small volume of data, and this is kept on some small, fast-access disk units.

Although it is desirable to have a fast response to all of the transactions, it is not thought to be worth the expense of duplicating *all* the file data. Most of the references to file could be delayed for two hours, say, in the event of a breakdown. This would cause inconvenience but would not be catastrophic providing that a summary of the *vital data* is always available. This will occupy the space of two disk units. Therefore it is duplicated as shown. The vital data can still be accessed if a file unit, a control unit, or a computer fails. The cost of the two extra file units is $52,000, which is a small proportion of the total system cost.

To end this chapter, let us summarize the technical considerations that apply to the hardware. The following are the main factors that should be examined when selecting random-access file equipment:

1. Capacity.
2. Speed of sequential data transfer.
3. Speed of access, lengths of seek, and rotational delays.
4. Spread of seek times. Some files take an almost equal time to access any record; others have a wide range of seek times, which may be more suitable for some applications.
5. How much data are available without a reseek.
6. Is scanning necessary in order to locate a record? If so, must this scan utilize the computer, or can it occur independently?
7. Failure rate. What is the mean time to failure? What is the mean time to repair when a failure occurs?
8. Security of data. Are the mechanisms fail safe? What is the chance that a mechanical failure may cause damage to data?
9. Checking. How thoroughly is a file/write operation checked? Does this need an extra scan of the recording surface? Does the mechanism check that a seek has, in fact, found the correct record? What redundancy checks are used?
10. Is it better to have one large file unit or several small ones? Several small ones permit parallel seeks, thus effectively reducing access times. They give a lower over-all mean time to failure, but only a portion of the file is lost at once.
11. Is the data-recording medium interchangeable?
12. Record format. Fixed or variable length? Are blocked records used? Is an efficient means of coding used? Can different tracks have different formats?
13. Can individual records be read, or must a whole track be used?
14. Does the mechanism perform efficiently with the mode of addressing that is to be used. Can index tracks be scanned quickly? With randomizing can an efficient pocket size be used? (Discussed further in Chapter 27.) Can an overflow area be accessed quickly?
15. Does the mechanism give suitable interrupts? Is there an interrupt at the end of a seek? Is there a "record ready" interrupt as the recording surface passes the read head, just before the record is in position? If the read/write operation is overlapped, is there an interrupt when it is complete?

DESIGN CALCULATIONS

23 THE CRITICAL FACTORS

This section describes the design calculations and estimating procedures that are necessary when planning and ordering a real-time system, and when programming and installing it. The chapters relate to an on-line real-time system for doing a specific set of functions, rather than to a time-sharing facility, which might be used by many different users for different purposes until it is fully utilized. Recommendations are made as to the techniques that should be employed.

It is intended that, with the techniques outlined in this section, a systems analyst familiar with conventional computing hardware will be able to make the required estimates. Where queuing and probability theory is used, it is reduced to sets of curves which a not-very-mathematical systems analyst should be able to employ.

Generally speaking, design calculations and estimates are far more difficult to carry out on a real-time system than on a conventional system. The hardware used is often more complex, and many more functions may be taking place simultaneously, or almost simultaneously. Furthermore, the input to the system is not constant or precisely predictable. Transactions will reach the system at random, usually at times determined by the needs of human operators. The load on the system will vary minute by minute. At times it will reach peak values, and occasionally the peaks will be so high that processing is delayed.

Different transactions will require different operations being carried out on them, and so the activities of the system will also vary minute by minute. On a system programmed in a multithread fashion there can be many permutations of simultaneous activities. On some systems there are an almost infinite number of different combinations of programs that may be in core at one

327

time. In addition to this, the program sizes and timings for individual functions have proved very difficult to estimate on some applications.

As well as the estimates being more difficult to make, the penalties of inaccuracy are greater. If the calculations are inaccurate on conventional systems and the programs take more time or core than was originally expected, the computer can usually still carry out its functions but will take more time to do so. On a real-time system, this latitude does not exist. The messages will flood into the system at a rate largely independent of the programming. If the estimates were too low, then the system may not be able to process these messages. It may be incapable of doing the work it was ordered for, without expensive additions to the hardware, such as an increase in core-storage or a faster processing unit.

Because a computer cannot expand its real-time capacity merely by extra-shift working, the estimates must be correct. A much greater depth of detail than on a conventional system is usually necessary in the design process before placing an order. It will often take several months to work through the estimating procedures described in this section. If, for some reason, the computer order is placed before the estimating is completed, as seems to happen in a surprising number of cases, then adequate contingency allowances should be used and high priority given to completing the estimating process before the order is frozen.

Furthermore, the procedures described should not cease after the first complete set of estimates are made. Almost always when the system is being programmed and preparations are being made for its installation, the design factors change. The programs are larger than anticipated. The volume of transactions is greater than was first thought. Extra files have to be added, and so on. A careful check should be kept as the scheme is being implemented, and the estimating procedures should be reiterated to ensure that no drift is occurring that will make the system unworkable.

NINE
BOTTLENECKS

In making the estimates for a real-time system a number of factors may become critical. There are a number of potential *bottlenecks* in the system. The estimating process must first establish what the critical factors are and then must evaluate each of them. On a typical system there are nine types of bottlenecks (Fig. 23.1).

1. Processing-unit core storage.
2. Processing time in the computer.
3. Peripheral file storage, for example, drums or disks.
4. Channel utilization.
5. Utilization of access mechanisms or read/write heads.

6. The multiplexor or line control unit and buffer storage.
7. Communication-line utilization.
8. Terminal utilization.
9. Capability of the terminal operators.

Some systems have more than one computer or several types of terminals or a message-switching center, and so there will be more factors than those listed.

In designing a system, each of these potential bottlenecks must be estimated with care, and the relationship between the factors must be examined. In some systems, one of these factors may be more critical than the others. In other systems several of them may be critical. But whether the system is large or small, these nine factors must be checked carefully in its design.

On a real-time system there is to some extent a *tradeoff* between these critical factors. If one of them becomes too tight, it may be possible to relieve it at the expense of some of the others. Designing a real-time system is, then, to a large extent, a matter of obtaining a balance between the factors. It is important to understand the nature of this balance.

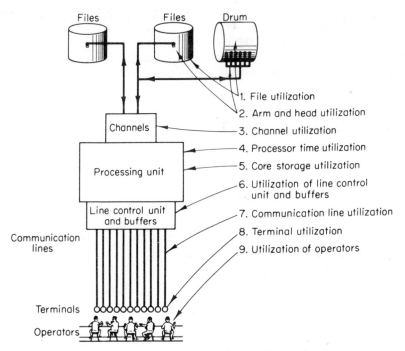

Fig. 23.1. The critical factors in the design of a real-time system. A balance must be achieved between these nine factors. Any one of them is a potential system bottleneck.

It is rather like planning traffic facilities in a city center. The traffic varies with time, and there will be peaks of certain types of traffic at certain times. A balance must be struck between the facilities provided. There is no point in building a large underpass if this will increase the traffic jam at either end of it. If roads into the city are improved, parking facilities must be built to balance this or the traffic in the center will be reduced to snarling chaos. Parking lots must be sufficiently close to shops, or the shops will lose business. If the facilities are not balanced, the response time of going shopping, for example, can increase drastically.

Before discussing methods for estimating the factors above, let us examine the tradeoff between the factors:

1. *Processing-unit Core Storage*

On a large system it will normally not be possible to hold all the Application Programs in core all the time. The core will not be large enough. It is therefore necessary to call some of them in from files when they are required. The less the core storage available, the more will be the programs called in from files. The calling-in of programs will be done at the expense of processing time, channel time, file-arm time if a disk with movable arms is used, and, to a negligible extent, file storage.

This is an illustration of the way the utilization of one critical factor can be relieved at the expense of other factors. There is obviously a limit to the extent that core-storage program space can be relieved by reading in programs from files.

2. *Processing Time in the Computer*

If the processing time is short, it may be possible to relieve it simply by "polishing" the programs. It may be relieved at the expense of other items in the following ways:

(a) Writing the programs so that they operate faster but use more core.

(b) Having more Application Programs in core.

(c) Designing the programming so that the Supervisory Programs are entered less frequently. This would probably lower the peak throughput that the system could handle.

(d) Using a fast tailor-made Supervisory Program rather than slow generalized software.

If the computer becomes overloaded momentarily from the timing point of view, this will result in queues building up and hence give an increase in core utilization. It will be seen that there is a balance here between core utilization and utilization of processing time.

3. Peripheral File Storage

At first sight it might appear that calculating the file requirements is merely a question of adding up the sizes of all the records to be stored there. However, two factors may complicate this:

(a) Minimizing the seek times. On most systems a prime reason for using Supervisory Programs which make multiprogramming possible is that the limiting factor on throughput is the seek mechanism. Multiprogramming keeps the file access mechanisms as busy as possible. Because this is the limiting factor, it is desirable to minimize the seek times. This may be done by placing the most frequently referenced records in such a position that a short seek is required, or even by putting very frequently read, but not frequently written, data in more than one place. Minimizing seek times may be done at the expense of tight file packing.

(b) Addressing. In order to obtain a record in a random file, its address must be obtained. If direct address calculation cannot be used, it must be found either by a randomizing method or by looking it up in index tracks as described briefly in Chapter 27, which may mean one or more additional file reads and maybe additional seeks. In either case, the file cannot be 100 per cent packed with data to be referenced.

In most methods of file organization, the file-reference time is longer, the higher the packing density of the file. If the reference time is long, there may then be larger queues in the system, occupying more core. The channel and access-mechanism utilization will be higher. The processing time used in making file references or doing address calculations will be somewhat higher. Here again is a balance between the factors.

4. Channel Utilization

The channel utilization may be lessened by having more Application Programs in core, by using re-entrant programs so that program blocks are read from the files less frequently, and possibly by having a better file organization, which may need more disk space or more processing time. If the channel utilization becomes too high, queues will build up, increasing core storage utilization. On some systems this can be a very significant factor.

5. Utilization of Access Mechanisms or Read/Write Heads

Arm utilization may be reduced by cutting down seek times, by better distribution of data between the arms, or by the considerations that apply to channel utilization. In particular, the file accesses may be sifted and executed in that sequence which minimizes the timing. This will increase the queue sizes and so increase the core needed. It will put up the response times. Again there can be a balance between the factors.

6. The Multiplexor or Line Control Unit and Buffer Storage

Where the communication lines are handled by a separate line-control computer, there are certain programs which could either be in this or in the main computer. To put them in the line-control computer would leave more room for processing in the main machine but would lessen the core that can be allocated for buffering input. If the buffering area is less, there is a greater chance of the system's delaying the acceptance of messages from the terminals or causing replies to be queued in the main computer.

The main computer may itself handle the control of communication lines and the buffering of input and output. This is at the expense of processing time and a considerable quantity of core. Here, if dynamic core allocation is used, as explained in detail in Chapter 32, the buffer area may be large or small. If it is small, it may be necessary for the computer to dump slices of long messages onto a backing file. This will be done at the expense of channel time and file head time.

7. Communication Line Utilization

When messages have to wait for a communication line until a previous message has finished using it, this will cause queuing at the terminal, in the core of the main computer, or in the line-control computer. The average length of these queues will depend upon the line utilization. With manually operated terminals this is likely to become critical only when there are a number of terminals on each line. The utilization, and hence the queues, may be lessened by increasing the number of lines or redistributing the terminals. In most systems an average line utilization of more than 65 per cent is too high and will occasionally cause large queues in the computer. Core storage may here be relieved at the expense of an increased number of lines.

8. Terminal Utilization

On systems in which the terminals are in very heavy use, these may become a system bottleneck. On some systems the cost of terminals is high, and it becomes important to optimize the use of them and minimize their number.

On certain systems the terminals are very heavily loaded during a peak period and may be in nonstop use. An example of this was a system studied for an Italian tax collection office with a very heavy peak four days in the year. In this case it is necessary that the work on the terminals should be as highly organized as in a keypunch room. Here the number of terminals could be reduced if the response time of the system was very fast. A fast response time in this case required more lines so that delay waiting for a line was avoided. In a more complex system the response time might be speeded up at the expense of core in the computer.

In the planning of certain types of system, Supervisory Programs might be designed which cycle through the Application Programs and give a response time which is long, perhaps thirty seconds. This might be adequate for the application and would give a more efficient use of core storage and processing time than a faster-responding multithread system. However, it might result in an excessive waiting time at the terminals, which would increase the number of terminals required at the peak hour. The response time could be brought down to five seconds, possibly, at the expense of core storage and perhaps processing time.

Here again a balance must be achieved.

9. Capability of the Terminal Operators

The operators of the terminals must be considered very carefully when the terminal utilization is high. They are very much part of the system because they are the means of getting the information to and from the computer. Computer specialists who are used to considering only the machinery are sometimes inclined to pay too little attention to real-time terminal operators.

An operator may take fifteen seconds to type a transaction into the terminal. The system may take five seconds to calculate and print the reply. The terminal is therefore in use for twenty seconds. However, the operator may take sixty seconds to deal with the transaction, and hence the terminal is excluded from other use for sixty seconds. Suppose that the location in question has more than one transaction per minute at peak periods. Arrangements may be made for two operators to use the same terminal. This may be slightly inconvenient for the operators, but it will lower the number of terminals needed.

Again, if the system is programmed to give a long response time, for example, thirty seconds, this may increase the number of operators as well as terminals needed to handle a given volume of transactions from one location. Core storage or file-access mechanism time may be saved at the cost of using more terminal operators and terminals.

The aim in designing a real-time system is to achieve a balance between the various bottlenecks that can occur. The relationship between the above nine factors must be clearly understood and their interplay evaluated.

Swinging the balance between the critical factors is to some extent a question of Supervisory Program design. Much of the estimating work will depend upon a basic knowledge of this and other mechanisms which control the flow of work through the system.

24   THE ESTIMATING PROCESS

Before work can begin on designing a system and making the necessary estimates, considerable study and data collection must have been carried out. The procedure that is described in these chapters will take place after a detailed analysis of the traffic that is to be processed.

It is necessary to determine factors such as the following:

1. What types of transaction will the system handle?
2. What functions will be needed for the processing of each of these?
3. What data files must be kept and in what form? What degree of accessibility?
4. How many transactions per hour of each type will there be at various times? In particular, what are the peak traffic volumes? What peaks must the system be designed to handle? For example, if a ten-minute peak occurs at a given time of day must this be handled as at other times?
5. How long are the transactions? If they vary in length, a histogram of message lengths will be required.
6. How long are the replies? Another histogram.
7. How many data records of each type are required on the files? How long are they?
8. What response time is needed for each type of transaction?
9. What degree of reliability is needed for the processing of each transaction; that is, what is the maximum allowable length and frequency of system interruption.

Such information will take some time to collect, and in many organizations it will be far from complete when the systems design is under way.

Often some of the data required for compiling these figure just do not exist. The gaps have to be bridged with sagacious guesswork.

If an information service is provided, how many people will make enquiries? If a fast telegram-switching system is set up, what increase in telegram traffic will take place? If a real-time system lessens the lunch-hour queues of customers in a bank, how many more people will come into the bank in their lunch hour? No one will really know the answer to these questions until the system is installed, and here lies a paradox of certain real-time systems. *The data needed to implement a system may not be available until the system is implemented.*

A good solution in this case is to install the system in two "models." Model 1 may not include all the functions of the final system. It will contain sufficient functions and collect enough data for the feedback of design information to make Model 2 as satisfactory as possible. With some real-time computers the first system is a nonprofit-making scheme which is largely designed to collect data for implementing the second system a year or so later. It is a good idea for Model 1 to be a rented, rather than purchased, system so that any desired changes can be made. Many systems have surprised their architects in being inadequate to cater to the increased use that people tried to make of them. More transactions than were estimated flooded into the system, constantly triggering overload procedures and making it difficult, if not impossible, to connect all the terminal points intended. It is better to anticipate such a load than to be caught by surprise. One way to do this is to omit some of the ultimate functions from Model 1 so that it has enough capacity to cater to a traffic larger than estimated.

Even when the design data are reasonably accurate and trustworthy, the estimating procedure will normally be an iterative process. At first a guess will be made at a possible system. Calculations will be done to see whether this system fulfills the requirements. If it does not, the system will be adjusted until it does fulfill them at the lowest cost. Figure 24.1 illustrates a possible iterative procedure.

Cost will no doubt be a determining factor, and, if, the earlier reiterations indicate that the cost is likely to be too high, the system functions may be cut down or modified somewhat. It may be possible to vary the processing procedures considerably. The degree of elegance with which the processing is done, or the number of exception conditions that are catered to, might be cut. The various reiterations of Fig. 24.1 will attempt to establish a balance between the critical factors in the manner described in the last chapter.

The person carrying out the design should, in its early stages, be broadly familiar with all the disciplines involved so that he can cycle through the appropriate reiterative loops. This involves a knowledge of the hardware, the Application Programs, basic Supervisory Program theory, file organization techniques, basic queuing theory as described in a subsequent chapter, and, usually, simulation. The ability to make an approximate set of estimates quickly, evaluate the cost of a design, and readjust the design and perhaps the system functions is likely to be very valuable in the early stages. The following chapters are intended to indicate to a systems analyst how this may be done.

After a system has been designed to a first approximation and appears acceptable, the design must then be done in greater detail. This may involve the use of specialized techniques, such as simulation, file analysis programs, and detailed Supervisory Program knowledge. The analyst may at this stage have to refer for help to specialized groups.

Many factors are likely to be uncertain in early days of the system design work. Even if the traffic volumes are firmly established, the details of the processing required may not yet be fully understood. The sizes of Application Programs will be far from certain. Many of the factors on Fig. 24.1 require a reiterative procedure themselves. As work progresses into greater depths of detail, these factors will come into focus steadily.

The most difficult part of the estimating process is often the determination of the requirements of the processing unit. This may be the most critical part, also, because while terminals, lines, and files can be added, the processing unit may be more difficult to change. On a large multiprogrammed system it is especially difficult to make the required estimates for the processing unit. Again this is likely to be a reiterative process. For example, an estimate will be made of the number of Application Program segments that may be in core at one time. From this the number of Application Programs read in from files is calculated. The length of queues in core is determined and the core storage requirements found. It may then be necessary to readjust the number of Application Programs in core and perform the calculations again. Figure 24.2 illustrates the type of iterative procedure that may be necessary for making the estimates for the processing unit.

As the work on the critical factors proceeds, the confidence with which a utilization figure can be placed on these will increase. It is a good idea to determine the critical bottlenecks of the system, to calculate a utilization figure for these, and to attach a confidence factor to it, saying, for example, that the channel utilization might in fact become 20 per cent greater than the estimate and that the core required might be 80 per cent greater.

Usually a characteristic of a real-time system is that the load on it will vary with time. The functions that it performs may also vary second by second, depending upon what transactions arrive for processing. The design calculations are therefore involved with *probability*. There is a certain probability that the system will be able to handle the load reaching it. During the peak hour the *average* channel utilization will be so-and-so. There will be peak hours and peak days in which the load is continuously heavier than average, and there will be peak seconds in which, by chance, many messages arrive at

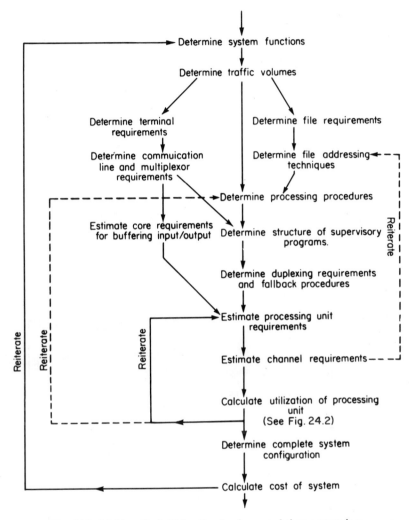

Fig. 24.1. Making the initial estimates for a real-time system is a reiterative procedure.

the system at almost the same time. It will not be economical to design the system to handle every instantaneous peak, but it is necessary when estimating to consider the variations in load and determine what effect these have on the system.

The question that the user will ask about the system is often, "What response time will I get at the terminals?" or "How long a delay will there be before I can enter a transaction?" The effect of a momentary peak greater than the system's capacity will be to lengthen the response time or the delay.

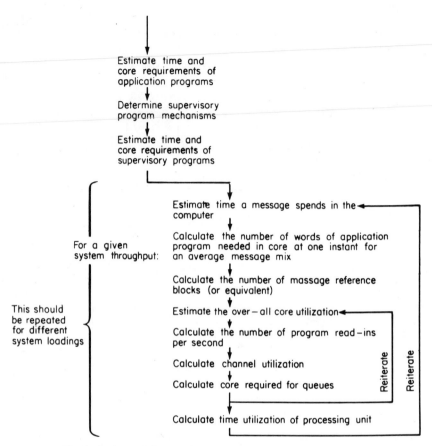

Fig. 24.2. A possible procedure for estimating the utilization of the processing unit of a multiprogrammed real-time system.

If everybody "pushes the button" at the same moment, the response time can be very long, though the likelihood of this happening is very small.

Figure 24.3 illustrates this. It shows the peaks in traffic reaching a real-time system. The system could be designed so its capacity is that represented by the line AB. It could then process all of the peaks without delay. This, however, would be wasteful, and normally systems are not designed to handle the largest peak in traffic. The system is more likely to be designed so that its capacity is represented by the line CD. In this the peaks cannot be processed as they occur but will be flattened by the system into the shaded areas under the line CD. This will lengthen the time of the system's response to these transactions, as indicated by the shading. The shaded area under the line CD is equal to that above it. If the capacity of the system was represented by line EF, then the system would be unable to process some of the transactions.

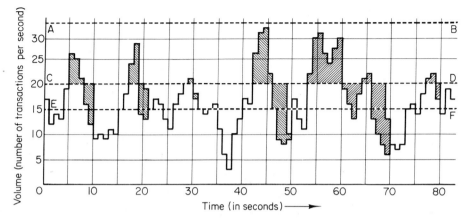

Fig. 24.3. Variation in volume of messages reaching the system. If the capacity of the system is AB, it can handle all the messages reaching it. If the capcity of the system is CD, the peaks of traffic can not be handled as they occur, but will be flattened as shown by the shaded areas below the line CD. This lengthens the response time as shown. If the capacity of the system is EF, it cannot handle all the messages reaching it.

When making statements or guarantees about the performance of a real-time system, a *probability statement* must be used. The contract for the American Airlines' SABRE system said, for example, that the system must be able to handle 90 per cent of the transactions reaching it with a response of three seconds or less. It is a statement such as this that will result from the estimating calculations.

The variation in load considerably complicates the estimating procedure. For some of the calculations in the following chapters, *this variable is removed, and the system performance for various fixed loads is examined.* Suppose that line *CD* on Fig. 24.3 represents the average load on the system in the peak hour of the peak day it is in use. This value may then be taken for evaluating channel utilization, core requirement, and so on. This calculation may need to be done for different loadings. As Fig. 24.2 suggests, the reiteration process should be cycled through for different load figures.

A load figure may be taken for the first iteration which will not be exceeded 90 per cent of the time. This load figure may be calculated, using Poisson tables, as described in Chapter 26.

Unfortunately the utilization of the various elements of the system are not directly proportional to the load. The Supervisory Programs may be written in such a way that the system degenerates, from the timing point of view, as the load increases. Similarly, the core requirement may become disproportionately high as the traffic builds up. Figures 24.4 and 24.5 illustrate this with graphs showing how the core and time are utilized on a system that uses multithread programs to give a fairly fast response time. Beyond a

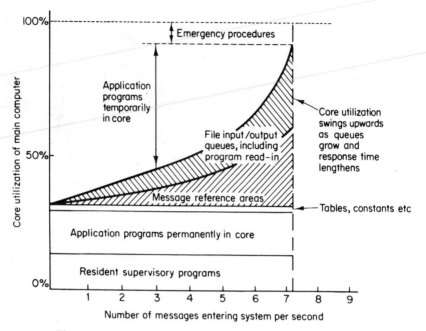

Fig. 24.4. Variation of core utilization with load on a typical system using multithread programs.

certain throughput the system degenerates, because the number of Application Programs that have to be called into core from the files increase and queues build up in core. It is important that this information should be known when designing the system, and it is suggested that curves, such as those in Figs. 24.4 and 24.5 should be drawn.

Such curves drawn for the file-response time, or the over-all response time obtained at the terminals, may take on a variety of different shapes. It is useful to plot a curve against throughput of the mean response time and also the standard deviation of response time of the over-all system or of subsystems within the whole. It is only by knowing the shape of such a curve that a designer will obtain a feel for the behavioral characteristics of the system he is putting together.

A skillful driver has an excellent feel for the behavioral characteristics of his car. He knows that if he depresses the accelerator too suddenly, the acceleration of the car will not immediately be proportional to the foot pressure. He knows that he can take a certain bend at 30 miles per hour in third gear, but if he drives at that speed in fourth gear he will end up in the ditch. We need similarly to have a feel for the behavior of the real-time computer system we are designing or thinking of purchasing. Unfortunately, we do not understand its behavioral characteristics instinctively. Often

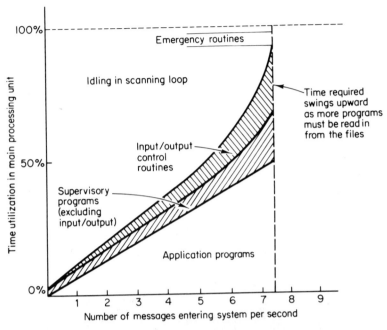

Fig. 24.5. Variation of time utilization of main processing unit with load, on a typical system using multithread programming.

indeed our intuitive feeling can lead us surprisingly astray. It improves with practice, of course, but in general it is not to be trusted. It can be observed that most people's intuition about the behavior of real-time systems leads them to make the wrong guess sufficiently frequently for it to be dangerous. We need to calculate how the system will behave and express the results of our calculations in such a way that the implications can be clearly grasped.

Figure 24.6 gives some typical curves that show how response times vary with the system throughput. The upper curves relate to file actions. The lower curves give the over-all response time obtained at the terminal. The curves all swing upward as the congestion in the system increases, just as the time to drive through a city increases with the number of vehicles on the streets. The times in the upper curves are for one file access. Many transactions will need more than one file access and so several of these times must be added together. The times in the lower curves are the over-all times to get a response from the system. A number of different elements of time will have been added together to obtain these figures.

The slope of the curves give an indication of the *stability* of the system. The system illustrated in diagram (1), for example, is fairly stable. Suppose that this is the system for an application which normally expects two transactions per second in the peak hour. If there is a sudden but temporary

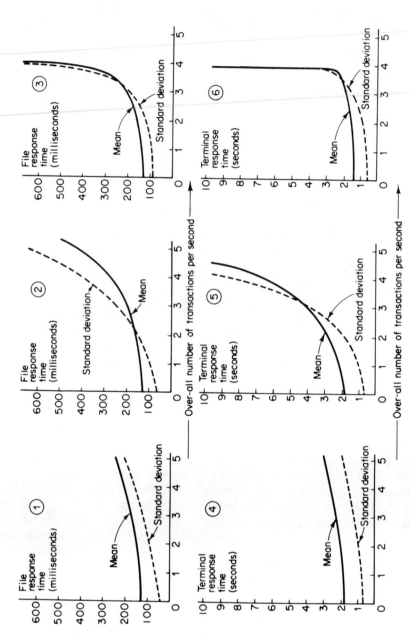

Fig. 24.6. System stability. Some typical examples of variation of response time with throughput.

rise in the demands on the system and for a period the throughput rises to 4 transactions per second, the system will be able to handle this without a noticeably bad degradation of performance. If the system in diagram (5), however, is planned for two transactions per second, this will be less stable. A temporary rise to four transactions per second will provide a decided rise in the mean response time. Also the standard deviation of response time has risen severely, and so now a significant proportion of transactions will have to wait a long time for a response. By a rough approximation, 10 per cent will have to wait more than 16 seconds; five per cent will have to wait more than 22 seconds.

With the system in diagram (6) the situation is still worse. Here two transactions per second are handled comfortably with a low response time, but if the throughput doubles temporarily the system will be completely unable to handle it. The traffic will back up endlessly like a Friday evening rush hour when the roads become blocked.

The system in diagram (6) is particularly dangerous if the designer has not investigated the whole shape of the curve. He may have explored that part between 1 and 3 transactions per second, perhaps using the simulation techniques discussed in the next chapter. In this case, his results will look good and he will be ignorant of the fact that the system is going to seize up between three and four transactions per second. (Many of the simulation studies the author has examined have investigated only one point on the curve.)

The shape of the curve in diagram (6), misleading though it is if you omit that part to the right of three transactions per second, is typical of many actual systems. The sudden swoop upwards is often caused by one particular bottleneck which does not contribute in a major way to the over-all response time when the throughput is low, but nevertheless reaches its maximum throughput at this point. The bottleneck might be a file system such as that in diagram (3).

It is also very important that the designer understand what the effect will be of errors in his basic assumptions or basic estimates. What will be the effect if the estimates of program size are off by 50 per cent? What if the messages are longer than estimated, or the number of file references greater? Sometimes the system behavior will change sharply when these figures are changed, and again this change is often not intuitively apparent to the designer. He should therefore do calculations to measure what changes might occur.

It is possible that any bottleneck in the system can cause the system to degenerate as the load increases. Which bottlenecks are likely to be critical depends upon the balance between the nine factors described in the last chapter. The aim in designing a system is to widen all bottlenecks so that transactions flow easily through the system without excessive queues forming. The result of any bottleneck is that queues form when the load on the system is high, just as they form in a cafeteria at lunch time. These queues may be inside the system or outside it, depending upon its mechanisms. On some systems it is acceptable to stop polling terminals when the load increases and so force the queues to be outside the system at the terminals. On other systems the queues may form inside the system and be temporarily stored in core or in an overflow file on disk, drum, or tape. With some types of Supervisory Programs the queues cause an increase in the use of core storage so that, when the load exceeds a certain level, the system becomes clogged and degenerates rapidly.

The results of the estimating process should be summarized so that management or senior systems analysts can quickly appraise the system and see which of the potential bottlenecks are dangerous. A table may be drawn up showing the facility utilization at different throughput figures of the various critical factors given in the last chapter. Table 24.1 gives an example of the way this can be done for a typical system. Such a table is used in monitoring the implementation progress.

The data in the right-hand column give the maximum values for the utilization of the various system facilities. If any of these are exceeded, then queues build up rapidly, the system becomes unstable, and the load will not be handled adequately. Note that the maximum utilization figures are not all the same. A large queue is more tolerable for some facilities than for others. If the facility takes a long time to handle each transaction, then a large queue will have a more serious effect on the system. Reasonable maximum values may be found in investigating the system with a simulation model as described in the next chapter.

Looking at the column in Table 24.1 for the peak hour of 1967, we see that a reasonably well-balanced system has been designed. The confidence associated with the estimate of the programs, however, is low. The person who has filled in the form has written that the program read-in area utilization could be 200 per cent higher. This is obviously, then, one area that needs to be watched carefully. Also disk A2 has 51.9 per cent utilization and a confidence factor which indicates that this could go up above its 60 per cent maximum. Similarly, the controller's cathode-ray tubes could go above their maximum. These items have been circled.

In the column for the peak hour of 1972 some items already exceed their maximum. If the system has the growth rate anticipated, additional lines, terminals, and disk files will apparently be necessary. It seems likely that more core will have to be added, although possibly a core reorganization will give more communication buffers. File I/O areas and message reference blocks will suffice.

To obtain estimates such as these on a complex system, simulation or the use of queuing theory will be needed. These are described and appraised in the next two chapters. The following chapters discuss in detail the evalua-

SYSTEM EVALUATION SUMMARY DATE: 1.1.66		Average 1967 CPU 1	CPU 2	Peak hour Peak day 1967 CPU 1	CPU 2	Peak hour Peak day 1972 CPU 1	CPU 2	Confidence factor (utilization could be higher) ....%	Recommended maximum for mean utilization (%) CPU 1	CPU 2
Processing unit	Processing time	14.8	8	22.2	12	33.3	18	150	80	80
	Processing time and file wait time	26.8	16	38.7	24	58.1	36	150	80	80
Core	Communication buffers	33.4	—	50.1	—	75.2	—	20	65	65
	File I/O area	32.1	15.6	48.2	23.1	72.3	34.7	30	70	70
	Program read-in area	27.1	20.5	40.7	30.8	61.1	46.2	200	70	70
	Message reference	33.5	—	50.3	—	75.5	—	50	70	70
	Fixed program area	50.0	20	50.0	20	50.0	20	150	95	95
	Total	31.4	17.4	47.2	26.2	70.8	39.3	80	70	70
File heads	Drum average	33.7		50.6		75.9		60	80	
	Disc A1	28.0		42.1		63.2		30	60	
	Disc A2	34.6		51.9		77.9		30	60	
	Disc B–G average	23.5		35.3		53.0		20	60	
	Mass storage file	13.6		20.4		30.6		20	60	
Channels	Selector 1	13.3		20.0		30.0		30	75	
	Selector 2	17.8		26.7		40.1		30	75	
	Multiplexor	9.0		13.5		20.1		20	70	
Lines	High speed A	36.2		54.4		81.6		20	75	
	High speed B	34.4		51.6		77.4		20	75	
	High speed C	20.5		30.8		46.2		20	75	
	Average low speed	27.6		41.4		62.1		20	60	
Concen‑trators	A	22.6		34.0		51.0		20	75	
	B	21.8		32.7		49.1		20	75	
	C	13.8		20.7		31.1		20	70	
Terminals (including human delays)	Controllers' cathode-ray tubes	33.3		50.0		75.0		40	60	
	Printers, London, average	37.4		56.2		84.3		20	70	
	Printers, Birmingham, average	27.2		40.8		61.2		20	70	
	Printers, Manchester, average	29.1		42.2		63.3		20	70	
	Printers, Glasgow, average	14.6		21.9		32.9		20	70	
	Printers, Northampton, average	17.2		25.9		38.9		20	70	
ram										

Table 24.1. A management summary, produced periodically, of estimated utilizations of various system facilities.

tion of various elements of the system, such as files, communication lines, core, processing time, and input/output buffers.

25 SIMULATION

One of the most powerful tools that can be used in estimating the requirements of a system is simulation.

A program is written on an existing computer to act as a *model* of the system in question. It behaves in some aspects like the system but vastly simplified. A few steps of program may represent, for example, transactions entering a buffer area and being allocated a core block; others represent file channels, seek arms, characters flowing on a communication line, or even customers walking into a bank. When the model is built, input will be fed to it for a period of time, which represents the volumes and types of traffic that the actual operational system will have to deal with. The simulation program then prints out certain statistics about the behavior of the model, such as what queues develop, what response times are obtained, how heavily the various critical factors are loaded.

A model may be built in this way of the entire system or of parts of the system. There may be a model of the communications network alone, of the file channels and read/write mechanism, and so on. The model will specify the speed or size of the various elements, the logical interaction between the units, the time transactions spend tying up various facilities, such as program times and seek times. The input will fluctuate in the same way as the input to the actual operational system, so that queue length and response times will vary from moment to moment. The model will produce statistics on how they vary, show what proportion of transactions are delayed, by what amount, and so on.

Typical of the output of a simulator program will be

1. The maximum and average queue sizes wherever queues occur.

2. A histogram of the transit or response times between selected points in the system.

3. The facility utilization, or extent to which various elements of the system are loaded.

4. The storage requirements for buffering or queuing.

5. The maximum throughput of the model.

The models, once built, can be adjusted and experimented with easily and endlessly. Different volumes and perhaps types of throughput can be fed to a model to see how it behaves. The effects of changes can be easily investigated. Extra communication lines can be added, core sizes can be changed, channels speeded up, programming mechanisms modified. The models can form a tool for deciding between alternative modes of operation. They may be used to settle arguments as to the merits of different programming techniques or file configurations. As the various design factors of the system come more sharply into focus, the models can be refined. More accurate program estimates become available and the models present an increasingly accurate representation of the behavior of the system.

Simulation is thus a very valuable technique for monitoring and assisting the *implementation* of a system. As programming work proceeds and the network design is refined, the effects on the system of any changes can be investigated by simulation.

At the *survey* stage, however, it is often difficult because of time pressures and manpower shortage to construct a model of sufficient detail to be worthwhile. Programming and debugging such a model can take a long time. Furthermore, in the early stages the input data may not be sufficiently good for this elaborate technique.

The following chapter discusses when in the estimating process simulation is warranted and when easier techniques are satisfactory. It describes how simple mathematical analysis can form an alternative to simulation in the early reiterations of the system survey. Meanwhile, this chapter outlines the techniques that are available for obtaining a suitable model and indicates some of the dangers inherent in this technique.

TYPES OF SIMULATOR PROGRAM
There are three levels of simulator program. *First*, a complete simulator program for the type of equipment in question may be available. By compiling it with appropriate parameter and control cards, the desired model is produced without any program writing. The traffic pattern under consideration is fed to it, and it will produce the required statistics.

Some computer manufacturers produce programs of this type for parts of their equipment. A number of simulators exist, for example, for examining the behavior of communication lines with different numbers of terminals, different positions of concentrators, and different traffic patterns.

If such a complete simulator exists, it can be used with little effort to produce the design figures for that part of the equipment it relates to. However, except for relatively simple systems, there is not likely at present to be such a program that covers the whole system. Possibly a communication-line simulator exists, but such programs for the file actions and processing unit may have to be written for individual cases. Often nothing exists that is applicable in detail. This is partly because of the great variety of design possibilities in real-time systems. No doubt as this technology matures, package simulators will become more common.

Second, at the other extreme, the model may have to be programmed in the normal computer language. This can be quite complicated and may take a long time. It usually needs some ingenuity to construct a satisfactory model in this way.

Third, a variety of *general-purpose simulation languages* are available. These are languages which permit the system to be described with relative ease and from which the model may be compiled. They can be highly flexible and can simulate almost any system mechanism. Adjustments to the logic of the flow of work through the system can be examined easily. A model written in such a language can be steadily increased in complexity or detail until it represents very accurately the behavior of a system.

Use of a simulation language is the most common method of tackling system simulations today, and it is worthwhile to describe the use of such a language in more detail. There are several such languages available. A commonly used one is IBM's GENERAL PURPOSE SYSTEMS SIMULATOR, GPSS III, the third of a series of languages—the first of which was known as the "Gordon simulator" after its designer Geoffrey Gordon. GPSS III is described below. Other simulation languages are referenced at the end of this chapter. They include SIMSCRIPT, SIMPAC, SIMULA, CSL, along with several others less widely used.

A GENERAL-PURPOSE SIMULATOR LANGUAGE

To produce a simulation model with GPSS III, a block diagram is first drawn using blocks, each having certain functions which help describe the behavior of the system. The most common block types are illustrated in Fig. 25.3, and a block diagram using them is given in Fig. 25.5. The mechanisms, capacities, and timings of the system to be simulated are built into this model.

The block diagram is coded into punched cards block by block, using coding sheets of a special format. Cards are included which specify the input to the system and say how long the model should be run. Certain transactions can be given priorities, and peak loads can be studied. The output of the program will give statistics about the utilization of the various parts of the system. It will say how many transactions occupy parts of the system at one time, what queues develop, what response times are obtained, and so on.

The simulator operates by effectively moving transactions through the model a block at a time. These events occur in the same time sequence as they would in the actual system. The program maintains a record of the elapsed clock time at which each event would occur on the working system. It thus updates a clock record appropriately.

Certain blocks have a time period associated with them. For example, a group of blocks which represent the seek action of a random-access file have a block which gives the time of this. This time may not be constant. It may not even be predictable, as it may depend upon the previous setting of the seek mechanism. The time may therefore, have a range of values, or it may be given by a function. It is often given as a *mean* and a *spread*; thus, for a seek time ranging from 40 to 120, it is 80 ± 40.

A transaction leaving one block normally passes to the next. However, a TRANSFER block can be used to direct the transaction to any other block. This may be an unvarying transfer or it may be a choice that is determined by a variety of conditions. For example, a certain *proportion* of the transactions may always go one way. Various logic conditions may determine the route taken: a route representing a "seek" may not be taken until both the arm and the channel required become free. A transaction may LOOP around a certain path several times as does a computer program. Again, the transaction may always go to Block *A*, but if Block *A* cannot accept it, it goes to Block *B*.

When a transaction enters a block, the particular event specified by that block occurs immediately. After this, the transaction attempts to move to the next block. However, if the program cannot execute the action called for in this next block, the transaction remains where it is until the condition causing the delay changes. It could in this way, for example, represent a car waiting for a traffic light to change, or an item in a computer waiting for a file reference to be completed. The transactions jerk their way through the model with the program simulating the delays and queues that would be found in actuality.

The items of equipment to be simulated are divided into two categories. Certain items can only handle one transaction at a time. For example, a computer channel can, in many cases, only transmit one record. This type of item is referred to as a *facility*. If a *facility* is occupied, other transactions for this facility have to wait, and so a queue forms.

Alternatively, an item of equipment may be able to have multiple occupancy. It is then referred to as a *storage*. A storage has a *capacity of so many* transactions. This capacity is stated in the cards defining the model. Examples of *storages* are an area of dynamically allocated core, and a message concentrator which can hold a limited number of messages.

A number of block types relate to *facilities*. A SEIZE block is one which initiates the use of the facility by a transaction. If the facility is already in use, the SEIZE block cannot be entered. The transaction must wait in the previous block until the facility becomes free, and it will then immediately enter the SEIZE block. Often the block immediately preceding a SEIZE block is a QUEUE block. This will measure statistics about the transactions queuing for the facility. The block after the SEIZE block will then normally be a DEPART block, saying that the transaction has obtained the facility and so is no longer in the queue. The transaction can, if so desired, hold the facility for a long period of time while other operations take place. When it eventually leaves the facility, this is denoted by a RELEASE block for that facility.

This procedure is illustrated simply in Fig. 25.1. Here Facility 5 may be the channel of a computer. A transaction needs to use the channel to write a record; however, the channel may be busy. It waits in Block 1 until the channel is free. It can then enter Block 2. It passes immediately through Block 3 to Block 4. Blocks 1 and 3 have measured the length of time the transaction queued the channel and statistics of this queue will be tabulated under the heading of Queue Number 3, as marked in the blocks. Block 4 represents the time taken to write the record. In this example, the mean time is 85 (probably milliseconds) and the time follows a distribution given by Function 6, as marked in Block 4. Function 6 is specified in detail elsewhere in the program. When the record is written, the channel is released by RELEASE Block 5. Facility 5 can then be used by other transactions. All of the blocks relating to a facility give the number of that facility.

Storages are handled in a similar manner. An ENTER block causes a transaction to enter a specified storage. If the storage is already full to capacity, the transaction must wait, and cannot enter the ENTER block until another

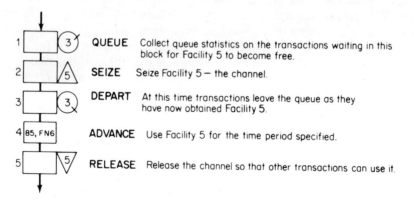

Figure 25.1

transaction leaves the storage. Again QUEUE and DEPART blocks may be used to measure the queues that form. A transaction may occupy a storage for some time while other operations go on, and then it leaves by means of a LEAVE block. As seen before, these blocks give the number of the storage in question.

Figure 25.2 illustrates the use of a storage. This might illustrate, for example, a remote buffer or concentrator relaying messages from a computer. The core of the device can hold, say, 20 messages. We, therefore, represent it by a storage of capacity 20. The messages try to enter Storage 1 in Block 2. If Storage 1 is already full, they will have to wait and so we again use QUEUE and DEPART Block 1 and 3 to collect statistics on the delay. Block 4 gives the time it takes the message to enter the concentrator. The mean time is 85 (milliseconds) and this is multiplied by Function 6 to represent the distribution of message lengths. When it is in the concentrator, it must SEIZE an outgoing line. This is done in Block 5. The line selected has the number in Parameter 2 of the message and this causes the appropriate facility to be seized. The facility may be already occupied by other traffic, possibly incoming traffic, and in this case the message waits in the concentrator until the facility becomes free. Block 6 gives the time it takes the message to be transmitted out. This is on a slower line and so the mean time is higher: 967 (milliseconds).

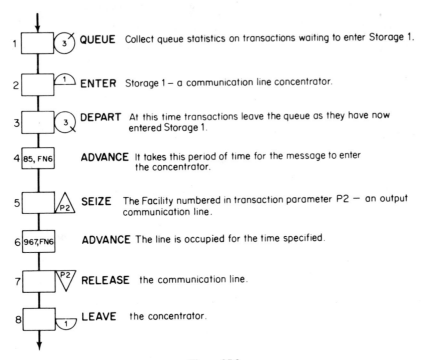

Figure 25.2

GENERATE	Creates new transactions and enters them into the system. A variety of ways of specifying time intervals are possible.
TERMINATE	Removes transactions from the system.
ADVANCE	A transaction can enter this block unconditionally and remains for the time period stated.
SEIZE	The transaction takes control of the stated facility if it is free.
RELEASE	The transaction releases control of the facility.
PREEMPT	The transaction takes control of the stated facility even if it was previously occupied by another transaction. It cannot do this if the occupying transaction had itself preempted the facility.
RETURN	The transaction which gained control of the facility with the PREEMPT block releases control. The preempt transaction resumed control.
ENTER	The transaction enters the stated store if there is room.
LEAVE	The transaction leaves the stated store.
QUEUE	These two blocks are used to gather queueing statistics The first is used when the transaction begins to queue, the second when it leaves the queue.
DEPART	
TRANSFER	The transaction may go to one of two blocks. A variety of criteria are permissible for specifying which path is taken.
LOOP	Causes the transaction to loop through a section of program a given number of times.
LOGIC	When a transaction enters this block, logic switches are set which may be tested elsewhere in the model.
GATE	A GATE block regulates the flow of transactions through the system depending upon certain logic conditions. A variety of logic conditions can be tested, for example, storage full or empty facility in use or not, facility preempted or not, logic switches set, and so on. One type of GATE block bars the path of transactions; another transfers them to specified blocks.
MARK	The time when the transaction enters this block is marked in it and can later be tabulated.
ASSIGN	This block assigns value to a parameter. For example it is used in Fig. 25.5 to select which file unit the transaction is to update.
SPLIT	One transaction enters this block. Two or more identical transactions leave it. The duplicates thus created go to the block specified.
ASSEMBLE	Re-combines duplicate transactions created by a SPLIT block. When a specified number of the identical transactions have arrived, one leaves and the others are destroyed.
GATHER	Similar to an ASSEMBLE block but all of the transactions leave.

352

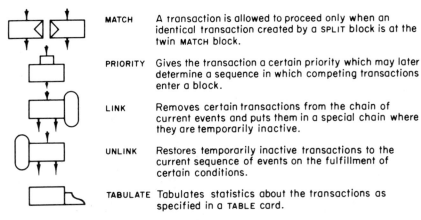

MATCH	A transaction is allowed to proceed only when an identical transaction created by a SPLIT block is at the twin MATCH block.
PRIORITY	Gives the transaction a certain priority which may later determine a sequence in which competing transactions enter a block.
LINK	Removes certain transactions from the chain of current events and puts them in a special chain where they are temporarily inactive.
UNLINK	Restores temporarily inactive transactions to the current sequence of events on the fulfillment of certain conditions.
TABULATE	Tabulates statistics about the transactions as specified in a TABLE card.

Fig. 25.3. Some of the block types used by IBM's GPSS III simulator language. The use of this is illustrated in the following three figures.

The mean time is multiplied by the same Function 6 representing the distribution of message lengths. The communication line is then released: Block 7, and the area the message occupied is freed for other use with a LEAVE block: Block 8. This of course, is an unrealistically simplified example of the mechanism of a concentrator. One message may occupy several relocatable core blocks, and considerations such as line control would complicate the model.

Other major block types are illustrated in Fig. 25.3. It is suggested that the reader examines these and then reads on to see how a file-access problem may be studied with GPSS III.

A FILE-ACCESS PROBLEM   Figure 25.4 represents the arrangement to be simulated. Transactions arriving at the computer must read a record from one of the three files, do some processing on it, and in 75 per cent of the cases update the record.

When the processing unit gives a file-read instruction, the relevant access arm will execute a seek if it is free. When the seek is complete, the record may be read, but only after the disk has rotated to the correct position and then only when the file channel shared by the other two files is free. If the channel is not free, the disk continues rotating and another attempt to read the record may be made one rotation later. Processing of the transaction can then take place when the processing unit is free. If the record is updated,

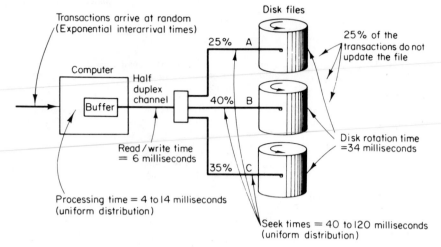

Transactions arrive at random
(Exponential interarrival times)

Disk files

Computer

Buffer

Half
duplex
channel

25% A

40% B

35% C

25% of the
transactions do not
update the file

Disk rotation time
=34 milliseconds

Read/write time
= 6 milliseconds

Processing time = 4 to 14 milliseconds
(uniform distribution)

Seek times = 40 to 120 milliseconds
(uniform distribution)

Fig. 25.4. The file access arrangement simulated in Figs. 25.5 and 25.6. This arrangement is also discussed using queuing theory in Chapter 28.

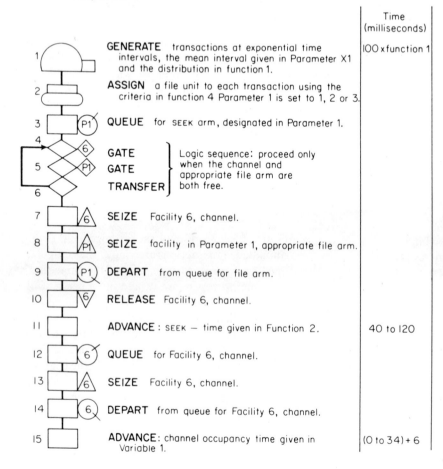

		Time (milliseconds)
1	GENERATE transactions at exponential time intervals, the mean interval given in Parameter X1 and the distribution in function 1.	100 × function 1
2	ASSIGN a file unit to each transaction using the criteria in function 4 Parameter 1 is set to 1, 2 or 3.	
3	QUEUE for SEEK arm, designated in Parameter 1.	
4	GATE	
5	GATE Logic sequence: proceed only when the channel and appropriate file arm are both free.	
6	TRANSFER	
7	SEIZE Facility 6, channel.	
8	SEIZE facility in Parameter 1, appropriate file arm.	
9	DEPART from queue for file arm.	
10	RELEASE Facility 6, channel.	
11	ADVANCE : SEEK − time given in Function 2.	40 to 120
12	QUEUE for Facility 6, channel.	
13	SEIZE Facility 6, channel.	
14	DEPART from queue for Facility 6, channel.	
15	ADVANCE: channel occupancy time given in Variable 1.	(0 to 34) + 6

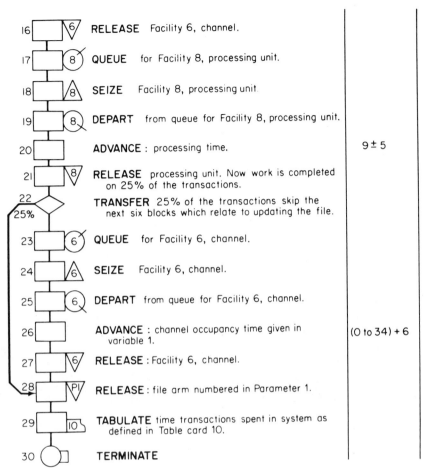

16	6 RELEASE	Facility 6, channel.	
17	8 QUEUE	for Facility 8, processing unit.	
18	8 SEIZE	Facility 8, processing unit.	
19	8 DEPART	from queue for Facility 8, processing unit.	
20	ADVANCE :	processing time.	9 ± 5
21	8 RELEASE	processing unit. Now work is completed on 25% of the transactions.	
22 25%	TRANSFER	25% of the transactions skip the next six blocks which relate to updating the file.	
23	6 QUEUE	for Facility 6, channel.	
24	6 SEIZE	Facility 6, channel.	
25	6 DEPART	from queue for Facility 6, channel.	
26	ADVANCE :	channel occupancy time given in variable 1.	$(0 \text{ to } 34) + 6$
27	6 RELEASE :	Facility 6, channel.	
28	P1 RELEASE :	file arm numbered in Parameter 1.	
29	10 TABULATE	time transactions spent in system as defined in Table card 10.	
30	TERMINATE		

Fig. 25.5. Block diagram for simulating the file system shown in Fig. 25.4.

no new seek will be necessary but the rest of the procedure will be similar to reading the record. Of the transactions, 25 per cent refer to file A, 40 per cent to file B and 35 per cent to file C. The timings for this are given in Fig. 25.4.

There will be queues of transactions in the computer waiting for the seeks. The simulation model will measure the sizes of the queues for the channel and for each arm by means of QUEUE and DEPART blocks. Statistics will be gathered about the over-all times that the process takes on the transactions. Figure 25.5 is the block diagram for this simulation, somewhat simplified. The GENERATE block creates the transactions at appropriate time intervals. The time intervals can be defined by any given *function*. In many simulations they are *exponentially distributed*, as is the case here. This means that individual transactions arrive at random times. It is an assumption that is discussed in the next chapter.

When the transactions are generated they are *marked* with the clock time so that statistics about timing can be gathered later by the TABULATE block, 29.

In this model, Facilities 1, 2, and 3 represent the three access arms A, B, and C. A file unit is assigned to each transaction by Block 2. This uses a function to assign Facility 1 to 25 per cent of the transactions, Facility 2 to 40 per cent and Facility 3 to 35 per cent. The relevant facility number is held

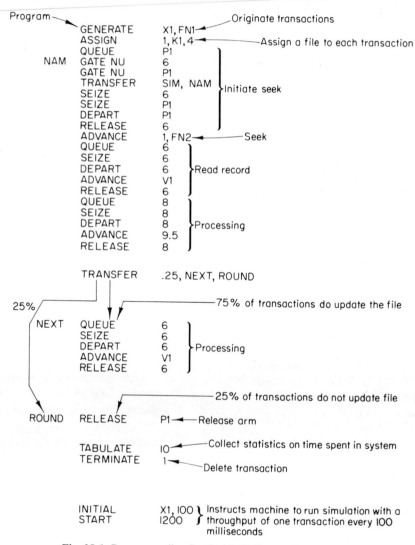

Fig. 25.6. Program coding for the block diagram in Fig. 25.5.

in a parameter P1, always associated with that transaction throughout its life in the system. In this way, Blocks 3, 5, 8, 9, and 28 know which file unit is refererred to.

Facility 6 represents the channel and Facility 8 represents the processing units. It will be seen that the model collects queue statistics for each of the facilities.

The transactions flow through the model as shown in Fig 25.5. The program for the model is shown in Fig. 25.6. The model will be run for a certain period of time to allow the system to fill up with transactions, and to allow the queues to stabilize. Then it will be run for another period to collect statistics.

OUTPUT OF
THE MODEL

When the model had stabilized, it was run with a mean input rate of one transaction every 100 milliseconds for a period which represents several minutes of actual operation. Examining the results, we find that 14,922 transactions had completely passed through the model, reaching Block 30.

Table 25.1 shows the utilization of the various facilities. If the utilization

Table 25.1. STATISTICS SHOWING THE UTILIZATION OF FACILITIES

	FACILITY NUMBER	AVERAGE UTILIZATION	NUMBER ENTRIES	AVERAGE TIME/TRANS
File-access arm A	1	0.337	3715	136.110
File-access arm B	2	0.525	5884	134.021
File-access arm C	3	0.477	5324	134.598
Channel	6	0.393	41034	14.381
Processing Unit	8	0.089	14922	9.024
		Fraction of the time the facility is utilized	Number of transactions using the facility. (Note: transaction SEIZES Facility 6 two or three times)	Average time a transaction occupies the facility (in milliseconds)

is high then the queues that build up will be greater, as is discussed mathematically in the next chapter. The QUEUE blocks give us statistics on these queues as is shown in Table 25.2. Note here that the number of items queuing for file-access arm B reaches a maximum of 9. With a higher transaction throughput the number will be higher than this. It is then apparent that we must think about the mechanisms of the Supervisory Program and ask: "Can we handle this number of items in the buffer areas allocated?" If not the model must be modified appropriately.

Table 25.2. STATISTICS OF THE QUEUES THAT BUILD UP

	QUEUE NUMBER	MAXIMUM CONTENTS	AVERAGE CONTENTS	TOTAL ENTRIES	ZERO ENTRIES	PER CENT ZEROS	AVERAGE TIME/TRANS	AVERAGE
File-access arm A	1	5	0.101	3,715	1,719	46.2	40.853	76.036
File-access arm B	2	9	0.344	5,884	2,022	34.3	87.875	133.884
File-access arm C	3	7	0.235	5,324	2,058	38.6	66.370	108.191
Channel	6	2	0.087	26,111	18,565	71.1	5.054	17.488
Processing Unit	8	1	0.001	14,922	14,681	98.3	0.053	3.302
		Maximum queue size at any one time	Average queue size	Total transactions that enter the QUEUE block	Total transactions passing through QUEUE block with no queuing	Percentage of transactions with no queuing	Average time a transaction waits in the queue	Average wait, not including transactions passing through without queuing.

Table 25.3. STATISTICS OF THE TRANSIT TIMES AS GATHERED BY TABULATE BLOCK 29

TABLE 10
ENTRIES IN TABLE
14,922

MEAN TRANSIT TIME
(milliseconds)
205.51

STANDARD DEVIATION OF
TRANSIT TIME
113.562

UPPER LIMIT	OBSERVED FREQUENCY	PER CENT OF TOTAL	CUMULATIVE PERCENTAGE	CUMULATIVE REMAINDER	MULTIPLE OF MEAN	DEVIATION FROM MEAN
100	1053	7.05	7.0	92.9	0.486	−0.929
150	4393	29.44	36.4	63.5	0.729	−0.489
200	4063	27.23	63.7	36.2	0.972	−0.048
250	1881	12.60	76.3	23.6	1.216	0.391
300	1311	8.78	85.1	14.8	1.459	0.831
350	821	5.50	90.6	9.3	1.702	1.271
400	483	3.23	93.8	6.1	1.945	1.712
450	299	2.00	95.8	4.1	2.189	2.152
500	202	1.35	97.2	2.7	2.432	2.592
550	129	0.86	98.0	1.9	2.675	3.033
600	93	0.62	98.7	1.2	2.918	3.473
650	57	0.38	99.0	0.9	3.162	3.913
700	48	0.32	99.4	0.5	3.405	4.353
750	19	0.12	99.5	0.4	3.648	4.794
800	24	0.16	99.6	0.3	3.891	5.234
850	10	0.06	99.7	0.2	4.135	5.674
900	12	0.08	99.8	0.1	4.378	6.115
950	7	0.04	99.8	0.1	4.621	6.555
1000	3	0.02	99.9	0	4.864	6.995
1050	5	0.03	99.9	0	5.108	7.435
1100	3	0.02	99.9	0	5.351	7.876
1150	1	0	99.9	0	5.594	8.316
1200	1	0	99.9	0	5.837	8.756
1250	1	0	99.9	0	6.081	9.197
1300	2	0.01	100.0	0	6.324	9.637

90 percentile level

90 per cent of the transactions have transit times less than 350 milliseconds.

Transit times

Frequency of those times occurring

Remaining frequencies are all zero.

359

Table 25.3A. A SECOND EXAMPLE OF TABLE NUMBER 10, IN WHICH THE THROUGHPUT HAS BEEN RAISED BY 50 PER CENT

TABLE NUMBER 10
ENTRIES IN TABLE
14,922

MEAN TRANSIT TIME
(milliseconds)
504.45

STANDARD DEVIATION OF
TRANSIT TIME
448.02

UPPER LIMIT	OBSERVED FREQUENCY	PER CENT OF TOTAL	CUMULATIVE PERCENTAGE	CUMULATIVE REMAINDER	MULTIPLE OF MEAN	DEVIATION FROM MEAN
1250	43	0.45	92.4	7.6	2.478	1.659
1300	42	0.44	92.8	7.2	2.577	1.772
1350	49	0.52	93.3	6.7	2.676	1.885
1400	43	0.45	93.7	6.3	2.775	1.997
1450	49	0.52	94.2	5.8	2.874	2.108
1500	47	0.50	94.7	5.3	2.973	2.220
1550	30	0.32	95.0	5.0	3.072	2.331
1600	46	0.49	95.5	4.5	3.172	2.443
1650	31	0.33	95.9	4.1	3.271	2.554
1700	27	0.28	96.1	3.9	3.370	2.666
1750	43	0.45	96.6	3.4	3.469	2.777
1800	30	0.32	96.9	3.1	3.568	2.889
1850	32	0.34	97.2	2.8	3.667	3.000
1900	31	0.33	97.6	2.4	3.766	3.112
1950	42	0.44	98.0	2.0	3.865	3.223
2000	26	0.27	98.3	1.7	3.964	3.335
2050	24	0.25	98.5	1.5	4.064	3.446
2100	35	0.37	98.9	1.1	4.163	3.558

Table 25.3A. (CONT.)

| | | | MEAN TRANSIT TIME (milliseconds) 504.45 | | | STANDARD DEVIATION OF TRANSIT TIME 448.02 | |
UPPER LIMIT	OBSERVED FREQUENCY	PER CENT OF TOTAL	CUMULATIVE PERCENTAGE	CUMULATIVE REMAINDER	MULTIPLE OF MEAN	DEVIATION FROM MEAN
2150	23	0.24	99.2	0.8	4.262	3.669
2200	27	0.28	99.4	0.6	4.361	3.781
2250	13	0.14	99.6	0.4	4.460	3.892
2300	7	0.07	99.7	0.3	4.559	4.004
2350	9	0.09	99.7	0.3	4.658	4.115
2400	7	0.07	99.8	0.2	4.757	4.227
2450	4	0.04	99.9	0.1	4.856	4.338
2500	2	0.02	99.9	0.1	4.956	4.450
2550	4	0.04	99.9	0.1	5.055	4.561
2600	3	0.03	100.0	0.0	5.154	4.673
2650	1	0.01	100.0	0.0	5.253	4.784
2700	1	0.01	100.0	0.0	5.352	4.896
2750	0	0.00	100.0	0.0	5.451	5.007
2800	1	0.01	100.0	0.0	5.550	5.119
2850	1	0.01	100.0	0.0	5.649	5.230

Remaining frequencies are all zero.

361

Table 25.4. SOME OF THE STATISTICS PRINTED ABOUT THE QUEUE FOR FILE ARM B

TABLE NUMBER 2
ENTRIES IN TABLE 2320
MEAN ARGUMENT 87.875
STANDARD DEVIATION 119.547

UPPER LIMIT	OBSERVED FREQUENCY	PER CENT OF TOTAL	CUMULATIVE PERCENTAGE	CUMULATIVE REMAINDER	MULTIPLE OF MEAN	DEVIATION FROM MEAN
0	841	36.25	36.2	63.8	0.000	−0.687
20	259	11.16	47.4	52.6	0.244	−0.519
40	179	7.72	55.1	44.9	0.487	−0.352
60	107	4.61	59.7	40.3	0.731	−0.185
80	101	4.35	64.1	35.9	0.975	−0.017
100	108	4.66	68.7	31.3	1.218	0.150
120	114	4.91	73.7	26.3	1.462	0.317
140	87	3.75	77.4	22.6	1.706	0.485
160	86	3.71	81.1	18.9	1.950	0.652
180	79	3.41	84.5	15.5	2.193	0.819
200	53	2.28	86.8	13.2	2.437	0.986
220	34	1.47	88.3	11.7	2.681	1.154
240	43	1.85	90.1	9.9	2.924	1.321
260	49	2.11	92.2	7.8	3.168	1.488
280	29	1.25	93.5	6.5	3.412	1.656
300	26	1.12	94.6	5.4	3.655	1.823
320	23	0.99	95.6	4.4	3.899	1.990
340	16	0.69	96.3	3.7	4.143	2.158
360	12	0.52	96.8	3.2	4.386	2.325
380	7	0.30	97.1	2.9	4.630	2.492
400	4	0.17	97.3	2.7	4.874	2.659
420	5	0.22	97.5	2.5	5.118	2.827
440	4	0.17	97.7	2.3	5.361	2.994
460	7	0.30	98.0	2.0	5.605	3.161
480	9	0.39	98.4	1.6	5.849	3.329

Annotations:

Time spent waiting for file arm B

Frequency of these times occurring

90 percentile level. Ten per cent of transactions using file arm B must wait 220 milliseconds to obtain it.

362

Table 25.4. (CONT.)

TABLE NUMBER 2
ENTRIES IN TABLE 3794

MEAN ARGUMENT 600.127

STANDARD DEVIATION 567.203

UPPER LIMIT	OBSERVED FREQUENCY	PER CENT OF TOTAL	CUMULATIVE PERCENTAGE	CUMULATIVE REMAINDER	MULTIPLE OF MEAN	DEVIATION FROM MEAN
500	6	0.26	98.6	1.4	6.092	3.496
520	5	0.22	98.8	1.2	6.336	3.663
540	1	0.04	98.9	1.1	6.580	3.831
560	2	0.09	99.0	1.0	6.823	3.998
580	3	0.13	99.1	0.9	7.067	4.165
600	3	0.13	99.2	0.8	7.311	4.332
620	2	0.09	99.3	0.7	7.554	4.500
640	3	0.13	99.4	0.6	7.798	4.667
660	3	0.13	99.6	0.4	8.042	4.834
680	1	0.04	99.6	0.4	8.285	5.002
700	1	0.04	99.7	0.3	8.529	5.169
720	1	0.04	99.7	0.3	8.773	5.336
740	2	0.09	99.8	0.2	9.017	5.504
760	1	0.04	99.8	0.2	9.260	5.671
780	1	0.04	99.9	0.1	9.504	5.838
800	1	0.04	99.9	0.1	9.748	6.005
820	0	0.00	99.9	0.1	9.991	6.173
840	0	0.00	99.9	0.1	10.235	6.340
860	1	0.04	100.0	0	10.479	6.507
880	0	0.00	100.0	0	10.722	6.675
900	0	0.00	100.0	0	10.966	6.842
920	0	0.00	100.0	0	11.210	7.009
940	1	0.04	100.0	0	11.453	7.176

Remaining frequencies are all zero.

Table 25.5. ON THE BRINK OF DISASTER*

16 Transactions per second:

FACILITY NUMBER	AVERAGE UTILI-ZATION	QUEUE NUMBER	MAXIMUM CONTENTS	AVERAGE CONTENTS	AVERAGE TIME/ TRANS
1	0.5779	1	8	0.51	125.68
2	0.8972	2	21	3.88	603.29
3	0.7978	3	19	2.05	363.56
6	0.6328	6	2	0.26	9.12
8	0.1446	8	1	0.00	0.08

TABLE NUMBER 10

	MEAN ARGUMENT 543.508		STANDARD DEVIATION 487.766	
UPPER LIMIT	OBSERVED FREQUENCY	PER CENT OF TOTAL	CUMULATIVE PERCENTAGE	CUMULATIVE REMAINDER
2000	37	0.38	98.0	2.0
2050	24	0.25	98.2	1.8
2100	13	0.13	98.4	1.6
2150	23	0.24	98.6	1.4
2200	19	0.20	98.8	1.2
2250	16	0.17	99.0	1.0
2300	16	0.17	99.1	0.9
2350	15	0.16	99.3	0.7
2400	11	0.11	99.4	0.6
2450	10	0.10	99.5	0.5
2500	3	0.03	99.5	0.5
2550	9	0.09	99.6	0.4
2600	6	0.06	99.7	0.3
2650	5	0.05	99.7	0.3
2700	5	0.05	99.8	0.2
2750	4	0.04	99.8	0.2
2800	4	0.04	99.9	0.1
2850	3	0.03	99.9	0.1
2900	2	0.02	99.9	0.1
2950	5	0.05	100.0	0.0
3000	0	0.00	100.0	0.0
3050	2	0.02	100.0	0.0

Remaining frequencies are all zero.

*The throughput is steadily increased until the system can no longer handle the load.

TABULATE Block 29 causes statistics of the transit times of the items to be listed in detail, as shown in Table 25.3. We see here that the mean transit time is 205.6 milliseconds, and standard deviation of the transit times is 113.6 milliseconds. Ninety per cent of the transactions have a transit time less than 350 milliseconds. Ninety-five per cent have a transit time of less than 450 milliseconds. The 99th percentile lies at about 650 milliseconds and the maximum time recorded for the 14,922 transactions is 1.3 seconds.

Table 25.5. (CONT.)

16.5 Transactions per second

FACILITY NUMBER	AVERAGE UTILI- ZATION	QUEUE NUMBER	MAXIMUM CONTENTS	AVERAGE CONTENTS	AVERAGE TIME/ TRANS
1	0.6190	1	9	0.64	150.77
2	0.9303	2	27	6.17	923.55
3	0.8041	3	16	1.96	332.36
6	0.6539	6	2	0.28	9.54
8	0.1492	8	1	0.00	0.09

TABLE NUMBER 10

	MEAN ARGUMENT 665.798		STANDARD DEVIATION 650.736	
UPPER LIMIT	OBSERVED FREQUENCY	PER CENT OF TOTAL	CUMULATIVE PERCENTAGE	CUMULATIVE REMAINDER
2750	22	0.22	98.0	2.0
2800	15	0.15	98.1	1.9
2850	22	0.22	98.3	1.7
2900	14	0.14	98.5	1.5
2950	17	0.17	98.7	1.3
3000	15	0.15	98.8	1.2
3050	17	0.17	99.0	1.0
3100	8	0.08	99.0	1.0
3150	13	0.13	99.2	0.8
3200	13	0.13	99.3	0.7
3250	9	0.09	99.4	0.6
3300	6	0.06	99.5	0.5
3350	5	0.05	99.5	0.5
3400	12	0.12	99.6	0.4
3450	8	0.08	99.7	0.3
3500	2	0.02	99.7	0.3
3550	6	0.06	99.8	0.2
3600	2	0.02	99.8	0.2
3650	4	0.04	99.8	0.2
3700	3	0.03	99.9	0.1
3750	2	0.02	99.9	0.1
3800	4	0.04	99.9	0.1
3850	1	0.01	99.9	0.1
3900	3	0.03	100.0	0.0
3950	1	0.01	100.0	0.0
4000	0	0.00	100.0	0.0
4050	2	0.02	100.0	0.0

Remaining frequencies are all zero.

In a similar fashion, the table cards shown in Fig. 25.6 give a detailed tabulation of the relevant queue statistics. The queue for file-access arm B is the critical one. Table 25.4 shows part of the statistics printed about this. We see that the mean time a transaction has to wait for this arm is 87.9

Table 25.5. (CONT.)

17 Transactions per second:

FACILITY NUMBER	AVERAGE UTILI-ZATION	QUEUE NUMBER	MAXIMUM CONTENTS	AVERAGE CONTENTS	AVERAGE TIME/ TRANS
1	0.6149	1	10	0.59	138.70
2	0.9406	2	33	6.70	1012.97
3	0.8363	3	17	1.99	349.68
6	0.6630	6	2	0.28	9.53
8	0.1512	8	1	0.00	0.09

TABLE NUMBER 10

MEAN ARGUMENT 704.755   STANDARD DEVIATION 780.979

UPPER LIMIT	OBSERVED FREQUENCY	PER CENT OF TOTAL	CUMULATIVE PERCENTAGE	CUMULATIVE REMAINDER
3200	21	0.21	98.0	2.0
3250	23	0.23	98.1	1.9
3300	13	0.13	98.2	1.8
3350	16	0.16	98.4	1.6
3400	16	0.16	98.5	1.5
3450	17	0.17	98.7	1.3
3500	15	0.15	98.9	1.1
3550	10	0.10	99.0	1.0
3600	11	0.11	99.1	0.9
3650	8	0.08	99.2	0.8
3700	4	0.04	99.2	0.8
3750	3	0.03	99.2	0.8
3800	4	0.04	99.3	0.7
3850	1	0.01	99.3	0.7
3900	0	0.00	99.3	0.7
3950	1	0.01	99.3	0.7
4000	0	0.00	99.3	0.7
4050	1	0.01	99.3	0.7
4100	2	0.02	99.3	0.7
4150	4	0.04	99.4	0.6
4200	4	0.04	99.4	0.6
4250	4	0.04	99.4	0.6
4300	9	0.09	99.5	0.5
4350	5	0.05	99.6	0.4
4400	4	0.04	99.6	0.4
4450	6	0.06	99.7	0.3
4500	2	0.02	99.7	0.3
4550	5	0.05	99.8	0.2
4600	6	0.06	99.8	0.2
4650	3	0.03	99.8	0.2
4700	5	0.05	99.9	0.1
4750	5	0.05	99.9	0.1
4800	3	0.03	100.0	0.0
4850	1	0.01	100.0	0.0
4900	1	0.01	100.0	0.0

Remaining frequencies are all zero.

Table 25.5. (CONT.)

17.5 Transactions per second:

FACILITY NUMBER	AVERAGE UTILI-ZATION	QUEUE NUMBER	MAXIMUM CONTENTS	AVERAGE CONTENTS	AVEAGE TIME/ TRANS
1	0.6319	1	8	0.68	156.76
2	0.9994	2	112	57.92	8097.59
3	0.8855	3	19	3.16	510.08
6	0.6923	6	2	0.31	10.08
8	0.1571	8	1	0.00	.09

TABLE NUMBER 10

	MEAN ARGUMENT 3609.910		STANDARD DEVIATION 4576.542	
UPPER LIMIT	OBSERVED FREQUENCY	PER CENT OF TOTAL	CUMULATIVE PERCENTAGE	CUMULATIVE REMAINDER
14050	9	0.09	98.0	2.0
14100	11	0.10	98.1	1.9
14150	10	0.10	98.2	1.8
14200	11	0.10	98.3	1.7
14250	9	0.09	98.4	1.6
14300	10	0.10	98.5	1.5
14350	10	0.10	98.6	1.4
14400	16	0.15	98.7	1.3
14450	8	0.08	98.8	1.2
14500	4	0.04	98.8	1.2
14550	5	0.05	98.9	1.1
14600	5	0.05	98.9	1.1
14650	7	0.07	99.0	1.0
14700	3	0.03	99.0	1.0
14750	18	0.17	99.2	0.8
14800	10	0.10	99.3	0.7
14850	10	0.10	99.4	0.6
14900	10	0.10	99.5	0.5
14950	16	0.15	99.6	0.4
15000	4	0.04	99.7	0.3
OVERFLOW	35	0.33	100.0	0.0

milliseconds (as was stated in Table 25.2). The standard deviation of this time is 119.5 milliseconds. Scanning down the table, we see that the 90th percentile level is about 240 milliseconds, and the 95th percentile level about 320 milliseconds of waiting.

This file arm is thus the worst bottleneck in the system and any systems design action which lessens its utilization slightly would be worth while.

We would also like to know how close the system is to its limit. Tables 25.1–25.4 are for an input rate of one transaction every 100 milliseconds, that is 10 transactions per second. Let us run the model with an input rate of 16, 16.5, 17 transactions per second, and so on. Table 25.5 shows the results of doing this. It shows the five facility utilizations, the queue content, and mean queuing times, and it prints the upper end of Table Number 10, the histogram of transit times. The 98th percentile and above are listed. We see that, although the system is becoming very tightly loaded at 17 transactions per second, no single transaction takes longer than 4.9 seconds. The maximum queue for arm B is large: 33 items, but the system is workable.

If we push the system just slightly harder to 17.5 transactions per second, then it fails to perform adequately. The transit time rises very sharply, the 98th percentile rising from 3.2 to 14.05 seconds. The *mean* queue size for arm B goes from 6.7 to 57.9 items. And the table of transit times overflows: 35 transactions taking longer than 15 seconds.

This system became jammed with transactions much as a city street can become jammed with cars at the rush hour. At 17 transactions per second it performed reasonably satisfactorily; at 17.5, it did not. If we could have kept the last 0.5 out of the system until after the peak everything would have been all right. This was the last straw. On this particular system the jam came suddenly. On others the deterioration is more gradual. On *any* system it is recommended that the designer should load it to its maximum and observe the nature of its death.

THE DANGERS OF SIMULATION   Simulations done on actual systems will usually be more complicated than that illustrated above, and they will provide information that is of more significance in the design process. They may, for example, help the design team to choose between different file configurations. However, they may take some time to write and debug. Collecting the data in the correct form may be lengthy and tedious, and the computer time to run and test the simulation is costly. Simulation is a powerful but expensive tool.

The simulation writer has to be familiar with all of the subtleties of the mechanisms, both of the hardware and of the programs of the system he is to simulate. He must ensure that these are all reproduced in the simulator model or that, where it is difficult to reproduce them exactly, the error caused by not doing so is negligible. The model in Fig. 25.5 does not reproduce the file mechanism quite correctly. When a record is updated after previously being read, this should occur an integral number of disk rotations after the read, which is not so on this model. However, disk rotational delay before the updating is allowed for, and averaging over a number of transactions, this gives a reasonably accurate answer. The effect of any such simplifying assumptions becomes more severe as the facility utilization rises. If the utilization of a facility is 0.85 or more, as is the case with file arm B in the example above, even minor approximations begin to have a significant effect.

Not too many liberties of this type can be taken or an argument will break out as to the validity of the model. There is always a danger that a model may be invalid, because of a logic error or an unjustified assumption, and that its results will be taken as correct. It is important for the simulation programmer to ascertain that the flow of transactions through his model is, in fact, exactly as he intended it. Program errors in a commercial program for payroll or billing manifest themselves only too clearly, but in a simulation program some may stay hidden. It is useful to check the model's queue estimates with the formulas given in the next chapter. Also the logic may be tested by varying the parameters in some way, and seeing if the model reacts as calculated.

It is important to run the simulation for long enough for the model to stabilize before results are collected. If one wanted to measure the queues at the cash desks of a supermarket, for example, one would start off with a model of an empty supermarket and allow people to flow through it for a few minutes until the queues had built up to a level at which they were steady enough to take measurements. A complex model might have to be run for quite a long period of time; first, to allow it to stabilize and then to avoid chance fluctuations in the statistics gathered.

The analyst who is planning the system will often not be the man who writes the simulation program. He should, however, have the ability to inspect its logic and ensure that it operates exactly in accordance with his own views. In verbal communication, the simulation programmer may well have failed to grasp some point that the analyst should have made about the system.

GARGABE IN/ GARBAGE OUT

In the early stages of a systems design there will be many factors that are not known. The volumes of traffic that the system is to process may be uncertain. Even more uncertain will be the size of programs needed. It may be known exactly how many records must be stored on the files, but exactly where they will be kept is a different question. How long will the seeks be for each type of record? How will the record be located? Must a table be read into core for this? Where from? How long will it take? Must a file area then be scanned? Will the required record be located at the first attempt?

On a complex system these questions and many others of a similar nature cannot be answered fully until well into the design process. On a large real-time system there may be several file accesses needed to process each transaction, but the complexity of the functions required is such that no exact estimate of the number can be made for some time. Again, the mechanisms chosen for the Supervisory Programs to route data through the system may remain uncertain until a considerable amount of design work has been done. Several man years of effort may be needed before all these questions are answered.

Even assuming the analyst is highly experienced and skilled, the problem he faces in obtaining realistic information for the model can be formidable. Both the volume of input and the logic with which it is processed may be in doubt. If this is so, the results of the simulation must be treated with an appropriate degree of caution. The term GIGO, used to mean "garbage in/garbage out," certainly applies here, but the garbage out may take on a *deceptively authentic and imposing appearance.*

Unfortunately, the large and impressive computer print-out tabulating the response times and the requirements of the system may tend to deceive persons not familiar with the basis of the model. The sponsors of the simulation may tend to use propaganda, such as, "To do this by hand would have taken 100 man years" or "We have had thirty-five runs on the 7094." The print-out needs to be treated with caution, especially perhaps, if it is used as a sales aid.

Simulation, then, is a very powerful tool. However, like a new drug, it can be tempting, expensive, and dangerous in the wrong hands, It needs to be prescribed by an expert and must be used with care and experience.

Bibliography

H. S. Krasnow, and R. Merikallio, "The Past, Present and Future of General Simulation Languages," *Management Science*, November 1964.

K. D. Tocher, *The Art of Simulation.* Princeton, N.J.: D. Van Nostrand, 1963.

C. W. Churchman, "An Analysis of the Concept of Simulation," *Symposium on Simulation Models.* Edited by Austin C. Hoggatt and Frederick E. Balderston. Cincinnati: South-Western Publishing Co., 1963.

J. M. Hammersley, and D. C. Handscomb, *Monte Carlo Methods.* New York: John Wiley and Sons, Inc., 1964.

Naylor, Balintfy, Burdick and Chu, *Computer Simulation Techniques.* New York: John Wiley and Sons, Inc., 1966.

General Purpose Systems Simulator III, *Introduction.* IBM Corporation Manual Number B20–0001–0.

General Purpose Systems Simulator III, *User's Manual.* IBM Corporation Manual Number H20–0163–1.

H. M. Markowitz, B. Hausner, and H. W. Karr, *SIMSCRIPT: A Simulation Programming Language.* The RAND Corporation RM-3310, November 1962. (An excellent FORTRAN-based language of more general applicability than GPSS.)

SIMPAC User's Manual. Santa Monica, California: Systems Development Corporation, TM 602/000/00, April 15, 1962.

O-J. Dahl, and K. Nygaard, *The Simula Language*, Norwegian Computing Centre, Oslo, 1964. A convenient language for simulating queuing processes.

C. C. Holt, R. W. Shirey, D. V. Steward, J. L. Midler, and A. Stroud, "Program SIMULATE, a User's and Programmer's Manual," Social Systems Research Institute, University of Wisconsin, May 1964 (Mimeographed).

J. N. Buxton and J. G. Laski, "Control and Simulation Language." *The Computer Journal*, October 1962. (A useful discrete simulation language comparable with SIMSCRIPT, widely used in Europe.)

K. Young, *A User's Experience with Three Simulation Languages* (*GPSS, SIMSCRIPT, and SIMPAC*), Santa Monica, California: System Development Corp., TM-1755/000/00, 1963.

Bibliography on Simulation (a KWIC index). International Business Machines Corporation, Manual Number 320–0924, 1966.

26

PROBABILITY AND
QUEUING THEORY

The team making a survey for a real-time system has to decide how much effort, tears, and computer hours it is worth spending on simulation. Sometimes the answer is none. If a proven simulation program already exists which the team simply feeds figures into, that is fine. But this is frequently not the case. More often the model has to be written and debugged. For a model of sufficient complexity to be worthwhile using, this often takes two or three months or longer.

In the first stages of the design, the systems engineer needs quick answers to a variety of questions, such as "What will be the effect on cost of tighter response time criteria?" "What will be the effect of having fewer lines or fewer terminals?" There will usually be a large variety of different possible configurations and a method much quicker than simulation is needed for exploring the possibilities. Later, when a configuration is tentatively selected, it can be simulated.

This chapter describes some basic methods that a systems analyst may use, without any knowledge of mathematics other than basic algebra, as an alternative to simulation. It is intended to give him a "cook book" of elementary formulas and curves with which he may size up a queuing situation. It is advocated that this *simple theory should always be used before simulation is considered.* A sense of perspective is needed in selecting the appropriate design tools. The chapter describes when simple queuing and probability theory is adequate and when it should be supplemented by simulation. This is a decision that must be made by the persons making design estimates for a system.

It is probable that, at the early stages of system design, the program estimates are only very approximate. In this case, if a simulation is made to give core, time, or channel requirements, its results will be as uncertain as are the program estimates. The results obtained by simple queuing theory might on some systems be as acceptable as an elaborate simulation. Decisions such as "Does this system require a computer type A or B?" or "Does this system require a machine with 64,000 or 128,000 positions of core?" may be more affected by a large error in program estimating than by the difference between the use of simulation and the use of less accurate techniques.

When simulation is done for a system on which the program estimates are uncertain or the Supervisory Program mechanics are not fully known, the possible effect of these uncertainties must be taken into account. It is only too easy to take the impressive output of a simulator as fact, when the input does not justify this. *The possible error of input must be translated into terms of possible error of results.*

When a complex real-time system is being installed or designed in fine detail, it is almost certain that simulation will be needed. This, for example, may affect the way the programs are written. But at the survey stage, simulation should be used only on those parts of the system where it may affect what hardware is proposed and will give a more certain answer to this than the simple analytical methods outlined below. Some systems, especially nonmultiprogrammed ones, will not benefit from simulation at the survey stage. On others, and especially those in which the utilization of the facilities is in the region of 80 per cent or higher, it will give a significantly more accurate answer. The designer must therefore be able to assess the validity of the formulas he employs.

There are basically two alternatives to writing a simulation model. First, manual methods may be used, such as drawing bar charts, totalling seek times with an adding machine, and drawing up long tables to calculate core block utilizations. These methods are effectively a type of hand simulation. Examples will be given in subsequent chapters. Second, probability and queuing theory formulas may be used which give an approximate description of the situation. These will indicate how much core is needed to hold queues, what delays will occur, what proportion of transactions will not achieve a given response time, and so on.

The basic concepts of queuing and probability theory that are applicable are stated below in terms that may be of value to a systems engineer without a great knowledge of mathematics. Curves are given that will enable a nonmathematician to obtain a quick estimate of queue sizes, probability of given delays, and so on. In some cases these curves are not applicable and will give a wrong answer. The limitations of such a method are stated below and should be noted carefully.

THE POISSON
DISTRIBUTION

The formulas and curves below are based on the assumption that the events causing input to the system occur *at random*. Let us clarify what we mean by this statement.

Suppose that at some random time in the future a customer walks into a bank and asks to withdraw some cash. This event causes a transaction to be sent to the computer. Ignore for the moment the question of lunchtime activity peaks, and assume we are considering a period during which the average customer activity is constant. This event could have occurred at any time during the period we are examining. The circumstances that cause it to happen are related to the individual's private life and, as far as we can assess, it happened *at random*. In other words, the probability of its happening in that second is the same as the probability of its happening at any other second.

Now the bank has many customers, and they all walk in to make transactions at *random* times. The probability of any one *particular* customer coming in any one minute is very low, but, because of the large number of customers, several will probably walk in during that one minute.

This situation is typical of the load on many real-time systems, but not all of them. A system may have ten transactions per second reaching it, say, on average. Although this system load is fairly high, the probability that any one *particular* transaction arrives in a given second is very low, and is equal to the probability of it arriving in any other second. This number of arrivals in a given time period may be described by a limiting case of the binomial distribution known as the *Poisson distribution*.

It can be shown mathematically that the probability of having n arrivals in a given time period is:

$$P(n) = \frac{e^{-\bar{n}} \times \bar{n}^n}{n!} \qquad (26.1)$$

where $P(n)$ is the probability of having n arrivals in the time period
$\bar{n}$ is the mean value of n for the time period
$n!$ is equal to $n \times (n-1) \times (n-2) \ldots \times 3 \times 2 \times 1$
e is equal to 2.71828

The reader should note that this arrival pattern may be described in a variety of different ways thus: "A Poisson arrival pattern." "The number of events per unit time follows the Poisson distribution." "A random arrival pattern." "The interarrival times follow an exponential distribution." "An exponential arrival pattern." "An Erlang 1 arrival pattern." These phrases, some of which are loosely worded, are all to be found in the literature and the reader is cautioned not to be confused by such terminology.

In this discussion, the probability of one *particular* customer entering the bank, or one *particular* event occurring in a given time period, follows *a uniform distribution.* In other words, the probability is the same regardless of which time period of that length is examined. The probability of having *n* such events occur in a given time period follows a *Poisson distribution.* And the probability that times between events are less than a certain figure follows an *exponential distribution.* These are all different descriptions of the same stochastic process. They are shown graphically in Fig. 26.1.

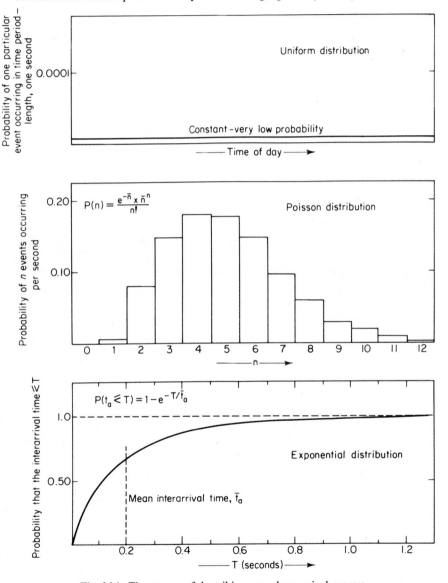

Fig. 26.1. Three ways of describing a random arrival process.

As an example of this, let us consider a real-time system with records relating to a large number of clients. During the peak hour of its activity, transactions are received at the average rate of two per second and follow a Poisson arrival pattern. Let us calculate the probability $P(n)$ of having n arrivals per second. In the formula above $\bar{n} = 2$. Therefore,

$$P(n) = \frac{2.71828^{-2} \times 2^n}{n!}$$

Substituting $n = 0, 1, 2, 3, \ldots$, we obtain the following probabilities rounded to four decimals:

Number of arrivals per second, n.	Probability
0	0.1353
1	0.2707
2	0.2707
3	0.1804
4	0.0902
5	0.0361
6	0.0120
7	0.0034
8	0.0009
9	0.0002

It is possible to get more than nine arrivals per second, but the probability of this is very small (about 0.000046).

This distribution may be plotted as a histogram, as shown in Fig. 26.2.

In this case, if the system is designed so that it can handle a maximum of three arrivals per second, the probability of its not being overloaded is

$$P(n \leqslant 3) = \sum_{n=0}^{n=3} \frac{2.71828^{-2} \times 2^n}{n!}$$
$$= 0.1353 + 0.2707 + 0.2707 + 0.1804 = 0.8571$$

In other words, 85.71 per cent of the arrivals will be handled immediately; 14.29 per cent will be delayed slightly. As is indicated by examination of Fig. 26.2, a delay greater than three times the time to handle one arrival will be very rare. The time to handle one arrival is on average one-third of a second. Therefore a delay greater than one second will be very rare, which on most systems is quite acceptable.

The system in this case can be regarded as a facility with a certain utilization factor. In this example it can handle a maximum of three arrivals per second but is in fact handling only two. It is therefore 66 $\frac{2}{3}$ per cent utilized. The concept of *facility utilization* is used frequently on the following pages. The closer the facility utilization is to 100 per cent, the greater the delays will become and the greater the queues that will build up.

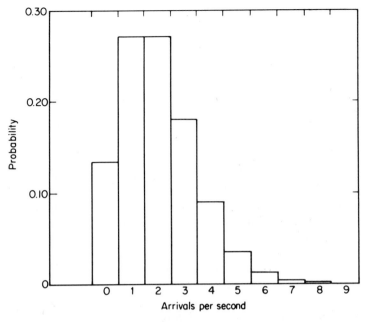

Figure 26.2

**THE USE
OF POISSON
TABLES**

Using the formula above, tables can be computed giving values of the Poisson function. Table 26.1 gives the probability of having X or more arrivals in a given time. For example, if the average arrival rate is 3.1 arrivals per second, (that is, $\bar{n} = 3.1$), then the probability of having five or more arrivals in a given second is 0.2018, from the table using $X = 5$. Mathematically this is

$$\sum_{n=5}^{n=\infty} \frac{e^{-\bar{n}} \bar{n}^n}{n!} \tag{26.2}$$

Using this the systems analyst may estimate the probability that the system will fail to handle a given throughput criterion.

Often *the initial estimates may be made using a load figure such that it will not be exceeded for 90 per cent of the time.* The figure may be obtained by using the Poisson tables.

Suppose that the average arrival rate $\bar{n}$ is 3.1 arrivals per second, again. From the tables the probability of having $X = 6$ arrivals per second or more is 0.0943. This might therefore be taken as the throughput for making the first estimates. Similarly, if a proposed system handles 17 transactions per second on average during the peak hour, there is a 0.0953 probability of having 23 or more transactions in one second. Therefore 23 transactions per second might be used as the preliminary design throughput, and for the first reiteration a system is designed that can handle this load.

**BASIC
QUEUING
THEORY**

When transactions arrive randomly at a facility in the manner described, and the facility takes a certain time to process, or serve, each transaction, queues will build up. Queues of bank customers wait for a teller and his terminal to become free. Queues of transactions in a computer input buffer wait for the attention of the processing unit. Queues of requests for file references wait for a file channel to become free. And so on. Queues may build up at any of the bottlenecks in a system.

The heavier the utilization of the facility in question, the longer the queues will become. As will be shown below, it may be satisfactory to design a system with a *facility utilization* of 70 per cent, but above 90 per cent it may be too risky or give too poor a service. Thus, if a file channel is 20 per cent loaded, there will be hardly any items waiting for it, on average. If it is 90 per cent loaded, there will normally be a queue, and at times this queue will become very large.

The facility utilization may be defined as:

$$\left(\frac{\text{the load on a facility}}{\text{the maximum load the facility can handle}} \right)$$

or

$$\left(\frac{\text{the time the facility is occupied}}{\text{the time available}} \right)$$

For example, if a bank teller is occupied 80 per cent of his time and the remainder of the time he stands idle waiting for the next customer, we can regard him as a facility with a facility utilization of 0.8. If a 2000-baud communication line is used to transmit six-bit characters so that it can transmit a maximum of 2000/6 characters per second, and we design a system in which a total of 12,000 characters from many different devices are sent down the line in a peak minute (including synchronization, end-of-message, control characters, etc.), then the facility utilization of the line during this minute is

$$\frac{12,000}{(2000/6) \times 60} = 0.6$$

Again, if a file arm makes 9000 file references in the peak hour and the arm is in use or held for an average of 300 milliseconds per reference, then

Table 26.1. SUMMED POISSON DISTRIBUTION FUNCTION*

This table contains values of:

$$P(n \geqslant X) = \sum_{n=X}^{n=\infty} \frac{e^{-\bar{n}} \times \bar{n}^n}{n!}$$

(probability of having X or more arrivals in a given time for which the mean arrival rate is $\bar{n}$)

For example, if $\bar{n} = 1.8$ arrivals per second, the probability of having four or more arrivals per second is 0.1087.

					$\bar{n}$					
X	0.1	0.2	0.3	0.4	0.5	0.6	0.7	0.8	0.9	1.0
0	1.0000	1.0000	1.0000	1.0000	1.0000	1.0000	1.0000	1.0000	1.0000	1.0000
1	.0952	.1813	.2592	.3297	.3935	.4512	.5034	.5507	.5934	.6321
2	.0047	.0175	.0369	.0616	.9002	.1219	.1558	.1912	.2275	.2642
3	.0002	.0011	.0036	.0079	.0144	.0231	.0341	.0474	.0629	.0803
4	.0000	.0001	.0003	.0008	.0018	.0034	.0058	.0091	.0135	.0190
5	.0000	.0000	.0000	.0001	.0002	.0004	.0008	.0014	.0023	.0037
6	.0000	.0000	.0000	.0000	.0000	.0000	.0001	.0002	.0003	.0006
7	.0000	.0000	.0000	.0000	.0000	.0000	.0000	.0000	.0000	.0001

					$\bar{n}$					
X	1.1	1.2	1.3	1.4	1.5	1.6	1.7	1.8	1.9	2.0
0	1.0000	1.0000	1.0000	1.0000	1.0000	1.0000	1.0000	1.0000	1.0000	1.0000
1	.6671	.6988	.7275	.7543	.7769	.7981	.8173	.8347	.8504	.8647
2	.3010	.3374	.3732	.4082	.4422	.4751	.5068	.5372	.5663	.5940
3	.0996	.1205	.1429	.1665	.1912	.2166	.2428	.2694	.2963	.3233
4	.0257	.0338	.0431	.0537	.0656	.0788	.0932	.1087	.1253	.1429
5	.0054	.0077	.0107	.0143	.0186	.0237	.0296	.0364	.0441	.0527
6	.0010	.0015	.0022	.0032	.0045	.0060	.0080	.0104	.0132	.0166
7	.0001	.0003	.0004	.0006	.0009	.0013	.0019	.0026	.0034	.0045
8	.0000	.0000	.0001	.0001	.0002	.0003	.0004	.0006	.0008	.0011
9	.0000	.0000	.0000	.0000	.0000	.0000	.0001	.0001	.0002	.0002

					$\bar{n}$					
X	2.1	2.2	2.3	2.4	2.5	2.6	2.7	2.8	2.9	3.0
0	1.0000	1.0000	1.0000	1.0000	1.0000	1.0000	1.0000	1.0000	1.0000	1.0000
1	.8775	.8892	.8997	.9093	.9179	.9257	.9328	.9392	.9450	.9502
2	.6204	.6454	.6691	.6916	.7127	.7326	.7513	.7689	.7854	.8009
3	.3504	.3773	.4040	.4303	.4562	.4816	.5064	.5305	.5540	.5768
4	.1614	.1806	.2007	.2213	.2424	.2640	.2859	.3081	.3304	.3528
5	.0621	.0725	.0838	.0959	.1088	.1226	.1371	.1523	.1682	.1847
6	.0204	.0249	.0300	.0357	.0420	.0490	.0567	.0651	.0742	.0839
7	.0059	.0075	.0094	.0116	.0142	.0172	.0206	.0244	.0287	.0335
8	.0015	.0020	.0026	.0033	.0042	.0053	.0066	.0081	.0099	.0119
9	.0003	.0005	.0006	.0009	.0011	.0015	.0019	.0024	.0031	.0038
10	.0001	.0001	.0001	.0002	.0003	.0004	.0005	.0007	.0009	.0011
11	.0000	.0000	.0000	.0000	.0001	.0001	.0001	.0002	.0002	.0003
12	.0000	.0000	.0000	.0000	.0000	.0000	.0000	.0000	.0001	.0001

*Reproduced from *Handbook of Mathematical Tables:* Chemical Rubber Company. (Reprinted by permission of the publisher.)

Table 26.1. (CONT.)

X	3.1	3.2	3.3	3.4	$\bar{n}$ 3.5	3.6	3.7	3.8	3.9	4.0
0	1.0000	1.0000	1.0000	1.0000	1.0000	1.0000	1.0000	1.0000	1.0000	1.0000
1	.9550	.9592	.9631	.9666	.9698	.9727	.9753	.9776	.9798	.9817
2	.8153	.8288	.8414	.8532	.8641	.8743	.8838	.8926	.9008	.9084
3	.5988	.6201	.6406	.6603	.6792	.6973	.7146	.7311	.7469	.7619
4	.3752	.3975	.4197	.4416	.4634	.4848	.5058	.5265	.5468	.5665
5	.2018	.2194	.2374	.2558	.2746	.2936	.3128	.3322	.3516	.3712
6	.0943	.1054	.1171	.1295	.1424	.1559	.1699	.1844	.1994	.2149
7	.0388	.0446	.0510	.0579	.0653	.0733	.0818	.0909	.1005	.1107
8	.0142	.0168	.0198	.0231	.0267	.0308	.0352	.0401	.0454	.0511
9	.0047	.0057	.0069	.0083	.0099	.0117	.0137	.0160	.0185	.0214
10	.0014	.0018	.0022	.0027	.0033	.0040	.0048	.0058	.0069	.0081
11	.0004	.0005	.0006	.0008	.0010	.0013	.0016	.0019	.0023	.0028
12	.0001	.0001	.0002	.0002	.0003	.0004	.0005	.0006	.0007	.0009
13	.0000	.0000	.0000	.0001	.0001	.0001	.0001	.0002	.0002	.0003
14	.0000	.0000	.0000	.0000	.0000	.0000	.0000	.0000	.0001	.0001

X	4.1	4.2	4.3	4.4	$\bar{n}$ 4.5	4.6	4.7	4.8	4.9	5.0
0	1.0000	1.0000	1.0000	1.0000	1.0000	1.0000	1.0000	1.0000	1.0000	1.0000
1	.9834	.9850	.9864	.9877	.9889	.9899	.9909	.9918	.9926	.9933
2	.9155	.9220	.9281	.9337	.9389	.9437	.9482	.9523	.9561	.9596
3	.7762	.7898	.8026	.8149	.8264	.8374	.8477	.8575	.8667	.8753
4	.5858	.6046	.6228	.6406	.6577	.6743	.6903	.7058	.7207	.7350
5	.3907	.4102	.4296	.4488	.4679	.4868	.5054	.5237	.5418	.5595
6	.2607	.2469	.2633	.2801	.2971	.3142	.3316	.3490	.3665	.3840
7	.1214	.1325	.1442	.1564	.1689	.1820	.1954	.2092	.2233	.2378
8	.0573	.0639	.0710	.0786	.0866	.0951	.1040	.1133	.1231	.1334
9	.0245	.0279	.0317	.0358	.0403	.0451	.0503	.0558	.0618	.0681
10	.0095	.0111	.0129	.0149	.0171	.0195	.0222	.0251	.0283	.0318
11	.0034	.0041	.0048	.0057	.0067	.0078	.0090	.0104	.0120	.0137
12	.0011	.0014	.0017	.0020	.0024	.0029	.0034	.0040	.0047	.0055
13	.0003	.0004	.0005	.0007	.0008	.0010	.0012	.0014	.0017	.0020
14	.0001	.0001	.0002	.0002	.0003	.0003	.0004	.0005	.0006	.0007
15	.0000	.0000	.0000	.0001	.0001	.0001	.0001	.0001	.0002	.0002
16	.0000	.0000	.0000	.0000	.0000	.0000	.0000	.0000	.0001	.0001

X	5.1	5.2	5.3	5.4	$\bar{n}$ 5.5	5.6	5.7	5.8	5.9	6.0
0	1.0000	1.0000	1.0000	1.0000	1.0000	1.0000	1.0000	1.0000	1.0000	1.0000
1	.9939	.9945	.9950	.9955	.9959	.9963	.9967	.9970	.9973	.9975
2	.9628	.9658	.9686	.9711	.9734	.9756	.9776	.9794	.9811	.9826
3	.8835	.8912	.8984	.9052	.9116	.9176	.9232	.9285	.9334	.9380
4	.7487	.7619	.7746	.7867	.7983	.8094	.8200	.8300	.8396	.8488

Table 26.1. (CONT.)

X	5.1	5.2	5.3	5.4	$\bar{n}$ 5.5	5.6	5.7	5.8	5.9	6.0
5	.5769	.5939	.6105	.6267	.6425	.6579	.6728	.6873	.7013	.7149
6	.4016	.4191	.4365	.4539	.4711	.4881	.5050	.5217	.5381	.5543
7	.2526	.2676	.2829	.2983	.3140	.3297	.3456	.3616	.3776	.3937
8	.1440	.1551	.1665	.1783	.1905	.2030	.2159	.2290	.2424	.2560
9	.0748	.0819	.0894	.0974	.1056	.1143	.1234	.1328	.1426	.1528
10	.0356	.0397	.0441	.0488	.0538	.0591	.0648	.0708	.0772	.0839
11	.0156	.0177	.0200	.0225	.0253	.0282	.0314	.0349	.0386	.0426
12	.0063	.0073	.0084	.0096	.0110	.0125	.0141	.0160	.0179	.0201
13	.0024	.0028	.0033	.0038	.0045	.0051	.0059	.0068	.0078	.0088
14	.0008	.0010	.0012	.0014	.0017	.0020	.0023	.0027	.0031	.0036
15	.0003	.0003	.0004	.0005	.0006	.0007	.0009	.0010	.0012	.0014
16	.0001	.0001	.0001	.0002	.0002	.0002	.0003	.0004	.0004	.0005
17	.0000	.0000	.0000	.0001	.0001	.0001	.0001	.0001	.0001	.0002
18	.0000	.0000	.0000	.0000	.0000	.0000	.0000	.0000	.0000	.0001

X	6.1	6.2	6.3	6.4	$\bar{n}$ 6.5	6.6	6.7	6.8	6.9	7.0
0	1.0000	1.0000	1.0000	1.0000	1.0000	1.0000	1.0000	1.0000	1.0000	1.0000
1	.9978	.9980	.9982	.9983	.9985	.9986	.9988	.9989	.9990	.9991
2	.9841	.9854	.9866	.9877	.9887	.9897	.9905	.9913	.9920	.9927
3	.9423	.9464	.9502	.9537	.9570	.9600	.9629	.9656	.9680	.9704
4	.8575	.8658	.8736	.8811	.8882	.8948	.9012	.9072	.9129	.9182
5	.7281	.7408	.7531	.7649	.7763	.7873	.7978	.8080	.8177	.8270
6	.5702	.5859	.6012	.6163	.6310	.6453	.6594	.6730	.6863	.6993
7	.4098	.4258	.4418	.4577	.4735	.4892	.5047	.5201	.5353	.5503
8	.2699	.2840	.2983	.3127	.3272	.3419	.3567	.3715	.3864	.4013
9	.1633	.1741	.1852	.1967	.2084	.2204	.2327	.2452	.2580	.2709
10	.0910	.0984	.1061	.1142	.1226	.1314	.1404	.1498	.1505	.1695
11	.0469	.0514	.0563	.0614	.0668	.0726	.0786	.0849	.0916	.0985
12	.0224	.0250	.0277	.0307	.0339	.0373	.0409	.0448	.0490	.0534
13	.0100	.0113	.0127	.0143	.0160	.0179	.0199	.0221	.0245	.0270
14	.0042	.0048	.0055	.0063	.0071	.0080	.0091	.0102	.0115	.0128
15	.0016	.0019	.0022	.0026	.0030	.0034	.0039	.0044	.0050	.0057
16	.0006	.0007	.0008	.0010	.0012	.0014	.0016	.0018	.0021	.0024
17	.0002	.0003	.0003	.0004	.0004	.0005	.0006	.0007	.0008	.0010
18	.0001	.0001	.0001	.0001	.0002	.0002	.0002	.0003	.0003	.0004
19	.0000	.0000	.0000	.0000	.0001	.0001	.0001	.0001	.0001	.0001

X	7.1	7.2	7.3	7.4	$\bar{n}$ 7.5	7.6	7.7	7.8	7.9	8.0
0	1.0000	1.0000	1.0000	1.0000	1.0000	1.0000	1.0000	1.0000	1.0000	1.0000
1	.9992	.9993	.9993	.9994	.9994	.9995	.9995	.9996	.9996	.9997
2	.9933	.9939	.9944	.9949	.9953	.9957	.9961	.9964	.9967	.9970
3	.9725	.9745	.9764	.9781	.9797	.9812	.9826	.9839	.9851	.9862
4	.9233	.9281	.9326	.9368	.9409	.9446	.9482	.9515	.9547	.9576

Table 26.1. (CONT.)

					$\bar{n}$					
X	7.1	7.2	7.3	7.4	7.5	7.6	7.7	7.8	7.9	8.0
5	.8359	.8445	.8527	.8605	.8679	.8751	.8819	.8883	.8945	.9004
6	.7119	.7241	.7360	.7474	.7586	.7693	.7797	.7897	.7994	.8088
7	.5651	.5796	.5940	.6080	.6218	.6354	.6486	.6616	.6743	.6866
8	.4162	.4311	.4459	.4607	.4754	.4900	.5044	.5188	.5330	.5470
9	.2840	.2973	.3108	.3243	.3380	.3518	.3657	.3796	.3935	.4075
10	.1798	.1904	.2012	.2123	.2236	.2351	.2469	.2589	.2710	.2834
11	.1058	.1133	.1212	.1293	.1378	.1465	.1555	.1648	.1743	.1841
12	.0580	.0629	.0681	.0735	.0792	.0852	.0915	.0980	.1048	.1119
13	.0297	.0327	.0358	.0391	.0427	.0464	.0504	.0546	.0591	.0638
14	.0143	.0159	.0176	.0195	.0216	.0238	.0261	.0286	.0313	.0342
15	.0065	.0073	.0082	.0092	.0101	.0114	.0127	.0141	.0156	.0173
16	.0028	.0031	.0036	.0041	.0046	.0052	.0059	.0066	.0074	.0082
17	.0011	.0013	.0015	.0017	.0020	.0022	.0026	.0029	.0033	.0037
18	.0004	.0005	.0006	.0007	.0008	.0009	.0011	.0012	.0014	.0016
19	.0002	.0002	.0002	.0003	.0003	.0004	.0004	.0005	.0006	.0006
20	.0001	.0001	.0001	.0001	.0001	.0001	.0002	.0002	.0002	.0003
21	.0000	.0000	.0000	.0000	.0000	.0000	.0001	.0001	.0001	.0001

					$\bar{n}$					
X	8.1	8.2	8.3	8.4	8.5	8.6	8.7	8.8	8.9	9.0
0	1.0000	1.0000	1.0000	1.0000	1.0000	1.0000	1.0000	1.0000	1.0000	1.0000
1	.9997	.9997	.9998	.9998	.9998	.9998	.9998	.9998	.9999	.9999
2	.9972	.9975	.9977	.9979	.9981	.9982	.9984	.9985	.9987	.9988
3	.9873	.9882	.9891	.9900	.9907	.9914	.9921	.9927	.9932	.9938
4	.9604	.9630	.9654	.9677	.9699	.9719	.9738	.9756	.9772	.9788
5	.9060	.9113	.9163	.9211	.9256	.9299	.9340	.9379	.9416	.9450
6	.8178	.8264	.8347	.8427	.8504	.8578	.8648	.8716	.8781	.8843
7	.6987	.7104	.7219	.7330	.7438	.7543	.7645	.7744	.7840	.7932
8	.5609	.5746	.5881	.6013	.6144	.6272	.6398	.6522	.6643	.6761
9	.4214	.4353	.4493	.4631	.4769	.4906	.5042	.5177	.5311	.5443
10	.2959	.3085	.3212	.3341	.3470	.3600	.3731	.3863	.3994	.4126
11	.1942	.2045	.2150	.2257	.2366	.2478	.2591	.2406	.2822	.2940
12	.1193	.1269	.1348	.1429	.1513	.1600	.1689	.1780	.1874	.1970
13	.0687	.0739	.0793	.0850	.0909	.0971	.1035	.1102	.1171	.1242
14	.0372	.0405	.0439	.0476	.0514	.0555	.0597	.0642	.0689	.0739
15	.0190	.0209	.0229	.0251	.0274	.0299	.0325	.0353	.0383	.0415
16	.0092	.0102	.0113	.0125	.0138	.0152	.0168	.0184	.0202	.0220
17	.0042	.0047	.0053	.0059	.0066	.0074	.0082	.0091	.0101	.0111
18	.0018	.0021	.0023	.0027	.0030	.0034	.0038	.0043	.0048	.0053
19	.0008	.0009	.0010	.0011	.0013	.0015	.0017	.0019	.0022	.0024
20	.0003	.0003	.0004	.0005	.0005	.0006	.0007	.0008	.0009	.0011
21	.0001	.0001	.0002	.0002	.0002	.0002	.0003	.0003	.0004	.0004
22	.0000	.0000	.0001	.0001	.0001	.0001	.0001	.0001	.0002	.0002
23	.0000	.0000	.0000	.0000	.0000	.0000	.0000	.0000	.0001	.0001

the facility utilization of the arm for the peak hour is

$$\frac{9000 \times 300}{3600 \times 1000} = 0.75$$

When we are designing a system we can usually produce an estimate for the utilization of the various facilities. Examples of this will be given in subsequent chapters. Knowing this utilization, we need to be able to estimate what queues of items build up to wait for the facility. How many items will there be in the queue and how long will they have to wait? These are the types of questions that queuing theory will sometimes be able to answer for us.

The queues that some of the formulas below deal with are "single server" queues, that is, items that are waiting to be serviced by *one* facility. They may be transactions in a new input queue (see Chapter 9) waiting for the Supervisory Program to cause work on them to commence. They may be items at terminals contending for a multidrop communication line, and so on. They wait for this facility in much the same way as automobiles arriving at a gas station wait for a solitary attendant. If, however, there were more than one attendant, this would constitute a *multiserver* queue, for which the analysis is rather more complex.

The formulas in the next section all relate to a situation in which the items arrive at random times. In other words, the interarrival times are exponentially distributed. The validity of this assumption is discussed later in the chapter.

DISTRIBUTION OF SERVICE TIMES   As well as making an assumption about the distribution of interarrival times, we also need to know something about the distribution of the service times. The service times may, like the interarrival times be exponentially distributed, as with the bottom curve of Fig. 26.1. If this is so, it leads to a relatively simple set of queuing formulas. Sometimes, on the other hand, the service times may be constant, as with the transmission times of constant-length messages. More often they do not fit into either of these patterns but follow a distribution characteristic of the particular application, file organization, or system procedures.

To take into account the distribution of service times, we may calculate their *standard deviation*. This does not tell us everything about the service time distribution but it will tell us enough to calculate the *mean* queue size and queuing times. Evaluating the standard deviation is a normal statistical method of expressing the dispersion in a set of values. It is the root-mean-square deviation of the values and is calculated as follows:

Suppose we have N values from which to do this calculation.

Table 26.2

S in milliseconds	$(S - \bar{S})$	$(S - \bar{S})^2$
30	−50	2500
50	−30	900
120	+40	1600
100	+20	400
70	−10	100
80	0	0
40	−40	1600
140	+60	3600
60	−20	400
100	+20	400
80	0	0
30	−50	2500
110	+30	900
90	+10	100
60	−20	400
70	−10	100
120	+40	1600
100	+20	400
70	−10	100
80	0	0
TOTAL 1600		TOTAL 17600

$$\text{MEAN, } \bar{S} = \frac{1600}{20} = 80 \qquad \frac{\Sigma(S - \bar{S})^2}{N} = 880$$

$$\sigma_s = \sqrt{880} = 29.66$$

Let S be an individual value.
Let σ_s represent the standard deviation of S.
Carry out the following steps:

1. Calculate $\bar{S}$, the mean value of S.
2. Calculate the deviation of each value of S from the mean,

$$(S - \bar{S}).$$

3. Calculate the mean value of the square of this deviation,

$$\frac{\Sigma(S - \bar{S})^2}{N}$$

4. Calculate the square root of this,

$$\sigma_s = \sqrt{\frac{\Sigma(S - \bar{S})^2}{N}} \qquad (26.3)$$

This process is illustrated in Table 26.2, in which the standard deviation of twenty representative file-reference times is calculated. The left-hand column gives the twenty file-reference times, and it will be seen that their mean is eighty milliseconds. The next columns calculate $(S - \bar{S})$ and $(S - \bar{S})^2$. Summing the right-hand column and dividing by 20 gives

$$\frac{\sum (S - \bar{S})^2}{N}$$

Hence σ_s is found to be 29.66 milliseconds. In an actual problem more than twenty values of the service time should be used, to give greater accuracy.

SINGLE-SERVER QUEUING FORMULAS

Knowing the facts above, the object of the queuing theory outlined here is to calculate the approximate average sizes of queues, and the average time that transactions are kept waiting in them. We also want to estimate how often the queues exceed certain values. This will enable us to calculate, for example, how much core storage is needed to hold the queues of transactions and associated programs, how many lines are needed, what size concentrator buffers are necessary, and so on. We will be able to estimate the response times. We will obtain an idea of how customers will be kept waiting at a bank counter, or how long we may have to wait if we telephone an airline to make a booking.

Most of the queue characteristics we are interested in are plotted in Figs. 26.9–26.24 at the end of this chapter. Each of these characteristics varies with the utilization of the facility in question. The horizontal scale of each set of curves is *facility utilization*.

It is suggested that *these curves, and the formulas behind them, should be a basic tool for making first approximation estimates of queue sizes in real-time systems.*

Let us first consider a queue with a single server as illustrated in Figure 26.3. In designing a computer system most of the queues that we will be able to apply formulas to will be of this type.

Let s be the service time of an item, and
σ_s be the standard deviation of all service times
Let w be the number of items waiting at a given time for service, and
q be the number of items in the system both waiting service or being served, at a given time.
Let t_w be the time an item waits before being served, and
t_q be the time it spends in the system both waiting and being served.

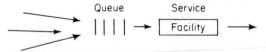

Mean of $\bar{n}$ arrivals per second   Mean service time $\bar{s}$ seconds

(Facility utilization, $\rho = \bar{n}\,\bar{s}$)

Fig. 26.3. A single-server queuing situation.

The mean values of w, q, t_w and t_q are represented by $\bar{w}$, $\bar{q}$, $\bar{t}_w$ and $\bar{t}_q$

$$t_q = t_w + s \tag{26.4}$$

$$\bar{t}_q = \bar{t}_w + \bar{s} \tag{26.5}$$

As $\bar{n}$ is the mean number of items being processed in unit time, and we are discussing a steady-state condition:

$$\bar{w} = \bar{n}\bar{t}_w \tag{26.6}$$

and

$$\bar{q} = \bar{n}\bar{t}_q \tag{26.7}$$

Let ρ be the facility utilization.

Then because we have a steady-state condition:

$$\rho = \bar{s}\bar{n} \tag{26.8}$$

This is the equation that is commonly used for calculating ρ. From Equations (26.5) and (26.7) we have

$$\bar{q} = \bar{n}\bar{t}_q = \bar{n}\bar{t}_w + \bar{n}\bar{s}$$

Substituting from Equations (26.6) and (26.8)

$$\bar{q} = \bar{w} + \rho \tag{26.9}$$

The basic theorem of single-server queuing theory was developed by Khintchine and Polloczek, and results in the following formula:

$$\bar{w} = \frac{\rho^2}{2(1-\rho)}\left[1 + \left(\frac{\sigma_s}{\bar{s}}\right)^2\right] \tag{26.10}$$

This is the formula that is used to make many of the queue size estimates in the design of computer systems. It applies to exponential interarrival times, any distribution of service times, and surprisingly perhaps, *any dispatching discipline provided that its selection of the next item to be serviced does not depend on the service time.*

By "dispatching discipline" we mean the rules governing the selection of the next item to be serviced. A common rule, for example, is "First in, first out (FIFO)"; less useful is "Last in, first out (LIFO)". The dispatching discipline may take *priority* into consideration and service the important items before others, or it may use selection criteria based upon the effect the item has on the system. Provided that the selection criterion does not depend upon the service time needed, the Khintchine-Polloczek formula applies. Illustrations will be given later in which this does not apply exactly.

Substituting Equation (26.10) into the previous equations we get

$$\bar{q} = \rho + \frac{\rho^2}{2(1 - \rho)}\left[1 + \left(\frac{\sigma_s}{\bar{s}}\right)^2\right] \tag{26.11}$$

$$\bar{t}_w = \frac{\rho\bar{s}}{2(1 - \rho)}\left[1 + \left(\frac{\sigma_s}{\bar{s}}\right)^2\right] \tag{26.12}$$

$$\bar{t}_q = \bar{s} + \frac{\rho\bar{s}}{2(1 - \rho)}\left[1 + \left(\frac{\sigma_s}{\bar{s}}\right)^2\right] \tag{26.13}$$

The term $1/2\,[1 + (\sigma_s/\bar{s})^2]$ appears in each of the equations describing mean queue characteristics. This term is dependent upon the dispersion of the service times. Two particular cases can be noted:

1. *When the service times are constant*

$$\sigma_s = 0$$

$$\therefore \quad \frac{1}{2}\left[1 + \left(\frac{\sigma_s}{\bar{s}}\right)^2\right] = \frac{1}{2}$$

$$\bar{q} = \rho + \frac{\rho^2}{2(1 - \rho)} \tag{26.14}$$

and

$$\bar{t}_q = \bar{s}\left[1 + \frac{\rho}{2(1 - \rho)}\right] \tag{26.15}$$

2. *When the service times are random, that is, exponentially distributed*

$$\sigma_s = \bar{s}$$

$$\therefore \quad \frac{1}{2}\left[1 + \left(\frac{\sigma_s}{\bar{s}}\right)^2\right] = 1$$

$$\bar{q} = \rho + \frac{\rho^2}{1 - \rho} = \frac{\rho}{1 - \rho} \tag{26.16}$$

and

$$\bar{t}_q = \bar{s}\left[1 + \frac{\rho}{(1 - \rho)}\right] = \frac{\bar{s}}{1 - \rho} \tag{26.17}$$

Most service times in computing systems lie somewhere between these two cases. We rarely find service times that are entirely constant. Even a drum access to read one complete track is not constant because of the varied rotational delay in waiting for the track to position itself. The occupancy of a communication line transmitting fixed-length messages may be one case where the service time is constant. On the other hand, we find that the dispersion of service times is not often as great as the case for random or exponentially distributed service times—σ_s is rarely as large as $\bar{s}$. This is sometimes regarded as a "worst case" and so the design is done with formulas relating to exponential service times. Such design may slightly overestimate the queue sizes and queuing times, but this can be regarded as a reasonable safety factor in the design.

Figure 26.9 on p. 411 gives curves plotting $\bar{q}$ against ρ for different values of σ_s. Figure 26.10 gives similar curves plotting $\bar{t}_q$ against ρ. The uppermost curve in each is for the "worst case" of exponential service times, and the lowest curve the best case of constant service times. Most cases fall between these two curves, and so some estimate of σ_s should be made.

Note that a circumstance which may make the queue size *worse* than the uppermost curve occurs when a small portion of the service times are much longer than the rest. If 80 per cent of the messages transmitted are 10 characters long, but the other 20 per cent are 100, and the service time, say line occupancy, is proportional to the number of characters, then we have a case where σ_s is greater than $\bar{s}$. It is not uncommon to find occasional long messages in a real-time system, and this is an indication that caution is needed in the use of queuing theory.

From these two sets of curves we can rapidly obtain our first estimate of certain of the queues that could build up in proposed systems. This applies to queues in the computer, in the concentrators and multiplexors, and to queues at the terminals. Examples of their use are given in subsequent chapters. Note that $\bar{t}_w$ may be obtained quickly from Fig. 26.10 using Equation (26.5): $\bar{t}_q = \bar{t}_w + \bar{s}$.

AMPLIFICATION FACTOR Inspecting the slope of the curves in Fig. 26.9 we see that *when the facility for which items are queuing becomes more than about 80 per cent utilized, the queues grow at an alarming rate*. This is a very important fact in the design of real-time systems. If we design a system with facility utilizations more than about 80 per cent then a small increase in traffic may cause severe degradation in system performance, or possibly cause the system to switch into the emergency procedures.

Substituting $\rho = \bar{s}\bar{n}$ into Equation (26.11), we get

$$\bar{q} = \bar{s}\bar{n} + \frac{\bar{s}^2\bar{n}^2}{2(1 - \bar{s}\bar{n})}\left[1 + \left(\frac{\sigma_s}{\bar{s}}\right)^2\right]$$

$$\therefore \quad \frac{d\bar{q}}{d\bar{n}} = \bar{s} + \frac{\bar{s}^2\bar{n}(2 - \bar{s}\bar{n})}{2(1 - \bar{s}\bar{n})^2}\left[1 + \left(\frac{\sigma_s}{\bar{s}}\right)^2\right]$$

$$\frac{d\bar{q}}{d\bar{n}} = \bar{s} + \frac{\bar{s}\rho(2-\rho)}{2(1-\rho)^2}\left[1 + \left(\frac{\sigma_s}{\bar{s}}\right)^2\right] \quad (26.18)$$

This indicates that a very small increase of x per cent in the input traffic will cause an increase of approximately

$$\left\{\bar{s} + \frac{\bar{s}\rho(2-\rho)}{2(1-\rho)^2}\left[1 + \left(\frac{\sigma_s}{\bar{s}}\right)^2\right]\right\} x$$

per cent in the queue size.

When the facility utilization is 50 per cent, this increase is $4\bar{s}x$ per cent for exponential service times. But when the facility utilization is 90 per cent, the increase is $100\bar{s}x$ per cent, that is 25 times greater. A small increase in throughput at 90 per cent utilization causes an effect on queue size 25 times greater than it would cause at a facility utilization of 50 per cent.

Similarly, the amplifying effect in queue time is given by

$$\frac{d\bar{t}_q}{d\bar{n}} = \frac{\bar{s}^2}{2(1-\rho)^2}\left[1 + \left(\frac{\sigma_s}{\bar{s}}\right)^2\right] \quad (26.19)$$

For exponential service times this is $4\bar{s}^2$ at a facility utilization of 50 per cent, but $100\bar{s}^2$ at a facility utilization of 90 per cent—again 25 times worse.

Furthermore, it will be seen that for low values of facility utilization the queue size is not greatly affected by differences in σ_s. However, for high facility utilizations, differences in σ_s make a large difference. It is, therefore, more desirable to obtain an accurate knowledge of σ_s if we are designing at high facility utilizations. The inaccuracy in an assumption that s is exponential will have more effect when ρ is high. Furthermore, if there is an occasional long service time as might be caused on a transmission line by a long message, this will cause heavy queuing when ρ is high.

STANDARD DEVIATION OF QUEUE SIZES

The previous formulas have given mean values for queue sizes and times. As well as knowing the mean, it is usually desirable to know something about the distribution of the queue sizes and times. We need to answer questions like "How many transactions will be delayed more than such-and-such an amount?" or "How much core do I need to hold the items in the queue (and possibly also the programs that are dealing with them)?"

Before we discuss these equations further we need to be able to evaluate the standard deviation of q or t_q, or the variance (which is the square of the standard deviation).

One way of doing this uses the *second and third moments* of service time. To calculate the second moment of a set of values of s, we take the mean of s^2 for these values. This is represented here by $\overline{s^2}$. To calculate the third moment of the set, we take the mean of s^3. This is represented here by $\overline{s^3}$.

The variance of s, Var (s) is $\overline{s^2} - \overline{s}^2$. And so σ_s is

$$\sqrt{\overline{s^2} - \overline{s}^2} \tag{26.20}$$

This gives us an alternative way of caluclating σ_s.

The variance of queue size was evaluated by Khintchine and Polloczek for a single-server queue with random arrivals and a *first-come, first-served, dispatching discipline*. The latter criterion did not apply to the earlier formulas.

The variance of q is

$$\text{Var}(q) = \frac{\bar{n}^3 \overline{s}^3}{3(1-\rho)} + \frac{\bar{n}^4 (\overline{s^2})^2}{4(1-\rho)^2} + \frac{\bar{n}^2 (3-2\rho)\overline{s^2}}{2(1-\rho)} + \rho(1-\rho) \tag{26.21}$$

The variance of t_q is

$$\text{Var}(t_q) = \frac{\bar{n}\overline{s}^3 + 3\overline{s^2}}{3(1-\rho)} + \frac{\bar{n}^2 (\overline{s^2})^2}{2(1-\rho)^2} - \bar{t}_q^2 \tag{26.22}$$

For exponential service times: $\overline{s^2} = 2\overline{s}^2$ and $\overline{s^3} = 6\overline{s}^3$

For constant service times: $\overline{s^2} = \overline{s}^2$ and $\overline{s^3} = \overline{s}^3$

In these two cases, the above formulas for variance simplify considerably. Table 26.4 lists the useful formulas for constant and exponential service times and gives the standard deviations of q, t_q, and t_w. Figures 26.11 and 26.12 plot standard deviations against ρ.

PROBABILITIES OF QUEUES EXCEEDING GIVEN SIZES

It is useful to be able to evaluate the probabilities that queues exceed certain sizes, and times exceed certain values. We frequently want an answer to questions, such as: "How often does the queue exceed six?" and "Will 90 per cent of the transactions be served in less than x seconds?" It is only possible to answer such questions by mathematical methods if we can fit the service times into a known distribution.

If the service time distribution is exponential, (normally our "worst case" assumption), then it can be shown that the distribution of q is

$$P(q = N) = (1-\rho)\rho^N$$

where $P(q = N)$ is the probability that $q = N$.

Hence the probability that q is greater than or equal to N is

$$P(q \geqslant N) = \sum_{q=N}^{\infty} (1-\rho)\rho^q \tag{26.23}$$

This is plotted in Fig. 26.15 for various values of N.

The probability of queuing time t_q being greater than time T can also be evaluated for exponential service times.

$$P(t_q > T) = e^{-[(1-\rho)T/\bar{s}]} \tag{26.24}$$

This is plotted in Fig. 26.14.

Where the service times can be approximated to an exponential distribution, Equations (26.23) and (26.24) can be used. Another set of distributions commonly used in queuing theory is the *Erlang distributions*. These are a family of functions referred to as Erlang 1, Erlang 2, Erlang 3 . . . Erlang E. E is an integer. Applied to service time, s the distributions are as follows:

$$P(s < T) = 1 - e^{-\frac{ET}{\bar{s}}} \sum_{K=0}^{E-1} \frac{(ET/\bar{s})^K}{K!}$$

where P is the probability that s is less than time T, and the factor $(\sigma_s/\bar{s})^2$ for the Erlang distribution is $1/E$.

As in the case of the earlier formulas $(\sigma_s/\bar{s})$ can range from 0 to 1. If it is higher than, 1, the Erlang approximation is invalid, but for most service times found in practice $(\sigma_s/\bar{s})$ does lie in this range.

To select the best Erlang function we use the formula

$$E = \left(\frac{\bar{s}}{\sigma_s}\right)^2 \tag{26.25}$$

and select the best integer, E, that will fulfill this.

As an example, if the service times are distributed as in Table 26.2, we then have $\bar{s} = 80$ and $\sigma_s = 29.66$.

$$\therefore \quad \frac{1}{(\sigma_s/\bar{s})^2} = \left(\frac{80}{29.66}\right)^2 = 7.27$$

We take E to be the nearest integer, 7, and use the assumption that the service times follow an Erlang 7 distribution.

Note that an Erlang 1 distribution is an exponential distribution. An Erlang ∞ distribution represents constant values with $\sigma_s = 0$. The larger E becomes, the closer the distribution is to a constant distribution.

Using this approximation we can now calculate the standard deviations of the queue sizes and the queuing times without knowing the third moments of service time. It can be shown that

$$\sigma_q^2 = \frac{1}{(1-\rho)^2}\left\{1 - \frac{\rho}{2}\left[3 - \frac{\rho(10-\rho)}{6} - \frac{3-3\rho+\rho^2}{E} - \frac{\rho(8-5\rho)}{6E^2}\right]\right\} \tag{26.26}$$

Also,

$$\sigma_{t_q}^2 = \left(\frac{\bar{s}}{1-\rho}\right)^2\left\{\left[1 - \frac{\rho}{6}(4-\rho)\left(1-\frac{1}{E}\right)\right]\left[1+\frac{1}{E}\right]\right.$$
$$\left. - \left[1 - \frac{\rho}{2}\left(1-\frac{1}{E}\right)\right]^2\right\} \tag{26.27}$$

This approximation enables us to plot σ_q and σ_{t_q} for different values of σ_q/s. These are plotted in Fig. 26.11 and 26.12. From these curves the systems engineer can obtain a very quick estimate of σ_q and σ_{t_q}.

To take an example, let the utilization of a multidrop contention line be 80 per cent, and the average message transmission time be 20 seconds, and the standard deviation 12 seconds. Then the average number of messages at a terminal waiting for transmission (including that being transmitted) is given by Fig. 26.9, using the curve for $\sigma_s = 0.6s$, as $\bar{q} = 2.98$ messages. The standard deviation of number of items queuing is given by Fig. 26.11. $(\bar{s}/\sigma_s)^2 = (\frac{20}{12})^2 = 2.78$, therefore interpolating between the Erlang 2 and Erlang 3 curves, we find that the standard deviation of q is approximately 3.2 messages.

We have now established a method of finding σ_q and σ_{t_q}. This is useful; it gives us an idea of the dispersion of q and t_q, but we need to know more than this to answer questions like "what proportion of the transactions will have a response time greater than three seconds?" Or, "what is the ninety percentile response time?" We need to fit a statistical distribution to these response times.

When we have a stream of transactions that arrive at random, the times between messages, as discussed earlier, are exponentially distributed. Many of the ways in which we could manipulate this stream of messages would result in an Erlang distribution. For example, suppose there is a two-way switch on an input line which carries messages with exponential interarrival times. This switch is operated in such a way that alternate messages go down different paths. The result of this (Fig. 26.4) is that the switched message stream has interarrival times which follow an Erlang 2 distribution.

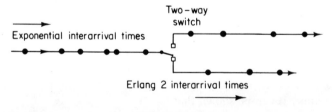

Figure 26.4

If we had used a three-way switch, and switched messages down paths A, B, C . . . successively, then the resulting message stream would have had Erlang 3 interarrival times (Fig. 26.5).

If we had switched them alternately down a very large number of paths, the resulting interarrival times would have become close to constant. An Erlang ∞ distribution of interarrival times means that the interarrival times are constant.

The Erlang distributions are specific cases of a more general family, *gamma distributions*. For an Erlang distribution of times, t, the ratio $(\bar{t}/\sigma_t)^2$ is

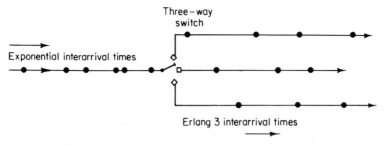

Figure 26.5

always an integer. For the gamma distribution it can have *any* value. The gamma distribution has a parameter, R, where:

$$R = \left(\frac{\bar{t}}{\sigma_t}\right)^2$$

For the gamma distribution the probability of t being less than a given time is

$$P(t \leqslant T) = \frac{\int_0^T \left(\frac{Rt}{\bar{t}}\right)^{(R-1)} e^{-(Rt/\bar{t})} \frac{R}{\bar{t}} \, dt}{\int_0^\infty \left(\frac{Rt}{\bar{t}}\right)^{(R-1)} e^{-(Rt/\bar{t})} \frac{R}{\bar{t}} \, dt}$$

The exponential distribution, the Erlang distributions, and a constant set of values, are all specific cases of the gamma distribution. Furthermore, if two or more independent variables follow a gamma distribution, it can be shown that the sum of these variables also follows a gamma distribution.

If we know the mean and standard deviation of a set of time values following a gamma distribution, then we can calculate R and use the equation above to find $P(t > T)$.

In most practical cases where we want to fit a known mathematical distribution to the response times of a real-time system, the gamma distribution gives a reasonable fit. In many cases in calculating the response time we have to add together times which themselves follow a gamma distribution. The queuing time for a facility with exponential service times, for example, is exponentially distributed. To this may be added another time which is always constant. These are two cases of gamma distributions, and adding them produces another gamma distribution with a different parameter, R.

It is suggested then, that when a system designer needs to estimate approximately the probabilities of obtaining different response times, he should calculate the mean and standard deviation of the response time and then use the appropriate gamma distribution. If, later, he needs to be more exact or more rigorous, he must either plunge into a *much* higher level of mathematics or else resort to simulation. The latter is probably the best approach.

The gamma distribution, unfortunately, is not so easy to handle for the purpose of calculations as are the other equations in this chapter. It is plotted

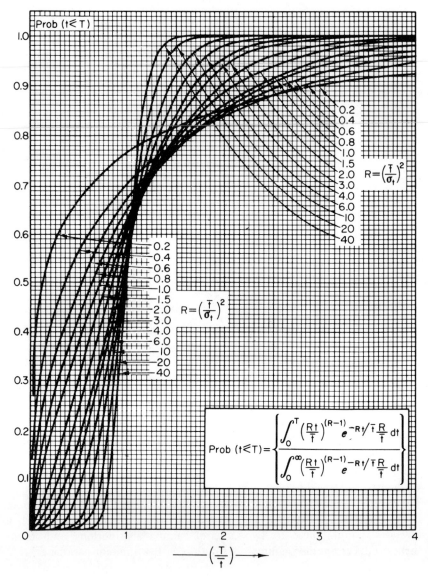

Fig. 26.6. A plot of the incomplete gamma function.

in Figs. 26.6 and 26.7. These two plots are intended to form a tool which the reader can use in estimating response times. The two plots are identical except that they are drawn with different scales.

Let us consider an example of the use of these curves: we have estimated the mean response time of a system to be three seconds and the standard

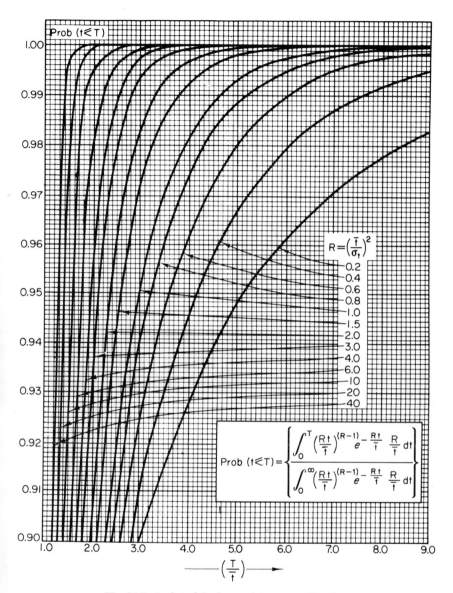

Fig. 26.7. A plot of the incomplete gamma function.

deviation to be 1.5 seconds. What fraction of the transactions will have a response time greater than six seconds?

In Figs. 26.6 or 26.7, $\bar{t}$ is now 3. Let us take T to be six seconds, so that the vertical axis reads: Prob $(t \leqslant 6)$. $(T/\bar{t})$ is then 2. $R = (\bar{t}/\sigma_t)^2 = 4$. When we use the R equals 4 curve on either figure, we can read the value of Prob.

$(t \leqslant 6)$ for $(T/\bar{t}) = 2$. It is approximately 0.955. In other words 0.955 trans-actions will have a response time of less than six seconds; 0.045 will take longer than six seconds.

How many will take longer than nine seconds? Repeat the process for $(T/\bar{t}) = 3$. Prob $(t \leqslant 9) = 0.998$. In other words only 0.2 per cent of the transactions will exceed nine seconds. How many will exceed 12 seconds? Practically none.

Fitting a gamma distribution to the response times is, of course, only an approximate method of answering these questions. The reader may like to re-examine Table 25.3 in the last chapter. This gives a distribution of response times for the file subsystem which was simulated there. The queues in this problem interact in a complex manner with each other as will be discussed in Chapter 28. It is by no means clear that the response times gathered by Table 10 of the simulation should fit a gamma distribution. If the reader plots a curve from the values in this table, he will find that it is approximately the same shape as the appropriate curve of Fig. 26.6 though it deviates somewhat from this curve at the bottom and at the very top. This is typical of actual systems. The reader may judge for himself whether this order of accuracy is sufficient for his design situation. Normally, Figs. 26.6 and 26.7 are very useful in the early stages of a design before enough is known for it to be worth while to write an exact simulation.

Further examples using these curves will be given in Chapter 33.

THE EFFECT OF DIFFERENT DISPATCHING DISCIPLINES

We noted above that the equations for $\bar{w}$, $\bar{q}$, $\bar{t}_w$, and $\bar{t}_q$ applied for any dispatching or scheduling discipline which chooses the next item to be served regardless of the service time. This is true of all the equations from Equation 26.4 to Equation 26.19 above. It is not true of Equation 26.21 and the following equations, which apply only to "first in, first out" dispatching.

The standard deviations of w, q, t_w, and t_q will be different for different dispatching disciplines. So also will be $P(q \geqslant N)$, $P(t_q > T)$ and other such measures. Only the *mean* values will be unaffected.

One dispatching discipline that is of interest is that in which the next item to be served is selected at *random* from the queue. This approximately corresponds to a polling situation in which a number of terminals are cyclically scanned to select the next item to be serviced. As might be expected, random dispatching gives a greater dispersion of queuing times than first-in, first-out dispatching. The difference in σ_q and σ_{t_q} between these two disciplines becomes larger as ρ becomes larger. This is shown in the curves in Fig. 26.13 for σ_{t_q}. These compare the two disciplines for constant service times, and also for exponential service times.

The equation equivalent to (26.22) for random dispatching is:

$$\text{var}\ (t_q) = \frac{2\bar{n}\overline{s^3}}{3(1-\rho)(2-\rho)} + \frac{\bar{n}^2(\overline{s^2})^2(2+\rho)}{4(1-\rho)^2(2-\rho)} + \overline{s^2} - \bar{s}^2 \qquad (26.28)$$

For exponential service times this becomes

$$\sigma_{t_q} = \frac{\bar{s}}{(1-\rho)}\sqrt{\frac{2\rho^2 + 2 - \rho}{2 - \rho}} \qquad (26.29)$$

and for constant service times

$$\sigma_{t_q} = \frac{\bar{s}}{(1-\rho)}\sqrt{\frac{8\rho - 2\rho^2 + 3\rho^3}{12(2-\rho)}} \qquad (26.30)$$

These two equations are plotted in Fig. 26.13.

QUEUES WITH PRIORITIES   Another class of dispatching discipline that we are likely to be interested in is that in which different items have different *priorities*. Let us consider the case in which Priority 1 items are always served before Priority 2 items, Priority 2 items before Priority 3, and so on. This case still obeys the formulas above for $\bar{w}$, $\bar{q}$, $\bar{t}_w$, and $\bar{t}_q$, if and only if the mean service time for each priority class is the same. If Priority 1 items require on average a shorter service time than Priority 2, then the dispatching discipline is no longer independent of service times, and we have disobeyed this condition which is necessary for the validity of the above equations. In fact *if we deliberately give high priority to the items with short service times, we can reduce the mean size of the queues and the queuing times.*

Let us suppose that items in a queue have k different priority levels: $1, 2, 3, \ldots, k$.

The mean arrival rate of Priority j items is $\bar{n}_j$.

If the items in each class arrive independently with Poisson arrival distributions, then the total arrival rate also follows a Poisson distribution with mean $\bar{n}$, such that:

$$\bar{n} = \bar{n}_1 + \bar{n}_2 + \bar{n}_3 + \cdots \bar{n}_k$$

Let the service time for the different priority levels be $s_1, s_2, s_3, \ldots, s_k$. Then:

$$\bar{s} = \frac{\bar{n}_1}{\bar{n}} \bar{s}_1 + \frac{\bar{n}_2}{\bar{n}} \bar{s}_2 + \frac{\bar{n}_3}{\bar{n}} \bar{s}_3 + \ldots \frac{\bar{n}_k}{\bar{n}} \bar{s}_k \qquad (26.31)$$

and

$$\overline{s^2} = \frac{\bar{n}_1}{\bar{n}} \overline{s_1^2} + \frac{\bar{n}_2}{\bar{n}} \overline{s_2^2} + \frac{\bar{n}_3}{\bar{n}} \overline{s_3^2} + \ldots \frac{\bar{n}_k}{\bar{n}} \overline{s_k^2} \qquad (26.32)$$

Let the fraction of facility utilization due to the Priority j items be ρ_j. Then

$$\rho_j = \bar{n}_j \bar{s}_j$$

and

$$\rho = \rho_1 + \rho_2 + \rho_3 + \ldots \rho_k \qquad (26.33)$$

The total number of items in the queue will be made up of the items of each separate priority stream.

Let the number in the queue for Priority j be q_j. Then the total number queuing is

$$q = q_1 + q_2 + \ldots q_k \qquad (26.34)$$

Let the mean queuing time for items of Priority j be $\bar{t}_q$. Then the over-all average queuing time is

$$\bar{t}_q = \frac{\bar{n}_1}{\bar{n}} \bar{t}_{q_1} + \frac{\bar{n}_2}{\bar{n}} \bar{t}_{q_2} + \ldots \frac{\bar{n}_k}{\bar{n}} \bar{t}_k \qquad (26.35)$$

Similar relationships apply to $\bar{w}$ and $\bar{t}_w$. It can be shown that the mean queuing time for Priority j items is

$$\bar{t}_{q_j} = \frac{\bar{n}\overline{s^2}}{2[1 - (\rho_1 + \rho_2 + \ldots \rho_{j-1})] \, [1 - (\rho_1 + \rho_2 + \ldots \rho_j)]} + \bar{s}_j \qquad (26.36)$$

The mean number of Priority j items in the queue is

$$\bar{q}_j = \bar{n}_j \bar{t}_{q_j}$$

$$\therefore \quad \bar{q}_j = \frac{\bar{n}\bar{n}_j \overline{s^2}}{2[1 - (\rho_1 + \rho_2 + \ldots \rho_{j-1})] \, [1 - (\rho_1 + \rho_2 + \ldots \rho_j)]} + \rho_j \qquad (26.37)$$

When there are only two priority levels, Equation (26.36) simplifies to

$$\bar{t}_{q_1} = \frac{\bar{n}\overline{s^2}}{2(1 - \rho_1)} + s_1 \qquad (26.38)$$

and

$$\bar{t}_{q_2} = \frac{\bar{n}\overline{s^2}}{2(1 - \rho_1)(1 - \rho)} + \bar{s}_2 \qquad (26.39)$$

If all of the service times are equal, $\overline{s^2} = \bar{s}^2$ and if all of the service times are exponential, $\overline{s^2} = 2\bar{s}^2$. Table 26.6 lists formulas for $\bar{t}_q$, $\bar{t}_w$, and $\bar{q}$ and $\bar{w}$ in these cases.

PREEMPTIVE
PRIORITIES

Formulas (26.36)–(26.39) relate to streams of transactions which do not interrupt each other.

We may also be interested in traffic streams in which an item *interrupts* the serving of any lower-priority item. High-priority items not only go to the head of the queue, but they cause the work on a lower-priority item to be stopped immediately. After an interruption ends, work recommences on a transaction at the point at which it ceased. This type of queuing theory might be useful, for example, in analyzing the work queuing for the attention of the processing unit in which certain events *interrupt* the processing of other items. There are often two levels of such priority, and there may be more than two.

Let us assume that all the priority streams arrive independently and with random arrival times. Equations (26.31)–(26.35) still hold. The mean queue size and queue time for the priority j items are

$$\bar{t}_{q_j} = \frac{1}{[1 - (\rho_1 + \rho_2 + \cdots \rho_{j-1})]} \left[\frac{(\bar{n}_1\bar{s}_1^2 + \bar{n}_2\bar{s}_2^2 + \cdots \bar{n}_j\bar{s}_j^2)}{2[1 - (\rho_1 + \rho_2 + \cdots \rho_j)]} + \bar{s}_j \right]$$

(26.40)

and

$$\bar{q}_j = \frac{1}{[1 - (\rho_1 + \rho_2 + \cdots \rho_{j-1})]} \left[\frac{\bar{n}_j(\bar{n}_1\bar{s}_1^2 + \bar{n}_2\bar{s}_2^2 + \cdots \bar{n}_j\bar{s}_j^2)}{2[1 - (\rho_1 + \rho_2 + \cdots \rho_j)]} + \rho_j \right]$$

(26.41)

For the top priority stream these condense to

$$\bar{t}_{q_1} = \frac{\bar{n}_1\bar{s}_1^2}{2(1 - \rho_1)} + \bar{s}_1$$

(26.42)

which is $\bar{t}_{q_1} = \dfrac{\bar{s}_1}{1 - \rho_1}$ when the service time   (26.43)
is exponential,

and $\bar{q}_1 = \dfrac{\bar{n}_1\bar{s}_1^2}{2(1 - \rho_1)} + \rho_1$ (26.44)

which is $\bar{q}_1 = \dfrac{\rho_1}{1 - \rho_1}$ when the service time   (26.45)
is exponential.

These last four equations are of the same form as the Khintchine-Polloczek equations for a single priority stream. For example for single-priority queues with exponential service times we have

$$\bar{t}_q = \frac{\bar{s}}{1 - \rho} \quad \text{and} \quad \bar{q} = \frac{\rho}{1 - \rho}$$

which are similar to Equations (26.43) and (26.45). This is to be expected, as the top priority items barge in front of all other items as if they did not exist.

Table 26.7 summarizes formulas for first and second-priority items, and constant and exponential service times, derived from Equations (26.40) and (26.41).

MULTISERVER	Lastly in this quick summary of basic queuing
QUEUES	formulas we will examine the situation in which
	more than one server tends the items.

Suppose now that our customer walking into a bank, at a randomly chosen time, is able to be serviced by any one of a group of tellers. He waits, with the other customers, for the first teller to become free. This situation is represented by the upper diagram in Fig. 26.8.

Multiserver queue

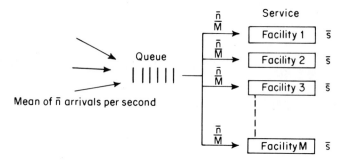

M identical servers

Each has mean service time $\bar{s}$ seconds

(Facility utilization of each server, $\rho = \dfrac{\bar{n}\,\bar{s}}{M}$)

Note that the queue time is less than if there were a separate queue for each server thus

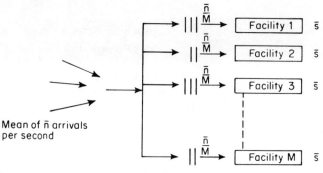

Figure 26.8

Note that he can go to any of the servers. If he could only go to his particular server, this would, in effect, be a single-server queue. The total queuing time for a group of items served by predetermined servers is greater than if they were able to choose the first of these servers who became free.

The formulas and curves below for multiserver queues make the following assumptions:

1. Arrival times follow a Poisson distribution, as before.
2. Items are served on a first-in, first-out basis.
3. The service times follow an exponential distribution.
4. All the servers have identical service time distributions. The latter two assumptions make these formulas more restricted in their use than the single-server formulas.

Let us suppose that there are M identical servers. The mean number of items being serviced is $\bar{n}$.

$$\therefore \quad \frac{\bar{n}}{M} \text{ items go to each server.}$$

The mean service time is $\bar{s}$. Therefore, the facility utilization of an individual server is

$$\rho = \frac{\bar{n}\bar{s}}{M} \tag{26.46}$$

As before, ρ must be less than 1. As ρ approaches 1, the queue sizes and times build up rapidly, though not quite as rapidly as in the single-server case with the same exponential service time.

The relationships in Equations (26.4)–(26.7) still hold:

$$t_q = t_w + s \tag{26.4}$$

$$\bar{t}_q = \bar{t}_w + \bar{s} \tag{26.5}$$

$$\bar{w} = \bar{n}\bar{t}_w \tag{26.6}$$

and

$$\bar{q} = \bar{n}\bar{t}_q \tag{26.7}$$

Now, t_w, t_q, w, and q relate to items waiting for any of the M servers, not just to one of them.

$$\bar{q} = \bar{n}\bar{t}_q = \bar{n}\bar{t}_w + \bar{n}\bar{s}.$$

Substituting from Equations (26.6) and (26.46), we get

$$\bar{q} = \bar{w} + M\rho \tag{26.47}$$

It can be shown that the probability of there being N items in the system at a given instant

$$P(q = N) = \frac{(M\rho)^N}{N!} P_o, \qquad \text{if } N < M$$

and

$$P(q = N) = \frac{(M\rho)^N}{M! \, M^{N-M}} P_o, \quad \text{if } N \geqslant M$$

where

$$P_o = \frac{1}{\sum\limits_{N=0}^{M-1} \dfrac{(M\rho)^N}{N!} + \dfrac{(M\rho)^M}{(1-\rho)M!}} \tag{26.48}$$

The probability of there being K or more than K items in the system at a given instant is

$$P(q \geqslant K) = \sum_{N=K}^{\infty} P(q = N)$$

This is plotted in Figs. 26.16 to 26.20 for two, three, four, five, and 20 servers, it is interesting to compare these with Fig. 26.15 for one server.

In particular, the probability of all the servers being busy at a given instant is

$$B = P(q \geqslant M) = \sum_{N=M}^{\infty} P(q = N)$$

This can be calculated to be

$$B = \frac{1 - \left(\dfrac{\sum\limits_{N=0}^{M-1} \dfrac{(M\rho)^N}{N!}}{\sum\limits_{N=0}^{M} \dfrac{(M\rho)^N}{N!}} \right)}{1 - \rho \left(\dfrac{\sum\limits_{N=0}^{M-1} \dfrac{(M\rho)^N}{N!}}{\sum\limits_{N=0}^{M} \dfrac{(M\rho)^N}{N!}} \right)} \tag{26.49}$$

This factor, B, appears in all of the remaining equations in this chapter (unfortunately!). It is plotted in Fig. 26.21. Note that this condenses to $B = \rho$ when $M = 1$.

It should be noted that B can be calculated fairly quickly from the *Summed Poisson Distribution* Table 26.1, early in this chapter, if we write it in the following form:

$$B = \frac{1 - \left(\dfrac{1 - \sum\limits_{N=M}^{\infty} \dfrac{e^{-(M\rho)}(M\rho)^N}{N!}}{1 - \sum\limits_{N=M+1}^{\infty} \dfrac{e^{-(M\rho)}(M\rho)^N}{N!}} \right)}{1 - \rho \left(\dfrac{1 - \sum\limits_{N=M}^{\infty} \dfrac{e^{-(M\rho)}(M\rho)^N}{N!}}{1 - \sum\limits_{M+1}^{\infty} \dfrac{e^{-(M\rho)}(M\rho)^N}{N!}} \right)}$$

This may be calculated from Table 26.1 if we replace $\bar{n}$ in the table by $(M\rho)$ and x by M or $(M+1)$ as required.

It can be shown that the mean number of items waiting before service begins in the multichannel queues described is

$$\bar{w} = B \frac{\rho}{1 - \rho} \tag{26.50}$$

$$\therefore \qquad \bar{q} = B \frac{\rho}{1 - \rho} + M\rho \tag{26.51}$$

The standard deviation of w is given by

$$\sigma_w = \frac{1}{1 - \rho} \sqrt{B\rho(1 + \rho - B\rho)} \tag{26.52}$$

The mean waiting time before service begins is

$$\bar{t}_w = \frac{B}{M} \frac{\bar{s}}{(1 - \rho)} \tag{26.53}$$

$$\therefore \qquad \bar{t}_q = \frac{B}{M} \frac{\bar{s}}{(1 - \rho)} + \bar{s} \tag{26.54}$$

The standard deviation of waiting time is

$$\sigma_{t_w} = \frac{\bar{s}}{M(1 - \rho)} \sqrt{B(2 - B)} \tag{26.55}$$

and

$$\sigma_{t_q} = \frac{\bar{s}}{M(1 - \rho)} \sqrt{B(2 - B) + M^2(1 - \rho)^2} \tag{26.56}$$

$\bar{q}$, $\bar{t}_q$, and σ_{t_q} are plotted against ρ in Figs. 26.22-26.24. The probability of waiting for a time longer than t is given by

$$P(t_w > t) = Be^{-(M/\bar{s})(1-\rho)t} \tag{26.57}$$

EXAMPLES OF THE USE OF THE CHARTS   *The curves in Figs. 26.9–26.24 constitute a basic tool which the not very mathematical systems engineer can use to give a first approximation of queue sizes and delays.*

Five examples of their use are given below. A number of more detailed examples will be included in the chapters that follow.

1. In the design of a banking system it is desirable to know how many customers will have to wait in a queue for a single bank teller at the peak hour.

The response time of the system and its standard deviation have been calculated, including the terminal key-in, printing, and document-insertion times.

The actions of the terminal operator have been timed. The "service time," s, is then the total time the teller takes in dealing with the transaction. The teller is the "facility" and so the "facility utilization," ρ, is the proportion of time the teller is occupied. If there are $\bar{n}$ transactions or customers in the peak hour, ρ for the teller $= \bar{n}\bar{s}$.

Let us suppose that there are 30 customers to be handled in the peak hour. On an average, the teller takes 1.5 minutes per customer.

$$\text{Then} \quad \rho = \frac{1.5 \times 30}{60} = 0.75$$

The teller is 75 per cent utilized.

From Fig. 26.9 we see that $\bar{q}$, the average number of people in the queue at the bank counter is between 1.88 and 3.0, depending upon the standard deviation of s, the time the teller takes to handle a transaction.

Suppose that we measure the standard deviation of s, and find it to be half a minute. Then $\sigma_s = 0.33\bar{s}$. Therefore, interpolating on Fig. 26.9 we find the $\bar{q} = 2.0$. On average, there will be two customers at the bank counter. Similarly using Fig. 26.10, or using the formula $\bar{q} = \bar{n}\bar{t}_q$, we find that $\bar{t}_q$, the total time the customer will be at the bank counter, on average, is 4.0 minutes.

Occasionally, however, the queues will become large. Figure 26.15 shows that the probability of there being more than ten customers at the counter with exponential service times is 0.05. For 5 per cent of the time, three minutes during the peak hour, there will, in this case, be more than ten customers queuing.

Similarly, using Fig. 26.14, we find that the probability of a customer having to wait more than 15 minutes ($T = 10\,\bar{s}$) is 0.08. However, as these curves relate to exponential service times they are on the high side. Let us try a different approach.

$$\sigma_s = 0.33\bar{s} \qquad \therefore \quad (\bar{s}/\sigma_s)^2 = 9$$

The service times approximate to an Erlang 9 distribution. Then from Fig. 26.12 we find that $\sigma_{t_q} = 2.1\bar{s} = 2.1 \times 1.5 = 3.15$ min. $(\bar{t}_q/\sigma_{t_q})^2 = (4/3.15)^2 = 1.51$. Let us therefore assume that queuing times follow a gamma distribution with parameter $R = 1.51$. This curve in Figs. 26.6 and 26.7 will give us the distribution of queuing times. For the figure above of 0.08 of the transactions, we can read off that $T/\bar{t}_q \simeq 2.3$, and $\bar{t}_q = 4$ min. Therefore 8 per cent of the customers have to wait $2.3 \times 4 = 9.2$ min. The figure of 15 minutes above was too pessimistic.

2. Now suppose that instead of one teller, there are five. Each teller has the same characteristics as the one teller described above. The customer is free to choose which teller he goes to.

The teller utilization now drops to one-fifth of its average value, i.e., 15 per cent. From Fig. 26.22 we see that the queue sizes are now very low.

If, however, there were five times as many customers so that the teller utilization was still 75 per cent, then from Fig. 26.22, or from Equations (26.51) and (26.49) we find that $\bar{q}$ is approximately 5.0 *if the service times are exponential*. In fact they are not exponential. Their dispersion is less than this and so the queues will be less. There is no convenient formula for evaluating the queue sizes exactly in this case. However, in the single-server case the queue size was two-thirds of that for the exponential case, and we may assume that *approximately* the same ratio will apply here. Similarly, Fig. 26.23 gives the queuing time.

From Fig. 26.19 we can evaluate the probability of exceeding certain queue sizes. As in the first example, this will give us an answer which overestimates the queue sizes because the service times are in fact better than exponentially distributed.

3. Next, consider a full duplex communication line with contention line control which transmits 15 characters per second. In the peak ten minutes it is estimated that 40 messages will be sent down the line to the computer. These have an average length of 100 characters, with standard deviation 50 characters. During this peak period, the facility utilization of the line will be

$$\frac{40 \times 100}{15 \times 60 \times 10} = 0.444$$

That part of the line going *to* the computer is 44.4 per cent utilized. A terminal on the line sending a message at a random point in time will have a waiting time t_w before it can start transmitting. Examining Fig. 26.10 we find that $\bar{t}_q = 1.50\bar{s}$.

We know that $\bar{t}_w = \bar{t}_q - \bar{s}$

$$\therefore \quad t_w = 0.50\,\bar{s} = \frac{0.50 \times 100}{15} = 3\tfrac{1}{3}$$

On average, a terminal will have to wait $3\tfrac{1}{3}$ seconds before transmission starts.

The standard deviation of t_q is found from Fig. 26.12 to be $0.97\,\bar{s} = 6.47$ seconds

$$t_q = t_w + s$$
$$\text{var}\,(t_q) = \text{var}\,(t_w) + \text{var}\,(s)$$
$$\therefore \quad \text{var}\,(t_w) = 6.47^2 - \left(\frac{50}{15}\right)^2$$

The standard deviation of t_w is 5.54 seconds.

4. The Supervisory Programs of a multithread system allow a number of message-reference blocks (see Chapter 9) to wait in a queue, or list, for the processing unit to start work on them. If details of program timings are known, the average size of these queues may be found from Fig. 26.9, and the standard deviation of these from Fig. 26.12. The facility utilization is the proportion of time the processing unit is in use and not in an idling loop or wait state.

If the items have more than one priority, then queue statistics can be found from the equations in Table 26.6. If there are two classes of items demanding the attention of the processing unit, one class will *interrupt* the other as soon as it needs the processing unit. This situation can be examined with the formulas in Table 26.7.

5. On a multiprogrammed system with many drums on one channel, references to these may be queued by the Supervisory Program. The "facility utilization" is now the channel utilization. The mean and standard deviation of the queue sizes and queue times may be obtained from Figs. 26.9–26.12.

In each of these cases use of the simple queuing theory illustrated above may lead only to an approximate answer. However, an approximate answer is often good enough to make the estimates of what hardware is required. The systems analyst must make the decision whether this simple queuing theory is good enough for his estimates, or whether he needs to use more elaborate mathematics or simulation.

CASES IN WHICH THE ABOVE THEORY IS INACCURATE

The formulas above, and indeed any mathematical analysis of this problem, are approximations of the more complex situations that exist in reality. In deriving the formulas certain assumptions were made, and the systems analyst should understand these. In most cases where they are applied they will give an answer that is slightly pessimistic. In other words, they will indicate rather longer queues and delays than are actually the case. This is because random arrivals and sometimes random service times are used. A live situation may be slightly better than random. However, the discrepancy is usually small and can well be regarded as a reasonable systems analyst's safety allowance.

There are, however, two types of situation when the queues and delays will be *worse* than those indicated by the above curves.

First, for some reason superimposed upon the normal behavior of the system, a sudden flood of items may arrive within a short period. For example, in a stockbroker's system certain news on the ticker-tape might trigger a sudden burst of transactions.

Second, on occasions the service time may be considerably longer than the normal range. For example, the system may handle a few exceptionally long messages which tie up the communication lines, buffers, core, and possibly file channels. In statistics when a small number of items in a group have values much higher than the rest, the mean is of little value and even the standard deviation is misleading. The queue sizes might, therefore, be evaluated ignoring the long service times, and the effect of these be investigated afterwards.

In some cases it will be incorrect to assume that the interarrival times follow a Poisson distribution. This assumption, however, usually does not introduce too great an inaccuracy. If non-Poisson interarrival times are to be considered in detail, simulation is necessary. It should be noted, however, that most simulations done for this kind of system have, themselves, a Poisson distribution of input.

In the case of messages entering a system, it will normally be sufficiently valid to assume a Poisson distribution. In the case of requests for file actions, this may not be true because the Supervisory Program mechanisms will have acted as a filter which, to some extent, evens out the distribution of events. At peak loads the interarrival times at the file channel will be more constant than a Poisson distribution. The degree of this effect will depend upon the Supervisory Program mechanisms. Some mechanisms will deliberately restrict the flow of work when the queues are becoming high. To estimate the behavior of such a mechanism in fine detail requires an elaborate simulation. At the survey stage, however, an approximate estimate of queues is usually enough to specify the core requirements of the system.

In general, any restricting element in a system, like a narrow section in a pipeline, tends to flatten the peaks of the traffic in the manner illustrated in Fig. 24.3. This traffic then reaching farther elements of the system has interarrival times slightly more constant than a Poisson distribution.

The structure of the queues may be more complex than those handled by the simple theory above. Customers telephoning or queuing at windows for service may give up if they have to wait too long. In some cases more elaborate theory may be required than that above. A bibliography is provided for the reader at the end of this chapter.

WHEN IS SIMULATION NEEDED?

To end this chapter let us reexamine the usefulness of simulation. As a tool for monitoring the implementation progress, simulation can be very valuable. During the survey stage of a real-time system it is thought that simulation is justified in the following circumstances:

1. *Communication Lines*

It is only when lines become heavily utilized that they are likely to need simulation. The average utilization of a line may be calculated from the average number of characters passing. It is generally true that, if the utilization is over 75 per cent and the input random, it can be stated without simulation that the line is too heavily utilized for safety. If it is below 30 per cent, it will cause no problem unless there are occasional very long messages, and the queues that these cause may be calculated arithmetically. If the utilization is between these figures, the resulting queues can often be predicted with sufficient accuracy for the initial system design from the curves in Figs. 26.9–26.15 if the message lengths are not too variable. These curves do not, however, take into account polling. On a polled line with short messages and many terminals on the line polling may need special consideration. With long messages and few terminals, however, polling will have only a minor effect on the waiting time, if all terminals are polled equally. An investigation of the effects of polling is best done with simulation. For a high line utilization and highly variable message lengths, simulation may be necessary with or without polling. This is particularly so if it is desirable to explore the merits of different polling disciplines.

2. Terminals

During the peak hours on certain types of system the terminals become very heavily loaded. Because of cost it is necessary to minimize the number of terminals used. On some systems the use of the terminals and their environment has been simulated; for example, the use of terminals in a bank at which customers are arriving at irregular time intervals during the lunch break. In general, however, the results obtained, such as those in the supermarket problems used in simulation classes, could be obtained with as much confidence without simulation. In the author's experience simulation has rarely been worthwhile in studying the terminals.

3. Processing Unit

On a nonmultiprogrammed system it is doubtful whether simulation is of value at the survey stage for making processing unit estimates. On a system with a low degree of multiprogramming which permits no more than two or three messages to be processed in parallel, it will commonly be possible to estimate the core utilization roughly without simulation and the time utilization with bar charts and simple queuing theory. Simulation is certainly valuable, however, to obtain a picture of what is happening when there is a high degree of multithread processing, or indeed in determining whether a high level of multiprogramming is in fact of value.

Simulation may be of great value in assessing the relative merits of certain supervisory mechanisms. The choice between different paging schemes, or, in general, the means of assessing new program blocks and determining the sequence in which operations are carried out, can be explored with simulation. Paging schemes and program read-in mechanisms are difficult to investigate analytically. However, this may be a long job, and it is often not investigated with this degree of thoroughness at the survey time.

4. *Files*

It is in the area of files that we sometimes have the most difficulty with analytical techniques. If there is only one file unit in operation on a channel at one time, then the above methods are excellent for evaluating the queue characteristics. This would be so if there were only drums on the channel. It would be so if there were only one file access mechanism on the channel. However, when we consider several "seek" mechanisms on one channel, as in the case that was simulated in the last chapter, then the queuing problems are compounded. We are queuing both for the channel, and for the "seek" mechanisms which can operate simultaneously. On some systems there are many file-access mechanisms and so the utilization of this mechanism is very low compared with the utilization of the channel. The channel then is the main factor determining the queue sizes. On the other hand, the system may have few file "arms" and long "seeks" so that the arm utilization is high compared with the channel. Then the arm is the main factor in determining queue sizes.

Furthermore, we sometimes have a situation in which many program and data segments are read in from file so that the channel and arm utilization will be dependent upon the core utilization. In this type of system only an approximate estimate can be made without resorting to simulation, and simulation is certainly needed if the facility utilizations are high. This will be discussed further in Chapter 28.

There is another form of simulation of a slightly different nature that may be needed for the files. Where an algorithm or randomizing process is needed to generate file addresses from a set of job-oriented identifications, such as part numbers or date and flight numbers, the packing density and average seek times associated with the various algorithms should be found. This may or may not require simulation and is discussed in the next chapter.

In general, queuing theory becomes inadequate when the message types or program functions are highly variable or when the way work is routed through the system is complex. Its inadequacies are more serious when the facility utilization is high, say more than 0.7. The need for simulation will depend upon the accuracy required in the estimates, and this can be indicated in part by how accurately the time and core requirements of the programs are known. Often the application of the curves in this chapter will indicate that there is no problem. Sometimes, however, it indicates that the conditions are marginal, and in such cases a more accurate means of making estimates will be needed.

Table 26.3. THE NOTATION USED IN THIS CHAPTER

n	Number of arrivals per second	
$\bar{n}$	Average number of arrivals per second	
$P(n = N)$	Probability of having N arrivals in a given second	
$P(n \geqslant N)$	Probability of having N or more arrivals in a given second	
t_a	Interarrival time	
$\bar{t}_a$	Mean Interarrival time	$\bar{t}_a = 1/\bar{n}$
s	Service time for an item	
$\bar{s}$	Mean service time for all items	
ρ	Facility utilization of one serving facility	$\rho = \bar{n}\bar{s}$ for a single server
M	The number of servers in parallel on a multiserver system.	$\rho = \bar{n}\bar{s}/M$ for multiple servers
t_ω	Time an item spends waiting for service (not including time being served)	
$\bar{t}_\omega$	Mean of t_w for all items	
w	Number of items waiting for service (not including item being served)	
$\bar{w}$	Mean of w for all items	$\bar{w} = \bar{n}\bar{t}_w$
t_q	Time an item spends in system, waiting and being served	$t_q = t_w + s$
$\bar{t}_q$	Mean of t_q for all items	$\bar{t}_q = \bar{t}_w + \bar{s}$
q	Number of items in system, waiting and being served.	
$\bar{q}$	Mean of q for all items	$\bar{q} = \bar{n}\bar{t}_q$
$P(q = N)$	Probability that N items are in the system	
$P(q \geqslant N)$	Probability that q equals or is greater than integer N	
$P(t_q > T)$	Probability that t_q is greater than a given time, T.	
B	Probability that all servers are busy on a multiserver system	
$\bar{x}$	The mean value of x	
$\overline{x^2}$	The second moment of x	
$\overline{x^3}$	The third moment of x	
σ_x	The standard deviation of x	$\sigma_x = \sqrt{\overline{x^2} - \bar{x}^2}$ $= \sqrt{\text{Mean}(\bar{x} - x)^2}$
$\text{var}(x)$	The variance of x	$\text{var}(x) = \sigma_x^2$
E_x	Parameter of an Erlang E distribution of x	$E_x = (\bar{x}/\sigma_x)^2$ to the nearest integer.

Table 26.4. FORMULAS FOR SINGLE-SERVER QUEUES

For random (Poisson) arrivals
General service times

$$\bar{w} = \frac{\rho^2}{2(1-\rho)}\left[1 + \left(\frac{\sigma_s}{\bar{s}}\right)^2\right]$$

$$\bar{q} = \rho + \frac{\rho^2}{2(1-\rho)}\left[1 + \left(\frac{\sigma_s}{\bar{s}}\right)^2\right]$$

$$\bar{t}_w = \frac{\rho\bar{s}}{2(1-\rho)}\left[1 + \left(\frac{\sigma_s}{\bar{s}}\right)^2\right]$$

$$\bar{t}_q = \bar{s} + \frac{\rho\bar{s}}{2(1-\rho)}\left[1 + \left(\frac{\sigma_s}{\bar{s}}\right)^2\right]$$

$$\text{var}\,(q) = \frac{\bar{n}^3\bar{s}^3}{3(1-\rho)} + \frac{\bar{n}^4(\overline{s^2})^2}{4(1-\rho)^2} + \frac{\bar{n}^2(3-2\rho)\overline{s^2}}{2(1-\rho)} + \rho(1-\rho)$$

$$\text{var}\,(t_q) = \frac{\bar{n}\bar{s}^3 + 3\bar{s}^2}{3(1-\rho)} + \frac{\bar{n}^2(\overline{s^2})^2}{2(1-\rho)^2} - \bar{t}_q^2$$

Random (Poisson) arrivals Random (exponential) service time	Random (Poisson) arrivals Constant service times
$$\bar{w} = \frac{\rho^2}{1-\rho}$$	$$\bar{w} = \frac{\rho^2}{2(1-\rho)}$$
$$\bar{q} = \frac{\rho}{1-\rho}$$	$$\bar{q} = \frac{\rho^2}{2(1-\rho)} + \rho$$
$$\sigma_q = \frac{1}{1-\rho}\sqrt{\rho}$$	$$\sigma_q = \frac{1}{1-\rho}\sqrt{\rho - \frac{3\rho^2}{2} + \frac{5\rho^3}{6} + \frac{\rho^4}{12}}$$
$$\bar{t}_w = \frac{\rho\bar{s}}{(1-\rho)}$$	$$\bar{t}_w = \frac{\rho\bar{s}}{2(1-\rho)}$$
$$\sigma_{t_w} = \frac{\bar{s}}{(1-\rho)}\sqrt{2\rho - \rho^2}$$	$$\sigma_{t_w} = \frac{\bar{s}}{(1-\rho)}\sqrt{\frac{\rho}{3} - \frac{\rho^2}{12}}$$
$$\bar{t}_q = \frac{\bar{s}}{(1-\rho)}$$	$$\bar{t}_q = \frac{\bar{s}(2-\rho)}{2(1-\rho)}$$
$$\sigma_{t_q} = \frac{\bar{s}}{(1-\rho)}$$	$$\sigma_{t_q} = \frac{\bar{s}}{(1-\rho)}\sqrt{\frac{\rho}{3} - \frac{\rho^2}{12}}$$
$$P(q = N) = (1-\rho)\rho^N$$	
$$P(q \lessgtr N) = \sum_{q=0}^{N}(1-\rho)\rho^q$$	
$$P(t_q \lessgtr t) = 1 - e^{-(1-\rho)t/\bar{s}}$$	

NOTE: The formulas for $\bar{w}$, $\bar{q}$, $\bar{t}_w$, and $\bar{t}_q$ apply for any dispatching discipline that is independent of service times. The other formulas apply only to first-in, first-out dispatching

Table 26.5. FORMULAS FOR MULTISERVER QUEUES

For random (Poisson) arrivals, random (exponential) service times, and M identical servers.

$$\rho = \frac{\bar{n}\bar{s}}{M}$$

Probability that all servers are busy

$$B = \frac{1 - \left(\dfrac{\sum_{N=0}^{M-1} \dfrac{(M\rho)^N}{N!}}{\sum_{N=0}^{M} \dfrac{(M\rho)^N}{N!}}\right)}{1 - \rho\left(\dfrac{\sum_{N=0}^{M-1} \dfrac{(M\rho)^N}{N!}}{\sum_{N=0}^{M} \dfrac{(M\rho)^N}{N!}}\right)}$$

$$\bar{w} = B\frac{\rho}{1-\rho}$$

$$\bar{q} = B\frac{\rho}{1-\rho} + M\rho$$

$$\sigma_w = \frac{1}{1-\rho}\sqrt{B\rho(1+\rho-B\rho)}$$

$$\bar{t}_w = \frac{B}{M}\frac{\bar{S}}{(1-\rho)}$$

$$\bar{t}_q = \frac{B}{M}\frac{\bar{S}}{(1-\rho)} + \bar{S}$$

$$\sigma_{t_w} = \frac{\bar{S}}{M(1-\rho)}\sqrt{B(2-B)}$$

$$\sigma_{t_q} = \frac{\bar{S}}{M(1-\rho)}\sqrt{B(2-B)+M^2(1-\rho)^2}$$

$$P(t_w > t) = Be^{-(M/\bar{S})(1-\rho)t}$$

$$P(q \leq k) = \sum_{N=0}^{k} P(q=N) \qquad \text{where}$$

$$P(q=N) = \begin{cases} \dfrac{\dfrac{(M\rho)^N}{N!}}{\displaystyle\sum_{N=0}^{M-1}\dfrac{(M\rho)^N}{N!} + \dfrac{(M\rho)^M}{(1-\rho)M!}}, & \text{if } N < M \\[4ex] \dfrac{\dfrac{(M\rho)^N}{M!\,M^{N-M}}}{\displaystyle\sum_{N=0}^{M-1}\dfrac{(M\rho)^N}{N!} + \dfrac{(M\rho)^M}{(1-\rho)M!}}, & \text{if } N \geq M \end{cases}$$

NOTE: These formulas apply only to first-in, first-out dispatching.

Table 26.6. FORMULAS FOR SINGLE-SERVER QUEUES WITH ITEMS OF DIFFERENT PRIORITIES. [PRIORITY j ITEMS ARE SERVED BEFORE PRIORITY $(j+1)$ ITEMS. NO ITEM IS INTERRUPTED WHILE BEING SERVED.]

Random (Poisson) arrivals	Random (Poisson) arrivals	Random (Poisson) arrivals
General service times	Random (exponential) service times	Constant service times

Column 1 (General service times):

$$\bar{q}_1 = \frac{\bar{n}\,\bar{n}_1\,\overline{s^2}}{2(1-\rho_1)} + \rho_1$$

$$\bar{q}_2 = \frac{\bar{n}\,\bar{n}_2\,\overline{s^2}}{2(1-\rho_1)(1-\rho)} + \rho_2$$

$$\bar{q} = \frac{\bar{n}\,\overline{s^2}}{2(1-\rho_1)}\left[\bar{n}_1 + \frac{\bar{n}_2}{1-\rho}\right] + \rho$$

$$\bar{w} = \frac{\bar{n}\,\overline{s^2}}{2(1-\rho_1)}\left[\bar{n}_1 + \frac{\bar{n}_2}{1-\rho}\right]$$

$$\bar{t}_{q_1} = \frac{\bar{n}\,\overline{s^2}}{2(1-\rho_1)} + \bar{s}_1$$

$$\bar{t}_{q_2} = \frac{\bar{n}\,\overline{s^2}}{2(1-\rho_1)(1-\rho)} + \bar{s}_2$$

$$\bar{t}_q = \frac{\overline{s^2}}{2(1-\rho_1)}\left[\bar{n}_1 + \frac{\bar{n}_2}{1-\rho}\right] + \bar{s}$$

$$\bar{t}_w = \frac{\overline{s^2}}{2(1-\rho_1)}\left[\bar{n}_1 + \frac{\bar{n}_2}{1-\rho}\right]$$

Column 2 (Random (exponential) service times):

$$\bar{q}_1 = \frac{\bar{n}_1\,\rho\,\bar{s}}{(1-\rho_1)} + \rho_1$$

$$\bar{q}_2 = \frac{\bar{n}_2\,\rho\,\bar{s}}{(1-\rho_1)(1-\rho)} + \rho_2$$

$$\bar{q} = \frac{\rho\,\bar{s}}{(1-\rho_1)}\left[\bar{n}_1 + \frac{\bar{n}_2}{1-\rho}\right] + \rho$$

$$\bar{w} = \frac{\rho\,\bar{s}}{(1-\rho_1)}\left[\bar{n}_1 + \frac{\bar{n}_2}{1-\rho}\right]$$

$$\bar{t}_{q_1} = \frac{\rho\,\bar{s}}{(1-\rho_1)} + \bar{s}_1$$

$$\bar{t}_{q_2} = \frac{\rho\,\bar{s}}{(1-\rho_1)(1-\rho)} + \bar{s}_2$$

$$\bar{t}_q = \frac{\overline{s^2}}{(1-\rho_1)}\left[\bar{n}_1 + \frac{\bar{n}_2}{1-\rho}\right] + \bar{s}$$

$$\bar{t}_w = \frac{\overline{s^2}}{(1-\rho_1)}\left[\bar{n}_1 + \frac{\bar{n}_2}{1-\rho}\right]$$

Column 3 (Constant service times):

$$\bar{q}_1 = \frac{\bar{n}_1\,\rho\,\bar{s}}{2(1-\rho_1)} + \rho_1$$

$$\bar{q}_2 = \frac{\bar{n}_2\,\rho\,\bar{s}}{2(1-\rho_1)(1-\rho)} + \rho_2$$

$$\bar{q} = \frac{\rho\,\bar{s}}{2(1-\rho_1)}\left[\bar{n}_1 + \frac{\bar{n}_2}{1-\rho}\right] + \rho$$

$$\bar{w} = \frac{\rho\,\bar{s}}{2(1-\rho_1)}\left[\bar{n}_1 + \frac{\bar{n}_2}{1-\rho}\right]$$

$$\bar{t}_{q_1} = \frac{\rho\,\bar{s}}{2(1-\rho_1)} + \bar{s}_1$$

$$\bar{t}_{q_2} = \frac{\rho\,\bar{s}}{2(1-\rho_1)(1-\rho)} + \bar{s}_2$$

$$\bar{t}_q = \frac{\overline{s^2}}{2(1-\rho_1)}\left[\bar{n}_1 + \frac{\bar{n}_2}{1-\rho}\right] + \bar{s}$$

$$\bar{t}_w = \frac{\overline{s^2}}{2(1-\rho_1)}\left[\bar{n}_1 + \frac{\bar{n}_2}{1-\rho}\right]$$

Formulas for single-server queues with items of two priorities: random (poisson) arrivals; general service times

$$\bar{q}_j = \frac{\bar{n}\,\bar{n}_j\,\overline{s^2}}{2[1-(\rho_1+\rho_2+\cdots\rho_{j-1})][1-(\rho_1+\rho_2+\cdots\rho_j)]} + \rho_j$$

$$\bar{w}_j = \frac{\bar{n}\,\bar{n}_j\,\overline{s^2}}{2[1-(\rho_1+\rho_2+\cdots\rho_{j-1})][1-(\rho_1+\rho_2+\cdots\rho_j)]}$$

$$\bar{t}_{qj} = \frac{\bar{n}\,\overline{s^2}}{2[1-(\rho_1+\rho_2+\cdots\rho_{j-1})][1-(\rho_1+\rho_2+\cdots\rho_j)]} + \bar{s}_j$$

$$\bar{t}_{wj} = \frac{\bar{n}\,\overline{s^2}}{2[1-(\rho_1+\rho_2+\cdots\rho_{j-1})][1-(\rho_1+\rho_2+\cdots\rho_j)]}$$

Formulas for Priority j items in a queue with many priorities

Table 26.7. FORMULAS FOR SINGLE-SERVER QUEUES WITH ITEMS OF DIFFERENT PRIORITIES AND IN WHICH ANY ITEM INTERRUPTS THE PROCESSING OF ITEMS OF LESSER PRIORITY. AFTER AN INTERRUPT, PROCESSING RESUMES WHERE IT STOPPED.

Random (Poisson) arrivals	Random (Poisson) arrivals	Random (Poisson) arrivals
General service times	Random (exponential) service times	Constant service times

Column 1 — General service times

$$\bar{q}_1 = \frac{\bar{n}_1^2 \bar{s}_1^2}{2(1-\rho_1)} + \rho_1$$

$$\bar{q}_2 = \frac{1}{(1-\rho_1)} \times \left[\frac{\bar{n}_1\bar{n}_2\bar{s}_1^2 + \bar{n}_2^2\bar{s}_2^2}{2(1-\rho)} + \rho_2\right]$$

$$\bar{q}_j = \frac{1}{[1-(\rho_1+\rho_2+\cdots\rho_{j-1})]} \times \left[\frac{\bar{n}_j(\bar{n}_1\bar{s}_1^2 + \bar{n}_2\bar{s}_2^2 + \cdots \bar{n}_j\bar{s}_j^2)}{2[1-(\rho_1+\rho_2+\cdots\rho_j)]} + \rho_j\right]$$

$$\bar{t}_{q1} = \frac{\bar{n}_1\bar{s}_1^2}{2(1-\rho_1)} + \bar{s}_1$$

$$\bar{t}_{q2} = \frac{1}{(1-\rho_1)} \times \left[\frac{\bar{n}_1\bar{s}_1^2 + \bar{n}_2\bar{s}_2^2}{2(1-\rho)} + \bar{s}_2\right]$$

$$\bar{t}_{qj} = \frac{1}{[1-(\rho_1+\rho_2+\cdots\rho_{j-1})]} \times \left[\frac{(\bar{n}_1\bar{s}_1^2 + \bar{n}_2\bar{s}_2^2 + \cdots \bar{n}_j\bar{s}_j^2)}{2[1-(\rho_1+\rho_2+\cdots\rho_j)]} + \bar{s}_j\right]$$

Column 2 — Random (exponential) service times

$$\bar{q}_1 = \frac{\rho_1}{1-\rho_1}$$

$$\bar{q}_2 = \frac{1}{(1-\rho)} \times \left[\frac{\bar{n}_2\bar{s}_1\rho_1}{(1-\rho_1)} + \rho_2\right]$$

$$\bar{q}_j = \frac{1}{[1-(\rho_1+\rho_2+\cdots\rho_{j-1})]} \times \left[\frac{\bar{n}_j(\rho_1\bar{s}_1 + \rho_2\bar{s}_2 + \cdots \rho_j\bar{s}_j)}{[1-(\rho_1+\rho_2+\cdots\rho_j)]} + \rho_j\right]$$

$$\bar{t}_{q1} = \frac{\bar{s}_1}{(1-\rho_1)}$$

$$\bar{t}_{q2} = \frac{1}{(1-\rho_1)} \times \left[\frac{\rho_1\bar{s}_1 + \rho_2\bar{s}_2}{(1-\rho)} + \bar{s}_2\right]$$

$$\bar{t}_{qj} = \frac{1}{[1-(\rho_1+\rho_2+\cdots\rho_{j-1})]} \times \left[\frac{\rho_1\bar{s}_1 + \rho_2\bar{s}_2 + \cdots \rho_j\bar{s}_j}{[1-(\rho_1+\rho_2+\cdots\rho_j)]} + \bar{s}_j\right]$$

Column 3 — Constant service times

$$\bar{q}_1 = \frac{\rho_1^2}{2(1-\rho_1)} + \rho_1$$

$$\bar{q}_2 = \frac{1}{(1-\rho_1)} \times \left[\frac{\bar{n}_2\bar{s}_1\rho_1 + \rho_2}{2(1-\rho)} + \rho_2\right]$$

$$\bar{q}_j = \frac{1}{[1-(\rho_1+\rho_2+\cdots\rho_{j-1})]} \times \left[\frac{\bar{n}_j(\rho_1\bar{s}_1 + \rho_2\bar{s}_2 + \cdots \rho_j\bar{s}_j)}{2[1-(\rho_1+\rho_2+\cdots\rho_j)]} + \rho_j\right]$$

$$\bar{t}_{q1} = \frac{\bar{s}_1(2-\rho_1)}{2(1-\rho_1)}$$

$$\bar{t}_{q2} = \frac{1}{(1-\rho_1)} \times \left[\frac{\rho_1\bar{s}_1 + \rho_2\bar{s}_2}{2(1-\rho)} + \bar{s}_2\right]$$

$$\bar{t}_{qj} = \frac{1}{[1-(\rho_1+\rho_2+\cdots\rho_{j-1})]} \times \left[\frac{\rho_1\bar{s}_1 + \rho_2\bar{s}_2 + \cdots \rho_j\bar{s}_j}{2[1-(\rho_1+\rho_2+\cdots\rho_j)]} + \bar{s}_j\right]$$

Total queue: $\qquad \bar{q} = \bar{q}_1 + \bar{q}_2 + \cdots \bar{q}_j + \cdots \bar{q}_k$

Average queue time: $\bar{t}_q = \frac{\bar{n}_1}{\bar{n}} \bar{t}_1 + \frac{\bar{n}_2}{\bar{n}} \bar{t}_2 + \cdots \frac{\bar{n}_j}{\bar{n}} \bar{t}_j + \cdots \frac{\bar{n}_k}{\bar{n}}\bar{t}_k$

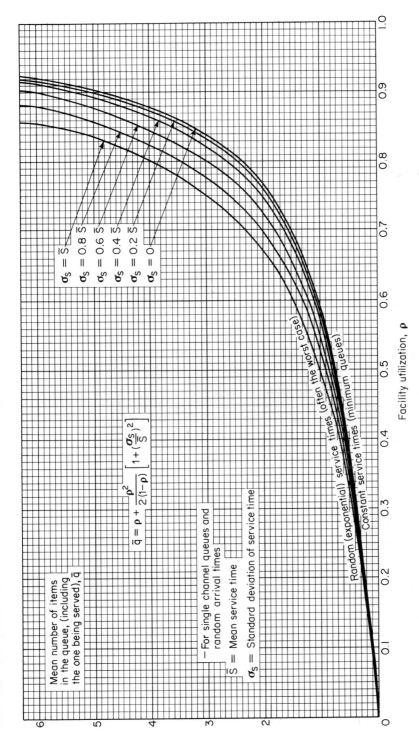

Fig. 26.9. Queue sizes with single-server queues.

411

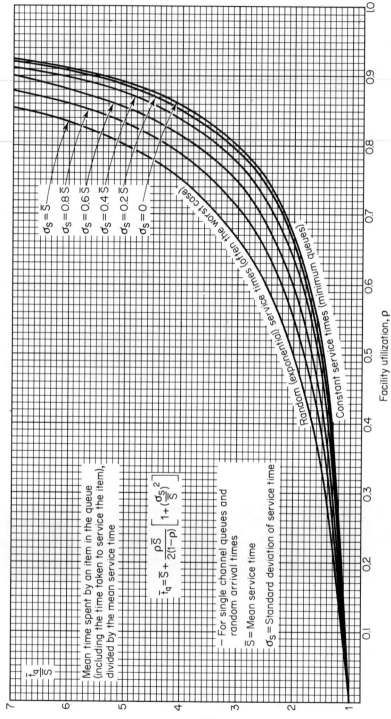

Fig. 26.10. Queuing times with single-server queues.

412

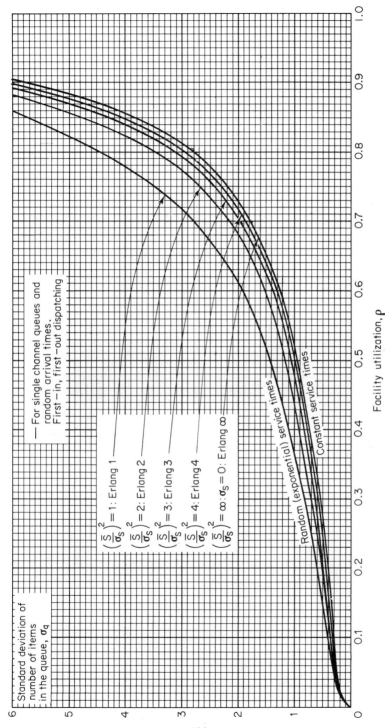

Fig. 26.11. Standard deviation of queue sizes in a single server queue.

413

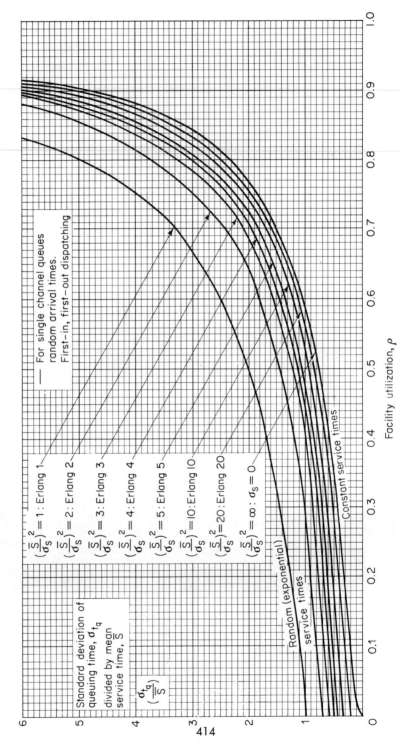

Fig. 26.12. Standard deviation of queuing times with single-server queues.

For single channel queues
random arrival times.
First–in, first–out dispatching

Standard deviation of
queuing time, σ_{t_q}
divided by mean
service time, $\overline{S}$

$\left(\dfrac{\sigma_{t_q}}{\overline{S}}\right)$

$\left(\dfrac{\overline{S}}{\sigma_S}\right)^2 = 1 : \text{Erlang 1}$
$\left(\dfrac{\overline{S}}{\sigma_S}\right)^2 = 2 : \text{Erlang 2}$
$\left(\dfrac{\overline{S}}{\sigma_S}\right)^2 = 3 : \text{Erlang 3}$
$\left(\dfrac{\overline{S}}{\sigma_S}\right)^2 = 4 : \text{Erlang 4}$
$\left(\dfrac{\overline{S}}{\sigma_S}\right)^2 = 5 : \text{Erlang 5}$
$\left(\dfrac{\overline{S}}{\sigma_S}\right)^2 = 10 : \text{Erlang 10}$
$\left(\dfrac{\overline{S}}{\sigma_S}\right)^2 = 20 : \text{Erlang 20}$
$\left(\dfrac{\overline{S}}{\sigma_S}\right)^2 = \infty : \sigma_S = 0$

Random (exponential)
service times

Constant service times

Facility utilization, ρ

414

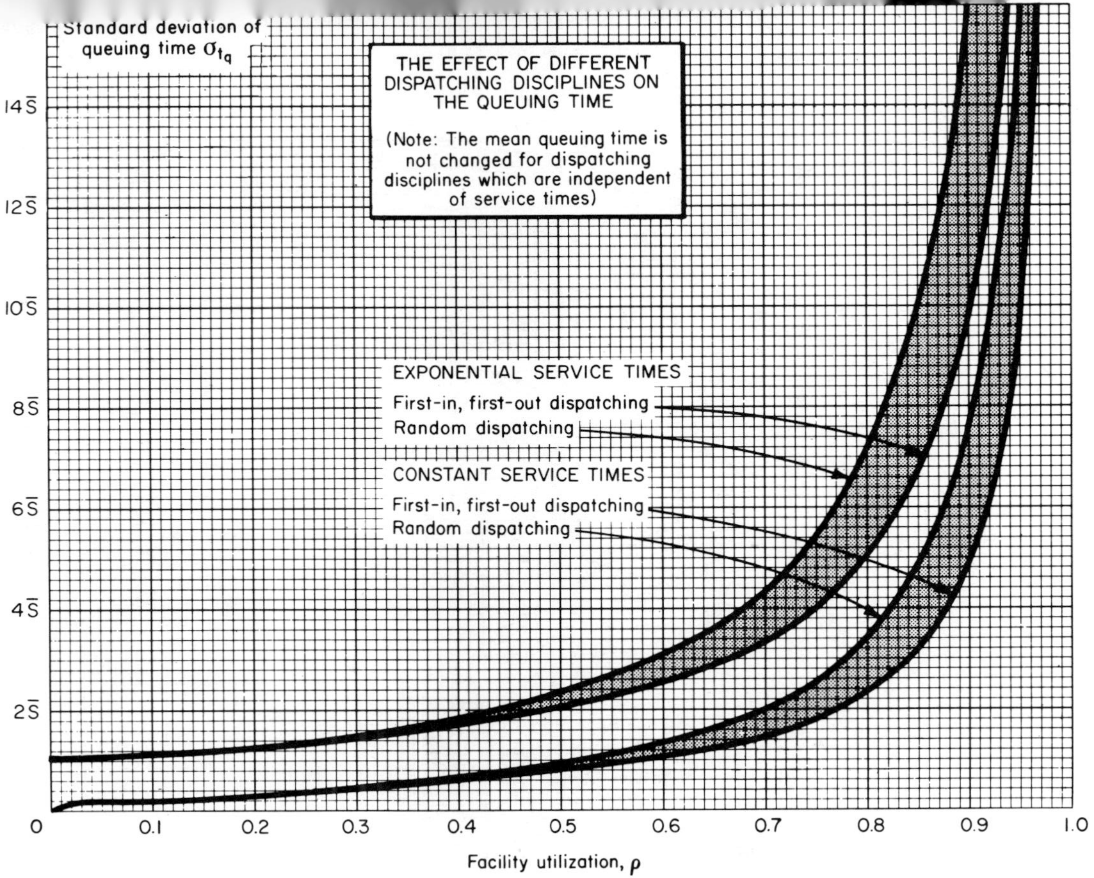
Standard deviation of queuing time σ_{t_q}
THE EFFECT OF DIFFERENT DISPATCHING DISCIPLINES ON THE QUEUING TIME
(Note: The mean queuing time is not changed for dispatching disciplines which are independent of service times)
EXPONENTIAL SERVICE TIMES
First-in, first-out dispatching
Random dispatching
CONSTANT SERVICE TIMES
First-in, first-out dispatching
Random dispatching
14$\bar{S}$
12$\bar{S}$
10$\bar{S}$
8$\bar{S}$
6$\bar{S}$
4$\bar{S}$
2$\bar{S}$
0
0.1
0.2
0.3
0.4
0.5
0.6
0.7
0.8
0.9
1.0
Facility utilization, ρ

Fig. 26.13. The effect of different dispatching disciplines on queuing time.

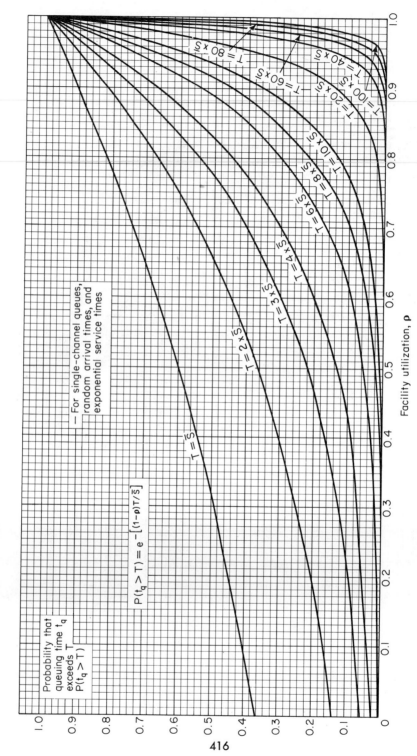

Fig. 26.14. Probability of exceeding certain queuing times.

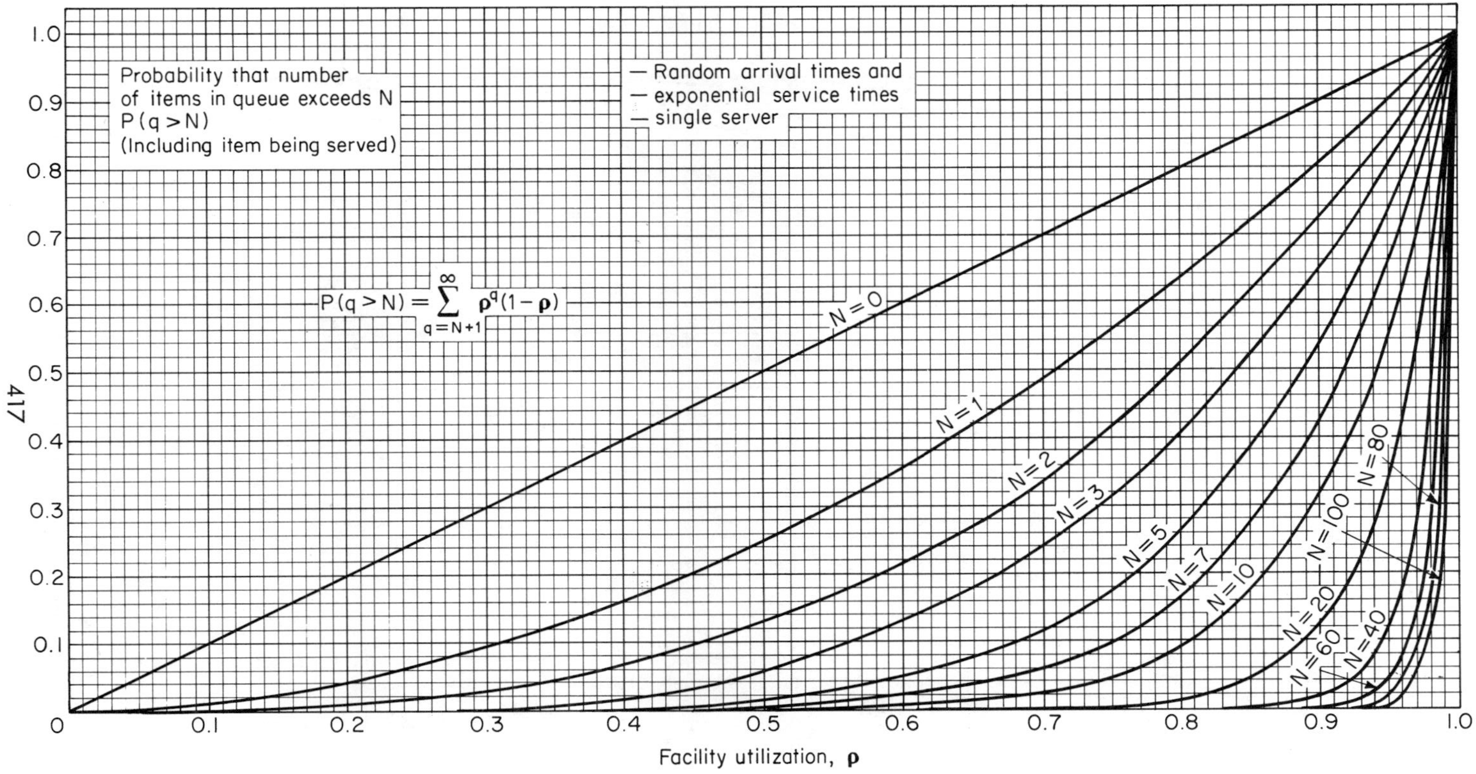

Probability that number of items in queue exceeds N P(q > N) (Including item being served)
— Random arrival times and
— exponential service times
— single server
$P(q>N)=\sum_{q=N+1}^{\infty}\rho^q(1-\rho)$
N = 0
N = 1
N = 2
N = 3
N = 5
N = 7
N = 10
N = 20
N = 40
N = 60
N = 80
N = 100
0
0.1
0.2
0.3
0.4
0.5
0.6
0.7
0.8
0.9
1.0
Facility utilization, ρ

Fig. 26.15. Probability of exceeding certain queue sizes in a single-server queue.

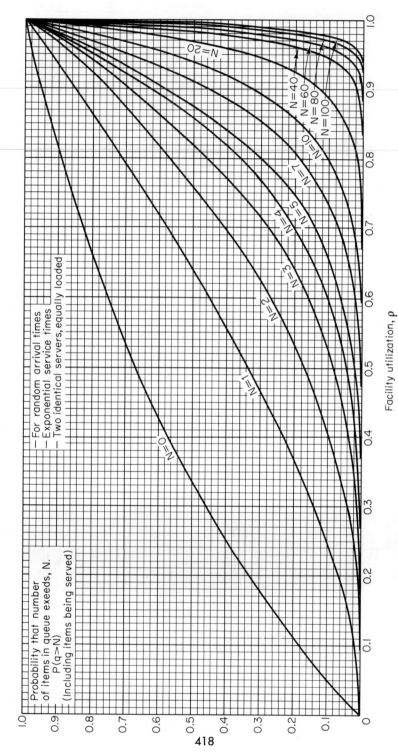

Fig. 26.16. Probability of exceeding certain queue sizes in a two-server queue.

418

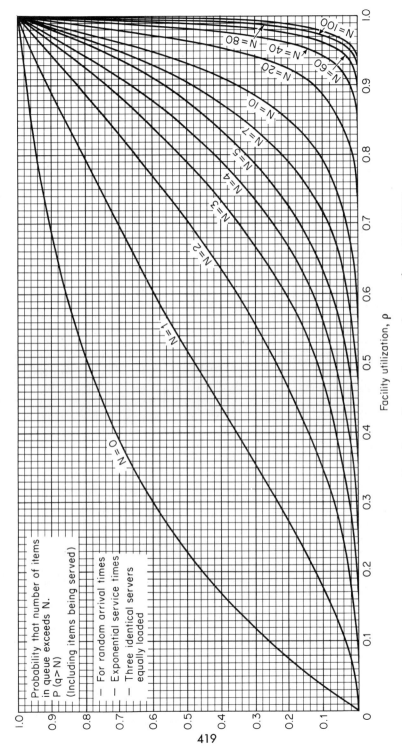

Probability that number of items
in queue exceeds N.
P (q > N)
(Including items being served)

— For random arrival times
— Exponential service times
— Three identical servers
  equally loaded

N = 0

N = 1

N = 2

N = 3

N = 4

N = 5

N = 7

N = 10

N = 20

N = 40

N = 60

N = 80

N = 100

Facility utilization, ρ

419

Fig. 26.17. Probability of exceeding certain queue sizes in a three-server queue.

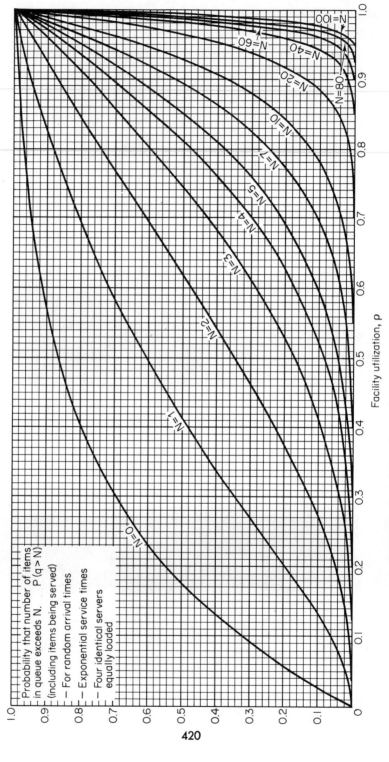

Fig. 26.18. Probability of exceeding certain queue sizes in a four-server queue.

420

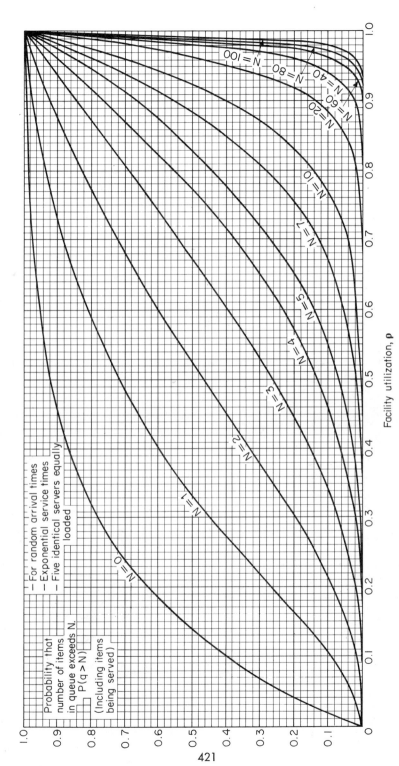

Fig. 26.19. Probability of exceeding certain queue sizes in a five-server queue.

Probability that
number of items
in queue exceeds N.

P(q > N)

(Including items
being served)

N = 0

N = 1

N = 2

N = 3

N = 4

N = 5

N = 7

N = 10

N = 20

N = 40

N = 60

N = 80

N = 100

— For random arrival times
— Exponential service times
— Five identical servers equally
     loaded

Facility utilization, ρ

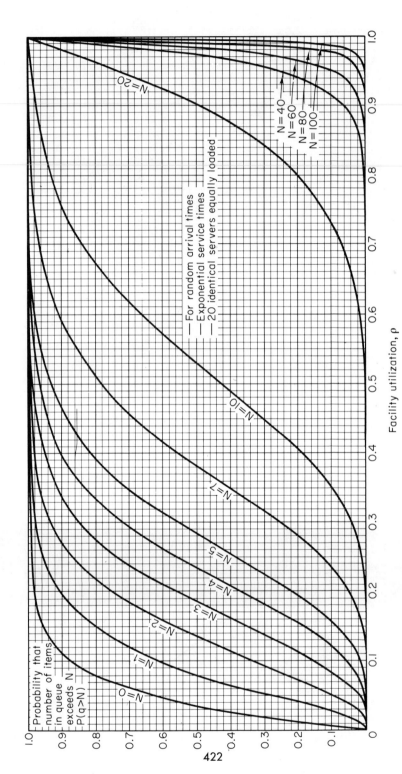

Fig. 26.20. Probability of exceeding certain queue sizes in a 20-server queue.

422

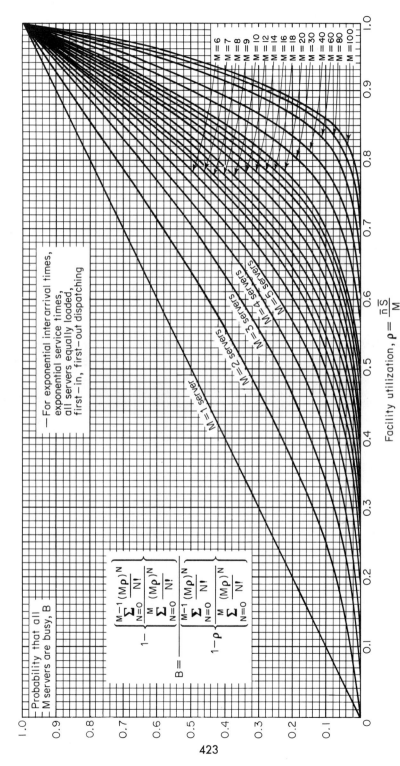

Fig. 26.21. Probability that all servers are busy in a multiserver queuing system.

Probability that all M servers are busy, B

— For exponential interarrival times, exponential service times, all servers equally loaded, first-in, first-out dispatching

$$B = \dfrac{\dfrac{(M\rho)^N}{N!}\Bigg|_{N=0}^{M-1}}{1 - \dfrac{\displaystyle\sum_{N=0}^{M-1}\dfrac{(M\rho)^N}{N!}}{\displaystyle\sum_{N=0}^{M}\dfrac{(M\rho)^N}{N!}}} = \dfrac{\dfrac{(M\rho)^N}{N!}\Bigg|_{N=0}^{M-1}}{1 - \rho\displaystyle\sum_{N=0}^{M}\dfrac{(M\rho)^N}{N!}}$$

M = 1 server

M = 2 servers

M = 3 servers

M = 4 servers

M = 5 servers

M = 6
M = 7
M = 8
M = 9
M = 10
M = 12
M = 14
M = 16
M = 18
M = 20
M = 30
M = 40
M = 60
M = 80
M = 100

Facility utilization, $\rho = \dfrac{\overline{n}\,\overline{S}}{M}$

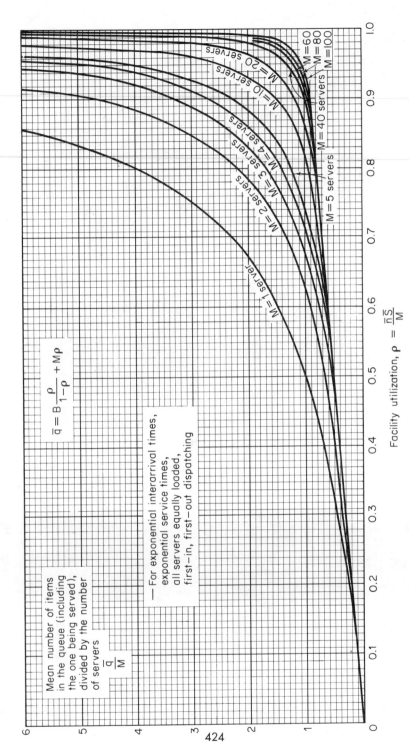

Fig. 26.22. Sizes of queues in a multiserver queuing system.

424

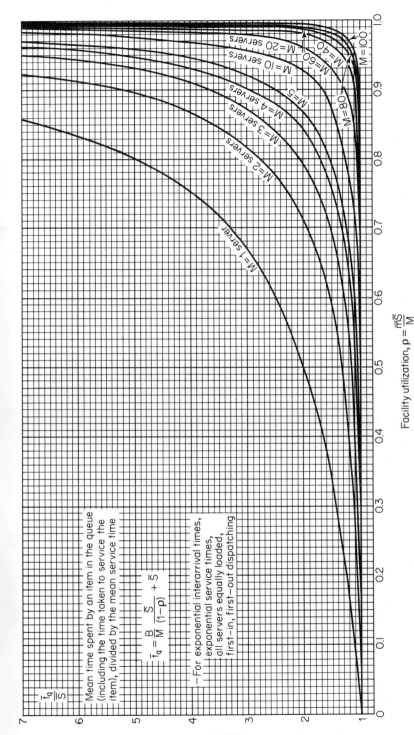

Fig. 26.23. Queuing times for multiserver queues.

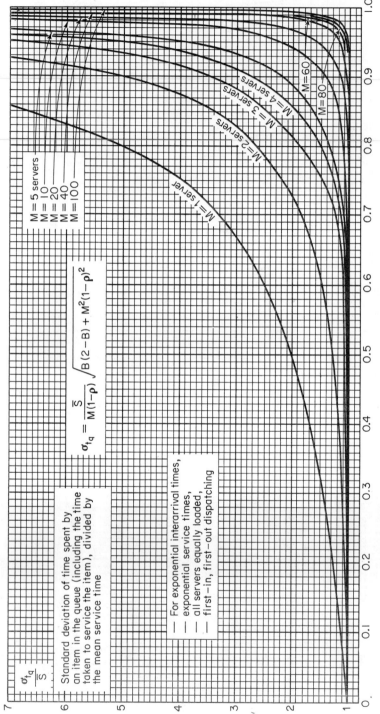

Fig. 26.24. Standard deviation of queuing times for multiserver queues.

M = 5 servers
M = 10
M = 20
M = 40
M = 100

$$\sigma_{t_q} = \frac{\overline{S}}{M(1-\rho)} \sqrt{B(2-B) + M^2(1-\rho)^2}$$

Standard deviation of time spent by an item in the queue (including the time taken to service the item), divided by the mean service time

— For exponential interarrival times,
— exponential service times,
— all servers equally loaded,
— first-in, first-out dispatching

M = 1 server

M = 2 servers

M = 3 servers

M = 4 servers

M = 60

M = 80

$\frac{\sigma_{t_q}}{\overline{S}}$

426

Bibliography

M. J. Moroney, *Facts From Figures*. London: Penguin Books, 1951. Delightfully readable nonmathematical survey of statistics. Paperback. Inexpensive.

J. E. Freund and F. J. Williams, *Modern Business Statistics*. Englewood Cliffs, N.J.: Prentice-Hall, Inc., 1958. Elementary introduction to statistics, nonmathematical.

A. M. Mood and F. A. Graybill, *Introduction to the Theory of Statistics*. New York: McGraw-Hill Book Company, Inc., 1963. More detailed introduction to statistics. Mathematics not too difficult.

K. A. Brownlee, *Statistical Theory and Methodology in Science and Engineering*. New York: John Wiley & Sons, Inc., 1965. Good general book on statistics. Many practical examples.

P. M. Morse, *Queues, Inventories and Maintenance*. New York: J. Wiley & Sons, Inc., 1958. Handles simple queuing theory in clear terms.

D. R. Cox and W. L. Smith, *Queues*. New York: J. Wiley & Sons, Inc., 1961. Brief, concise survey of queuing theory.

J. Riordan, *Stochastic Service Systems*. New York: J. Wiley & Sons, Inc., 1962. Moderately mathematical queuing book by a staff member of Bell Telephone Laboratory.

A. Y. Khintchine., *Mathematical Methods in the Theory of Queuing*. New York: Hafner, 1960. Mathematical treatment of queuing fundamentals.

W. Feller, *An Introduction to Probability Theory and Its Applications*, 2nd edition. New York: J. Wiley & Sons, Inc., 1957. Short but clear derivations of the multiserver queue problems.

T. L. Saaty, *Elements of Queuing Theory*. New York: McGraw-Hill, Book Company, Inc., 1961. Collection of techniques and results for queuing problems, very mathematical.

L. Takacs, *Introduction to the Theory of Queues*. New York: Oxford University Press, 1962. Strictly for mathematicians.

D. Nee, *Application of Queuing Theory to Information System Design*, Stanford Research Institute Technical Documentary Report. No. ESD-TDR-64-428. A report classifying a wide variety of queuing models and queuing literature.

Analysis of Some Queuing Models in Real-Time Systems, IBM Manual Number F20-0007-0. Published by IBM, Poughkeepsie, New York, 1965. Very useful application of queuing theory to computer systems.

27 ESTIMATING THE RANDOM-ACCESS FILE SIZES

The considerations necessary in selecting file units for a computer system were discussed in Chapter 22. When the types of unit have been chosen, the decision must be made on how many modules of the file in question are needed for the application. Because of the size of the units, excess capacity may be available, On the other hand, the data to be stored may be near the limits of the system, and care is needed to ensure that the files are, in fact, large enough.

The main work in making estimates of the space required in random-access files is in deciding what records are to be stored and how many characters or words they contain. All the logical files needed for the application must be specified in detail.

From the numbers and sizes of records that must be simultaneously on line, the volume required for their storage may be found. There are, however, a number of factors which complicate this:

1. Should any records be duplicated for fallback reasons?
2. Is an extra file needed for fallback and recovery?
3. What allowance should be made for future growth and increased complexity of the application?
4. Are there any ways of compressing the space requirements using coding or tables?
5. Are variable-length records used? If so, how are they loaded?
6. Are any records repeated to minimize seek time?
7. What allowance must be made for additions and deletions?
8. Is a spare file needed for program testing purposes?
9. How are records addressed and located? This might add an extra 20 or even 40 per cent onto the space required.

This chapter discusses the above points. To some extent they are tied up with file-reference time which is the subject of the following chapter. There is a compromise to be achieved between minimizing space requirements and minimizing timing. The balance between these must be determined by what pressures are on the system.

1. *Fallback*

Some of the real-time systems now in operation duplicate all of their random-access file records. Some duplicate only a portion. Some duplicate none. The question must be answered, "What happens when a file mechanism fails to operate?" When this happens, it may take, perhaps, two hours to repair. Can the application manage without these records for that period of time, or is it worth the expense of duplicating them?

As indicated in earlier chapters, the answer to this question on many commercial applications is that the majority of the records *can* be lost for two hours or so with only moderate inconvenience; however a certain nucleus of them are vital and must not be lost. If the recording medium is interchangeable between one file and another, a spare unit may be included. When one file unit fails, its cartridge or disk pack is transferred to the spare unit.

If the records are duplicated, when one copy is lost for a time, it will not be updated as it should be. There are two ways to deal with this situation. *Firstly*, all records updated during the time one copy is inaccessible may be noted or written on a spare file. The duplicate will be updated from these when it is back on the air. *Secondly*, the available copy may itself be duplicated in real time onto a spare file unit and the lost copy ignored. The file that failed then becomes the spare file when it is repaired.

It is important to think about the fallback needs at the time the system is planned, rather than as an afterthought halfway through implementation.

2. *Future Growth*

There are a number of different ways in which the file requirements can grow. First, there may be a growth in the size of the business handled. A bank may increase its number of customers and hence customer records. A factory may increase the number of types of stock it holds. On a message-switching system where the files are used almost entirely for holding messages, the volume of messages may increase and on some systems has increased drastically because the users of the system found it a valuable service.

Secondly, the functions performed by the system may increase. An airline booking system with passenger name records on line may not initially contain the passengers' addresses and telephone numbers, these being still filed at the agents' offices. Later it may be decided to automate this filing.

Thirdly, there may possibly be changes in the formats of the records. The method of classifying tracks on a railroad-track control system may be amplified. The codes needed for specifying operations on a production control application may be increased. On at least one airline system the records were designed to handle only two classes of flight, first class and tourist class. When some carriers introduced a third class, this constituted a severe problem.

Last, and this is usually the biggest worry at the design stage, the planners are likely not to have thought of all the complications that will become apparent as the system is implemented. What safety factor should be left for this? That depends upon how much detail has been gone into, but the more experienced systems analysts, who perhaps may have had their fingers burnt once, usually leave as many empty characters in a record as they reasonably can in anticipation of unthought-of complexities.

To a large extent the files and their organization are a foundation stone on which the system implementation rests. It is better to overestimate them than underestimate. If their organization has to be changed at a late stage, this can cause great difficulties. Where it is known that expansion will occur or that other functions will be added, the file organization should be planned so that this can take place with as little upheaval as possible. If a phase-by-phase system build-up is used, the files, at least, should be compatible.

3. *Record Compaction*

On the credit side of this account, the space required for records may be reduced by compressing the records, using special formatting or coding. The data will be reformatted or coded and decoded by a programmed routine. Record compaction will reduce the file size and reduce channel utilization at the expense of processing time and core storage. The balance of critical factors on the system will determine whether or not various types of compaction are worthwhile.

Typical compaction techniques include using combinations of bits to code possible alternatives; substituting code for names, places, identity characteristics, or dates, etc.; converting numeric fields into binary, and so on. Sometimes table look-up operations or even a second access to an index file is needed for unscrambling compacted data.

4. *Variable-length Records*

The records to be stored on many systems, especially for commercial applications, are of variable length. Some files are designed to handle variable-length records with ease by using a "format track" or record header which indicates the length. Others are not.

However, variable-length records can play havoc with some addressing schemes. Because of the addressing requirements it might not be possible to have records as completely variable as they would be on magnetic tape or on a serial file. Often it is necessary to take a fixed-length area, such as a disk track, as a unit of file space and *block* variable-length records within this area. The entire track may have to be read into core and scanned to obtain the requisite record. On some machines it is possible to scan for the record in question without reading the entire track into core.

Another possibility is to divide the record into a fixed part and a variable part. The fixed part is stored and addressed in a normal manner. The variable part is stored in an area which can then be quickly accessible and which has its address stored in the fixed part,

These factors need to be thought about in adding up the total file requirements.

5. *Repeated Records*

Records which are referred to very frequently need to be in such a position on the files as to be accessible very quickly. In some cases records which are not constantly being updated are written in several different places to minimize the reading time. This is commonly done with tables and with programs. Two variations of this are as follows:

(a) Programs or tables may be stored on a backing disk file. If the disk rotation time, is say, twenty milliseconds, there will be a delay of an average ten milliseconds and maximum twenty milliseconds before the item begins to be read in. Therefore each item may be stored, say, four times identically on each track. The delay is then an average two and a half and maximum five milliseconds.

(b) A disk file may have one access mechanism which takes at least fifty milliseconds to change its position. At worst, it may take perhaps 250 milliseconds. However, at each setting it can read from ten to perhaps twenty-five, different tracks. Information which is referred to very frequently may be stored on one track for every different arm setting. If the arm has 250 different settings, it will be written 250 times on the file. An example of this is given below in considering the indexing method of file addressing.

6. *Additions and Deletions*

In some file applications, the records loaded initially are a fairly stable set, such as bank customer records or manufacturing product specifications. New records may be added to the file and old records deleted at a rate of less than 0.1 per cent per day. On other types of application, however, records, such as passenger name records on an airline may have an addition and deletion rate as high as 25 per cent per day. This may mean that periodically the file must be reorganized, as the additions have not filled the space left by the deletions. On a sequentially organized file it may be necessary to batch additions and deletions and sort them into the file when the system is not on line. This and other considerations will probably mean that the system cannot be on line twenty-four hours a day.

To assess the additional space required for additions and deletions, it is necessary to decide how these will be organized. It must be decided what type of addressing scheme will be used and how often the file will be reorganized.

7. *Program and System Testing*

On some applications an extra file has had to be added for program testing. Much testing will usually still be required when the system is in operation. There may not be time to remove the operational data and replace it when the testing is finished. The testing requirement may be such that it has to go on while the system is operating with suitable storage protection.

It is important to define the needs of testing early enough to obtain any extra file capacity that may be needed. If the need is not realized until the system is under test, this may be too late to obtain the extra equipment.

8. *File Addressing*

Most addressing schemes that have to be used for random-access files result in far from 100 per cent utilization of the space available. With some, 90 per cent of space utilization can be achieved. With others, 70 per cent is a safer figure to plan for.

The basic problem of file addressing is this: Records in the logical files are identified to persons using the system by a number or key which is determined by the application. This may be, for example, an account number in a bank, a part number in a factory, a flight number and date in an airline reservation system, or a passenger name. It is this number or key which will reach the processing unit in the input transaction, and from this the machine address of the record must be determined so that the record can be read.

There are a number of possible methods of obtaining the file address. Any one application may use more than one of these possible techniques. Four of the commonest methods are described below:

(a) *Direct Addressing.* The easiest and often the most economical way to solve this problem is to make the input transaction contain the machine address of the record in question. For example, in some banking applications the account numbers have been changed so that the number, or part of the number, is the file address of that account.

On many applications this is not possible. For example, the part numbers in a factory or warehouse could not normally be changed, as they have significance to the organization in question. In some cases this method can be used even though it is inconvenient to change the reference numbers in question. For example, in an application for updating savings bank passbooks, the file address of the account record may be written on the passbook and this be keyed in by the clerk operating the terminals.

Where direct addressing can be used, it gives a *high file packing* and generally a *low file reference time*, though it is sometimes possible to obtain lower average file references with randomizing described below. No additional file requirements are needed because of inefficient addressing, and the space required can be calculated in a straightforward manner.

(b) *Algorithm*. It may be possible to organize a logical file so that the addresses within that file may be calculated from the reference information such as account number or flight number and date. This is not possible in the majority of applications, but where it is, a *simple and fast method of addressing* the files results. It is often, however, *inefficient in its use of file space*. An airline, for example, may have perhaps 100 flight numbers.

The algorithm uses these and the date to calculate the file address. However, not every flight flies on every day; hence some of the addresses generated will not contain a record. There will be gaps in the file layout. The same space would have been needed if every flight flew on every day.

Because of this wastefulness in the use of file space, this addressing method may be used only for small portions of the data to which very frequent reference is made. It requires completely individual assessment for each application.

(c) *Table Look-up or Indexing*. On most systems there will be no logical relationship between the reference number (part number, account number, and so on) and the machine address of its location on the files. The records may however be arranged on the file sequentially by reference number. If any sequential processing of a file is done, as well as single-transaction enquiries or updating, this method gives the advantage that the *sequential processing can be much quicker* and easier.

The addressing problem of locating an item at random now becomes rather like finding a person's telephone number in a telephone directory. To do this with our fingers, we may execute a crude binary search and then, after locating the correct page, scan a relatively small number of names sequentially. The same method may be used with random-access files, but it is slow. More often an index is used like the index of this book. Instead of directing the reader to the correct page, it directs the program to the right file-unit "cylinder" or track.

An index is a table on which a table look-up operation must be executed. With large files the table may be too big for all of it to be in core at once, and so multiple tables are used. The primary table gives the file location of the secondary table. The secondary table is read in from the file and gives the file location of the record being sought. With two levels of table like this, two seek operations may be needed to find the record. This is a disadvantage because a seek is a lengthy mechanical operation. Because of this the secondary table may be stored on a file which gives a low seek time, or it may be stored repetitively, so that only one seek is needed.

Figure 27.1 shows a disk file on which an index is stored repetitively so that it may be read without a seek whatever the location of the access mechanism. The tracks which can be read at one access setting may be described as a "cylinder." Each position of the access mechanism enables it to read

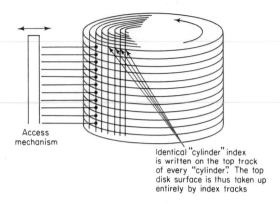

Access
mechanism

Identical "cylinder" index
is written on the top track
of every "cylinder". The top
disk surface is thus taken up
entirely by index tracks

Fig. 27.1. Space required for index tracks.

another cylinder. Suppose that a system has several disk files organized in this manner. To locate a record at random, a table in core is first examined to find which disk file the record is on. The cylinder index is then read into core from the top disk surface, as shown. This can be done without moving the access mechanism, because the cylinder index is stored identically on each cylinder. The cylinder index is scanned to find which cylinder contains the record in question. The machine then seeks that cylinder. It still does not know which track the record is on, and that must be found from another index, again stored on the upper disk surface. Finally the record address is obtained, and the record read.

It thus takes three read operations and one seek operation to obtain a record. The whole of one disk surface is needed for storing the index records. If such a system had ten disk surfaces per file unit, 10 per cent of the available space would be used for this purpose. If the cylinder-index records were not repetitively stored, this figure would be less, but two seeks would be needed.

This method can used with any file, which the previous two methods cannot. In general it is *more economical in file space than randomizing*, described below, but *needs greater access times*. In estimating the file packing on a system of this type, the space for the tables must be taken into account. Methods of handling file additions must be considered also. These cannot immediately be stored on the file in sequence with the other records.

(d) *Randomizing.* This is a common method of addressing. It requires a much more extensive analysis before file requirements can be estimated exactly. The first step in this type of addressing is to convert the item's reference number into a random (approximately) number that lies within the range of the file addresses where the record is to be located. There are many methods of generating this random number, and these must be evaluated for each specific application.

The random number is used as the machine address of that record, or of a *pocket* containing several records. A pocket may be, for example, a track on a disk or magnetic card or tape strip. It may be half a track or two tracks, and so on. When the record is first loaded onto the file, the program seeks that location. In most cases, with a suitably chosen method of generating the random number, the location will be empty if it is the address of a single record or it will have available space if it is a pocket. The record to be loaded will thus be stored at this address. Sometimes, however, there will be no space left at the address because other items' reference numbers generated the same random number. In this case the record must be stored in an overflow location, and the address of the overflow record or pocket will be stored in the original one. When it is necessary to obtain a record stored in this way, the same procedure will be followed. The same random number will be produced and hence the same location found.

The transform for generating the random number must have two properties:

(1) It must have an almost equal probability of generating any address in the desired range.

(2) In some cases two or more reference numbers will generate the same machine address. The quantity of such "synonyms," which cause overflows, must be as low as possible.

There are a variety of methods of generating the required random number. The method best suited to the application in question must be selected, and this usually means a detailed examination of many alternatives. A computer program is needed to do this examination. All of the reference numbers to be used (part numbers, account numbers, and so on) will be operated on by each transform being considered. This will produce a long list of machine addresses which must then be scanned to see how many overflows would result. The transform selected will probably be that which produces the minimum number of overflows.

Some computer manufacturers and consultants provide programs for helping to select the randomizing technique. These programs print statistics on the resulting file-packing density and the number of overflows. They are therefore of value in estimating the file-space requirements. A high file-packing density giving an efficient use of space will also give a large number of overflows. To lower the number of overflows and hence improve the file-reference times, the file-packing density must be lowered. There is always a compromise between these factors.

Figure 27.2 illustrates this with reference to a system on which one track is used as a pocket and the records are of such a size that a track can contain ten of them. The solid curve in this figure relates to an efficient randomizing transform. It gives the probability that overflows will occur or that tracks will have empty space on them. If a smaller file area were used so that there could be less unused space, the number of overflows would be greater. On the

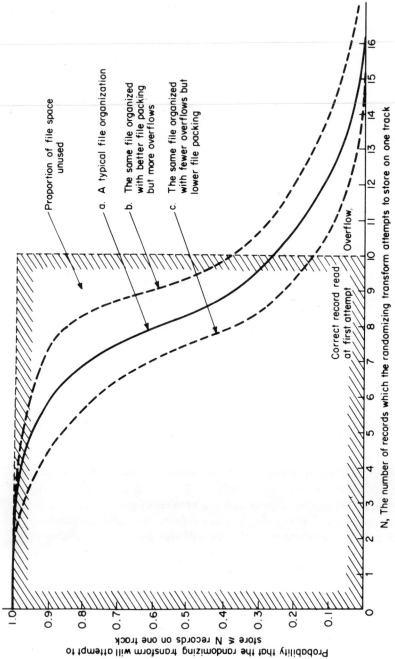

Fig. 27.2. Space utilization of a file in which randomizing is used for addressing. This diagram relates to a file that can have a maximum of 10 records per track, and a track is used as one address. If the randomizing process attempts to load more than 10 records on a track, the excess must be stored in an overflow area. The shaded rectangle therefore represents the main file area. The section to the right of this represents the overflow area.

Labels within the figure:

Proportion of file space unused

a. A typical file organization

b. The same file organized with better file packing but more overflows

c. The same file organized with fewer overflows but lower file packing

Correct record read at first attempt

Overflow.

N, The number of records which the randomizing transform attempts to store on one track

Probability that the randomizing transform will attempt to store ≤ N records on one track

1.0
0.9
0.8
0.7
0.6
0.5
0.4
0.3
0.2
0.1

other hand, increasing the space available for the main file would decrease the number of overflows.

At the survey stage it may not be possible or desirable to obtain enough information to select a transform and analyze its performance in detail. A shortcut is required in order to make suitable estimates. A straightforward way to make approximate initial estimates is to assume that the transform selected will produce a random disbursement within the required range of addresses. Any actual randomizing transform will not produce a completely random disbursement, though it should be possible to find one that is close to it.

Let N be   the total number of records to be stored, that is, the total number of reference numbers.

Let M be   the total number of address locations in the range above.

Each address location then has a probability $1/M$ of being generated in a single trial. The probability that it will fail to be generated in a single trial is $[1 - (1/M)]$. Using the binomial distribution, the probability that it will be generated x times in N trials is

$$P(x) = \frac{N!}{x!(N - x)!} \left(\frac{1}{M}\right)^x \left(1 - \frac{1}{M}\right)^{N - x}$$

If N is large and $1/M$ is very small, which is so in this case, then $P(x)$ is given approximately by the Poisson distribution.

$$P(x) = \frac{\left(\frac{N}{M}\right)^x e^{-(N/M)}}{x!}$$

The probability of an address being generated more than x times may, therefore, be evaluated from the summed Poisson distribution tables facing page 378.

For quick reference, a set of curves has been drawn using the above formulas (Fig. 27.3). A reader with no mathematical knowledge may use these to estimate how many records are in the overflow area. The same curves are also used for timing purposes in the next chapter. These were drawn assuming a completely random disbursement of records. As an actual transform will not give this, it is suggested that, when making the initial estimates, a *safety factor of 20 per cent should be added to the number of overflows given by these curves or the above formulas.*

One more decision that remains to be made is, "Where will the overflow records be kept?" As indicated in Fig. 27.3, some empty space remains in the main file which is not filled by the randomizing transform. This space may be big enough to hold all the overflow records, and use should be made of it if possible. On some systems, however, a separate overflow area has been used.

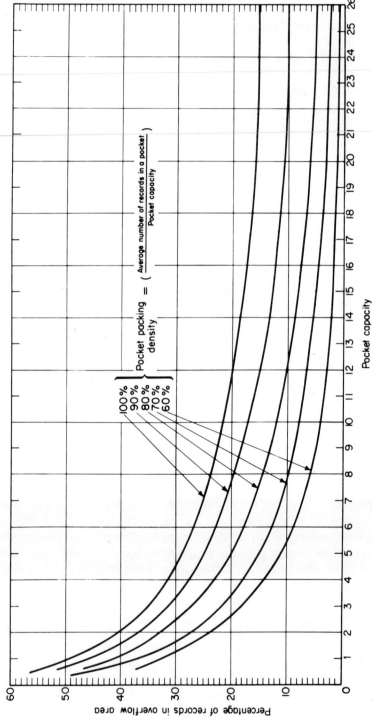

Fig. 27.3. The percentage of records in the overflow area. These curves provide a quick means of making the first approximate estimates for a file addressed by randomizing.

438

28 ESTIMATING FILE REFERENCE TIMES AND QUEUES

To estimate the time needed to read or write a file item, the following factors must be considered:

1. How many read operations will be necessary? With some forms of addressing, more than one will be needed.

2. How many seek operations will be necessary? With some forms of addressing, more than one will be needed.

3. How long will the seeks and reads be?

4. Will a checking operation, which takes extra time, be needed to verify that the data have been written correctly? On some systems, each track written is read back to ensure that it has been written correctly.

5. Is any additional control time needed for the file operation—for example, time to select the appropriate read/write head?

6. What will be the queuing time waiting for the appropriate computer channel?

7. Will there also be queuing time waiting for the file arm or read/write mechanism? To what extent are the separate operations overlapped?

8. On a file reference with more than one seek, read, or write, will there be queuing for each of these separately or merely for the entire file reference? This depends upon the Supervisory Program mechanisms.

The time for one solitary file reference to a record of known address may consist of the times for a seek, read, write, and possibly check operation. Some file units take an extra read operation to check what has been written. The times will usually include also a delay time, separate from the seek, which is the time the recording medium takes to come into position under the read/write head. For example, on a drum or disk, this will be rotation time. When the unit is ready to read or write, the head waits for the record to revolve into position under it.

The sequence will be as shown in Fig. 28.1.

If, for example, the seek takes 80 milliseconds, the read or write takes 6, and the rotation time of the disk or drum is 34, the total time will be as follows:

Seek	80 milliseconds
Rotation (minimum)	0
(maximum)	34 milliseconds
Read	6 milliseconds
Processing	overlapped with rotation
Rotation and write	34 milliseconds
Rotation and check	34 milliseconds
TOTAL (minimum)	154 milliseconds
(maximum)	188 milliseconds
(average)	171 milliseconds

This example could relate to the file system which was discussed and simulated in Chapter 25 (Fig. 25.4). Here the seek time could vary from 40 to 120 milliseconds. It would be necessary to calculate the *average* seek time and hence the average file reference time.

As was seen in Chapter 25, however, there are two other elements of time which are important. Because many items will be using the files, one particular item may not be able to obtain the seek arm, or the channel, as soon as it requests it. Queues will build up and some items will have to *wait* for the file arm and also wait for the channel. In the model in Chapter 25, it was assumed that the seek arm, once allocated to one file updating operation, was not released until the operation was complete; the channel, however,

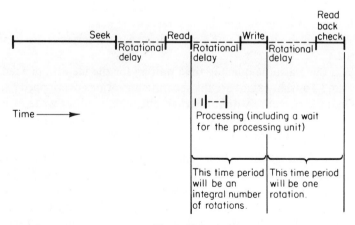

Figure 28.1

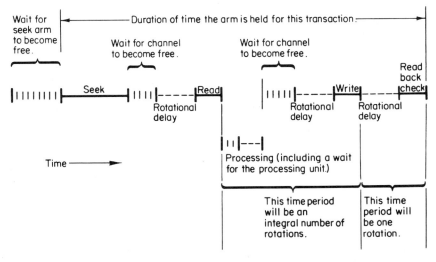

Figure 28.2

was released as soon as the read operation was completed. The times involved in the file operation then appear as in Fig. 28.2. We have to evaluate not only the average seek times but also the average waiting times.

SEEK TIMES

Let us first examine the question of seek times. On a disk unit, if the arm is positioned over one track and we move it to another track, the time taken for this "seek" will depend upon the number of tracks traversed between the initial and final resting places of the arm. On some file units, if we can estimate the number of tracks traversed on average, this will enable us to evaluate the average seek time. Manufacturers commonly provide a table or graph giving the relation between number of tracks traversed and the seek times. Figure 28.3 gives such a curve for the IBM 2314 disk unit.

Equipped with this information we now need to be able to calculate the number of tracks that the arm will traverse on an average seek. This depends upon how the data are laid out on the disks. Often, at the design stage, the best we can say about how the data are laid out is to assume that it will be scattered evenly over a given part of the file. With this assumption we can calculate the probability of different seek lengths and evaluate the average seek time.

Let us suppose that the data are scattered evenly over N tracks or "cylinders." We wish to calculate the average number of gaps between tracks that the arm will pass over. The arm movement will depend firstly on the previous

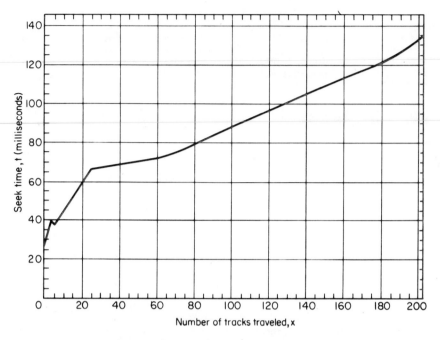

Fig. 28.3. On some disk files there is a direct relationship between the number of tracks the "seek" arm travels over in executing its seek, and the time the seek takes. This curve, for example, gives such a relationship for the IBM 2314 disk file. (Reproduced from IBM 2314 Reference Manual—Form Number A26-3599-1. Published by IBM, 1966.)

position of the arm, and secondly on the new position to which we are moving it. If we instruct the arm to, say, access track Number 3, the probability of its not having to move at all (i.e., the probability of its already being on track Number 3) is $1/N$. The probability of it having to move over one gap between tracks (i.e., the probability of it previously being on track Number 2 or 4) is $2 \times (1/N)$, and so on.

Table 28.1 shows the tabulation of the probabilities of different arm movements for a disk area of six tracks:

In general, extending this to N tracks, the probability that x gaps between tracks are traversed is

$$P_x = \frac{2x}{N} \times \frac{1}{N} + \frac{(N - 2x)}{N} \times \frac{2}{N}$$

$$= \frac{2(N - x)}{N^2}$$

The mean number of gaps traversed is given by

Table 28.1

	Starting at track number 1	Starting at track number 2	Starting at track number 3	Starting at track number 4	Starting at track number 5	Starting at track number 6	
Probability of traversing 1 gap between tracks =	$\frac{1}{6}\times\frac{1}{6}$	$+\frac{1}{6}\times\frac{2}{6}$	$+\frac{1}{6}\times\frac{2}{6}$	$+\frac{1}{6}+\frac{2}{6}$	$+\frac{1}{6}+\frac{2}{6}$	$+\frac{1}{6}\times\frac{1}{6}$	$=\frac{10}{36}$
Probability of traversing 2 gaps between tracks =	$\frac{1}{6}\times\frac{1}{6}$	$+\frac{1}{6}\times\frac{1}{6}$	$+\frac{1}{6}\times\frac{2}{6}$	$+\frac{1}{6}\times\frac{2}{6}$	$+\frac{1}{6}\times\frac{1}{6}$	$+\frac{1}{6}\times\frac{1}{6}$	$=\frac{8}{36}$
Probability of traversing 3 gaps between tracks =	$\frac{1}{6}\times\frac{1}{6}$	$+\frac{1}{6}\times\frac{1}{6}$	$+\frac{1}{6}\times\frac{1}{6}$	$+\frac{1}{6}\times\frac{1}{6}$	$+\frac{1}{6}\times\frac{1}{6}$	$+\frac{1}{6}\times\frac{1}{6}$	$=\frac{6}{36}$
Probability of traversing 4 gaps between tracks =	$\frac{1}{6}\times\frac{1}{6}$	$+\frac{1}{6}\times\frac{1}{6}$	$+\ 0$	$+\ 0$	$+\frac{1}{6}\times\frac{1}{6}$	$+\frac{1}{6}\times\frac{1}{6}$	$=\frac{4}{36}$
Probability of traversing 5 gaps between tracks =	$\frac{1}{6}\times\frac{1}{6}$	$+\ 0$	$+\ 0$	$+\ 0$	$+\ 0$	$+\frac{1}{6}\times\frac{1}{6}$	$=\frac{2}{36}$

Probability of arm not moving $=\frac{1}{6}$

Total $=1$

$$\bar{x} = \sum_{x=1}^{N} x P_x$$

$$= \sum_{x=1}^{N} \frac{2x(N-x)}{N^2} = \frac{2}{N} \sum_{x=1}^{N} x - \frac{2}{N^2} \sum_{x=1}^{N} x^2$$

$$= (N+1) - \frac{2(N+1)(2N+1)}{6N}$$

$$= \frac{N^2 - 1}{3N}$$

Similarly, the variance of x is equal to

$$\sigma_x^2 = \sum_{x=1}^{N} x^2 P_x - \bar{x}^2$$

$$= \sum_{x=1}^{N} \frac{2(N-x)x^2}{N^2} - \bar{x}^2$$

$$= \frac{2}{N} \sum_{x=1}^{N} x^2 - \frac{2}{N^2} \sum_{x=1}^{N} x^3 - \bar{x}^2$$

$$= \frac{2(N+1)(2N+1)}{6} - \frac{1}{2}(N+1)^2 - \left(\frac{N^2-1}{3N}\right)^2$$

$$= \frac{N^4 + N^2 - 2}{18N^2}$$

These are two generally useful results: the *mean* number of gaps traversed is

$$\bar{x} = \frac{N^2 - 1}{3N} \simeq \frac{N}{3} \qquad \text{when } N \text{ is large} \tag{28.1}$$

and the *variance* of the number of gaps traversed is

$$\sigma_x^2 = \frac{N^4 + N^2 - 2}{18N^2} \simeq \frac{N^2}{18} \quad \text{when } N \text{ is large} \tag{28.2}$$

In a similar manner, if the relationship between the seek time and the number of gaps traversed is known, as in Fig. 28.3, the mean seek time and its variance may be found.

If seek time, t, is a function of x, $t = F(x)$, then the mean seek time is

$$\bar{t} = \sum_{x=1}^{N} F(x) P_x \tag{28.3}$$

The variance of seek time is

$$\sigma_t^2 = \sum_{x=1}^{N} [F(x)]^2 P_x - \bar{t}^2 \tag{28.4}$$

To simplify the calculation, the curve in Fig. 28.3 or a similar curve for other files may be assumed to be a straight line. If we are using the whole disk surface to store data, a line with a slope of $\frac{86}{200}$ and crossing the vertical axis at 45 may be used as shown in Fig. 28.4. If, on the other hand, we are referring to a small group of cylinders such that the arm will never normally move more than 25 tracks, then a line of slope $\frac{105}{80}$ and crossing the vertical axis at 29 may be used (Fig. 28.4).

Let us suppose that we are using almost the whole disk area for storing records, and so we take the equation

$$t = 45 + 0.43\,x$$

Then

$$\bar{t} = 45 + 0.43\,\bar{x} \quad \text{and} \quad \sigma_t = 0.43\,\sigma_x$$

Therefore, substituting from Equations (28.1) and (28.2):

$$\bar{t} = 45 + 0.43 \left(\frac{N^2 - 1}{3N}\right) \tag{28.5}$$

and

$$\sigma_t = 0.43 \sqrt{\frac{N^4 + N^2 - 2}{18N^2}} \tag{28.6}$$

If our data file is such that, say, it actually occupies 186 cylinders, then we can substitute $N = 186$ into these equations and find that the mean seek time is 71.7 milliseconds, and its standard deviation is 18.9 milliseconds.

On some files, the equations for seek time would be different from those

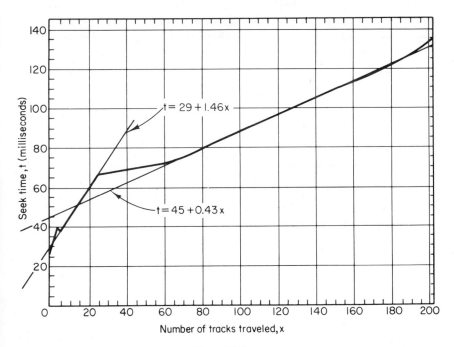

Figure 28.4

above. On some devices, the arm returns to a home location between seeks. In this case, the seek time would be easy to calculate. Sometimes, on the other hand, the problem is made much more complicated because there is no direct relationship between the number of tracks traversed and the seek time. It depends upon the specific starting and ending points of the seek.

FILE-	To evaluate total times for locating and reading
ADDRESSING	or updating, it is necessary to take the file-
CONSIDERATIONS	addressing and queuing mechanisms into con-
	sideration.

The common types of file-addressing mechanisms were indicated in the last chapter. Once the addressing mechanisms are decided upon for the various parts of the file, it is possible to determine the number of reads and seeks required to have access to a record, and their average lengths may be estimated. It is desirable to minimize the number of seeks and the lengths of seeks as far as is possible. However, this will normally be done at the expense of file packing. As previously shown, a balance between these must be obtained.

If an indexing or table-look-up method of addressing is used, there are two main methods of minimizing the file-reference times. Firstly the positioning of the tables is important. Tables containing a cylinder or strip or track index should be placed so that they can be referred to in the minimum time. As described in the last chapter, a disk-unit cylinder index may be duplicated on every cylinder of one unit, so that, wherever the arm is located, no seek will be needed to find the cylinder index.

Secondly the data should be placed in the best position. On many commercial files the majority of file references are to a small proportion of the data. Seventy per cent of the seeks may refer to 5 or 10 per cent of the file. This frequently referred-to portion should be placed, as far as possible, where short seeks will be required to locate it. To some extent this is possible with an indexing method of addressing. With randomizing, the frequently used item should be loaded first so that there will be no overflows in obtaining these.

When random addressing is used, it is important to take into account the number of overflows and the time taken to gain access to overflow records. Figure 27.3 will enable a systems analyst to estimate the number of overflows on the assumption that the randomizing process generates a truly random set of numbers. The randomizing process used on an actual application will not be this efficient. How far it deviates from the theoretical may be assessed if the transform to be used is decided upon; however, when estimates are being made at the survey stage, it will probably not be desirable to go into this level of detail. It was therefore suggested that 20 per cent should be added as a safety factor to the number of overflows indicated in Fig. 27.3.

SPECIMEN
CALCULATION
FOR A
RANDOM FILE

An illustration of the use of these curves is given below:

Suppose that a file system is being designed which can hold a maximum of ten records per track. One part of the file consisting of 64,000 records is to be randomly addressed. Suppose that at the first iteration you assume that 8000 tracks will be used for the main file (excluding overflow for the moment). Then,

$$\frac{\text{average records per track}}{\text{maximum records per track}} =$$

$$\frac{(64,000/8000)}{10} = 0.80$$

Figure 27.3 then gives an overflow percentage of 12 per cent. Adding a safety factor of 20 per cent to this to allow for possible nonrandom bias, this becomes 14.4 per cent. The overflow records which must be relocated then total $64,000 \times 0.144 = 9216$.

These would occupy 922 fully packed tracks. They may be tightly packed in a separate overflow area of this size or rather larger. However, space for $80,000 - (64,000 - 9216) = 25,216$ records is still unoccupied in the main file area, and so it is probable that this will be used.

How then do we locate the overflow records? Possibly one of the records on each track will contain an index of the overflow records, but this may mean that only nine records per track can be stored. The packing density is now

$$\frac{(64,000/8000)}{9} = 0.889$$

Using this and a pocket capacity of 9, Fig. 27.3 gives an overflow percentage of 17 per cent. Adding the safety factor, this gives 20.4 per cent, which means 13,056 overflow records to be relocated. There is still room to hold them.

We may assume that the overflows need no new seek in the majority of cases, and so 20.4 per cent of the file accesses need one extra read operation. This will be a read of the entire track. If the channel or file arm utilization is high on a real-time system, it will be desirable to have a low number of overflows. Let us suppose that the above figure of 20.4 per cent overflows is too high; 6 per cent may be a more desirable figure.

Referring again to Fig. 27.3, after the 20 per cent safety margin is removed, this leaves a 5 per cent overflow on a truly random system and this, for a pocket capacity of 9, gives a packing density of 61 per cent, or 9×0.61 = 5.49 records per track on average. $64{,}000/5.49 = 11{,}658$ tracks will be required for the file, as opposed to 8000 tracks in the previous example.

In this way a systems analyst can adjust his estimates up and down until a suitable balance is found.

NOTE: The above calculations assume that all records in the file are used equally frequently. This is often not the case, and, if the file is arranged so that the frequently referred-to items are in nonoverflow positions, that is, they were loaded first, the number of overflows would be considerably lower.

QUEUE SIZES

When the addressing techniques have been determined and the seek times estimated, one last problem remains: how long do the transactions have to wait in queues for the channel and for the file arm?

If we know how long the file arm is held by each transaction we can then use the equations in Chapter 26 to calculate the "facility utilization" ρ of the arm and hence find $\bar{t}_w$ or $\bar{t}_q$ for the arm. This tells us the over-all response time of the file subsystem. Figure 26.11 can be used to read off t_q, knowing ρ, $\bar{s}$, and σ_s for the arm. Figure 26.13 gives the standard deviation of t_q.

In using the queuing formulas of Chapter 26, we are making the assumption that the transactions attempting to use the arm arrive at random in the manner described in Chapter 26. This may be a slightly pessimistic assumption. The queues that result from this assumption may be *slightly* larger than what is actually the case, but, at least, we will be erring on the side of safety.

Unfortunately, however, the calculation of how long the arm is held is not straightforward. As can be seen from Fig. 28.2, this time period *itself* includes two queues. The queuing times waiting for the channel must be included in the arm "service time."

Let us make use of the vocabulary of Chapter 26 and employ the following notation.

$\bar{t}_{q_{arm}}$	is the mean queuing time for arm	(including the service
$\bar{t}_{q_{chan}}$	is the mean queuing time for channel	time of the item in
$\bar{t}_{q_{proc}}$	is the mean queuing time for processor	question)
Rot	is the disk rotation time	
W	is the time to write a record which equals the time to read a record	
$\bar{t}_{w_{chan}}$	is the waiting time for channel {i.e., $\bar{t}_{w_{chan}} = \bar{t}_{q_{chan}} - [W + (Rot/2)]$}	
ρ_{arm}	is the facility utilization of the arm	
ρ_{cham}	is the facility utilization of the channel	
ρ_{proc}	is the facility utilization of the processor	
$\bar{s}_{arm}$	is the mean service time for the arm	

$\bar{s}_{cham}$ is the mean service time for the channel

$\bar{s}_{proc}$ is the mean service time for the processor.

We, then, want to calculate $\bar{t}_{q_{arm}}$. Employing Equation (26.13) we find that this is

$$\bar{t}_{q_{arm}} = \bar{s}_{arm} + \frac{\rho_{arm}\bar{s}_{arm}}{2(1 - \rho_{arm})}\left[1 + \left(\frac{\sigma_{s_{arm}}}{\bar{s}_{arm}}\right)^2\right] \tag{28.7}$$

But,

$$\rho_{arm} = \bar{n}_{arm}\bar{s}_{arm} \qquad \text{from Equation (26.8)}$$

We, presumably know $\bar{n}_{arm}$, the number of transactions using each arm. Therefore, if we can evaluate $\bar{s}_{arm}$ and $\sigma_{s_{arm}}$, we have solved the problem. s_{arm} is the sum of the following factors:

1. The seek time.
2. The time waiting for the channel so that the item can be read.
3. Disk rotational delay, as the item rotates to a position under the read head.
4. The read time.

The sum of these is $\bar{t}_{q_{chan}}$

And for the items which update the same record:

5. The time the arm waits while the item is being processed. } This is $\bar{t}_{q_{proc}}$
6. The time waiting for the channel so that the item can be written.
7. Disk rotational delay (again).
8. The write time.

These must total an integral number of disk rotations

And, if a write check is used:

9. One disk rotation while the updated record is read for checking.

These items with the exception of the write check are illustrated in Fig. 28.5.

Let us take the file system that was simulated in Chapter 25 and evaluate the queuing times involved. We can then compare the results of this analytical approach with the simulation and see what is the effect of the approximations we will have to make. Let us consider 10 transactions per second arriving at random and updating the file in Fig. 25.4. Ten transactions per second was the throughput used for Tables 25.1 to 25.4, so we shall be able to compare this calculation with these, directly.

The mean seek time is 80 milliseconds. The seek time is uniformly dis-

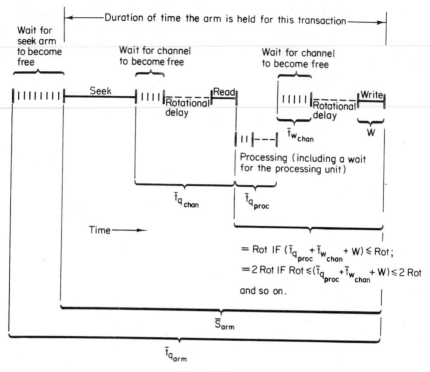

Figure 28.5

tributed between 40 and 120 milliseconds. It can be shown that the variance, σ_x^2, for a *uniform distribution* of values spreading from x_1 to x_2 is $(x_2 - x_1)^2/12$.

In this case then, $\sigma_{seek}^2 = \dfrac{80^2}{12}$

The mean processing time, $\bar{s}_{proc}$, is 9 milliseconds. The processing time is *uniformly* distributed between 4 and 14 milliseconds. Therefore,

$$\sigma_{s_{proc}}^2 = \frac{10^2}{12}$$

If we assume that no processing time is used other than this (this is a highly simplified problem), then

$$\rho_{proc} = \bar{s}_{proc} \cdot \bar{n} = 0.009 \times 10 = 0.09$$

In actual systems other processing time would almost certainly be used and ρ_{proc} would be evaluated taking all of this into account.

When we need to use the processing unit to process the items read from the file, we may have to queue for it. Assuming that all of the requests for the processing occur at random, we may again use the Khintchine-Polloczek formula, with some degree of approximation to calculate $t_{q_{proc}}$

$$\bar{t}_{q_{proc}} = \bar{s}_{proc} + \frac{\rho_{proc}\bar{s}_{proc}}{2(1 - \rho_{proc})}\left[1 + \left(\frac{\sigma_{s_{proc}}}{\bar{s}_{proc}}\right)^2\right]$$

If $\rho_{proc} = 0.09$, then

$$\bar{t}_{q_{proc}} = 9 + \frac{0.09 \times 9}{2(1 - 0.09)}\left[1 + \frac{100}{12 \times 81}\right] = 9.49 \text{ milliseconds}$$

Similarly, using Equation (26. 27), we can calculate that the variance of $t_{q_{proc}}$ is 12.12 milliseconds^2.

All of the transactions *read* a file record. This takes 6 milliseconds, but it also occupies the channel for a rotational delay time varying from 0 to 34 milliseconds. The average time the channel is occupied will, then, be $6 + 17 = 23$ milliseconds. In one second, the total time the channel is in use for reading will be $10 \times 23 = 230$ milliseconds.

Seventy-five per cent of the transactions write a file record, again taking 6 milliseconds plus rotational delay. We are not too sure this time how long the rotational delay will be. It might be slightly different from the average of 17 milliseconds because the write must start an integral number of rotations after the start of the read. In absence of more detailed information, as yet, about what occurs between the read and write, let us assume that the average rotational delay is 17 milliseconds, as it would be if it started at a random point in time. Then, in one second, the total time the channel is in use for writing is $0.75 \times 10 \times 23 = 172.5$ milliseconds.

For the channel, then,

$$\rho_{chan} = \frac{230 + 172.5}{1000} = 0.4025$$

The mean channel service time, $\bar{s}_{chan}$ is 23 milliseconds. Because of the rotation of the disk, both the reading and writing times are *uniformly* distributed between $6 + 0$ and $6 + 34$ milliseconds. The variance of the channel service time is then

$$\sigma^2_{s_{chan}} = \frac{34^2}{12}$$

It might be tempting to again use the Khintchine-Polloczek formula for evaluating $\bar{t}_{q_{chan}}$:

$$\bar{t}_{q_{chan}} = \bar{s}_{chan} + \frac{\rho_{chan}\bar{s}_{chan}}{2(1 - \rho_{chan})}\left[1 + \left(\frac{\sigma_{s_{chan}}}{\bar{s}_{chan}}\right)^2\right] = 30.75 \text{ milliseconds}$$

and, using Equation (26.27), the variance of $t_{q_{chan}} = 371.75$ milliseconds^2.

However, it is not valid to use these formulas because they assume an infinite population of items that could possibly join the queue. All of the curves for $\bar{q}$ and $\bar{t}_q$ in Chapter 26 swing upwards as ρ approaches 1, and continue to travel upwards to infinity.

In assessing the channel queue, we do not have an infinite population of items that could join the queue. The only items contending for use of the channel, in fact, are items connected with the reading or writing from one of the file arms. In this problem, we only have three file arms, so the maximum number of items in the channel queue is 3 (including the item in service). The maximum possible value of $\bar{q}$ is 3 and the maximum possible value of $\bar{t}_q/\bar{s}$ is 3, not infinity as in the curves of Figs. 26.9 and 26.10.

This situation can be analyzed by assuming that the channel is fed by K arms with identical usage. The channel service time is assumed to be exponentially distributed and the arm usage between channel operations is also assumed to be exponentially distributed.

It can be shown that*

$$\frac{\bar{t}_{q_{chan}}}{\bar{s}_{chan}} = \frac{K}{\rho_{chan}} - Z$$

where Z is the unique positive solution to

$$\rho_{chan} = \frac{\sum\limits_{i=0}^{K-1} \dfrac{z^i}{i!}}{\sum\limits_{i=0}^{K} \dfrac{z^i}{i!}} \tag{28.8}$$

With this formula, $\bar{t}_q$ is harder to calculate than in the previous cases. It is plotted in Fig. 28.6. The reader may use this set of curves in conjunction with those in Figs. 26.10 and 26.12 when doing file calculations.

Note that in the case we are discussing, $K = 3$, and the maximum value of $\bar{t}_q/\bar{s}$ on the curve is 3, whereas the curve in Fig. 26.10 rises to infinity.

We are still making assumptions that sound hardly justifiable. For example, we know that the distribution of channel service time is far from exponential. However, it is found that $t_{q_{chan}}$ is not very sensitive to this distribution. In fact, if the channel service was constant the curves on Fig. 28.6 would only be moved slightly. Also, we have assumed that all arms are equally loaded, which could also be far from the truth.

However, in spite of its deficiencies, this method gives fairly good results —of an order of accuracy usually *greater than the accuracy of the input data* when such systems are being designed. It was once said that it is the hallmark of good systems engineering to use models and theories but not to believe in them!

To return to our problem, using the method above we find that:

$$\frac{\bar{t}_{q_{chan}}}{\bar{s}_{chan}} = 1.31$$

Therefore,

$$\bar{t}_{q_{chan}} = 30.2 \text{ milliseconds}$$

$$\bar{t}_{w_{chan}} = 7.2 \text{ milliseconds}$$

*IBM Manual Number F20-0007-0: *Analysis of Some Queuing Models in Real-Time Systems*. Published by IBM, Poughkeepsie, 1965.

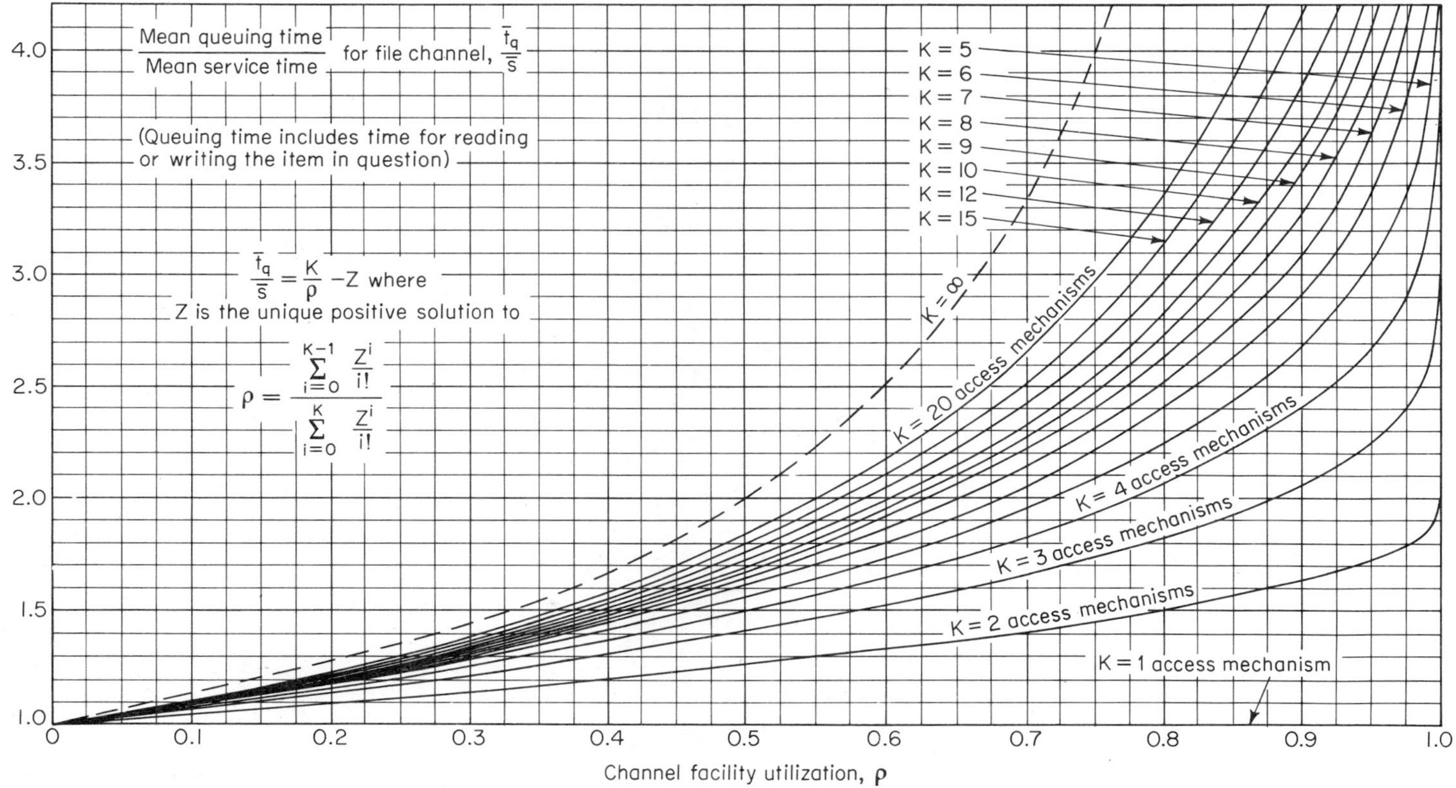

Mean queuing time / Mean service time for file channel, $\frac{\bar{t}_q}{s}$
(Queuing time includes time for reading or writing the item in question)
$\frac{\bar{t}_q}{s} = \frac{K}{\rho} - Z$ where
Z is the unique positive solution to
$\rho = \frac{\sum_{i=0}^{K-1} \frac{Z^i}{i!}}{\sum_{i=0}^{K} \frac{Z^i}{i!}}$
K = 5
K = 6
K = 7
K = 8
K = 9
K = 10
K = 12
K = 15
K = ∞
K = 20 access mechanisms
K = 4 access mechanisms
K = 3 access mechanisms
K = 2 access mechanisms
K = 1 access mechanism
4.0
3.5
3.0
2.5
2.0
1.5
1.0
0
0.1
0.2
0.3
0.4
0.5
0.6
0.7
0.8
0.9
1.0
Channel facility utilization, ρ

Fig. 28.6. Channel queues.

Note that these are only slightly lower than the figures obtained with the Khintchine-Polloczek formula above. Hence

$$(\bar{t}_{q_{proc}} + \bar{t}_{w_{chan}} + W) = 22.7 \text{ milliseconds}$$

This is less than one disk rotation, so we will take the interval between the end of the read operation and the end of the write to be one disk rotation.

We are now in a position to calculate $\bar{s}_{arm}$. Referring to Fig. 28.5, it will be seen that the time the arm is held is the mean seek time plus $t_{q_{chan}}$ for transactions which do not update it. Therefore:

$$\bar{s}_{arm} = 80 + 30.2 + (0.75 \times 34) = 135.7 \text{ milliseconds}$$

Assuming that the one disk rotation between reading and writing does not vary, then the variance of s_{arm} is the sum of the variance of the seek time + the variance of $\bar{t}_{q_{chan}}$.

We do not know the latter exactly if we have used the second method of calculating $\bar{t}_{q_{chan}}$, so we will assume that $\bar{t}_{w_{chan}}$ is exponential. It is almost certain to be somewhat lower than this. In absence of more accurate figures, we will assume the worst. The variance of $\bar{t}_{w_{chan}}$ is then $(7.2)^2$.

$$\therefore \quad \text{Variance of} \quad \bar{s}_{arm} = \sigma^2_{S_{eek}} + (7.2)^2$$

$$= \frac{80^2}{12} + (7.2)^2 = 585 \text{ milliseconds}^2$$

The three arms take 25 per cent, 40 per cent, and 35 per cent of the throughput, respectively. They therefore have the following values of ρ:

$$\rho_{arm\text{-}A} = 0.25 \times 10 \times 0.1357 = 0.34$$
$$\rho_{armB} = 0.40 \times 10 \times 0.1357 = 0.54$$
$$\rho_{armC} = 0.35 \times 10 \times 0.1357 = 0.47$$

Substituting these figures into Equation (28.7), we get, respectively,

$$\bar{t}_{q_{arm\text{-}A}} = 177.6$$
$$\bar{t}_{q_{armB}} = 232.8$$
$$\bar{t}_{q_{armC}} = 209.6$$

The mean value of $\bar{t}_{q_{arm}}$ is then

$$0.25\,\bar{t}_{q_{arm\text{-}A}} + 0.40\,\bar{t}_{q_{armB}} + 0.35\,\bar{t}_{q_{armC}} = 210.8 \text{ milliseconds}$$

There is one last factor we should add to this if we assume that the channel was needed in order to initiate a seek. It would be a useful type of file design if the seek instruction was conveyed to the seek mechanism by a path other than the data channel. In this case the answer above would be final. However, our simulation assumed that the seek command went down the same path as the data, as on most file systems in practice. We therefore may have to wait for both the channel and the arm before a seek can begin. The channel is only utilized for 0.4025 of the total time, so only 0.4025 of the seeks will encounter this small additional delay. How long will this delay be, on average?

Assuming that the mean channel occupancy $\bar{s}_{chan}$, for data, is 23 milliseconds, the transaction will have to wait between 0 and 23 milliseconds before it can attempt to begin a seek. The mean length of the wait is

$$\frac{1}{2}\left[\bar{s}_{chan} + \frac{\mathrm{Var}\,(s_{chan})}{\bar{s}_{chan}}\right]$$

As only 0.4025 transactions (ρ_{chan}) encounter this delay, the mean delay for all transactions is

$$\rho_{chan} \times \frac{1}{2}\left[\bar{s}_{chan} + \frac{\mathrm{Var}\,(s_{chan})}{\bar{s}_{chan}}\right] = 0.4025 \times \frac{1}{2}\left[23 + \frac{34^2}{23 \times 12}\right] = 5.5 \quad (28.9)$$

It will be approximately correct to add this delay factor to this value of $\bar{t}_{q_{arm}}$ above. This gives

$$210.8 + 5.5 = 216.3 \text{ milliseconds.}$$

This is the answer we were requiring. Note that the simulation in Chapter 25 gave this as 205.6 milliseconds.

The steps in this calculation are summarized by Fig. 28.7. The file response may be evaluated by referring to curves listed in Fig. 28.7.

We have had to make a number of approximations in this calculation regardless of which method we have used. The answer, then, is not exact. How inaccurate is it as a result of our assumptions? Let us compare the various methods of tackling the problem.

Figure 28.8 plots the file response time, $\bar{t}_q$, against $\bar{n}$, the mean number of transactions per second. The thick curve gives the result obtained by simulation, which is the most accurate of all the methods provided that the model is allowed to run with a very large number of transactions. The curve to the left of this is obtained by the method used in this chapter. It will be seen that it closely approximates the simulation curve. A variety of other file systems gave similarly close concurrence. The other solid curve also follows the method discussed above, but uses the Khintchine-Polloczek equation [Equation (26.27)] —invalidly— to calculate the channel queue. The computation is easier: the result is slightly less accurate, but there is not much in it—especially when the queue buildup is not too great. If the channel utilization had been much greater than the highest arm utilization then there would have been more difference between these two methods and the one outlined above would have been the better.

The dotted curves on the extreme left and extreme right represent the results of assumptions which have a more major effect on the accuracy of the calculation, and the reader is cautioned against using them. The leftmost curve was obtained by assuming all of the various service times were exponential. This is not true, and although it makes the calculation easier, it is hardly justified.

The rightmost curve is worse still. This ignores the channel queue. The

Table 28.2*

Time and Arrival	Account Number	File Unit	Seek Duration	Arv. this File Free?	Time Seek Started	Time Seek Completed	Time Channel Operation Starts	Time Read Completed	Time Processing Starts	Time Processing Completed	Time Channel Operation Starts	Time Write Completed
0	658230	A	100	Yes	0	100	100	123	123	132	153	191
50	127006	B	80	Yes	50	130	130	153	153	162	191	221
110	445189	C	40	Yes	123	163	221	244	244	253	253	278
190	782871	A	90	Yes	191	281	281	304	304	313	313	338
250	564742	C	120	No	278	398	398	421	421	430	444	455
320	217423	B	80	Yes	338	418	421	444	444	453	455	478
420	433267	C	70	No	455	525	525	548	548	557	557	582
460	276234	B	100	No	478	578	582	605	605	614	614	639
520	774695	A	110	Yes	520	630	639	662	662	671	671	696
620	380556	B	40	No	639	679	696	719	719	728	728	753
700	699978	A	100	Yes	719	819	819	842	842	851	865	876
760	409359	C	80	Yes	760	840	842	865	865	874	876	899
870	318057	B	40	Yes	876	916	916	939	939	948	948	973
880	666129	A	90	Yes	899	989	989	1012	1012	1021	1021	1046
950	107411	B	120	No	973	1093	1093	1116	1116	1125	1125	1150
1080	521315	C	80	Yes	1080	1160	1160	1183	1183	1192	1192	1217
1100	535024	C	70	No	1217	1287	1306	1329	1329	1338	1340	1363
1170	294233	B	100	Yes	1183	1283	1283	1306	1306	1315	1329	1340
1240	473819	C	110	No	1363	1473	1497	1520	1520	1529	1529	1554
1300	332628	B	40	No	1340	1380	1380	1403	1403	1412	1412	1437
1370	647776	A	70	Yes	1370	1440	1440	1463	1463	1472	1472	1497
1470	518967	C	110	No	1497	1607	1607	1630	1630	1639	1639	1664
1580	300412	B	60	Yes	1580	1640	1664	1687	1687	1696	1696	1721
1600	496258	C	100	No	1664	1764	1780	1803	1803	1812	1814	1837
1680	669149	A	70	Yes	1687	1757	1757	1780	1780	1789	1803	1814

* See p. 460.

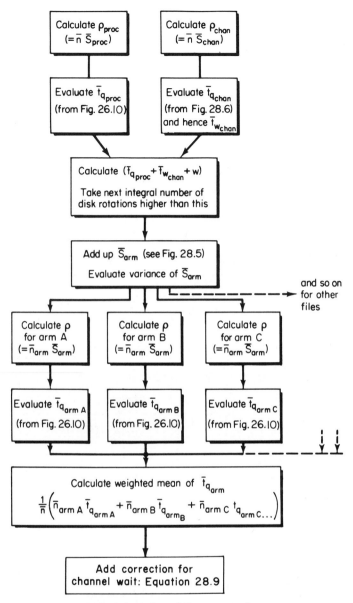

Fig. 28.7. Calculation of file response time.

one just to the left of it is obtained by using the Khintchine-Polloczek equations to calculate separately the channel queue (neglecting the effect of the arms) and the arm queue (neglecting the effect of the channel). The two wait times are then added. This gives a misleading result, which, unlike the others, does not err on the side of safety.

It is interesting also to compare the standard deviations from the various approaches that are plotted in Figure 28.9.

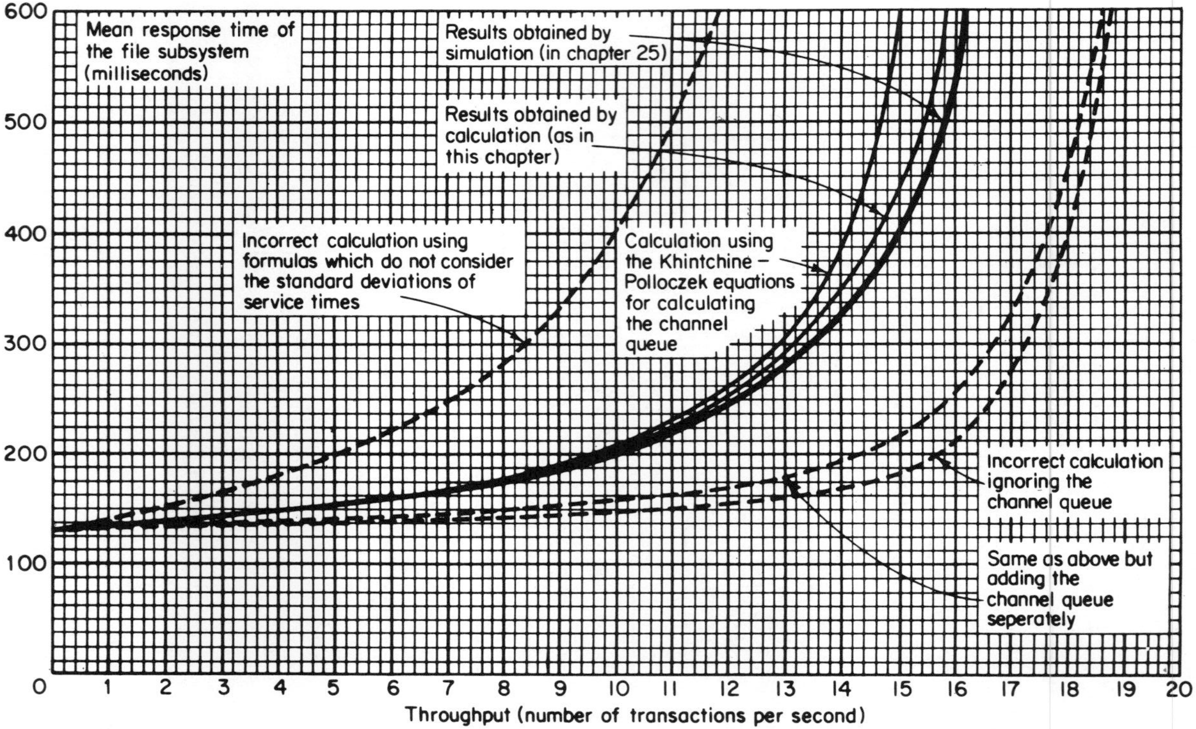
600
500
400
300
200
100
0
Mean response time of the file subsystem (milliseconds)
Results obtained by simulation (in chapter 25)
Results obtained by calculation (as in this chapter)
Incorrect calculation using formulas which do not consider the standard deviations of service times
Calculation using the Khintchine – Polloczek equations for calculating the channel queue
Incorrect calculation ignoring the channel queue
Same as above but adding the channel queue seperately
1 2 3 4 5 6 7 8 9 10 11 12 13 14 15 16 17 18 19 20
Throughput (number of transactions per second)

Fig. 28.8. The results of calculations of the response time of the file system in Fig. 25.4.

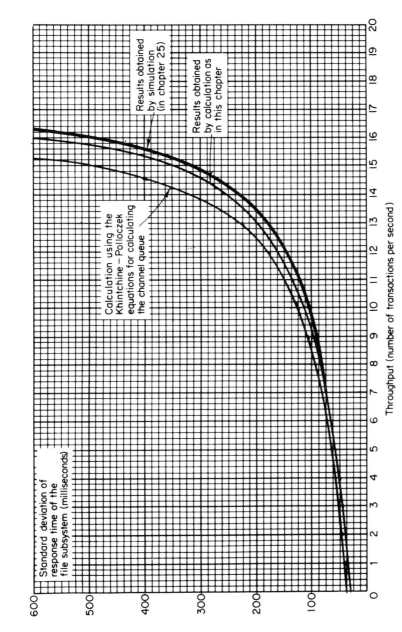

Fig. 28.9. The results of calculations of the standard deviation of response time of the file system in Fig. 25.4.

The following text labels appear within the figure:

Standard deviation of response time of the file subsystem (milliseconds)

Calculation using the Khintchine – Polloczek equations for calculating the channel queue

Results obtained by simulation (in chapter 25)

Results obtained by calculation as in this chapter

Throughput (number of transactions per second)

HAND
SIMULATION

The author has observed systems analysts, for want of a better method, tackle problems like this by tabulating the times at which events occur. This, in effect, is a kind of simulation by hand. Table 28.2 gives an illustration of this, again for the system in Fig. 25.4.

This approach might start by writing a string of reference numbers, account numbers, for example, in a sequence in which they could be processed by the system. Knowing the file organization, the unit to which these relate is then written down, and the lengths of the seeks involved. In the far left column the times at which the transactions are ready to begin processing are written down. These might follow a Poisson interarrival time obtained from Poisson tables. The times that various events, such as seeks and reads, take place are then written down, noting any delays due to conflicting requirements. These times must all be written in the sequence in which they occur.

This method is not recommended. It is laborious, inaccurate, and involves a surprisingly large number of events that must be tabulated before the system "stabilizes" and gives a reasonable result.

29 ESTIMATING THE PROGRAM SIZES

In most on-line systems the core will not be large enough to hold all the programs at once. Many of the programs will be kept in files, or second-level storage, and called into core when they are required in convenient-sized blocks.

The blocks of programs will usually be relocatable, that is, they can be operated from any position in core. The only routines which may not be in blocks but which will be be packed into a fixed core location are those that are permanently required core or used too frequently to be read in from files each time. This will include part of the Supervisory Programs.

The following decisions therefore must be made in the estimating process:

1. How large are the blocks?
2. How many blocks of program are there in total?
3. What size are the programs permanently in core and not in blocks?
4. How many blocks will normally be in core?

BLOCK SIZES

The answer to the first question will, to some extent, be dependent upon the characteristics of the computer and its files. Is the machine specifically designed for program relocation? If so, does the mechanism give any preferred block size? Do the file characteristics indicate any preferred block size; for example, does the file have fixed record lengths? Should the block size be related to the size of a track on disk or drum?

Generally speaking, as core storage is very much more expensive than file storage, it should be core considerations that determine this, rather than factors such as disk-track length. The nature of the programs themselves will do much to determine it. It will be inconvenient, for example, to split a long program with elaborate branching into a number of relatively short blocks. On the other hand, a system handling a wide variety of relatively simple actions may use small blocks. Very complex airline reservation systems have used program blocks as small as 256 characters, because many of the individual actions only needed a short piece of program. As in this case, the core allocation may be such that blocks can be used interchangeably either for data or programs, and this may determine the economic block size.

Consideration of the programs themselves can be divided into two categories, Supervisory Programs and Applications Programs.

ESTIMATING SUPERVISORY PROGRAMS

The Supervisory Programs may be specially written for an application, or they may be package programs provided by a manufacturer. Some of them may be routines taken from another application. In many applications with a high degree of real-time operation it seems that the supervisory routines available from some manufactures do not solve all of the user's problems. And so the routines already available, if used, are often modified or added to. A supervisory package, for a real-time system will often end up consisting of some standard routines but much coding written specially for the application.

Nevertheless, considerable data are available on sizes of certain types of supervisory routines, and this will usually enable the estimates made in this area to be rather more reliable than the estimates of the Application Programs. Unfortunately, for estimating purposes, some of the mechanisms of Supervisory Programs are likely to differ from one application to another.

There are two types of reasons for Supervisory Program differences. Firstly, there may be differences in the hardware, including:

1. Different types of processing unit.
2. Special engineering changes on the computer.
3. Different input/output configurations, communication line types, and so on.
4. Different core sizes.
5. Different line control units.
6. Different switchover hardware.

Secondly, there may be differences inherent in the application itself:

1. Differences in throughput.
2. Differences in the required response time.
3. Differences in the number of Application Programs in use.

4. Differences in the size and complexity of the Application Programs.

5. Differences in the message mix; for example, some applications will have a much broader spread of message length or message type than others.

6. Differences in message priority considerations.

7. Differences in fallback procedures.

8. In some applications, the processing may be shared between more than one computer.

9. In some systems non-real-time jobs are a major part of the work load.

These differences in requirements lead to differences in the mechanisms of the Supervisory Program, which will affect the estimating of program requirements. The differences in mechanisms will include the following:

1. Differences in the functions performed by the Supervisory Programs.

2. Differences in the macroinstructions provided.

3. Differences in the degree of multiprogramming, that is, the number of messages that can be processed in parallel at one time.

4. Differences in the block sizes required for storage of programs, data, and messages.

5. Differences in the manner in which Application Programs are obtained from files ready for processing the message.

6. Differences in the way linkages are made between programs and between subroutines.

7. Differences in input/output control routines.

8. Differences in the queuing structure.

9. Differences in switchover and fallback procedures.

Before an accurate estimate of Supervisory Program sizes and core and timing requirements, in general, can be made, it must be decided what the basic structure and mechanisms of the Supervisory Programs will be.* Figures 31.1–31.4 give core figures typical of certain types of system. It is recommended that the reader, if making estimates for a system, should obtain similar figures in greater detail for the computer and application that he is concerned with.

ESTIMATING APPLICATION PROGRAMS

The estimating of the Application Programs is the area in which a book of this type will be of least help. The Application Programs are unique to their particular application, and estimates can only be made from a detailed knowledge of this application.

---

*James Martin, *Programming Real-Time Computer Systems*. Englewood Cliffs, N.J.: Prentice-Hall, Inc., 1965.

The estimating of Application Programs corresponds to the estimating of the number of data-processing instructions on a batch-processing application. It is, however, desirable that it should be done more accurately than on a batch-processing application because the penalties of making low estimates are greater. On a conventional system, the time of the computer run expands as required to complete the job. This cannot occur on a real-time system. Also, if a bad core estimate is made, the conventional run can normally be divided into two runs to compensate for this. As is illustrated in Chapter 34, the mechanism for compensation on a real-time system is far less expandable.

Probably the most dangerous area in the whole estimating procedure is estimating the size of the Application Programs. On some systems that have been installed, the original estimates for these were too small by a factor of 6 or even higher. Looking back to find the reason for this, it becomes apparent that the complications of the systems grew far beyond those originally anticipated.

The complications increase in two ways. Firstly, unless a tight restriction is imposed, there is a tendency for the user's requirements to increase beyond those originally listed. It is tempting on any data-processing system to add sophistications before the difficulties of implementing these sophistications are realized. On a real-time system, this temptation may be even greater, as there is a tendency among the uninitiated to see the potentialities of these systems without seeing the difficulties equally clearly. To avoid this, the system should be designed to a clearly defined set of customer requirements, and these should not be allowed to increase without a reappraisal of the estimates.

Secondly, the programming that is needed for one specific customer requirement tends to be underestimated. Programming for an electronic data-processing installation is more complicated than that for the equivalent unit-record installation. This is because more work is done manually in the unit-record installation, such as sorting and moving cards from one machine to another. Similarly, the change from an electronic batch-processing system to a real-time system means that the programming will be more complicated, because more human functions are being taken on by the machine. It is a change to a higher degree of automation. Program functions are now required which were not needed on a batch-processing system. These include program selection and read-in, elaborate checking of input data and appropriate error procedures, the calculation of addresses of records in a large random-access file, fallback procedures for use when units of equipment fail, procedures for recovering from a period of fallback operation when, for instance, records have been stored in a different place in the file, a large variety of possible computer responses in a man-machine conversation, and routines which can recognize or reject the enormous variety of possible human input messages, including those that are erroneous.

Many of the Application Program actions related to a certain function may be omitted if the function is not examined in sufficient detail. On an airline reservation system processing passenger name and detail information, the programming needed for handling reservation information can easily be underestimated because there are many types and combinations of such requests—many different possible journeys, interconnections with other carriers, inventory control problems on flights with multiple stopping points, requests to book passengers who are already booked or cancel passengers not booked, and all manner of elaborate changes of booking. It is easy to omit in the estimate much of the coding necessary for these if the problem is not analyzed in sufficient detail by persons fully familiar with all the peculiarities of the reservations process. Similarly, actions needed to display information from the files may be correctly assessed, but programs needed to change this information have been neglected on the initial estimates of some systems.

If an Application Program is underestimated, the damage that this causes depends upon the frequency of use of the program in question. There are some programs which may only be used very infrequently, but which contain many lines of coding, such as the change of flight schedules on an airline. If these programs are underestimated or even neglected, it will make little or no difference to the performance of the system and will only affect the estimates of manpower requirements. If, however, the program is frequently used, it is much more important that the estimates should be correct.

On one type of application with, say, 100,000 lines of real-time coding, broken into something like 1000 segments, perhaps 10 per cent of these would be sufficiently frequently used to need detailed, accurate estimating. On other systems, the frequency-of-use distribution might be different, some having a small number of actions almost always in use and a large number of very infrequently used programs; others have a more even spread. A class of routines with a high usage that are often grossly underestimated are those needed for handling the man-machine conversation.

In view of the above difficulties in estimating Application Programs, the following suggestions are offered:

1. Every attempt should be made to foresee all the complications that are likely to be required. Attention should be paid to the following questions:

Have all possible message types been considered?

Have all the variations possible on each message been considered?

Have all the functions required to process each message been taken into account?

Have all the housekeeping functions been considered, such as error routines, file-addressing methods, end transaction, and ignore transaction?

Have all the actions necessary for updating, changing, and maintaining the file been considered?

2. To assist in this, it would be worthwhile to check through a listing of all the Application Programs required on a previous similar system, if this is possible, or even a system for a different type of application.

To make this easier, it is desirable to have experienced programmers or systems analysts on the team that draws up the functional requirements of the system. This sounds obvious, but it is surprising how often functional requirements are drawn up without this experience.

3. Those programs which are most frequently used should be block diagrammed in as much detail as possible, and portions of them should be coded.

4. Even with these precautions, it is worthwhile to heed the serious expansions in Application Program estimates that have taken place on other systems and to design new systems with such an expansion in view. Can the system still function if the Application Programs expand by a factor of 2? If not, then the safety margin in the design is probably inadequate.

5. The estimating process should include the calculation of what will happen if the Application Programs do become larger than the estimates by various amounts.

6. Having designed the system using certain Application Program figures, every means should be used to ensure that the programs do not expand beyond these figures. In a number of systems within the author's experience, the user requirements expanded considerably beyond those used in making the original estimates. If this is allowed to happen, then, almost certainly, the system will become short of core and possibly other additional hardware will be needed.

7. To cater for future expansion, as well as to cater for misestimates, the system should be designed in such a way that its core can be increased.

WHERE ARE THE PROGRAMS STORED?
When an estimate, probably at first an approximate estimate, has been made of the sizes of all the various programs, the decision has then to be made where the programs will normally be stored: in core or on files. Normally the volume of programs will be too large for it to be economic to keep all the programs in core all of the time. On complex commercial systems, only a small fraction of the programs may be in core at one time.

The programs, then, fall into one of the following categories:

1. *Programs which are always in core*, whatever the system status, These are the only programs that are likely to not be written in blocks, not to be written in a relocatable manner, because they are never read in from the files.

2. *Programs which are normally in core*, but may be read in from files under exceptional circumstances, such as when switchover to a standby computer occurs. During normal processing the Supervisory Programs will assume that these programs are in core.

3. *Programs which may not be in core*. When such a program is required, a Supervisory Routine must determine whether it is in core or not. This will require a list of programs in core to be scanned, perhaps in a table look-up operation which determines their location.

4. *Programs which are not normally in core*. These are programs for processing infrequently occurring message types or rare exception conditions, such as error routines. It will not be worthwhile scanning a list to see whether they are in core.

Table 29.1. AN ESTIMATE OF THE FREQUENCY OF USAGE OF THE BLOCKS OF PROGRAMS.

Average number times a block used in peak hour	Number blocks with this usage	Permanently in core	Read in from files if not already in core	Always read in from files
Less than 1				✓
1– 2	507			✓
	192			
2– 4	286			✓
4– 8	210			
8– 16	180		✓	
16– 32	103		✓	
32– 64	67		✓	
64– 128	59		✓	
128– 256	43		✓	
256– 512	96		✓	
512– 1024	64		✓	
1024– 2048	50		✓	
2048– 4096	33	✓	✓	
4096– 8192	5	✓		
8192–16384	42	✓		

Total: 1937

NOTE: A table of this type is used in the following two chapters for estimation of core storage utilization and timing. Such figures are always very approximate when estimating is initially done but improve in accuracy as the project proceeds.

After determining the program sizes, a table can be made to indicate their frequency of use. The frequency of use of a program block will determine whether it is kept in core or not. To estimate the frequency of use of a program block in the peak hour, it is necessary to know the number of types of transactions that will be processed in that time. Table 29.1 is an illustration of this type of estimate. Such a table will be used for estimating core storage requirements and processing time as described in the next two chapters.

30   ESTIMATING THE SYSTEM TIMING

On a batch-processing computer, the utilization of time can usually be mapped out in detail when the programs are designed. This is not so on a real-time system because events happen at times which are not exactly known beforehand. For example, the times of completion of input/output actions, especially of references to random-access files, are not known exactly. Messages are entered by human operators at times dependent upon human events. The sequence of message types or functions to be performed may be unpredictable.

Because of this unpredictability, the computer cannot follow a repetitive cycle of events but must allocate the time on its various units according to requirements. This allocation of time may be done in a simple, serial fashion or may be very complex with a high degree of multiprogramming and overlapping of operations. On some systems the processing unit utilization is so slack in timing that there is no need to work out the timing in great detail. However, on other systems timing is tight, and great attention must be paid to it.

The work of estimating the timing on a real-time system is intended to ensure that the system is fast enough to handle the transactions it will receive at periods of peak traffic. It will be necessary to estimate how much slack there is. How can the system expand? Are the estimates tight? How much more traffic could be handled, other factors permitting? If it is a hybrid system handling non-real-time work as well as real-time, what is the capacity of the processing unit left for this other work?

BASIC TYPES OF TIMING PATTERN

Before any timing estimates can be attempted, it is necessary to determine the mechanisms by which traffic is routed through the system. To what extent will file references be overlapped with processing? To what extent will they be overlapped with one another? Will transactions be sifted to any degree to minimize file-seeking actions? Will long messages be chopped into slices? It is necessary, in other words, to understand those mechanisms of the Supervisory Programs which have an effect on the timing. Figures 30.1–30.5 provide illustrations of this. These diagrams all oversimplify the actions that occur but indicate some of the basic timing patterns that are possible. It is necessary to establish the basic pattern before estimating begins.

In Fig. 30.1 the processor is idling most of the time waiting for file-reference operations to be completed. Here the seek, read, and write actions cannot be overlapped.

Figures 30.2 and 30.3 indicate how the throughput may be increased when file actions are overlapped. Transactions which need the processing shown in Fig. 30.2 are handled in parallel as shown in Fig. 30.3. The transactions to be processed arrive at random times. The pattern of events in an actual system may be very much more complex than in this simplified diagram. As the degree of multiprogramming increases, so the Supervisory Programs, as opposed to Application Programs, take up a higher proportion of the processing unit's time.

Figure 30.4 shows the timing pattern of a two-computer system in which a small and relatively inexpensive computer collects transactions which, at intervals, a large computer processes in a batch.

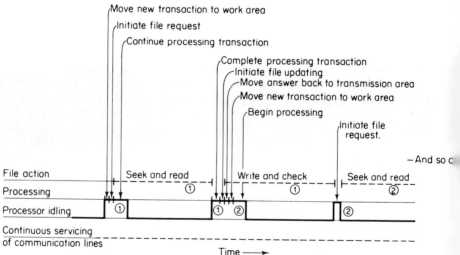

Fig. 30.1. A timing diagram for a system with serial processing —e.g., a savings bank system.

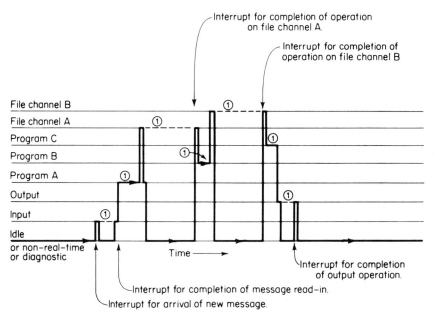

Fig. 30.2. A timing diagram to be used in conjunction with Fig. 30.3, which shows transactions of this type being processed in parallel.

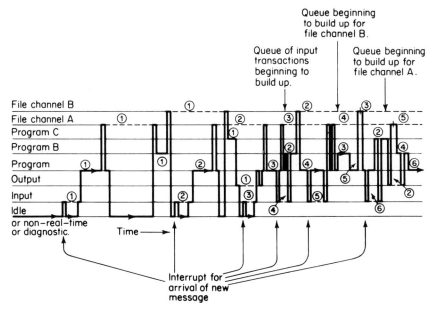

Fig. 30.3. A timing diagram showing the utilization of time on a simple multiprogrammed system processing transactions of the type illustrated in Fig. 30.2.

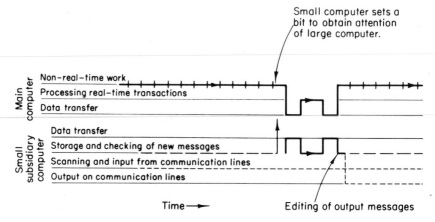

Fig. 30.4. A timing diagram for a two-computer system on which a small proportion of the work is real-time.

Figure 30.5 shows the timing on a process control application in which a repetitive cycle of events occurs. The cycle is started at intervals by a pulse from a real-time clock, which interrupts the computer. The system then collects readings from instruments and goes through a cycle of events which may be timed with much more detail than on a computer in which the input arrives at random. The repetitive cycle may, however, be interrupted by a relatively exceptional event which does occur at random and which needs fairly quick attention.

FACTORS THAT DETERMINE THE TIMING PATTERN

In planning the pattern of timing in a system, the following factors need attention:

1. *What overlapping of input/output and file actions occurs?* This is to some extent a function of the hardware, but on a system on which timing is slack too much overlapping of operations may be avoided for the sake of simplicity.

2. *What is the degree of multiprogramming?* In other words, how many transactions can be processed in parallel? Some systems restrict the number of transactions that can be handled in parallel. The Supervisory Programs may be designed so that not more than two or three items are being processed at once. In other systems the degree of multiprogramming will not be limited except by the limits of time or core available. This directly affects the timing pattern.

3. *The Queuing Mechanism.* Items flowing through the system have to wait in queues. They wait, for example, for the attention of the processing

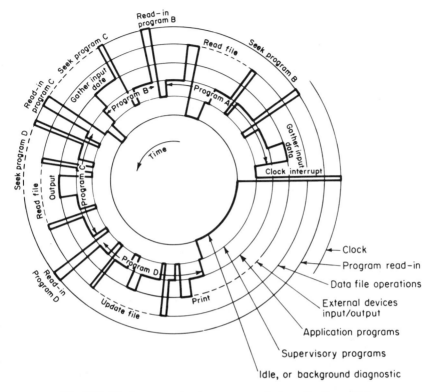

Fig. 30.5. Timing on a simple process-control application which cycles through its application programs sequentially. When a clock interrupt occurs, the computer scans a set of instruments and processes the readings. It changes settings and prints out information accordingly. To do this, it must make references to records on files and update them. Occasionally interrupts will be caused by exceptional external events which cause additional times, not shown on this diagram, to be utilized.

unit, for the file channels, for the read/write mechanisms, and for the output channels. The types of queues must be specified along with the criteria causing items to enter and leave them. The average time an item waits in queue, dependent of course on the number of items in the queue, must be estimated. This affects the over-all pattern of events in the system, and in particular it affects the response times of the system.

4. *The Priority Structure.* Some items may have higher priorities than others, enabling them, for example, to jump the queues or even break into the processing of other items. The priority arrangements need to be known.

5. *The Mechanism of Program Read-in.* This factor may considerably

affect the timing pattern. If programs have to be called in from outside the core, the method of doing this may be determined to a large extent by the timing factors involved and, particularly, by the response times that are needed. Programs may be read in in serial, or cyclic, fashion, and a transaction will wait until its particular program is in core or they might be called in at random when required. If the response time is to be a few seconds or less, the program read-in will probably have to be random. This is discussed more fully later in the chapter.

6. *Other Read-in.* The factors determining the method of program read-in apply also to obtaining data from the files. Is the response time such that data required must be obtained immediately, or can file actions be delayed and sifted in such a way as to minimize seek times and increase file arm utilization?

7. *Line Control.* What time factors are involved in the performance of the line control unit? Can all lines operate at the same time? Can data be sent at the same time as received on a line? On some small systems processing cannot take place at the same time as operating the lines because the message buffering and the line control program take up all or most of the available core. There will therefore be intermittent bursts of processing, line activity, processing, and so on.

ELEMENTS COMPRISING THE PROCESSING TIME

The use of the computer processing time is made up of the following elements:

1. Application Program time. The processing time utilized in executing the segments of Application Program.

2. Supervisory Program time. The processing time utilized for supervisory functions, such as input/output control, scheduling work, transferring control between programs, initiating the read-in of programs, and handling interrupts.

3. Input/output time on a computer in which input/output operations are not completely overlapped with processing. On many machines data coming into the computer or leaving it snatch processing cycles away from the main programs. This must be added up.

4. Time when the computer is forced to idle in a Supervisory Program scanning loop, waiting for an input request to be completed or a new message to arrive.

In assessing the computer processing unit time of a proposed system, it is necessary to calculate what proportion of the total time is taken up by 1, 2, and 3 above. This will give an indication of the speed of computer necessary for the application.

1. *The Application Program Times*

On most applications, a relatively small number of message *types* represent the majority of the processing time used by the system. The only safe way to obtain Application Program timings and to evaluate such factors as segment size and core utilization is to study the processing on these most frequently occurring messages in as much detail as possible and to program them where possible. One of the main causes of inaccuracy in timing estimates for existing systems has again been a failure to foresee all the complications in the Application Programs. It is difficult to see any way around this danger other than to look at the frequently used programs in depth.

Timing the Application Programs corresponds to the timing of programs on a conventional data-processing job. On some systems it is made a little easier than this conventional timing by the fact that input/output operations, buffering, and so on, need not be considered here. They are part of the Supervisory Programs. However, on many systems this factor is an added complication. Above all, the timing needs to be more accurate because the penalties for errors in estimating on a real-time system are greater. On a conventional system, if the timing estimates were low, the run merely takes longer than was anticipated. On a real-time system, the input arrives at a rate largely independent of the programs and so may result in the building up of queues, which will cause the response time to increase. When the queues become large, the system degenerates rapidly.

A real-time system is less able to yield to take account of too low an estimate, and so the safety factor left in the assessment of the Application Programs should be high.

2. *The Supervisory Program Estimates*

The Supervisory Program times vary from one application to another, depending upon the mechanisms for scheduling work, controlling input/output, allocating priorities, and so on. The basic mechanisms for routing work through the system must be determined before an attempt can be made at Supervisory Program timing.

The safest way to estimate these times is to work from times for similar functions on existing systems, making modifications where required. Often, the computer manufacturer provides these times. Usually, the supervisory routines can be timed, if sufficient investigation is done, much more accurately than the Application Program timings.

The following elements are typical ones for which times must be estimated and illustrate the degree of breakdown that is needed. Knowing these times and the number of input, output, and file actions, the number of programs read in, the number of interrupts, and so on, the total Supervisory Program time can be added up.

(a) *Times for Message Input*

(i) *Interrupts.* The processing unit will be interrupted at times as messages are received from the communications equipment. On some computers an interrupt occurs at the start of the message and when its reception is complete. This may be the case if a separate line control unit or line control computer is used for assembling and checking characters from the lines. On other computers an interrupt is needed for every character received.

The time taken for these interrupts will vary with the design of the computer. On some machines the interrupt and its associated functions will be largely automatic, and not many machine cycles will be taken away from the main processing. Others will need small program routines to be executed when the interrupt occurs, and the time taken is greater.

(ii) *Editing and code-converting the incoming message.* It will be necessary to eliminate backspace and control characters from the message and to remove "tabs" and arbitrary spacing done on a typewriter keyboard. The computer may convert the code of the characters from that used on the communication lines, such as BAUDOT code, to that used in the computer, for example, BCD. This may be an automatic hardware function, or it may, again, be done by programming. It may, as with other message input functions, be performed in a line control computer separate from the main machine. It may scan the message, interpreting the language of the human user.

(iii) *Error checking.* Longitudinal redundancy characters in the message may be analyzed, again by programming on some machines, by hardware on others. Another form of checking commonly used is for the operators to put serial numbers on the messages. The computer checks these to ensure that no messages have been lost.

(iv) *Storage allocation.* When dynamic core allocation is used for input messages, blocks of core are allocated as they are required to store the message. A complete and lengthy message may thus be scattered around in blocks in different parts of core, these blocks being appropriately chained together. Using this technique can make the over-all core utilization much lower, but a small amount of processing time is needed to allocate the blocks and chain them together.

(v) *Message logging.* It may be necessary to log the incoming message onto magnetic tape or some other form of storage.

(vi) *Setting up message-reference block.* When the reception of a message is complete, an area may be set up in which it will be processed, In a multi-thread application it is desirable to have an area of core unique to each message for its life in the system. The areas containing input messages effectively form a queue of items waiting to be processed. Time may be required to allocate a block, move the message into it, and chain it to form a queue.

(vii) *Line scanning*. The communication lines must be constantly scanned for the computer to maintain an awareness of their status. On a *polling* network, constant requests must be sent to the terminals asking if they have anything to transmit. On some machines these functions take time from the central processor. On others they are handled by a separate line control unit.

(b) *Times for Message Output*

(i) *Interrupts*. As with message input, the processing unit may be interrupted as messages are sent. On some machines this happens for each character; on others, at the end of each message.

(ii) *Editing and code-converting the outgoing message*. The converse of the input process must occur. Characters must be converted, for example, from BCD to BAUDOT code. Space, line control, and other control characters must be added.

(iii) *Time to initiate the output*. When a macroinstruction is given, stating that the output message is to be sent, time is needed to interpret this and initiate the action.

(iv) *Storage allocation*. Dynamically allocated blocks of core may be used for output. When such a block becomes free, it is rechained to an available-storage chain.

(c) *Elements of Time Needed for Each File Event*

When a record is sought and read from a random-access or other file, the following Supervisory Program times are needed for this:

(i) *Time to process the macroinstruction* requesting the file action. The request may be placed in a queue of requests for that channel or file head.

(ii) *Interrupt time*. Normally an interrupt will occur when the file action is complete. An interrupt may also occur when a seek is complete, and a read instruction should be given. An interrupt may also occur on some machines when, as the drum, disk, or recording medium rotates, the record is about to pass over the read/write head, This interrupt will be used to initiate the read-in or writing of characters.

When an interrupt occurs indicating the completion of a file action, a file- or channel-scheduling routine will see whether there is another request for this file or channel and, if so, initiate the new operation.

(iii) *Return of the transaction in question to the work-in-progress queue*. In a multithread system where many messages are being processed in parallel, processing may be temporarily suspended on one transaction while lengthy file references associated with it are made. It may be necessary to complete one file action, or more than one, before processing can continue. A message-reference block containing all details of the processing of this message must be inspected and updated after a file action; and, if this reveals that processing can continue on the message because the reason for its wait is now satisfied, it will be placed in a queue of work-in-progress items. These are half-processed items waiting again for the attention of the main processing programs.

Time is needed to examine the message-reference block and update the requisite indicators so that the scheduling programs can continue processing this transaction.

(iv) *File-addressing routines.* When data are to be sought in the files, the address of those data must be calculated or obtained before the file action can be executed. This may be a lengthy process. Various means of calculating file addresses are discussed in Chapter 22. The file organization must be determined before this time can be assessed, as there are many different methods of converting a key in the data into a file address.

(d) *Time for Transfers between Programs*

On a system with many small segments of program, the marshalling of these segments and the transfer of control between them will occupy a significant amount of Supervisory Program time. If, on the other hand, the segments are large and run for a long time, the time for switching between them will be very small compared with the Application Program operating time. On many real-time systems, however, a large amount of activity uses relatively simple segments of Application Program, and the proportion of time spent in the Supervisory Programs is high. The main types of transfer time between programs are as follows:

(i) *Time for entry macroinstructions.* This is the transfer from the Supervisory Programs to a segment of Application Program. Certain entry macroinstructions are usually given in the Supervisory Programs to effect this.

(ii) *Time for departure macroinstructions.* This is the transfer from an Application Program to the Supervisory Program. It is usually given when the processing using that Application Program is complete or when it must be suspended until a file or other overlapped action is complete. Certain departure macroinstructions are usually given in the Application Program to effect this.

(iii) *Time for direct transfers to a subroutine and back.* This is a simple, direct transfer between blocks of Application Program, which does not need reference to the Supervisory Programs. In a system with a high degree of multiprogramming it is limited in its use, but in less complex systems it is frequently used.

(iv) *Selection of application program segments.* On most systems the segments of program cannot all be in core at once as there are too many. They will have to be read in from the files. When a segment is needed a list may be scanned to see whether it is in core already or not. If it is not, its address on the files must be determined and it must be read in. The transaction being processed has to wait until the read-in operation is completed. During this wait, work on other transactions may continue if the system is designed to handle that degree of multiprogramming.

(e) *Interrupt Routines*

Various types of interrupts have been referred to above. Types of interrupts commonly found are:

(i)   Start of input/output operation.

(ii) End of input/output operation.

(iii) Start or end of any other overlapped function.

(iv) External event, such as when the closing or opening of two contacts has been sensed.

(v)   Clock interrupts at preset times or intervals. This may, for example occur if a time-sharing technique is used to divide the time between different users.

(vi) Errors or abnormal conditions.

When interrupts occur, the following times are needed to process them:

(i) *Time to store current conditions.* Control may be snatched away from an operating program at almost any point in its execution. That program may be using accumulators, registers, or almost any of the computer facilities. So that control may be returned to the program without upsetting its execution, the contents of the accumulators or registers, switches being used, latches such as high-low-equal compare, and so on, must be stored. On some machines this is done automatically, on some semiautomatically, on others entirely by programming. On one machine with a cycle time of 4.5 microseconds per character and no automatic features for storing conditions when an interrupt occurs, the storing and replacing of these conditions takes about one-half millisecond per interrupt.

(ii) *Time to replace conditions after interrupt routine.* This is the time taken to return everything that was stored above, so that the interrupted program can continue where it left off. Again on some machines this is automatic and takes very little time.

(iii) *Time to analyze the cause of the interrupt.* The cause of the interrupt must be analyzed so that control can be transferred to the appropriate program for processing it.

(iv) *Execution of the interrupt program.* Finally the time for executing the interrupt program, whatever it may be, must be considered.

(f) *Scheduling the Work*

The Supervisory Program makes the decision continuously on which operations to do next. What channel operation should be done next when the channel becomes free? What Application Program segment should be executed next when one transfers control to the Supervisory Programs?

The former scheduling decision, input/output scheduling, is in the timing given above. The latter, Application Program scheduling, is one of the main routines of a multithread Supervisory System. It is brief but frequently in use. The greater the degree of multiprogramming, the greater the use.

On a multiprogrammed system with many short Application Programs, the timing of this routine should be worked out in some detail and an estimate made of the number of times it is entered.

(g) Other Miscellaneous Times

Many real-time Supervisory Programs have other minor actions which consume some time. These are often characteristic of a specific application. Examples are time-initiated actions to be carried out at a certain time of day or at a certain time some other action, statistics-gathering routines, routines to keep a lookout for a certain type of message, overload routines, and so on. The number of characters from each terminal might be counted for billing or monitoring purposes. Certain messages might be intercepted and exception action taken on them, such as rerouting. Traffic may be rerouted when a line fails or processing modified when a file fails.

During estimating the systems analyst must think what functions might be required that are peculiar to his particular application.

3. Nonoverlapped Input/Output Times

On machines on which input and output of characters are not completely overlapped with processing, it is necessary to add a factor representing this to the processing-unit timings. Processing cycles will be delayed or taken away from the programs for this purpose. Fast input and output, such as reading and writing tapes, disks, and drums, may have to be considered separately from slow input and output, such as data on communication lines, as a different technique of data transfer may be used.

A knowledge of the number of characters transmitted from each type of device will enable this time to be calculated.

4. Forced Idling Time

If all the processing times above are added together for all the messages passing through the system, at the maximum design throughput, this will give a figure for the proportion of the central-processing-unit time usefully utilized. This figure will give an indication of the speed of processing unit needed. The remainder of the time, the processing unit will be idling, waiting for an interrupt. Some machines will idle in an interruptable "wait" state. Others will loop continuously in their central scanning loop. Both will be waiting for a new message to enter the system or for a wait macro-instruction in an Application Program to be satisfied, by a file request's being executed, for example.

Unfortunately, on a system with other than the lowest degree of multi-programming, it will be very difficult to calculate how much time can be usefully employed while waiting for the completion of an input/output request. This can be estimated on a system with purely serial processing or one in which only two, or perhaps three, messages are handled in parallel, but, for more complex systems than this, it is probably desirable to resort to simulation techniques to obtain the over-all timing of the system.

In general, the higher the degree of multiprogramimng, the lower will be the proportion of time that has to be spent idling while waiting for input/output requests to be satisfied. If the total processing-unit time, as calculated above, is low compared with the time available for the maximum message throughput, it will be apparent without simulation that the utilization of computer time is not dangerously high. However, if it is critical or if a figure for the maximum possible throughput is required, then simulation might have to be resorted to, to ensure that time does not become too tight.

THE READING IN
OF PROGRAMS

The reading in of programs from outside the core can become a critical factor in timing these systems. A careful assessment of the programs to be read in must be made.

To evaluate this, timings for program segments may be worked out in the manner shown in Table 30.1. This is an extension of the table in the previous chapter.

This table calculates the channel utilization in reading the programs from a backing file. It makes the assumption, which can later be modified, that the programs are either permanently resident in core, or else are read in every time they are needed. This assumption will enable us, at a first reiteration, to calculate both the core needed to hold the programs, and the channel utilization in reading them in.

The table refers to the programs in terms of fixed-length blocks. One request for program may cause the reading in of one block or it may reference several blocks. It has been calculated that the reading in of one block occupies the channel for ten milliseconds.

Taking the number and mix of messages reaching the computer during the peak hour, the first two columns in Table 30.1 were calculated. We have decided (and this may be changed on later reiterations) that 80 blocks of program will be permanently in core. The remainder will be read in as required. We then multiply the mean value in the first column by the second, and multiply this by ten milliseconds to get the time the channel is occupied, in the third column. The third column is added to give us the total number of seconds the channel is in use in the peak hour. Divided by 3600 seconds, this gives the channel utilization. The channel utilization in this case is 52 per

Table 30.1. EXAMPLE OF TIMING AND CHANNEL ESTIMATES FOR READING IN PROGRAMS

Average number of times a block is used in the peak hour	Number of blocks with this usage	Total channel utilization in peak hour, in seconds (assuming ten milliseconds per block)	Time, in milliseconds, this block is in core for one transaction*	Total time, in seconds, this block is in core in the peak hour
less than 1	507	2.5	2000	1
1– 2	192	2.9	2000	3
2– 4	286	8.6	2000	6
4– 8	210	12.6	1000	6
8– 16	180	21.6	1000	12
16– 32	103	24.7	1000	24
32– 64	67	32.2	1000	48
64– 128	{ 20 39	} 56.6	1000 500	96 48
128– 256	{ 23 20	} 82.6	1000 500	192 96
256– 512	{ 48 48	}368.6	1000 500	384 192
512– 1024	{ 24 20 20	}491.5	2000 1000 500	1536 768 384
1024– 2048	{ 20 20 10	}768.0	2000 1000 500	3072 1536 768
2048– 4096	33	0.0	}Permanently in core Total: 80 blocks	
4096– 8192	5	0.0		
8192–16334	42	0.0		

1872.4 sec

$$\therefore \quad \text{Channel utilization} = \frac{1872.4 \times 100\%}{3600} = 52\%$$

This estimate of the channel utilization assumes that each block is read into core when it is needed (with the exception of those permanently in core). If, however, blocks are already sometimes in core and so not read in, the channel utilization will be lower and the figures in the two right-hand columns will be higher. The channel utilization must be multiplied by a factor which represents the probability of a block of program being already available in core.

*These will initially be very crude estimates. They depend on the number of file references made while a block waits in core and on the *queue sizes*. They will become more accurate with successive reiterations.

cent. It would generally be inadvisable to design a system with this channel utilization for program read-in because if the programs in fact turn out to be considerably larger than our estimates (and on how many systems is this not true), then the channel utilization will grow so that a large waiting time could be necessary for program read-in.

This may, of course, only be part of the utilization of this channel. The channel may also be used for certain data and the data utilization will be added to the utilization for program blocks to give the total utilization. In this example, the channel utilization is already becoming high. Not much can be added to it without causing queues to build up waiting for program accesses, as shown in Fig. 26.9. It is probable however that we do not need to read in a program block every time we use it. It may be in core already, depending upon how much core we have. This subject will be taken up again in the next chapter when core is discussed.

The fourth column in Table 30.1 lists the time we must keep the block in core for the processing of one transaction. These initially are somewhat crude estimates. We know how long it will take to execute the program, but we do not yet know as accurately how long the waiting time in the queues for the file accesses and for processing unit will be, or how long we have to wait to obtain other program blocks. We may attempt to estimate these as discussed in previous chapters. The estimate will become more accurate when the channel utilization for program read-in becomes known more accurately.

Column 4 is now multiplied by the mean value in Column 1 to obtain Column 5, which in this example is the total time each block of program is in core during the peak hour. The third figure from the bottom in Column 5 is 3072 seconds. There are 20 blocks to which this figure applies. This suggests that these 20 blocks might be *permanently* in core. Possibly others should also be permanently in core, which would lessen the channel load.

For many systems this would be an unrealistic calculation, implying, as it does, that each operation other than the most frequent has a block of programs read into core especially for it. On many systems *some* of the operations have a block of programs read in for them. There are clearly many variations on this theme, depending upon the volumes and nature of the program read-in. There are a variety of different program read-in mechanisms. On a system with a high degree of multiprogramming it will often become desirable to simulate the program read-in. On the not-so-complicated system, or one with only a small degree of program read-in, it can be estimated satisfactorily without simulation.

ESTIMATING THE OVER-ALL TIMING

Having established a timing pattern for the events in the system, as in the figures earlier in this chapter, and having estimated the processing times, as above, and the input/output and file times, as in previous chapters, the over-all timing of the system can be worked out.

The over-all timing cannot be obtained merely by adding together the various processing times or file times, but must fit them together into a pattern, for example, like that in Fig. 30.3. It is necessary to take into account the times the processing unit is forced to be idle because a program is waiting for an input/output or file action to be completed. At the same time the file channels will not be fully utilized because situations will occur when they are waiting for the processing unit.

On a system without multiprogramming, it is possible, by means of a simple bar chart, to take the input/output operations into account and evaluate the over-all timing of the system. Similarly on a system with a very low degree of multiprogramming, such as one in which only two messages may be processed in parallel, it is still possible to obtain these figures arithmetically or by means of a bar chart. However, on a system with a high degree of multiprogramming, the timing becomes very complex to analyze by hand. To obtain accurate estimates, it is desirable to resort to a simulation method.

A similar consideration applies to the over-all core utilization. On a system without multiprogramming, the core storage requirements can easily be added together. On a system with a high degree of multiprogramming, it is necessary to know the average contents of various queues. In order to determine this, it is necessary to know how long items have to wait for file arms and channels and how long an item spends in the system. Mathematical techniques may become too complicated or insufficiently accurate, and it is desirable to resort to a simulation method.

As with core utilization, processing-unit time utilization will vary with the load on the system. This is illustrated in Fig. 24.5. For many systems this increase will not be linear. Beyond a certain point the system becomes degenerate, and a small peak in traffic will exceed the capacity of the system.

The shape of the time utilization curve in Fig. 24.5 will vary from one type of Supervisory Program to another, as does the core utilization curve in Fig 24.4. In making estimates for the design of a system, it is important to know the effect of peaks in load on the time and core utilization in order to know what peaks the system can handle. Unless the system is obviously in the clear from the timing point of view, it will be desirable to estimate the computer time usage for different loads and plot a curve as in Fig. 24.5.

31 ESTIMATING THE CORE STORAGE REQUIREMENTS

Experience of systems installed to date seems to indicate that, of the nine critical design factors given in Chapter 23, the one that is most critical is the core storage.

Many users have ordered real-time computers only to find that, as programming and systems design proceed, it becomes apparent that the core is insufficient. The only way to avoid such an error is to go into a considerable amount of detail in planning the use of core storage before the order is placed. On a complex real-time system it is usually necessary to go into much more detail before the specifications of the hardware are frozen than is done on a conventional or batch-processing system. It may take many months to obtain this level of detail. Block diagrams of programs will be needed. So will a detailed analysis of buffering techniques and program read-in from files. Queue sizes must be estimated and attention paid to overload and emergency situations.

Even with this level of detailed design it would be very unwise to order a complex real-time system using computers which cannot easily increase their core size. A computer using the upper limit of core available to it is a dangerous machine to order for the types of applications discussed in this book.

USES OF CORE STORAGE

Core storage may be used for the following items:

1. *Programs permanently in core storage.*
2. *Programs read into core when required.* The majority of segments of

program are not likely to be in core permanently but are stored on files of some type. However, there may be many of these temporary segments of program required in core at one time. The space available for them must be assessed.

3. *Tables* permanently in core or areas for read-in of tables from files. Tables may be needed for file-addressing purposes, line control, message routing, and so on. Examples are given below.

4. *Buffer areas for input and output.* Transactions may be received or transmitted on many communication lines or subchannels at once. Buffers for these will either be in the core of the main computer or possibly in the core of a subsidiary line control machine.

5. *Queues.* In addition to the items in buffer areas, queues of transactions will build up in a multithread system. There will be queues of items waiting for processing, waiting for file actions, and waiting for output channels.

6. *Message-reference blocks.* When several transactions are being processed in parallel, an area will be needed that is unique to each transaction, just as an envelope in a broker's filing cabinet might be unique to one customer. All details related to the transaction are kept in this area, including the transaction itself. When processing of the transaction is complete, the area is released for other use.

7. *Work areas.* The programs may need a work area in which to manipulate data. This may or may not be included in the message-reference block.

8. *Constants and operator messages.* Some messages for indicating system conditions or errors may be kept permanently in core. Others will be in the files.

Every different set of Supervisory Programs or computer manufacturer's "Operating System" is likely to have its own list of core requirements including some of the above items, and sometimes many others.

On a "single thread" application, the two items, queues and message-reference blocks, may not be needed. As only one message is processed at a time, a work area for that message may replace the message-reference blocks of a multiprogrammed system. Queues are likely to consist only of a buffer area for input messages waiting to be processed and an area for output messages waiting for transmission, as calculated later in this chapter. These areas may be limited in size.

However, in a multiprogrammed real-time system the core required for other queues must be included. Also there will be a varying number of program segments temporarily read in from files. The core area required for each of these will depend upon how long a transaction remains in the system or upon how many transactions are in process at one time.

The utilization of core storage will vary with the load on the system.

This is illustrated in Fig. 24.4. On most multithread systems the increase in core utilization with load will not be linear. Beyond a certain point the system becomes degenerate, and a small peak in traffic will exceed the capacity of the system.

The shape of the core utilization curve in Fig. 24.4 will vary from one set of Supervisory Programs to another. In making estimates for the design of a system it is important to know the effect of peaks in load on the core utilization in order to know what peaks the system can handle. It is normally desirable to estimate the core usage for different loads and to plot a curve as in Fig. 24.4.

DYNAMIC CORE ALLOCATION

The usage of core on most real-time systems varies from moment to moment because different messages arrive requiring different operations and occupying different amounts of space.

There are two ways in which core can be allocated, *fixed core allocation* and *dynamic core allocation*. With the former, specific areas are set aside for specific tasks. There are fixed areas into which new messages may be read, fixed areas into which records are read from file, fixed areas from programs, and so on. If the capacity of any of these areas is exceeded, the work using that area stops until space becomes free again.

Dynamic core allocation does not impose this restriction but allocates blocks of core as they are needed. Only when all of the blocks available are used up does work stop. In buffering communication lines, for example, there is not a fixed core area for each line. If the messages differ widely in length, this would be uneconomic. Suppose that the average message length was 50 characters but that some messages require 200, 300, or 400 characters. Occasional long messages require 1000 characters. It would be uneconomic to allocate fixed areas of 1000 characters to each line or even 400 characters. Instead, the core might be allocated in blocks of, say, 30 characters as it is required.

Similarly with programs, relocatable program segments, usually of fixed length, are read into blocks anywhere within a given core area. The Supervisory Program allocates core dynamically as required.

A block of core might be used *only* for programs, only for message-reference blocks, only for file queues, or the concept of dynamic core allocation, might be taken one step further. Blocks are sometimes used interchangeably for different purposes. Figure 31.2 gives the core layout on a system in which blocks are used for input/output queues, data storage, and programs. This is only possible when it is convenient or, more to the point, economical to use the same *size* blocks for these different purposes.

In doing calculations of dynamic core requirements it is necessary to decide what size blocks will be used and how many of these will be needed.

A pool of blocks must be provided, and not all of them will be in use at once except during momentary peaks. A *facility utilization* for the pool of blocks can therefore be worked out and made to balance, as far as possible, with the other facility utilization figures on the system.

The examples that follow in this chapter calculate the total *number* of blocks of various types that will be used in an hour of peak traffic. They estimate the average time that these blocks will be occupied. Multiplying these figures, the total core used in the peak hour *in block-seconds* is found. For example, three blocks used for two seconds are quoted as six block-seconds. The total number of block-seconds used in an hour of steady-state operation, equivalent to the peak load, is divided by 3600 to give the average number of blocks in use during this period. Hence the number of blocks required is estimated.

SUPERVISORY
MECHANISMS

Figures 31.1–31.4 give four typical core layout maps. *All are for systems in which the Supervisory Programs were tailor-made to a given application or set of applications*, rather than ones which used a very broadly general-purpose Operating System. As will be seen, some of the areas on these maps use dynamic core allocation, others, fixed allocation. The first step in estimating core storage requirements is to decide what areas would be on a map of this type. The second step is to evaluate the sizes of the various areas.

Before any reasonable attempt can be made to do this, there must, as with timing estimates, be a broad understanding of the way the Supervisory Programs for the particular application will route work through the system. Differences in the mechanisms of the Supervisory Program can make a large difference to the core requirements of the system, especially in a system with a high degree of multiprogramming. On some multithread systems, for example, the pool of core blocks required for temporary programs can be more than half the total core in the main computer (Fig. 31.4). The supervisory mechanisms affect the length of time a transaction stays in the system and so affect the time each program block is required in core. They can increase or decrease the core required for this by a factor of 3 or possibly much higher.

It is suggested that before core estimating can begin, the following minimum should be established about the Supervisory Program mechanisms:

1. *Method of program read-in.* On some systems this is the most sensitive factor affecting core estimation. On one real-time system the initial working estimate of the number of program segments read into core was one per second. By the time the programs were half developed, little more than a year later, this had risen to eighty-one per second. The core size and the peripheral hardware for program storage had to be changed.

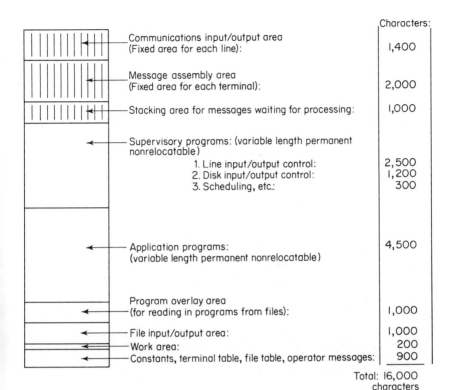

Fig. 31.1. First example of a core map. Typical core allocation on a savings-bank system: 15 communication lines; 1 or 2 terminals per line; small files; single-thread processing; relatively simple programs; about 2000 transactions per hour. (The areas on the figure are drawn roughly to scale so that they are proportional to the core areas they represent.) Note: This and the following three examples are all for systems using Supervisory Programs tailor-made to a given set of real-time applications, rather than a general purpose Operating System.

The program read-in mechanism should be dependent upon the nature, size, and frequency of use of the Application Programs. A system with a long response time, say, five minutes, can use a more economical method of read-in than a system with a short response time, say, three seconds. The latter will have to read the program, as soon as it is wanted, at random from the files. The former may possibly cycle the programs into core in a serial fashion, and the transaction will wait until the appropriate program is there.

The possibility that two transactions being processed in parallel may need the same block of program must be considered. Can they both use it

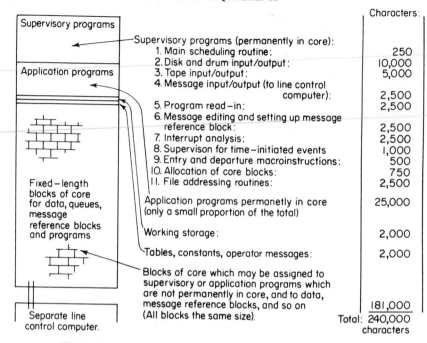

Characters:

Supervisory programs (permanently in core):	
1. Main scheduling routine:	250
2. Disk and drum input/output:	10,000
3. Tape input/output:	5,000
4. Message input/output (to line control computer):	2,500
5. Program read–in:	2,500
6. Message editing and setting up message reference block:	2,500
7. Interrupt analysis:	2,500
8. Supervison for time–initiated events	1,000
9. Entry and departure macroinstructions:	500
10. Allocation of core blocks:	750
11. File addressing routines:	2,500
Application programs permanetly in core (only a small proportion of the total)	25,000
Working storage:	2,000
Tables, constants, operator messages:	2,000
Blocks of core which may be assigned to supervisory or application programs which are not permanently in core, and to data, message reference blocks, and so on (All blocks the same size).	181,000
	Total: 240,000 characters

Fig. 31.2. Second example of a core map. Typical core allocation for a large reservation system: many communication lines; several hundred terminals; large random-access file; high degree of multiprogramming; many application programs; 5000 to 20,000 transactions per hour.

without interfering with one another? Or must it be read in separately for each transaction?

On some existing systems a program segment will be read into core when needed, regardless of whether it is there already. With others, the program will check first to see whether it is in core. Such a difference will affect the number of program segments in core.

2. *The degree of multiprogramming.* Some Supervisory Programs that have been written restrict the number of items that can be in process at one time or restrict the number of programs that can be partially completed at one time. Other programs do not restrict the degree of multiprogramming, and the limit is imposed only by such factors as available storage and available processor time. Many small systems are likely to have no multiprogramming but to handle items strictly serially. Whatever the case, the degree of multiprogramming in the system must be ascertained, as it directly affects the queue sizes and number of message-reference blocks in the system.

3. *Queuing mechanism.* The nature of the queues must be understood and, in particular, the amount of storage an item takes up when it is in a queue. Each message, for example, has a message-reference block allocated

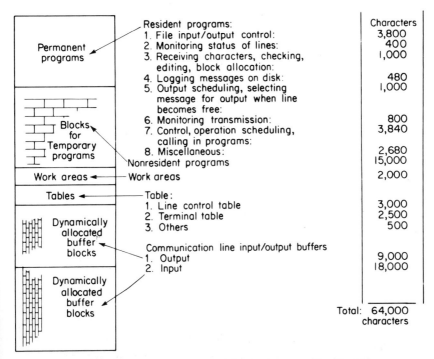

		Characters
	Resident programs:	
	1. File input/output control:	3,800
	2. Monitoring status of lines:	400
	3. Receiving characters, checking, editing, block allocation:	1,000
	4. Logging messages on disk:	480
	5. Output scheduling, selecting message for output when line becomes free:	1,000
	6. Monitoring transmission:	800
	7. Control, operation scheduling, calling in programs:	3,840
	8. Miscellaneous:	2,680
	Nonresident programs	15,000
	Work areas	2,000
	Table:	
	1. Line control table	3,000
	2. Terminal table	2,500
	3. Others	500
	Communication line input/output buffers	
	1. Output	9,000
	2. Input	18,000
	Total:	64,000 characters

Fig. 31.3. Third example of core map. Typical core allocation for a message-switching system: 1000 terminals; 10,000-20,000 messages per day stored and forwarded; tailor-made Supervisory Programs. (The areas on the figure are drawn roughly to scale so that they are proportional to the core areas they represent.)

to it for the duration of its life in the system. The size of the message-reference blocks must be known, and, to determine this, it is necessary to know something about their structure. This is discussed below. The queues on many existing systems consist of items in core blocks of fixed size with a chained linkage between them, but this may not necessarily always be true. Some systems may restrict the number of items that can be in a given queue.

4. *The block sizes.* Blocks of core are likely to be allocated for buffering input and output messages on the communication lines, for storing data in use in the processing—for example, the queues of transactions partially processed or waiting for file action—and also for temporary programs.

The desirable sizes of these blocks must be determined before an attempt is made to count them. This will depend upon certain characteristics of the hardware and upon the sizes of the data and programs to be manipulated. On some systems all the blocks are the same size (Fig. 31.2). This gives a very neat mechanism for dynamic core allocation. A block from anywhere in the pool of available blocks may be used for either data or programs.

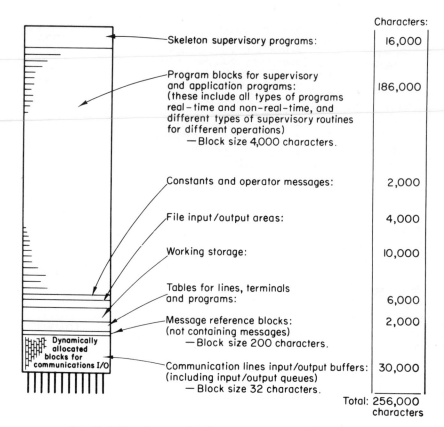

Characters:

Skeleton supervisory programs: 16,000

Program blocks for supervisory
and application programs: 186,000
(these include all types of programs
real-time and non-real-time, and
different types of supervisory routines
for different operations)
— Block size 4,000 characters.

Constants and operator messages: 2,000

File input/output areas: 4,000

Working storage: 10,000

Tables for lines, terminals
and programs: 6,000

Message reference blocks: 2,000
(not containing messages)
— Block size 200 characters.

Dynamically
allocated
blocks for
communications I/O

Communication lines input/output buffers: 30,000
(including input/output queues)
— Block size 32 characters.

Total: 256,000
characters

Fig. 31.4. Fourth example of a core map. Core allocation for a stores and production control system: many terminals; random-access files and tapes; real-time processing and batch processing combined; complex programs with different types of action and different times. (The areas on the figure are drawn roughly to scale so that they are proportional to the core areas they represent.)

However, on many systems the sizes of data and programs are such that this cannot be done. Different areas and perhaps different mechanisms may be used for programs.

5. *Priority of processing.* In order to estimate the number of core blocks in use, it is necessary to know what time messages spend in the system taking up core. This will depend in part upon the priority with which they are processed. The priority mechanisms of the Supervisory Programs must be known.

It is beyond the scope of this book to go into the details of the supervisory mechanisms that may be used.* The remainder of this chapter discus-

*James Martin, *Programming Real-Time Computer Systems.* Englewood Cliffs, N.J.: Prentice-Hall, Inc., 1965.

ses the items for which core is used and how estimates for this use may be made. The core required for input/output buffering is discussed in the following chapter. Often when a computer manufacturer produces software for a system, he writes a guide to estimating the core as well as time required for use with his Supervisory Package. When such a guide exists it will clearly be of more use than anything that this necessarily generalized chapter can say.

1. *Storage Required for Programs*

Chapter 29 discussed the estimating of program sizes. In attempting to estimate that part of the core occupied by programs, a decision must be made about which programs are to be in core permanently and which are to be stored in files and called into core when required. Those programs which are used very frequently will be in core permanently. Programs which are in core all the time or a large proportion of the time need to be estimated very carefully. The ones which are infrequently used are less critical, though there may be a large number of these.

Programs which are always in core and never read in from files during operational running may be nonrelocatable programs and not divided up into segments of fixed length. Programs which may be called from files even if they are normally kept in core will usually be divided into fixed-length segments. A decision as to the lengths of these segments should be made before estimates are attempted.

The length of program segments may be determined partly by file characteristics, such as the length of a track on a drum, but stronger factors will be the internal organization of the system and the nature of the programs themselves. One airline reservation system has program segments of 119 and 237 instructions each, because these block sizes are used for all types of core activity. If the individual programs were more complex and had program loops of more than 237 instructions, it would be disadvantageous to have this small segment size.

The reasons for not having programs in core are that core is an expensive form of storage and to put all of the programs in it would be uneconomic, even if it were possible on the computer in question.

However, the advantages of having a program segment in core are:

(a) The macro time to enter it is reduced. Therefore, the processing-unit time utilization is increased and the message-processing time speeded up slightly.

(b) Message-waiting time for access to the program is considerably reduced, reducing the time the message spends in core and thereby reducing core utilization.

(c) File utilization is reduced, and therefore the waiting times for other accesses are speeded up, again reducing the times messages spend in core and hence reducing storage utilization.

It will be seen that having the segment in core effects a saving in processing-unit time and file-channel utilization. It effects a core saving in reduced queues which may or may not offset the core storage required for the segment itself. There is thus a break-even point depending upon the frequency of use of the segment.

It is suggested that, when making an estimate of file-channel utilization, processing-time utilization, and core utilization on a proposed system, a reasonable but arbitrary mix should be selected as a starting point. The estimate should be made with this figure and then the mix should be adjusted to see the effect on the estimate of different numbers of programs permanently in core.

Let us look again at Table 30.1. In this, we calculate the total time, in seconds, that each program block was in core during the peak hour. To begin with, this figure may be somewhat approximate because it depends upon the length of time spent queuing for the file accesses and for the processing unit, and this in turn depends in part on the reading in of programs, on a system such as that described.

Table 31.1 gives the core estimates. Its first four columns repeat the data evaluated in Table 30.1. The fifth column estimates the total core utilization in *block-seconds*. This is obtained by multiplying the figures in Column 4 for the total time that each block is in core during the peak hour, by Column 2—the number of blocks with this usage.

Adding up Column 5 we get the total number of block-seconds used for programs during the peak hour. We divide this by 3600 seconds and get the total number of *blocks* for the programs read in. To this, the number of blocks for programs not read in is added. This gives a total of 139 blocks. We may deliberately increase this number, giving more blocks permanently in core, in order to lower the channel utilization. The figures in this table, as with the data in Table 30.1, were worked out assuming a steady state equivalent to the peak throughput. A larger core area than this will probably be used to take into account throughput fluctuations about the mean. The summed Poisson function tables in Chapter 26 give an indication of the factor that should be added to the area for temporary programs.

Table 30.1 assumes that each program block is either always read into core from the file when needed or else is permanently in core. A third category is possible—programs which are sometimes in core and are read in if they are not. This third category lowers the required channel utilization but will increase the number of core blocks used. One further factor must now be considered: can messages from different terminals use the *same* program blocks in parallel if by chance they need to or must each transaction have its own copy of the block in question in core? If the programs are written in a re-entrant fashion, different messages can use the same blocks. With a large number of different types of message it becomes complex to calculate the probability of having a program block already available when needed. Once again, simulation may be resorted to. During the implementation

Table 31.1. EXAMPLE OF CORE ESTIMATES

Average number of times a block is used in the peak hour	Number of blocks with this usage	Time, in milliseconds, this block is in core for one trans- action*	Total time, in seconds, this block is in core in the peak hour	Total core utilization in peak hour, in block- seconds
less than 1	507	2000	1	507
1– 2	192	2000	3	576
2– 4	286	2000	6	1,716
4– 8	210	1000	6	1,260
8– 16	180	1000	12	2,160
16– 32	103	1000	24	2,472
32– 64	67	1000	48	3,216
64– 128	{ 20	1000	96	1,920
	39	500	48	1,872
128– 256	{ 23	1000	192	4,416
	20	500	96	1,920
256– 512	{ 48	1000	384	18,432
	48	500	192	9,216
512– 1024	{ 24	2000	1536	36,864
	20	1000	768	15,360
	20	500	384	7,680
1024– 2048	{ 20	2000	3072	61,440
	20	1000	1536	30,720
	10	500	768	7,680
2048– 4096	33	}Permanently in core		{118,800
4096– 8192	5	Total: 80 blocks		18,000
8192–16384	42			151,200

TOTAL for temporary programs   209,427
block-seconds used in the peak hour

$$\frac{209{,}427 \text{ block-seconds}}{3600 \text{ seconds}} = 58.2 \text{ blocks}$$

59 blocks required for temporary programs
+ 80 blocks required for permanent programs

TOTAL: 139 blocks

This estimate assumes that each block is read into core when it is needed (with the exception of those permanently in core). If, however, blocks are already sometimes in core and so not read in, the number of core blocks needed will be higher (and the channel utilization lower). Often, the total number of blocks available in core determines the channel utilization.

*These will initially be very crude estimates. They depend on the number of file refer- ences made while a block waits in core and on the *queue sizes*. They will become more accurate with successive reiterations.

phase, it is useful to have a simulation model of the program read-in. As the programs are written, the model can be adjusted to see how the system will behave, or to optimize the read-in method. It is desirable on the program read-in model also to simulate the other file accesses, because the queues they cause affect the length of time programs are in core. The model can thus become a complex one.

If the programs called in from outside core are in *varying-length segments*, the calculation is a little more complicated. The break-even point for core utilization will depend upon the segment length as well as its frequency of use. It is suggested that the ratio (frequency of usage/segment length) should be calculated as accurately as possible for each program segment. This will then be the criterion for determining whether a segment is kept permanently in core or not, segments with a high value for this ratio being permanently in core.

2. Core Required for Tables

Tables which may be needed for the control of a real-time system with random-access files and telecommunication links are as follows:

(a) *File-addressing tables.* Given a reference key to some data stored on the files, the machine address of these data must be located so that they can be read or updated. A client's name or a part number or a flight number and date might be the reference key for which a machine address must be found. There are various ways of locating or generating this address, as indicated in Chapter 27. Some of these involve table look-up.

Most random-access files are too large for a complete indexing table of the file to be in core. Sections of the table will be read from the file as required. An area should be provided in core large enough for these tables to be read into.

(b) *Program table.* When a segment of program is required, it may be in core or on file. In this case, when a transfer is made to the program, a table of programs in core at that moment must be scanned. If the program is in core, its address will be found. If not, some means of locating it in the files must be used so that it can be read in.

(c) *Transfer table.* Some computers have special hardware for making a transfer (branch, jump) to a program which is not at a fixed core address because it is relocatable. If this is not the case, a device such as a "transfer table" is needed. It may be combined with the program table mentioned above. It will contain one instruction for each of the programs in core. Each of these instructions will be an unconditional branch to an entry point of the program. There may be two or more instructions for two or more entry points to each program. All references between relocatable programs will pass through the transfer table,

(d) *Communication line control table.* This table may contain one entry for each communication line. A different record may be used for incoming and outgoing lines. The table will contain information necessary for controlling the operation of the communication lines. It will contain data, such as the status of the lines (receiving, transmitting, or scanning), the line and terminal characteristics, and the count of errors on the line. In this table the number of characters sent may be counted. The addresses of the start and end of the core-block chain allocated to the line may be kept.

The address in the files at which an incoming line's traffic is stored may be recorded in the table. Similarly an outgoing line may have a file area associated with it as a form of buffer, and the address of that will be in the table, along with an indication whether there is anything waiting to be transmitted.

(e) *Terminal table.* This table contains information about each terminal connected to the system. A code may represent a terminal on the system, for example, JFK may mean Kennedy Airport; MAN 2, terminal no. 2 in the Manchester branch office. The table may give a machine line and terminal address for each of these codes. It may give information about the status of the terminal. If a terminal is temporarily not working, it may give an alternative to which messages are sent as a means of fallback. The serial number of the last message received from, or sent to, the terminal may be recorded. If a timer is used to check that no terminal is off the air for more than a certain time, the timer count may be recorded in this table.

This and the above line table may be part of the same table. This will usually be so if nonmultidrop lines are used.

3. *Core Required for Message-reference Areas*

When a message enters a multiprogrammed system, an area of storage is allocated to it. On most such systems this area of storage will belong to that message for the entire life of the message in the computer. It contains the message itself and indicators and working data related to that message. It provides continuity between the programs that process the message at different times. This area is referred to in this book as a message-reference area, or block. On some systems, it is more than one area but nevertheless performs the same functions.

A message-reference block area is set up when an interrupt indicates that a new message has entered, or is about to enter, the computer. It may also be created by a macroinstruction in a program by means of which a transaction being processed may create other transactions, so that more than one reply message is sent.

The message-reference block may be destroyed (that is, the core area may be made available for other work) when the processing of the transaction is finally completed and the sending of the reply checked out.

The average length of time transactions spend in the system occupying message-reference areas may be multiplied by the maximum design through-put to give the maximum number of these areas. This figure multiplied by the size of the area will give the core storage required or the number of blocks in a pool of blocks used for this purpose. It is thus necessary to determine the average time a transaction spends in the system. On a multiprogrammed system, this will vary with the size of the queues and hence with the file-channel utilization. This estimate will be very approximate at first, but on successive reiterations of the estimating process it will become more ac-curate.

A system with no multiprogramming, in which transactions are handled entirely serially, will not require a number of message-reference blocks. There will just be one work area and the processing of another transaction will not start until this is finished with. This is the case on a large number of small systems, for example, systems used in banks.

For convenience, the message-reference blocks may be allocated along with the blocks of program segments. This may mean that a block larger than necessary is used, but the means for allocating and controlling blocks is not duplicated.

The size of the area or block needed for this purpose will be determined by the length of the message and by control data, and other data are needed in the area. Typical contents of a message-reference area are:

(a) The message itself.
(b) The address of the line and terminal from which it originated.
(c) A reply message that is being constructed.
(d) Working storage that is to be preserved, if required, for the active life of the message.
(e) (Possibly) a list of input/output requests awaiting execution for this message.
(f) (Possibly) the area into which desired records from the files are read.
(g) Scheduling indicators telling the Supervisory Program the status of the processing on the message.

4. *Core Storage Required for Queues*

The queues may consist solely of message-reference blocks, discussed above, and input/output buffering areas, discussed in the next chapter. If this is so, then it is necessary to estimate how long the message-reference block or input/output areas will be occupied. The total core utilization in *block-seconds* can then be estimated.

Other areas of core may, however, be used for queuing. For example, on some systems messages received for the communication lines are taken from the input/output buffers into a *stacking area* awaiting processing. This may be necessary because of the nature of a standard input/output control program being used. Again records from the *files* may go into the message-reference areas or into a stacking area awaiting use. In a similar manner the output messages may be queued while waiting for a line or channel to become free.

The nature of the queues must be determined before this part of the estimating process can be carried out, and it must be ascertained what types of delay can occur in the processing of a message. When it is determined, the number of items in the queues must be evaluated, so that the core storage needed for them can be worked out. In estimating the number of items in the queues, curves such as those in Chapter 26 may be used initially. Later it may be necessary to do this more accurately using simulation techniques.

The blocks used for queuing may be the same as the blocks required for programs if these are small. Some systems read *file records* into these blocks, for example. This simplifies block allocation and lessens the chance of a shortage of blocks for file records. However, it can only be done if the sizes can be made roughly similar.

Generally, the greater the degree of multiprogramming, the greater the attention that has to be paid to queues in the estimating process. On single-thread systems the queues will be relatively simple in structure. It will not be difficult to make estimates for them by hand, that is, without resorting to simulation. Normally only communication input and output queues will be needed, and core may be set aside for the maximum size of these.

Wherever queues are used consideration must be given to chaining the blocks together and organizing their usage. Sometimes as many as ten or twenty characters are used for this in each block. These characters will give the address of the next block and possibly the previous block in the chain. They may give priority indications, indications of which message they relate to, and so on.

5. *Other Core Storage Requirements*

Core is required for input/output operations. This is discussed in detail in the next chapter. Areas are required for reading in file records, buffering output to printers, and so on. Such an operation may be done in areas used for other purposes, or it may need a separate area. A considerable amount of core may be needed for buffering input and output on the communication lines. This may be in a separate line control computer or in the main machine.

Core must include a work area where data can be manipulated. This may be in the message-reference area or the input/output areas, or a separate work area may be provided.

Certain constants and prefixed messages to operators may be permanently in core.

It may be necessary to save records or data during the processing of a transaction while new programs or records are called. Data may be saved in the message-reference area, or special storage may be set aside for this.

OVERLOADS   Wherever *dynamic core allocation* is used there arises the possibility of an overload. In other words, the blocks available for allocating to various functions run out. In certain circumstances this could mean that work is started which *cannot* be completed.

The overload that causes this is a temporary one and may only last a second or a few seconds. If a number of tasks are started on a multiprogrammed system and twenty core blocks are needed to complete them, the computer must have this number available or at least release this number in sufficient time to complete the work. If it has only fifteen blocks available or released on time, then all of the tasks cannot be finished. The situation can arise when each of the tasks needs more core before it can be completed and none is available. In this case the work on one of the tasks must be destroyed. In some circumstances the message itself must be destroyed, and the computer must ask the terminal in question for retransmission when the temporary overload has passed. Whatever happens, the computer must be capable of taking *some* action if core blocks run out.

The core allocation scheme may be designed so that it is impossible to run out of blocks. The Supervisory Program will keep control of the blocks as a storekeeper keeps records of his stock. When the stock falls below a certain level, he reorders. If it falls below a further level, he takes expediting action. With core allocation the Supervisory Program keeps a count of the blocks remaining. If this count falls below a certain level, emergency action will be taken, and possibly a stronger action if it falls below a second, lower level. The types of action possible are:

1. Dump some of the blocks on the files and return them later when the temporary overload has passed.

2. Seal off the communication lines so that messages under transmission are fully received, but no more messages will be accepted until the overload has passed.

And more extreme:

3. Destroy work on a message and release the blocks tied up, but preserve the original message.

4. Destroy the message and all work connected with it. When the overload has passed, the terminal operator will be requested to retransmit the message.

In calculating core storage requirements, overloads must be considered, as some extra core will be needed for dealing with them. If messages are destroyed or communication lines sealed off, it is desirable to work out how often this will occur.

32   ESTIMATING STORAGE
        FOR INPUT/OUTPUT BUFFERING

On systems in which speed of operation is important, buffering is required for all input and output devices. It is only on systems with a very small load that an input/output device in frequent use can be allowed to be unbuffered.

The buffering may be external to the computer, but on most modern machines the computer's core storage constitutes the buffers. There will be an output area for devices such as a high-speed printer or magnetic-tape units. There will be an input area for card readers, files, and so on. These areas may be part of the work areas used for processing. They are relatively easy to allow for in the core storage calculations. The size of the areas will generally be the size of the records being written or read. As these devices are fast and not very numerous, they will not tie up too great a part of the computer's core.

The buffering for communication lines and terminals, however, may not be so easy to assess. Unless the system has only a small number of these, it will not be economic to allow an input and an output area for each terminal or each line equal to the maximum length of message transmitted.

In addition to normal buffering, the buffer areas may be used to queue messages waiting for processing or to file records waiting to be used or messages waiting to be transmitted. Queues of this type are not included in the calculations in this chapter. They should be considered separately in evaluating core utilization.

USE OF
PERIPHERAL MEDIA
FOR BUFFERING

On many communication-based computer systems the core storage alone is sufficient for input/output buffering of messages. This may be core in the main computer or in a subsidiary line-control computer. However, on some systems it is desirable to supplement the core with other, cheaper storage media. Disk files, drums, or magnetic tape, for example, may be used for buffering.

It is normal to use peripheral storage on a message-switching system. Here the processing needed is slight, and the traffic volumes fairly large. The computer is relatively inexpensive, and to buffer this number of messages in core would be uneconomic. As messages are received into core, they are written on a peripheral medium, commonly on disk files. As output messages are sent, they are read, as required, from the files into core for transmission.

Peripheral storage may be used like this for normal traffic flow, or it may be used only for temporary overloads. The core may be able to handle the average traffic, but, when by chance every terminal sends a long message or more terminals than normal transmit at once, then tape or disks may be used as a temporary dumping area to prevent core's becoming clogged.

The economies of using peripheral storage can be strong where multi-drop lines are used for output. If messages are prepared for a number of terminals on the same line, only one of these can be sent at once. Rather than waiting in core for their turn, they may wait on drums, disks, or tape.

Such storage devices sometimes add little or nothing to the cost of the system, as they are already used for other purposes. Most real-time data-processing systems have large random-access files. Many have serial files, such as tape, for logging traffic. External files may be used for fallback, to store messages for later transmission when a terminal breaks down. Similarly they may be used for rerouting messages, storing messages with many addresses, and giving terminals a facility to retrieve messages if this is desirable.

CALCULATION OF CORE REQUIRED FOR BUFFERING   Planning the storage area required for buffering on peripheral media is not, generally, a critical or difficult calculation, as the areas available are large. Core storage, on the other hand, is usually at a premium, and buffering calculations for it need to be done with care.

A message arriving at the computer and being processed may occupy core for the following periods of time:

1. While it is being received (which may take several seconds).
2. When it has been received completely and is queuing, waiting for the processor.
3. While it is being processed.
4. After processing is complete and the reply is queuing, waiting for the output line.
5. While the reply is being transmitted.

With some methods of core allocation, when one message has finished with an area of core, another, possibly from a different communication line, will use it. The length of time the area is tied up is therefore important in the calculations. The term *block-second* is used, as with relocatable program blocks, to mean one block occupied for one second.

Knowing how much core one message takes up, the times for 2 and 4 above may be calculated from queuing theory, as described in Chapter 26. To do this, the line utilization, the throughput, and the processing times must be known.

Let us now examine more closely the times used during periods 1 and 5 above.

THREE
METHODS OF
CORE ALLOCATION

There are three common methods of allocating core storage for buffering on communication lines. The user may not, however, be free to choose that method which gives the most economic use of core as calculated below. He may be bound by other considerations; for example, he may be using a standard communication-line input/output control program which dictates how buffer core is allocated. Even if this does not give the optimum usage of core, he may still wish to use it because to rewrite such a program would involve much work. In making core storage estimates it must be known how such a program operates.

The three common techniques are as follows:

Method 1. A fixed input and output area may be permanently associated with each communication line.

Method 2. As soon as a message is to be transmitted or received, a block of storage corresponding to the size of the message is taken from a pool and reserved for the message. It is held until the message is completely transmitted or received and then becomes part of the pool again. With messages of fixed length, this technique is common. With messages that vary in length, it can be used for output but cannot easily be used for input.

Method 3. A pool of blocks, each smaller than the size of most messages, is used. A block is assigned to a line when the computer starts to receive a message from the line. If the block fills with characters, another block from the pool is chained to it. Blocks are assigned in this way until the complete message is received. The converse is done on transmission.

Figure 32.1, illustrates these three methods. It will be seen that method 3 uses the least storage.

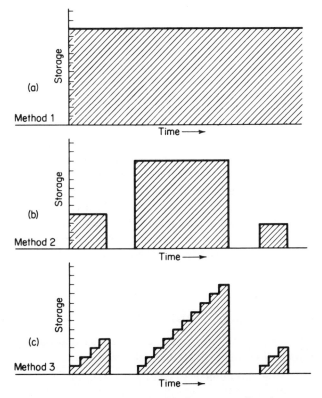

Fig. 32.1. Three methods of buffer storage allocations.

CALCULATIONS FOR FIXED MESSAGE LENGTHS

Let us suppose, initially, that the system handles messages of fixed length and calculate the core requirements for buffering with the above three methods.

The calculations in this chapter assume that as soon as the reception of a message is complete, the message is removed from the buffer area into a queue, either waiting for processing or for logging on files or tape. Similarly, on output, the message is not placed in the buffer area until the line is free, ready for transmission. This may not be so. If a message is received and cannot be processed immediately, it may be queued in the buffering area. Similarly with output. If this is so, the core utilization is greater than that used below, and the addition may be evaluated when the queue sizes are estimated.

Method 1

Suppose that there are N lines and that the length of a message is l characters.

NOTE: The length of a message must include all the necessary control characters that are stored in the buffer. This will include the terminal address but may not include start- and end-of-message indicators.

The storage required for input is *Nl characters*.

The same storage will be required also for output, unless input and output share a half-duplexed line, in which case input and output may share the same buffer area.

Method 2

Suppose that the speed of the lines is s characters per second and that the length of a message again is l characters. Then the message will occupy the line for l/s seconds. If a block of core storage of l characters is allocated when a message begins to be received and is released when reception is complete, the l characters will be occupied for l/s seconds.

Suppose the frequency of reception in the peak period, for which the design is done, is such that on average f messages per hour are received. Then f blocks of l characters will be occupied for l/s seconds each. Therefore the core required on average is

$$\frac{fl(l/s)}{3600} = \frac{fl^2}{3600\,s} \quad \text{characters}$$

The choice between method 1 and method 2 may depend upon the line utilization. Suppose that the over-all line utilization is ρ:

$$\rho = \frac{\text{actual number of characters transmitted}}{\text{maximum possible number of characters transmitted}}$$

$$= \frac{(fl/3600)}{Ns} = \frac{fl}{3600Ns}$$

Then

$$\frac{\text{core required for method 2}}{\text{core required for method 1}} = \frac{N\rho l}{Nl} = \rho$$

Thus, if the line utilization is near to 100 per cent, method 1 may be used, as it is simple to program. The lower the line utilization, the greater the disadvantage of using an input/output control program which operates in method 1, as certain of the standardized programs made available by manufacturers do operate.

Method 3

Suppose the characters arriving on the communication lines are read into a block of core which can hold B characters. When this block is full, the characters are read into another block which is chained to this one. On a machine with binary capabilities, space equivalent to one character might be sufficient for this chaining. On a machine without binary capabilities, two or more characters might be needed. On a typical system, blocks capable of holding thirty-two characters are used, but only thirty message characters are placed in one block, the remaining space being used for chaining.

Suppose that space equivalent to $(B + 2)$ characters is occupied by the block. For the receipt of one message,

$$(B + 2) \text{ characters are occupied for } \frac{B}{s} \text{ seconds}$$

for another $(B + 2)$ characters are occupied for $\dfrac{2B}{s}$ seconds

and so on,

$$\vdots$$

$$(B + 2) \quad \text{characters are occupied for} \quad \left\lceil \frac{l}{B} \right\rceil \frac{B}{s} \quad \text{seconds*}$$

Therefore the total occupancy of core for one message is

$$\frac{1}{2} \left\lceil \frac{l}{B} \right\rceil \left(\left\lceil \frac{l}{B} \right\rceil + 1 \right) \frac{B}{s} (B + 2) \quad \text{character-seconds}$$

Therefore the core required on average is

$$\frac{\lceil l/B \rceil (\lceil l/B \rceil + 1)(B/s)(B + 2)f}{2 \times 3600} \quad \text{characters}$$

The ratio of core utilization between method 2 and method 3 is as follows:

$$\frac{\text{core required for method 3}}{\text{core required for method 2}} = \frac{\lceil l/B \rceil (\lceil l/B \rceil + 1)B(B + 2)}{2l^2}$$

To illustrate this with values from a typical system, suppose that blocks of 32 characters are used, giving $B = 30$, and that the messages are all 200 characters in length.

$$\frac{\text{core required for method 3}}{\text{core required for method 2}} = \frac{\left\lceil \dfrac{200}{30} \right\rceil \left(\left\lceil \dfrac{200}{30} \right\rceil + 1 \right) \times 30 \times 32}{2 \times 200^2} = 0.672$$

FACTORS AFFECTING CORE REQUIREMENTS

Note that with short fixed-length messages, method 3 could possibly take more core than method 2, for example if $B = 30$ and $l = 91$. Method 3 becomes decidedly better when l is large with respect to B.

Two points should be noticed about the core requirement for buffering. For methods 2 and 3 the following factors affect this:

Firstly, the core requirement is inversely proportional to the speed at which the data arrive. If fast transmission is used, it will reduce the core storage needed. This might be aided by use of a concentrator, as described in

---

*($\lceil l/B \rceil$ is used to mean l/B rounded up to the nearest integer, this being the total number of blocks used to contain a message of length l.)

Chapter 20, for concentrating the traffic from several slow lines onto one fast line to the computer. It may also be helped by using a terminal with a buffer so that there is relatively fast buffer-to-core transmission, rather than transmission at the speed of an operator pressing the keys. An operator may, alternatively, punch a message into paper tape and then transmit this, using a relatively fast paper tape reader. This is often done on message-switching systems.

Secondly, the core requirement is still more strongly affected by the message length. It is proportional in method 2, or nearly proportional in method 3, to the *square* of message length, l^2. Therefore it saves core if long messages are split up into parts and the parts sent separately. This may not be possible on systems with fixed message lengths but is an important consideration on systems which have variable message lengths and where a proportion of messages can be quite long. In a system in which messages are logged directly onto a second-level store or read from a second-level store for transmission, the splitting of messages may be done automatically in the core of the computer under program control.

CALCULATIONS
FOR VARIABLE
MESSAGE LENGTHS

The calculations above are done for systems on which all messages are the same length. On the majority of systems messages vary in length. If there are two or three discrete message lengths, methods like those above may be used and the calculations done by adding together the results for each message length.

Where the message lengths vary widely, the advantages of using method 3 above become more pronounced. In collecting the data for this system's design a histogram showing the numbers of messages of different lengths is needed, as in Fig. 32.2. Where the block size is known or can be assumed, the messages can be counted according to the numbers of blocks they occupy. The block utilization can be evaluated then for messages occupying one block, two blocks, three blocks, and so on. A table like Table 32.1 can be used to evaluate the average core requirement.

In the example in the table there is a wide spread of message lengths. It is assumed that blocks of thirty-two characters, or bytes, are used and that these can hold thirty message characters each. It is assumed that fifty baud lines are used, working at a speed of 6.6 characters per second. It will therefore take $30/6.6 = 4.55$ seconds to fill up one block. A message which fills one block will tie up one block for 4.55 seconds. A message which fills two blocks will tie up one block for 2×4.55 seconds and another block for 4.55 seconds, giving a total occupancy of 3×4.55 block-seconds, and so on. This is how the third column in the table was evaluated.

It will be seen from the table that the long messages cause a much larger

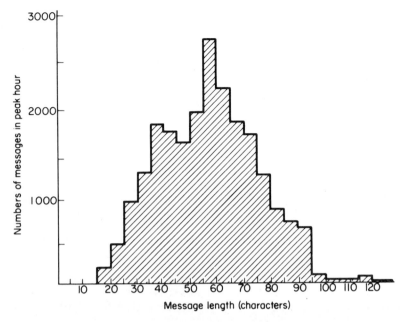

Fig. 32.2. Histogram showing distribution of message lengths.

core occupancy than they would if split into shorter messages. The exceptional messages of 100 blocks, that is, about 3100 characters, increase the average core requirement by nearly 1000 characters.

OVERLOADS When using method 3 for allocating buffer storage, a temporary overload can cause a problem, as described in the last chapter. Suppose that the system starts receiving and allocating blocks of core to a number of input messages. By chance all of these are long messages so that the total number of blocks available for buffering are insufficient to store them all.

As these messages flow into the computer, a state will be reached when no more blocks are available to store them. At the start of their transmission, the computer has no way of knowing their lengths and so cannot foresee this situation. Unless some emergency action is taken, one or more of the messages will be cut off before it is fully received. If this is so, an estimate must be made of the number of messages that will be cut off. The computer will have to notify the terminal operator of its action and request that the message in question be retransmitted.

The overload condition might also be dealt with by temporarily dumping part of the used block chains onto an external file or tape. The computer

Table 32.1

Message length $\left\lceil \dfrac{l}{B} \right\rceil$ Blocks	Number of messages in peak hour f	Block utilization per message, in block seconds $\dfrac{\left\lceil \frac{l}{B} \right\rceil\left(\left\lceil \frac{l}{B} \right\rceil + 1\right)}{2}\dfrac{B}{s}$	∴ Total block utilization for messages in peak hour; in block seconds $\dfrac{\left\lceil \frac{l}{B} \right\rceil\left(\left\lceil \frac{l}{B} \right\rceil + 1\right)}{2}\dfrac{B}{s}f$
1 block	407	1×4.55	407×4.55
2 blocks	2112	3×4.55	$6,336 \times 4.55$
3 blocks	4350	6×4.55	$26,100 \times 4.55$
4 blocks	3151	10×4.55	$31,510 \times 4.55$
5 blocks	2711	15×4.55	$40,665 \times 4.55$
6 blocks	1090	21×4.55	$22,890 \times 4.55$
7 blocks	381	28×4.55	$10,668 \times 4.55$
8 blocks	140	36×4.55	$5,040 \times 4.55$
9 blocks	201	45×4.55	$9,045 \times 4.55$
10 blocks	64	55×4.55	$3,520 \times 4.55$
15 blocks	8	120×4.55	960×4.55
20 blocks	8	210×4.55	$1,680 \times 4.55$
50 blocks	4	1275×4.55	$5,100 \times 4.55$
100 blocks	4	5050×4.55	$20,200 \times 4.55$

Total for all messages,

$$\sum \frac{\left\lceil \frac{l}{B} \right\rceil\left(\left\lceil \frac{l}{B} \right\rceil + 1\right)\frac{B}{s}f}{2} = 184,121 \times 4.55$$

∴ Average core requirement,

$$\sum \frac{\left\lceil \frac{l}{B} \right\rceil\left(\left\lceil \frac{l}{B} \right\rceil + 1\right)\frac{B}{s}f(B+2)}{2 \times 3600} = \frac{184,121 \times 4.55 \times 32}{3600}$$

$$= 7443 \text{ characters}$$

will do this before it completely runs out of blocks, thereby releasing core blocks to hold further message characters.

VARIATION IN BUFFER REQUIREMENT

We have discussed buffer calculation in which the throughput is constant. The number of messages passing will, however, vary from moment to moment. As was indicated in Chapter 26, the variation may follow a Poisson distribution and Poisson tables will indicate the proportion of messages delayed if the system is designed to a given throughput figure.

33 ESTIMATING LINE AND TERMINAL REQUIREMENTS

Three main types of calculation need to be done in estimating the line and terminal requirements:

1. An estimate of what terminals are needed to handle the volume and message lengths in question. This must take into account what actions the operator has to perform besides working the terminal. If a man-machine conversation takes place the estimate is much affected by the nature of the conversation and by the language used.

2. An estimate of what number and speed of communication lines are needed to carry the traffic without undue delays.

3. An evaluation of the most economic layout of these lines. This might involve the suitable placing of exchanges, concentrators, remote multiplexors or other devices.

Having determined the number and speed of the communication lines, a suitable line control computer or set of line control units can be selected for connecting the communication lines to the computer. The buffer storage needed for receiving and transmitting messages must be calculated, as discussed in the previous chapter. The line control device and buffer storage used may have some effect on the planning of lines. A line control computer or line control unit has the capacity of handling a given number of lines. If this number is exceeded, the cost of the system will go up as a step function. The line control equipment may be cheaper if only one type of terminal is used or only one speed of communication line. Some devices can only handle one type of line. If high-speed lines are used, the core requirements for buffering will be considerably less, as indicated in Chapter 32.

511

The balance between the communication lines and other equipment may be dominated by the lines if these are long and therefore expensive. If the lines are short, as with a system, for example, which covers the financial area of a city like London or New York, single-terminal, point-to-point lines will usually be used to reduce the cost of the line control equipment. In the latter case the line layout and loading calculations described below will not be needed.

There can be a very wide variety of line and terminal configurations to choose from. On some systems the range of choices is immense. Determining the number and types of terminals, the number and types of lines and their facilities, and the layout of the lines will usually involve several iterations. Each proposed layout must be costed, and sometimes the requirements then need to be reexamined.

TERMINALS   The choice of terminals, so important because these are the human link with the system, was discussed in Chapter 21. The main factors that affect the design calculations are as follows:

1. *Fast enough terminal?* Where a bulk of continuous transmission takes place, the required terminal speed can be calculated from the volume to be transmitted and the time limitations. Where the terminals are used for individual transactions or for enquiries and responses, other factors enter into the calculations: Does the terminal give the answer back quickly enough to satisfy the operator? If a reply message consists of a long listing which the operator must scan, a teleprinter or typewriter may be too slow; a fast display screen device would be preferable. If a display screen is used, can the operator change the contents of the screen quickly if what he is searching for is not there?

2. *Large enough display screen?* Where a screen or other display device is used, is it large enough to hold the longest message? If not, is it convenient to have the message broken into two parts, or must all the information be inspected at one time.

3. *Human delays?* It is important to consider the behavior of the operators of the terminals. With terminals handling individual transactions or enquiries, the operator will usually be carrying out some other actions simultaneously and the terminal can only be used for a portion of the time. The terminal is a tool to be used when it is needed by an operator, for example, an airline booking clerk, a bank teller, or a factory foreman. In order to ascertain how many terminals are needed at a location, the human operations carried out must be examined in detail. Often it is the operators who are the bottleneck, not the terminal. Consider an office full of terminals such as that shown in Fig. 33.1. The terminals here are expensive, and it is desirable to have as few of them as possible. Calls from the public are received (with a

Fig. 33.1. A multiserver queuing situation. Outside telephone calls are routed to the first operator free in the American Airlines reservation office. There is little or no waiting other than during exceptional peaks.

Poisson distribution) and are routed to any terminal operator who is free. The average time an operator takes to deal with a call can be estimated. This might be, say, ninety seconds talking and twenty seconds using the machine. The terminal is, then, underutilized, and it would save money if two operators could share one terminal. This would be difficult to organize with the terminals in Fig. 31.1, but some terminal arrangements on other applications permit multiple operators.

4. *Multidrop facility?* To save communication line costs, it is often desirable to have more than one terminal on a line. Some terminals can be used in this manner, others cannot.

5. *Buffer storage in terminal?* If a human operator keys characters into a terminal which does not have a buffer, the communication line is tied up for the duration of that keying process. To use a voice grade line may be wasteful of the line capacity. Some terminals have a buffer storage to overcome this. The message or a segment of a message, if it is long, is keyed into the buffer and checked for accuracy. The contents of the buffer are then transmitted at high speed over the line. This can lessen the communication line requirements and the core needed for buffering in the computer. An alternative approach is to use a remote concentrator or control unit which itself buffers the messages of several terminals, and sends them at high speed on the line to the computer.

SIMULATING THE MAN-MACHINE CONVERSATION

When a conversation between an operator and the computer is necessary in order to carry out a certain process, as for example with the operators in Fig. 33.1, an important part of the design calculation is a study of the conversation that takes place. It is necessary to know the numbers of characters in the various responses both of the man and the machine. This can vary widely depending upon the design of the language, as will be seen by a study of conversations in Chapter 8. It is also necessary to know how long the man is likely to wait between the continuing segments of a conversation, how many errors he will make, and so on.

For a simple operation like that of a savings bank teller updating passbooks the number of characters is easy to estimate. There is no multisegment conversation, and the minimum wait between transactions is determined by the other actions that the teller performs. By studying the conversations between tellers and bank customers figures can be established for the mean and standard deviation of the time a teller takes to handle a customer. Often, however, a more complex conversation takes place. An airline journey being booked on a terminal needs several, answer-backs before it is complete. Other conversations, including many now being planned for visual display terminals are much lengthier than this. A fairly complicated administrative process such as the ordering of a computer or the changing of a production schedule may require the terminal to "talk" to the computer for about a half an hour.

In all of these cases, and particularly in the more complex ones, it is desirable to simulate what will happen by rigging up a device something like the terminal that will eventually be used, and observing the performance of operators using it. This is more difficult with the more complex conversations but it is here that it is most needed. Where it is planned that the operator should carry on a long conversation at a display terminal it is desirable to see this conversation taking place, to measure the typical lengths of messages, to observe the operator's errors and "think" time. Practical experience of first seeing an operator working with a live display terminal using a language that has been devised for a particular application almost always makes the designer see his language differently, and introduce several changes to it. It also reveals figures that are useful in the terminal design calculations.

Some organizations have a *conversation simulator language* which enables them to specify details of a terminal conversation with many possible branching paths. This can then be punched into cards. A program processes the cards and enables an operator to sit at a terminal and converse with it as he would on an actual operational system. He can practice until he becomes slick on the keyboard, and his actions can be observed in detail. This is extremely useful in improving the language that would be used, and this is likely to be its main purpose. The actual people the terminal is intended for can use it in advance of the major programming work, for example, shop foreman, managers, or airline agents. They will doubtless have many comments about its suitability for their work. In addition such a program can collect statistics about number of characters and operator "think time."

Typical of the output of such a program would be a histogram of the numbers of characters sent for each message type, the average and the standard deviation of these. This would be done both for the operator-generated and computer-generated messages. In addition the times spent by the operator to respond to the various situations presented to him, would be printed. From these figures a realistic assessment can be made of the message lengths and operator delay times.

THE LOCATION OF BOTTLENECKS   The points at which queues build up must be determined. Knowing the traffic volumes, speeds of lines, and so on, the percentage utilization of the various facilities on the system may be calculated, as illustrated in Fig. 33.2. *In calculating the utilization, it is important to take polling and control messages into account.* Let us examine this figure along with the curves in Chapter 26. In general these curves indicate that it is only when the facility utilization is more than about 50 per cent that large queues build up. (This assumes that the messages arrive more or less at random times and that no extraordinary conditions exist, such as very long messages.)

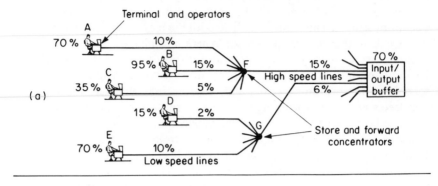

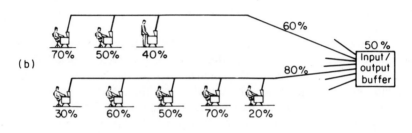

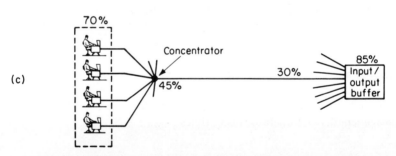

Fig. 33.2. Percentage utilization figures to be used in queue estimating.

In the first illustration in Fig. 33.2, all the communication lines have a fairly low utilization and these are not going to cause very big queues. Some of the operators, however, do have a high utilization and will occasionally keep their clients waiting. A is utilized 70 per cent, and so Fig. 26.9 indicates, taking the top curve, that on average he has 2.3 clients in a queue waiting for his attention, including the client now being served. The curves in Fig. 26.15 indicate that 10 per cent of the time he will have just over five clients in the queue, and the queue will become as long as ten clients about 2 per cent of the time. B, who is perhaps in a busier office, seems to be severely overworked. Using the formula $\bar{q} = \rho/(1 - \rho)$ we see that, with a utilization ρ of 95 per cent, he is likely to be keeping nineteen clients waiting. Ten per cent of the time his queue will grow very large indeed. Furthermore, a minor increase in the number of customers will raise the queue sizes enormously. It becomes apparent immediately that this is unacceptable and some better arrangement will have to be provided in this office.

The figure for the utilization of the operator will depend upon how much delay there is from the system in responding to his messages. This, in turn will depend upon what queues build up at other points in the system.

In a multidrop system the communication lines are likely to be more heavily loaded, as in Fig. 33.2(b). Here the terminals will be held up in trying to obtain a line, and this waiting time must be added into the calculations of the terminal utilization.

How long they will be held up waiting for a line depends upon the transmission speed of the line. The line utilization, in fact, depends upon the transmission speed. In Fig. 33.2(b) the utilization of the bottom line is marked as 80 per cent. Figure 26.10 indicates (using the upper curve again) that the queuing time $\bar{t}_q$, including the time taken in transmission, is 5 times the mean transmission time. Suppose, now, that the mean number of characters transmitted in a message is 100, and that the line speed is 150 characters per second. If the full line speed can be utilized then the mean transmission time is $\frac{100}{150} = 0.67$ seconds. However, the full transmission speed can only be realized *if the terminal has a buffer*. In this case, if the buffer is to hold the longest message it would have to be a large buffer. The long messages may use a smaller buffer and be transmitted from this in slices, one buffer full at a time. Often, however, the terminal has no buffer. One might suspect that this is the case here because the line utilization is so high. If this is so, then transmission will take place, not at the full line speed, but at the much lower speed of the operator's manual keying. Suppose it has been observed that the operators in question are likely to type data into the terminal at about two keystrokes per second. One hundred characters will then take 50 seconds to transmit instead of 0.67 seconds. The queuing for the line, 5 times this, is then 250 seconds instead of $(5 \times 100)/150 = 3.33$ seconds. In other words, the 80 per cent line utilization is much more serious if the terminal is unbuffered than if it is buffered.

In either case it is inadvisable to work at such a high line loading because a temporary increase of 10 or 15 per cent would drastically increase the response times. If the operators who were assumed to type at two keystrokes per second, actually only managed 1.5 keystrokes per second, then the unbuffered line could not handle the load.

Figure 33.2(c) shows a room full of terminal operators organized in such a way that, when a call comes in, it is routed to the first free terminal, as in Fig. 31.1. In this case, multiserver queuing theory must be used. If there are four terminal operators with a utilization of 70 per cent as in the diagram, then Fig. 26.22 tells us that the average queue size will be 3.8. As this includes the clients being served by the four servers the number waiting for a server is low. $\bar{q} = \bar{w} + M\rho$—Equation 26.47. Therefore, $\bar{w}$ the mean number waiting is $3.8 - (4 \times 0.7) = 1.0$. The mean number of customers waiting before being served is 1. This has assumed an exponential distribution of service times as in the examples above. Actual service times might give a result slightly better than this.

Making the same assumption, Fig. 26.18 shows that $\bar{q}$ will grow to 5 ($\bar{w} = 2.2$) about 21 per cent of the time. It will grow to 10 ($\bar{w} = 7.2$) about 4 per cent of the time, and will hardly ever grow to 20.

In assessing response time the delay caused by waiting for the concentrator and the input/output buffer must also be included. In Fig. 33.2(c) the utilization of the input/output buffer is marked as 85 per cent. This seems high. The input/output buffer also may be regarded as a multiserver queue. Suppose that it contains 60 dynamically-allocatable blocks of core. When a message requires buffering, any one of the 60 blocks may be given to it. This is, in effect, like a multiserver queue with 60 servers. Glancing at Fig. 26.23 we see that for $m = 60$, and $\rho = 0.85$, $\bar{t}_q$ is approximately equal to $\bar{s}$. In other words although the facility utilization is as high as 85 per cent, transactions are not kept waiting for this facility significantly longer than the normal service time. If a simulation was done using the same throughput as in Fig. 33.2(c) it would not show up the input/output buffer as a cause of trouble. However, if the input volume increased by 15 per cent then, as is seen in Fig. 26.23, the delay caused by the input/output buffer would rise quickly to an unacceptably high figure. Beyond this, the system would seize up unless some means of automatically supplementing the buffer or closing down selected lines was built in. The input/output buffer, then, makes this system design unstable. As in diagram 6 of Fig. 24.6 the curve of response time against throughput would suddenly turn a sharp corner. In this case it would pay to increase the number of buffer segments.

QUEUES OF CUSTOMERS AT THE TERMINALS

Often in the design of a real-time system for commercial usage one finds that the terminals and their operators are planned to have a high facility utilization. Sometimes the reasoning behind this is that terminals and operator positions are expensive and should therefore be kept to the minimum. Furthermore, if an unusually high burst of customers come in, or telephone, they can always wait. It may be better to keep the queues at the terminals, outside the system, than to let them up in the computer. Extra terminals can always be added later if this will give better service, whereas other parts of the system cannot so easily be expanded.

It is useful to be able to assess how long the new system may keep customers waiting. When a passenger telephones an airline during a peak period, for example, to enquire about his reservation, how long will he have to wait before he can talk to the reservation agent who will help him? The queues may be multiserver queues and the queue sizes estimated approximately from curves in Figs. 26.21 to 26.24. On the other hand, on some systems although there is more than one server, the customer may not have a free choice of which server he deals with. In some banks with real-time systems, for example, the teller windows are still marked with alphabetic groupings so that the customer must go to one or two particular tellers. (Why?) Comparing the curves in Figs. 26.21 to 26.24 it will be seen that this increases the over-all queues and it would have been better to have given the customer a free choice. Similarly at a highway toll-booth with several gates for toll collection the cars might be thought to have a free choice of gate, but often one lane has more cars than the others and queues build up somewhat higher than those in Fig. 26.22. In estimating the customer queues the designer must decide whether there is a complete freedom of choice between operators.

QUEUES FOR THE COMMUNICATION LINES   The queues for lines can be assessed easily with the formulas and curves given if a *contention* system of line control is used. That is, each device contends openly, though possibly with different priorities, for the line. Output from the computer often has a higher priority than input to it on a contention system. Polling in which the computer sends a signal to each specific terminal telling it when to send, is not used.

Let us examine a situation using a contention line to a computer. Suppose that the line is full duplex so that input messages to the computer queue for a different facility, in effect, from output messages to the terminal. Each line has many small cathode-ray tube terminals. A study has been made of the man-machine conversation for which they will be used. The average length of input messages is 20 characters with a standard deviation of 10 characters. The output message is.frequently almost a complete screen full of data. Its average length is 400 characters with a standard deviation of 200. The line speed is 150 characters per second and the line is buffered so that the full speed can be achieved. In studying this proposed arrangement we would like to make a plot of the mean response time and its standard deviation, against the line loading. We would also like to know the probabilities of obtaining long response times. A convenient way to define response time here is as *that period between the completion of the keying of the input message and the completion of the reply filling the screen.* To calculate the response time it is necessary to know the response time of the computer system. To begin with, in absence of any other knowledge, let us assume that this has a mean of two seconds and is exponentially distributed.

Let us start with a mean transaction rate of one transaction in five seconds, assuming as in all of these calculations that the input occurs at random times (Poisson). The mean number of characters per second travelling on the input line is then $\frac{20}{5} = 4$. The standard deviation of this is $\frac{10}{5} = 2$. The mean service time for the input line is then $\frac{20}{150}$ seconds and the standard deviation of this is $\frac{10}{150}$ seconds. $\bar{s}/\sigma_s = 2$, $(\bar{s}/\sigma_s)^2 = 4$ (Erlang 4). The facility utilization, ρ, for the input line is $20/(150 \times 5) = 0.0267$.

Figure 26.10 tells us that $\bar{t}_q$ for the input line is only slightly higher than the service time $\bar{s}$. More exactly, Equation 26.13 gives it as 0.136 seconds. Similarly Equation 26.26 gives the variance of t_q for the input line to be 0.00475 seconds.[2]

For the output line, the mean number of transactions travelling is the same as on the input line. The mean service time for the output line is then $\frac{400}{150}$ seconds and the standard deviation of this is $\frac{200}{150}$ seconds. $(\bar{s}/\sigma_s) = 2$, $(\bar{s}/\sigma_s)^2 = 4$ (Erlang 4). The facility utilization, ρ, for the output line is then $400/(150 \times 5) = 0.533$.

Figure 26.10 tells us that $\bar{t}_q$ for the output line is $1.7\bar{s}$. More exactly, Equation 26.13 gives it as 4.571 seconds. Figure 26.12 gives the standard deviation of t_q, or more exactly Equation 26.27 gives its variance to be 10.485 seconds.[2]

The total response time as we have chosen to define it in this case is the sum of $\bar{t}_q$ for the input line, $\bar{t}_q$ for the output line, and the two-second response time assumed for the computer.

$$0.136 + 4.571 + 2 = 6.707 \text{ seconds}$$

The variance of this is the variance of t_q for the input line, the variance of t_q for the output line, *plus* the variance of the computer response time, 4.

$$0.00475 + 10.485 + 4 \simeq 14.490 \text{ seconds}^2$$

Therefore, the standard deviation of response time is 3.807 seconds.

These values are plotted for other throughputs in Fig. 33.3. If our expected input is as in the calculation above, the curves of Fig. 33.3 appear to give a reasonable and stable system.

Let us now suppose, however, that these transactions read and sometimes update the file system that was discussed in Chapters 25 and 26, the file system of Fig. 25.4. Let us insert this file problem into the middle of the line problem we have just discussed. Assume that no more computing time is needed than that in the file problem (the reader can easily add some if he wishes). The response time of the file problem therefore replaces the two-seconds compute time assumed above. Let us suppose that the line we have

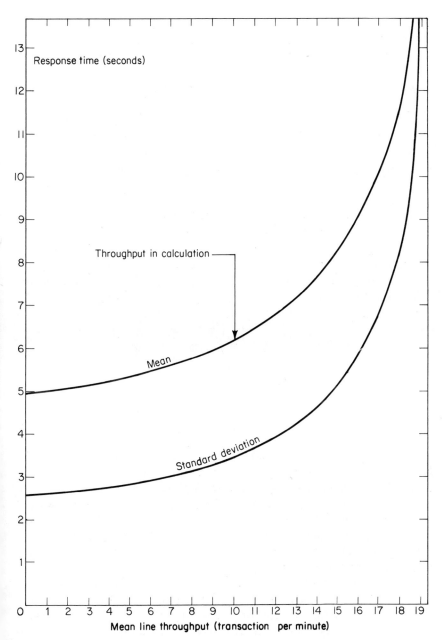

Fig. 33.3. Results of response time calculation on contention line system discussed in this chapter.

just discussed carries 0.0125 of the total transactions into the computer, all transactions being the same length as those discussed. The file response time is low compared with the total line response time at lower throughputs, but the file queue builds up more rapidly than the line queue.

The results of this calculation are shown in Fig. 33.4. If the expected input is as before (marked by an arrow in Fig. 33.4) then the system no longer looks like a good stable design. It cannot survive a throughput increase of more than about 20 per cent. It would be a more balanced design if the file response time could be prevented from building up so rapidly. This could be done by lessening the seek time or spreading the data over four files instead of three.

When systems such as this are being designed the question always arises: What percentage of transactions will have response times greater than five seconds, 10 seconds, and so on. How often will an operator have to wait 15 seconds before he has his reply on the screen. A delay greater than 10 seconds might be regarded as unacceptable for this particular system.

To obtain a clear picture of the probabilities of response times exceeding different values we would like to draw a curve of the probability that response time, t, is less than or equal to a given value T, Prob $(t \ll T)$, against T. We will assume, as discussed in Chapter 26 that this curve fits a gamma distribution such that:

$$\text{Prob}\,(t \ll T) = \left\{ \frac{\int_0^T \left(\frac{Rt}{\bar{t}}\right)^{(R-1)} e^{-Rt/\bar{t}} \frac{R}{\bar{t}}\, dt}{\int_0^\infty \left(\frac{Rt}{\bar{t}}\right)^{(R-1)} e^{-Rt/\bar{t}} \frac{R}{t}\, dt} \right\}$$

where

$$R = \left(\frac{\text{mean response time}}{\text{standard deviation of response time}}\right)^2$$

This can either be computed for different values of T, or can be obtained from the curves in Figs. 26.6 and 26.7. We know that this is only an approximate calculation, and so using the curves is probably a good enough way to obtain an answer. It is certainly good enough for most practical purposes.

It was desirable to calculate the mean and standard deviation at different throughputs. Here again we would like to calculate Prob $(t \ll T)$ for different throughputs, and produce a family of curves. Such a family of curves for the line problem, above, is given in Fig. 33.5, and when the assumption about computer response time being 2 seconds is replaced by the file calculation of Chapter 28, the curves are those of Fig. 33.6. In any calculation of response times, curves Fig. 33.3 to 33.6 form a useful way of expressing the results so that the behavior characteristics of the system are quickly apparent to management and system designers.

In an actual system there may be certain additional elements of time that

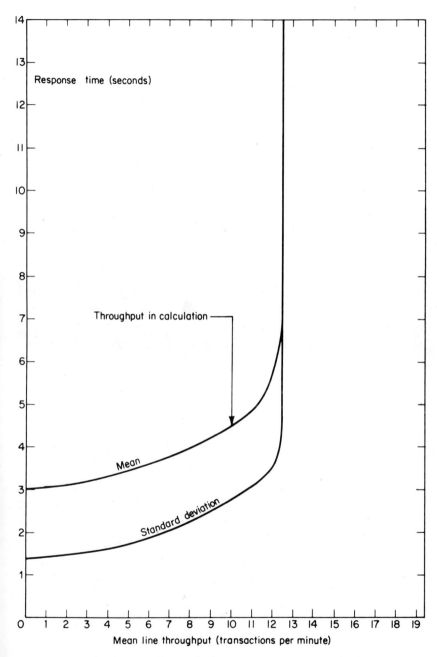

Fig. 33.4. Results of response time calculation on contention line system updating the file system of Fig. 25.4.

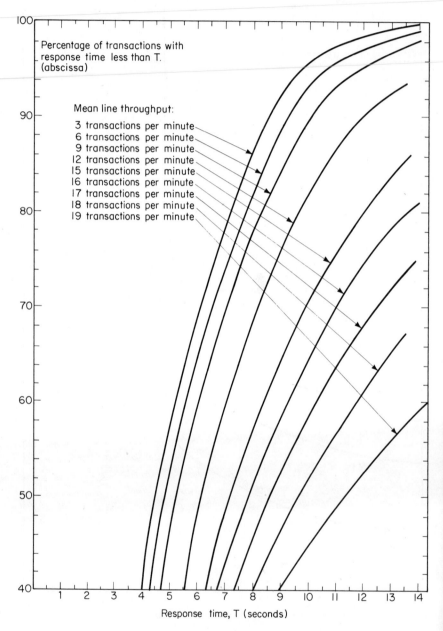

Fig. 33.5. Results of response time calculation on contention line system discussed in this chapter.

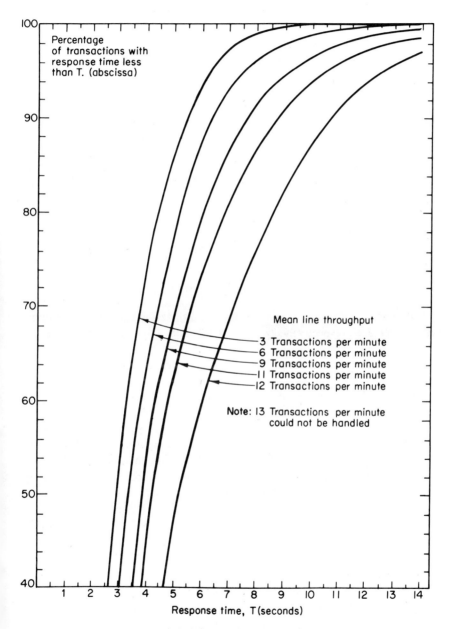

Fig. 33.6. Results of response time calculation on contention line updating the file system of Fig. 25.4.

need to be added to these calculated here. Modems, or other devices, may for example have a small turn-around time.

The calculations above related to a full-duplex line. The equations in Chapter 26 could have been applied equally well to a half-duplex line. Here the line is regarded as *one* facility with input both at the computer and at the terminals contending for service. Sometimes different transactions or different terminals have different priorities. This situation can be examined with the equations in Table 26.6. In particular, transactions sent by the computer may always take priority on a half-duplex line over transactions sent by the terminals. In this case there are two priorities and so we can use the equations in the upper part of Table 26.6.

Where the output messages have a constant length such that they occupy the line for a time $\bar{s}_o$, for example, and the input messages have a constant length such that they occupy the line for a time $\bar{s}_I$, then the queuing time at the computer end of the line is given by:

$$\bar{t}_{q_0} = \frac{\rho \bar{s}}{2(1 - \rho_0)} + \bar{s}_0$$

and for the terminal end of the line:

$$\bar{t}_{q_1} = \frac{\rho \bar{s}}{2(1 - \rho_I)} + \bar{s}_I$$

Where ρ_o and ρ_I are the part of the line utilization caused by output and input messages respectively, $(\rho = \rho_o + \rho_I)$, and $\bar{s}$ is the mean service time for all messages.

Where the message lengths vary, then the equations using $\overline{s^2}$, must be used $(\overline{s^2} = \text{Var}(s) + \bar{s}^2 = \sigma_s^2 + \bar{s}^2)$.

How do these computed curves compare with simulation results? They are, as we might have expected, *slightly* pessimistic. The actual response times will be *slightly* lower than on these curves in general. The difference between the two methods is very small. The computation, which is quick and can be done with a slide-rule and the curves in this book, are close enough for most practical systems, and its slight inaccuracies err on the side of safety.

There is one type of case in which caution is needed in using the method above. That is when the communication line carries a few messages which are much longer than the remainder. This is sometimes the case on actual systems and when the long message occupies the line, the others will be delayed more than normal. This is a special case and is probably best examined by using simulation. In general the designer should examine the ratio

$$\left(\frac{\text{standard deviation of number of characters}}{\text{mean number of characters}} \right)^2$$

for the messages in question. If this is greater than 1 the queuing times will be worse than those given by the upper curve of Fig. 26.10. If it is greater than 1.3 it would probably be better to use simulation rather than the calculations above.

LINES WITH POLLING The reason why we were able to perform the line calculation above was that we were discussing *contention* line control. The transactions competed freely for the line facility. Most line control schemes with a large number of terminals on the line use a *polling* scheme of line control, not contention. This is especially likely to be true if the line utilization is high.

Mathematical methods for considering polling on the line are much more complex than those above. The easiest way of examining the delays on a polled line is probably to use simulation. Fortunately, a simulation program which examines the performance of *one line* can be written so that it has very wide general applicability. It will give the same form of results as the queue calculations above. The systems designer can carry it in his kit of tools and use it instead of queuing theory whenever he meets a polled communication line. He will plug into it the number of terminals, the polling sequence that is used, the distribution of line "service times" and so on. A variety of such programs exist and typically they print tables of the response time distribution for a given throughput.

When a system has several lines which are differently configured, the methods above must be used for each separate line. Using the simulation method this could be expensive and could run up a bill for many hours on a fast computer. It may therefore be desirable to examine only the worst and average lines and make an estimate of the performance of the others.

How much does the performance of a polled line differ from a contention line analyzed with the queuing curves as above? This depends upon the polling rate and the numbers of terminals to be polled. If the line utilization is fairly low there will be a close proximity between the results obtained using queuing curves and those taking polling into consideration.

If the time taken by the line control system to do the polling was negligible, then the line could be regarded as a single server with messages at many different places queuing for its attention. We would not have a first-come, first-served queue, but as indicated in Chapter 26, provided that the polling sequence was independent of the message lengths, this would not affect the mean queuing time. It would, somewhat, affect the standard deviation of queuing time, as illustrated in Fig. 26.13. Consequently, it would affect the gamma-distribution parameter R for queuing time, $R = (\bar{t}_q/\sigma_{t_q})^2$. However, on the majority of systems it would not change R by more than about 20 per cent and so the curves in Figs. 26.6 and 26.7 still give an estimate of the distribution of response times which is of value in most practical cases. The dispatching discipline for a polled line may be assumed to be random. This is a reasonable assumption as terminal operators enter transactions largely independent of the line scanning cycles. If anything it will be a pessimistic assumption erring on the side of safety, because once a terminal has sent a message it is usually less likely to demand attention on the subsequent cycles than other active terminals. Using the assumption of random dispatching, Equation 26.28 gives the variance of queuing time:

$$\text{Var } (t_q) = \frac{2\bar{n}s^3}{2(1-\rho)(2-\rho)} + \frac{\bar{n}^2(\overline{s^2})^2(2+\rho)}{4(1-\rho)^2(2-\rho)} + \overline{s^2} - \bar{s}^2$$

For constant message lengths this condenses to:

$$\text{Var } (t_q) = \frac{\bar{s}^2(8\rho - 2\rho^2 + 3\rho^3)}{12(1-\rho)^2(2-\rho)}$$

For lines in which the polling time is very small compared with the message transmission time the above equations and curves give a good answer. Let us see what happens when this is not the case.

We will define a ratio—

$$\frac{\text{mean poll time}}{\text{mean message transmission time}}$$

—and call this the *poll time ratio*. In this ratio, the poll time is the mean total time the line is occupied by a polling message and the reply to it. The message transmission time is the mean total of the times involved in transmitting a message, and this includes the time for the successful poll which initiates the transmission.

On one typical system the poll time is equivalent to the transmission time for eight characters. If the mean message length is 100 characters, then the poll time ratio $= 8/(100 + 8) = 0.0747$. If the mean message length is 250 characters, then the poll time ratio is $8/(250 + 8) = 0.0310$.

Let us suppose, as an illustration, that the message transmission time is exponentially distributed, and that the mean input message length equals the mean output length. The response time, as defined in the previous example, will be equal to the queuing time for the input messages, $\bar{t}_{q_I}$, plus the queuing time for the output messages, $\bar{t}_{q_o}$, plus the computer response time. Let us ignore the latter as we do not know what it is and make a plot of the queuing times against the line utilization. To obtain the total response time, the computer response time must be added to this. We have not stated the mean message length or line speed so we will plot $(\bar{t}_{q_I} + \bar{t}_{q_o})/\bar{s}$ against ρ for the line. The curve will be closely related to the upper curve in Fig. 26.10 when poll time ratio is low. If we ignore the poll time, then $(\bar{t}_{q_I} + \bar{t}_{q_o})/\bar{s}$ is equal to $2(\bar{t}_q/\bar{s})$ from Fig. 26.10. This is plotted in Fig. 33.7.

Figure 33.7 also plots the response times obtained by examining this line with simulation; first for a case in which the poll time ratio is 0.0310

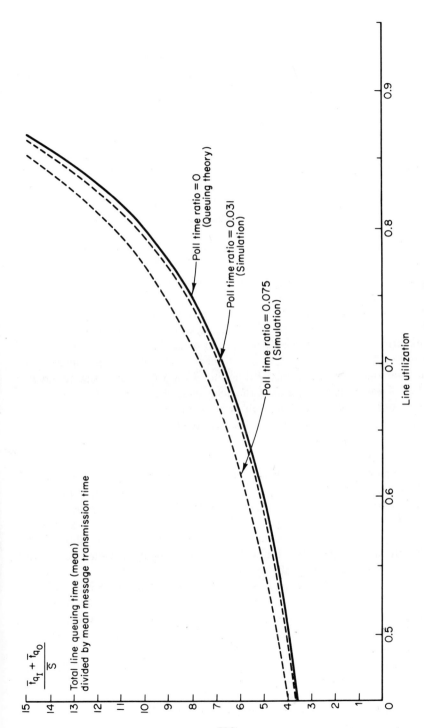

Fig. 33.7. Queues on a polled multidrop line.

529

as with the 250 character messages above, and secondly for a case in which the poll time ratio is 0.0747, as with the 100 character messages above.

It will be seen that the result with a poll time ratio of 0.0310 gives a result very close to the queuing calculation with a poll time ratio of zero. In general where the number of characters in the message transmitted is 10 times the number in the poll, it is hardly worth while resorting to simulation to improve upon a calculation such as that above.

If the output messages had been longer than the input messages, as is often the case in man-machine communication, this would have moved the simulation curves closer to the calculation curve. If the output messages have a mean length twice or more that of the input ones, which is very often true, these curves become close enough together to allow the queuing equations above to be usable up to a poll time ratio of 0.1 or even higher.

Simulation may be worth while, when message lengths are very dispersed, when special messages are associated with particular terminals, or when the terminal polling priorities follow a distinctive pattern.

Figure 33.2(c) shows a room full of terminal operators organized in such a way that, when a call comes in, it is routed to the first free terminal, as in Fig. 33.1. In this case, multiserver queuing theory must be used. If there are four terminal operators with a utilization of 70 per cent as in the diagram, then Fig 26.22 tells us that average queue size will be 3.8. Figure 26.18 indicates that 10 per cent of the time the queue will become slightly greater than 7. In assessing service time, the delay caused by waiting for the concentrator must be included. This itself depends upon queue sizes, which may be found from the knowledge that the concentrator is 70 per cent utilized.

ESTIMATING QUEUE SIZES AND RESPONSE TIMES

It can be seen that there may be a string of elements in the system that can cause queues, or delays in giving a response. The most accurate way to investigate the behavior of a string of queues is to use simulation. An approximate solution can, however, be obtained without simulation using the above methods, and this is probably good enough for the earlier iterations of the system design. It will enable a systems analyst to determine, for example, possible locations of concentrators and whether a possible system is within the right order of price. To evaluate the service times at each of the queuing points, it is best to start at the "inside" of the system and work out toward the terminals.

Examine the configuration in Fig. 33.8. The calculation on this system may proceed as follows:

1. Evaluate the file-reference times, as described in Chapter 28. In particular, evaluate:

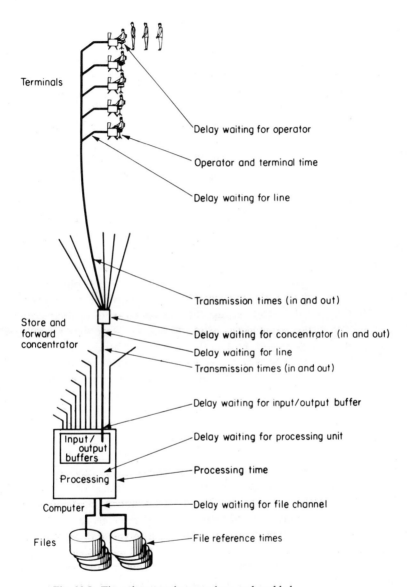

Fig. 33.8. Time elements that may have to be added.

$\bar{t}_F$, the average file-reference time, and

σ_{t_F}, the standard deviation of the file-reference times.

2. Evaluate the file channel, and then arm, utilization ρ_F. From this the length of queues and hence the average time in queues may be evaluated, as in Chapter 28. Let us refer to this time as $\bar{t}_{q_F}$

3. Evaluate $\bar{t}_{\text{proc}}$, the processing time not overlapped with file-reference time. The total mean service time of the computer may thus be $\bar{s}_C = \bar{t}_{\text{proc}} + \Sigma \bar{t}_{q_F}$ if the file-reference times are not overlapped with one another. If they are overlapped or if multiprogramming is used, this must be taken into account and the service time at the computer estimated. This will usually be short compared with the transmission times and if so, in this first-approximation calculation, need not be evaluated too accurately unless it reaches a point at which queues build up excessively.

4. The time that a transaction waits for processing, possibly in the input/output buffer, must be estimated. Again simulation is the accurate way to obtain this, especially on a multithread system. However, again the queuing curves give an approximate answer, the service times as calculated above being known.

5. There may be a delay waiting for output if the communication line to the concentrator is heavily utilized. The utilization of this line may be found if its speed and the quantity of traffic are known. Again from the queuing curves the delay is evaluated approximately.

6. The total time to send a message from the concentrator to the computer and receive the answer back is the sum of the above delays plus the transmission times to and from the computer. There is, however, a complication here if the concentrator sends groups of messages to the computer rather than single messages, as is sometimes the case. In this case the timings must be worked out for a group rather than for individual messages.

7. The total time evaluated above will enable the reader to work out how long a transaction stays in the concentrator. The entire system on the computer side of the concentrator may be regarded as a facility, the utilization of which is

$$\rho = \frac{\bar{n}\bar{t}_R}{3600}$$

where $\bar{n} =$ mean number of transactions per hour transmitted to the computer by the concentrator

$\bar{t}_R =$ mean total time from when a transaction starts to be sent by the concentrator to when its reply is completely received

Again the queue sizes may be found if $\bar{n}$, $\bar{t}_R$, and the standard deviation of $\bar{t}_R$ are known.

8. In a similar manner, working back to the terminal, the delays at the terminal due to waiting for a line can be found.

9. Knowing the full extent of the delays at the terminal, the total time to receive an answer back at the terminal may be estimated. The other actions of the operator are then taken into account to evaluate the service time that the clients receive from the operator.

10. From this the queues of clients waiting for service may be estimated.

If they queue for more than one terminal, multiserver queuing theory would be used.

A method like that above becomes more inaccurate, the greater the number of stages in the chain. This is because each stage tends to smooth out the pattern of interarrival times and the pattern of service times, so that the queuing theory formula slightly exaggerates the delays. Often, however, the situations to be tackled by a systems analyst are simpler than that above, because concentrators may not be used or lines may not be multidrop. In any case, if the queuing curves are too pessimistic, this might be regarded as a prudent systems analyst's safety factor. Often the approach above will indicate simply that the delays are acceptably small and that there is no need to use more elaborate evaluation techniques.

TYPES OF COMMUNICATION LINES   The calculations on communication-line volumes and usage will indicate what types of lines are needed. The following choices must be made from the available facilities:

1. Multidrop or point-to-point lines?
2. What speed of lines?
3. Simplex, half duplex, or full duplex?
4. Leased lines or switched lines?
5. Any private exchanges, concentrators, multiplexors, or switching centers?

Multidrop lines will be cheaper than equivalent point-to-point lines but will increase the line loading. A high traffic volume or a short response time criterion will favor point-to-point lines. Multidrop lines also increase the cost of the terminal and control equipment.

A full-duplex line is in some countries only slightly more expensive than a half-duplex line. However, many applications cannot take advantage of traffic moving in both directions at the same time. Again full-duplex lines increase the cost of terminal and control equipment.

If a terminal is lightly used, it may be more economical to put it on a switched line rather than a leased line. However, if it is near other locations on the system, it may be better to include it on a multidrop line. There is a break-even point beyond which a leased line is cheaper than switched lines. A terminal on a switched line may present an advantage in that it can be directly connected to other terminals in the organization. The time taken in dialing may have to be considered in a switched system. It can take about thirty seconds to dial and establish a connection. The probability that the line will be busy should be assessed.

In all of these considerations it will be seen that line cost enters into the design calculations. The tariffs of the various carriers must be used.

**LINE
LAYOUT**

The physical layout of leased lines can have a considerable effect on the cost of the system if the lines are long. With a complex network of multidrop lines there can be a vast number of routes by which the terminals are connected to the computer.

The calculation of the minimum-cost line layout can be done by hand or with the aid of a computer program. On a system with many locations it becomes too complex to obtain the optimum solution by hand.

Consider the locations in the diagram in Fig. 33.9. Suppose that it is necessary to connect all of these to the data-processing center in New York City by means of half-duplex lines. One line may have terminals in several locations connected to it. Which locations can be on the same line will depend upon the volumes of traffic from the locations. The procedure for working out a line layout by hand can be as follows:

1. The maximum load permissible on a line is determined either by the methods above or by simulation.

2. The load from each location is determined in the same units.

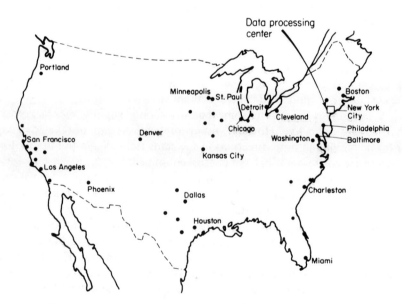

Fig. 33.9. Example of locations to be connected to data processing center.

3. A small-scale map of the area in question may be used. The projection and drawing must be such that the scale is accurate in all directions (for example, *conformal conic* projection).

4. Starting at the farthest points from the computer, the locations may be linked together until those linked have the maximum permitted load. The group will then be linked to the computer. The total line distance in doing this will be kept to a minimum. Different combinations should be tried in an attempt to minimize the total line mileage.

5. Having established a reasonable set of interconnections, the exact distances and costs may be obtained from suitable tables.

A solution such as that in Fig. 33.10 may be obtained. However, the problem is further complicated if concentrators or exchanges can be used, as in Fig. 33.11. Again a map may be used as a crude and perhaps laborious method of obtaining a minimum-cost network.

NETWORK
DESIGN PROGRAMS
A number of computer programs are available, or are used confidentially, in different organizations for tackling the problem of laying down a minimum cost communication network. These may or may not take into consideration the placing of concentrators, remote buffers, multiplexors or exchanges in the network. In general, no program the author has yet examined

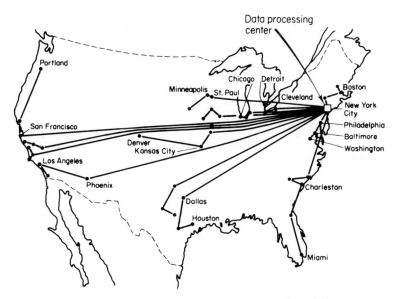

Fig. 33.10. The network in Fig. 33.9 connected with multidrop lines.

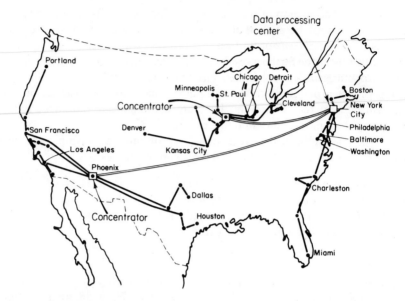

Fig. 33.11. The network in Fig. 33.9 connected using concentrators.

is sufficiently comprehensive to choose between these possible approaches. As with other such programs they form a tool which needs to be employed with intelligence where and when it is useful. It is always dangerous to use such devices as a blind panacea.

The input to the program may be a distribution of message lengths, and details of the geographical locations from which they originate and to which they go. If the input is in terms of message lengths or message transmission times, and a desired response time, then the program is presumably working out the queues in some way similar to those discussed above. It may, however, have to be fed with figures for acceptable line utilizations, which means that the above calculations have to be done externally.

The program for laying down the line network may have details of the common carriers' tarrifs built into it or it may have to be provided with these. Working from input figures for the horizontal and vertical coordinates of the terminal locations (which are listed for most towns in common carriers' tarrif literature), the program will compute the cost of different approaches or layouts and optimize the network accordingly.

34 THE REASONS FOR WRONG ESTIMATES

It is not a new phenomenon for the cost of complex technical projects to exceed their estimates. This has happened ever since the building of the pyramids. However, it is still the aim of systems analysts and management to estimate correctly. A number of real-time projects have notoriously overshot their design estimates, and, as was remarked earlier, this is dangerous because it could result in an *unworkable* system rather than one that merely needs extra shift operation.

There are basically three causes of wrong estimates:

Firstly, the data collection carried out for the system may prove incorrect. There may be more messages sent to the system than originally counted. This may sound easy to control, but in fact a large proportion of the systems in operation have found themselves processing or being required to process substantially more transactions than were written down in the original estimates.

One of the reasons for this is that terminal operators of certain types of system tend to use the terminal just because it is there, without realizing the effect they are having on the system as a whole. This needs to be foreseen and carefully controlled. Operators must not be allowed to press keys for the sake of pressing keys. However, many systems are used more than anticipated because they are *useful.* Experience on some systems for storing and forwarding administrative messages has been that, after the system has been in operation for a time, the number of administrative messages is double that before the system was used. Enquiry terminals on other systems are likely to be used far more frequently than data collection based on previous facilities would indicate.

One might formulate a Parkinson's law of real-time systems saying that, "If operator terminals provide a useful service, their utilization will

537

expand to fill the system capacity." This has no doubt been foreseen by the computer manufacturers wishing to sell more equipment, but it can make a mockery of the design calculations. Indeed, it appears that, with many systems, the traffic being handled by the system *cannot* be assessed with any accuracy until after the system has been installed! This paradoxical situation can only be resolved by installing equipment that can be expanded, or possibly contracted, easily. The ranges of computers now available that are *truly* modular are essential in this field.

A business system may be deliberately planned in two models. The first may be partially an experimental system and will collect data of its own actual operation for design of the second system. In installing a system for switching administrative traffic, for example, the system may be such that it can handle what is thought to be the present-day volumes. When this is installed, measurements will be made of the load passing through it and of any extra use that may be made of it. Its network or core storage or number of files may then be increased as required to increase the throughput, lessen the waiting times, or increase the message-storage facilities. A real-time business system should always be designed to maintain statistics about its own operation so that, when a further model of the system is installed, the best design data will be available.

The second cause of wrong estimates is that the functions which the system must perform are ill defined. It is often the case that a system must be ordered without knowing all the details of all the functions the system is to perform or all the operations that are necessary to carry out a certain action. This is very dangerous as it will almost certainly lead to underestimating the Application Programs. Complications in the functions of a real-time system can often not be seen until its operation has been specified in considerable detail.

If an order is placed without a detailed analysis of the computer's operation, for example, preliminary specifications of the programs, then this order should be treated as provisional. Before it is finally confirmed, six months detailed work will probably be needed to specify exactly what the input and output are, how the files are to be organized and addressed, how the Supervisory Programs route work through the system, what the mechanism of the Application Programs is, and so on. Record layouts should be worked out in detail. The communication facilities should be planned. Fallback programs and standby procedures should be planned. All the estimating procedures described in the previous chapters should be worked through.

To evaluate the hardware requirements of a real-time system it is normally necessary to go further into the detailed systems analysis than is necessary on a batch-processing system. If an order is placed without such a detailed analysis a contingency allowance for possible additional costs should be borne in mind. As additional details are worked out the hardware requirements almost always increase rather than decrease.

The third reason for wrong estimates is that, given a set of functions and a set of throughput figures, the system was designed inadequately. This is less excusable. It may be that insufficient detail has been worked out. It may be that certain of the critical factors in Chapter 23 have been evaluated but not others. Possibly a balance between the critical factors has not been achieved, and one factor is going to upset the evaluation of the others.

Inadequate design may be due to inability to foresee all the complications that will arise in the processing or inability to estimate the number of program steps required. Often it is very difficult to estimate the core or time required for programs without actually writing part of them, and this is not possible in the time available before an order is placed. If similar programs exist on another system, the best method may be a critical comparison with these. A likely cause of inadequate design is insufficient understanding of the mechanisms for routing work through the system, such as the Supervisory Programs, file-addressing routines, and so on.

Of the critical factors described in Chapter 23 the most dangerous in estimating appears to be the core storage requirements. It is common to find that this is drastically underestimated. However, because of the balance between the critical factors, a shortage of core commonly leads to an excessive channel or file arm utilization as more programs are read in from files. It may lead to an excessive use of processing-unit time.

Another area that appears to be dangerous is estimating the utilization of terminals with human operators, such as typewriters, cathode-ray tubes, voice answer-back telephones, and so on. Here due allowance must be made for the behavior of the persons using the system. Human errors will be made. Delays will occur. The conversation between man and machine may be lengthier than anticipated. A terminal operator may be handling other documents or talking on the telephone at the same time. Several telephone calls may have to be distributed to a number of terminal operators. The organization and timing of such actions must be evaluated. It is wrong to think about the terminal utilization without detailed consideration of the actions of its operator.

Terminals are sometimes fairly expensive, perhaps $10,000 each, and every effort is made to reduce the numbers of these on the system. Careful planning of the human usage is needed to do this, especially where volumes are such that there are several terminals in one location. Skilled technical men sometimes make core and timing calculations but neglect the human factors that may slow up the system or necessitate the adding of extra terminals.

Looking back at the calculations of some systems that have suffered from severe underestimating, the only factor that was *grossly* inaccurate

Table 34.1. A FICTIONAL ILLUSTRATION OF THE TYPES OF ERROR THAT TYPICALLY OCCUR IN PROGRAM ESTIMATING

	No. of times executed in peak hour	Estimates at time of ordering		Estimates 18 months later	
		No. of instructions	File events per action	No. of instructions	File events per action
Supervisory Programs		3000		3400	
Application Programs					
Function 1	10,000	2000	9	2500	10
Function 2	9,000	800	2	4000	5–7
Function 3	8,000	Not in Estimate		1000	2
Function 4	5,000	5000	3	5000	2
Function 5	3,000	2500	4	3000	4–6
Function 6	3,000	Not in Estimate		9000	3
Function 7	1,000	600	2	3500	6
End of transaction	14,000	5000	16	8500	20
Ignore transaction	1,000	1500	...	500	
Cancel previous transaction	200	Not in Estimate		1200	5–7
Change file data	200	Not in Estimate		800	3–4
Delete file record	50	600	3	800	3–4
Error procedures	50	Not in Estimate		1200	
Edit input	14,000	Not in Estimate		1500	

Two Types of Error Occur:
1. Certain functions are omitted completely.
2. Others are underestimated because not all the complexities are foreseen.

was the Application Programs. It is not too difficult with the data available today to achieve reasonably accurate estimates for the Supervisory Programs, both in core utilization and time utilization. Given adequate throughput figures and data volumes, the communication line utilization and file requirements should not be far out. However, the total size of the Application Programs, when written, has sometimes proved to be several times the estimated figure.

It is suggested that this is likely to be the most dangerous factor on future systems also. Table 34.1 gives a fictional illustration to indicate the two types of error that should be guarded against. Firstly, some *types* of Application Programs may not be included in the original estimates, and, secondly, some of those that are included may be underestimated because not all the complexities are foreseen. Underestimates in the infrequently used programs are not serious if these are stored on files, but underestimates in the frequently used programs may be very serious.

One danger that must be resisted is the adding of further system functions or details after the original estimates have been made. It is tempting to do this, and on some systems it has happened without a reappraisal of the original estimates. The job complications must not be allowed to expand in this way. Additional functions should be held back until a later model of the system, as described in Chapter 38. It is essential for programming reasons to have a *freeze point* in the design process, and estimates should be based on the functions agreed upon at the freeze point.

Inflation of the functions of the Application Programs or an error in estimating their core requirements can have far-reaching effects that upset the balance of the system. To illustrate this, an example is given below of a system in which the core storage utilization is high.

The system processes messages of different types requiring many different programs. Not all of the programs can be in core at once, and many of them are kept in segments on the files, as is often the case on real-time systems. It is a multithread system and consequently has queues of transactions waiting for the attention of the processor, waiting for the file channels, and waiting for output. It has a core storage map like that in Fig. 31.2.

Consider such a system designed to handle at its peak period eight actions per second. Let us suppose that the programs are in fixed-length segments and that an estimate of Application Program size indicates that ninety different program segments will be required for processing the messages arriving in an average second of the peak hour. Suppose also that a calculation of core storage requirements reveals that there will be space for only eighty of these in core. There will then be *ten* program segments read in from file per second. Suppose that on average an action requires three file events for its processing, excluding the reading in of programs. There will then be $3 \times 8 + 10 = 34$ file events per second. Suppose that the system has two file channels. Knowing the length of the records read in, it may be calculated that the average channel utilization is, say, on a system without a record-ready interrupt, 30 per cent. With this facility utilization, it may be seen from the uppermost curve in Fig. 26.9 that the number of items in the queue for each file channel is about 0.45.

These figures appear to be reasonable with no facility overloaded. But now suppose that the estimates for core storage required for the Application Programs were *one-third below what was actually required*. The effect of this is that 135 program segments are needed in one second instead of the estimate of 90. The effect of this turns out to be that 55 will have to read in in one second. There will then be $3 \times 8 + 55 = 79$ file events per second. This gives a channel utilization of 73 per cent, say. The curve in Fig. 26.9 now indicates that the number of items in a queue for each channel will be about 2.7. Before, each action required an average 3 long seeks to data records and 1.25 short file references to programs. The channel queue that these had to wait for was 0.45 items on average. Now each action has 3 long file references, and $55/8 = 6.875$ file references to programs, with a queue of 2.7 items.

This means that every message will spend longer in core having to wait for program segments to be pulled in from file and also having to wait while queues averaging 2.7 items are depleted. At any one instant, there will be more messages in the core, utilizing more storage for message-reference blocks, file-record blocks, and data saved in core.

The figures in this example were used in a simple simulation, using hardware and Supervisory Program timings taken from an actual application typical of this type. An average file-reference time to data of 160 milliseconds was used, and a file-reference time to programs of 30 milliseconds. The simulation indicated that with the first estimate there would be on the average 2.4 messages in core at one instant. With the increase in size of Application Programs, there would be fifteen messages in core at one instant. Because of this, it was wrong, in fact, to assume that there would still be room for eighty Application Program segments in core. Less than this could now be accommodated, and there would be more program segments read in from files than indicated above.

In this example, the original estimate for Application Program storage was one-third lower than it should have been. It should be noted that, if the actual requirements had been higher than this, the channel utilization would have risen above 73 per cent and the queues would have become very large. If the actual requirements had been double the estimate, it would have been impossible to read in the required programs.

A relatively small inaccuracy in program estimating is *magnified by the nature of the system* in this example. Such an error will result in more core having to be added to the system. In real life much greater errors than this are common in estimating Application Programs. Sometimes on real-time systems the Application Programs have turned out to be several times greater than the original estimates.

The designer should examine his system to see whether it will also magnify the effect of any misestimates he may have made.

If when designing the system there is uncertainty about any estimates, as there normally will be, then the question must be asked, "How far is this likely to be out, and what precautions can be taken to accommodate an error?" The system may be designed with the possibility of adding extra core or keeping more Application Programs on drums. However, *a safety margin must be built into the design*, and, to some extent, this should depend upon the certainty of the estimates.

Furthermore, during the implementation process the design should be constantly monitored as its details come more sharply into focus. Any drift or uncertainties should be noted, and the design summarized on charts such as that on page 345.

SECTION **VI**

IMPLEMENTATION

35 ACCURACY AND SECURITY CONTROLS

The controls that are placed on a batch-processing system to ensure that no transactions are accidentally lost, double-processed, or garbled, and to prevent fraud, are now well-known computer practice. It is vitally important that such controls are applied from the start in any commercial computer installation. In an on-line system it can be even more important, because there is more scope for error. However, the methods of batch processing are no longer applicable to most systems, and so new types of controls must be thought out.

PURPOSES
Controls are needed for the following reasons:

1. *To detect and prevent terminal operator errors.* However infallible the computer, its operators and the staff preparing data ready for processing will always make mistakes. An on-line system may have many more operators than a batch system and so the scope for error is great. However, the on-line system acquires its data closer to its source, and so, if it can quickly detect errors, the data source can be better controlled. Fewer human beings handle a transaction before it reaches the machine. Quick detection of operator errors enables the source of errors to be better disciplined.

2. *To prevent abuse and embezzlement.* Controls are needed on any system where money or goods are handled, to prevent theft by the staff or outsiders. It is generally more difficult to embezzle money from a tightly controlled computer system than from a system which is largely manual. On an on-line system the controls can be made very tight indeed.

3. *To prevent hardware or program errors' damaging or losing data.* If the

545

machine should drop bits, add digits incorrectly, mistakenly overwrite data, or make other errors, these must be detected. External controls will reinforce the already rigorous checks that should be built into the hardware. A likely source of errors is the programs, which on complex multithread systems usually contain traces of rarely occurring errors. As the programs become more complex they seem to be becoming a more likely source of errors than the hardware.

4. *To ensure that nothing is lost or double-entered when outages occur.* If a computer, file, communication line, or other part of the system fails, transactions passing through the system at the instant may not be completely processed. The terminal operator must be aware of this, but he may not know whether the item has updated the requisite records or not. Controls must ensure that the transaction is completely processed. If the operator reenters an item because of a failure, care must be taken that it does not update a file twice because of this.

5. *To reconstruct any records that may be accidentally lost.* It is always the intention that no records *can* become lost accidentally. Indeed on systems with tight controls, elaborate file protection, and well-designed hardware they may not. But many systems so far have lost or damaged single records, because of a rare and unforeseen program error, or multiple records, because of operator faults.

6. *To prevent computer-room operator errors*, such as operators' loading the wrong tapes or files.

7. *To permit auditing* that satisfies the firm's auditors.

BATCH CONTROLS

Controls on card and tape systems are mostly based on taking *batch* totals. Checks, invoices, or other documents may pass through a control point where a girl groups them into batches and adds up on an adding machine the total sum of money in the batch. Or a *hash total* may be taken by adding all the account numbers or customer numbers, or those of other fields.

These batch totals accompany the group of work as it goes to the punch room and later goes into the computer. The computer will check the totals to make sure that all the items have been correctly punched into cards. Where these small batches are combined to form large decks of work, appropriate totals will be built up and used to ensure that no items are lost, for example, in sorts or merges, and that all the required documents are printed.

Where transactions are sent to an on-line machine in batches, similar totals will be accumulated. A depot may, for example, punch items into paper tape as they arise. When about a hundred items, say, have been accumulated, the tape will be put into a reader and transmitted to a distant computer.

This batch will be totalled with an adding machine and the batch total punched as the last item in the tape. The computer receiving this will check the total *immediately*, although it may not process the batch at the time. It sends a reply stating whether the batch was correct. If not, it ignores it; if it is correct, it puts it in a stack of jobs waiting to be processed and maintains totals for control purposes in a similar way to that of a conventional system.

Some line-control computers or multiplexors built to collect data of this type, but without the power to process it, have an instruction set capable of making this check. They accumulate and check the data ready for a larger computer to process.

SINGLE TRANSACTION CONTROLS On systems that need a real-time response, a single transaction is sent to the computer and completely processed before the next one is sent. Batch controls cannot be applied *before* the processing takes place. On some systems they can, however, be used afterwards. The operator or a separate control desk may make a total of the account numbers, quantities, or other significant items. Sometimes the terminal is designed so that it can automatically add these at the end of the day or after every hundred transactions or so or possibly every time there is a lull in the traffic being handled.

If the terminal maintains totals and these are compared with a computer's totals, this serves only as a check that the transmission between the terminal and the computer has been correct. There are better ways of checking the accuracy of transmission, as discussed in Chapter 21. If an unchecked teleprinter or other device is used as the terminal, such totals could be of value, but it is extremely inadvisable to use an unchecked terminal for work that needs this kind of check. Terminal totals thus provide a slight extra security but generally are of little value. They can, however, form very useful controls during periods of equipment failure when bypass procedures are used, as discussed later in this chapter.

On any given system, it is possible to calculate the probability of an error's not being detected. Line test information will indicate the number of errors that may be expected. If this estimate does not give a high enough reliability for the application in question, other checks, such as terminal totals, may be built into the system.

There are a variety of checks that can be built into the system to check a single, individual transaction. These are largely planned to check the accuracy of the operator, who might press a wrong key, type in a wrong account number, interchange two digits, and so on. The computer should have built into its Application Programs whatever means are reasonable and necessary for checking the operators. Incorrect keying and internal contradictions will be tested for as far as possible and the operator notified immediately. *Self-checking numbers* or codes should be used to rapidly detect invalid keying. In these, the last character or characters will be derived from the others in such a way as to check that no wrong key has been depressed. Thus, bad keying of account numbers or of other checkable fields will be picked up immediately it occurs and the operator notified.

Different applications will have different ways of checking the validity of an input message. When the computer examines the files, it will test that this customer does have *this* old balance, this man does have a booking on *this* flight, this railroad car is in *this* location, this payment is the expected amount. Such on-the-spot detection of miskeying is likely to reduce its occurrence. The computer can record every operator mistake it detects, and these statistics can be sent to the proper supervisors.

When enquiries are being made, the computer may print an *alphabetic description* to assure the operator that it is referring to the correct items. For example, if enquiring about the stock of a given part number, the operator may key in a wrong part number by mistake, perhaps 16049 instead of 16409. He detects this quickly when the computer prints back "16049 hexagonal bracket 5 inch, 125 dozen," instead of "16049 electric motor $\frac{1}{4}$ hp. . . ." Particularly when voice answer-back is used, the computer should speak back a description of the items or shares or locations in question, to confirm that it has interpreted the dialling correctly.

When the operator is building up information relating to a new transaction or event, as is the case on many real-time systems, the computer may check that all the desired facts have been entered. It may check that there are no inconsistencies in the facts. Checks on facts entered in this way may be of two categories: first *definite* errors or omissions, which must be corrected before the transaction is accepted by the system, and, second, possible errors or omissions, which the computer asks the operator about in case something is wrong or additional data can be obtained.

In an airline system which stores passenger details, there are certain facts about the passenger which the computer *must* have before it files that record. There are certain fields which the airline agent must fill in, even if she writes "NIL" in them. She may write NIL for the telephone number, for example. The computer will check the date/time continuity of a booking for a journey with more than one flight. The date of each flight requested should be equal to, or later than, the date of the previous flight, for example, though this may be overridden if the international date line is crossed. The location continuity of the journey may also be checked. The board point of each continuing flight will be compared with the off point of the previous one. The passenger may, of course, travel part of his itinerary by a means other than plane or mode of transport booked. If this is so, the operator will use a code to indicate this.

WHEN
OUTAGES
OCCUR

When a communication line fails, or other part of the equipment, it is essential that the operator knows and will take the appropriate corrective action. When the computer has received an item, it should send a *message acknowledgment* of some sort, possibly the reply after processing, to the terminal so that the operator knows his message has reached the computer. On a well-designed system, this check will often be a programmed, rather than an automatic, hardware function because the computer withholds message acknowledgment until the message is in the core of the main processor or, better, until it is written on a logging tape or file. It may withhold acknowledgment until file records have been updated. Doing this ensures that, if a fault occurs, then either the operator will have had no acknowledgment and so will repeat the message, or the computer will have reached such a point that, when a restart or switchover occurs, it can finish processing the message.

There is a danger when a transaction updates a file that an outage may occur at such an instant that the record is not updated. The above answer-back removes this danger but leaves the equally undesirable possibility that the operator may reenter the transaction and cause the record to be updated twice, for example, a bank withdrawal subtracted from the customer's account record twice.

When an abrupt outage occurs, it will probably not be possible to tell how far the Application Programs had gone in handling their message or messages. They may or may not have updated the relevant files. It is, therefore, necessary to place some form of indication on the files at the time they are updated so that either the programs or the operator can tell whether the record in question has been updated. This may be a sequential number allocated either by the computer or by the operator. Sometimes the operator can tell from the data itself. In a savings bank system, for example, he will record the old balance that was on the record before the transaction in question was made. After the outage is repaired he will again key in this transaction along with the old balance and, if there is disagreement, he will know that the record was in fact updated before. He must then check whether the teller total on a separate record is correct. Similarly an airline agent can tell whether his booking for Mr. So-and-So was in fact recorded, by attempting to display the passenger name record for this passenger.

Sometimes, when a piece of equipment fails, a switchover to a substitute occurs. This may be automatic or manual. The switchover process must be planned so that no item is lost or double-entered, and to do this may involve the terminal operator, depending upon the system. Generally in a multiprocessing system where each transaction is held in more than one computer, possibly first in a line-control computer and then in the main processing computer, a switchover procedure can be devised that *automatically* prevents loss or double updating. Where this is not so, the terminal operator will be involved and must have a *rigorously* laid down set of instructions to follow. In general, if good error detection procedures are used, the entry of transactions on line should give rise to fewer errors than similar keying off line onto cards or paper tape, or the writing of documents. The entry of transactions at their source with immediate checking enables errors to be controlled and minimized.

OPERATOR-ADDED SERIAL NUMBERS

On some systems control against loss is achieved by giving serial numbers to the transactions. This is commonly the case, for example, on message-switching systems. Each operator gives a sequential number, of not more than three digits, to each message she sends. On receiving messages, the computer checks that the number from that operator is in fact one higher than the last and stores the message along with the address of the sender. If a breakdown occurs and the system restarts after a period of down time, each operator will resend his last message .The computer will check that there is no gap in the number sequences and no messages stored twice. Conversely on output, the machine will maintain a sequential number for each operator it sends messages to. The operator must check that all the messages he receives are sequentially numbered. If an outage occurs he must be particularly careful to ensure that there is no break in the number sequence.

COMPUTER-ADDED SERIAL NUMBERS

In other systems it is not the operator who gives the item a serial number but the computer itself. The sequential number is written temporarily on the file records which this message causes to be updated. If the question then arises in the restart procedures, "Has such-and-such a record been updated by message no. XXX?" this can be answered. If a duplexed system is used, a scheme such as this will be used to protect the transactions when a switchover occurs, assuring that none are lost or entered twice.

A further variation on the theme is for the computer to compose transaction numbers and send these to the operator. Consider a system in which transactions are read into core by a programmed communication-transmission control computer and then, when checked out, are passed to a main processing computer as it asks for them. The sequence of events might be as follows (Fig. 35.1):

1. The terminal operator sends the message.

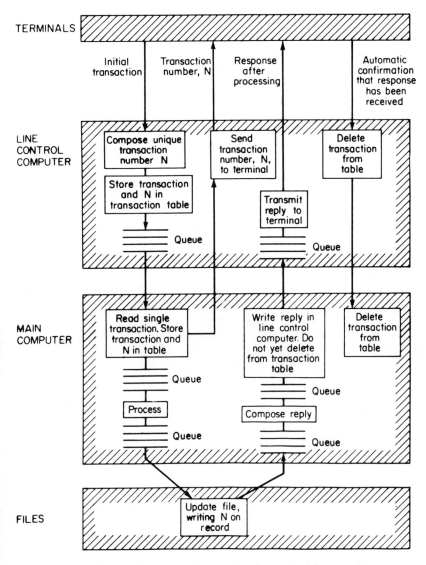

Fig. 35.1. Use of a transaction number for maintaining security.

2. It is received in the transmission control computer. This adds a unique number to it and stores the transaction and its number in a table.

3. The items are checked, edited, and then queued in the transmission control computer. The main computer reads them from the transmission control computer one at a time.

4. The main computer stores the transaction with its number, in a table or message-reference block.

5. As soon as the transmission control computer receives confirmation that the main computer has received the transaction correctly, it sends the transaction number to the terminal operator.

6. The main computer processes the transaction and prepares to update the files.

7. The unique transaction number is written on each file record updated, and remains there until it is again updated by another different transaction.

8. The main computer composes the reply.

9. The transmission control computer transmits the reply, noting this in its transaction table.

10. When the hardware signals that the terminal has correctly received the answer-back, the transaction number is deleted in the transmission control computer's table and the message is deleted from the core of the main computer.

The terminal operator is given the following instructions on what to do if a breakdown occurs: If she has received (or partially received) a reply giving the number of the transaction, she should not enter it again. If she has not received this, she should enter it when the system returns to operation. With this rule the system can be programmed to recover from the failure of a *single* unit without risk of not updating or double updating the file. This is so wherever the failure occurs in the above sequence of events.

If, however, *both* the main computer *and* the transmission control computer fail at once—if, for example, there is a power failure at the computer room, then the recovery procedure is different. If the terminal operator has received the message number but not the answer-back, then she must key in both the message number and the message. All the terminal operators involved do this, and again the system can be programmed to resume in safety.

Schemes such as this, but differing in detail, must be thought out for each system that updates vital files in an on-line manner.

LOGGING   The accuracy control on some systems is built around a *log* which is kept constantly to record the transactions being processed. In its simpler form, the log may record merely the input transactions received by the computer. Each item is written out on tape, drum, or on disk before it is processed, or at least before any critical files are updated.

In order that restart procedures or reconstruction procedures may be facilitated, it is useful to write a serial number also on the log. After a computer failure has occurred the restart procedures center around the use of the log.

It may not be necessary to log the entire message, but only those parts used in updating the record, so that a smaller volume has to be stored. On some systems, information about the file updating is also stored on the log. For example, in an inventory system a note of all the records updated would be kept giving the item number, old balance, and new balance. The terminal number or operator number will be recorded, and sometimes the date and time are recorded. Sometimes the file action log is kept separately from the transaction log as in Fig. 35.2.

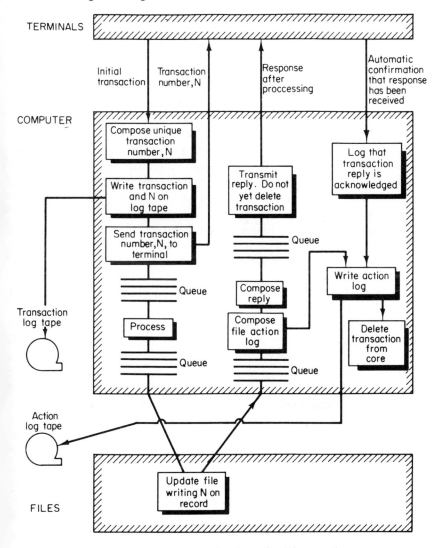

Fig. 35.2. Use of tape logging for maintaining security.

The transaction log may be kept by the transmission control computer if this is separate from the main computer. It is generally desirable that the writing of the log should be the first action that is taken when a message is received, and this action may be taken by a priority routine which deals with the message when its transmission into the computer is completed. Figure 35.2 shows a typical logging procedure.

CHECKPOINTS   The taking of checkpoints is common practice on batch-processing systems. At intervals the status of the run in question is recorded on tape or file. If then a failure occurs, or the run is stopped for some reason, the operation returns to the previous checkpoint and can be restarted from there.

Checkpoints are still useful for some on-line and real-time systems, although on many they are a clumsy and unsatisfactory way of maintaining control. Certainly, when batches of work are sent over communication links it is a good idea to have checkpoints at fairly frequent intervals in the processing so that not too much has to be reprocessed, or possibly retransmitted, when a failure occurs. Where single transactions are sent it is more difficult. However some single transaction systems do maintain checkpoints.

As transactions flow through a typical system, the programs maintain tables giving the status of various lines and terminals, and recording the stage of processing that the various transactions have reached. One way of maintaining checkpoints is to dump these tables onto tape, drum, or disk at regular intervals, perhaps every thirty seconds or so. The tables may be dumped onto two alternating areas of a drum, for example, at time intervals determined by a real-time clock. This will be fast and will not use much drum space. If a computer failure or stoppage occurs, the restart procedures will return to the previous checkpoint and examine what was on the tables at that time. The latest checkpoint tables will be reloaded into core and the programs will determine which messages had been processed or are in such a state that the processing can be completed. The computer will complete the processing on these and will send messages to the terminal operators telling them to retransmit all messages sent after the message with such-and-such a serial number. Using the serial numbers, it will check carefully that it is not causing a file to be updated twice.

It will be noticed that the message logging method gives more immediate control than a thirty-second checkpoint, and will normally not require so many messages to be retransmitted. Checkpoint recording, on the other hand, uses rather less machine and channel time.

CONTROLS ON
BYPASS
PROCEDURES

On many systems, especially those that operate in real time, some sort of bypass procedure must be devised for when the system fails. This is particularly so when the equipment is not duplexed and so may go off the air for two hours or more, occasionally. In a savings bank, for example, customers walking in must be dealt with, and so a bypass procedure is necessary. It is especially important that the system controls do not allow errors to occur during this brief period of difficulty.

The computer may send each location a listing, perhaps at night, which will enable it to operate, albeit in a less controlled fashion, when the equipment fails. The clerks will accumulate their transactions for entry into the terminal when it is on-line again.

In the savings bank, as discussed in Chapter 16, the bank teller uses the same terminal to record transactions off line on its printed tape. When the computer failure occurs, the teller makes the terminal print out control totals, kept in its own accumulators, showing net cash. These will also have been recorded in the computer up to the time when the failure occurred. The terminal counters go on accumulating net cash totals during the period of off-line operation, and, when the computer becomes usable again, the operator prints the totals. He then enters all the transactions into the computer, which updates its files accordingly. The computer totals are then printed and must agree with the terminal's off-line ones. Thus continuity of the use of control totals is maintained throughout the period of bypass operation.

FILE
SCANNING

Another type of a control on the system's operation that may be built in uses an off-line scanning of the files. The run may balance cash or other quantities, check that no records have been damaged, search for accidental duplicates, and so on. It may be necessary to scan the records daily, inspecting them for other conditions, and so this run may be combined with a control run.

In a system dealing with cash the total sum of all of the accounts may be added on the file scan. This must equal yesterday night's grand total *plus* the cash that has been added to records today *minus* the cash subtracted from records today. The last two figures are totalled as the day goes by from transactions dealt with and then are checked against the totals kept by the terminal operators. A tight network of totals can thus be maintained daily.

The records may be divided into groups for the purpose of such totalling so that errors can be pinned down somewhat more quickly if any are found. If it is felt that there is a risk of records' being accidentally overwritten, the daily scan may total the account numbers or other data on records that will indicate that this has not happened.

A problem on airline systems is that one passenger may be booked twice by accident (or deliberately, if he is worried about not having a seat). This happens very often and constitutes a loss of revenue for most airlines. Here the flights may be scanned off line to see whether there are any suspected duplicates. Some airlines want to search for duplicates in real time when the booking is made, but this uses more processing time and may need a bigger or faster computer for peak periods.

A variety of other undesirable conditions may be checked for by non-real-time runs at night or during nonpeak periods. The type of conditions that may be sought differ widely from one application to another. *Off-line policing* can often be devised to keep a check on the validity of the data or the files and also to scan a log of the input received.

FILE
RECONSTRUCTION

Records have occasionally become damaged on the real-time systems in operation, especially the large multithread ones which still contain traces of program errors even years after cutover. Occasionally, a single record will be found to be overwritten and will need reconstructing. Worse than this, it is possible that a complete file or portion of a file might be accidentally destroyed. This is a *very* unlikely event, but it might happen, as in one case when a computer room used the wrong file load tapes after a weary night of testing program changes. It needs some sort of insurance policy in the form of a file reconstruction procedure.

There are thus two types of reconstruction that might be needed: the relatively quick reconstruction of single records, and reconstruction of a major part of the file following a catastrophe that one hopes will never happen.

The means for file reconstruction will be firstly a dump, possibly on to magnetic tape, of the files at certain intervals, and secondly a log of all the transactions that cause a modification to the file. When an installation is first cut over, the files might be dumped every night and then less frequently when it settles down. Programs should be written so that, by scanning these two sets of data, a record can be reconstructed fairly quickly, and, after inspection, substituted for the one that is in error. Possibly a slightly different program will be written for doing a major file reconstruction from this data.

Some on-line systems have a hierarchy of different files—a fast access file of low volume, a slower access file of larger volume, and so on, with magnetic tape being used for the slowest but largest volume file of the hierarchy. On this type of system the smaller file may have its contents duplicated on the larger one, and so on, for reasons of backup in case of failure and file-reconstruction because of accident.

AUDITING

The implementation of these new techniques for financial data, as with the use of batch-processing methods before them, will require a change in the auditor's procedures. It is usually worthwhile, indeed often essential, to bring in the auditor when designing the system. His experience can ensure that the controls are adequate and that suitable data are recorded to permit the necessary audits.

On some systems he will want certain hard-copy data to be recorded at the terminals and possibly certain nightly print-outs to be made in the computer room. Generally speaking, the totals and balances described above, along with tight controls over operator misentry or misuse of terminals, can make the auditing power of an on-line system greater than that of a batch-processing system.

CONTROLS ON OPERATORS

Tight discipline on the operators of an on-line system is one of the important factors. This should be maintained by programmed checks and strong supervision. The ability of the computer to detect many types of errors as soon as they are made and to check for the completeness of transactions will aid this.

During periods when part of the equipment fails, detailed and well-rehearsed instructions to operators are vital. Fallback and bypass tactics to meet all circumstances should be mapped out in advance and documented clearly. The operators must be trained carefully in fallback procedures. When on-line terminals are used for training, this should include operation in the various fallback modes. A remote office must not panic when the personnel discover that they are cut off from their source of information.

During periods of switchover or computer outages it may be especially important to have tight controls on the terminal operators. Where the terminals are being used merely for enquiries there is normally no problem about transactions being lost. If the user wants an answer to his enquiry he will re-enter it when the computer is back "on the air." However, if he is entering data that *must* not be lost, it is worthwhile to derive checks on each individual operator. In a banking system, for example, the daily totals entered by the teller are added up first by the teller and also by the machine. The totals are compared to ensure that nothing has been lost, and the methods for totalling bridge any period of switchover or outage. On other systems, totals of this type are kept but are compared at much more frequent intervals, say, every hour. In this case, if any discrepancy is discovered it will not take so long to put it right. The system may be designed so that the operator can check every time he has an idle period to ensure that the computer's total agrees with his; however, such a check left to the operator should not replace an enforced periodic check.

Computer center operators of high ability are needed who can deal with the various emergencies that may arise. They must be able to initiate the correct type of fallback and recovery action. However, human operators in the computer room make the system vulnerable to some extent, and controls should be devised to check *their* actions. They may load the wrong disks or tape, execute incorrect routines that could destroy data on file, and so on. The computers must, where possible, examine what their operators do and check that the right disks and tapes have been loaded.

The system designers should try to anticipate all possible sources of trouble and tie the system down with a network of controls that will make it safe from hardware or software errors, from terminal operator mistakes and clerical errors, and from the staff in its own computer room. A well-planned commercial system should be locked in a straight-jacket of carefully designed controls on accuracy.

36 THE PROGRAMMING WORK

As has been seen, the programming of on-line computer systems brings many problems and challenges not usually encountered on conventional computers. Perhaps the greatest of the problems lies in the management of a team putting together a complex system with the constraints of real time. More rigorous disciplines and a different order of management control are needed.

The main difficulties on such a system arise because the work of many programmers is no longer largely independent as it may have been on batch-processing or scientific systems. The programs often relate to each other in a complex way. There are tight logical interactions between the work of a programmer and that of his many colleagues. Like the components of an intricate piece of machinery, the programs, written by many different people, must mesh together to form a smoothly working whole.

The work of one programmer thus considerably affects the work of others. To illustrate this, one might imagine a chart in which small blocks are drawn to represent segments of program and other items in the design, such as file records, input transactions, and so on. If the equipment configuration or design is not completely frozen from the start, the blocks might also be used to represent hardware elements on which design is proceeding. Each block therefore represents something that will be produced and will develop in the design process. Now imagine lines with arrows on the chart to represent logical interactions between the blocks. Even in a small real-time system, such as that for a savings bank, there will be quite a large number of blocks. In a major real-time system it might be possible to draw many hundreds or even thousands of blocks. The number of links between them is great and the pattern of interactions very complex. In the eventual system these items must fit together and are closely interdependent.

If a programmer makes a change in his program or in his data specifications, this is likely to affect the work of a number of other programmers, and these must all be notified of the changes. In reality, in the course of his work the programmer constantly makes changes of this type. Programs tend to grow and develop rather like the growth of a city. To communicate all of these changes to all of the other programmers who need to know about them on a large system becomes a severe problem.

The problem, then, which must be faced on such a system may be stated thus: How can the programs that make up a tightly interwoven system be developed concurrently by separate programmers when there are so many interactions between them? How can control over the interactions be maintained?

TO ACHIEVE PROGRAMMER INDEPENDENCE   This is not a severe problem on all on-line systems. Some are specifically designed so that the programmers of the Application Programs are totally independent and so that their work will not interfere with other programs. Many time-sharing systems, for example, are designed for complete programmer independence. The Supervisory Programs are written so that, with the help of certain hardware features, they prevent a user's program that is full of errors from damaging the work of other programs or seriously holding up the system. All on-line and real-time systems must be protected from their operators. They must be made foolproof. In this case the operator writes and executes programs on line, and so the system must be protected from these.

Two hardware features, discussed in Chapter 19, are important in protecting the system. These are a *memory protection* feature and a *watchdog timer*. The former confines the user's program to a certain area of core. If the program attempts to make any reference beyond this area, possibly owing to the program's "running wild," an interrupt will occur and the program will be stopped. Similarly a watchdog timer or interval timer can be set to interrupt the program if it takes too long a period of time and so holds up other users, possibly because it is looping. On most time-sharing systems the program is interrupted after a certain interval if it runs that long, say, a quarter of a second, so that other users may be given a good response time. It will then be returned to core later to continue running. If, however, it runs for longer than its expected time, it may be stopped for investigation. Many commercial systems have programs written in segments which do not take long to execute, and at the end of each segment control passes back to a main scheduling routine. In the main scheduling routine the watchdog timer can be reset as in Fig. 9.4, p.129. The device may be set to time for an interval of, say, 500 milliseconds. If it reaches the end of that interval, this indicates that something is wrong because the main scheduling routine has not been entered and some program has been hogging the machine 500 milliseconds. It therefore causes the program in question to be interrupted.

Other devices besides memory protection and a watchdog timer are needed to ensure complete independence of operation of separate users' programs. They must be prevented, for example, from interfering with each other's file areas. They must be prevented from using registers needed by the Supervisory Programs. The Supervisory Programs must ensure that, when control passes from one Application Program to another, possibly following a timer interrupt, no vital data are left in registers, accumulators, or other common parts of the machine.

On many time-sharing systems in which the operators write programs, the problem of noninterference is tackled in the language, or languages, used and by the compilers of these languages. The compilers ensure that the object programs they produce use the correct registers, do not access files they should not, and so on. In other words, they keep the separate programs rigorously separated. It is, of course, necessary to ensure that the compilers do not interfere with each other. Careful control and much debugging will be needed to ensure that these and other tools fit together into a system that works without producing errors.

INTERACTIONS BETWEEN PROGRAMS   On time-sharing systems where all the programs and their data are strictly independent, there is little problem of interaction between different programmers, once the system and its tools, such as on-line compilers, are set up. On commercial and military real-time systems, however, the labors of separate programmers are usually not independent, because they relate to different aspects of the same job. Different programs, written by different people, for example, may use the same data records, same subroutines, same tables in core, possibly at the same time in a multithread manner.

On one large airline reservation system it is estimated that the handling of one transaction may need about six messages processing in real time. In other words, if a potential customer is on the telephone for two minutes, or standing in front of a sales agent in the airline office, the sales agent will send about six messages to the computer, getting a reply to each in a second or so. An average message causes about 12,000 computer instructions to be executed in its processing. Twenty or so such messages may be in the computer at one time being handled in a multithread manner. There are about 150,000 instructions in the system that *could* be executed in real time. It has been estimated that there are no less than 250 million possible paths through which the input may go before a response message is sent. The work of the many programmers who specified and coded this thus fits together in a very tight manner. If a program is modified, the effects of this change can echo through the system, causing minor modifications to be needed in the work of many other programmers.

On many of the complex military, government, and commercial systems now being installed or contemplated, the units of program cannot be written independently because they affect the functioning of each other in an intricate fashion. Work on a large system will usually start with a small and competent group of systems analysts who understand well the problems of the application. These people may be selected from the different areas with which the computer will become involved. When this team has produced a tentative design plan, programmers will be brought in to begin working out the details of the plan. They will draw up programming specifications and block diagrams and eventually will start coding. The programs will be written in separate units small enough for one man to handle. The size of the units is often determined by the size of blocks of program that the supervisory system can read into core. The system may have many separate blocks written at different times by different people. The blocks of program will be tested individually for logic errors and then, later, will be made to work in conjunction with each other, so that the complete system is slowly built up and tested.

As the development is proceeding, the need to make changes will constantly arise. The number of changes should be minimized. The specifications of the system need to be frozen fairly early in its development and the pressure for changes from the outside resisted. However, numerous changes will be needed for internal reasons. The programmers steadily improve upon or correct the logic of the system. The exact usage of characters and bits in the data fields becomes specified and refined. The interactions between programs are steadily clarified and modified, and complications that were not foreseen in detail at the outset are constantly being revealed.

It is interesting to pursue the analogy between this type of system and a complex piece of mechanical or electrical engineering. Some of the techniques that have become traditional in conventional engineering point the way here also.

DOCUMENTATION   First, the level of documentation used in engineering is very much greater than that normally found in the programming world. Before work starts on the components of a new piece of computer circuitry or a section of a chemical plant, it is planned in fine detail on paper. Elaborate specifications are drawn up for the components and for the over-all layout. If, during the construction, any deviation occurs from the specifications, this again is documented in detail and replanned with care

Without doubt, real-time systems need a higher degree of documentation than is found in conventional systems. Part of the solution to the problem of programmer interactions is to draw up detailed specifications for each program segment and data record in the system. The same discipline that is used in engineering documentation should be applied here in programming. There are several reasons why detailed specifications are essential; they can be summarized in one word, *constraints*. If a complex piece of machinery is being built and different components are being made by different people, the specifications for these components must be drawn up very carefully so that they fit together when the machinery is assembled. Once the specifications are drawn up, they must be adhered to exactly or the parts will not fit. A relatively simple piece of mechanical engineering has this type of discipline, and yet many highly complex pieces of data processing have been attempted without it.

A basic difference between programming and engineering construction exists, however, in the number of changes that are constantly needed as the logic develops. In view of the *constraints* that apply and because the programmer's work must fit in with all the other parts of the programming, he must be careful in the changes he makes. He must not modify items that will upset the work of other programmers without consulting them, and the changes must be documented very carefully; otherwise the whole system will get out of hand, and one programmer will not know what the others are doing. In this environment of constant change there must be careful control of the documentation; otherwise there is no hope that the parts of the machine will fit together when the time comes to assemble it.

The documentation and the channels of flow for documentation must therefore be designed so that changes, where essential, can occur and be communicated easily to the programmers who need to know about them.

The arrows on the imaginary chart described at the start of this chapter can thus indicate the flow of paperwork. The flow of such paperwork can indeed become too great to be reasonably manageable in a large system, unless it is controlled somehow. The programmers become deluged with so many tedious documents that they do not read them all or do not assimilate their significance. Programmers almost invariably dislike this large amount of paperwork. Generally they do not like writing specifications. Any means of cutting down the number of interactions should be used so that the paperwork can be lessened. Where interactions of the type described do occur, they must be documented, especially in a large system, or serious confusion can occur, bringing in its wake chaos at system testing time.

DIVISION INTO SUBSYSTEMS

The number of interactions between programs or between programmers can be cut down by dividing the system programs into subsystems. This is rather like making subassemblies in mechanical engineering. The behavior of the subassembly is clearly defined, and the way it fits into the rest of the machinery is specified in detail. This done, the subassemby can be made independently of the remainder. Subsystems of program might be the main scheduling routine, the communication-line input/output control, message-editing routines, self-contained groups of Application Programs, and so on. These units are small enough for two or three men, or even one man, to handle them. The interactions within this unit are then relatively easy to control. The unit is insulated as completely as possible from the other units. The interface between the unit and the rest of the system must be very clearly defined.

Every attempt will be made not to modify the interfaces between the units. This means that, before programming begins, the functions of the units must be very clearly thought out. It will, however, be inevitable that the interface needs some modification as the system develops. When this occurs, it must be documented thoroughly, and all programmers concerned must know about it.

PACKAGE PROGRAMS

There is a possibility that some of the subsystems may be obtainable as working, fully debugged programs. This is particularly so of the Supervisory Programs. It would be very useful to be able to employ standardized software for the Supervisory Programs. With some computers this is possible, especially on smaller systems or systems without too high a degree of real-time activity. On very complex or special-purpose real-time systems it may become more difficult or inefficient to use standardized packages. There are many differences between complex real-time systems. These systems have many specialties of their own or are unique in some way, so that it might be difficult to use an off-the-shelf set of Supervisory Programs. Sometimes certain routines of such Supervisory Programs can be rewritten or added to.

There are many other advantages in using an existing and proven set of Supervisory Programs besides the one that this difficult area of programming with which every programmer must interface is then defined at the start of the development. A system which uses debugged and error-free Supervisory Programs is likely to have far fewer installation problems. The Application Programs will be made to work with the actual Supervisory Programs at an early stage. There will be less doubt as to whether program errors here are caused by the Application Programs or the Supervisory Programs. The types of program errors that are likely to occur will be understood early.

If no Supervisory Programs were complete at that stage, as has often been the case, they would have to be simulated in some way.

The design of the system around an existing set of Supervisory Programs would also be easier. Another powerful reason for using standardized Supervisory Programs is the cost involved in writing them specially for an application. Major applications are likely to have twelve or more man years in the writing and testing of specially designed Supervisory Programs. At least some of the men must be highly skilled. If the support programs needed to accompany these Supervisory Programs are included, the bill is likely to be more than $200,000.

The disadvantages of using generalized Supervisory Programs, if they are available, may be that they consume more core and time than would a set written specifically for the application in question. However, this is often a small price to pay for the saving in programming difficulty and, often, earlier implementation.

For some of the better-known uses of on-line and real-time systems, Application Programs as well as Supervisory Programs are available from some computer manufacturers. This is so, for example, in banking, message-switching, and airline reservations. Often such packaged Application Programs need modifying before use, but nevertheless they can make the overall programming work much easier.

In addition to obtaining packaged programs from manufacturers, programs or specifications can be obtained from other users. Even if the other user does not employ the same machine, it may be valuable to buy his specifications. Half of the programming work is specification writing, and much time could be saved.

It is often very tempting for skilled programmers to devise their own ways of doing the job rather than use existing ones which were "not invented here." An expert may have a strong desire to produce his own Supervisory Programs or testing techniques. Resisting such temptations may save much manpower, headaches, and time.

CONTROLLING CHANGES   An engineering project, once the plan of what is to be built has been laid down, will not normally change from the original plan. In programming, however, it is often thought by those not directly involved that changes can easily be made. Persons often think that the functions can be modified slightly as the programming proceeds, as this is only a matter of altering lines of coding on a piece of paper. This may be a reasonable view for a conventional system for billing, or payroll, or doing engineering calculations. Here changes can easily be made. However, when a complex real-time system is fitted together, it causes endless trouble if the requirements of the system are changed now and then as it is being programmed.

Any requirements for changes that do arise should be noted and left for incorporation in a later model. As soon as the writing of operational programs for one model begins, this model and its functional specifications should be *frozen*. When this model is working, the programmers may then begin a second version of the system which will incorporate any improvements thought of while the first was being developed. Using the word "model" here does not imply, necessarily, that the computer or other hardware is changed; only the programs need be.

MODEL-BY-MODEL BUILDUP
The changes built into the second model may include additional functions and modifications required by the users of the system and, sometimes more important, modifications desired by the programmers themselves. It is rare that a good programmer reaches the end of a piece of coding without wanting to rewrite it. He sees ways of cleaning up the logic, speeding up the program, making it perform better. In a large system written with a team of many coders, this is much more true, There will be many deficiencies in the first working model, many areas which could be simplified and improved. The testing phase, when the work of several programmers is first made to perform as one system, normally suggests many possibilities for improvement. It is likely that the first model of a multiprogrammed system will have a number of elements in the combined logic which slow it down. The second model of most such systems is considerably faster than the first. The Supervisory Programs, in particular, may be capable of being speeded up.

Saving all the possible changes for a new model, rather than tearing the present coding to pieces as soon as improvements are thought of, will enable one model to go on the air fairly quickly so that experience can be gained in using it. Furthermore, the second model will certainly benefit from a joint planning of the improvements incorporated in it.

The freezing of each model and the model-by-model buildup is desirable, then, to protect the system both from external pressures for change and from its own programmers' desire for change. The programmers will generally be happier if they know that they can incorporate the modifications they invent in the next model.

In engineering development it is common to build a prototype designed to investigate the functioning of the system, or part of the system, before the final working product is built. Design feedback from the prototype is used to improve the final system. This technique is useful also in a complex programming system. Subunits of the system may be programmed and tested experimentally, often using simulation, before the coding of the final product begins. The first of the models may be designed to be not an operational model, but an experimental prototype.

CONTROL GROUP

A management problem that can become very difficult with an inventive programming team is deciding which of the many features they devise should be incorporated. To add them all could run the system out of core storage or processing time. It can be difficult to decide whether a programming proposal is worthwhile when it is considered on its own. However, when all the various ideas are discussed together in deciding on the features of a new model, their relative merits can be compared. The decisions can be made which are practical and economical. The core storage, processing time, and, possibly, money available for improvements can be assessed.

Some decisions must be made as the system is being programmed. They concern changes which cannot wait for the next model. To approve and help handle these, it is suggested that a separate control group should be set up. For a small system this may be one man. On a larger system the function may need six or eight people full time.

The control group would read all program specifications before they are handed to programmers to work on. It would thus build up a complete knowledge of the system under development. The control group would evaluate the core storage utilization, processor time utilization, file utilization, and other critical factors. It would monitor the progress of the program writing to ensure that these figures did not exceed the allowable values. Any changes to the specifications that programmers need to make would be referred to the control group. This group would modify the specifications as needed and so relieve the programmers of a task they generally dislike. It would communicate all changes to the persons who need to know about them.

On a large and complex system a control group of this type has proved most valuable in directing the progress of what can otherwise be a most unwieldy monster. It monitors what is happening and channels the design down the right paths. The control group needs to be planned in such a way that it will not itself become a bottleneck. If it is unable to read, assimilate, and approve of specifications fast enough, a queue of work builds up which can become an annoying delay.

It is important that there should be only one control group for the whole system and, indeed, only one over-all management. Some systems have suffered from split management, with part of the programs being done by one group and part by another, and no one person with over-all authority. For example, in some cases a computer manufacturer or consultant has specially written the Supervisory Programs and sometimes also the Support

Programs, while the system user has written the Application Programs. Sometimes the groups, with no combined management, have even been in different countries. Not to have an over-all control group and an over-all manager with power of veto is to impose a grave difficulty on a system that is already difficult enough. Tight management and very tight over-all control is needed on these systems. Split management is a grave and unnecessary hazard.

TEAMWORK　　　　　To summarize the main difference between the programming effort for a real-time system and that for a batch-processing or conventional system of similar complexity is that the former must be a tightly integrated piece of *teamwork*. The programming group must be built up as a team and managed as a team. Each individual piece of programming craftsmanship must fit exactly with the rest to contribute to the over-all result. The members of the programming team must recognize each other's problems. They should be encouraged to strive for careful cooperation and should be made to understand the importance of the separate elements' meshing together cleanly. Simplicity of individual programming mechanisms is often a key factor in fitting together a complex system. As good team members, the programmers should know that the ease with which the components fit together is more important than individual brilliance.

Each programmer must see his role in the system clearly and understand the concept of teamwork in constructing the system. He must understand the roles of the other programmers and how he fits in with them. General system education for all programmers will pay dividends.

The specifications and interface documents will help greatly in this. These represent a *formal* means of control of interactions. *Informal* contact between the programmers must also be encouraged to the full. It should be a point of pride with programmers to know as much as they can about the system as a whole. They should know exactly how their own work fits in with other parts of the system. They should understand the nature of the interactions as fully as possible.

Parochialism is a fault that occurs only too easily on a large programming team, especially if parts of it are in different locations, as is sometimes the case. A programmer can become so immersed in the problems of his own program or subsystem that he tends to lose contact with the rest of the system and its environment. Regular exposure to the problems and viewpoints of other personnel is essential. This may be done by periodic seminars which the whole programming team attends. Selected programmers or systems analysts should speak to the group about their work or aspects of the system.

An external consultant or person not connected with part of the system can be of value. Programming groups may periodically discuss their approaches with such a person. Exposure to a completely external or over-all viewpoint can improve their work or remove deficiencies that result from shortsightedness.

To a large extent the understanding of the interactions with other programmers requires good *teamwork*. Not all programmers work well in close teamwork. Some of the best programmers are creative persons who feel they need more freedom than such work offers them. Careful consideration should be given to this in recruiting and building up the team. Being a member of a real-time programming team may not be the right place for a programming prima donna. But, on the other hand, it is a great advantage to have very bright and fast working men on the project. With a small number of bright men the interaction problem will be much less than with twice the number of men of half the productivity.

A well-knit team that is managed efficiently and moves fast, as a team, to tackle the problems that confront it is the ideal to aim at.

37 SYSTEM TESTING

On the large real-time systems installed to date, the testing, first of programs and then of the over-all system has proved extremely difficult. Crises and delays in testing have been considerable. This is one of the fundamental problems of real time, and techniques more advanced than those used on conventional systems are required.

These techniques will differ widely between a simple and a complex system. There is a great difference in complexity between the programs for a savings bank system with 4000 lines of coding, single-thread processing, and perhaps 20 operator sets and a large airline reservation system with 140,000 lines of coding, 1000 operator sets, and a high order of multiprogramming. The comments in this chapter will be aimed mainly at the larger system and can be trimmed down as appropriate for smaller systems.

THE PROBLEMS   The problems of real-time program testing are caused by six factors not normally found on conventional systems:

1. Use of terminals and lines for input and output.
2. Use of specially engineered equipment that is not on an off-the-shelf computer.
3. Multiprogramming and multiprocessing.
4. Unpredictability.
5. An added reliability requirement.
6. A very complex interrelation between the programs.

1. *Input and output.* The input will be from many terminals or remote devices. When testing, it will be necessary to use predetermined input to the programs being tested. It will, however, be impractical to use terminals, because this would be too slow and because the terminals probably will not be available in the early testing phases. For this reason the input must be simulated. For example, it may be stored on tape and fed to the programs being tested by means of a Test Supervisor Program. On a technical application, input signals from radars or other devices must be simulated.

Terminals, displays, or other remote devices are also used for output. For the same reasons it is not desirable to use actual displays or terminals. Some means of replacing these is required, such as recording the output on magnetic tape and later printing it. The input rate of conventional systems is fixed by computers reading cards onto tape as required. On real-time systems the input rate will fluctuate. There will be a probability of the system's becoming overloaded at times. When an overload occurs, the system may have to take emergency action. A means of varying the input must be devised, and means of feeding enough messages to the system to test its overload action must be devised.

2. *Special equipment.* Equipment specially engineered for an application is commonly used in real-time systems. Because this equipment may not be ready for early phases of testing, the first testing may have to be done using a specially written program to simulate the system on an existing computer configuration.

3. *Multiprogramming and multiprocessing.* On a complex system, specially written Supervisory Programs may be used. Probably these will not be completely debugged when in use with the data-processing programs. Controversy may arise as to whether an error resulted from a fault in a Supervisory Program or a fault in a data-processing program. This may be specially troublesome if one team writes the Supervisory Programs and another writes the data-processing programs, as often happens. It will be especially troublesome if the interface between the Supervisory Programs and data-processing programs is not clearly defined. A way is needed to determine whether an error is caused by a Supervisory Program or a data-processing program.

When two data-processing programs are in core at the same time, it may be difficult to tell which caused an error. One may write incorrectly on file records used by another and so cause trouble later without giving an indication of the cause of the trouble.

When Supervisory Programs are written specially for an application, it may be desirable to start testing the data-processing programs before the Supervisory Programs are fully developed. Macroinstructions which simulate Supervisory Program macroinstructions in a simple manner will be required.

4. *Unpredictability*. In a large real-time system, messages enter the system at random and many messages will be in core at one time, partially processed. Where in batch processing the sequence of events follows one of a small number of preplanned routes, in a real-time multiprogrammed system there is an almost infinite number of possible combinations. It is therefore very difficult to remove the last traces of errors from a system.

The supervisory system is designed so that interrupts (traps) occur frequently—more than 100 times a second on some large systems. The exact time when an interrupt occurs cannot be predicted before the test nor easily ascertained after the test. Because of the interrupts, the sequence of events in the test is not repeatable. If an attempt is made to repeat a test exactly, the file interrupts alone will prevent this, because the end-of-record or ready-made signals may be many milliseconds different in time from the previous run. This means that some errors will not be *solid*. An error may occur once but defy further investigations. Furthermore, an attempt to pin down such an error by using techniques for logging interrupts will probably destroy the timing relationships that cause the error.

Another nonsolid error will be caused by noise on transmission lines. In some cases it may be difficult to differentiate between a random transmission error and an unrepeatable program error.

In the later stages of testing, when the input is from remote terminals, an error may exhibit itself only very infrequently because of the slow rate of input. An error which appears only once a day at unpredictable times could be very difficult to track down. Yet a number of such errors in the operational system could cause much trouble, especially if there is a risk of their damaging file data.

5. *Added reliability requirements*. In a batch-processing system it is possible to begin operational running before all the most remote errors are removed. If an error occurs during operational running, it is possible to stop the run and look for the cause of the error. The day's work will end later than scheduled.

This is not possible on a real-time system, and, because of the changing time relationships, more remote errors will exist in a real-time system. In general, if program errors occur after operational cutover, they will be much more difficult to find than on a conventional system and cause much more trouble. The precutover debugging must therefore be very thorough on a real-time system.

However thorough the testing, it is almost certain that there will be some requirements for testing during operational running. Some errors will slip through, and program modifications will be demanded throughout the life of the system. Testing during operational running will be difficult. Only such time as is left over from the main work of the system can be made available for other functions, such as testing, and that only perhaps in small instalments. Some systems will have no such time available.

A program error may cause the program to run wild. In ordinary data processing, this risk may be tolerated, since the loss of time or data can easily be repaired. In real-time systems, unless the functioning part of the system can be protected by rigorous hardware measures, the risk is far more serious.

6. *Added complexity.* A large number of programmers may be involved in producing a real-time system. Because of the difficulty in recruiting a big team suddenly, these may be beginners at programming. The work of one programmer will intermesh tightly with the work of others. Individual contributions will be much more highly interdependent than on a conventional system, and so every time a programmer makes changes he may be affecting the work of others.

Because of the difficulty of combining the work of so many people, the program testing effort is not directly proportional to the size of the system. On a large system many discrepancies are likely to be found when, finally, all the bits and pieces are put together.

THE TECHNIQUES To tackle these problems, modifications to the programs and modifications to the equipment may be needed.

The data-transmission lines in the earlier stages of testing will normally terminate in the same room as the computer. They may have the normal terminals attached to them, but usually these slow units will be simulated using devices such as paper-tape or magnetic-tape units for providing the input to, and capturing the output from, the testing (Fig. 37.1). The lines may be "wrapped around" as in Fig. 37.2, so that the computer provides its own messages for testing and captures its own output. Where a duplexed system is to be used, one computer can feed messages to the other and analyze the test results (Fig. 37.3). One computer can, in fact, become a real-time system for testing the other computer. When the programs are largely debugged, communication lines and terminals must be included in the testing.

On a complex system a formidable array of programs may be needed as testing aids. Some of these may be built into the

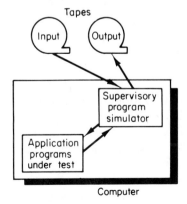

Figure 37.1

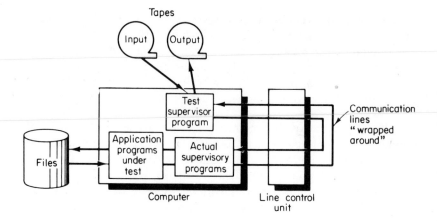

Figure 37.2

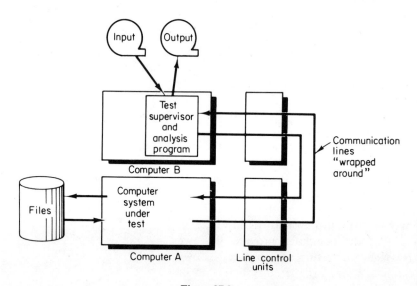

Figure 37.3

Supervisory Programs. Some may be added to the Application Programs. When the Supervisory Programs are planned, detailed consideration should be given to system testing.

The types of program needed are indicated below:

1. *Simulators*

(a) *Equipment simulators,* for simulating hardware not available; for simulating lines and terminal devices.

(b) *Program simulators*, to bridge a gap when programs are not yet available or debugged. Supervisory Program simulators may be needed; also pseudo-data-processing programs, pseudo-file-addressing routines, and so on.

(c) *Overload simulators*, to test the system behavior under peak conditions without actually flooding a peak volume of transactions into it.

2. *Test Supervisory Program*

The input data will probably be read in from tape rather than from the actual terminal devices of the system. Similarly, the output will go to tape. Input will be read in at appropriate times by a test Supervisory Program which makes the input appear as though it had come from terminals. Entering data from an *actual* terminal would usually be too slow. The test Supervisory Program would also log the output on tapes and be used to enter control cards and batches and to set up the test.

3. *Error Detection Aids*

(a) *Tracing.* Three levels of trace are possible: an instruction trace, which operates on every instruction executed, a branch trace, which records only transfers, and a macro trace, which records pertinent information when certain macroinstructions are executed or possibly only when control enters or leaves a data-processing program via the Supervisory Programs. The instruction trace and branch trace are too lengthy in operation and not really needed, but the macro trace will be extremely valuable. Without it, there can be great difficulty in following what happened on some programs that operate in a multiprogrammed fashion.

There can be several levels of macro trace depending upon how much information is printed out. It is suggested that two levels might be used, one which merely records the macroinstruction, and the other which records it and also dumps working storage and pertinent registers on each occasion.

(b) *Interrupt loggings.* When testing in a real-time mode, interrupts will occur at random times. Errors will probably arise because data-processing programs have been interrupted and control returned to them after priority routines were executed. It is therefore essential to know what priority interrupts occurred during the execution of each program segment.

A trace, similar to the macro trace, for interrupts would be useful. However, as there are many different types of interrupt, this would require many instructions in core. Furthermore, the timing relationships would be upset by the duration of the trace routines. Instead, it is suggested that each priority routine should contain one instruction which sets a bit in a core location characteristic of that routine. The area where the bits are set is then dumped by the macro trace program. This method is simple, quick to program, and does not upset the timing relationships. However, if the same type of interrupt occurs twice during the execution of one program segment, it will give no indication of this.

A slightly more complicated variation of this might be to store the return address for that priority routine, thereby indicating that such an interrupt has occurred. However, it is thought that merely setting a bit will be adequate and that this one instruction might be left permanently in the program even during operational running.

(c) *Debug macros.* The macro trace, message logging, and interrrupt logging routines described above would be built into the framework of the supervisory system. It is possible to allow the other programmers to build some aids into their programs if they wish, also. By using debugging macros at a predetermined point they might be able to take such actions as dumping core, working storage, or registers.

(d) *Priority error dump.* When an error occurs on a real-time system, it is normal to interrupt with a priority error routine rather than stop the machine. It would be advantageous to make this priority routine dump all information required for debugging.

4. *Saturation Testing*

Because of the many permutations and combinations of random events that can occur on all but the simplest real-time applications, the system must be thoroughly *exercised* or combinations of events will occur in operational running that did not occur during testing. *Bulk* or *saturation* testing is needed. This may require the following:

(a) *Data generators,* to generate the bulk of input data that are required or capture it at its source.

(b) *Test output processors,* to analyze the mass of output resulting from bulk testing and inspect it for errors.

(c) *A macro exerciser,* for repetitively utilizing the macroinstructions of the system in different combinations.

5. *Utilities*

Core dumps, file dumps, core and file loaders, library programs, and so on.

BUILDING UP A SYSTEM

If program testing is to be successful and move rapidly, it must proceed in small, logical steps. If too large a step is attempted at one time, the program testers become lost in complications and progress slows down. This is true in simple batch processing. It is very much more important in real-time processing with a high degree of multiprogramming and sometimes more than one processing unit.

A complex system needs to be built up piece by piece. Different programmers or groups of programmers will write different programs, with varying
degrees of independence. As the programs are produced, they always drift
away from their original idealistic concept. Each segment of the programs
will be debugged by the person or group who writes it, until on its own,
it is logically correct. When all the various segments are put together, each
tested by itself, there will be new errors because the segments do not interface
together exactly. Part of the work of system testing is to straighten out these
interface problems, making sure that the component parts of the programs
fit together.

The various sections of programs should be put together one at a time so
that the system is built up stage by stage. When several program segments
are used in the processing of a message, these segments must be tested first
singly and then in sequence. When several programs interface to form a
system, these programs must be tested first individually and then linked
together stage by stage. When several processing units are involved, these
must be tested one at a time and then jointly. Lastly, when multiprogramming is used, the programs must be tested first sequentially or single thread
(where a thread is all the actions associated with one input message) and then
in parallel or multithread.

This is illustrated in Fig. 37.4. The various segments of program will

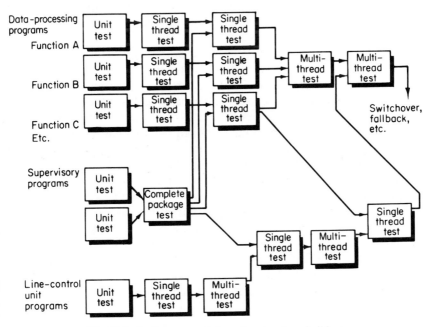

Fig. 37.4. Testing proceeds in a stage-by-stage build-up.

be fed through a logically planned process for building up the system. As more segments are added to the tested system, earlier segments should be recycled through the tests, as interactions with the new programs may reveal new errors. In general it is necessary to progress from simple short batches of input, designed by the programmer, to bulk data for *saturation testing*. Similarly it is necessary to progress from generated data to actual data and from a simulated environment (that is, input and output on magnetic tape using a special program) to a real environment, such as terminal sets in remote offices. When a very complex system is designed, it is difficult to install the entire system in one cutover. It is difficult to install a system of, for example, 100,000 instructions of tightly integrated real-time coding in one cutover. It would be much easier if the system could be split up into a succession of models. A relatively simple model would be installed first. This at a later date would be replaced by a more complex model, and in this way the system would develop to its final concept.

NETWORK TESTING   As the program testing is proceeding, the communication links forming the network will be set up. Terminals, control units, modems, concentrators, and other telecommunications equipment will be installed, linked up, and tested by the engineers. The communications network must then be made to operate linked up to the computer with its Supervisory Programs for handling input and output. The interface between the Supervisory Programs and the communications network usually throws up new errors.

During this period, a variety of small problems usually arise. Program errors are expected and looked for, but other faults quite unanticipated crop up as well. If more than one manufacturer is involved, interface problems between their process of equipment may be discovered, although every attempt has been made to check this out before. In one system the terminals would recognize their own address in messages satisfactorily but would not accept a broadcast code. In another, some terminals constantly gave an incorrect answer-back signal. The communication line to one location in Europe proved periodically noisy and interfered with terminals on that line in other cities. A simulator of a computer input/output control, used in developing communication channels, proved to have not simulated it exactly because the model produced pulses that were finer than those in actual operation. Interference from an airport radar scanner caused baffling logic errors in transistor circuitry. Terminal potentiometers were incorrectly set. Unexpected faults of this type will always occur and are straightened out during the installation and system test period.

When the data links are working, a further interface that must be tested is that between the system, particularly its programs, and the terminal operators. On a complex system, almost certainly the operators working the terminals will do things that were unanticipated. The ingenuity of the relatively unintelligent terminal girls in making mistakes can often exceed that of graduate programmers in devising error procedures. They produce all combinations of wrong formats. They discover empirically that the pressing of certain keys can cause actions they were not intended to. If the response from the computer is slow, indicating that it is at that moment heavily loaded, they may repetitively pound the keys with impatience, which on some systems can grossly aggravate the overload by making the computer accept these key thumpings as messages.

Operator actions which cause malfunctions or misunderstandings may at this stage give rise to small changes in the programs.

TEST
PLANNING
It will be seen that much planning is required for the testing of a large real-time system. The schedule for testing both the programs and the over-all system needs to be planned from the outset. The testing of the system needs to be thought about at each stage in the design and implementation. The tools necessary for testing must be produced to a well-planned schedule. A large number of programs are required, and, if these are not ready when wanted, the implementation will be held up. Similarly a massive amount of data needs to be collected or produced which relates to the system in question.

Both the hardware configuration and the programs must be planned so that they are suitable for testing. The Supervisory Programs in particular need testing aids built into them so that selective tracing or logging of events may be done. A design policy that concentrates solely on the final working system and neglects its suitability for testing will lead to chaos at installation time.

38 CUTTING OVER THE SYSTEM

It would be pleasant if an on-line system could be cut over at the flick of a switch, one moment not in use and the next on the air fully operational. However, except with the simplest system, this is not the case. There is usually a period of building up the system, altering the procedures, training and changing the working habits of many personnel members. It is often a period filled with organizational, human, and technical problems. Careful design of the cutover phase can minimize these difficulties. As with the testing of such systems, certain Support Programs or interim Application Programs will be needed to enable the organization to go through the transition period. Cutover planning, like testing, must not be left until the last minute, or the necessary programs and facilities will not be available and chaos will result.

In most commercial data-processing installations it is desirable to work for the first few days or weeks of a computer system's life with the old system still running. This will help to discover errors in the new system and provide a backup in case the computer should fail. It is not always possible to do this in a straightforward way on a real-time system, because the volume of work involved in entering every transaction into a terminal as well as handling it by the old method would be very great. Furthermore, a real-time system servicing many locations cannot easily be stopped when an error is found. For this reason very thorough system testing is needed, as described in the last chapter, followed by a planned buildup of the system into operational running.

SYSTEM BUILDUP

So many factors are involved in the conversion of a large on-line system that the complications would be quite overwhelming if the system were all cut over at once. Therefore it is necessary to break down the conversion into relatively simple stages.

The conversion of a system may proceed in the following possible ways:

1. *Location by location.* One branch or terminal location may be installed at first. When this is working satisfactorily, others are added. Concentrators, exchanges, subsidiary computers, and other equipment are installed, initially servicing limited numbers of terminals, and are built up until the whole network is on line. The buildup period may be anything from a few weeks to a few years. An integrated system which is part on-line and part off-line often has to have special procedures and programs to bridge the interim period.

2. *Function by function.* When a terminal location goes on-line, the terminals may not at first carry out all of the operations that they will in the ultimate system. The terminal may initially execute a small number of relatively simple actions. When these work problem free and the hardware, Supervisory Programs, and communication facilities are well proven, other functions may be added. This type of buildup needs the facility for program testing the new functions without interfering with the operational system.

3. *Model by model.* The first version of a working system may be designed so that it is on the air for a period of time and then gives way to a more complex, and where necessary, re-thought-out version. This second model may use rewritten programs, improved or expanded hardware, an improved file organization, and so on. The time interval between the inceptions of model 1 and model 2 should be such that information about the functioning of model 1 will be used in the design of model 2. Most programmers when they have finished a complex program want to rewrite it afresh with cleaner logic, and this can also be so with a complete system. Model 2 cleans up the logic of model 1, improves areas where the man-machine relationship is not as smooth as it could be, and adds new features. Model 2 may give way to subsequent models, each planned so that *design feedback* from one improves the next.

4. *Combinations of these.* The buildup of a large system may be planned to take place over several years, different parts of the work and different terminal locations being added in a planned fashion. There should be a carefully phased and carefully thought-out development plan for such a system, designed so that each development learns the maximum from the steps that have gone before it, and each cutover of new terminals or new operations can be done with the least disruption.

CUTOVER OF A MESSAGE-SWITCHING SYSTEM Some systems are of such a nature that they *should* be cut over quickly, all at once. The replacement of an existing message-switching center is an example of this. If a torn paper-tape center, such as that in Figs. 17.5 to 17.8, is computerized, there must be no disruption in the sending of traffic. Normally the computer when it comes into operation will take over all of the terminals of the network in a relatively short period. The existing teleprinters may be replaced by different terminals or may be kept.

Program testing and system testing on the computer and its network will be carried to a point when there is sufficient confidence in the system for cutover to be attempted. Communication lines will have been checked out on line to the computer. Terminals in each of the remote offices will have sent messages to, and received messages from, the computer under control of the Supervisory Programs. The technical faults, missing cables, telecommunication problems, and so on, that occur will be cleared up, and then actual operators will begin to use some of the terminals.

This can sometimes reveal the need for modifications to the programs, but, as it also usually reveals the need for improvements in the operators' training, it should be done early enough in the schedule to permit this. Prior to the cutover period then, all operators will have a session operating the terminal in a training mode, on line to the computer, either at their own office or at a central training location.

Terminals will be installed at their remote locations, and, when the operators are all sufficiently familiar with their operation and the system is sufficiently debugged, some locations will send live traffic to the computer. They will also send the same transactions via their normal routing, and so the system will be run in parallel with the old methods for a period and the results compared.

If errors are still being found at a considerable rate, say five or ten per day, the number of terminals in use will probably be kept very small until these bugs are mostly eradicated. As the errors are removed, terminals will be added, cautiously at first and then, as confidence builds up, rapidly, until the whole system is on line. There may be periods when the system has to be taken off line during the parallel running to correct some fundamental fault.

On one system, probably typical, it was found that the amount of traffic at the computer center was not as great as expected. On investigation it was discovered that operators trying to get messages processed were having difficulties and, because of format problems and being insufficiently trained, were abandoning the new system and using the old one. This problem was dealt with, and the operators were given further operating instruction. Two weeks later it was found that there were now *more* terminals on line than there should have been, presumably indicating that the operators were becoming enthused.

Eventually a point will be reached when all terminals are on line and in use. There may still be occasional errors occurring, but by now they should be few and infrequent on a relatively simple system such as message switching. A more complex real-time system will have a large number of rarely occurring bugs, and most complex systems *never* become fully debugged. If the computer has replaced a torn-tape switching center, this may now become idle. As soon as sufficient confidence has been built up in the new system, the torn-tape center will be disbanded.

CUTOVER OF A SYSTEM WITH CENTRAL FILES
In a system in which the terminal operators update and use information in central files, an important step in the cutover is the storing of live data on the files. On some systems the data records will be created at the terminals, in others at the computer center. On some systems it is a normal part of terminal operation to create records, for example, for a new customer or a new job, and so these records can be made by the office that originates or stores them now. It will take some time to enter all of the data into the system, and after they are entered they will possibly need updating. When a customer walks into a savings bank, for example, and makes a transaction during the cutover period, the terminal operator must establish whether this customer's account record is yet on the files and, if so, update it.

Building up the files is relatively easy when each location has its own set of files and they cannot be updated from any other location. This is so in the beginning in a savings bank system. The customer must always go to his own branch to deposit or withdraw cash, and no other branch will update his account record on line. Later, when all the files are loaded and the system is working well, customers can be told that they can now make transactions at any branch that is equipped with terminals.

Where the data in the files are used in an integrated fashion by many terminal locations from the start, the problem is more difficult. Either the · files must be loaded in a brief, concentrated period when the data are not in use, such as a weekend, and all the terminals which update them cut over at once, or else some means must be devised of bridging the gap. In the former case, as much data as possible may be loaded into the files while the old system is working. As this may take several days, some of these transactions will need updating prior to the moment of cutover. This updating may be done from the terminals on a weekend or at night when work is not proceeding. It will need a special program to make the computer use the normal checks when updating files from terminal actions but not take other actions which it would if it were dealing with a live transaction.

INTERIM OPERATIONS
On a large system it is too difficult a job to cut over all the terminals at once. There would be too many different people and different actions to coordinate. Furthermore, it is undesirable, because the programs cannot be debugged to fullest confidence until some locations are cut over

and using them. A procedure for interim operations must therefore be devised in which some locations are off line and others on line. The cutover procedure in which an off-line location goes on line must be planned carefully.

Let us consider a system in which transactions are originated at many separate locations. A file of the details of the transactions is kept, before mechanization, at each transaction location, but also a central location must control and coordinate the transactions. Certain facts about each transaction are sent to the controlling location where they are processed and filed and where certain actions may be taken. The controlling location will send messages to the transaction locations, at times, to give them information and to control their actions. The whole process is to be tightened up and made more efficient by installing a real-time system.

A transaction location, possibly one of the branch offices of the organization, establishes a *cutover date* after which all transactions will be handled in an on-line fashion and the file of transaction details will then be kept in the distant computer. Some weeks before this date the first terminal will be installed, and terminal operators will be able to use it for training on line. If the control location is on line (and where possible it will be the first one to go on line), any messages controlling the operations of the transaction location will now be transmitted to its terminal directly.

When there are sufficient terminals installed and sufficient operators fully trained, new transactions relating to the period beyond the cutover date will be entered into the terminals instead of being filed and handled in the normal way. The terminal will print out a record of the transaction as it is checked and accepted by the computer. This may be printed out on a sprocket-fed card, for example. The print-outs will be used by the office during the interim period as a record of the transactions. The computer will take any action that is necessary when these items are entered as it would with any new transactions.

There will be some items which must be entered because they relate to a period after the cutover date, but which were made before this terminal operation began. These will be filed by the computer, but it will not take any action on them as they have already been processed by the old system. Again a print-out of the transactions will be produced. Eventually all the transactions relating to the period after the cutover date will be in the system. The office will have had a file of these transactions printed out and any further modifications to the transactions will be stored in this manual file as well as in the computer. However, only transactions for the period before the cutover date will now be processed manually. By the time the cutover date arrives all the transactions will be processed by the new system. If by now confidence in the system is sufficiently high, the office's manual filing may be dispensed with, and the terminal may no longer print out details of each item given to it. The location is then fully cut over.

The situation is further complicated if there is more than one control location. This is the case, for example, in an airline reservation system. The selling and cancelling of seats for one flight is controlled at one location for that flight. However, before full mechanization, different flights are controlled at many different locations. After mechanization, control of some flights may be moved to the location of the computer center, or at least to an on-line location. On a world-wide airline, however, it may be necessary to keep the control of certain flights in cities that will not be directly on line because telecommunication facilities are too poor or too expensive. This gap must be bridged by the sending of teletype messages.

Before mechanization, the selling office will send a teletype message to the control point saying what it has sold and giving the names of the passengers. It will receive messages from the control point placing restrictions on what it can sell and informing it when the flight is full. After mechanization of that office, the computer will inform it what it can sell, and, if the computer itself does not control the flight in question, it will send appropriate messages to the control point. If the control point is off line and reached via teletype links, the control point must send teletype messages to the computer informing it of what restrictions to place on selling.

In this case cutover of an airline sales office may proceed as follows:

Step 1. First terminals installed. On-line training of sales agents proceeds.

Step 2. A specific "cutover date" is agreed upon. New transactions arising for flights after this cutover date are entered on line. The computer sends the requisite teletype messages to the control points. The terminal prints a record of the transaction for storing in the office files. (Transactions for flights prior to the cutover date are still handled by premechanization methods.)

Step 3. Transactions already on the office files relating to flights after the cutover date are entered on line. The computer must not send teletype messages relating to these transactions, as the office will have already done this.

Step 4. The office's teletype code-directing character is changed to that of the computer. The computer then receives all the office teletype messages. It will process those relating to beyond the cutover date and place appropriate limits on the office's selling. Those relating to flights prior to cutover will be relayed to the office.

Step 5. The cutover date is reached. All transactions should now be in the computer's files. If a sufficient degree of confidence has been reached, the terminal will stop printing back details of transactions for the office file. Certain minor functions may still be done in the sales office at this time, for example, allocation of passengers from a waiting list. These may now be turned over to the computer. Until the completion of step 3, only the sales office had a complete file of all the postcutover transactions, and so only the sales office could carry out such functions as servicing the waiting list.

PROGRAMS NEEDED FOR CUTOVER   Programs are needed during the conversion phase to assist in obtaining and loading the necessary data on the files and to bridge the gap between the old methods and the new during interim operations. On some systems it is possible to load the files, using the system's Application Programs or minor modifications of them. Off-line programs, such as card-to-tape converters, data editors, or programs for converting data existing in another form may be used. On some real-time systems the files are largely built up by operators using the terminals in a normal manner. Programs may have been used to determine the best file-addressing algorithms, especially if randomizing is used, and the addressing routines for loading the files will be the same as those used in the operation system. Sometimes the programs for cutover are similar to those used in recovering from a period of system failure and may be so combined.

During the cutover process the computer needs to know which cities it has on line and which it must contact in other ways. It may have to examine a table to determine this until the whole system is cut over. As the conversion proceeds, the computer must vary its actions somewhat at various critical points. In the above airline example these would be:

1. When the first terminal is installed in a city and training commences.
2. When new transactions are first entered.
3. When transactions already on the office files are entered. These may be entered by a special agent whom the computer recognizes as a meshing agent.
4. When the city's code-directing character is changed.
5. When the terminal finally stops printing records for filing.

OPERATOR TRAINING   Mistakes made by terminal operators and lack of control over operators have been a major cause of difficulty during cutover of many of the real-time and on-line systems installed to date. The importance of giving the operators very thorough training, indeed, cannot be stressed too strongly. There will be enough problems at cutover time without their being compounded by all manner of operator errors.

There may be some interim method of making the operators familiar with their terminals before the cutover period. In one such system, for example, it was necessary to introduce a new and complex set of codes for sending machinable information by teletype. These teletype transactions were to enter the computer along with other, real-time work, and from past experience, a large number of operator errors were anticipated. Elaborate format-checking programs were to be written, and a semi-real-time section of operators was planned at the computer center to handle teletype rejects. In this case it was planned to bring the new teletype codes into operation a year before the main system. The teletype messages were processed by a relatively simple and temporary off-line installation. Paper tape was captured and analyzed off line to determine sources of error. It was fed through programs which simulated the format checking of the final system and produced statistics of operator errors, which proved indeed to be as bad as the most pessimistic estimate. For some months a campaign of discipline and extra training was waged to reduce the error rate. By the time the real-time system was cut over, the operators were at least familiar with teletype codes.

Many terminals are designed so that they can be operated off line. Banking terminals, for example, as described in Chapter 16, are designed for off-line operation during a period of computer or line failure. The IBM 1050 series can operate off line, one terminal communicating on a "home loop" to other terminals. Where these facilities exist, fullest use should be made of them in making the operators familiar with their terminals.

Whether or not off-line or interim operation is possible to train the operators, a *training mode* for running the system should be programmed into the on-line system. On-line training can be programmed in an elaborate fashion, or it can be made a simple variation of the normal Application Programs. Often the latter is good enough. Some real-time systems, however, have contained a form of teaching program for instructing the operators.

The training programs should allow the operators to use the terminals before or after cutover without damaging the working data in the system. They may use a small area of the files of their own which contains training records, or they may use the working data of the system but without the facility to modify it. It is usually desirable that the training mode should be able to operate after cutover while the system is in actual use by other operators. The training mode must then obey the following rules:

1. It must not interfere with the work of the other operators.

2. It should permit the trainee operator to perform as many functions as possible.

3. It must prevent the trainee from creating or changing any working data.

4. It must not activate any function which takes a relatively long processing time.

In some systems the user has a working area which is allocated uniquely to him. Into this he reads data from the files, displays them, modifies them, adds new data, and processes that. Only when the computer and he are satisfied that this has been completed without error is the data written back onto the data files. In this type of system, the training mode can permit him to do everything except the last step of writing the results back onto the file. The program which completes the transaction needs to be modified, but few of the others.

The systems analyst, preoccupied largely with the technicalities of the system, can easily neglect the training of the operators. On a real-time system, however, it is vitally important. A long enough period of training and familiarization must be allowed to prevent the cutover phase from being inflamed with operator errors and inability. As with other aspects of testing and cutover, it needs to be planned well in advance.

TYPES OF TERMINAL OPERATORS

During the cutover phase the Application Programs respond differently to different types of terminal operators. Four types of operator are common:

1. The normal terminal operator.
2. The supervisor, who can take certain actions which the normal operator cannot.
3. The trainee operator, who must not modify any of the working data.
4. The interim operator who is entering data or carrying out some operation prior to cutover which needs a different action than normal from the computer.

On a system which is cut over office by office, as is usually the case, all of these types of operator may be using the computer at the same time. There may also be other types of operator, for example, operators for handling different functions, for dealing with teletype or reject messages, or for dealing with a period of recovery from fallback or computer failure.

There must be a way for the operators to identify themselves to the computer programs. The computer may have a table of which type of operator is at which terminal. Alternatively it may have in its files a separate working or assembly block for each terminal or each operator, and this will identify the type of operator. A common practice is for the operator to have to sign in each day before using the terminal and sign out when leaving it. The method of signing in will identify the operator type and enable any operator to use any terminal. It needs to be carefully controlled, however, or a trainee or other unauthorized person may modify the files. Use of a machine-read identification card or a sign-in code number for each operator or a key can prevent this.

**INSTALLATION
TIME**

On a batch-processing system or computer for scientific use, the period between machine delivery and operational running can be short. It is sometimes only a few days or one week-end. On an on-line system it will be longer. With simple on-line data transmission, it may be a month; with a small real-time system, such as that of a savings bank, it may be three months; with a large and complex real-time system, six months. The reason for this is that the actual system needs to be installed for the final phases of program testing, network testing, and operator training.

It is only at cutover time that the validity of the system design is really tested. The moment of truth has arrived for the systems analysts. It is possible that something fundamentally wrong may be discovered at this time. The processing unit may be overloaded; the volumes of certain types of transaction may be greater than in the design statistics and (the simulation); one file arm may be taking a higher proportion of the activity than expected and causing overlarge queues. Some error may be found now, that was not apparent in earlier testing and that necessitates a major change, such as increasing the core size, reorganizing the file layout, or adding a faster file module.

If major programming changes are needed or an engineering modification has to be made or the manufacturer has to deliver some new hardware, this may take time. It will mean that some of the system testing has to be done again. At worst it may mean that locations already cut over have to be taken off the air.

Often during the installation of real-time systems, a *test cell* is set up before the complete system is delivered. This will contain the computers, or possibly only one of them, and enough peripheral equipment to test almost all of the hardware and program interfaces. Often it is possible to go only part of the way using conventional test center facilities. A test cell is particularly needed for testing and exercising the Supervisory Programs, for example. On a large and complex system the test cell may be in use six months before the equipment is installed in its final form, and after installation it is another six months before cutover is complete.

During the period before cutover the new equipment may be installed at the same time the old operating methods are in use. It is necessary to plan that there is enough physical *space* for both.

**PRINCIPLES IN
PLANNING CUTOVER
PROCEDURES**

In conclusion let us summarize some principles which should be adopted when cutover is being planned:

1. Design the procedures so that no data can be accidentally lost during the cutover process.

2. Design the procedures so that no files can be accidentally updated twice with the same data, especially during parallel running.

3. Design the procedures so as to cause the minimum upheaval in the offices affected.

4. Minimize those operator procedures which are used *only* for interim operation during cutover.

5. Plan well in advance and ensure that all programs are written and tested for setting up the records, interim operations, and training.

6. Ensure that the various telecommunication facilities are ready and tested on time.

7. Carry out the operator training and familiarization very thoroughly indeed and well in advance. Ensure that the operators use the terminals off line or on line in the training mode for some time before cutover.

8. Plan the cutover to take place step by step where possible rather than to take too large a bite at the apple at one time.

39 A QUESTIONNAIRE FOR PLANNING

There is so much that could be written about the planning of a large system that it could occupy another book of this size. The intention of the last two chapters of this book is to list certain key steps that may be progressed through, key functions that may be performed, and key questions that should be answered in planning and implementing a system. This chapter suggests points that should be examined before the system's design is complete or the final go-ahead given. The next chapter gives examples of PERT and planning charts that may be used during the implementation. It is hoped that these two chapters will form, not exactly a check list, but at least a list of points that those involved in system planning may examine with the possibility of finding suggestions for items they may have forgotten.

First, in setting up the *study* for an on-line system, the entire organization may be examined to determine which areas are to be tackled. The following steps may be progressed through:

1. Examine the organization to determine areas to be tackled.
2. Define the objectives of the system.
3. Determine the structure of the study.
4. Divide the study into parts or teams.
5. Determine what data must be collected.
6. Determine who in the organization can help in the data collection.
7. Establish documentation formats.

Ideally, the initial study should progress without consideration of available hardware, determining what would be best for the organization if it were available. In reality, the study needs to be tempered by a knowledge of what is broadly practical and economic and usually by what techniques have been made to work to date. However, in the initial study stage one should not be bound by questions such as, "Is such and such a terminal available?" or "Can such and such a computer have this attached to it?"

The following *functional objectives* of the system should be determined and evaluated:

1. Describe the jobs to be done.
2. Specify the input sources and locations.
3. Specify the output requirements and locations.
4. Specify the data that are to be stored on direct-access files.
5. Specify the data that are to be stored on non-direct-access files (for example, tapes).
6. Specify any real-time man-machine interactions that are needed.
7. Specify response times for different actions.
8. Specify turn-around times or times for completion of processing.

The *throughput* and *peak load conditions* should be determined, along with *availability objective;*

1. What are the total loadings on the system?
2. What are the peak load conditions?
3. When do peak loads occur on different jobs and what is their duration?
4. What response times and turn-around times are needed at times of momentary or sustained peaks? A probability statement is often used, such as

> 50 per cent of transactions, response time less than   3 seconds
> 90 per cent of transactions, response time less than 10 seconds
> 100 per cent of transactions, response time less than 15 seconds

5. What future growth is envisaged in throughput?
6. What future growth is envisaged in file requirements?
7. What future growth is envisaged in added functions?
8. What hours of operation are planned per day, week, month?
9. What system outages can be tolerated by the various functions performed?
10. What total down-time is acceptable?
11. What down-time is tolerable in real-time work? Mean time to failure and mean time to repair might be used to specify this.
12. What are the permissible fallback modes?
13. What functions can be omitted during degraded operation?
14. What functions can be omitted during peak periods?
15. What partial outages can be tolerated per occurrence, per day, per week?
16. Should any specific guarantees be sought on down-time?

17. Should any penalty clauses be planned for the contract or any insurance policy be considered?

A most critical input to the system design is the cost objective. The economic justification may cause much of the above study to be reevaluated. What is the cost of obtaining a certain reliability? What is the cost of a fast response and what is its economic justification?

Having made this study and determined the above factors, the available hardware may be examined. The design calculations will be done and probably reiterated, as discussed in Section V of this book.

Hardware considerations to be decided and evaluated include the following:

1. The Computers

(a) Determine the final computer configuration.
(b) Ensure that the software provided with these computers is satisfactory.
(c) Determine the core requirements, average and peak.
(d) Determine the processor time requirements, average and peak.
(e) Specify standby, backup, and spare components, and the interconnections between components.
(f) Determine modes of switchover.
(g) Determine action when each and any component fails.
(h) Carry out reliability analysis.
(i) If equipment of different manufacturers is used, check that these interface together exactly.

2. The Files

(a) Determine the categories of data to be stored.
(b) Determine the volumes of these.
(c) Determine the access times required to these, average and peak.
(d) Determine what hardware will be used for primary and secondary storage, on-line and off-line files, direct-access files
(e) Determine the direct-access file layouts.
(f) Specify file-addressing techniques.
(g) Determine how additions and deletions are to be handled.
(h) Determine total file-access or update times, file-passing times, sort times where applicable.
(i) Determine means of file protection.
(j) Determine management controls to be used on files, for example, file-scanning or -balancing runs.
(k) Determine file reconstruction in case of damage to records.
(l) Plan audit trails.

3. *The Communications Network*

(a) Determine the total volumes of input traffic, average and peak.

(b) Determine the total volumes of output traffic, average and peak.

(c) Determine requirements of the man-machine interface.

(d) Plan details of the input/output hardware.

(e) Evaluate printing requirements.

(f) Determine desirable terminal characteristics.

(g) Select terminals.

(h) Determine whether any special engineering, perhaps unique to the application, is needed on the terminals.

(i) Establish locations and numbers of terminals.

(j) Determine operating procedures.

(k) Plan communications network—types of lines, speeds, tariffs, terminal assignments, and loads, peak and average.

(l) Plan other equipment used in the communications network—multiplexors, concentrators, transmission-control units, multidrop facilities, channels, and so on.

(m) Establish means of error detection and correction.

(n) Plan management controls on the data transmission.

(o) Plan alternate routings or other backup.

(p) Evaluate queue buildup on this network.

(q) Carry out reliability analysis.

(r) Determine what negotiations are needed with the common carriers.

(s) Establish whether the required communication lines can be obtained.

In considering the *flow of work through the system* and *the way data are organized* in it, questions such as the following should be answered:

1. How are priorities of work assigned?

2. How will the attention of the processor be shared between contending tasks?

3. Will the system be controlled by one processor or more than one?

4. Does each processor select its next job or are selections made by another unit?

5. Is the allocation of core storage static or dynamic?

6. What form of memory protection is needed?

7. What form of watchdog timer is needed?

8. How will time-initated actions be handled?

9. What over-all system controls will be used?

10. What logging of messages or system behavior will occur?

11. What fault diagnostics are needed?

12. What on-line diagnostics will be used?

13. What plans are there for switchover, fallback, and recovery?

14. Will this be manual or automatic?

15. Will it be necessary to dump the files in real time?

16. What management controls will be used during periods of fallback or standby?

17. What manual backup procedures are planned?

18. What provisions are planned for manual intervention?

19. How can the system be expanded to meet growth requirements?

The programming of the system also needs careful consideration:

1. Will the Supervisory Programs be written for this application or will available ones be used?

2. If the latter, will these need modification?

3. What programming languages will be used, and will they be compatible with the use of the Supervisory Programs?

4. On which programs can a higher-level language, such as COBOL or PL 1, be used and on which would this be too imprecise?

5. Will any modifications be needed to the manufacturer's programming systems?

6. What utility programs and Support Programs are needed—library, file organization, loaders, dumps, training programs?

7. What plans are there for program testing?

8. What special programs will be needed for testing—simulators, data generators, pseudo Supervisory Programs, test Supervisory Programs, debugging aids, traces, selective macro traces, dumps, test output-analysis programs, and so on?

9. How many lines of code are involved in each type of program?

10. How many man-years will be needed to write these, and is the manpower available?

At the design stage when questions like these are being answered, *the testing and cutover phase* probably seems for away. However, "We'll worry about that when we get to it" is a viewpoint that will lead to trouble, because features needed for cutover and testing usually have to be in the system design from the start.

1. Plan what equipment is needed for testing in addition to that for a working system—printers, tapes, extra files, simulators, line wraparound, computer-to-computer connections.

2. Plan what equipment will need early installation for testing. Will a test cell be set up?

3. Plan what programs will need to be produced early for the testing of other programs.

4. What modifications will be made to the Supervisory Programs for testing?

5. What modifications will be made to the Application Programs for testing?

6. Determine who will provide the programs and other tools needed for testing. Will the manufacturer provide them?

7. Plan the cutover procedures

8. Plan what programs will be needed to bridge the gaps during cutover.

9. Is a period of parallel running planned?

10. Will there be space enough for both systems to operate at once?

11. Plan what pilot operation will occur. Using what input/output? What file data? What other facilities?

12. What operator training will be needed?

13. Will the computer assist in this on line? What programs are needed? Is enough processing time available?

14. What other hardware will be needed for training—terminal with off-line or for a loop operation?

15. Plan the growth to the complete system.

16. Plan how testing will be done and modifications made when the system is on the air. Possibly extra hardware, for example, a file unit, will be needed for this.

17. Will the system be maintainable when it is installed? Does it contain all the components required to perform diagnostics?

18. Will enough engineers be available to service all the remote equipment?

19. How will the remote equipment be checked out and faults diagnosed?

20. Will problems arise because more than one manufacturer or common carrier is involved? When faults occur how will it be known which manufacturer or carrier is responsible?

40 IMPLEMENTATION CHARTS

In conclusion, this chapter gives illustrations of the types of planning charts in use for the installation of complex computer systems. Careful planning and progress monitoring can be more important on a complex on-line system than for conventional computer installations because there are more factors which link together and which can hold up the project if delayed or forgotten.

A schedule is needed for the programming and also for the other factors, such as physical installation, planning the environment in which the system will work, planning deliveries, buildings, communication facilities, and so on. It is valuable to have a check list of points to be considered in planning the installation, as seemingly insignificant items have often caused holdups.

The schedule will be used both for planning and for monitoring the implementation progress. It will indicate how much emphasis should be placed on which items, at various points in time. It should be used in planning the manpower requirements and the other resources that are needed, such as computer time. Measuring the progress on various parts of the schedule will help to evaluate the quality of the manpower and so plan its usage better.

On some installations a simple bar chart is used for the installation planning. This may, however, be too clumsy a tool because of the intricate relationships that exist between different events. Progress on one element of the work is dependent upon certain other jobs having been completed or decisions having been made.

Figure 40.1 gives an over-all bar chart of the work needed for the main system on a typical not-too-complex on-line system. The vertical lines on the chart indicate relationships between the activities, that is, the need for one program or specification before a certain activity can begin. For example, the supervisory package I must be completed and debugged before opera-

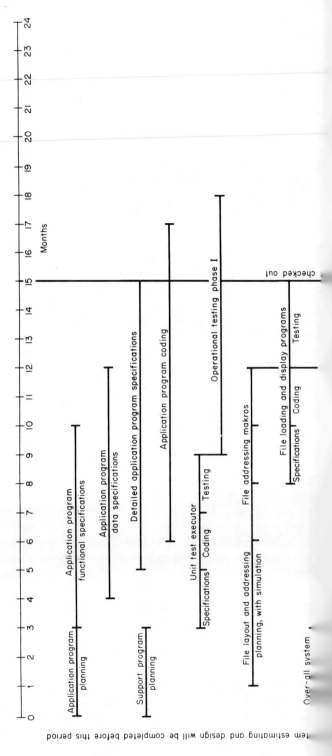

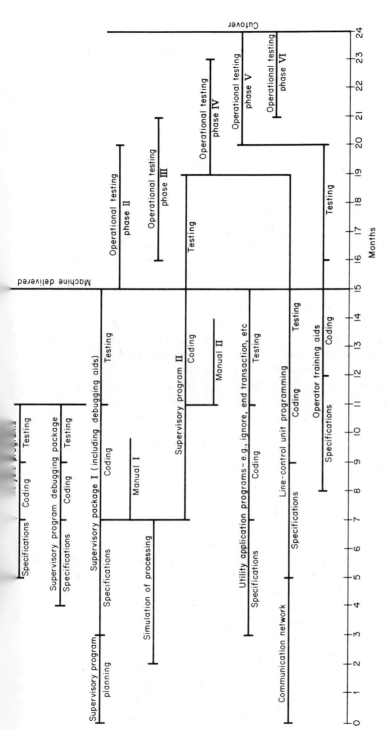

Fig. 40.1. An illustration of a programming schedule for a system with a 24-month installation period.

599

tional testing phase I can begin; the Supervisory Program debugging package must be completed before the supervisory package can be debugged; and so on. This chart shows only broad categories. If it showed details, such as individual programs, there would be many more vertical interrelations. One Application Program must be specified before another is written. Macro instructions must be specified in detail before programs using them are written. They must be debugged before the program that uses them, can be perfected. File organization and addressing need to be planned early.

Many separate programs must be tested, all working in conjunction with one another. The work of many programs must be fitted together to form a tightly integrated whole, and the sequence in which the pieces must be fitted together needs to be scheduled. Testing aids for various types of test must be ready on time. Data generators must produce test data in time for the tests. File-addressing routines must be ready and debugged before they are needed for routines that use them. The Supervisory Programs must be written and debugged with appropriate diagnostics before being interfaced with the Application Programs. On an actual installation the planning chart would be broken down into greater detail in the Application Program area. Individual packages of Application Program and their interrelation would be shown. A model-by-model approach may be used in producing the system as a whole or in producing individual packages.

Various means have been devised for showing linkages between interrelated activities and events on bar charts. Figure 40.2 shows an illustration from a PLANNET planning network chart used during the implementation of Pan American's reservation system. Schedule charts of this type were reproduced at intervals and arrows marked on them to show how far various activities were behind or ahead of schedule.

CRITICAL-PATH SCHEDULING   Rather than bar charts, other projects have preferred to use PERT, or some means of critical-path scheduling, which can be run periodically on a computer to produce appropriate reports for management. PERT emphasizes the interaction between different events and highlights those parts of the schedule that may become critical if not watched. In drawing a PERT arrow diagram, the lengths of the lines, unlike those on a bar chart, are not proportional to the time taken to complete the item. This is helpful because the initial estimates are often little better than guesswork, and as the work proceeds the estimates will change constantly.

Packaged computer programs are readily available for producing PERT reports. These are simple to run, and, once the arrow diagram has been drawn, they give an easy way of keeping the installation schedule up to date. Diagrams, such as those in Figs. 40.3–40.8, are described for the computer

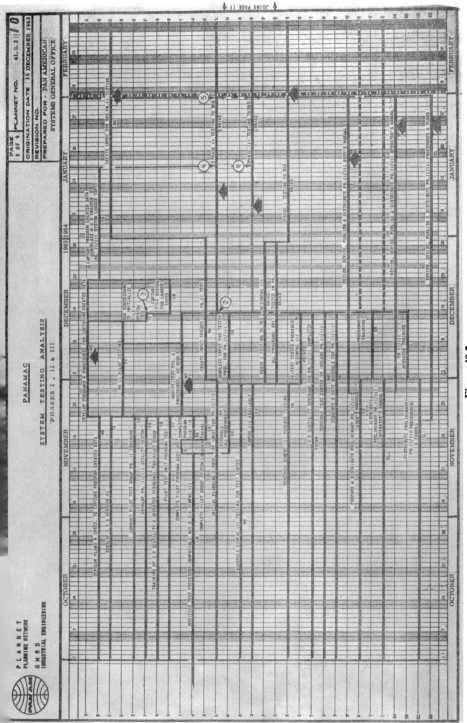

Figure 40.2

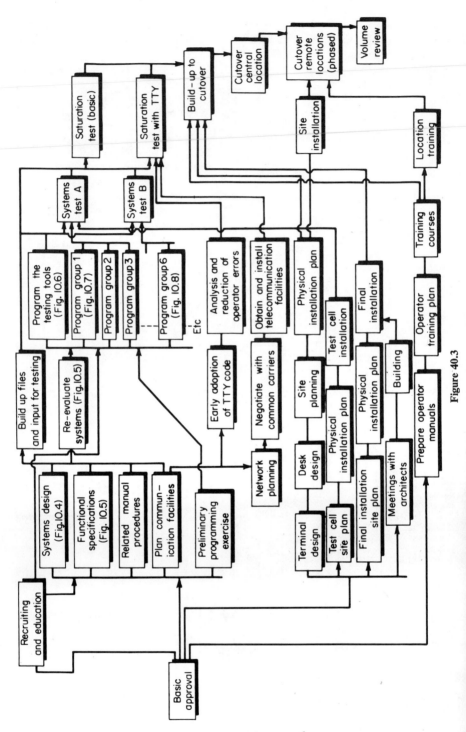

Figure 40.3

602

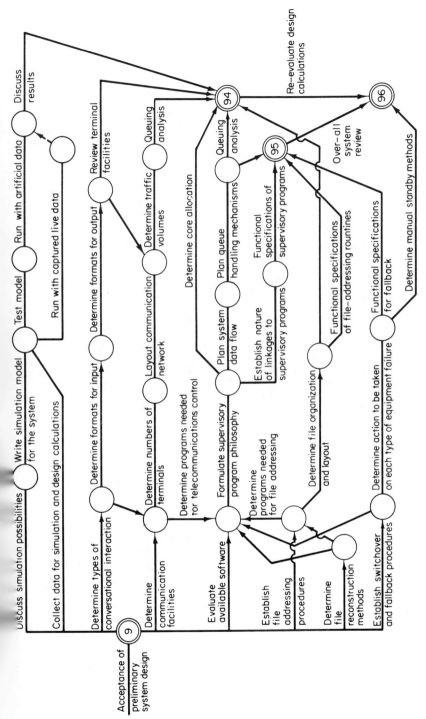

Figure 40.4

603

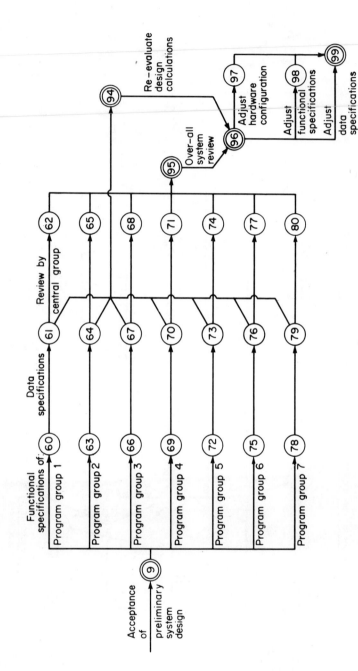

Figure 40.5

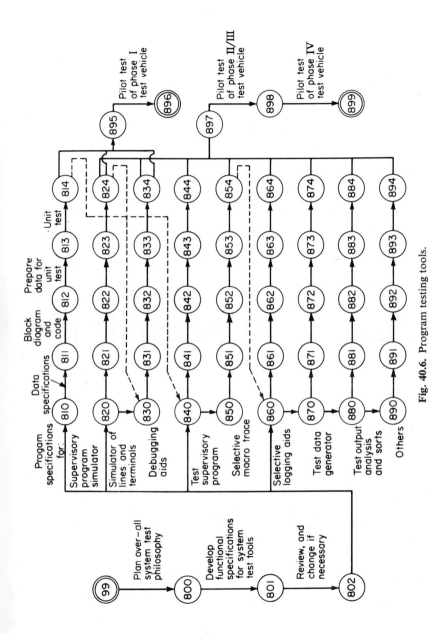

Fig. 40.6. Program testing tools.

605

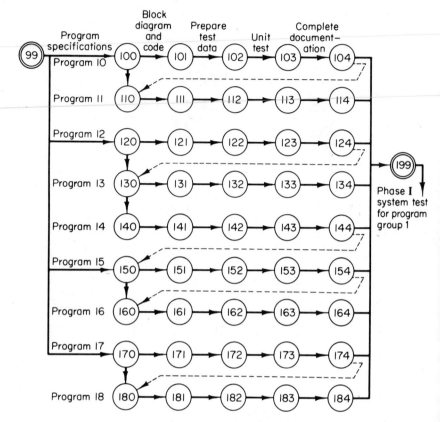

Fig. 40.7. Program Group 1.

program by punching cards representing each line on the chart. The card will contain the name of the activity, its estimated duration, and, if it has already been started or finished, the actual start or finish date. As the project proceeds this information may be updated, where it needs to be, perhaps once a month.

The program will produce management reports which highlight any slippages. It will indicate which items are the most critical and list them in order of criticality, taking into account how one item can delay others throughout the project. This should be a useful guide for telling management where extra effort is needed.

PERT is more difficult to use than less mechanical techniques such as PLANNET charts. The former usually needs a man who will spend all or most of his time on the PERT network. Some installations have set off enthusiastically PERTing their progress and later have abandoned this technique because it got out of control or needed too much work. Its main

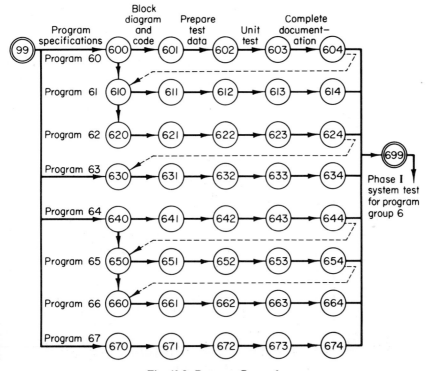

Fig. 40.8. Program Group 6.

value is that it can emphatically highlight, to management, the areas that need attention. It is not unknown for PERT to be used as a political weapon. If there is one area that you feel sure is going to give trouble, get it on the critical path regardless! A higher management progress review sometimes starts with the items at the top of the periodic PERT listing and works down.

It is not always possible to advance an element of a programming project by pouring additional effort into it. It may already have as many men as it can usefully employ. There is thus a degree to which a critical item in the schedule can be relieved with extra manpower, but a point past which it is beyond help. If any item on the arrow diagram reaches this degree of criticality, it will delay the completion of the project.

One commonly finds PERT networks drawn in the form of a very large and complex-looking chart containing all of the activities needed for the project. It is much more manageable to break them into separate interlinked pages relating to different activities. Figure 40.3 gives an over-all map of a PERT chart for system installation. Each block refers to a page or set of pages of the chart. Some of these pages are shown in Figs. 40.4–40.8. The

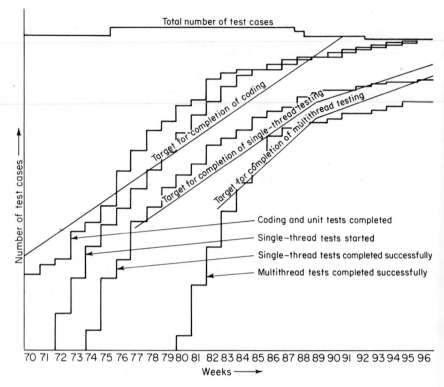

Figure 40.9

separate pages or groups of pages may then be reviewed by separate managers and changed in detail without necessitating redrawing other parts of the chart.

In the later part of a project, as the coding is being completed and the testing carried out, some means is needed to monitor this. Various landmarks in the progress of writing a package may be used and charted, such as:

Cards punched ready for running.
Test data ready.
One nontrivial test case works correctly, as a unit test.
One nontrivial test works in single-thread real-time running.
Complete set of test cases completed in single-thread running.

The chart illustrated in Fig. 40.9 relates the progress of program writing and testing to the number of test cases completed. In some installations this method has been found preferable to charting the numbers of programs or packages completed.

GLOSSARY OF PROGRAMMING TERMS USED IN THIS BOOK.

The programming terms used in real-time applications differ considerably from one system to another, and from one computer manufacturer to another. The terminology in this book has been consistent throughout, in order to avoid confusion. The programming terms used are defined below.

Analysis Block. This is a relocatable segment of the computer storage in which data are stored which can later be used to analyze the performance of the system. These may be program testing data or statistical data. There may be an Analysis Block for each transaction in the system during program testing. When the transaction leaves the system this block is dumped on tape or onto a file. The Analysis Block may be chained to the Message Reference Block.

Analysis Mode. This is a mode of operation in which the performance of the system is monitored by special programs for subsequent analysis. When the system is running in Analysis Mode, program testing data or statistical data may be automatically recorded.

Any-Sequence Queue. This is a group of items in the system waiting for the attention of the processor. They are organized in such a way that items may be removed from the group regardless of the sequence in which they entered it.

Application Program. The working programs in a system may be classed as Application Programs and Supervisory Programs. The Application Programs are the main data-processing programs. They contain no input/output coding except in the form of macro-instructions which transfer control to the Supervisory Programs.

Automatic Recovery Program. This is a program which enables a system to carry on its function when a piece of equipment has failed. It may bring into play duplex circuitry or a standby computer, or it may switch to a mode of degraded operation.

Block-Chaining. A block of data in core is associated with another block so that an item or queue of items may occupy more than one block. The linkage between the blocks may be by programming or, on some machines, it may be automatic.

Central Scanning Loop. The nucleus of a set of Supervisory Programs is a loop of instructions which determines what work is to be done next. When one item of work is completed, control will be transferred to the Central Scanning Loop which will scan requests for processing to determine the next item to be processed. When no item requires the attention of the computer, it may cycle idly in this loop. Alternatively, it may go into a WAIT state which can be interrupted if the need arises.

Chaining (in file addressing). When a randomizing technique is being used for file addressing, a file address may be created which does not in fact contain the item that is being sought. The location sought will instead give another file address in which the item may be stored. This second address also may not contain the item but may refer the computer to a third address, and so on.

Channel Scheduler. A list of requests for input/output operations on a channel are executed in a desirable sequence by a Channel Scheduler Program. When one operation on a channel is completed, the Channel Scheduler Program initiates the next on the list.

Channel Waiting Queue. This is a group of items in the system waiting for the attention of the Channel Scheduler Program.

Close-down, orderly. If the system is forced to stop it should execute an orderly close-down, if possible. This ensures that a restart can be made in an orderly fashion and that no messages are lost. All records are updated that should be updated, and no records are accidentally updated a second time when the restart is made. All incoming and outgoing transmissions are completed, and an administrative message is sent to the terminals to notify the operators of the close-down.

Close-down, disorderly. This may occur when the system stops because of an equipment error which prevents it from doing an orderly close-down. When this occurs special precautions are needed to ensure that no messages are lost and that no records are updated twice.

Contention. This is a method of line control in which the terminals request to transmit. If the channel in question is free, transmission goes ahead; if it is not free the terminal will have to wait until it becomes free. The queue of contention requests may be built up by the computer, and this can either be in a prearranged sequence or in the sequence in which the requests are made.

Debug Macro-instruction. A macro-instruction placed in a program which records certain data or programs or other facts that are subsequently used for program testing analysis.

Degree of Multi-programming. Where several transactions are being handled in parallel by the systems in a multi-programming fashion, the degree of multi-programming refers to the number of these transactions.

Departure Time. When a segment of an Application Program is completed and control is returned to the Supervisory Programs, the time at which this happens is referred to as the Departure Time.

Diagnostic Programs. These are used to check equipment malfunctions and to pinpoint faulty components. They may be used by the computer engineer or be called in by the Supervisory Programs automatically.

Diagnostics, Unit. These are used on a conventional computer to detect faults in the various units. Separate unit diagnostics will check such items as arithmetic circuitry, transfer instructions, each input/output unit, and so on.

Diagnostics, System. Rather than checking one individual component, system diagnostics utilize the whole system in a manner similar to its operational running. Programs resembling the operational programs will be used rather than systematic programs that run logical patterns. These will normally detect overall system malfunctions but will not isolate faulty components.

Duplexing. The use of duplicate computers, files or circuitry, so that in the event of one component failing an alternative one can enable the system to carry on its work.

Dynamic Core Allocation. The allocation of storage in a computer in such a way that at one time a piece of work may occupy one part of storage and at another time it may occupy another, depending on the circumstances. It is used to give a more efficient utilization of core when multi-programming takes place.

Dynamic Scheduling. The decision which piece of work to do next is made by the computer from moment to moment, depending upon the circumstances. In conventional applications the computer has a fixed and preset schedule. This is often not so in a real-time system, where the schedule is determined as the transactions arrive and work proceeds.

Entry Time. When control is transferred from the Supervisory Programs to an Application Program, the time at which this transfer is made is referred to as Entry Time.

Errors, intermittent. Equipment errors which occur intermittently but not constantly. These are difficult to reproduce, and diagnostics may not detect such faults because they may not occur when the diagnostic is being run.

Errors, solid. Equipment errors which always occur when a particular piece of equipment is used. They are repeatable and therefore relatively easy to detect.

Errors, transient. A type of error which occurs only once and cannot be made to repeat itself.

Exit Macro-instruction. This is the last macro-instruction of each and every Application Program. It causes the blocks of storage used by that program to be released, including the Message Reference Block, so that the other programs may use them. If necessary, conditions associated with the transaction in question are reset.

Fall-back Procedures. When the equipment develops a fault the programs operate in such a way as to circumvent this fault. This may or may not give a degraded service. Procedures necessary for fall-back may include those to switch over to an alternative computer or file, to change file addresses, to send output to a typewriter instead of a printer, and so on.

Fall-back, double. Fall-back in which two separate equipment failures have to be contended with.

Fail softly. When a piece of equipment fails, the programs let the system fall back to a degraded mode of operation rather than let it fail catastrophically and give no response to its users.

File Addressing. A data or a file record have a key which uniquely identifies those data. Given this key, the programs must locate the address of a file record associated with these data. There are a variety of techniques for converting such a key into a machine file address.

File Packing Density. A ratio of amount of space (in words or characters) on a file, available for storing data to the total amount of data that are stored in the file.

File Reconstruction Procedures. There is a remote possibility that vital data on the files will be accidentally destroyed by an equipment failure, or a program or operator error. The means of reconstructing the file must be devised should such an unfortunate circumstance occur. Vital data must be dumped onto tape or some other media, and programs must be written so that the file may be reconstructed from these data if necessary.

Initializer Routine. When a message enters the system certain functions must be performed upon it before the Application Programs begin processing it. These functions are checking for errors in the message, erasing backspace characters, analyzing the action code, and so on. They may be performed by an Initializer Routine.

Input/Output Control Program. That part of the Supervisory Programs which executes and controls all input and output operations.

Interrupt. Various external events, such as the arrival of a new message or the completion of an input/output operation, may interrupt the program that is presently in progress. This means that the central processing unit leaves this program, stores any working data that it needs to continue the program at a later time, and executes a different program which deals with the cause of the interrupt. After the cause of the interrupt has been dealt with, control will return to the original program that was interrupted.

Interrupt Control Routine. When an interrupt occurs this routine may be entered. It may take action such as storing the working details of the program that was interrupted so that control may be returned to it, and analyzing the cause of the interrupt to decide what action should be taken.

Interrupt Logging. When program testing or monitoring the behavior of the system, the interrupts that occur may be logged. An interrupt occuring at an unpredictable time during the execution of a program may possibly cause a program error. It is therefore important during testing to know what type of interrupt occurred.

Interrupt Log Word. An indication of what interrupt occurred during the running of each segment of program may be made in an Interrupt Log Word. As each interrupt occurs a bit is set in this word, characteristic of that type of interrupt. The Interrupt Log Word is written onto tape or some other medium for later analysis.

Interrupt Priority Table. For machines which do not handle interrupts in a fully automatic manner this table may list the sequence in which interrupt indicators should be tested.

Introspective Program. A program which monitors its own behavior. It may record program testing or statistical data in an Analysis Block.

List. This word means the same as Queue. It refers to a group of items in the system waiting for the attention of the processor. The number of items in the list will vary from time to time. Normally queues are "dynamic", which means that they consist of storage areas which can be anywhere within part of the core and which are chained together by means of words in each area, containing addresses of consecutive areas in the queue.

Load Sharing. Two computers which normally form a duplexed pair may share the load of the system during peak periods. During non-peak periods one of the two computers can handle the entire load with the other one acting as the standby.

Macro Exerciser. A means of testing the Supervisory Programs and other macro-instructions. The macro-instruction routines are made to operate repeatedly with varying conditions in an attempt to discover any program errors.

Macro-Instruction. One line of program code which generates a program routine rather than one program instruction.

Main Scheduling Routine. The nucleus of a set of Supervisory Programs is a loop of instructions which determines what is to be done next when one item of work is completed. Control will be transferred to the Central Scanning Loop which will scan requests for processing to determine the next item to be processed. When no item requires the attention of the computer, the computer may cycle idly in this loop. Alternatively it may go into a "wait" state which can be interrupted if the need arises.

Master and Slave Computers. Where two or more computers are working jointly, one of these is sometimes a master computer and the others are slaves. The master can interrupt the slaves and send data to them when it needs to. When data pass from the slaves to the master it will be at the master's request.

Mean Time to Failure. The average length of time for which the system, or a component of the system, works without fault.

Mean Time to Repair. When the system, or a component of the system, develops a fault, this is the average time taken to correct the fault.

Memory Protection. This is a hardware device which prevents a program from entering areas of memory that are beyond certain boundaries. It is useful in a multi-programmed system. Different programs in that system will be confined within different boundaries, and thus cannot do damage to each other.

Message Reference Block. When more than one message in the system is being processed in parallel, an area of storage is allocated to each message and remains uniquely associated with that message for the duration of its stay in the computer. This is called the Message Reference Block. It will normally contain the message and data associated with it that are required for its processing. In most systems it contains an area of working storage uniquely reserved for that message.

Multiplexor. A device which uses several communication channels at the same time, transmitting and receiving messages and controlling the communication lines. This device itself may or may not be a stored-program computer. It will always be attached to a stored-program computer.

Multipriority Queue. This is a group of items in the system waiting for the attention of the processor. The items have different priorities and form in effect a number of queues of different priority from which items may be extracted on a first-come-first-served basis.

Multiprocessing. Multi-processing means that more than one computer is used in the processing of one transaction.

Multiprogramming. Multi-programming means that more than one item is in one computer, with the items being processed in parallel.

Multithread Processing. A thread refers to a sequence of events or programs which are needed for the complete processing of a message. In some systems all of these programs or events will be completed before work begins on a new message. This is referred to as single-thread processing. In other systems a thread for one message may be broken while a thread for another message continues. In this way several threads may be handled in parallel. This is referred to as multi-thread processing.

New Input Queue. This is a group of new messages which have arrived in the system and which are waiting for the computer to begin processing. The New Input Queue will be scanned, along with the Work-In-Progress Queue and possible other queues, by the Main Scheduling Routine.

Next-Available-Block Register. This is a facility on a line control computer which automatically allocates storage to new characters arriving on the communication lines. When one block of core is filled, the next characters go automatically to the next block. The address of the next block is contained in a register referred to as the Next-Available-Block Register. The available blocks of storage are all chained together. When one block from a chain of available blocks is assigned, the address of the next block is automatically stored in the register.

On-Line. An on-line system may be defined as one in which the input data enter the computer directly from their point of origin and/or output data are transmitted directly to where they are used. The intermediate stages such as punching data into cards or paper tape, writing magnetic tape, or off-line printing, are largely avoided.

Overflow Areas in a File. When randomizing is used for file addressing, the addresses generated refer to pockets where one or more file records are stored. The pocket may however already be full, having a different item stored in it. In this case the item in question must be stored in an overflow location in the file which is chained to the location first found.

Overloads. The rate of input to some real-time systems will vary from one moment to another. At times a momentary overload may occur because all the communications lines transmit data to the computer at once, and the computer is not fast enough to process this sudden flood of messages. There are various types of emergency action possible for dealing with this type of overload.

Overload Simulator. It is necessary to program test the system under overload conditions. However, it is usually undesirable to use for such a test as many messages as would be needed to produce a genuine overflow. Therefore, the system is modified in some artificial way to produce a condition which makes the programs behave as they would during an overload, but which does not actually need this number of transactions.

Output Queue. This is a group of output messages which have been produced by the system and which are waiting for the Output Scheduler to transmit them down the communication lines.

Pilot Model. This is a model of the system used for program testing purposes which is less complex than the complete model, e.g., the files used on a pilot model may contain a much smaller number of records than the operational files.

Pilot Tape. This is a tape used for loading the files. It contains all the data used on the pilot model.

Pockets (in file addressing). When randomizing is used for file addressing, this technique locates a small area in the file in which one or more records are kept. This area is referred to as a pocket. It is usually economical to have a small number of records in a pocket. A pocket may, for example, correspond to one track on a disk file containing perhaps 20 records.

Polling. This is a means of controlling communication lines. The communication control device will send signals to a terminal saying, "Terminal A. Have you anything to send?" if not, "Terminal B. Have you anything to send?" and so on. Polling is an alternative to contention. It makes sure that no terminal is kept waiting for a long time as could conceivably happen with a contention network.

Polling List. The polling signals will usually be sent under program control. The program will have in core a list for each channel which tells the sequence in which the terminals are to be polled.

Priority Error Dump. In some systems equipment errors, or program errors, cause an interrupt which makes the system execute a priority program. This priority program may dump onto tape, or other media, areas of core storage or other information which enables programmers or engineers to assess the cause of the error.

Priority Routine. When an interrupt occurs the program in use at that time will be left and a different program will be executed to deal with interrupt. This new program is sometimes referred to as a Priority Routine.

Program Relocation. This means that programs can operate in different locations in core. In most systems Application Programs are in segments which may be read into different locations of core and operated from these locations. This can be achieved by programming or by a circuitry device. Normally, special circuitry is needed for program relocation.

Pseudo File Address. The Application Program, when giving an address for obtaining a record from the files, may not give an actual machine address but a false address which is converted by the Supervisory Programs into an actual machine address. The reason for this is that the actual machine address may change from one time to another because different file units may be used as part of a duplexing or fall-back process.

Push-down Queue. This is a group of items or areas in the system chained together and organized in such a way that the last item to be attached to the group is the first one to be withdrawn from it, giving a last-in-first-out priority.

Queue. This is a group of items in the system waiting for the attention of the processor. Normally, queues are "dynamic" which means that they consist of storage areas which can be anywhere within part of the core, and which are chained together by means of words in each area, containing addresses of consecutive areas in the queue.

Random-access Files. These are storage media holding a large amount of information in such a way that any item may be read or written at random with a short access time, i.e., usually less than one second. Example of random-access files are disk storages, drums, and magnetic tape or strip files.

Randomizing (for file addressing). A means by which a record may be located in a large random-access file, given a key set of characters which immediately identifies this record. The key is converted into a random number by means of an algorithm, and the random number is converted into the machine address of a pocket where the item may be stored. If the item is not stored in that pocket, the pocket will contain the address of an overflow pocket which should be examined in the search for the item.

Real-time. A real-time computer system may be defined as one that controls an environment by receiving data, processing them and returning the results sufficiently quickly to affect the functioning of the environment at that time.

Reasonableness Checks. Tests made on information reaching a real-time system or being transmitted from it to ensure that the data in question lie within a given reasonable range.

Recovery from Fall-back. When the system has switched to a fall-back mode of operation and the cause of the fall-back has been removed, the system must be restored to its former condition. This is referred to as Recovery from Fall-back. The recovery process may involve updating information on the files to produce two duplicate copies of the file.

Relocatable Programs. A relocatable program is one that can operate from different locations in core. In most systems Application Programs are in segments which may be read into different locations of core and operated from these locations. This can be achieved by programming or a circuitry device. Normally, special circuitry is needed for program relocation.

Resident Executive. That part of the Supervisory Programs which must remain permanently in core, i.e., this is not to be stored on the files, to be called in when required, as are other parts of the Supervisory Programs.

Response Time. This is the time the system takes to react to a given input. If a message is keyed into a terminal by an operator and the reply from the computer, when it comes, is typed at the same terminal, response times may be defined as the time interval between the operator pressing the last key and the terminal typing the first letter of the reply. For different types of terminal, response time may be defined similarly. It is the interval between an event and the system's response to the event.

Saturation Testing. Program testing with a large bulk of messages intended to bring to light those errors which will only occur very infrequently and which may be triggered by rare coincidences such as two different messages arriving at the same time.

Seek. A mechanical movement involved in locating a record in a random-access file. This may, for example, be the movement of an arm and head mechanism that is necessary before a read instruction can be given to read data in a certain location on the file.

Self-checking Numbers. Numbers which contain redundant information so that an error in them, caused, for example, by noise on a transmission line, may be detected. A number may, for example, contain two additional digits which are produced from the other digits in the number by means of an arithmetical process. If these two digits are not correct it will indicate that the number has in some way been garbled. The two additional digits may be checked by the computer as a safeguard against this.

Sequential Queue. This is a group of items in the system waiting for the attention of the processor, and organized in such a way that the first item to gain attention will be the first one placed in the group, i.e., priority first-in-first-out.

Set-up Services. When a message enters the system certain functions must be performed upon it before the Application Program begins processing it. These functions are checking for errors in the message, erasing back-space characters, analyzing the action code, and so on. These are referred to as Set-up Services.

Simulation. This is a word which is sometimes confusing as it has three entirely different meanings, namely:

Simulation (for Design and Monitoring). This is a technique whereby a model of the working system can be built in the form of a computer program. Special computer languages are available for producing this model. A complete system may be described by a succession of different models. These models can then be adjusted easily and endlessly, and the system that is being designed or monitored can be experimented with to test the effect of any proposed changes. The simulation model is a program that is run on a computer separate from the system that is being designed.

Simulation of Input Devices. This is a program testing aid. For various reasons it is undesirable to use actual lines and terminals for some of the program testing. Therefore, magnetic tape or other media may be used and read in by a special program which makes the data appear as if they came from actual lines and terminals. Simulation in this sense is the replacement of one set of equipment by another set of equipment and programs, so that the behavior is similar.

Simulation of Supervisory Programs. This is used for program testing purposes when the actual Supervisory Programs are not yet available. A comparitively simple program to bridge the gap is used instead. This type of simulation is the replacement of one set of programs by another set which imitates it.

Status Maps. Tables which give the status of various programs, devices or input/output operations.

Supervisory Programs. Those computer programs designed to coordinate service and augment the machine components of the system, and coordinate and service Application Programs. They handle work scheduling, input/output operations, error actions, and other functions.

Supervisory System. The complete set of Supervisory Programs used on a given system.

Support Programs. The ultimate operational system consists of Supervisory Programs and Application Programs. However, a third set of programs are needed to install the system, including diagnostics, testing aids, data generator programs, terminal simulators, and so on. These are referred to as Support Programs.

Switchover. When a failure occurs in the equipment a switch may occur to an alternative component. This may be, for example, an alternative file unit, an alternative communication line or an alternative computer. The switchover process may be automatic under program control or it may be manual.

Single-thread Processing. See Multi-thread Processing.

System Utilization Loggers. A device, frequently a program, designed to gather statistics about the operation of the system. These may, for example, indicate how many messages the system is handling at a given time and how much processing time remains available.

Terminals. The means by which data are entered into the system and by which the decisions of the system are communicated to the environment it affects. A wide variety of terminal devices have been built, including teleprinters, special keyboards, light displays, cathode tubes, thermocouples, pressure gauges and other instrumentation, radar units, telephones, and so on.

Test Supervisor Program. The Supervisory Program used solely for testing purposes. It may read the input to the test at appropriate moments and log the output from the test. It may be controlled by a timing device.

Transfer Vector. This is a means of transferring control from one relocatable program to another. This cannot be done by a simple branch or transfer, instruction because the location of the program to which the control is being transferred is not known at the time of writing the programs. The Transfer Vector is a table which may contain a list of transfer or branch instructions, enabling transfers to be made to the entry points of the various programs in core. This table must be updated when new programs are brought into core.

Uncommited Storage List. When dynamic storage allocation is used, those blocks of storage which are not at a given moment allocated will be chained together. When a block is needed for a specific purpose it will be taken from this chain of blocks. The chain of blocks is referred to as the Uncommitted Storage List.

Violation Subroutines. Subroutines which are executed when the input to the system does not conform to specific criteria, e.g., a gauge reading may not lie within certain limits, or it may have changed too much since the last time it was read, or an operator may have transmitted an invalid message, and so on.

WAIT, Macro-instruction. When an Application Program is processing a message and a request is given which causes a delay so that no further processing can continue, e.g., an input/output request, a WAIT Macro-instruction is given. This causes control to be transferred to a Supervisory Program. Processing continues on other messages, but it will continue on this message only when the cause of the delay has been removed and the processor is ready to continue work on this message. This type of Macro-instruction is needed for Multi-thread Processing.

Watchdog Timer. This is a timer which is set by the program. It interrupts the program after a given period of time, e.g., one second. This will prevent the system from going into an endless loop due to a program error, or becoming idle because of an equipment fault. The Watchdog timer may sound a horn if such a fault is detected.

Work-In-Progress queue. This is a queue of items on which processing has been started and interrupted. These items are waiting for the computer to complete their processing.

INDEX

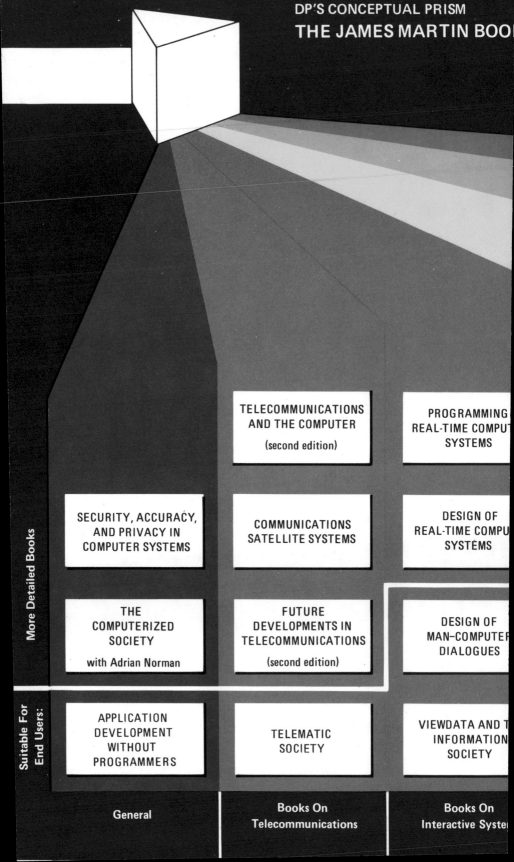